The Works
of
Sir William Gilbert
and
Sir Arthur Sullivan

BLACK'S READERS SERVICE COMPANY
NEW YORK, N. Y.

Printed in the United States of America

CONTENTS

THE MIKADO
OR
THE TOWN OF TITIPU

DRAMATIS PERSONÆ

THE MIKADO OF JAPAN

NANKI-POO (*his Son, disguised as a wandering minstrel, and in love with* YUM-YUM)

KO-KO (*Lord High Executioner of Titipu*)

POOH-BAH (*Lord High Everything Else*)

PISH-TUSH (*a Noble Lord*)

YUM-YUM ⎫
PITTI-SING ⎬ *Three Sisters—Wards of* KO-KO
PEEP-BO ⎭

KATISHA (*an elderly Lady, in love with* NANKI-POO)

Chorus of School-girls, Nobles, Guards, and Coolies

ACT I

SCENE.—*Courtyard of* KO-KO's *Palace in Titipu. Japanese nobles discovered standing and sitting in attitudes suggested by native drawings.*

CHORUS OF NOBLES

If you want to know who we are,
  We are gentlemen of Japan;
On many a vase and jar—
  On many a screen and fan,
  We figure in lively paint:
  Our attitude's queer and quaint—
  You're wrong if you think it ain't, oh!
If you think we are worked by strings,
  Like a Japanese marionette,
You don't understand these things:
  It is simply Court etiquette.
  Perhaps you suppose this throng
  Can't keep it up all day long?
  If that's your idea, you're wrong, oh!

Enter NANKI-POO *in great excitement. He carries a native guitar on his back and a bundle of ballads in his hand*

RECIT—NANKI-POO

Gentlemen, I pray you tell me
Where a gentle maiden dwelleth,
Named Yum-Yum, the ward of Ko-Ko?
In pity speak—oh, speak, I pray you!

A Noble

Why, who are you who ask this question?

Nank.

Come gather round me, and I'll tell you.

SONG AND CHORUS—NANKI-POO

A wandering minstrel I—
  A thing of shreds and patches,
  Of ballads, songs and snatches,
And dreamy lullaby!
My catalogue is long,
  Through every passion ranging,
  And to your humours changing
I tune my supple song!
  Are you in sentimental mood?
  I'll sigh with you,
    Oh, sorrow, sorrow!
  On maiden's coldness do you brood?
  I'll do so, too—
    Oh, sorrow, sorrow!
  I'll charm your willing ears
  With songs of lovers' fears,
  While sympathetic tears
    My cheeks bedew—
    Oh, sorrow, sorrow!
But if patriotic sentiment is wanted,
  I've patriotic ballads cut and dried;
For where'er our country's banner may be planted,
  All other local banners are defied!

1

Our warriors, in serried ranks assembled,
  Never quail—or they conceal it if they
      do—
And I shouldn't be surprised if nations
  trembled
  Before the mighty troops of Titipu!
        Chorus
We shouldn't be surprised, etc.
        Nank.

And if you call for a song of the sea,
  We'll heave the capstan round,
With a yeo heave ho, for the wind is free,
Her anchor's a-trip and her helm's a-lee,
  Hurrah for the homeward bound!
        Chorus
  Yeo-ho—heave ho—
Hurrah for the homeward bound!
To lay aloft in a howling breeze
May tickle a landsman's taste,
But the happiest hour a sailor sees
  Is when he's down
  At an inland town,
With his Nancy on his knees, yeo ho!
And his arm around her waist!
        Chorus
  Then man the capstan—off we go,
    As a fiddler swings us round,
  With a yeo heave ho,
  And a rumbelow,
    Hurrah for the homeward bound!
A wandering minstrel I, etc.
      Enter PISH-TUSH

Pish. And what may be your business
with Yum-Yum?

Nank. I'll tell you. A year ago I was a
member of the Titipu town band. It was
my duty to take the cap round for contri-
butions. While discharging this delicate office, I saw Yum-Yum. We loved each other
at once, but she was betrothed to her
guardian Ko-Ko, a cheap tailor, and I saw
that my suit was hopeless. Overwhelmed
with despair, I quitted the town. Judge of
my delight when I heard, a month ago, that
Ko-Ko had been condemned to death for
flirting! I hurried back at once, in the hope
of finding Yum-Yum at liberty to listen to
my protestations.

Pish. It is true that Ko-Ko was condemned to death for flirting, but he was
reprieved at the last moment, and raised to
the exalted rank of Lord High Executioner
under the following remarkable circumstances:

SONG—PISH-TUSH *and* CHORUS

Our great Mikado, virtuous man,
When he to rule our land began,
  Resolved to try
  A plan whereby
Young men might best be steadied.
So he decreed, in words succinct,
That all who flirted, leered or winked
(Unless connubially linked),
  Should forthwith be beheaded.
    And I expect you'll all agree
    That he was right to so decree.
    And I am right,
    And you are right,
    And all is right as right can be!
        Chorus
    And you are right,
    And we are right, etc.
This stern decree, you'll understand,
Caused great dismay throughout the land!
  For young and old
  And shy and bold
Were equally affected.
The youth who winked a roving eye,
Or breathed a non-connubial sigh,
Was thereupon condemned to die—
  He usually objected.
    And you'll allow, as I expect,
    That he was right to so object.
    And I am right,
    And you are right,
    And everything is quite correct!
        Chorus
    And you are right,
    And we are right, etc.
And so we straight let out on bail,
A convict from the county jail,
  Whose head was next
  On some pretext
Condemnèd to be mown off,
And made *him* Headsman, for we said,
"Who's next to be decapited
Cannot cut off another's head
  Until he's cut his own off."
    And we are right, I think you'll say,
    To argue in this kind of way;
    And I am right,
    And you are right,
    And all is right—too-looral-lay!
        Chorus
    And you are right,
    And we are right, etc.
          [*Exeunt* CHORUS.

Enter POOH-BAH

Nank. Ko-ko, the cheap tailor, Lord High Executioner of Titipu! Why, that's the highest rank a citizen can attain!

Pooh. It is. Our logical Mikado, seeing no moral difference between the dignified judge who condemns a criminal to die, and the industrious mechanic who carries out the sentence, has rolled the two offices into one, and every judge is now his own executioner.

Nank. But how good of you (for I see that you are a nobleman of the highest rank) to condescend to tell all this to me, a mere strolling minstrel!

Pooh. Don't mention it. I am, in point of fact, a particularly haughty and exclusive person, of pre-Adamite ancestral descent. You will understand this when I tell you that I can trace my ancestry back to a protoplasmal primordial atomic globule. Consequently, my family pride is something inconceivable. I can't help it. I was born sneering. But I struggle hard to overcome this defect. I mortify my pride continually. When all the great officers of State resigned in a body, because they were too proud to serve under an ex-tailor, did I not unhesitatingly accept all their posts at once?

Pish. And the salaries attached to them? You did.

Pooh. It is consequently my degrading duty to serve this upstart as First Lord of the Treasury, Lord Chief Justice, Commander-in-Chief, Lord High Admiral, Master of the Buckhounds, Groom of the Back Stairs, Archbishop of Titipu, and Lord Mayor, both acting and elect, all rolled into one. And at a salary! A Pooh-Bah paid for his services! I a salaried minion! But I do it! It revolts me, but I do it!

Nank. And it does you credit.

Pooh. But I don't stop at that. I go and dine with middle-class people on reasonable terms. I dance at cheap suburban parties for a moderate fee. I accept refreshment at any hands, however lowly. I also retail State secrets at a very low figure. For instance, any further information about Yum-Yum would come under the head of a State secret. (NANKI-POO *takes the hint, and gives him money*.) (*Aside.*) Another insult, and, I think, a light one!

SONG—POOH-BAH *with* NANKI-POO *and* PISH-TUSH

Young man, despair,
    Likewise go to,
Yum-Yum the fair
    You must not woo.
    It will not do:
    I'm sorry for you,
You very imperfect ablutioner!
    This very day
    From school Yum-Yum
Will wend her way,
    And homeward come,
    With beat of drum
    And a rum-tum-tum,
To wed the Lord High Executioner!
And the brass will crash,
    And the trumpets bray,
    And they'll cut a dash
    On their wedding day.
She'll toddle away, as all aver,
With the Lord High Executioner!

Nank. and Pooh.

And the brass will crash, etc.
    It's a hopeless case,
    As you may see,
And in your place
    Away I'd flee;
    But don't blame me—
    I'm sorry to be
Of your pleasure a diminutioner.
    They'll vow their pact
    Extremely soon,
In point of fact
    This afternoon.
    Her honeymoon
    With that buffoon
At seven commences, so *you* shun her!

All

And the brass will crash, etc.
                                    [*Exit* PISH-TUSH.

RECIT NANKI-POO *and* POOH-BAH

Nank.

And I have journeyed for a month, or nearl ,
To learn that Yum-Yum, whom I love so dearly,
This day to Ko-Ko is to be united!

Pooh.

The fact appears to be as you've recited:
But here he comes, equipped as suits his station;
He'll give you any further information.
                        [*Exeunt* POOH-BAH *and* NANKI-POO.

Enter CHORUS OF NOBLES

Behold the Lord High Executioner
    A personage of noble rank and title—
A dignified and potent officer,
    Whose functions are particularly vital!
      Defer, defer,
    To the Lord High Executioner!
    Enter KO-KO *attended*

SOLO—KO-KO

Taken from the county jail
    By a set of curious chances;
Liberated then on bail,
    On my own recognizances;
Wafted by a favouring gale
    As one sometimes is in trances,
To a height that few can scale,
    Save by long and weary dances;
Surely, never had a male
    Under such like circumstances
So adventurous a tale
    Which may rank with most romances.

Chorus

    Defer, defer,
    To the Lord High Executioner, etc.

Ko. Gentlemen, I'm much touched by
this reception. I can only trust that by
strict attention to duty I shall ensure a
continuance of those favours which it will
ever be my study to deserve. If I should
ever be called upon to act professionally,
I am happy to think that there will be no
difficulty in finding plenty of people whose
loss will be a distinct gain to society at
large.

SONG—KO-KO *with* CHORUS OF MEN

As some day it may happen that a victim
    must be found,
    I've got a little list—I've got a little list
Of society offenders who might well be
    underground,
    And who never would be missed—who
      never would be missed!
There's the pestilential nuisances who write
    for autographs—
All people who have flabby hands and
    irritating laughs—
All children who are up in dates, and floor
    you with 'em flat—
All persons who in shaking hands, shake
    hands with you like *that*—
And all third persons who on spoiling *tête-
    à-têtes* insist—
    They'd none of 'em be missed—they'd
      none of 'em be missed!

Chorus

He's got 'em on the list—he's got 'em on
    the list;
    And they'll none of 'em be missed—
      they'll none of 'em be missed.
There's the nigger serenader, and the others
    of his race,
    And the piano-organist—I've got him on
      the list!
And the people who eat peppermint and
    puff it in your face,
    They never would be missed—they never
      would be missed!
Then the idiot who praises, with enthusi-
    astic tone,
All centuries but this, and every country
    but his own;
    And the lady from the provinces, who
      dresses like a guy,
And who "doesn't think she waltzes, but
    would rather like to try";
And that singular anomaly, the lady nov-
    elist—
    I don't think she'd be missed—I'm *sure*
      she'd not be missed!

Chorus

He's got her on the list—he's got her on
    the list;
    And I don't think she'll be missed—I'm
      sure she'll not be missed!
And that *Nisi Prius* nuisance, who just now
    is rather rife,
    The Judicial humorist—I've got *him* on
      the list!
All funny fellows, comic men, and clowns
    of private life—
    They'd none of 'em be missed—they'd
      none of 'em be missed.
And apologetic statesmen of a compromis-
    ing kind,
Such as—What d'ye call him—Thing'em-
    bob, and likewise—Never-mind,
And 'St—'st—'st—and What's-his-name,
    and also You-know-who—
The task of filling up the blanks I'd rather
    leave to *you*.
But it really doesn't matter whom you put
    upon the list,
    For they'd none of 'em be missed—they'd
      none of 'em be missed!

Chorus

You may put 'em on the list—you may put
    'em on the list;

And they'll none of 'em be missed—
they'll none of 'em be missed!

Enter POOH-BAH

Ko. Pooh-Bah, it seems that the festivities in connection with my approaching marriage must last a week. I should like to do it handsomely, and I want to consult you as to the amount I ought to spend upon them.

Pooh. Certainly. In which of my capacities? As first Lord of the Treasury, Lord Chamberlain, Attorney-General, Chancellor of the Exchequer, Privy Purse, or Private Secretary?

Ko. Suppose we say as Private Secretary.

Pooh. Speaking as your Private Secretary, I should say that, as the city will have to pay for it, don't stint yourself, do it well.

Ko. Exactly—as the city will have to pay for it. That is your advice.

Pooh. As Private Secretary. Of course you will understand that, as Chancellor of the Exchequer, I am bound to see that due economy is observed.

Ko. Oh! But you said just now "Don't stint yourself, do it well."

Pooh. As Private Secretary.

Ko. And now you say that due economy must be observed.

Pooh. As Chancellor of the Exchequer.

Ko. I see. Come over here, where the Chancellor can't hear us. (*They cross the stage.*) Now, as my Solicitor, how do you advise me to deal with this difficulty?

Pooh. Oh, as your Solicitor, I should have no hesitation in saying "Chance it——"

Ko. Thank you. (*Shaking his hand.*) I will.

Pooh. If it were not that, as Lord Chief Justice, I am bound to see that the law isn't violated.

Ko. I see. Come over here where the Chief Justice can't hear us. (*They cross the stage.*) Now, then, as First Lord of the Treasury?

Pooh. Of course, as First Lord of the Treasury, I could propose a special vote that would cover all expenses, if it were not that, as Leader of the Opposition, it would be my duty to resist it, tooth and nail. Or, as Paymaster-General, I could so cook the accounts that, as Lord High Auditor, I should never discover the fraud. But then, as Archbishop of Titipu, it would be my duty to denounce my dishonesty and give myself into my own custody as First Commissioner of Police.

Ko. That's extremely awkward.

Pooh. I don't say that all these distinguished people couldn't be squared; but it is right to tell you that they wouldn't be sufficiently degraded in their own estimation unless they were insulted with a very considerable bribe.

Ko. The matter shall have my careful consideration. But my bride and her sisters approach, and any little compliment on your part, such as an abject grovel in a characteristic Japanese attitude, would be esteemed a favour.

[*Exeunt together.*

Enter procession of YUM-YUM'S *schoolfellows, heralding* YUM-YUM, PEEP-BO, *and* PITTI-SING.

CHORUS OF GIRLS

Comes a train of little ladies
  From scholastic trammels free,
Each a little bit afraid is,
  Wondering what the world can be!
Is it but a world of trouble—
  Sadness set to song?
Is its beauty but a bubble
  Bound to break ere long?
Are its palaces and pleasures
  Fantasies that fade?
And the glory of its treasures
  Shadow of a shade?
Schoolgirls we, eighteen and under,
  From scholastic trammels free,
And we wonder—how we wonder!—
  What on earth the world can be!

TRIO

YUM-YUM, PEEP-BO *and* PITTI-SING, *with*
CHORUS OF GIRLS

The Three

Three little maids from school are we,
Pert as a school-girl well can be,
Filled to the brim with girlish glee,
  Three little maids from school!

Yum-Yum

Everything is a source of fun. (*Chuckle*)

Peep-Bo

Nobody's safe, for we care for none!
  (*Chuckle*)

Pitti-Sing

Life is a joke that's just begun! (*Chuckle*)

The Three

Three little maids from school!

ALL (*dancing*)

Three little maids who, all unwary,
Come from a ladies' seminary,
Freed from its genius tutelary—

THE THREE (*suddenly demure*)

Three little maids from school!

Yum-Yum

One little maid is a bride, Yum-Yum—

Peep-Bo

Two little maids in attendance come—

Pitti-Sing

Three little maids is the total sum.

The Three

Three little maids from school!

Yum-Yum

From three little maids take one away.

Peep-Bo

Two little maids remain, and they—

Pitti-Sing

Won't have to wait very long, they say—

The Three

Three little maids from school!

ALL (*dancing*)

Three little maids who, all unwary,
Come from a ladies' seminary,
Freed from its genius tutelary—

THE THREE (*suddenly demure*). Three little maids from school!

Enter KO-KO *and* POOH-BAH

Ko. At last, my bride that is to be! (*About to embrace her.*)

Yum. You're not going to kiss me before all these people?

Ko. Well, that was the idea.

Yum. (*aside to* PEEP-BO). It seems odd, doesn't it?

Peep. It's rather peculiar.

Pitti. Oh, I expect it's all right. Must have a beginning, you know.

Yum. Well, of course I know nothing about these things; but I've no objection if it's usual.

Ko. Oh, it's quite usual, I think. Eh, Lord Chamberlain? (*Appealing to* POO-BAH.)

Pooh. I have known it done. (KO-KO *embraces her.*)

Yum. Thank goodness that's over! (*Sees* NANKI-POO, *and rushes to him.*) Why, that's never you? (*The Three Girls rush to him and shake his hands, all speaking at once.*)

Yum. Oh, I'm so glad! I haven't seen you for ever so long, and I'm right at the top of the school, and I've got three prizes, and I've come home for good, and I'm not going back any more!

Peep. And have you got an engagement? —Yum-Yum's got one, but she doesn't like it, and she'd ever so much rather it was you! I've come home for good, and I'm not going back any more!

Pitti. Now tell us all the news, because you go about everywhere, and we've been at school, but, thank goodness, that's all over now, and we've come home for good, and we're not going back any more!

(*These three speeches are spoken together in one breath.*)

Ko. I beg your pardon. Will you present me?

Yum. Oh, this is the musician who used—

Peep. Oh, this is the gentleman who used—

Pitti. Oh, it is only Nanki-Poo who used—

Ko. One at a time, if you please.

Yum. Oh, if you please, he's the gentleman who used to play so beautifully on the—on the—

Pitti. On the Marine Parade.

Yum. Yes, I think that was the name of the instrument.

Nank. Sir, I have the misfortune to love your ward, Yum-Yum—oh, I know I deserve your anger!

Ko. Anger! not a bit, my boy. Why, I love her myself. Charming little girl, isn't she? Pretty eyes, nice hair. Taking little thing, altogether. Very glad to hear my opinion backed by a competent authority. Thank you very much. Good-bye. (*To* PISH-TUSH.) Take him away. (PISH-TUSH *removes him.*)

Pitti. (*who has been examining* POOH-BAH). I beg your pardon, but what is this? Customer come to try on?

Ko. That is a Tremendous Swell.

Pitti. Oh, it's alive. (*She starts back in alarm.*)

Pooh. Go away, little girls. Can't talk to little girls like you. Go away, there's dears.

Ko. Allow me to present you, Pooh-Bah. These are my three wards. The one in the middle is my bride elect.

Pooh. What do you want me to do to them? Mind, I *will not* kiss them.

Ko. No, no, you shan't kiss them; a little bow—a mere nothing—you needn't mean it, you know.

Pooh. It goes against the grain. They are not young ladies, they are young persons.

Ko. Come, come, make an effort, there's a good nobleman.

Pooh. (*aside to* KO-KO). Well, I shan't mean it. (*With a great effort.*) How de do, little girls, how de do? (*Aside.*) Oh, my protoplasmal ancestor!

Ko. That's very good. (*Girls indulge in suppressed laughter.*)

Pooh. I see nothing to laugh at. It is very painful to me to have to say "How de do, little girls, how de do?" to young persons. I'm not in the habit of saying "How de do, little girls, how de do?" to anybody under the rank of a Stockbroker.

Ko. (*aside to girls*). Don't laugh at him, he can't help it—he's under treatment for it. (*Aside to* POOH-BAH.) Never mind them, they don't understand the delicacy of your position.

Pooh. We know how delicate it is, don't we?

Ko. I should think we did! How a nobleman of your importance can do it at all is a thing I never can, never shall understand.

[KO-KO *retires up and goes off.*

QUARTET AND CHORUS OF GIRLS

YUM-YUM, PEEP-BO, PITTI-SING, *and* POOH-BAH

Yum, Peep and Pitti

So please you, Sir, we much regret
If we have failed in etiquette
Towards a man of rank so high—
We shall know better by and by.

Yum.

But youth, of course, must have its fling,
So pardon us,
So pardon us,

Pitti.

And don't, in girlhood's happy spring,
Be hard on us,
Be hard on us,
If we're inclined to dance and sing.
Tra la la, etc. (*Dancing.*)

CHORUS OF GIRLS

But youth, of course, etc.

Pooh.

I think you ought to recollect

You cannot show too much respect
Towards the highly titled few;
But nobody does, and why should you?
That youth at us should have its fling,
Is hard on us,
Is hard on us;
To our prerogative we cling—
So pardon us,
So pardon us,
If we decline to dance and sing.
Tra la la, etc. (*Dancing.*)

CHORUS OF GIRLS

But youth, of course, must have its fling, etc.

[*Exeunt all but* YUM-YUM.

Enter NANKI-POO

Nank. Yum-Yum, at last we are alone! I have sought you night and day for three weeks, in the belief that your guardian was beheaded, and I find that you are about to be married to him this afternoon!

Yum. Alas, yes!

Nank. But you do not love him?

Yum. Alas, no!

Nank. Modified rapture! But why do you not refuse him?

Yum. What good would that do? He's my guardian, and he wouldn't let me marry you!

Nank. But I would wait until you were of age!

Yum. You forget that in Japan girls do not arrive at years of discretion until they are fifty.

Nank. True; from seventeen to forty-nine are considered years of indiscretion.

Yum. Besides — a wandering minstrel, who plays a wind instrument outside tea-houses, is hardly a fitting husband for the ward of a Lord High Executioner.

Nank. But—— (*Aside.*) Shall I tell her? Yes! She will not betray me! (*Aloud.*) What if it should prove that, after all, I am no musician?

Yum. There! I was certain of it, directly I heard you play!

Nank. What if it should prove that I am no other than the son of his Majesty the Mikado?

Yum. The son of the Mikado! But why is your Highness disguised? And what has your Highness done? And will your Highness promise never to do it again?

Nank. Some years ago I had the misfortune to captivate Katisha, an elderly lady of my father's Court. She misconstrued my customary affability into expressions of affection, and claimed me in marriage, under my father's law. My father, the Lucius Junius Brutus of his race, ordered me to marry her within a week, or perish ignominiously on the scaffold. That night I fled his Court, and, assuming the disguise of a Second Trombone, I joined the band in which you found me when I had the happiness of seeing you! (*Approaching her.*)

Yum. (*retreating*). If you please, I think your Highness had better not come too near. The laws against flirting are excessively severe.

Nank. But we are quite alone, and nobody can see us.

Yum. Still, that doesn't make it right. To flirt is capital.

Nank. It *is* capital!

Yum. And we must obey the law.

Nank. Deuce take the law!

Yum. I wish it would, but it won't!

Nank. If it were not for that, how happy we might be!

Yum. Happy indeed!

Nank. If it were not for the law, we should now be sitting side by side, like that. (*Sits by her.*)

Yum. Instead of being obliged to sit half a mile off, like that. (*Crosses and sits at other side of stage.*)

Nank. We should be gazing into each other's eyes, like that. (*Gazing at her sentimentally.*)

Yum. Breathing sighs of unutterable love —like that. (*Sighing and gazing lovingly at him.*)

Nank. With our arms round each other's waists, like that. (*Embracing her.*)

Yum. Yes, if it wasn't for the law.

Nank. If it wasn't for the law.

Yum. As it is, of course we couldn't do anything of th kind.

Nank. Not for worlds!

Yum. Being engaged to Ko-Ko, you know!

Nank. Being engaged to Ko-Ko!

DUET—YUM-YUM *and* NANKI-POO

Nank.

Were you not to Ko-Ko plighted,

I would say in tender tone,
"Loved one, let us be united—
Let us be each other's own!"
I would merge all rank and station,
  Worldly sneers are nought to us,
And, to mark my admiration,
  I would kiss you fondly thus—
                              (*Kisses her.*)

Both

$\left.\begin{array}{c}I\\He\end{array}\right\}$ would kiss $\left\{\begin{array}{c}you\\me\end{array}\right\}$ fondly thus—(*Kiss.*)

Yum.

But as I'm engaged to Ko-Ko,
To embrace you thus, *con fuoco,*
Would be distinctly no *giuoco,*
And for yam I should get toko—
                Both
Toko, toko, toko, toko!
                Nank.
So, in spite of all temptation,
  Such a theme I'll not discuss,
And on no consideration
  Will I kiss you fondly thus—
                              (*Kissing her.*)
Let me make it clear to you,
This is what I'll never do!
  This, oh, this, oh, this, oh, this—
                              (*Kissing her.*)

Together

This, oh, this, etc.
        [*Exeunt in opposite directions.*
            Enter KO-KO

Ko. (*looking after* YUM-YUM). There she goes! To think how entirely my future happiness is wrapped up in that little parcel! Really, it hardly seems worth while! Oh, matrimony!— (*Enter* POOH-BAH *and* PISH-TUSH.) Now then, what is it? Can't you see I'm soliloquizing? You have interrupted an apostrophe, sir!

Pish. I am the bearer of a letter from his Majesty the Mikado.

Ko. (*taking it from him reverentially*). A letter from the Mikado! What in the world can he have to say to me? (*Reads letter.*) Ah, here it is at last! I thought it would come sooner or later! The Mikado is struck by the fact that no executions have taken place in Titipu for a year and decrees that unless somebody is beheaded within one month the post of Lord High Executioner shall be abolished, and the city reduced to the rank of a village!

Pish. But that will involve us all in irretrievable ruin!

Ko. Yes. There is no help for it, I shall have to execute somebody at once. The only question is, who shall it be?

Pooh. Well, it seems unkind to say so, but as you're already under sentence of death for flirting, everything seems to point to *you.*

Ko. To me? What are you talking about? I can't execute myself.

Pooh. Why not?

Ko. Why not? Because, in the first place, self-decapitation is an extremely difficult, not to say dangerous, thing to attempt; and, in the second, it's suicide, and suicide is a capital offence.

Pooh. That is so, no doubt.

Pish. We might reserve that point.

Pooh. True, it could be argued six months hence, before the full Court.

Ko. Besides, I don't see how a man *can* cut off his own head.

Pooh. A man might try.

Pish. Even if you only succeeded in cutting it half off, that would be something.

Pooh. It would be taken as an earnest of your desire to comply with the Imperial will.

Ko. No. Pardon me, but there I am adamant. As official Headsman, my reputation is at stake, and I can't consent to embark on a professional operation unless I see my way to a successful result.

Pooh. This professional conscientiousness is highly creditable to *you,* but it places us in a very awkward position.

Ko. My good sir, the awkwardness of your position is grace itself compared with that of a man engaged in the act of cutting off his own head.

Pish. I am afraid that, unless you can obtain a substitute——

Ko. A substitute? Oh, certainly—nothing easier. (*To* POOH-BAH.) I appoint you Lord High Substitute.

Pooh. I should be delighted. Such an appointment would realize my fondest dreams. But no, at any sacrifice, I must set bounds to my insatiable ambition!

TRIO

KO-KO	POOH-BAH	PISH-TUSH
My brain it teems	I am so proud	I heard one day
With endless schemes	If I allowed	A gentleman say
Both good and new	My family pride	That criminals who
For Titipu;	To be my guide,	Are cut in two
But if I flit,	I'd volunteer	Can hardly feel
The benefit	To quit this sphere	The fatal steel,
That I'd diffuse	Instead of you,	And so are slain
The town would lose!	In a minute or two.	Without much pain.
Now every man	But family pride	If this is true,
To aid his clan	Must be denied,	It's jolly for you;
Should plot and plan	And set aside,	Your courage screw
As best he can,	And mortified.	To bid us adieu,
And so,	And so,	And go
Although	Although	And show
I'm ready to go,	I wish to go,	Both friend and foe
Yet recollect	And greatly pine	How much you dare.
'Twere disrespect	To brightly shine,	I'm quite aware
Did I neglect	And take the line	It's your affair,
To thus effect	Of a hero fine,	Yet I declare
This aim direct,	With grief condign	I'd take your share,
So I object—	I must decline—	But I don't much care—
So I object—	I must decline—	I don't much care—
So I object—	I must decline—	I don't much care—

All

To sit in solemn silence in a dull, dark
    dock,
In a pestilential prison, with a life-long
    lock,
Awaiting the sensation of a short, sharp
    shock,
From a cheap and chippy chopper on a
    big black block!

               [*Exeunt* POOH *and* PISH.

Ko. This is simply appalling! I, who allowed myself to be respited at the last moment, simply in order to benefit my native town, am now required to die within a month, and that by a man whom I have loaded with honours! Is this public gratitude? Is this—— (*Enter* NANKI-POO, *with a rope in his hands.*) Go away, sir! How dare you? Am I never to be permitted to soliloquize?

Nank. Oh, go on—don't mind me.

Ko. What are you going to do with that rope?

Nank. I am about to terminate an unendurable existence.

Ko. Terminate your existence? Oh, nonsense! What for?

Nank. Because you are going to marry the girl I adore.

Ko. Nonsense, sir. I won't permit it. I am a humane man, and if you attempt anything of the kind I shall order your instant arrest. Come, sir, desist at once or I summon my guard.

Nank. That's absurd. If you attempt to raise an alarm, I instantly perform the Happy Despatch with this dagger.

Ko. No, no, don't do that. This is horrible! (*Suddenly.*) Why, you cold-blooded scoundrel, are you aware that, in taking your life, you are committing a crime which—which—which is—— Oh! (*Struck by an idea.*) Substitute!

Nank. What's the matter?

Ko. Is it *absolutely certain* that you are resolved to die?

Nank. Absolutely!

Ko. Will *nothing* shake your resolution?

Nank. Nothing.

Ko. Threats, entreaties, prayers—all useless?

Nank. All! My mind is made up.

Ko. Then, if you really mean what you say, and if you are absolutely resolved to die, and if nothing whatever will shake your determination—don't spoil yourself by committing suicide, but be beheaded handsomely at the hands of the Public Executioner!

Nank. I don't see how that would benefit me.

Ko. You don't? Observe: you'll have a month to live, and you'll live like a fighting-cock at my expense. When the day comes there'll be a grand public ceremonial —you'll be the central figure—no one will attempt to deprive you of that distinction. There'll be a procession — bands — dead march—bells tolling—all the girls in tears —Yum-Yum distracted—then, when it's all over, general rejoicings, and a display of fireworks in the evening. *You* won't see them, but they'll be there all the same.

Nank. Do you think Yum-Yum would really be distracted at my death?

Ko. I am convinced of it. Bless you, she's the most tender-hearted little creature alive.

Nank. I should be sorry to cause her pain. Perhaps, after all, if I were to withdraw from Japan, and travel in Europe for a couple of years, I might contrive to forget her.

Ko. Oh, I don't think you could forget Yum-Yum so easily; and, after all, what is more miserable than a love-blighted life?

Nank. True.

Ko. Life without Yum-Yum—why, it seems absurd!

Nank. And yet there are a good many people in the world who have to endure it.

Ko. Poor devils, yes! You are quite right not to be of their number.

Nank. (*suddenly*). I *won't* be of their number!

Ko. Noble fellow!

Nank. I'll tell you how we'll manage it Let me marry Yum-Yum to-morrow, and in a month you may behead me.

Ko. No, no. I draw the line at Yum-Yum.

Nank. Very good. If you can draw the line, so can I. (*Preparing rope.*)

Ko. Stop, stop—listen one moment—be reasonable. How can I consent to your marrying Yum-Yum if I'm going to marry her myself?

Nank. My good friend, she'll be a widow

in a month, and you can marry her then.

Ko. That's true, of course. I quite see that. But, dear me! my position during the next month will be most unpleasant—most unpleasant.

Nank. Not half so unpleasant as my position at the end of it.

Ko. But—dear me!—well—I agree—after all, it's only putting off my wedding for a month. But you won't prejudice her against me, will you? You see, I've educated her to be my wife; she's been taught to regard me as a wise and good man. Now I shouldn't like her views on that point disturbed.

Nank. Trust me, she shall never learn the truth from me.

FINALE

Enter CHORUS, POOH-BAH, *and* PISH-TUSH

Chorus
With aspect stern
  And gloomy stride,
We come to learn
  How you decide.
Don't hesitate
  Your choice to name,
A dreadful fate
  You'll suffer all the same.

Pooh.
To ask you what you mean to do we punctually appear.

Ko.
Congratulate me, gentlemen, I've found a Volunteer!

All
The Japanese equivalent for Hear, Hear, Hear!

Ko (*presenting him*).
'Tis Nanki-Poo!

All
Hail, Nanki-Poo!

Ko.
I think he'll do!

All
Yes, yes, he'll do!
He yields his life if I'll Yum-Yum surrender.
Now I adore that girl with passion tender,
And could not yield her with a ready will,
  Or her allot
  If I did not
Adore myself with passion tenderer still!
Enter YUM-YUM, PEEP-BO, *and* PITTI-SING

All
Ah, yes!
  He loves himself with passion tenderer still!

Ko. (*to* NANKI-POO)
Take her—she's yours!

            [*Exit* KO-KO.

ENSEMBLE

Nanki-Poo
The threatened cloud has passed away,
Yum-Yum
And brightly shines the dawning day;
Nanki-Poo
What though the night may come too soon,
Yum-Yum
There's yet a month of afternoon!

NANKI-POO, POOH-BAH, YUM-YUM, PITTI-SING, *and* PEEP-BO
  Then let the throng
  Our joy advance,
  With laughing song
  And merry dance,

Chorus
With joyous shout and ringing cheer,
Inaugurate our brief career!
Pitti-Sing
A day, a week, a month, a year—
Yum.
Or far or near, or far or near,
Pooh.
Life's eventime comes much too soon,
Pitti-Sing
You'll live at least a honeymoon!
All
Then let the throng, etc.

Chorus
With joyous shout, etc.

SOLO—POOH-BAH
As in a month you've got to die,
  If Ko-Ko tells us true,
'Twere empty compliment to cry
  "Long life to Nanki-Poo!"
But as one month you have to live
  As fellow-citizen,
This toast with three times three we'll give—
  "Long life to you—till then!"

           [*Exit* POOH-BAH.

Chorus
May all good fortune prosper you,
May you have health and riches, too,
May you succeed in all you do!
  Long life to you—till then!

(Dance)
Enter KATISHA *melodramatically*
Kat.
Your revels cease! Assist me, all of you!
Chorus
Why, who is this whose evil eyes
Rain blight on our festivities?
Kat.
I claim my perjured lover, Nanki-Poo!
Oh, fool! to shun delights that never cloy!
Chorus
Go, leave thy deadly work undone!
Kat.
Come back, oh, shallow fool! come back
to joy!
Chorus
Away, away! ill-favoured one!
Nank (aside to YUM-YUM)
Ah!
'Tis Katisha!
The maid of whom I told you.
(About to go)
Kat. (detaining him)
No!
You shall not go,
These arms shall thus enfold you!
SONG—KATISHA
Kat. (addressing NANKI-POO)
Oh fool, that fleest
My hallowed joys!
Oh blind, that seest
No equipoise!
Oh rash, that judgest
From half, the whole!
Oh base, that grudgest
Love's lightest dole!
Thy heart unbind,
Oh fool, oh blind!
Give me my place,
Oh rash, oh base!
Chorus
If she's thy bride, restore her place,
Oh fool, oh blind, oh rash, oh base!
Kat. (addressing YUM-YUM)
Pink cheek, that rulest
Where wisdom serves!
Bright eye, that foolest
Heroic nerves!
Rose lip, that scornest
Lore-laden years!
Smooth tongue, that warnest
Who rightly hears!
Thy doom is nigh,
Pink cheek, bright eye!

Thy knell is rung,
Rose lip, smooth tongue!
Chorus
If true her tale, thy knell is rung,
Pink cheek, bright eye, rose lip, smooth
tongue!
Pitti-Sing
Away, nor prosecute your quest—
From our intention, well expressed,
You cannot turn us!
The state of your connubial views
Towards the person you accuse
Does not concern us!
For he's going to marry Yum-Yum—
All
Yum-Yum!

Pitti.
Your anger pray bury,
For all will be merry,
I think you had better succumb—
All
'Cumb—'cumb!
Pitti.
And join our expressions of glee.
On this subject I pray you be dumb—
All
Dumb—dumb.
Pitti.
You'll find there are many
Who'll wed for a penny—
The word for your guidance is "Mum"—
All
Mum—mum!
Pitti.
There's lots of good fish in the sea!
All
On this subject we pray you be dumb, etc.
SOLO—KATISHA
The hour of gladness
Is dead and gone;
In silent sadness
I live alone!
The hope I cherished
All lifeless lies,
And all has perished
Save love, which never dies!
Oh, faithless one, this insult you shall rue!
In vain for mercy on your knees you'll sue.
I'll tear the mask from your disguising!
Nank. (aside)
Now comes the blow!
Kat.
Prepare yourselves for news surprising!

Nank. (aside)
How foil my foe?
Kat.
No minstrel he, despite bravado!
Yum (aside, struck by an idea)
Ha! ha! I know!
Kat.
He is the son of your——
[NANKI-POO, YUM-YUM, *and* CHORUS, IN-
*terrupting, sing Japanese words, to
drown her voice.*
O ni! bikkuri shakkuri to!
Kat.
In vain you interrupt with this tornado!
He is the only son of your——
All
O ni! bikkuri shakkuri to!

Kat.
I'll spoil——
All
O ni! bikkuri shakkuri to!
Kat.
Your gay gambado!
He is the son——
All
O ni! bikkuri shakkuri to!
Of your——
All
O ni! bikkuri shakkuri to!
Kat.
The son of your——
All
O ni! bikkuri shakkuri to! oya! oya!

ENSEMBLE

KATISHA

Ye torrents roar!
Ye tempests howl!
Your wrath outpour
With angry growl!
Do ye your worst, my vengeance call
Shall rise triumphant over all!
Prepare for woe,
Ye haughty lords,
At once I go
Mikado-wards,
My wrongs with vengeance shall be
crowned!
My wrongs with vengeance shall be
crowned!

THE OTHERS

We'll hear no more,
Ill-omened owl,
To joy we soar,
Despite your scowl!
The echoes of our festival
Shall rise triumphant over all!
Away you go,
Collect your hordes;
Proclaim your woe
In dismal chords;
We do not heed their dismal sound,
For joy reigns everywhere around.
[KATISHA *rushes furiously up stage, clear-
ing the crowd away right and left,
finishing on steps at the back of stage.*

END OF ACT I

ACT II

SCENE.—KO-KO'S *Garden*
YUM-YUM *discovered seated at her bridal
toilet, surrounded by maidens, who
are dressing her hair and painting her
face and lips, as she judges of the
effect in a mirror.*
SOLO—PITTI-SING *and* CHORUS OF GIRLS
Chorus
Braid the raven hair—
Weave the supple tress—
Deck the maiden fair,
In her loveliness—
Paint the pretty face—
Dye the coral lip—

Emphasize the grace
Of her ladyship!
Art and nature, thus allied,
Go to make a pretty bride.
SOLO—PITTI-SING
Sit with downcast eye—
Let it brim with dew—
Try if you can cry—
We will do so, too.
When you're summoned, start
Like a frightened roe—
Flutter, little heart,
Colour, come and go!
Modesty at marriage-tide
Well becomes a pretty bride!

Chorus

Braid the raven hair, etc.

[*Exeunt* PITTI-SING, PEEP-BO, *and* CHORUS.

Yum. Yes, I am indeed beautiful! Sometimes I sit and wonder, in my artless Japanese way, why it is that I am so much more attractive than anybody else in the whole world. Can this be vanity? No! Nature is lovely and rejoices in her loveliness. I am a child of Nature, and take after my mother.

SONG—YUM-YUM

The sun, whose rays
Are all ablaze
  With ever-living glory,
Does not deny
His majesty—
  He scorns to tell a story!
He don't exclaim,
"I blush for shame,
  So kindly be indulgent."
But, fierce and bold,
In fiery gold,
  He glories all effulgent!
    I mean to rule the earth,
    As he the sky—
    We really know our worth,
    The sun and I!
Observe his flame,
That placid dame,
  The moon's Celestial Highness;
There's not a trace
Upon her face
  Of diffidence or shyness:
She borrows light
That, through the night,
  Mankind may all acclaim her!
And, truth to tell,
She lights up well,
  So I, for one, don't blame her!
    Ah, pray make no mistake,
    We are not shy;
    We're very wide awake,
    The moon and I!

Enter PITTI-SING *and* BEEP-BO

Yum. Yes, everything seems to smile upon me. I am to be married to-day to the man I love best, and believe I am the very happiest girl in Japan!

Peep. The happiest girl indeed, for she is indeed to be envied who has attained happiness in all but perfection.

Yum. In "all but" perfection?

Peep. Well, dear, it can't be denied that the fact that your husband is to be beheaded in a month, is, in its way, a drawback. It does seem to take the top off it, you know.

Pitti. I don't know about that. It all depends!

Peep. At all events, *he* will find it a drawback.

Pitti. Not necessarily. Bless you, it all depends!

Yum. (*in tears*). I think it very indelicate of you to refer to such a subject on such a day. If my married happiness *is* to be—to be——

Peep. Cut short.

Yum. Well, cut short—in a month, can't you let me forget it? (*Weeping.*)

Enter NANKI-POO, *followed by* PISH-TUSH

Nank. Yum-Yum in tears—and on her wedding morn!

Yum. (*sobbing*). They've been reminding me that in a month you're to be beheaded! (*Bursts into tears.*)

Pitti. Yes, we've been reminding her that you're to be beheaded. (*Bursts into tears.*)

Peep. It's quite true, you know, you *are* to be beheaded! (*Bursts into tears.*)

Nank. (*aside*). Humph! Now, some bridegrooms would be depressed by this sort of thing! (*Aloud.*) A month? Well, what's a month? Bah! These divisions of time are purely arbitrary. Who says twenty-four hours make a day?

Pitti. There's a popular impression to that effect.

Nank. Then we'll efface it. We'll call each second a minute—each minute an hour—each hour a day—and each day a year. At that rate we've about thirty years of married happiness before us!

Peep. And, at that rate, this interview has already lasted four hours and three-quarters!

[*Exit* PEEP-BO.

Yum. (*still sobbing*). Yes. How time flies when one is thoroughly enjoying oneself.

Nank. That's the way to look at it! Don't let's be downhearted! There's a silver lining to every cloud.

Yum. Certainly. Let's—let's be perfectly happy! (*Almost in tears.*)

Pish-Tush. By all means. Let's — let's thoroughly enjoy ourselves.

Pitti. It's—it's absurd to cry. (*Trying to force a laugh.*)

Yum. Quite ridiculous! (*Trying to laugh.*)

[*All break into a forced and melancholy laugh.*

MADRIGAL

YUM-YUM, PITTI-SING, NANKI-POO, *and* PISH-TUSH

Brightly dawns our wedding day;
    Joyous hour, we give thee greeting!
    Whither, whither art thou fleeting?
Fickle moment, prithee stay!
    What though mortal joys be hollow?
    Pleasures come, if sorrows follow:
Though the tocsin sound, ere long,
    Ding dong! Ding dong!
Yet until the shadows fall
Over one and over all,
Sing a merry madrigal—
        A madrigal!
Fal-la—fal-la! etc. (*Ending in tears.*)
Let us dry the ready tear,
    Though the hours are surely creeping
    Little need for woeful weeping,
Till the sad sundown is near.
    All must sip the cup of sorrow—
    I to-day and thou to-morrow;
This the close of every song—
    Ding dong! Ding dong!
What, though solemn shadows fall,
Sooner, later, over all?
Sing a merry madrigal—
        A madrigal!
Fal-la—fal-la! etc. (*Ending in tears.*)

[*Exeunt* PITTI-SING *and* PISH-TUSH.

[NANKI-POO *embraces* YUM-YUM. *Enter* KO-KO. NANKI-POO *releases* YUM-YUM.

Ko. Go on—don't mind me.

Nank. I'm afraid we're distressing you.

Ko. Never mind, I must get used to it. Only please do it by degrees. Begin by putting your arm around her waist. (NANKI-POO *does so.*) There; let me get used to that first.

Yum. Oh, wouldn't you like to retire? It must pain you to see us so affectionate together!

Ko. No, I must learn to bear it! Now oblige me by allowing her head to rest on your shoulder.

Nank. Like that? (*He does so.* KO-KO *much affected.*)

Ko. I am much obliged to you. Now—

kiss her! (*He does so.* KO-KO *writhes with anguish.*) Thank you—it's simple torture!

Yum. Come, come, bear up. After all, it's only for a month.

Ko. No. It's no use deluding oneself with false hopes.

Nank. ⎫ What do you mean?
Yum.   ⎭

Ko. (*to* YUM-YUM). My child—my poor child! (*Aside.*) How shall I break it to her? (*Aloud.*) My little bride that was to have been?

Yum. (*delighted*). *Was* to have been?

Ko. Yes, you never can be mine!

Nank. ⎫ (*in ecstasy*). ⎧ What!
Yum. ⎭   ⎩ I'm so glad!

Ko. I've just ascertained that, by the Mikado's law, when a married man is beheaded his wife is buried alive.

Nank. ⎫ Buried alive!
Yum. ⎭

Ko. Buried alive. It's a most unpleasant death.

Nank. But whom did you get that from?

Ko. Oh, from Pooh-Bah. He's my Solicitor.

Yum. But he may be mistaken!

Ko. So I thought; so I consulted the Attorney-General, the Lord Chief Justice, the Master of the Rolls, the Judge Ordinary, and the Lord Chancellor. They're all of the same opinion. Never knew such unanimity on a point of law in my life!

Nank. But stop a bit! This law has never been put in force.

Ko. Not yet. You see, flirting is the only crime punishable with decapitation, and married men never flirt.

Nank. Of course, they don't. I quite forgot that! Well, I suppose I may take it that my dream of happiness is at an end!

Yum. Darling—I don't want to appear selfish, and I love you with all my heart— I don't suppose I shall ever love anybody else half as much—but when I agreed to marry you—my own—I had no idea—pet —that I should have to be buried alive in a month!

Nank. Nor I! It's the very first I've heard of it!

Yum. It—it makes a difference, doesn't it?

Nank. It *does* make a difference, of course.

Yum. You see—burial alive—it's such a stuffy death!

Nank. I call it a beast of a death.

Yum. You see my difficulty, don't you?

Nank. Yes, and I see my own. If I insist on your carrying out your promise, I doom you to a hideous death; if I release you, you marry KO-KO at once!

TRIO.—YUM-YUM, NANKI-POO, *and* KO-KO

Yum.

Here's a how-de-do!
If I marry you,
When your time has come to perish,
When the maiden whom you cherish
  Must be slaughtered, too!

Here's a how-de-do!
Nank.

Here's a pretty mess!
In a month, or less,
I must die without a wedding!
Let the bitter tears I'm shedding
  Witness my distress,
Here's a pretty mess!
Ko.

Here's a state of things!
To her life she clings!
Matrimonial devotion
Doesn't seem to suit her notion—
  Burial it brings!
Here's a state of things!

ENSEMBLE

YUM-YUM *and* NANKI-POO

With a passion that's intense
  I worship and adore,
But the laws of common sense
  We oughtn't to ignore.
If what he says is true,
  'Tis death to marry you!
Here's a pretty state of things!
  Here's a pretty how-de-do!

KO-KO

With a passion that's intense
  You worship and adore,
But the laws of common sense
  You oughtn't to ignore.
If what I say is true,
  'Tis death to marry you!
Here's a pretty state of things¡
  Here's a pretty how-de-do!

[*Exeunt* YUM-YUM.

Ko. (*going up to* NANKI-POO). My poor boy, I'm really very sorry for you.

Nank. Thanks, old fellow. I'm sure you are.

Ko. You see I'm quite helpless.

Nank. I quite see that.

Ko. I can't conceive anything more distressing than to have one's marriage broken off at the last moment. But you shan't be disappointed of a wedding—you shall come to mine.

Nank. It's awfully kind of you, but that's impossible.

Ko. Why so?

Nank. To-day I die.

Ko. What do you mean?

Nank. I can't live without Yum-Yum. This afternoon I perform the Happy Despatch.

Ko. No, no—pardon me—I can't allow that.

Nank. Why not?

Ko. Why, hang it all, you're under contract to die by the hand of the Public Executioner in a month's time! If you kill yourself, what's to become of me? Why, I shall have to be executed in your place!

Nank. It would certainly seem so!

Enter POOH-BAH

Ko. Now then, Lord Mayor, what is it?

Pooh. The Mikado and his suite are approaching the city and will be here in ten minutes.

Ko. The Mikado! He's coming to see whether his orders have been carried out! (*To* NANKI-POO.) Now look here, you know —this is getting serious—a bargain's a bargain, and you really mustn't frustrate the ends of justice by committing suicide. As a man of honour and a gentleman, you are bound to die ignominiously by the hands of the Public Executioner.

Nank. Very well, then—behead me.

Ko. What, now?

Nank. Certainly; at once.

Pooh. Chop it off! Chop it off!

Ko. My good sir, I don't go about prepared to execute gentlemen at a moment's notice. Why, I never even killed a bluebottle!

Pooh. Still, as Lord High Executioner—

Ko. My good sir, as Lord High Executioner, I've got to behead him in a month. I'm not ready yet. I don't know how it's done. I'm going to take lessons. I mean to begin with a guinea pig, and work my way through the animal kingdom till I come to a Second Trombone. Why, you don't suppose that, as a humane man, I'd have accepted the post of Lord High Executioner if I hadn't thought the duties were purely nominal? I *can't* kill you—I can't kill anything! I can't kill anybody! (*Weeps.*)

Nank. Come, my poor fellow, we all have unpleasant duties to discharge at times; after all, what is it? If I don't mind, why should you? Remember, sooner or later it must be done.

Ko. (*springing up suddenly.*) *Must it?* I'm not so sure about that!

Nank. What do you mean?

Ko. Why should I kill you when making an affidavit that you've been executed will do just as well? Here are plenty of witnesses—the Lord Chief Justice, Lord High Admiral, Commander-in-Chief, Secretary of State for the Home Department, First Lord of the Treasury, and Chief Commissioner of Police.

Nank. But where are they?

Ko. There they are. They'll all swear to it—won't you? (*To* POOH-BAH.)

Pooh. Am I to understand that all of us high Officers of State are required to perjure ourselves to ensure your safety?

Ko. Why not? You'll be grossly insulted, as usual.

Pooh. Will the insult be cash down, or at a date?

Ko. It will be a ready-money transaction.

Pooh. (*Aside*). Well, it will be a useful discipline. (*Aloud.*) Very good. Choose your fiction, and I'll endorse it! (*Aside.*) Ha! ha! Family Pride, how do you like *that,* my buck?

Nank. But I tell you that life without Yum-Yum——

Ko. Oh, Yum-Yum, Yum-Yum! Bother Yum-Yum! Here, Commissionaire (*to* POOH-BAH), go and fetch Yum-Yum. (*Exit* POOH-BAH.) Take Yum-Yum and marry Yum-Yum, only go away and never come back again. (*Enter* POOH-BAH *with* YUM-YUM.) Here she is. Yum-Yum, are you particularly busy?

Yum. Not particularly.

Ko. You've five minutes to spare?

Yum. Yes.

Ko. Then go along with his Grace the Archbishop of Titipu; he'll marry you at once.

Yum. But if I'm to be buried alive?

Ko. Now, don't ask any questions, but do as I tell you, and Nanki-Poo will explain all.

Nank. But one moment——

Ko. Not for worlds. Here comes the Mikado, no doubt to ascertain whether I've obeyed his decree, and if he finds you alive I shall have the greatest difficulty in persuading him that I've beheaded you. (*Exeunt* NANKI-POO *and* YUM-YUM, *followed by* POOH-BAH.) Close thing that, for here he comes! [*Exit* KO-KO

March.—Enter procession, heralding MIKADO, *with* KATISHA

Entrance of MIKADO *and* KATISHA

("*March of the Mikado's troops.*")

Chorus

Miya sama, miya sama,
On n'm-ma no mayé ni
Pira-Pira suru no wa
Nan gia na
Toko tonyaré tonyaré na?

DUET—MIKADO *and* KATISHA

Mikado

From every kind of man
   Obedience I expect;
I'm the Emperor of Japan—

Katisha

And I'm his daughter-in-law elect!
   He'll marry his son
   (He's only got one)
To his daughter-in-law elect.

Mikado

My morals have been declared
   Particularly correct;

Katisha

But they're nothing at all, compared
   With those of his daughter-in-law elect!
   Bow—Bow—
To his daughter-in-law elect!

All

Bow—Bow—
To his daughter-in-law elect!

Mikado
In a fatherly kind of way
    I govern each tribe and sect,
All cheerfully own my sway—
            Katisha
Except his daughter-in-law elect!
    As tough as a bone,
    With a will of her own,
Is his daughter-in-law elect!
            Mikado
My nature is love and light—
    My freedom from all defect—
            Katisha
Is insignificant quite,
    Compared with his daughter-in-law elect!
        Bow—Bow—
    To his daughter-in-law elect!
            All
        Bow—Bow—
    To his daughter-in-law elect!
        SONG—MIKADO *and* CHORUS
A more humane Mikado never
    Did in Japan exist,
    To nobody second,
    I'm certainly reckoned
A true philanthropist.
It is my very humane endeavour
    To make, to some extent,
    Each evil liver
    A running river
Of harmless merriment.
        My object all sublime
        I shall achieve in time—
    To let the punishment fit the crime—
        The punishment fit the crime;
    And make each prisoner pent
    Unwillingly represent
    A source of innocent merriment!
        Of innocent merriment!
All prosy dull society sinners,
    Who chatter and bleat and bore,
    Are sent to hear sermons
    From mystical Germans
Who preach from ten till four.
The amateur tenor, whose vocal villainies
    All desire to shirk,
    Shall, during off-hours,
    Exhibit his powers
To Madame Tussaud's waxwork.
The lady who dyes a chemical yellow
    Or stains her grey hair puce,
    Or pinches her figger,
    Is blacked like a nigger
With permanent walnut juice.

The idiot who, in railway carriages,
    Scribbles on window-panes,
        We only suffer
        To ride on a buffer
    In Parliamentary trains.
        My object all sublime, etc.
            Chorus
        His object all sublime, etc.
The advertising quack who wearies
    With tales of countless cures,
        His teeth, I've enacted,
        Shall all be extracted
    By terrified amateurs.
The music-hall singer attends a series
    Of masses and fugues and "ops"
        By Bach, interwoven
        With Spohr and Beethoven,
    At classical Monday Pops.
The billiard sharp whom any one catches,
    His doom's extremely hard—
        He's made to dwell—
        In a dungeon cell
    On a spot that's always barred.
And there he plays extravagant matches
    In fitless finger-stalls
        On a cloth untrue,
        With a twisted cue
    And elliptical billiard balls!
        My object all sublime, etc.

            Chorus
        His object all sublime, etc.
Enter POOH-BAH, KO-KO, *and* PITTI-SING.
        All kneel.
    (POOH-BAH *hands a paper to* KO-KO.)
Ko. I am honoured in being permitted
to welcome your Majesty. I guess the object of your Majesty's visit—your wishes
have been attended to. The execution has
taken place.
Mik. Oh, you've had an execution, have
you?
Ko. Yes. The Coroner has just handed
me his certificate.
Pooh. I am the Coroner. (KO-KO *hands
certificate to* MIKADO.)
Mik. And this is the certificate of his
death. (*Reads.*) "At Titipu, in the presence
of the Lord Chancellor, Lord Chief Justice,
Attorney-General, Secretary of State for
the Home Department, Lord Mayor, and
Groom of the Second Floor Front——"
Pooh. They were all present, your Majesty. I counted them myself.

Mik. Very good house. I wish I'd been in time for the performance.

Ko. A tough fellow he was, too—a man of gigantic strength. His struggles were terrific. It was really a remarkable scene.

Mik. Describe it.

TRIO AND CHORUS

KO-KO, PITTI-SING, POO-BAH *and* CHORUS

Ko.

The criminal cried, as he dropped him
    down,
  In a state of wild alarm—
With a frightful, frantic, fearful frown,
  I bared my big right arm.
I seized him by his little pig-tail,
  And on his knees fell he,
    As he squirmed and struggled,
    And gurgled and guggled,
  I drew my snickersnee!
    Oh, never shall I
    Forget the cry,
Or the shriek that shriekèd he,
    As I gnashed my teeth,
    When from its sheath
  I drew my snickersnee!

Chorus

  We know him well,
  He cannot tell
Untrue or groundless tales—
  He always tries
  To utter lies,
And every time he fails.

Pitti.

He shivered and shook as he gave the sign
  For the stroke he didn't deserve;
When all of a sudden his eye met mine,
  And it seemd to brace his nerve;
For he nodded his head and kissed his hand,
  And he whistled an air, did he,
    As the sabre true
    Cut cleanly through
His cervical vertebræ!
    When a man's afraid,
    A beautiful maid
Is a cheering sight to see;
    And it's oh, I'm glad
    That moment sad
Was soothed by sight of me!

Chorus

  Her terrible tale
  You can't assail,
With truth it quite agrees:
  Her taste exact
  For faultless fact

Amounts to a disease.

Pooh.

Now though you'd have said that head was
  dead
  (For its owner dead was he),
It stood on its neck, with a smile well-bred.
  And bowed three times to me!
It was none of your impudent off-hand
  nods,
  But as humble as could be;
    For it clearly knew
    The deference due
To a man of pedigree!
    And it's oh, I vow,
    This deathly bow
Was a touching sight to see;
    Though trunkless, yet
    It couldn't forget
The deference due to me!

Chorus

  This haughty youth,
  He speaks the truth
Whenever he finds it pays:
  And in this case
  It all took place
Exactly as he says!

        [Exeunt CHORUS.

Mik. All this is very interesting, and I should like to have seen it. But we came about a totally different matter. A year ago my son, the heir to the throne of Japan, bolted from our Imperial Court.

Ko. Indeed! Had he any reason to be dissatisfied with his position?

Kat. None whatever. On the contrary, I was going to marry him—yet he fled!

Pooh. I am surprised that he should have fled from one so lovely!

Kat. That's not true.

Pooh. No!

Kat. You hold that I am not beautiful because my face is plain. But you know nothing; you are still unenlightened. Learn, then, that it is not in the face alone that beauty is to be sought. My face is unattractive!

Pooh. It is.

Kat. But I have a left shoulder-blade that is a miracle of loveliness. People come miles to see it. My right elbow has a fascination that few can resist.

Pooh. Allow me!

Kat. It is on view Tuesdays and Fridays, on presentation of visiting card. As for my circulation, it is the largest in the world.

Ko. And yet he fled!

Mik. And is now masquerading in this town, disguised as a Second Trombone.

Ko.
Pooh. } A Second Trombone!
Pitti.

Mik. Yes; would it be troubling you too much if I asked you to produce him? He goes by the name of——

Kat. Nanki-Poo.

Mik. Nanki-Poo.

Ko. It's quite easy. That is, it's rather difficult. In point of fact, he's gone abroad!

Mik. Gone abroad! His address.

Ko. Knightsbridge!

Kat. (*who is reading certificate of death*). Ha!

Mik. What's the matter?

Kat. See here—his name—Nanki-Poo—beheaded this morning. Oh, where shall I find another? Where shall I find another?

[KO-KO, POOH-BAH, *and* PITTI-SING
fall on their knees.

Mik. (*looking at paper*). Dear, dear, dear! this is very tiresome. (*To* KO-KO.) My poor fellow, in your anxiety to carry out my wishes you have beheaded the heir to the throne of Japan!

Ko. I beg to offer an unqualified apology.

Pooh. I desire to associate myself with that expression of regret.

Pitti. We really hadn't the least notion——

Mik. Of course you hadn't. How could you? Come, come, my good fellow, don't distress yourself—it was no fault of yours. If a man of exalted rank chooses to disguise himself as a Second Trombone, he must take the consequences. It really distresses me to see you take on so. I've no doubt he thoroughly deserved all he got. (*They rise.*)

Ko. We are infinitely obliged to your Majesty——

Pitti. Much obliged, your Majesty.

Pooh. Very much obliged, your Majesty.

Mik. Obliged? not a bit. Don't mention it. How *could* you tell?

Pooh. No, of course we couldn't tell who the gentleman really was.

Pitti. It wasn't written on his forehead, you know.

Ko. It might have been on his pocket-handkerchief, but Japanese don't use pocket-handkerchiefs! Ha! ha! ha!

Mik. Ha! ha ha! (*To* KATISHA.) I forget the punishment for compassing the death of the Heir Apparent.

Ko.
Pooh. } Punishment. (*They drop down
Pitti. } on their knees again.*)

Mik. Yes. Something lingering, with boiling oil in it, I fancy. Something of that sort. I think boiling oil occurs in it, but I'm not sure. I know it's something humorous, but lingering, with either boiling oil or melted lead. Come, come, don't fret—I'm not a bit angry.

Ko. (*in abject terror*). If your Majesty will accept our assurance, we had no idea——

Mik. Of course——

Pitti. I knew nothing about it.

Pooh. I wasn't there.

Mik. That's the pathetic part of. Unfortunately, the fool of an Act says "compassing the death of the Heir Apparent." There's not a word about a mistake——

Ko., Pitti., and Pooh. No!

Mik. Or not knowing——

Ko. No!

Mik. Or having no notion——

Pitti. No!

Mik. Or not being there——

Pooh. No!

Mik. There should be, of course——

Ko., Pitti., and Pooh. Yes!

Mik. But there isn't.

Ko., Pitti., and Pooh. Oh!

Mik. That's the slovenly way in which these Acts are always drawn. However, cheer up, it'll be all right. I'll have it altered next session. Now, let's see about your execution—will after luncheon suit you? Can you wait till then?

Ko., Pitti., and Pooh. Oh, yes—we can wait till then!

Mik. Then we'll make it after luncheon.

Pooh. I don't want any lunch.

Mik. I'm really very sorry for you all, but it's an unjust world, and virtue is triumphant only in theatrical performances.

Glee

PITTI-SING, KATISHA, KO-KO, POOH-BAH,
and MIKADO

Mikado

See how the Fates their gifts allot,
For A is happy—B is not.
Yet B is worthy, I dare say,
Of more prosperity than A!

Ko., Pooh., and Pitti. Is B more worthy?

Katisha

I should say
He's worth a great deal more than A

Ensemble

Yet A is happy!
Oh, so happy!
Laughing, Ha! ha!
Chaffing, Ha! ha!
Nectar quaffing, Ha! ha! ha!
Ever joyous, ever gay,
Happy, undeserving A!

Ko., Pooh., and Pitti.

If I were Fortune—which I'm not—
B should enjoy A's happy lot,
And A should die in miserie—
That is, assuming I am B.

Mikado and Katisha

But *should* A perish?

Ko., Pooh., and Pitti.

That should he
(Of course, assuming I am B).
B should be happy!
Oh, so happy!
Laughing, Ha! ha!
Chaffing, Ha! ha!
Nectar quaffing, Ha! ha! ha!
But condemned to die is he,
Wretched meritorious B!

[*Exeunt* MIKADO *and* KATISHA.

Ko. Well, a nice mess you've got us into, with your nodding head and the deference due to a man of pedigree!

Pooh. Merely corroborative detail, intended to give artistic verisimilitude to an otherwise bald and unconvincing narrative.

Pitti. Corroborative detail indeed! Corroborative fiddlestick!

Ko. And you're just as bad as he is with your cock-and-a-bull stories about catching his eye and his whistling an air. But that's so like you! You must put in your oar!

Pooh. But how about your big right arm?

Pitti. Yes, and your snickersnee!

Ko. Well, well, never mind that now. There's only one thing to be done. Nanki-Poo hasn't started yet—he must come to life again at once. (*Enter* NANKI-POO *and*

YUM-YUM *prepared for journey.*) Here he comes. Here, Nanki-Poo, I've good news for you—you're reprieved.

Nank. Oh, but it's too late. I'm a dead man, and I'm off for my honeymoon.

Ko. Nonsense! A terrible thing has just happened. It seems you're the son of the Mikado.

Nank. Yes, but that happened some time ago.

Ko. Is this a time for airy persiflage? Your father is here, and with Katisha!

Nank. My father! And with Katisha!

Ko. Yes, he wants you particularly.

Pooh. So does she.

Yum. Oh, but he's married now.

Ko. But, bless my heart! what has that to do with it?

Nank. Katisha claims me in marriage, but I can't marry her because I'm married already—consequently she will insist on my execution, and if I'm executed, my wife will have to be buried alive.

Yum. You see our difficulty.

Ko. Yes. I don't know what's to be done.

Nank. There's one chance for you. If you could persuade Katisha to marry you, she would have no further claim on me, and in that case I could come to life without any fear of being put to death.

Ko. I marry Katisha!

Yum. I really think it's the only course.

Ko. But, my good girl, have you seen her? She's something appalling!

Pitti. Ah! that's only her face. She has a left elbow which people come miles to see!

Pooh. I am told that her right heel is much admired by connoisseurs.

Ko. My good sir, I decline to pin my heart upon any lady's right heel.

Nank. It comes to this: While Katisha is single, I prefer to be a disembodied spirit. When Katisha is married, existence will be as welcome as the flowers in spring.

DUET—NANKI-POO *and* KO-KO

(*With* YUM-YUM, PITTI-SING *and*

POOH-BAH)

Nanki-Poo

The flowers that bloom in the spring,
Tra la,
Breathe promise of merry sunshine—
As we merrily dance and we sing,
Tra la,
We welcome the hope that they bring,

Tra la,
Of a summer of roses and wine.
And that's what we mean when we
    say that a thing
Is welcome as flowers that bloom in
    the spring.
          Tra la la la la la, etc.

All

Tra la la la la, etc.
          Ko-Ko
The flowers that bloom in the spring,
          Tra la,
Have nothing to do with the case.
I've got to take under my wing,
          Tra la,
A most unattractive old thing,
          Tra la,
With a caricature of a face
And that's what I mean when I say, or
    I sing,
"Oh, bother the flowers that bloom in
    the spring."
          Tra la la la la la, etc.

All

Tra la la la, Tra la la la, etc.
          [*Dance and exeunt* NANKI-POO,
          YUM-YUM, POOH-BAH, PITTI-
          SING, *and* KO-KO.
          Enter KATISHA

RECITATIVE *and* SONG—KATISHA
Alone, and yet alive! Oh, sepulchre!
My soul is still my body's prisoner!
Remote the peace that Death alone can
    give—
My doom, to wait! my punishment, to
    live!

          SONG
Hearts do not break!
They sting and ache
For old love's sake,
    But do not die,
Though with each breath
They long for death
As witnesseth
          The living I!
          Oh, living I!
          Come, tell me why,
          When hope is gone,
          Dost thou stay on?
          Why linger here,
          Where all is drear?
          Oh, living I!
          Come, tell me why,

          When hope is gone,
          Dost thou stay on?
          May not a cheated maiden die?

Ko. (*entering and approaching her timidly*). Katisha!

Kat. The miscreant who robbed me of
my love! But vengeance pursues—they are
heating the cauldron!

Ko. Katisha—behold a suppliant at your
feet! Katisha—mercy!

Kat. Mercy? Had you mercy on him?
See here, you! You have slain my love. He
did not love me, but he would have loved
me in time. I am an acquired taste—only
the educated palate can appreciate *me*. I
was educating *his* palate when he left me.
Well, he is dead, and where shall I find
another? It takes years to train a man to
love me. Am I to go through the weary
round again, and, at the same time, implore mercy for you who robbed me of my
prey—I mean my pupil—just as his education was on the point of completion? Oh,
where shall I find another?

Ko. (*suddenly, and with great vehemence*). Here!—Here!

Kat. What!!!

Ko. (*with intense passion*). Katisha, for
years I have loved you with a white-hot
passion that is slowly but surely consum-
ing my very vitals! Ah, shrink not from
me! If there is aught of woman's mercy
in your heart, turn not away from a love-
sick suppliant whose every fibre thrills at
your tiniest touch! True it is, that under
a poor mask of disgust, I have endeavoured
to conceal a passion whose inner fires are
broiling the soul within me! But the fire
will not be smothered—it defies all attempts at extinction, and, breaking forth,
all the more eagerly for its long restraint,
it declares itself in words that will not be
weighed—that cannot be schooled—that
should not be too severely criticised. Katisha, I dare not hope for your love—but
I will not live without it! Darling!

Kat. You, whose hands still reek with
the blood of my betrothed, dare to address
words of passion to the woman you have
so foully wronged!

Ko. I do—accept my love, or I perish on
the spot!

Kat. Go to! Who knows so well as I

that no one ever yet died of a broken heart!

Ko. You know not what you say. Listen!

SONG—KO-KO

On a tree by a river a little tom-tit
    Sang "Willow, titwillow, titwillow!"
And I said to him, "Dicky-bird, why do you sit
    Singing 'Willow, titwillow, titwillow'?"
"Is it weakness of intellect, birdie?" I cried,
"Or a rather tough worm in your little inside?"
With a shake of his poor little head, he replied,
    "Oh, willow, titwillow, titwillow!"

He slapped at his chest, as he sat on that bough,
    Singing "Willow, titwillow, titwillow!"
And a cold perspiration bespangled his brow,
    Oh, willow, titwillow, titwillow!
He sobbed and he sighed, and a gurgle he gave,
Then he plunged himself into the billowy wave,
And an echo arose from the suicide's grave—
    "Oh, willow, titwillow, titwillow!"

Now I feel just as sure as I'm sure that my name
    Isn't Willow, titwillow, titwillow,
That 'twas blighted affection that made him exclaim
    "Oh, willow, titwillow, titwillow!"
And if you remain callous and obdurate, I
Shall perish as he did, and you will know why,
Though I probably shall not exclaim as I die,
    "Oh, willow, titwillow, titwillow!"

    [*During this song* KATISHA *has been greatly affected, and at the end is almost in tears.*

Kat. (*whimpering*). Did he really die of love?

Ko. He really did.

Kat. All on account of a cruel little hen?

Ko. Yes.

Kat. Poor little chap!

Ko. It's an affecting tale, and quite true. I knew the bird intimately.

Kat. Did you? He must have been very fond of her.

Ko. His devotion was something extraordinary.

Kat. (*still whimpering*). Poor little chap! And—and if I refuse you, will you go and do the same?

Ko. At once.

Kat. No, no—you musn't! Anything but that! (*Falls on his breast.*) Oh, I'm a silly little goose!

Ko. (*making a wry face*). You are!

Kat. And you won't hate me because I'm just a little teeny weeny wee bit bloodthirsty, will you?

Ko. Hate you? Oh, Katisha! Is there not beauty even in bloodthirstiness?

Kat. My idea exactly.

DUET—KATISHA *and* KO-KO

Katisha

There is beauty in the bellow of the blast,
    There is grandeur in the growling of the gale,
        There is eloquent outpouring
        When the lion is a-roaring,
    And the tiger is a-lashing of his tail!

Ko-Ko

        Yes, I like to see a tiger
        From the Congo or the Niger,
    And especially when lashing of his tail!

Katisha

Volcanoes have a splendour that is grim,
    And earthquakes only terrify the dolts,
        But to him who's scientific
        There's nothing that's terrific
    In the falling of a flight of thunderbolts!

Ko-Ko

        Yes, in spite of all my meekness,
        If I have a little weakness,
    It's a passion for a flight of thunderbolts!

Both

    If that is so,
        Sing derry down derry!
        It's evident, very,
            Our tastes are one.
    Away we'll go,
        And merrily marry,
        Nor tardily tarry
            Till day is done!

Ko-Ko

There is beauty in extreme old age—
    Do you fancy you are elderly enough?
    Information I'm requesting

On a subject interesting:
Is a maiden all the better when she's
    tough?

Katisha

Throughout this wide dominion
It's the general opinion
That she'll last a good deal longer when
    she's tough.

Ko-Ko

Are you old enough to marry, do you
    think?
Won't you wait till you are eighty in the
    shade?
There's a fascination frantic
In a ruin that's romantic;
Do you think you are sufficiently de-
    cayed?

Katisha

To the matter that you mention
I have given some attention,
And I think I am sufficiently decayed.

Both

If that is so,
        Sing derry down derry!
        It's evident, very,
            Our tastes are one!
Away we'll go,
        And merrily marry,
        Nor tardily tarry
            Till day is done!

    [*Exeunt together.*
Flourish. Enter the MIKADO, *attended by*
    PISH-TUSH *and Court*

Mik. Now then, we've had a capital
lunch, and we're quite ready. Have all the
painful preparations been made?

Pish. Your Majesty, all is prepared.

Mik. Then produce the unfortunate gentleman and his two well-meaning but misguided accomplices.

Enter KO-KO, KATISHA, POOH-BAH, *and*
    PITTI-SING

They throw themselves at the MIKADO'S *feet*

Kat. Mercy! Mercy for Ko-Ko! Mercy
for Pitti-Sing! Mercy even for Pooh-Bah!

Mik. I beg your pardon, I don't think I
quite caught that remark.

Pooh. Mercy even for Pooh-Bah.

Kat. Mercy! My husband that was to
have been is dead, and I have just married
this miserable object.

Mik. Oh! You've not been long about it!

Ko. We were married before the Registrar.

Pooh. I am the Registrar.

Mik. I see. But my difficulty is that, as
you have slain the Heir Apparent—

Enter NANKI-POO *and* YUM-YUM.

They kneel

Nanki. The Heir Apparent is *not* slain.

Mik. Bless my heart, my son!

Yum. And your daughter-in-law elected!

Kat. (*seizing Ko-Ko*). Traitor, you have
deceived me!

Mik. Yes, you are entitled to a little explanation, but I think he will give it better
whole than in pieces.

Ko. Your Majesty, it's like this: It is
true that I stated that I had killed Nanki-
Poo——

Mik. Yes, with most affecting particulars.

Pooh. Merely corroborative detail intended to give artistic verisimilitude to a
bald and——

Ko. Will you refrain from putting in
your oar? (*To* MIKADO.) It's like this:
When your Majesty says, "Let a thing be
done, it's as good as done—practically, it *is*
done—because your Majesty's will is law.
Your Majesty says, "Kill a gentleman,"
and a gentleman is told off to be killed.
Consequently, that gentleman is as good as
dead—practically, he *is* dead—and if he is
dead, why not say so?

Mik. I see. Nothing could possibly be
more satisfactory!

FINALE

Pitti-Sing

For he's gone and married Yum-Yum—

All

Yum-Yum!

Pitti-Sing

Your anger pray bury,
For all will be merry,
I think you had better succumb—

All

'Cumb—'cumb!

Pitti-Sing

And join our expressions of glee!

Ko-Ko

On this subject I pray you be dumb—

All

Dumb—dumb!

Ko-Ko

Your notions, though many,
Are not worth a penny,
The word for your guidance is "Mum"—

All

Mum—Mum!

Ko-Ko

You've a very good bargain in me.

All

On this subject we pray you be dumb—
Dumb—dumb!
We think you had better succumb—
'Cumb—'cumb!
You'll find there are many
Who'll wed for a penny,
There are lots of good fish in the sea.

Yum-Yum and Nanki-Poo

The threatened cloud has passed away,
And brightly shines the dawning day;
What though the night may come too soon,
We've years and years of afternoon!

All

Then let the throng
Our joy advance,
With laughing song
And merry dance,
With joyous shout and ringing cheer,
Inaugurate our new career!
Then let the throng, etc.

CURTAIN

H.M.S. PINAFORE

OR

THE LASS THAT LOVED A SAILOR

DRAMATIS PERSONÆ

THE RT. HON. SIR JOSEPH PORTER, K.C.B. (*First Lord of the Admiralty*)

CAPTAIN CORCORAN (*Commanding H.M.S. Pinafore*)

TOM TUCKER (*Midshipmite*)

RALPH RACKSTRAW (*Able Seaman*)

DICK DEADEYE (*Able Seaman*)

BILL BOBSTAY (*Boatswain's Mate*)

BOB BECKET (*Carpenter's Mate*)

JOSEPHINE (*the Captain's Daughter*)

HEBE (*Sir Joseph's First Cousin*)

MRS. CRIPPS (LITTLE BUTTERCUP) (*a Portsmouth Bumboat Woman*)

First Lord's Sisters, his Cousins, his Aunts, Sailors, Marines, etc.

ACT I.—*Noon*

ACT II.—*Night*

ACT I

SCENE.—*Quarter-deck of H.M.S. Pinafore. Sailors, led by* BOATSWAIN, *discovered cleaning brasswork, splicing rope, etc.*

CHORUS

We sail the ocean blue,
And our saucy ship's a beauty;
We're sober men and true,
And attentive to our duty.
When the balls whistle free
O'er the bright blue sea,
We stand to our guns all day;
When at anchor we ride
On the Portsmouth tide,
We have plenty of time to play.
Enter LITTLE BUTTERCUP, *with large basket on her arm*

RECIT

Hail, men-o'-war's men—safeguards of your nation,
Here is an end, at last, of all privation;
You've got your pay—spare all you can afford
To welcome Little Buttercup on board.

ARIA

For I'm called Little Buttercup—dear Little Buttercup,
Though I could never tell why,
But still I'm called Buttercup—poor little Buttercup,
Sweet Little Buttercup I!

I've snuff and tobaccy, and excellent jacky,
I've scissors, and watches, and knives;
I've ribbons and laces to set off the faces
Of pretty young sweethearts and wives.

I've treacle and toffee, I've tea and I've coffee,
Soft tommy and succulent chops;
I've chickens and conies, and pretty polonies,
And excellent peppermint drops.

Then buy of your Buttercup—dear Little Buttercup;
Sailors should never be shy;
So, buy of your Buttercup—poor Little Buttercup;
Come, of your Buttercup buy!

26

Boat. Aye, Little Buttercup—and well called—for you're the rosiest, the roundest, and the reddest beauty in all Spithead.

But. Red, am I? and round—and rosy! Maybe, for I have dissembled well! But mark ye, my merry friend—hast ever thought that beneath a gay and frivolous exterior there may lurk a canker-worm which is slowly but surely eating its way into one's very heart?

Boat. No, my lass, I can't say I've ever thought that.

Enter DICK DEADEYE. *He pushes through sailors, and comes down*

Dick. I have thought it often. (*All recoil from him.*)

But. Yes, you look like it! What's the matter with the man? Isn't he well?

Boat. Don't take no heed of *him;* that's only poor Dick Deadeye.

Dick. I say—it's a beast of a name, ain't it—Dick Deadeye?

But. It's not a nice name.

Dick. I'm ugly too, ain't I?

But. You are certainly plain.

Dick. And I'm three-cornered too, ain't I?

But. You are rather triangular.

Dick. Ha! ha! That's it. I'm ugly, and they hate me for it; for you all hate me, don't you?

All. We do!

Dick. There!

Boat. Well, Dick, we wouldn't go for to hurt any fellow-creature's feelings, but you can't expect a chap with such a name as Dick Deadeye to be a popular character—now can you?

Dick. No.

Boat. It's asking too much, ain't it?

Dick. It is. From such a face and form like mine the noblest sentiments sound like the black utterances of a depraved imagination. It is human nature—I am resigned.

RECIT

But. (*looking down hatchway*).
But, tell me—who's the youth whose faltering feet
    With difficulty bear him on his course?
Boat. That is the smartest lad in all the fleet—Ralph Rackstraw!
But. Ha! That name! Remorse! remorse!

Enter RALPH *from hatchway*
MADRIGAL—RALPH
The Nightingale
Sighed for the moon's bright ray,
    And told his tale
In his own melodious way!
He sang "Ah, well-a-day!"
        All
He sang "Ah, well-a-day!"
    The lowly vale
For the mountain vainly sighed,
    To his humble wail
The echoing hills replied.
    They sang "Ah, well-a-day!"
        All
    They sang "Ah, well-a-day!"

RECIT

I know the value of a kindly chorus,
    But choruses yield little consolation
When we have pain and sorrow too before us!
    I love—and love, alas, above my station!
But. (*aside*). He loves—and loves a lass above his station!
All (*aside*). Yes, yes, the lass is much above his station!
                    [*Exit* LITTLE BUTTERCUP
BALLAD—RALPH
A maiden fair to see,
The pearl of minstrelsy,
    A bud of blushing beauty;
For whom proud nobles sigh,
And with each other vie
    To do her menial's duty.
        All
To do her menial's duty.
A suitor, lowly born,
With hopeless passion torn,
    And poor beyond denying,
Has dared for her to pine
At whose exalted shrine
    A world of wealth is sighing.
        All
A world of wealth is sighing.
Unlearned he in aught
Save that which love has taught
    (For love had been his tutor);
Oh, pity, pity me—
Our captain's daughter she,
    And I that lowly suitor!
        All
And he that lowly suitor!
Boat. Ah, my poor lad, you've climbed too high: our worthy captain's child won't

have nothin' to say to a poor chap like you. Will she, lads?

All. No, no.

Dick. No, no, captains' daughters don't marry foremast hands.

All (*recoiling from him*). Shame! shame!

Boat. Dick Deadeye, them sentiments o' yourn are a disgrace to our common natur'.

Ralph. But it's a strange anomaly, that the daughter of a man who hails from the quarter-deck may not love another who lays out on the fore-yard arm. For a man is but a man, whether he hoists his flag at the main-truck or his slacks on the main-deck.

Dick. Ah, it's a queer world!

Ralph. Dick Deadeye, I have no desire to press hardly on you, but such a revolutionary sentiment is enough to make an honest sailor shudder.

Boat. My lads, our gallant captain has come on deck; let us greet him as so brave an officer and so gallant a seaman deserves.

Enter CAPTAIN CORCORAN

RECIT

Capt. My gallant crew, good morning.

All (*saluting*). Sir, good morning!

Capt. I hope you're all quite well.

All (*as before*). Quite well; and you, sir?

Capt. I am in reasonable health, and happy
    To meet you all once more.

All (*as before*). You do us proud, sir!

SONG—*Captain*

Captain

I am the Captain of the *Pinafore;*
          All
And a right good captain, too!
          Captain
    You're very, very good,
    And be it understood,
I command a right good crew.
          All
    We're very, very good,
    And be it understood,
He commands a right good crew.
          Captain
Though related to a peer,
I can hand, reef, and steer,
    And ship a selvagee;
I am never known to quail
At the fury of a gale,
    And I'm never, never sick at sea!

          All
What, never?
          Captain
No, never!
          All
What, *never?*
          Captain
Hardly ever!
          All
He's hardly ever sick at sea!
Then give three cheers, and one cheer more,
For the hardy Captain of the *Pinafore!*
          Captain
    I do my best to satisfy you all—
          All
And with you we're quite content.
          Captain
    You're exceedingly polite,
    And I think it only right
To return the compliment.
          All
    We're exceedingly polite,
    And he thinks it's only right
To return the compliment.
          Captain
Bad language or abuse,
    I never, never use.
Whatever the emergency;
    Though "Bother it" I may
Occasionally say,
I never use a big, big D—
          All
What, never?
          Captain
No, never!
          All
What, *never?*
          Captain
Hardly ever!
          All
Hardly ever swears a big, big D—
Then give three cheers, and one cheer more,
For the well-bred Captain of the *Pinafore.*
      [*After song exeunt all but* CAPTAIN
      Enter LITTLE BUTTERCUP

RECITATIVE

Buttercup

Sir, you are sad! The silent eloquence
Of yonder tear that trembles on your eye-lash
Proclaims a sorrow far more deep than common;
Confide in me—fear not—I am a mother!

Captain

Yes, Little Buttercup, I'm sad and sorry—
My daughter, Josephine, the fairest flower
That ever blossomed on ancestral timber,
Is sought in marriage by Sir Joseph Porter,
Our Admiralty's First Lord, but for some
    reason
She does not seem to tackle kindly to it.

Buttercup (with emotion)

Ah, poor Sir Joseph! Ah, I know too well
The anguish of a heart that loves but
    vainly!
But see, here comes your most attractive
    daughter.
I go—Farewell!

                  [*Exit*

Capt. (*looking after her*). A plump and
pleasing person!

                  [*Exit*

Enter JOSEPHINE, *twining some flowers
which she carries in a small basket*

BALLAD—*Josephine*

Sorry her lot who loves too well,
Heavy the heart that hopes but vainly,
Sad are the sighs that own the spell,
    Uttered by eyes that speak too plainly;
    Heavy the sorrow that bows the head
When love is alive and hope is dead!
Sad is the hour when sets the sun—
    Dark is the night to earth's poor daugh-
        ters,
When to the ark the wearied one
    Flies from the empty waste of waters!
    Heavy the sorrow that bows the head
    When love is alive and hope is dead!

Enter CAPTAIN

Capt. My child, I grieve to see that you
are a prey to melancholy. You should look
your best to-day, for Sir Joseph Porter,
K.C.B., will be here this afternoon to claim
your promised hand.

Jos. Ah, father, your words cut me to
the quick. I can esteem—reverence—ven-
erate Sir Joseph, for he is a great and good
man; but oh, I cannot love him! My heart
is already given.

Capt. (*aside*). It is then as I feared.
(*Aloud.*) Given? And to whom? Not to
some gilded lordling?

Jos. No, father—the object of my love is
no lordling. Oh, pity me, for he is but a
humble sailor on board your own ship!

Capt. Impossible!

Jos. Yes, it is true—too true.

Capt. A common sailor? Oh fie!

Jos. I blush for the weakness that allows
me to cherish such a passion. I hate myself
when I think of the depth to which I have
stooped in permitting myself to think tenderly of one so ignobly born, but I love
him! I love him! I love him! (*Weeps.*)

Capt. Come, my child, let us talk this
over. In a matter of the heart I would not
coerce my daughter—I attach but little
value to rank or wealth, but the line must
be drawn somewhere. A man in that station may be brave and worthy, but at
every step he would commit solecisms that
society would never pardon.

Jos. Oh, I have thought of this night
and day. But fear not, father, I have a
heart, and therefore I love; but I am your
daughter, and therefore I am proud.
Though I carry my love with me to the
tomb, he shall never, never know it.

Capt. You *are* my daughter after all. But
see, Sir Joseph's barge approaches, manned
by twelve trusty oarsmen and accompanied
by the admiring crowd of sisters, cousins,
and aunts that attend him wherever he
goes. Retire, my daughter, to your cabin—
take this, his photograph, with you—it
may help to bring you to a more reasonable frame of mind.

Jos. My own thoughtful father!

    [*Exit* JOSEPHINE. CAPTAIN *remains and
    ascends the poop-deck.*

BARCAROLLE (*invisible*)

Over the bright blue sea
Comes Sir Joseph Porter, K.C.B.,
    Wherever he may go
Bang-bang the loud nine-pounders go!
    Shout o'er the bright blue sea
For Sir Joseph Porter, K.C.B.

[*During this the Crew have entered on
tiptoe, listening attentively to the song.*

CHORUS OF SAILORS

Sir Joseph's barge is seen,
    And its crowd of blushing beauties,
We hope he'll find us clean,
    And attentive to our duties.
We sail, we sail the ocean blue,
    And our saucy ship's a beauty.
We're sober, sober men and true
    And attentive to our duty.
We're smart and sober men,
    And quite devoid of fe-ar,

In all the Royal N.
  None are so smart as we are.
  Enter SIR JOSEPH'S FEMALE RELATIVES
    (*They dance round stage*)
        Relatives
Gaily tripping,
Lightly skipping,
Flock the maidens to the shipping.
        Sailors
Flags and guns and pennants dipping!
All the ladies love the shipping.
        Relatives
Sailors sprightly
Always rightly
Welcome ladies so politely.
        Sailors
Ladies who can smile so brightly,
Sailors welcome most politely.
    Captain (*from poop*)
Now give three cheers, I'll lead the way
        All
Hurrah! hurrah! hurrah! hurray!
  Enter SIR JOSEPH *with* COUSIN HEBE
        SONG—*Sir Joseph*
I am the monarch of the sea,
  The ruler of the Queen's Navee,
Whose praise Great Britain loudly chants.
        Cousin Hebe
And we are his sisters, and his cousins
    and his aunts!
        Relatives
And we are his sisters, and his cousins
    and his aunts!
        Sir Joseph
When at anchor here I ride,
  My bosom swells with pride,
And I snap my fingers at a foeman's
    taunts;
        Cousin Hebe
And so do his sisters, and his cousins,
    and his aunts!
        All
And so do his sisters, and his cousins,
    and his aunts!
        Sir Joseph
But when the breezes blow,
  I generally go below,
And seek the seclusion that a cabin grants;
        Cousin Hebe
And so do his sisters, and his cousins,
    and his aunts!
        All
And so do his sisters, and his cousins,
    and his aunts!

His sisters and his cousins,
  Whom he reckons up by dozens,
    And his aunts!
        SONG—*Sir Joseph*
When I was a lad I served a term
As office boy to an Attorney's firm.
I cleaned the windows and I swept the
    floor,
And I polished up the handle of the big
    front door.
    I polished up that handle so carefullee
    That now I am the Ruler of the Queen's
      Navee!
        Chorus.—He polished, etc.
As office boy I made such a mark
That they gave me the post of a junior
    clerk.
I served the writs with a smile so bland,
And I copied all the letters in a big round
    hand—
    I copied all the letters in a hand so free,
    That now I am the Ruler of the Queen's
      Navee!
        Chorus.—He copied, etc.
In serving writs I made such a name
That an articled clerk I soon became;
I wore clean collars and a brand-new suit
For the pass examination at the Institute,
    And that pass examination did so well
      for me,
    That now I am the Ruler of the Queen's
      Navee!
Chorus.—And that pass examination, etc.
Of legal knowledge I acquired such a grip
That they took me into the partnership.
And that junior partnership, I ween,
Was the only ship that I ever had seen.
    But that kind of ship so suited me,
    That now I am the Ruler of the Queen's
      Navee!
        Chorus.—But that kind, etc.
I grew so rich that I was sent
By a pocket borough into Parliament.
I always voted at my party's call,
And I never thought of thinking for my-
    self at all.
    I thought so little, they rewarded me
    By making me the Ruler of the Queen's
      Navee!
        Chorus.—He thought so little, etc.
Now landsmen all, whoever you may be,
If you want to rise to the top of the tree,
If your soul isn't fettered to an office stool,

Be careful to be guided by this golden
rule—
Stick close to your desks and never go
to sea,
And you all may be Rulers of the Queen's
Navee!

  Chorus.—Stick close, etc.

Sir Joseph. You've a remarkably fine
crew, Captain Corcoran.

Capt. It *is* a fine crew, Sir Joseph.

Sir Joseph (*examining a very small mid-
shipman*). A British sailor is a splendid
fellow, Captain Corcoran.

Capt. A splendid fellow indeed, Sir
Joseph.

Sir Joseph. I hope you treat your crew
kindly, Captain Corcoran.

Capt. Indeed I hope so, Sir Joseph.

Sir Joseph. Never forget that they are
the bulwarks of England's greatness, Captain Corcoran.

Capt. So I have always considered them,
Sir Joseph.

Sir Joseph. No bullying, I trust—no
strong language of any kind, eh?

Capt. Oh, never, Sir Joseph.

Sir Joseph. What, *never?*

Capt. Hardly ever, Sir Joseph. They are
an excellent crew, and do their work thoroughly without it.

Sir Joseph. Don't patronise them, sir—
pray, don't patronise them.

Capt. Certainly not, Sir Joseph.

Sir Joseph. That you are their captain
is an accident of birth. I cannot permit
these noble fellows to be patronised because an accident of birth has placed you
above them and them below you.

Capt. I am the last person to insult a
British sailor, Sir Joseph.

Sir Joseph. You are the last person who
did, Captain Corcoran. Desire that splendid seaman to step forward.

   (DICK *comes forward.*)

Sir Joseph. No, no, the other splendid
seaman.

Capt. Ralph Rackstraw, three paces to
the front—march!

Sir Joseph (*sternly*). If what?

Capt. I beg your pardon—I don't think
I understand you.

Sir Joseph. If you *please.*

Capt. Oh, yes, of course. If you please.
(RALPH *steps forward.*)

Sir Joseph. You're a remarkably fine
fellow.

Ralph. Yes, your honour.

Sir Joseph. And a first-rate seaman, I'll
be bound.

Ralph. There's not a smarter topman in
the Navy, your honour, though I say it
who shouldn't.

Sir Joseph. Not at all. Proper self-respect,
nothing more. Can you dance a hornpipe?

Ralph. No, your honour.

Sir Joseph. That's a pity: all sailors
should dance hornpipes. I will teach you
one this evening, after dinner. Now tell
me—don't be afraid—how does your captain treat you, eh?

Ralph. A better captain don't walk the
deck, your honour.

All. Aye, Aye!

Sir Joseph. Good. I like to hear you
speak well of your commanding officer; I
daresay he don't deserve it, but still it
does you credit. Can you sing?

Ralph. I can hum a little, your honour.

Sir Joseph. Then hum this at your
leisure. (*Giving him MS. music.*) It is a
song that I have composed for the use of
the Royal Navy. It is designed to encour-
age independence of thought and action in
the lower branches of the service, and to
teach the principle that a British sailor
is any man's equal, excepting mine. Now,
Captain Corcoran, a word with you in
your cabin, on a tender and sentimental
subject.

Capt. Aye, aye, Sir Joseph. (*Crossing.*)
Boatswain, in commemoration of this joyous occasion, see that extra grog is served
out to the ship's company at seven bells.

Boat. Beg pardon. If what, your honour?

Capt. If what? I don't think I understand you.

Boat. If you *please*, your honour.

Capt. What!

Sir Joseph. The gentleman is quite right.
If you *please.*

Capt. (*stamping his foot impatiently*).
If you *please!*

         [*Exit.*

    Sir Joseph
For I hold that on the seas
The expression, "if you please",

A particularly gentlemanly tone implants.

Cousin Hebe

And so do his sisters, and his cousins, and his aunts!

All

And so do his sisters, and his cousins, and his aunts!

[*Exeunt* SIR JOSEPH *and* RELATIVES

Boat. Ah! Sir Joseph's a true gentleman; courteous and considerate to the very humblest.

Ralph. True, Boatswain, but we are not the very humblest. Sir Joseph has explained our true position to us. As he says, a British seaman is any man's equal excepting his, and if Sir Joseph says that, is it not our duty to believe him?

All. Well spoke! well spoke!

Dick. You're on a wrong tack, and so is he. He means well, but he don't know. When people have to obey other people's orders, equality's out of the question.

All (recoiling). Horrible! horrible!

Boat. Dick Deadeye, if you go for to infuriate this here ship's company too far, I won't answer for being able to hold 'em in. I'm shocked! that's what I am—shocked!

Ralph. Messmates, my mind's made up. I'll speak to the captain's daughter, and tell her, like an honest man, of the honest love I have for her.

All. Aye, aye!

Ralph. Is not my love as good as another's? Is not my heart as true as another's? Have I not hands and eyes and ears and limbs like another?

All. Aye, Aye!

Ralph. True, I lack birth——

Boat. You've a berth on board this very ship.

Ralph. Well said—I had forotten that. Messmates—what do you say? Do you approve my determination?

All. We do.

Dick. I don't.

Boat. What is to be done with this here hopeless chap? Let us sing him the song that Sir Joseph has kindly composed for us. Perhaps it will bring this here miserable creetur to a proper state of mind.

GLEE—RALPH, BOATSWAIN, BOATSWAIN'S
MATE, *and* CHORUS

A British tar is a soaring soul,
    As free as a mountain bird,
His energetic fist should be ready to resist
    A dictatorial word.
His nose should pant and his lip should
        curl,
His cheeks should flame and his brow
        should furl,
His bosom should heave and his heart
        should glow,
And his fist be ever ready for a knock-
        down blow.

CHORUS.—His nose should pant, etc.

His eyes should flash with an inborn fire,
    His brow with scorn be wrung;
He never should bow down to a domineer-
        ing frown,
    Or the tang of a tyrant tongue.
His foot should stamp and his throat
        should growl,
His hair should twirl and his face should
        scowl;
His eyes should flash and his breast pro-
        trude.
And this should be his customary attitude
        —(*pose*).

CHORUS.—His foot should stamp, etc.

[*All dance off excepting* RALPH, *who remains
leaning pensively against bulwark.*

Enter JOSEPHINE *from cabin*

Jos. It is useless—Sir Joseph's attentions nauseate me. I know that he is a truly great and good man, for he told me so himself, but to me he seems tedious, fretful, and dictatorial. Yet his must be a mind of no common order, or he would not dare to teach my dear father to dance a hornpipe on the cabin table. (*Sees* RALPH.) Ralph Rackstraw! (*Overcome by emotion.*)

Ralph. Aye, lady—no other than poor Ralph Rackstraw!

Jos. (*aside*). How my heart beats! (*Aloud.*) And why poor, Ralph?

Ralph. I am poor in the essence of happiness, lady—rich only in never-ending unrest. In me there meet a combination of antithetical elements which are at eternal war with one another. Driven hither by objective influences—thither by subjective emotions—wafted one moment into blazing day, by mocking hope—plunged the next into the Cimmerian darkness of tangible despair, I am but a living ganglion of irreconcilable antagonisms. I hope I make myself clear, lady?

Jos. Perfectly. (*Aside.*) His simple eloquence goes to my heart. Oh, if I dared—but no, the thought is madness! (*Aloud.*) Dismiss these foolish fancies, they torture you but needlessly. Come, make one effort.

Ralph (*aside*). I will—one. (*Aloud.*) Josephine!

Jos. (indignantly). Sir!

Ralph. Aye, even though Jove's armoury were launched at the head of the audacious mortal whose lips, unhallowed by relationship, dared to breathe that precious word, yet would I breathe it once, and then perchance be silent evermore. Josephine, in one brief breath I will concentrate the hopes, the doubts, the anxious fears of six weary months. Josephine, I am a British sailor, and I love you!

Jos. Sir, this audacity! (*Aside.*) Oh, my heart, my beating heart! (*Aloud.*) This unwarrantable presumption on the part of a common sailor! (*Aside.*) Common! oh, the irony of the word! (*Crossing, aloud.*) Oh, sir, you forget the disparity in our ranks.

Ralph. I forget nothing, haughty lady. I love you desperately, my life is in your hand—I lay it at your feet! Give me hope, and what I lack in education and polite accomplishments, that I will endeavour to acquire. Drive me to despair, and in death alone I shall look for consolation. I am proud and cannot stoop to implore. I have spoken and I wait your word.

Jos. You shall not wait long. Your proffered love I haughtily reject. Go, sir, and learn to cast your eyes on some village maiden in your own poor rank—they should be lowered before your captain's daughter.

DUET—JOSEPHINE *and* RALPH
Josephine

Refrain, audacious tar,
  Your suit from pressing,
Remember what you are,
  And whom addressing!
      (*Aside*)
I'd laugh my rank to scorn
  In union holy,

Were he more highly born
  Or I more lowly!
      Ralph
Proud lady, have your way,
  Unfeeling beauty!
You speak and I obey,
  It is my duty!
I am the lowliest tar
  That sails the water,
And you, proud maiden, are
  My captain's daughter!

      (*Aside*)
My heart with anguish torn
  Bows down before her,
She laughs my love to scorn,
  Yet I adore her!
      [*Repeat refrain, ensemble, then
        exit* JOSEPHINE *into cabin.*
      Ralph (*Recit.*)
Can I survive this overbearing
Or live a life of mad despairing,
My proffered love despised, rejected?
No, no, it's not to be expected!
      (*Calling off*)
Messmates, ahoy!
Come here! Come here!
      Enter SAILORS, HEBE, *and* RELATIVES
            All
Aye, aye, my boy,
What cheer, what cheer?
  Now tell us, pray,
  Without delay,
  What does she say—
What cheer, what cheer?
      Ralph (*to cousin Hebe*)
The maiden treats my suit with scorn,
  Rejects my humble gift, my lady;
She says I am ignobly born,
  And cuts my hopes adrift, my lady.
            All
    Oh, cruel one.
            Dick
She spurns your suit? Oho! Oho!
I told you so, I told you so.
      Sailors and Relatives
Shall we submit? Are we but slaves?
Shall they submit? Are they but slaves?
  Love comes alike to high and low—
Britannia's sailors rule the waves,
  And shall they stoop to insult? No!
            Dick
You must submit, you are but slaves;
  A lady she! Oho! Oho!

You lowly toilers of the waves,
    She spurns you all—I told you so!
                    Ralph
My friends, my leave of life I'm taking,
For oh, my heart, my heart is breaking.
When I am gone, oh, prithee tell
The maid that, as I died, I loved her well!
        All (turning away, weeping)
Of life, alas! his leave he's taking,
For ah! his faithful heart is breaking;
When he is gone we'll surely tell
The maid that, as he died, he loved her
    well.
    [*During Chorus* BOATSWAIN *has loaded
        pistol, which he hands to* RALPH.
                    Ralph
Be warned, my messmates all
    Who love in rank above you—
For Josephine I fall!
            [*Puts pistol to his head. All the
                sailors stop their ears.
            Enter* JOSEPHINE *on deck*
                    Josephine
Ah! stay your hand! I love you!
                    All
Ah! stay your hand—she loves you!
    Ralph (incredulously). Loves me?
                    Josephine
Loves you!
                    All
Yes, yes—ah, yes,—she loves you!
                    Ensemble
    SAILORS *and* RELATIVES *and* JOSEPHINE
Oh joy, oh rapture unforeseen,
For now the sky is all serene;
The god of day—the orb of love—
Has hung his ensign high above,
    The sky is all ablaze.
With wooing words and loving song,
We'll chase the lagging hours along,
And if $\left\{\begin{array}{l}\text{I find}\\\text{We find}\end{array}\right\}$ the maiden coy,

$\left.\begin{array}{l}\text{I'll}\\\text{We'll}\end{array}\right\}$ murmur forth decorous joy

    In dreamy roundelays!
                Dick Deadeye
He thinks he's won his Josephine,
But though the sky is now serene,
A frowning thunderbolt above
May end their ill-assorted love
    Which now is all ablaze.
Our captain, ere the day is gone,
Will be extremely down upon
The wicked men who art employ

To make his Josephine less coy
    In many various ways.
                    [*Exit* DICK.
                Josephine
This very night,
                Hebe
With bated breath
                Ralph
And muffled oar—
                Josephine
Without a light,
                Hebe
As still as death,
                Ralph
We'll steal ashore
                Josephine
A clergyman
                Ralph
Shall make us one
                Boatswain
At half-past ten,
                Josephine
And then we can
                Ralph
Return, for none
                Boatswain
Can part them then!

                All
This very night, etc.
        (DICK *appears at hatchway*)

                Dick
Forbear, nor carry out the scheme you've
    planned;
She is a lady—you a foremost hand!
Remember, she's your gallant captain's
    daughter,
And you the meanest slave that crawls the
    water!

                All
    Back, vermin, back,
        Nor mock us!
    Back, vermin, back,
        You shock us!
                    [*Exit* DICK.
Let's give three cheers for the sailor's bride
Who casts all thought of rank aside—
Who gives up home and fortune too
For the honest love of a sailor true!
    For a British tar is a soaring soul
        As free as a mountain bird!
    His energetic fist should be ready to
        resist
        A dictatorial word!

His foot should stamp and his throat
    should growl,
His hair should twirl and his face should
    scowl,
His eyes should flash and his breast pro-
    trude,
And this should be his customary attitude—
    (*pose*).

GENERAL DANCE
END OF ACT I

ACT II

*Same Scene. Night. Awning removed.
Moonlight.* CAPTAIN *discovered singing
on poop-deck, and accompanying himself on a mandolin.* LITTLE BUTTERCUP
*seated on quarter-deck, gazing senti-
mentally at him.*

SONG—CAPTAIN

Fair moon, to thee I sing,
    Bright regent of the heavens,
Say, why is everything
Either at sixes or at sevens?
I have lived hitherto
Free from breath of slander,
Beloved by all my crew—
A really popular commander.
But now my kindly crew rebel,
    My daughter to a tar is partial,
Sir Joseph storms, and, sad to tell,
    He threatens a court martial!
    Fair moon, to thee I sing,
      Bright regent of the heavens,
    Say, why is everything
    Either at sixes or at sevens?

But. How sweetly he carols forth his
melody to the unconscious moon! Of whom
is he thinking? Of some high-born beauty?
It may be! Who is poor Little Buttercup
that she should expect his glance to fall
on one so lowly! And yet if he knew—if
he only knew!

Capt. (*coming down*). Ah! Little Buttercup, still on board? That is not quite
right, little one. It would have been more
respectable to have gone on shore at dusk.

But. True, dear Captain—but the recol-
lection of your sad pale face seemed to
chain me to the ship. I would fain see you
smile before I go.

Capt. Ah! Little Buttercup, I fear it will
be long before I recover my accustomed
cheerfulness, for misfortunes crowd upon
me, and all my old friends seem to have
turned against me!

But. Oh no—do not say "all", dear Captain. That were unjust to one, at least.

Capt. True, for you are staunch to me.
(*Aside.*) If ever I gave my heart again,
methinks it would be to such a one as
this! (*Aloud.*) I am touched to the heart
by your innocent regard for me, and were
we differently situated, I think I could
have returned it. But as it is, I fear I can
never be more to you than a friend.

But. I understand! You hold aloof from
me because you are rich and lofty—and I
poor and lowly. But take care! The poor
bumboat woman has gipsy blood in her
veins, and she can read destinies.

Capt. Destinies?

But. There is a change in store for you!

Capt. A change?

But. Aye—be prepared!

DUET—LITTLE BUTTERCUP *and* CAPTAIN

Buttercup

Things are seldom what they seem,
Skim milk masquerades as cream;
Highlows pass as patent leathers;
Jackdaws strut in peacock's feathers.

Captain (*puzzled*)

    Very true,
    So they do.

Buttercup

Black sheep dwell in every fold;
All that glitters is not gold;
Storks turn out to be but logs;
Bulls are but inflated frogs.

Captain (*puzzled*)

    So they be,
    Frequentlee.

Buttercup

Drops the wind and stops the mill;
Turbot is ambitious brill;
Gild the farthing if you will,
Yet it is a farthing still.

Captain (*puzzled*)

    Yes, I know.
    That is so.
Though to catch your drift I'm striving,
    It is shady—it is shady;
I don't see at what you're driving,
    Mystic lady—mystic lady,

(*Aside*)

Stern conviction's o'er me stealing,
That the mystic lady's dealing
In oracular revealing.

Buttercup (*aside*)

Stern conviction's o'er him stealing,

That the mystic lady's dealing
In oracular revealing.
Both
Yes, I know—
That is so!
Captain
Though I'm anything but clever,
I could talk like that for ever:
Once a cat was killed by care;
Only brave deserve the fair.
Buttercup
Very true,
So they do.
Captain
Wink is often good as nod;
Spoils the child who spares the rod;
Thirsty lambs run foxy dangers;
Dogs are found in many mangers.
Buttercup
Frequentlee,
I agree.
Captain
Paw of cat the chestnut snatches;
Worn-out garments show new patches;
Only count the chick that hatches;
Men are grown-up catchy-catchies.
Buttercup
Yes, I know,
That is so.
(*Aside*)
Though to catch my drift he's striving,
I'll dissemble—I'll dissemble;
When he sees at what I'm driving,
Let him tremble—let him tremble!
Ensemble
Though a mystic tone $\left\{\begin{array}{l}\text{I}\\\text{you}\end{array}\right\}$ borrow,

$\left.\begin{array}{l}\text{You will}\\\text{I shall}\end{array}\right\}$ learn the truth with sorrow,

Here today and gone to-morrow;
Yes, I know—
That is so!

[*At the end exit* LITTLE BUTTERCUP
melodramatically.

Capt. Incomprehensible as her utterances are, I nevertheless feel that they are dictated by a sincere regard for me. But to what new misery is she referring? Time alone can tell!

Enter SIR JOSEPH
Sir Joseph. Captain Corcoran, I am much disappointed with your daughter. In fact, I don't think she will do.
Capt. She won't do, Sir Joseph!

Sir Joseph. I'm afraid not. The fact is, that although I have urged my suit with as much eloquence as is consistent with an official utterance, I have done so hitherto without success. How do you account for this?
Capt. Really, Sir Joseph, I hardly know. Josephine is of course sensible of your condescension.
Sir Joseph. She naturally would be.
Capt. But perhaps your exalted rank dazzles her.
Sir Joseph. You think it does?
Capt. I can hardly say; but she is a modest girl, and her social position is far below your own. It may be that she feels she is not worthy of you.
Sir Joseph. That is really a very sensible suggestion, and displays more knowledge of human nature than I had given you credit for.
Capt. See, she comes. If your lordship would kindly reason with her and assure her officially that it is a standing rule at the Admiralty that love levels all ranks, her respect for an official utterance might induce her to look upon your offer in its proper light.
Sir Joseph. It is not unlikely. I will adopt your suggestion. But soft, she is here. Let us withdraw, and watch our opportunity.
Enter JOSEPHINE *from cabin.* FIRST LORD
and CAPTAIN *retire*

JOSEPHINE

The hours creep on apace,
    My guilty heart is quaking!
Oh, that I might retrace
    The step that I am taking!
Its folly it were easy to be showing,
What I am giving up and whither going.
On the one hand, papa's luxurious home,
    Hung with ancestral armour and old brasses,
Carved oak and tapestry from distant Rome,
    Rare "blue and white" Venetian finger-glasses,
Rich oriental rugs, luxurious sofa pillows,
And everything that isn't old, from Gillow's.
And on the other, a dark and dingy room,
    In some black street with stuffy children crying,

Where organs yell, and clacking housewives
    fume
  And clothes are hanging out all day a-
    drying.
With one cracked looking-glass to see your
    face in,
And dinner served up in a pudding basin!
  A simple sailor, lowly born,
    Unlettered and unknown,
  Who toils for bread from early morn
    Till half the night has flown!
  No golden rank can he impart—
    No wealth of house or land—
  No fortune save his trusty heart
    And honest brown right hand!
  And yet he is so wondrous fair
  That love for one so passing rare,
  So peerless in his manly beauty,
  Were little else than solemn duty!
Oh, god of love, and god of reason, say,
Which of you twain shall my poor heart
    obey!

SIR JOSEPH *and* CAPTAIN *enter*

Sir Joseph. Madam, it has been repre-
sented to me that you are appalled by my
exalted rank. I desire to convey to you
officially my assurance, that if your hesitation is attributable to that circumstance, it
is uncalled for.

Jos. Oh! then your lordship is of opinion
that married happiness is *not* inconsistent
with discrepancy in rank?

Sir Joseph. I am officially of that opinion.

Jos. That the high and the lowly may be
truly happy together, provided that they
truly love one another?

Sir Joseph. Madam, I desire to convey
to you officially my opinion that love is a
platform upon which all ranks meet.

Jos. I thank you, Sir Joseph. I *did* hesitate, but I will hesitate no longer. (*Aside.*)
He little thinks how eloquently he has
pleaded his rival's cause!

Trio

FIRST LORD, CAPTAIN, *and* JOSEPHINE

Captain

Never mind the why and wherefore,
Love can level ranks, and therefore,
Though his lordship's station's mighty,
  Though stupendous be his brain,
Though your tastes are mean and flighty
  And your fortune poor and plain,

Captain and Sir Joseph

Ring the merry bells on board-ship,
  Rend the air with warbling wild,
For the union of $\begin{Bmatrix} my \\ his \end{Bmatrix}$ lordship
  With a humble captain's child!

Captain

For a humble captain's daughter—

Josephine

For a gallant captain's daughter—

Sir Joseph

And a lord who rules the water—

Josephine (*aside*)

And a *tar* who ploughs the water!

All

Let the air with joy be laden,
  Rend with songs the air above,
For the union of a maiden
  With the man who owns her love!

Sir Joseph

Never mind the why and wherefore,
Love can level ranks, and therefore,
Though your nautical relation (*alluding to*
                    CAPT.)
In my set could scarcely pass—
Though you occupy a station
  In the lower middle class—

Captain and Sir Joseph

Ring the merry bells on board-ship,
  Rend the air with warbling wild,
For the union of $\begin{Bmatrix} my \\ his \end{Bmatrix}$ lordship
  With a humble captain's child!

Captain

For a humble captain's daughter—

Josephine

For a gallant captain's daughter—

Sir Joseph

And a lord who rules the water—

Josephine (*aside*)

And a *tar* who ploughs the water!

All

Let the air with joy be laden,
  Rend with songs the air above,
For the union of a maiden
  With the man who owns her love!

Josephine

Never mind the why and wherefore,
Love can level ranks, and therefore
I admit the jurisdiction;
  Ably have you played your part;
You have carried firm conviction
  To my hesitating heart.

Captain and Sir Joseph
Ring the merry bells on board-ship,
  Rend the air with warbling wild,
For the union of $\left\{\begin{array}{l} \text{my} \\ \text{his} \end{array}\right\}$ lordship
  With a humble captain's child!
Captain
For a humble captain's daughter—
Josephine
For a gallant captain's daughter—
Sir Joseph
And a lord who rules the water—
Josephine (aside)
And a *tar* who ploughs the water!
(Aloud)
Let the air with joy be laden.
Captain and Sir Joseph
Ring the merry bells on board-ship—
Josephine
For the union of a maiden—
Captain and Sir Joseph
For her union with his lordship.

All
Rend with songs the air above
For the man who owns her love!

                                   [*Exit* JOS.

Capt. Sir Joseph, I cannot express to you my delight at the happy result of your eloquence. Your argument was unanswerable.

Sir Joseph. Captain Corcoran, it is one of the happiest characteristics of this glorious country that official utterances are invariably regarded as unanswerable.

                   [*Exit* SIR JOSEPH.

Capt. At last my fond hopes are to be crowned. My only daughter is to be the bride of a Cabinet Minister. The prospect is Elysian. (*During this speech* DICK DEADEYE *has entered.*)

Dick. Captain.

Capt. Deadeye! You here? Don't (*Recoiling from him.*)

Dick. Ah, don't shrink from me, Captain, I'm unpleasant to look at, and my name's agin me, but I ain't as bad as I seem.

Capt. What would you with me?

Dick (*mysteriously*). I'm come to give you warning.

Capt. Indeed! do you propose to leave the Navy then?

Dick. No, no, you misunderstand me; listen!

Duet
CAPTAIN *and* DICK DEADEYE

Dick
Kind Captain, I've important information,
  Sing hey, the kind commander that you are,
About a certain intimate relation,
  Sing hey, the merry maiden and the tar.
Both
  The merry maiden and the tar.

Captain
Good fellow, in conundrums you are speaking,
  Sing hey, the mystic sailor that you are;
The answer to them vainly I am seeking;
  Sing hey, the merry maiden and the tar.
Both
  The merry maiden and the tar.

Dick
Kind Captain, your young lady is a-sighing,
  Sing hey, the simple captain that you are,
This very night with Rackstraw to be flying;
  Sing hey, the merry maiden and the tar.
Both
  The merry maiden and the tar.

Captain
Good fellow, you have given timely warning,
  Sing hey, the thoughtful sailor that you are,
I'll talk to Master Rackstraw in the morning:
  Sing hey, the cat-o'-nine-tails and the tar.

           (*Producing a "cat".*)

Both
The merry cat-o'-nine-tails and the tar!

Capt. Dick Deadeye—I thank you for your warning—I will at once take means to arrest their flight. This boat cloak will afford me ample disguise—So! (*Envelops himself in a mysterious cloak, holding it before his face.*)

Dick. Ha, ha! They are foiled—foiled—foiled!

Enter Crew on tiptoe, with RALPH *and* BOATSWAIN *meeting* JOSEPHINE, *who enters from cabin on tiptoe, with bundle of necessaries, and accompanied by* LITTLE BUTTERCUP.

Ensemble

Carefully on tiptoe stealing,
  Breathing gently as we may,
Every step with caution feeling,
  We will softly steal away.
    (CAPTAIN *stamps*.)—*Chord*
      All (*much alarmed*)
Goodness me—
  Why, what was that?
        Dick
Silent be,
  It was the cat!
      All (*reassured*)
It was—it was the cat!
Captain (*producing cat-o'-nine-tails*)
They're right, it was the cat!

        All

Pull ashore, in fashion steady,
  Hymen will defray the fare,
For a clergyman is ready
  To unite the happy pair!
    (*Stamp as before, and Chord*.)
        All

Goodness me,
  Why, what was that?
        Dick

Silent be,
  Again the cat!
        All

It was again that cat!
      Captain (*aside*)
They're right, it was the cat!
  Captain (*throwing off cloak*)
Hold! (*All start*.)
Pretty daughter of mine,
  I insist upon knowing
  Where you may be going
With these sons of the brine,
For my excellent crew,
Though foes they could thump any,
Are scarcely fit company,
  My daughter, for you.
        Crew

Now, hark at that, do!
Though foes we could thump any,
We are scarcely fit company
  For a lady like you!

        Ralph

Proud officer, that haughty lip uncurl!
Vain man, suppress that supercilious
  sneer,
For I have dared to love your matchless
  girl,

A fact well known to all my messmates
  here!

        Captain
Oh, horror!
      Ralph and Josephine

$\left.\begin{array}{l} \text{I,} \\ \text{He,} \end{array}\right\}$ humble, poor, and lowly born,
The meanest in the port division—
  The butt of epauletted scorn—
The mark of quarter-deck derision—
$\left.\begin{array}{l} \text{Have} \\ \text{Has} \end{array}\right\}$ dared to raise $\left\{\begin{array}{l} \text{my} \\ \text{his} \end{array}\right\}$ wormy eyes

Above the dust to which you'd mould $\left\{\begin{array}{l} \text{me} \\ \text{him} \end{array}\right.$

In manhood's glorious pride to rise,
$\left.\begin{array}{l} \text{I am} \\ \text{He is} \end{array}\right\}$ an Englishman—behold $\left\{\begin{array}{l} \text{me!} \\ \text{him!} \end{array}\right.$

        All
He is an Englishman!
      Boatswain
He is an Englishman!
  For he himself has said it,
  And it's greatly to his credit,
That he is an Englishman!

        All
That he is an Englishman!
      Boatswain
For he might have been a Roosian,
A French, or Turk, or Proosian,
Or perhaps Itali-an!

        All
Or perhaps Itali-an!
      Boatswain
But in spite of all temptations
To belong to other nations,
  He remains an Englishman!

        All
For in spite of all temptations, etc.
  Captain (*trying to repress his anger*)
In uttering a reprobation
  To any British tar,
I try to speak with moderation,
  But you have gone too far.
I'm very sorry to disparage
  A humble foremast lad,
But to seek your captain's child in mar·
  riage,
  Why damme, it's too bad!
      [*During this*, COUSIN HEBE *and*
        FEMALE RELATIVES *have entered.*

All (shocked)

Oh!

Captain

Yes, damme, it's too bad!

All

Oh!

Captain and Dick Deadeye

Yes, damme, it's too bad.

[*During this,* SIR JOSEPH *has appeared
on poop-deck. He is horrified at the
bad language.*

Hebe

Did you hear him—did you hear him?
　Oh, the monster overbearing!
Don't go near him—don't go near him—
　He is swearing—he is swearing!

Sir Joseph

My pain and my distress,
　I find it is not easy to express;
My amazement—my surprise—
　You may learn from the expression of
　　my eyes!

Captain

My lord—one word—the facts are not
　before you
　The word was injudicious, I allow—
But hear my explanation, I implore you,
　And you will be indignant too, I vow!

Sir Joseph

I will hear of no defence,
　Attempt none if you're sensible.
That word of evil sense
　Is wholly indefensible.
Go, ribald, get you hence
　To your cabin with celerity.
This is the consequence
　Of ill-advised asperity!

[*Exit* CAPTAIN, *disgraced,
followed by* JOSEPHINE.

All

This is the consequence
　Of ill-advised asperity!

Sir Joseph

For I'll teach you all, ere long,
　To refrain from language strong
For I haven't any sympathy for ill-bred
　taunts!

Hebe

No more have his sisters, nor his cousins,
　nor his aunts.

All

For he is an Englishman, etc.

Sir Joseph. Now, tell me, my fine fellow—for you *are* a fine fellow——

Ralph. Yes, your honour.

Sir Joseph. How came your captain so
far to forget himself? I am quite sure you
had given him no cause for annoyance.

Ralph. Please your honour, it was thus-
wise. You see I'm only a topman—a mere
foremast hand——

Sir Joseph. Don't be ashamed of that.
Your position as a topman is a very exalted
one.

Ralph. Well, your honour, love burns as
brightly in the fo'c'sle as it does on the
quarter-deck, and Josephine is the fairest
bud that ever blossomed upon the tree of
a poor fellow's wildest hopes.

Enter JOSEPHINE; *she rushes to* RALPH'S
　arms.

Jos. Darling! (SIR JOSEPH *horrified.*)

Ralph. She is the figurehead of my ship
of life—the bright beacon that guides me
into my port of happiness—that the rarest,
the purest gem that ever sparkled on a
poor but worthy fellow's trusting brow!

All. Very pretty, very pretty!

Sir Joseph. Insolent sailor, you shall repent this outrage. Seize him!

(*Two Marines seize him and handcuff
him.*)

Jos. Oh, Sir Joseph, spare him, for I
love him tenderly.

Sir Joseph. Pray, don't. I will teach this
presumptuous mariner to discipline his affections. Have you such a thing as a
dungeon on board?

All. We have!

Dick. They have!

Sir Joseph. Then load him with chains
and take him there at once!

OCTETTE

Ralph

Farewell, my own,
　Light of my life, farewell!
For crime unknown
　I go to a dungeon cell.

Josephine

I will atone.
　In the meantime farewell!
And all alone
　Rejoice in your dungeon cell!

Sir Joseph

A bone, a bone
　I'll pick with this sailor fell;
Let him be shown
　At once to his dungeon cell.

Boatswain, Dick Deadeye, and Cousin Hebe
He'll hear no tone
  Of the maiden he loves so well!
No telephone
  Communicates with his cell!

Buttercup (mysteriously)
But when is known
  The secret I have to tell,
Wide will be thrown
  The door of his dungeon cell.

All
For crime unknown
  He goes to a dungeon cell!

[RALPH *is led off in custody.*

Sir Joseph
My pain and my distress
Again it is not easy to express.
My amazement, my surprise,
Again you may discover from my eyes.

All
How terrible the aspect of his eyes!

Buttercup
Hold! Ere upon your loss
  You lay much stress,
A long-concealèd crime
  I would confess.

SONG—BUTTERCUP
A many years ago,
When I was young and charming,
  As some of you may know,
I practised baby-farming.

All
Now this is most alarming!
When she was young and charming,
  She practised baby-farming,
A many years ago.

Buttercup
Two tender babes I nussed:
  One was of low condition,
The other, upper crust,
  A regular patrician.

All (explaining to each other)
Now, this is the position:
One was of low condition,
  The other a patrician,
A many years ago.

Buttercup
Oh, bitter is my cup!
  However could I do it?
I mixed those children up,
  And not a creature knew it!

All
However could you do it?
Some day, no doubt, you'll rue it,

Although no creature knew it,
  So many years ago.

Buttercup
In time each little waif
  Forsook his foster-mother,
The well-born babe was Ralph—
  Your captain was the other!!!

All

They left their foster-mother,
The one was Ralph, our brother,
Our captain was the other,
  A many years ago.

Sir Joseph. Then I am to understand that Captain Corcoran and Ralph were exchanged in childhood's happy hour—that Ralph is really the Captain, and the Captain is Ralph?

But. That is the idea I intended to convey, officially!

Sir Joseph. And very well you have conveyed it.

But. Aye! aye! yer 'onour.

Sir Joseph. Dear me! Let them appear before me, at once!

RALPH *enters as* CAPTAIN; CAPTAIN *as a common sailor.* JOSEPHINE *rushes to his arms.*

Jos. My father—a common sailor!

Capt. It is hard, is it not, my dear?

Sir Joseph. This is a very singular occurrence; I congratulate you both. (*To* RALPH.) Desire that remarkably fine seaman to step forward.

Ralph. Corcoran. Three paces to the front—march!

Capt. If what?

Ralph. If what? I don't think I understand you.

Capt. If you please.

Sir Joseph. The gentleman is quite right. If you *please.*

Ralph. Oh! If you *please.* (CAPTAIN *steps forward.*)

Sir Joseph (to CAPTAIN). You are an extremely fine fellow.

Capt. Yes, your honour.

Sir Joseph. So it seems that you were Ralph, and Ralph was you.

Capt. So it seems, your honour.

Sir Joseph. Well, I need not tell you that after this change in your condition, a marriage with your daughter will be out of the question.

Capt. Don't say that, your honour—love levels all ranks.

Sir Joseph. It does to a considerable extent, but it does not level them as much as that. (*Handing* JOSEPHINE *to* RALPH.) Here—take her, sir, and mind you treat her kindly.

Ralph and Jos. Oh bliss, oh rapture!
Capt. and But. Oh rapture, oh bliss!

Sir Joseph

Sad my lot and sorry,
What shall I do? I cannot live alone!

Hebe

Fear nothing—while I live I'll not desert you.
I'll soothe and comfort your declining days.

Sir Joseph

No, don't do that.

Hebe

Yes, but indeed I'd rather—

Sir Joseph (*resigned*)

To-morrow morn our vows shall all be plighted,
Three loving pairs on the same day united!

Quartette

JOSEPHINE, HEBE, RALPH, *and* DEADEYE

Oh joy, oh rapture unforeseen,
The clouded sky is now serene,
The god of day—the orb of love,
Has hung his ensign high above,
  The sky is all ablaze.
With wooing words and loving song,
We'll chase the lagging hours along,
And if $\begin{Bmatrix} \text{he finds} \\ \text{I find} \end{Bmatrix}$ the maiden coy,
We'll murmur forth decorous joy,
  In dreamy roundelay.

Captain

For he's the Captain of the *Pinafore*.

All

And a right good captain too!

Captain

And though before my fall
I was captain of you all,
I'm a member of the crew.

All

Although before his fall, etc.

Captain

I shall marry with a wife,
In my humble rank of life! (*turning to* BUT.)
  And you, my own, are she—
I must wander to and fro;
But wherever I may go,
  I shall never be untrue to thee!

All

What, never?

Captain

No, never!

All

What, *never?*

Captain

Hardly ever!

All

Hardly ever be untrue to thee.
Then give three cheers, and one cheer more
For the former Captain of the *Pinafore*.

Buttercup

For he loves Little Buttercup, dear Little Buttercup,
  Though I could never tell why;
But still he loves Buttercup, poor Little Buttercup,
  Sweet Little Buttercup, aye!

All

  For he loves, etc.

Sir Joseph

I'm the monarch of the sea,
And when I've married thee (*to* HEBE),
I'll be true to the devotion that my love implants,

Hebe

Then good-bye to his sisters, and his cousins, and his aunts,
Especially his cousins,
Whom he reckons up by dozens,
His sisters, and his cousins, and his aunts!

All

For he is an Englishman,
  And he himself hath said it,
  And it's greatly to his credit
That he is an Englishman!

CURTAIN

THE PIRATES OF PENZANCE

OR

THE SLAVE OF DUTY

DRAMATIS PERSONÆ

MAJOR-GENERAL STANLEY

THE PIRATE KING

SAMUEL (*his Lieutenant*)

FREDERIC (*the Pirate Apprentice*)

SERGEANT OF POLICE

MABEL

EDITH

KATE

ISABEL } (*General Stanley's Daughters*)

RUTH (*a Pirate Maid of all Work*)

Chorus of Pirates, Police, and General Stanley's Daughters

ACT I

SCENE.—*A rocky sea-shore on the coast of Cornwall. In the distance is a calm sea, on which a schooner is lying at anchor. As the curtain rises groups of pirates are discovered, some drinking, some playing cards.* SAMUEL, *the Pirate Lieutenant, is going from one group to another, filling the cups from a flask.* FREDERIC *is seated in a despondent attitude at the back of the scene.*

Opening Chorus

Pour, oh, pour the pirate sherry;
  Fill, oh, fill the pirate glass;
And, to make us more than merry,
  Let the pirate bumper pass.

Samuel

For to-day our pirate 'prentice
  Rises from indenture freed;
Strong his arm and keen his scent is,
  He's a pirate now indeed!

All

Here's good luck to Frederic's ventures!
Frederic's out of his indentures.

Samuel

Two-and-twenty now he's rising,
  And alone he's fit to fly,
Which we're bent on signalizing
  With unusual revelry.

All

Here's good luck to Frederic's ventures!

Frederic's out of his indentures.
Pour, oh, pour the pirate sherry, etc.

FREDERIC *rises and comes forward with*

PIRATE KING, *who enters.*

King. Yes, Frederic, from to-day you rank as a full-blown member of our band.

All. Hurrah.

Fred. My friends, I thank you all, from my heart, for your kindly wishes. Would that I could repay them as they deserve!

King. What do you mean?

Fred. To-day I am out of my indentures, and to-day I leave you for ever.

King. But this is quite unaccountable; a keener hand at scuttling a Cunarder or cutting out a P. & O. never shipped a handspike.

Fred. Yes, I have done my best for you. And why? It was my duty under my indentures, and I am the slave of duty. As a child I was regularly apprenticed to your band. It was through an error—no matter, the mistake was ours, not yours, and I was in honour bound by it.

Sam. An error? What error?

RUTH *enters*

Fred. I may not tell you; it would reflect upon my well-loved Ruth.

Ruth. Nay, dear master, my mind has long been gnawed by the cankering tooth of mystery. Better have it out at once.

43

SONG—RUTH

When Frederic was a little lad he proved
    so brave and daring,
His father thought he'd 'prentice him to
    some career sea-faring.
I was, alas! his nurserymaid, and so it fell
    to *my* lot
To take and bind the promising boy ap-
    prentice to a *pilot*—
A life not bad for a hardy lad, though
    surely not a high lot,
Though I'm a nurse, you might do worse
    than make your boy a pilot.
I was a stupid nurserymaid, on breakers
    always steering,
And I did not catch the word aright,
    through being hard of hearing;
Mistaking my instructions, which within
    my brain did gyrate,
I took and bound this promising boy ap-
    prentice to a *pirate*.
A sad mistake it was to make and doom
    him to a vile lot.
I bound him to a pirate—you—instead of
    to a pilot.
I soon found out, beyond all doubt, the
    scope of this disaster,
But I hadn't the face to return to my place,
    and break it to my master.
A nurserymaid is not afraid of what you
    people *call* work,
So I made up my mind to go as a kind
    of piratical maid-of-all-work.
And that is how you find me now, a
    member of your shy lot,
Which you wouldn't have found, had he
    been bound apprentice to a pilot.

Ruth. Oh, pardon! Frederic, pardon!
(*Kneels.*)

Fred. Rise, sweet one, I have long pardoned you.

Ruth (*rises*). The two words were so
much alike!

Fred. They were. They still are, though
years have rolled over their heads. But this
afternoon my obligation ceases. Individu-
ally, I love you all with affection unspeak-
able, but, collectively, I look upon you with
a disgust that amounts to absolute detestation. Oh! pity me, my beloved friends, for
such is my sense of duty that, once out
of my indentures, I shall feel myself bound
to devote myself heart and soul to your
extermination!

All. Poor lad—poor lad! (*All weep.*)

King. Well, Frederic, if you conscientiously feel that it is your duty to destroy
us, we cannot blame you for acting on
that conviction. Always act in accordance
with the dictates of your conscience, my
boy, and chance the consequences.

Sam. Besides, we can offer you but little
temptation to remain with us. We don't
seem to make piracy pay. I'm sure I don't
know why, but we don't.

Fred. I know why, but, alas! I mustn't
tell you; it wouldn't be right.

King. Why not, my boy? It's only half-
past eleven, and you are one of us until
the clock strikes twelve.

Sam. True, and until then you are bound
to protect our interests.

All. Hear, hear!

Fred. Well, then, it is my duty, as a
pirate, to tell you that you are too tender-
hearted. For instance, you make a point
of never attacking a weaker party than
yourselves, and when you attack a stronger
party you invariably get thrashed.

King. There is some truth in that.

Fred. Then, again, you make a point of
never molesting an orphan!

Sam. Of course: we are orphans ourselves, and know what it is.

Fred. Yes, but it has got about, and
what is the consequence? Every one we
capture says he's an orphan. The last three
ships we took proved to be manned entirely by orphans, and so we had to let
them go. One would think that Great
Britain's mercantile navy was recruited
solely from her orphan asylums—which we
know is not the case.

Sam. But, hang it all! you wouldn't
have us absolutely merciless?

Fred. There's my difficulty; until twelve
o'clock I would, after twelve I wouldn't.
Was ever a man placed in so delicate a
situation.

Ruth. And Ruth, your own Ruth, whom
you love so well, and who has won her
middle-aged way into your boyish heart,
what is to become of *her*?

King. Oh, he will take you with him.

Fred. Well, Ruth, I feel some little difficulty about you. It is true that I admire
you very much, but I have been constantly at sea since I was eight years old,

and yours is the only woman's face I have seen during that time. I think it is a sweet face.

Ruth. It is—oh, it is!

Fred. I say I *think* it is; that is my impression. But as I have never had an opportunity of comparing you with other women, it is just possible I may be mistaken.

King. True.

Fred. What a terrible thing it would be if I were to marry this innocent person, and then find out that she is, on the whole, plain!

King. Oh, Ruth is very well, very well indeed.

Sam. Yes, there are the remains of a fine woman about Ruth.

Fred. Do you really think so?

Sam. I do.

Fred. Then I will not be so selfish as to take her from you. In justice to her, and in consideration for you, I will leave her behind. (*Hands* RUTH *to* KING.)

King. No, Frederic, this must not be. We are rough men who lead a rough life, but we are not so utterly heartless as to deprive thee of thy love. I think I am right in saying that there is not one here who would rob thee of this inestimable treasure for all the world holds dear.

All (loudly). Not one!

King. No, I thought there wasn't. Keep thy love, Frederic, keep thy love. (*Hands her back to* FREDERIC.)

Fred. You're very good, I'm sure.

[*Exit* RUTH.

King. Well, it's the top of the tide, and we must be off. Farewell, Frederic. When your process of extermination begins, let our deaths be as swift and painless as you can conveniently make them.

Fred. I will! By the love I have for you, I swear it! Would that you could render this extermination unnecessary by accompanying me back to civilization!

King. No, Frederic, it cannot be. I don't think much of our profession, but, contrasted with respectability, it is comparatively honest. No, Frederic, I shall live and die a Pirate King.

SONG—PIRATE KING

Oh, better far to live and die
Under the brave black flag I fly,
Than play a sanctimonious part,
With a pirate head and a pirate heart.
Away to the cheating world go you,
Where pirates all are well-to-do;
But I'll be true to the song I sing,
And live and die a Pirate King.
　For I am a Pirate King.

All

　　You are!
Hurrah for our Pirate King!
King
And it is, it is a glorious thing
To be a Pirate King.

All

　　Hurrah!
Hurrah for our Pirate King!

King

When I sally forth to seek my prey
I help myself in a royal way:
I sink a few more ships, it's true,
Than a well-bred monarch ought to do;
But many a king on a first-class throne,
If he wants to call his crown his own,
Must manage somehow to get through
More dirty work than ever *I* do,
　Though I am a Pirate King.

All

　　You are!
Hurrah for our Pirate King!
King
And it is, it is a glorious thing
To be a Pirate King!

All

　　It is!
Hurrah for our Pirate King!
　　[*Exeunt all except* FREDERIC.

Enter RUTH

Ruth. Oh, take me with you! I cannot live if I am left behind.

Fred. Ruth, I will be quite candid with you. You are very dear to me, as you know, but I must be circumspect. You see, you are considerably older than I. A lad of twenty-one usually looks for a wife of seventeen.

Ruth. A wife of seventeen! You will find me a wife of a thousand!

Fred. No, but I shall find you a wife of forty-seven, and that is quite enough. Ruth, tell me candidly, and without reserve: compared with other women—how are *you?*

Ruth. I will answer you truthfully,

master—I have a slight cold, but otherwise
I am quite well.

Fred. I am sorry for your cold, but I
was referring rather to your personal appearance. Compared with other women, are
you beautiful?

Ruth (*bashfully*). I have been told so,
dear master.

Fred. Ah, but lately?

Ruth. Oh, no, years and years ago.

Fred. What do you think of yourself?

Ruth. It is a delicate question to answer,
but I think I am a fine woman.

Fred. That is your candid opinion?

Ruth. Yes, I should be deceiving you
if I told you otherwise.

Fred. Thank you, Ruth, I believe you,
for I am sure you would not practise on
my inexperience; I wish to do the right
thing, and if—I say *if*—you are really a
fine woman, your age shall be no obstacle
to our union! (*Chorus of Girls heard in
the distance.*) Hark! Surely I hear voices!
Who has ventured to approach our all but
inaccessible lair? Can it be Custom House?
No, it does not sound like Custom House.

Ruth (*aside*). Confusion! it is the voices
of young girls! If he should see them I
am lost.

Fred. (*looking off*). By all that's marvellous, a bevy of beautiful maidens!

Ruth (*aside*). Lost! lost! lost!

Fred. How lovely! how surpassingly
lovely is the plainest of them! What grace
—what delicacy—what refinement! And
Ruth—Ruth told me she was beautiful!

RECIT
Frederic
Oh, false one, you have deceived me!
Ruth
I have deceived you?

Frederic
Yes, deceived me!
         (*Denouncing her.*)
DUET—FRED. *and* RUTH
Frederic
You told me you were fair as gold!
Ruth (*wildly*)
And, master, am I not so?
Frederic
And now I see you're plain and old.
Ruth
I am sure I am not a jot so.
Frederic
Upon my innocence you play.
Ruth
I'm not the one to plot so.
Frederic
Your face is lined, your hair is grey.
Ruth
It's gradually got so.
Frederic
Faithless woman, to deceive me,
    I who trusted so!
Ruth
Master, master, do not leave me!
    Hear me, ere you go!
    My love without reflecting,
    Oh, do not be rejecting.
Take a maiden tender—her affection raw
      and green,
    At very highest rating,
    Has been accumulating
Summers seventeen—summers seventeen.
    Don't, beloved master,
    Crush me with disaster.
What is such a dower to the dower I
    have here?
    My love unabating
    Has been accumulating
Forty-seven year—forty-seven year!

ENSEMBLE

RUTH	FRED.
Don't, beloved master,	Yes, your former master
Crush me with disaster.	Saves you from disaster.
What is such a dower to the dower	Your love would be uncomfortably fervid,
I have here?	it is clear,
My love unabating	If, as you are stating,
Has been accumulating	It's been accumulating
Forty-seven year—forty-seven year!	Forty-seven year—forty-seven year!

[*At the end he renounces her, and she goes off in despair.*

RECIT—FRED.

What shall I do? Before these gentle
maidens
I dare not show in this alarming costume.
No, no, I must remain in close conceal-
ment
Until I can appear in decent clothing!
(*Hides in cave as they enter climbing over
the rocks.*)

Girls

Climbing over rocky mountain,
Skipping rivulet and fountain,
Passing where the willows quiver
By the ever-rolling river,
　Swollen with the summer rain;
Threading long and leafy mazes
Dotted with unnumbered daisies;
Scaling rough and rugged passes,
Climb the hardy little lasses,
　Till the bright sea-shore they gain!

Edith

Let us gaily tread the measure,
Make the most of fleeting leisure;
Hail it as a true ally,
Though it perish by and by.

All

　Hail it as a true ally,
　Though it perish by and by.

Edith

Every moment brings a treasure
Of its own especial pleasure,
Though the moments quickly die,
Greet them gaily as they fly.

Kate.

Far away from toil and care,
Revelling in fresh sea air,
Here we live and reign alone
In a world that's all our own.
Here in this our rocky den,
Far away from mortal men,
We'll be queens, and make decrees—
They may honour them who please.

All

Let us gaily tread the measure, etc.

Kate. What a picturesque spot! I wonder
where we are!

Edith. And I wonder where papa is. We
have left him ever so far behind.

Isabel. Oh, he will be here presently!
Remember poor papa is not as young as
we are, and we have come over a rather
difficult country.

Kate. But how thoroughly delightful it
is to be so entirely alone! Why, in all probability we are the first human beings who
ever set foot on this enchanting spot.

Isabel. Except the mermaids — it's the
very place for mermaids.

Kate. Who are only human beings down
to the waist!

Edith. And who can't be said strictly
to set *foot* anywhere. Tails they may, but
feet they *cannot*.

Kate. But what shall we do until papa
and the servants arrive with the luncheon?

Edith. We are quite alone, and the sea
is as smooth as glass. Suppose we take
off our shoes and stockings and paddle?

All. Yes, yes! The very thing! (*They
prepare to carry out the suggestion. They
have all taken off one shoe, when* FREDERIC
comes forward from cave.)

Frederic (*recitative*)

Stop, ladies, pray!
　　All (*hopping on one foot*)
　A man!

Frederic

I had intended
Not to intrude myself upon your notice
In this effective but alarming costume,
But under these peculiar circumstances
It is my bounden duty to inform you
That your proceedings will not be unwit-
nessed!

Edith

But who are you, sir? Speak! (*All
hopping.*)

Frederic

I am a pirate!
　　All (*recoiling, hopping*)
　A pirate! Horror!

Frederic

Ladies, do not shun me!
This evening I renounce my wild profession;
And to that end, oh, pure and peerless
maidens!
Oh, blushing buds of ever-blooming
beauty!
I, sore at heart, implore your kind assistance.

Edith

How pitiful his tale!

Kate

How rare his beauty!

All

How pitiful his tale! How rare his beauty!
SONG—FRED.

Oh, is there not one maiden breast
  Which does not feel the moral beauty
Of making worldly interest
  Subordinate to sense of duty?
Who would not give up willingly
  All matrimonial ambition,
To rescue such a one as I
  From his unfortunate position?

All

Alas! there's not one maiden breast
  Which seems to feel the moral beauty
Of making worldly interest
  Subordinate to sense of duty!

Frederic

Oh, is there not one maiden here
  Whose homely face and bad complexion
Have caused all hopes to disappear
  Of ever winning man's affection?
To such a one, if such there be,
  I swear by Heaven's arch above you,
If you will cast your eyes on me—
  However plain you be—I'll love you!

All

Alas! there's not one maiden here
  Whose homely face and bad complexion
Have caused all hope to disappear
  Of ever winning man's affection!

Frederic (in despair)

Not one?

All

No, no—not one!

Frederic

Not one?

All

No, no!

MABEL *enters*

Mabel

Yes, one!

All

'Tis Mabel!

Mabel

Yes, 'tis Mabel!
RECIT—MABEL

Oh, sisters, deaf to pity's name,
  For shame!
It's true that he has gone astray,
  But pray
Is that a reason good and true
  Why you
Should all be deaf to pity's name?

All (aside)

The question is, had he not been
  A thing of beauty,
Would she be swayed by quite as keen
  A sense of duty?

Mabel

For shame, for shame, for shame!
SONG—MABEL

Poor wandering one!
Though thou hast surely strayed,
  Take heart of grace,
  Thy steps retrace,
Poor wandering one!
Poor wandering one!
If such poor love as mine
  Can help thee find
  True peace of mind—
Why, take it, it is thine!
  Take heart, fair days will shine;
  Take any heart—take mine!

All

Take heart; no danger lowers;
Take any heart—but ours!
  [*Exeunt* MABEL *and* FREDERIC.
(*Edith beckons her sisters, who form in a
    semicircle around her.*)

Edith

What ought we to do,
  Gentle sisters, say?
Propriety, we know,
  Says we ought to stay;
While sympathy exclaims,
  "Free them from your tether—
Play at other games—
  Leave them here together."

Kate

Her case may, any day,
  Be yours, my dear, or mine.
Let her make her hay
  While the sun doth shine.
Let us compromise,
  (Our hearts are not of leather.)
Let us shut our eyes,
  And talk about the weather.

Girls

Yes, yes, let's talk about the weather.
Chattering chorus

How beautifully blue the sky,
The glass is rising very high,
Continue fine I hope it may,
And yet it rained but yesterday.
To-morrow it may pour again
(I hear the country wants some rain),
Yet people say, I know not why,

That we shall have a warm July.

Enter MABEL *and* FREDERIC

[*During* MABEL'S *solo the* GIRLS *continue chatter pianissimo, but listening eagerly all the time.*

SOLO—MABEL

Did ever maiden wake
　From dream of homely duty,
To find her daylight break
　With such exceeding beauty?
Did ever maiden close
　Her eyes on waking sadness,
To dream of such exceeding gladness?

Frederic

Oh, yes! ah, yes! this is exceeding gladness,

Girls

How beautifully blue the sky, etc.

SOLO—FRED

[*During this,* GIRLS *continue their chatter pianissimo as before, but listening intently all the time.*

Did ever pirate roll
　His soul in guilty dreaming,
And wake to find that soul
　With peace and virtue beaming?

ENSEMBLE

Mabel	*Fred*	*Girls*
Did ever maiden wake, etc.	Did ever pirate roll, etc.	How beautifully blue the sky, etc.

RECIT—FRED

Stay, we must not lose our senses;
　Men who stick at no offences
　　Will anon be here.
Piracy their dreadful trade is;
　Pray you, get you hence, young ladies,
　　While the coast is clear.

[FREDERIC *and* MABEL *retire.*

Girls

No, we must not lose our senses,
　If they stick at no offences
　　We should not be here.
Piracy their dreadful trade is—
Nice companions for the young ladies!
　Let us disappear.

[*During this chorus the* PIRATES *have entered stealthily, and formed in a semi-circle behind the* GIRLS. *As the* GIRLS *move to go off each* PIRATE *seizes a girl.* KING *seizes* EDITH *and* ISABEL, SAMUEL *seizes* KATE.

All
Too late!
Pirates
Ha! Ha!
All
Too late!
Pirates
Ha! Ha!
Ha! ha! ha! ha! Ha! ha! ha! ha!

ENSEMBLE

(*Pirates pass in front of Girls.*)
Pirates

Here's a first-rate opportunity
To get married with impunity,
And indulge in the felicity
Of unbounded domesticity.
You shall quickly be parsonified,
Conjugally matrimonified,
By a doctor of divinity,
Who resides in this vicinity.

(*Girls pass in front of Pirates.*)
Girls

We have missed our opportunity
Of escaping with impunity;
So farewell to the felicity
Of our maiden domesticity!
We shall quickly be parsonified,
Conjugally matrimonified,
By a doctor of divinity,
Who resides in this vicinity.

And father is a Major-General!
Sam. (*cowed*)
We'd better pause, or danger may befall,
Their father is a Major-General.

Girls

Yes, yes; he is a Major-General!

Mabel (*coming forward*).
RECIT

Hold, monsters! Ere your pirate caravan-
　　serai
　Proceed, against our will, to wed us all,
Just bear in mind that we are Wards in
　Chancery.

The MAJOR-GENERAL *has entered unnoticed,*
on rock
General
Yes, I am a Major-General!
Samuel
For he is a Major-General!
All
He is! Hurrah for the Major-General!
General
And it is—it is a glorious thing
To be a Major-General!
All
It is! Hurrah for the Major-General!
SONG—MAJOR-GENERAL
I am the very model of a modern Major-
General,
I've information vegetable, animal, and
mineral,
I know the kings of England, and I quote
the fights historical,
From Marathon to Waterloo, in order cate-
gorical;
I'm very well acquainted too with mat-
ters mathematical,
I understand equations, both the simple
and quadratical,
About binomial theorem I'm teeming with
a lot o' news—
With many cheerful facts about the square
of the hypotenuse.
All
With many cheerful facts, etc.
General
I'm very good at integral and differential
calculus,
I know the scientific names of beings ani-
malculous;
In short, in matters vegetable, animal, and
mineral,
I am the very model of a modern Major-
General.
All
In short, in matters vegetable, animal, and
mineral,
He is the very model of a modern Major-
General.
General
I know our mythic history, King Arthur's
and Sir Caradoc's,
I answer hard acrostics, I've a pretty taste
for paradox,
I quote in elegiacs all the crimes of Helio-
gabalus,

In conics I can floor peculiarities para-
bolous.
I can tell undoubted Raphaels from Ger-
ard Dows and Zoffanies,
I know the croaking chorus from the
Frogs of Aristophanes,
Then I can hum a fugue of which I've
heard the music's din afore,
And whistle all the airs from that infernal
nonsense *Pinafore*.
All
And whistle all the airs, etc.
General
Then I can write a washing bill in Baby-
lonic cuneiform,
And tell you every detail of Caractacus's
uniform;
In short, in matters vegetable, animal and
mineral,
I am the very model of a modern Major-
General.
All
In short, in matters vegetable, animal, and
mineral,
He is the very model of a modern Major-
General.
General
In fact, when I know what is meant by
"mamelon" and "ravelin,"
When I can tell at sight a chassepôt rifle
from a javelin,
When such affairs as sorties and surprises
I'm more wary at,
And when I know precisely what is meant
by "commissariat",
When I have learnt what progress has
been made in modern gunnery,
When I know more of tactics than a novice
in a nunnery:
In short, when I've a smattering of ele-
mental strategy,
You'll say a better Major-Gener*al* has
never *sat* a gee—
All
You'll say a better, etc.
General
For my military knowledge, though I'm
plucky and adventury,
Has only been brought down to the be-
ginning of the century;
But still in matters vegetable, animal, and
mineral,
I am the very model of a modern Major-
General.

All

But still in matters vegetable, animal, and
    mineral,
He is the very model of a modern Major-
    General.

Gen. And now that I've introduced myself I should like to have some idea of
what's going on.

Kate. Oh, papa—we——

Sam. Permit me, I'll explain in two
words: we propose to marry your daughters.

Girls. Dear me!

Girls. Against our wills, papa—against
our wills!

Gen. Oh, but you mustn't do that! May
I ask—this is a picturesuqe uniform, but
I'm not familiar with it. What are you?

King. We are all single gentlemen.

Gen. Yes, I gathered that—anything
else?

King. No, nothing else.

Edith. Papa, don't believe them; they
are pirates—the famous Pirates of Penzance!

Gen. The Pirates of Penzance! I have
often heard of them.

Mabel. All except this gentleman—(*indicating* FREDERIC)—who was a pirate
once, but who is out of his indentures to-
day, and who means to lead a blameless
life evermore.

Gen. But wait a bit. I object to pirates
as sons-in-law.

King. We object to Major-Generals as
fathers-in-law. But we waive that point.
We do not press it. We look over it.

Gen. (*aside*). Hah! an idea! (*Aloud.*)
And do you mean to say that you would
deliberately rob me of these, the sole remaining props of my old age, and leave
me to go through the remainder of my
life unfriended, unprotected, and alone?

King. Well, yes, that's the idea.

Gen. Tell me, have you ever known
what it is to be an orphan?

Pirates (*disgusted*). Oh, dash it all!

King. Here we are again!

Gen. I ask you, have you ever known
what it is to be an orphan?

King. Often!

Gen. Yes, orphan. Have you ever known
what is to be one?

King. I say, often.

All (*disgusted*). Often, often, often.
(*Turning away.*)

Gen. I don't think we quite understand
one another. I ask you, have you ever
known what it is to be an orphan, and
you say "orphan". As I understand you,
you are merely repeating the word "orphan" to show that you understand me.

King. I didn't repeat the word often.

Gen. Pardon me, you did indeed.

King. I only repeated it once.

Gen. True, but you repeated it.

King. But not often.

Gen. Stop: I think I see where we are
getting confused. When you said "orphan",
did you mean "orphan"—a person who has
lost his parents, or "often"—frequently?

King. Ah! I beg pardon—I see what you
mean—frequently.

Gen. Ah! you said often—frequently.

King. No, only once.

Gen. (*irritated*). Exactly—you said often,
frequently, only once.

RECIT—GENERAL

Oh, men of dark and dismal fate,
    Forgo your cruel employ,
Have pity on my lonely state,
    I am an orphan boy!

King and Samuel

An orphan boy?

General

An orphan boy!

Pirates

How sad—an orphan boy.

SOLO—GENERAL

These children whom you see
    Are all that I can call my own!

Pirates

    Poor fellow!

General

Take them away from me
    And I shall be indeed alone.

Pirates

    Poor fellow!

General

If pity you can feel,
    Leave me my sole remaining joy—
See, at your feet they kneel;
    Your hearts you cannot steel
Against the sad, sad tale of the lonely
    orphan boy!

Pirates (*sobbing*).

    Poor fellow!
See at our feet they kneel;

Our hearts we cannot steel
Against the sad, sad tale of the lonely
    orphan boy!
King
The orphan boy!

Samuel
The orphan boy!

All
The lonely orphan boy! Poor fellow!

ENSEMBLE

General (aside)

I'm telling a terrible story,
But it doesn't diminish my
    glory;
For they would have taken
    my daughters
Over the billowy waters.

If I hadn't, in elegant dic-
    tion,
Indulged in an innocent fic-
    tion;
Which is not in the same
    cate*gory*
As a regular terrible story.

Girls (aside)

He's telling a terrible story,
Which will tend to diminish
    his glory;
Though they would have
    taken his daughters
Over the billowy waters.

It's easy, in elegant diction,

To call it an innocent fic-
    tion,
But it comes in the same
    cate*gory*
As a regular terrible story.

Pirates (aside)

If he's telling a terrible
    story,
He shall die by a death that
    is gory,
One of the cruellest slaugh-
    ters
That ever were known in
    these waters;
And we'll finish his moral
    affliction
By a very complete male-
    diction,
As a compliment valedic-
    tory,
If he's telling a terrible
    story.

King
Although our dark career
    Sometimes involves the crime of steal-
      ing,
We rather think that we're
    Not altogether void of feeling.
Although we live by strife,
    We're always sorry to begin it,
For what, we ask, is life
    Without a touch of Poetry in it?
All (kneeling)
Hail, Poetry, thou heaven-born maid!
Thou gildest e'en the pirate's trade:
Hail, flowing fount of sentiment!
All hail, Divine Emollient! (*All rise.*)
King
You may go, for you're at liberty, our
    pirate rules protect you,
And honorary members of our band we
    do elect you!
Samuel
For he is an orphan boy.
Chorus
He is! Hurrah for the orphan boy.
General
And it sometimes is a useful thing
    To be an orphan boy.
Chorus
It is! Hurrah for the orphan boy!

Oh, happy day, with joyous glee
They will away and married be;
Should it befall auspiciously,
Our sisters all will bridesmaids be!
RUTH *enters and comes down to* FREDERIC
Ruth
Oh, master, hear one word, I do implore
    you!
Remember Ruth, your Ruth, who kneels
    before you!
Chorus
Yes, yes, remember Ruth, who kneels be-
    fore you!
Frederic (Pirates threaten Ruth)
Away, you did deceive me!
Chorus
Away, you did deceive him!
Ruth
Oh, do not leave me!
Chorus
Oh, do not leave her!
Frederic
Away, you grieve me!
Chorus
Away, you grieve him!
Frederic
I wish you'd leave me!
    (FREDERIC *casts* RUTH *from him.*)

Chorus

We wish you'd leave him!

Ensemble

Pray observe the magnanimity
(We) (They) display to lace and dimity!
Never was such opportunity
To get married with impunity,
But (we) (they) give up the felicity
Of unbounded domesticity,
Though a doctor of divinity
Resides in this vicinity.

[GIRLS *and* GENERAL *go up rocks, while*
PIRATES *indulge in a wild dance of delight on stage. The* GENERAL *produces a
British flag, and the* PIRATE KING *produces
a black flag with skull and cross-bones.
Enter* RUTH, *who makes a final appeal
to* FREDERIC, *who casts her from him.*

END OF ACT I

ACT II

SCENE.—*A Ruined Chapel by Moonlight.
Ruined Gothic windows at back.* GEN-
ERAL STANLEY *discovered seated pensive-
ly, surrounded by his daughters.*

Chorus

Oh, dry the glistening tear
    That dews that martial cheek;
Thy loving children hear,
    In them thy comfort seek.
With sympathetic care
    Their arms around thee creep,
For oh, they cannot bear
    To see their father weep!

Enter MABEL

SOLO—MABEL

Dear father, why leave your bed
    At this untimely hour,
When happy daylight is dead,
    And darksome dangers lower?
See heaven has lit her lamp,
    The midnight hour is past,
The chilly night air is damp,
    And the dews are falling fast!
Dear father, why leave your bed
When happy daylight is dead?

FREDERIC *enters*

Mabel. Oh, Frederic, cannot you, in the
calm excellence of your wisdom, reconcile
it with your conscience to say something
that will relieve my father's sorrow?

Fred. I will try, dear Mabel. But why
does he sit, night after night, in this
draughty old ruin?

Gen. Why do I sit here? To escape from
the pirates' clutches, I described myself
as an orphan, and, heaven help me, I am
no orphan! I come here to humble myself
before the tombs of my ancestors, and
to implore their pardon for having brought
dishonour on the family escutcheon.

Fred. But you forget, sir, you only
bought the property a year ago, and the
stucco in your baronial hall is scarcely dry.

Gen. Frederic, in this chapel are ancestors: you cannot deny that. With the estate, I bought the chapel and its contents.
I don't know whose ancestors they *were*,
but I know whose ancestors they *are*,
and I shudder to think that their descend-
ant by purchase (if I may so describe
myself) should have brought disgrace upon
what, I have no doubt, was an unstained
escutcheon.

Fred. Be comforted. Had you not acted
as you did, these reckless men would assuredly have called in the nearest clergyman, and have married your large family
on the spot.

Gen. I thank you for your proffered
solace, but it is unavailing. I assure you,
Frederic, that such is the anguish and remorse I feel at the abominable falsehood
by which I escaped these easily deluded
pirates, that I would go to their simple-
minded chief this very night and confess
all, did I not fear that the consequences
would be most disastrous to myself. At
what time does your expedition march
against these scoundrels?

Fred. At eleven, and before midnight I
hope to have atoned for my involuntary
association with the pestilent scourges by
sweeping them from the face of the earth
—and then, dear Mabel, you will be mine!

Gen. Are your devoted followers at hand?

Fred. They are, they only wait my orders.

RECIT—GENERAL

Then, Frederic, let your escort lion-hearted
Be summoned to receive a General's bless-
    ing,
Ere they depart upon their dread adven-
    ture.

Fred. Dear sir, they come.

Enter POLICE, *marching in single file. They
form in line, facing audience*

SONG—SERGEANT

When the foeman bares his steel,
    Tarantara! tarantara!
We uncomfortable feel,
    Tarantara!
And we find the wisest thing,
    Tarantara! tarantara!
Is to slap our chests and sing
    Tarantara!
For when threatened with emeutes,
    Tarantara! tarantara!
And your heart is in your boots,
    Tarantara!
There is nothing brings it round,
    Tarantara! tarantara!
Like the trumpet's martial sound,
    Tarantara! tarantara!
Tarantara–ra–ra–ra–ra!

All

Tarantara–ra–ra–ra–ra!

Mabel

Go, ye heroes, go to glory,
Though you die in combat gory,
Ye shall live in song and story.
    Go to immortality!
Go to death, and go to slaughter;
Die, and every Cornish daughter
With her tears your grave shall water.
    Go, ye heroes, go and die!

All

Go, ye heroes, go and die!

Police

Though to us it's evident,
    Tarantara! tarantara!
These intentions are well meant,
    Tarantara!

Chorus of all but Police

Go and do your best endeavour,
And before all links we sever
We will say farewell for ever.
    Go to glory and the grave!
For your foes are fierce and ruthless,
False, unmerciful, and truthless.
Young and tender, old and toothless,
    All in vain their mercy crave.

Such expressions don't appear,
    Tarantara! tarantara!
Calculated men to cheer,
    Tarantara!
Who are going to meet their fate
In a highly nervous state,
    Tarantara!
Still to us it's evident
These intentions are well meant.
    Tarantara!

Edith

Go and do your best endeavour,
And before all links we sever,
We will say farewell for ever.
    Go to glory and the grave!

Girls

For your foes are fierce and ruthless,
False, unmerciful, and truthless.
Young and tender, old and toothless,
    All in vain their mercy crave.

Sergeant

We observe too great a stress,
On the risks that on us press,
And of reference a lack
To our chance of coming back.
Still, perhaps it would be wise
Not to carp or criticise,
For it's very evident
These attentions are well meant.

All

Yes, to them it's evident
Our attentions are well meant.
    Tarantara–ra–ra–ra–ra!
Go, ye heroes, go to glory, etc.

ENSEMBLE

Chorus of Police

Such expressions don't appear,
    Tarantara, tarantara!
Calculated men to cheer,
    Tarantara!
Who are going to their fate,
    Tarantara, tarantara!
In a highly nervous state—
    Tarantara!
We observe too great a stress,
    Tarantara, tarantara!
On the risks that on us press,
    Tarantara!
And of reference a lack,
    Tarantara, tarantara!
To our chance of coming back,
    Tarantara!

General

Away, away!

POLICE (*without moving*)

Yes, yes, we go.

General

These pirates slay.

Police

Tarantara!

General

Then do not stay.

Police

Tarantara!

General

Then why this delay?

Police

All right—we go.

Yes, forward on the foe!

General

Yes, but you *don't* go!

Police

We go, we go!

Yes, forward on the foe!

General

Yes, but you *don't* go!

All

At last they really go.

[MABEL *tears herself from* FREDERIC *and
exit, followed by her sisters, consoling
her. The* GENERAL *and others follow.*
FREDERIC *remains.*

RECIT—FRED

Now for the pirates' lair! Oh, joy unbounded!

Oh, sweet relief! Oh, rapture unexampled!

At last I may atone, in some slight
measure,

For the repeated acts of theft and pillage

Which, at a sense of duty's stern dictation,

I, circumstance's victim, have been guilty.

(KING *and* RUTH *appear at the window,
armed.*)

King

Young Frederic! (*Covering him with
pistol.*)

Frederic

Who calls?

King

Your late commander!

Ruth

And I, your little Ruth! (*Covering him
with pistol.*)

Frederic

Oh, mad intruders,

How dare ye face me? Know ye not, oh
rash ones,

That I have doomed you to extermination?

(KING *and* RUTH *hold a pistol to each ear.*)

King

Have mercy on us, hear us, ere you slaughter.

Frederic

I do not think I ought to listen to you.

Yet, mercy should alloy our stern resent-
ment,

And so I will be merciful—say on!

TRIO—RUTH, KING, *and* FRED

Ruth

When you had left our pirate fold

  We tried to raise our spirits faint,

According to our customs old,

  With quips and quibbles quaint.

But all in vain the quips we heard,

  We lay and sobbed upon the rocks,

Until to somebody occurred

  A startling paradox.

Frederic

  A paradox?

KING (*laughing*).

  A paradox!

Ruth

A most ingenious paradox!

We've quips and quibbles heard in flocks,

But none to beat this paradox!

  Ha! ha! ha! ha! Ho! ho! ho! ho!

King

We knew your taste for curious quips,

  For cranks and contradictions queer,

And with the laughter on our lips,

  We wished you there to hear.

We said, "If we could tell it him,

  How Frederic would the joke enjoy!"

And so we've risked both life and limb

  To tell it to our boy.

Frederic (*interested*).

That paradox? That paradox?

King and Ruth (*laughing*).

That most ingenious paradox!

We've quips and quibbles heard in flocks,

But none to beat that paradox!

  Ha! ha! ha! ha! Ho! ho! ho! ho!

CHANT—KING

For some ridiculous reason, to which, however, I've no desire to be disloyal,

Some person in authority, I don't know
who, very likely the Astronomer Royal,

Has decided that, although for such a
beastly month as February, twenty-eight
days as a rule are plenty.
One year in every four his days shall be
reckoned as nine-and-twenty.
Through some singular coincidence — I
shouldn't be surprised if it were owing
to the agency of an ill-natured fairy—
You are the victim of this clumsy arrangement, having been born in leap-year,
on the twenty-ninth of February,
And so, by a simple arithmetical process,
you'll easily discover,
That though you've lived twenty-one years,
yet, if we go by birthdays, you're only
five and a little bit over!

Ruth

Ha! ha! ha! ha!

King

Ho! ho! ho! ho!

Frederic

Dear me!
Let's see! (*counting on fingers*).
Yes, yes; with yours my figures do
agree!

All

Ha! ha! ha! Ho! ho! ho! ho! (FRED-
ERIC *more amused than any.*)

Frederic

How quaint the ways of Paradox!
At common sense she gaily mocks!
Though counting in the usual way,
   Years twenty-one I've been alive,
Yet, reckoning by my natal day,
   I am a little boy of five!

All

He is a little boy of five! Ha! ha!
A paradox, a paradox,
A most ingenious paradox!
Ha! ha! ha! Ho! ho! ho! ho! (RUTH
   and KING *throw themselves back on
   seats, exhausted with laughter.*)

Fred. Upon my word, this is most curious—most absurdly whimsical. Five-and-
a-quarter! No one would think it to look
at me!

Ruth. You are glad now, I'll be bound,
that you spared us. You would never have
forgiven yourself when you discovered
that you had killed *two of your comrades.*

Fred. My comrades?

King (*rises*). I'm afraid you don't appreciate the delicacy of your position. You
were apprenticed to us——

Fred. Until I reached my twenty-first
year.

King. No, until you reached your twenty-first *birthday* (*producing document*),
and, going by birthdays, you are as yet
only five-and-a-quarter.

Fred. You don't mean to say you are
going to hold me to that?

King. No, we merely remind you of the
fact, and leave the rest to your sense of
duty.

Ruth. Your sense of duty!

Fred. (*wildly*). Don't put it on that
footing! As I was merciful to you just
now, be merciful to me! I implore you not
to insist on the letter of your bond just
as the cup of happiness is at my lips!

Ruth. We insist on nothing; we content
ourselves with pointing out to you *your
duty.*

King. Your duty!

Fred. (*after a pause*). Well, you have
appealed to my sense of duty, and my duty
is only too clear. I abhor your infamous
calling; I shudder at the thought that I
have ever been mixed up with it; but duty
is before all—at any price I will do my
duty.

King. Bravely spoken! Come, you are
one of us once more.

Fred. Lead on, I follow. (*Suddenly.*)
Oh, horror!

King. Ruth. What is the matter?

Fred. Ought I to tell you? No, no, I
cannot do it; and yet, as one of your
band——

King. Speak out, I charge you by that
sense of conscientiousness to which we have
never yet appealed in vain.

Fred. General Stanley, the father of my
Mabel——

King. Ruth. Yes, yes!

Fred. He escaped from you on the plea
that he was an orphan!

King. He did!

Fred. It breaks my heart to betray the
honoured father of the girl I adore, but
as your apprentice I have no alternative.
It is my duty to tell you that General
Stanley is no orphan!

King. Ruth. What!

Fred. More than that, he never was one!

King. Am I to understand that, to save

his contemptible life, he dared to practise on our credulous simplicity? (FREDERIC *nods as he weeps.*) Our revenge shall be swift and terrible. We will go and collect our band and attack Tremorden Castle this very night.

Fred. But—stay——

King. Not a word! He is doomed!

TRIO

King and Ruth

Away, away! my heart's on fire,
  I burn this base deception to repay,
This very night my vengeance dire
  Shall glut itself in gore. Away, away!

King

With falsehood foul
He tricked us of our brides.
Let vengeance howl;
The Pirate so decides.
Our nature stern
He softened with his lies,
  And, in return,
Tonight the traitor dies.

All

Yes, yes! to-night the traitor dies.

Ruth

To-night he dies!

King

Yes, or early to-morrow.

Frederic

His girls likewise?

Ruth

They will welter in sorrow.

King

The one soft spot

Frederic

In their natures they cherish—

Ruth

And all who plot

King

To abuse it shall perish!

All

Yes, all who plot
To abuse it shall perish!
Away, away! etc.

[*Exeunt* KING *and* RUTH.
Enter MABEL
RECIT—MABEL

All is prepared, your gallant crew await
    you.
My Frederic in tears? It cannot be
That lion-heart quails at the coming con-
    flict?

Frederic

No, Mabel, no. A terrible disclosure
Has just been made! Mabel, my dearly-
    loved one,

Frederic

Away, away! ere I expire—
  I find my duty hard to do today!
My heart is filled with anguish dire,
  It strikes me to the core. Away, away!

I bound myself to serve the pirate captain
Until I reached my one-and-twentieth
    birthday—

Mabel

But you *are* twenty-one?

Frederic

I've just discovered
That I was born in leap-year, and that
    birthday
Will not be reached by me till 1940.

Mabel

Oh, horrible! catastrophe appalling!

Frederic

And so, farewell!

Mabel

No, no! Ah, Frederic, hear me.
DUET—MABEL *and* FREDERIC

Mabel

Stay, Frederic, stay!
  They have no legal claim,
  No shadow of a shame
  Will fall upon thy name.
Stay, Frederic, stay!

Frederic

Nay, Mabel, nay!
  To-night I quit these walls,
  The thought of my soul appals,
  But when stern Duty calls,
I must obey.

Mabel

Stay, Frederic, stay!

Frederic

Nay, Mabel, nay!

Mabel

They have no claim—

Frederic

But Duty's name!
  The thought of my soul appals,
  But when stern Duty calls,
I must obey.

BALLAD—MABEL

Ah, leave me not to pine
  Alone and desolate;

No fate seemed fair as mine,
  No happiness so great!
And nature, day by day,
  Has sung, in accents clear,
This joyous roundelay,
  "He loves thee—he is here.
    Fa-la, fa-la, fa-la."
           Frederic
Ah, must I leave thee here
  In endless night to dream,
Where joy is dark and drear,
  And sorrow all supreme!
Where nature, day by day,
  Will sing, in altered tone,
This weary roundelay,
  "He loves thee—he is gone.
    Fa-la, fa-la, fa-la."
           Frederic
In 1940 I of age shall be,
I'll then return, and claim you—I declare
    it!

           Mabel
It seems so long!
           Frederic
Swear that, till then, you will be true to
    me.
           Mabel
  Yes, I'll be strong!
By all the Stanleys dead and gone, I
    swear it!

           ENSEMBLE

Oh, here is love, and here is truth,
  And here is food for joyous laughter.
He ⎱ will be faithful to ⎱ his ⎰ sooth
She ⎰   ⎰ her ⎰
Till we are wed, and even after.
[FREDERIC *rushes to window and leaps out.*
    MABEL (*almost fainting*).
No, I am brave! Oh, family descent,
How great thy charm, thy sway how ex-
    cellent!
Come, one and all, undaunted men in blue,
A crisis now, affairs are coming to!
    Enter Police, marching in single file
           Sergeant
  Though in body and in mind,
    Tarantara, tarantara!
  We are timidly inclined,
    Tarantara!
  And anything but blind,
    Tarantara, tarantara!
  To the danger that's behind,
    Tarantara!

Yet, when the danger's near,
    Tarantara, tarantara!
  We manage to appear,
    Tarantara!
  As insensible to fear
  As anybody here.
    Tarantara, tarantara–ra–ra–ra–ra!
  Mabel. Sergeant, approach! Young Fred-
eric was to have led you to death and
glory.
  All. That is not a pleasant way of put-
ting it.
  Mabel. No matter; he will not so lead
you, for he has allied himself once more
with his old associates.
  All. He has acted shamefully!
  Mabel. You speak falsely. You know
nothing about it. He has acted nobly.
  All. He has acted nobly!
  Mabel. Dearly as I loved him before, his
heroic sacrifice to his sense of duty has en-
deared him to me tenfold. He has done
his duty. I will do mine. Go ye and do
yours.   [*Exit* MABEL.
  All. Right oh!
  Serg. This is perplexing.
  All. We cannot understand it at all.
  Serg. Still, as he is actuated by a sense
of duty——
  All. That makes a difference, of course.
At the same time we repeat, we cannot
understand it at all.
  Serg. No matter; our course is clear.
We must do our best to capture these
pirates alone. It is most distressing to us
to be the agents whereby our erring fellow-
creatures are deprived of that liberty which
is so dear to all—but we should have
thought of that before we joined the Force
  All. We should!
  Serg. It is too late now!
  All. It is!
           SONG—SERGEANT
           Sergeant
When a felon's not engaged in his employ-
    ment—
           All
           His employment,
           Sergeant
Or maturing his felonious little plans—
           All
           Little plans,
           Sergeant
His capacity for innocent enjoyment—

All
'Cent enjoyment
Sergeant
Is just as great as any honest man's—
All
Honest man's.
Sergeant
Our feelings we with difficulty smother—
All
'Culty smother
Sergeant
When constabulary duty's to be done—
All
To be done.
Sergeant
Ah, take one consideration with another—
All
With another,
Sergeant
A policeman's lot is not a happy one.
All
When constabulary duty's to be done—
To be done,
The policeman's lot is not a happy one.
Sergeant
When the enterprising burglar's not
a-burgling—
All
Not a-burgling,
Sergeant
When the cut-throat isn't occupied in
crime—
All
'Pied in crime,
Sergeant
He loves to hear the little brook a-gur-
gling—
All
Brook a-gurgling,
Sergeant
And listen to the merry village chime—
All
Village chime.
Sergeant
When the coster's finished jumping on his
mother—
All
On his mother,
Sergeant
He loves to lie a-basking in the sun—
All
In the sun.
Sergeant
Ah, take one consideration with another—

All
With another,
Sergeant
The policeman's lot is not a happy one.
All
When constabulary duty's to be done—
To be done,
The policeman's lot is not a happy one—
Happy one.
(*Chorus of Pirates without, in the
distance.*)
A rollicking band of pirates we,
Who, tired of tossing on the sea,
Are trying their hand at a burglaree,
With weapons grim and gory.
Sergeant
Hush, hush! I hear them on the manor
poaching,
With stealthy step the pirates are ap-
proaching.
(*Chorus of Pirates, resumed nearer.*)
We are not coming for plate or gold—
A story General Stanley's told—
We seek a penalty fifty-fold,
For General Stanley's story.
Police
They seek a penalty—
Pirates (*without*)
Fifty-fold,
We seek a penalty—
Police
Fifty-fold,
All
We }
They } seek a penalty fifty-fold,
For General Stanley's story.
Sergeant
They come in force, with stealthy stride,
Our obvious course is now—to hide.
[*Police conceal themselves. As they do so,
the Pirates are seen appearing at ruined
window. They enter cautiously, and
come down stage.* SAMUEL *is laden with
burglarious tools and pistols, etc.*
Chorus—Pirates (*very loud*)
With cat-like tread,
Upon our prey we steal,
In silence dread
Our cautious way we feel.
No sound at all,
We never speak a word,
A fly's foot-fall
Would be distinctly heard—
Police (*pianissimo*).

Tarantara, tarantara!
Pirates
So stealthily the pirate creeps,
While all the household soundly sleeps.
Come, friends, who plough the sea,
    Truce to navigation,
    Take another station;
Let's vary piracee
With a little burglaree!
Police (*pianissimo*)
Tarantara, tarantara!
Sam. (*distributing implements to various
    members of the gang*).
Here's your crowbar and your centrebit,
Your life-preserver—you may want to hit;
Your silent matches, your dark lantern
    seize,
Take your file and your skeletonic keys.
Enter KING, FREDERIC, *and* RUTH
All (*fortissimo*).
With cat-like tread, etc.
RECIT
Frederic
Hush, hush, not a word! I see a light in-
    side!
The Major-General comes, so quickly hide!
Pirates
Yes, yes, the Major-General comes!
    [*Exeunt* KING, FREDERIC, SAMUEL,
    and RUTH.

Police
Yes, yes, the Major-General comes!
General (*entering in dressing-gown, carry-
    ing a light*).
Yes, yes, the Major-General comes!
SOLO—GENERAL
Tormented with the anguish dread
Of falsehood unatoned,
I lay upon my sleepless bed,
    And tossed and turned and groaned.
The man who finds his conscience ache
No peace at all enjoys,
And as I lay in bed awake
    I thought I heard a noise.
Pirates
He thought he heard a noise—ha! ha!
Police
He thought he heard a noise—ha! ha!
    (*Very loud.*)
General
    No, all is still
    In dale, on hill;
My mind is set at ease.
    So still the scene—

It must have been
The sighing of the breeze.
BALLAD—GENERAL
Sighing softly to the river
    Comes the loving breeze,
Setting nature all a-quiver,
    Rustling through the trees—
All
    Through the trees.
General
And the brook, in rippling measure,
    Laughs for very love,
While the poplars, in their pleasure,
    Wave their arms above.
Police and Pirates
Yes, the trees, for very love,
Wave their leafy arms above,
River, river, little river,
May thy loving prosper ever.
Heaven speed thee, poplar tree,
May thy wooing happy be.
General
Yet, the breeze is but a rover;
    When he wings away,
Brook and poplar mourn a lover!
    Sighing well-a-day!
All
    Well-a-day!
General
Ah! the doing and undoing,
    That the rogue could tell!
When the breeze is out a-wooing,
    Who can woo so well?
Police and Pirates
Shocking tales the rogue could tell
Nobody can woo so well.
    Pretty brook, thy dream is over,
    For thy love is but a rover!
    Sad the lot of poplar trees,
    Courted by the fickle breeze!
    [*Enter the* GENERAL'S *daughters, all in
    white peignoirs and night-caps, and
    carrying lighted candles.*
Girls
Now what is this, and what is that, and
    why does father leave his rest
At such a time of night as this, so very in-
    completely dressed?
Dear father is, and always was, the most
    methodical of men!
It's his invariable rule to go to bed at
    half-past ten.
What strange occurrence can it be that
    calls dear father from his rest

At such a time of night as this, so very in-
completely dressed?

[Enter KING, SAMUEL, *and* FREDERIC

King

Forward, my men, and seize that General
there!

(They seize the GENERAL*)*

Girls

The pirates! the pirates! Oh, despair!

Pirates

Yes, we're the pirates, so despair!

General

Frederic here! Oh, joy! Oh, rapture!
Summon your men and effect their capture!

Mabel

Frederic, save us!

Frederic

Beautiful Mabel,
I would if I could, but I am not able.

Pirates

He's telling the truth, he is not able.

King

With base deceit
You worked upon our feelings!
Revenge is sweet,
And flavours all our dealings!
With courage rare
And resolution manly,
For death prepare,
Unhappy General Stanley.

Mabel (wildly)

Is he to die, unshriven—unannealed?

Girls

Oh, spare him!

Mabel

Will no one in his cause a weapon wield?

Girls

Oh, spare him!

Police (springing up)

Yes, we are here, though hitherto concealed!

Girls

Oh, rapture!

Police

So to the Constabulary, pirates, yield!

Girls

Oh, rapture!

*[A struggle ensues between Pirates and
Police. Eventually the Police are overcome, and fall prostrate, the Pirates
standing over them with drawn swords.*

CHORUS OF POLICE AND PIRATES

You ⎱
We ⎰ triumph now, for well we trow

Our mortal career's cut short,
No pirate band will take its stand
At the Central Criminal Court.

Sergeant

To gain a brief advantage you've contrived,
But your proud triumph will not be long-
lived.

King

Don't say you are orphans, for we know
that game.

Sergeant

On your allegiance we've a stronger
claim—
We charge you yield, in Queen Victoria's
name!

King (baffled)

You do!

Police

We do!
We charge you yield, in Queen Victoria's
name!

*[Pirates kneel, Police stand over them
triumphantly.*

King

We yield at once, with humbled mien,
Because, with all our faults, we love our
Queen.

Police

Yes, yes, with all their faults, they love
their Queen.

Girls

Yes, yes, with all, etc.

*[Police, holding Pirates by the collar,
take out handkerchiefs and weep.*

General

Away with them, and place them at the
bar!

Enter RUTH

Ruth

One moment! let me tell you who they
are.
They are no members of the common
throng;
They are all noblemen who have gone
wrong!

General

No Englishman unmoved that statement
hears,
Because, with all our faults, we love our
House of Peers.

RECIT—GENERAL

I pray you, pardon me, ex-Pirate King,
Peers will be peers, and youth will have
    its fling.
Resume your ranks and legislative duties,
And take my daughters, all of whom are
    beauties.

FINALE

Poor wandering ones!
   Though ye have surely strayed,

Take heart of grace.
Your steps retrace,
Poor wandering ones!
Poor wandering ones!
   If such poor love as ours
   Can help you find
   True peace of mind,
Why, take it, it is yours!
   Poor wandering ones! etc.
            CURTAIN

THE YEOMEN OF THE GUARD

OR

THE MERRYMAN AND HIS MAID

DRAMATIS PERSONÆ

SIR RICHARD CHOLMONDELEY (*Lieutenant of the Tower*)

COLONEL FAIRFAX (*under sentence of death*)

SERGEANT MERYLL (*of the Yeomen of the Guard*)

LEONARD MERYLL (*his Son*)

JACK POINT (*a Strolling Jester*)

WILFRED SHADBOLT (*Head Jailer and Assistant Tormentor*)

THE HEADSMAN

FIRST YEOMAN

SECOND YEOMAN

FIRST CITIZEN

SECOND CITIZEN

ELSIE MAYNARD (*a Strolling Singer*)

PHOEBE MERYLL (*Sergeant Meryll's Daughter*)

DAME CARRUTHERS (*Housekeeper to the Tower*)

KATE (*her Niece*)

Chorus of Yeomen of the Guard, Gentlemen, Citizens, etc.

Date, 16th Century.

ACT I

SCENE.—*Tower Green*
PHOEBE *discovered spinning*
SONG—PHOEBE

When maiden loves, she sits and sighs,
   She wanders to and fro;
Unbidden tear-drops fill her eyes,
And to all questions she replies
   With a sad "heigho!"
'Tis but a little word—"heigho!"
So soft, 'tis scarcely heard—"heigho!"
   An idle breath—
   Yet life and death
May hang upon a maid's "heigho!"
When maiden loves, she mopes apart,
   As owl mopes on a tree;
Although she keenly feels the smart,
She cannot tell what ails her heart,
   With its sad "Ah me!"
'Tis but a foolish sigh—"Ah me!"
Born but to droop and die—"Ah me!"
   Yet all the sense
   Of eloquence

Lies hidden in a maid's "Ah me!"
   (*Weeps.*)
      Enter WILFRED
Wil. Mistress Meryll!
Phoe. (*looking up*). Eh! Oh! it's you, is it? You may go away, if you like. Because I don't want you, you know.
Wil. Haven't you anything to say to me?
Phoe. Oh yes! Are the birds all caged? The wild beasts all littered down? All the locks, chains, bolts, and bars in good order? Is the Little Ease sufficiently uncomfortable? The racks, pincers, and thumbscrews all ready for work? Ugh! you brute!
Wil. These allusions to my professional duties are in doubtful taste. I didn't become a head-jailer because I like head-jailing. I didn't become an assistant-tormentor because I like assistant-tormenting. We can't *all* be sorcerers, you know. (PHOEBE, *annoyed.*) Ah! you brought that upon yourself.
Phoe. Colonel Fairfax is *not* a sorcerer.

63

He's a man of science and an alchemist.

Wil. Well, whatever he is, he won't be one long, for he's to be beheaded to-day for dealings with the devil. His master nearly had him last night, when the fire broke out in the Beauchamp Tower.

Phoe. Oh! how I wish he had escaped in the confusion! But take care; there's still time for a reply to his petition for mercy.

Wil. Ah! I'm content to chance that. This evening at half-past seven—ah!

Phoe. You're a cruel monster to speak so unfeelingly of the death of a young and handsome soldier.

Wil. Young and handsome! How do *you* know he's young and handsome?

Phoe. Because I've seen him every day for weeks past taking his exercise on the Beauchamp Tower.

Wil. Curse him!

Phoe. There, I believe you're jealous of *him,* now. Jealous of a man I've never spoken to! Jealous of a poor soul who's to die in an hour!

Wil. I am! I'm jealous of everybody and everything. I'm jealous of the very words I speak to you—because they reach your ears—and I mustn't go near 'em!

Phoe. How unjust you are! Jealous of the words you speak to me! Why, you know as well as I do that I don't even like them.

Wil. You used to like 'em.

Phoe. I used to *pretend* I liked them. It was mere politeness to comparative strangers.

[*Exit* PHOEBE, *with spinning wheel.*

Wil. I don't believe you know what jealousy is! I don't believe you know how it eats into a man's heart—and disorders his digestion—and turns his interior into boiling lead. Oh, you are a heartless jade to trifle with the delicate organization of the human interior!

[*Exit* WILFRED.

Enter Crowd of Men and Women, followed by Yeomen of the Guard.

CHORUS (*as Yeomen march on*)
Tower Warders,
    Under orders,
Gallant pikemen, valiant sworders!
    Brave in bearing,
    Foemen scaring,

In their bygone days of daring!
    Ne'er a stranger
    There to danger—
Each was o'er the world a ranger;
    To the story
    Of our glory
Each a bold contributory!

CHORUS OF YEOMEN
In the autumn of our life,
    Here at rest in ample clover,
We rejoice in telling over
    Our impetuous May and June.
In the evening of our day,
    With the sun of life declining,
We recall without repining
    All the heat of bygone noon.

SOLO—2ND YEOMAN
This the autumn of our life,
    This the evening of our day;
Weary we of battle strife,
    Weary we of mortal fray.
But our year is not so spent,
    And our days are not so faded,
But that we with one consent,
    Were our lovèd land invaded,
    Still would face a foreign foe,
    As in days of long ago.

Chorus
    Still would face a foreign foe,
    As in days of long ago.

PEOPLE
Tower Warders,
Under orders, etc.

YEOMEN

This the autumn of our life, etc.
[*Exeunt Crowd. Manent Yeomen*
    Enter DAME CARRUTHERS

Dame. A good day to you!

2nd Yeoman. Good day, Dame Carruthers. Busy to-day?

Dame. Busy, aye! the fire in the Beauchamp last night has given me work enough. A dozen poor prisoners—Richard Colfax, Sir Martin Byfleet, Colonel Fairfax, Warren the preacher-poet, and half a-score others—all packed into one small cell, not six feet square. Poor Colonel Fairfax, who's to die to-day, is to be removed to No. 14 in the Cold Harbour that he may have his last hour alone with his confessor; and I've to see to that.

2nd Yeo. Poor gentleman! He'll die bravely. I fought under him two year since, and he valued his life as it were a feather!

Phoe. He's the bravest, the handsomest, and the best young gentleman in England! He twice saved my father's life; and it's a cruel thing, a wicked thing, and a barbarous thing that so gallant a hero should lose his head—for it's the handsomest head in England!

Dame. For dealings with the devil. Aye! if all were beheaded who dealt with *him*, there'd be busy doings on Tower Green.

Phoe. You know very well that Colonel Fairfax is a student of alchemy—nothing more, and nothing less; but this wicked Tower, like a cruel giant in a fairy-tale, must be fed with blood, and that blood must be the best and bravest in England, or it's not good enough for the old Blunderbore. Ugh!

Dame. Silence, you silly girl; you know not what you say. I was born in the old keep, and I've grown grey in it, and, please God, I shall die and be buried in it; and there's not a stone in its walls that is not as dear to me as my own right hand.

SONG WITH CHORUS—DAME CARRUTHERS *and* YEOMEN

When our gallant Norman foes
  Made our merry land their own,
    And the Saxons from the Conqueror
    were flying,
At his bidding it arose,
  In its panoply of stone,
    A sentinel unliving and undying.
Insensible, I trow,
  As a sentinel should be,
    Though a queen to save her head
    should come a-suing.
There's a legend on its brow
  That is eloquent to me,
    And it tells of duty done and duty
    doing.
"The screw may twist and the rack
  may turn,
And men may bleed and men may
  burn,
O'er London town and its golden
  hoard
I keep my silent watch and ward!"

Chorus
  The screw may twist, etc.
Within its wall of rock
  The flower of the brave

Have perished with a constancy unshaken.
From the dungeon to the block,
  From the scaffold to the grave,
    Is a journey many gallant hearts have
    taken.
And the wicked flames may hiss
  Round the heroes who have fought
    For conscience and for home in all its
    beauty,
But the grim old fortalice
  Takes little heed of aught
    That comes not in the measure of its
    duty.
"The screw may twist and the rack
  may turn,
And men may bleed and men may
  burn,
O'er London town and its golden hoard
I keep my silent watch and ward!"

Chorus
  The screw may twist, etc.

    [*Exeunt all but* PHOEBE.
    Enter SERGEANT MERYLL.

Phoe. Father! Has no reprieve arrived for the poor gentleman?

Mer. No, my lass; but there's one hope yet. Thy brother Leonard, who, as a reward for his valour in saving his standard and cutting his way through fifty foes who would have hanged him, has been appointed a Yeoman of the Guard, will arrive to-day; and as he comes straight from Windsor, where the Court is, it may be— it *may* be—that he will bring the expected reprieve with him.

Phoe. Oh, that he may!

Mer. Amen to that! For the Colonel twice saved my life, and I'd give the rest of my life to save his! And wilt thou not be glad to welcome thy brave brother, with the fame of whose exploits all England is a-ringing?

Phoe. Aye, truly, if he brings the reprieve.

Mer. And not otherwise?

Phoe. Well, he's a brave fellow indeed, and I love brave men.

Mer. *All* brave men?

Phoe. Most of them, I verily believe! But I hope Leonard will not be too strict with me—they say he is a very dragon of virtue and circumspection! Now, my dear old father is kindness itself, and——

Mer. And leaves thee pretty well to thine own ways, eh? Well, I've no fears for thee; thou hast a featherbrain, but thou'rt a good lass.

Phoe. Yes, that's all very well, but if Leonard is going to tell me that I may not do this and I may not do that, and I must not talk to this one, or walk with that one, but go through the world with my lips pursed up and my eyes cast down, like a poor nun who has renounced mankind—why, as I have *not* renounced mankind, and don't mean to renounce mankind, I won't have it—there!

Mer. Nay, he'll not check thee more than is good for thee, Phoebe! He's a brave fellow, and bravest among brave fellows, and yet it seems but yesterday that he robbed the Lieutenant's orchard.

Enter LEONARD MERYLL

Leon. Father!

Mer. Leonard! my brave boy! I'm right glad to see thee, and so is Phoebe!

Phoe. Aye—hast thou brought Colonel Fairfax's reprieve?

Leon. Nay, I have here a despatch for the Lieutenant, but no reprieve for the Colonel!

Phoe. Poor gentleman! poor gentleman!

Leon. Aye, I would I had brought better news. I'd give my right hand—nay, my body—my life, to save his!

Mer. Dost thou speak in earnest, my lad?

Leon. Aye, father—I'm no braggart. Did he not save thy life? and am I not his foster-brother?

Mer. Then hearken to me. Thou hast come to join the Yeomen of the Guard!

Leon. Well?

Mer. None has seen thee but ourselves?

Leon. And a sentry, who took but scant notice of me.

Mer. Now to prove thy words. Give me the despatch, and get thee hence at once! Here is money, and I'll send thee more. Lie hidden for a space, and let no one know. I'll convey a suit of Yeoman's uniform to the Colonel's cell—he shall shave off his beard, so that none shall know him, and I'll own him as my son, the brave Leonard Meryll, who saved his flag and cut his way through fifty foes who thirsted for his life. He will be welcomed without ques-

tion by my brother-Yeomen, I'll warrant that. Now, to get access to the Colonel's cell? (*To* PHOEBE.) The key is with thy sour-faced admirer, Wilfred Shadbolt

Phoe. (*demurely*). I think—I say, I *think*—I can get anything I want from Wilfred. I think—mind I say, I *think*—you may leave that to me.

Mer. Then get thee hence at once, lad—and bless thee for this sacrifice.

Phoe. And take my blessing, too, dear dear Leonard!

Leon. And thine, eh? Humph! Thy love is newborn; wrap it up carefully, lest it take cold and die.

TRIO—PHOEBE, LEONARD, MERYLL

Phoebe

Alas! I waver to and fro!
Dark danger hangs upon the deed!

All

Dark danger hangs upon the deed!

All

Leonard

The scheme is rash and well may fail,
But ours are not the hearts that quail,
The hands that shrink, the cheeks that pale
In hours of need!

All

No, ours are not the hearts that quail,
The hands that shrink, the cheeks that pale
In hours of need!

Meryll

The air I breathe to him I owe:
My life is his—I count it naught!
Phoebe and Leonard
That life is his—so count it naught!

Meryll

And shall I reckon risks I run
When services are to be done
To save the life of such an one?
Unworthy thought!
Phoebe and Leonard
And shall we reckon risks we run
To save the life of such an one?

All

Unworthy thought!
We may succeed—who can foretell?
May heaven help our hope—farewell!

[LEONARD *embraces* MERYLL *and* PHOEBE *and then exit.* PHOEBE *weeping.*

Mer. Nay, lass, be of good cheer, we may save him yet.

Phoe. Oh! see, father—they bring the

oor gentleman from the Beauchamp! Oh, ather! his hour is not yet come?

Mer. No, no,—they lead him to the Cold Harbour Tower to await his end in solitude. But softly—the Lieutenant aproaches! He should not see thee weep. *Enter* FAIRFAX, *guarded. The* LIEUTENANT *enters, meeting him.*

Lieut. Halt! Colonel Fairfax, my old riend, we meet but sadly.

Fair. Sir, I greet you with all good-will; nd I thank you for the zealous care with which you have guarded me from the pesilent dangers which threaten human life utside. In this happy little community, Death, when he comes, doth so in punctual nd business-like fashion; and, like a ourtly gentleman, giveth due notice of his dvent, that one may not be taken unwares.

Lieut. Sir, you bear this bravely, as a rave man should.

Fair. Why, sir, it is no light boon to lie swiftly and surely at a given hour nd in a given fashion! Truth to tell, I would gladly have my life; but if that may ot be, I have the next best thing to it, which is death. Believe me, sir, my lot is ot so much amiss!

Phoe. (*aside to* MERYLL). Oh, father, ather, I cannot bear it!

Mer. My poor lass!

Fair. Nay, pretty one, why weepest hou? Come, be comforted. Such a life as nine is not worth weeping for. (*Sees* Meryll.*) Sergeant Meryll, is it not? (*To* LIEUT.) May I greet my old friend? *Shakes* MERYLL'S *hand.*) Why, man, what's ll this? Thou and I have faced the grim ld king a dozen times, and never has ais majesty come to me in such goodly 'ashion. Keep a stout heart, good fellow— ve are soldiers, and we know how to die, hou and I. Take my word for it, it is asier to die well than to live well—for, n sooth, I have tried both.

BALLAD—FAIRFAX

s life a boon?
  If so, it must befall,
  That Death, whene'er he call,
Must call too soon.
  Though fourscore years he give,
  Yet one would pray to live
Another moon!

What kind of plaint have I,
Who perish in July?
I might have had to die,
Perchance, in June!
Is life a thorn?
  Then count it not a whit!
  Man is well done with it;
Soon as he's born
  He should all means essay
  To put the plague away;
And I, war-worn,
  Poor captured fugitive,
  My life most gladly give—
I might have had to live
Another morn!
  [*At the end,* PHOEBE *is led off, weeping, by* MERYLL.

Fair. And now, Sir Richard, I have a boon to beg. I am in this strait for no better reason than because my kinsman, Sir Clarence Poltwhistle, one of the Secretaries of State, has charged me with sorcery, in order that he may succeed to my estate, which devolves to him provided I die unmarried.

Lieut. As thou wilt most surely do.

Fair. Nay, as I will most surely *not* do, by your worship's grace! I have a mind to thwart this good cousin of mine.

Lieut. How?

Fair. By marrying forthwith, to be sure!

Lieut. But heaven ha' mercy, whom wouldst thou marry?

Fair. Nay, I am indifferent on that score. Coming Death hath made of me a true and chivalrous knight, who holds all womankind in such esteem that the oldest, and the meanest, and the worst-favoured of them is good enough for him. So, my good Lieutenant, if thou wouldst serve a poor soldier who has but an hour to live, find me the first that comes—my confessor shall marry us, and her dower shall be my dishonoured name and a hundred crowns to boot. No such poor dower for an hour of matrimony!

Lieut. A strange request. I doubt that I should be warranted in granting it.

Fair. There never was a marriage fraught with so little of evil to the contracting parties. In an hour she'll be a widow, and I—a bachelor again for aught I know!

Lieut. Well, I will see what can be done, for I hold thy kinsman in abhorrence for the scurvy trick he has played thee.

Fair. A thousand thanks, good sir; we meet again on this spot in an hour or so. I shall be a bridegroom then, and your worship will wish me joy. Till then, farewell. (*To Guard.*) I am ready, good fellows.

[*Exit with Guard into Cold Harbour Tower.*

Lieut. He is a brave fellow, and it is a pity that he should die. Now, how to find him a bride at such short notice? Well, the task should be easy! [*Exit.*

Enter JACK POINT *and* ELSIE MAYNARD, *pursued by a crowd of men and women.* POINT *and* ELSIE *are much terrified;* POINT, *however, assuming an appearance of self-possession.*

Chorus

Heres a man of jollity,
Jibe, joke, jollify!
Give us of your quality,
Come, fool, follify!
If you vapour vapidly,
River runneth rapidly,
Into it we fling
Bird who doesn't sing!
Give us an experiment
In the art of merriment;
Into it we throw
Cock who doesn't crow!
Banish your timidity,
And with all rapidity
Give us quip and quiddity—
Willy-nilly, O!
River none can mollify;—
Into it we throw
Fool who doesn't follify,
Cock who doesn't crow!

Point (*alarmed*). My masters, I pray you bear with us, and we will satisfy you, for we are merry folk who would make all merry as ourselves. For, look you, there is humour in all things, and the true philosophy is that which teaches us to find it and to make the most of it.

Elsie (*struggling with one of the crowd*). Hands off, I say, unmannerly fellow!

Point (*to 1st Citizen*). Ha! Didst thou hear her say, "Hands off"?

1st Cit. Aye, I heard her say it, and I felt her do it! What then?

Point. Thou dost not see the humour of that?

1st Cit. Nay, if I do, hang me!

Point. Thou dost not? Now observe. She said, "Hands off!" Whose hands? Thine. Off whom? Off *her.* Why? Because she is a woman. Now, had she *not* been a woman, thine hands had not been set upon her at all. So the reason for the laying on of hands is the reason for the taking off of hands, and herein is contradiction contradicted! It is the very marriage of *pro* with *con;* and no such lopsided union either, as times go, for *pro* is not more unlike *con* than man is unlike woman—yet men and women marry every day with none to say, "Oh, the pity of it!" but I and fools like me! Now wherewithal shall we please you? We can rhyme you couplet, triolet, quatrain, sonnet, rondolet, ballade, what you will. Or we can dance you saraband, gondolet, carole, pimpernel, or Jumping Joan.

Elsie. Let us give them the singing farce of the Merryman and his Maid—therein is song and dance too.

All. Aye, the Merryman and his Maid!

DUET—ELSIE *and* POINT

Point

I have a song to sing, O!

Elsie

Sing me your song, O!
It is sung to the moon
By a love-lorn loon,
Who fled from the mocking throng, O!
It's a song of a merryman, moping mum,
Whose soul was sad, and whose glance was glum,
Who sipped no sup, and who craved no crumb,
As he sighed for the love of a ladye.
Heighdy! heighdy!
Misery me, lackadaydee!
He sipped no sup, and he craved no crumb,
As he sighed for the love of a ladye.

Elsie

I have a song to sing, O!

Point

What is your song, O?

Elsie

It is sung with the ring
Of the songs maids sing
Who love with a love life-long, O!
It's the song of a merrymaid, peerly proud,
Who loved a lord and who laughed aloud
At the moan of the merryman, moping mum,

Whose soul was sad, and whose glance was
glum,
Who sipped no sup, and who craved no
crumb,
  As he sighed for the love of a ladye.
    Heighdy! heighdy!
  Misery me, lackadaydee!
    He sipped no sup, etc.
          Point
I have a song to sing, O!
          Elsie
Sing me your song, O!
          Point
It is sung to the knell
Of a churchyard bell,
And a doleful dirge, ding dong, O!
It's a song of a popinjay, bravely born,
Who turned up his noble nose with scorn
At the humble merrymaid, peerly proud,
Who loved a lord, and who laughed aloud
At the moan of a merryman, moping mum,
Whose soul was sad, and whose glance was
glum,
Who sipped no sup, and who craved no
crumb,
  As he sighed for the love of a ladye.
          Both
    Heighdy! heighdy!
  Misery me, lackadaydee!
    He sipped no sup, etc.
          Elsie
I have a song to sing, O!
          Point
Sing me your song, O!
          Elsie
It is sung with a sigh
And a tear in the eye,
For it tells of a righted wrong, O!
It's a song of the merrymaid, once so gay,
Who turned on her heel and tripped away
From the peacock popinjay, bravely born,
Who turned up his noble nose with scorn
At the humble heart that he did not prize:
So she begged on her knees, with downcast
eyes,
For the love of the merryman, moping
mum,
Whose soul was sad, and whose glance was
glum,
Who sipped no sup, and who craved no
crumb,
  As he sighed for the love of a ladye.
          Both
    Heighdy! heighdy!

  Misery me, lackadaydee!
His pains were o'er, and he sighed **no more**,
For he lived in the love of a ladye.
  1st Cit. Well sung and well danced!
  2nd Cit. A kiss for that, pretty maid!
  All. Aye, a kiss all round.
  Elsie. (*drawing dagger*). Best beware! I
am armed!
  Point. Back, sirs—back! This is going
too far.
  2nd Cit. Thou dost not see the humour
of it, eh? Yet there is humour in all things
—even in this. (*Trying to kiss her.*)
  Elsie. Help! help!
Enter LIEUTENANT *with Guard. Crowd falls
back.*
  Lieut. What is this pother?
  Elsie. Sir, we sang to these folk, and they
would have repaid us with gross courtesy,
but for your honour's coming.
  Lieut. (*to Mob.*) Away with ye! Clear
the rabble. (*Guards push Crowd off, and
go off with them.*) Now, my girl, who are
you, and what do you here?
  Elsie. May it please you, sir, we are two
strolling players, Jack Point and I, Elsie
Maynard, at your worship's service. We
go from fair to fair, singing, and dancing,
and playing brief interludes; and so we
make a poor living.
  Lieut. You two eh? Are ye man and
wife?
  Point. No, sir; for though I'm a fool,
there is a limit to my folly. Her mother,
old Bridget Maynard, travels with us (for
Elsie is a good girl), but the old woman
is a-bed with fever, and we have come
here to pick up some silver to buy an
electuary for her.
  Lieut. Hark ye, my girl! Your mother
is ill?
  Elsie. Sorely ill, sir.
  Lieut. And needs good food, and many
things that thou canst not buy?
  Elsie. Alas! sir, it is too true.
  Lieut. Wouldst thou earn an hundred
crowns?
  Elsie. An hundred crowns! They might
save her life!
  Lieut. Then listen! A worthy but unhappy gentleman is to be beheaded in an
hour on this very spot. For sufficient reasons, he desires to marry before he dies, and

he hath asked me to find him a wife. Wilt
thou be that wife?

Elsie. The wife of a man I have never
seen!

Point. Why, sir, look you, I am concerned in this; for though I am not yet
wedded to Elsie Maynard, time works wonders, and there's no knowing what may be
in store for us. Have we your worship's
word for it that this gentleman will die
to-day?

Lieut. Nothing is more certain, I grieve
to say.

Point. And that the maiden will be allowed to depart the very instant the ceremony is at an end?

Lieut. The very instant. I pledge my
honour that it shall be so.

Point. An hundred crowns?

Lieut. An hundred crowns!

Point. For my part, I consent. It is for
Elsie to speak.

TRIO—ELSIE, POINT, *and* LIEUTENANT

Lieutenant

How say you, maiden, will you wed
A man about to lose his head?
   For half an hour
     You'll be a wife,
   And then the dower
     Is yours for life.
A headless bridegroom why refuse?
If truth the poets tell,
Most bridegrooms, ere they marry, lose
Both head and heart as well!

Elsie

A strange proposal you reveal,
It almost makes my senses reel.
Alas! I'm very poor indeed,
And such a sum I sorely need.
   My mother, sir, is like to die,
     This money life may bring.
   Bear this in mind, I pray, if I
     Consent to do this thing!

Point

Though as a general rule of life
I don't allow my promised wife,
My lovely bride that is to be,
To marry any one but me,
   Yet if the fee is promptly paid,
     And he, in well-earned grave,
   Within the hour is duly laid,
     Objection I will waive!
     Yes, objection I will waive!

All

Temptation, oh, temptation,
   Were we, I pray, intended
To shun, whate'er our station,
   Your fascinations splendid;
Or fall, whene'er we view you,
   Head over heels into you?
Temptation, oh, temptation, etc.

[*During this, the lieutenant has whispered
to* WILFRED (*who has entered*). WIL-
FRED *binds* ELSIE's *eyes with a kerchief,
and leads her into the Cold Harbour
Tower.*

Lieut. And so, good fellow, you are a
jester?

Point. Aye, sir, and like some of my
jests, out of place.

Lieut. I have a vacancy for such an one.
Tell me, what are your qualifications for
such a post?

Point. Marry, sir, I have a pretty wit. I
can rhyme you extempore; I can convulse
you with quip and conundrum; I have the
lighter philosophies at my tongue's tip; I
can be merry, wise quaint, grim, and sar-
donic, one by one, or all at once; I have
a pretty turn for anecdote; I know all the
jests—ancient and modern—past, present,
and to come; I can riddle you from dawn
of day to set of sun, and, if that content
you not, well on to midnight and the small
hours. Oh, sir, a pretty wit, I warrant you
—a pretty, pretty wit!

RECITATIVE AND SONG—POINT

I've jibe and joke
   And quip and crank
For lowly folk
   And men of rank.
I ply my craft
   And know no fear,
But aim my shaft
   At prince or peer.
At peer or prince—at prince or peer,
I aim my shaft and know no fear!
I've wisdom from the East and from the
   West,
   That's subject to no academic rule;
You may find it in the jeering of a jest,
   Or distil it from the folly of a fool.
I can teach you with a quip, if I've a
   mind;
   I can trick you into learning with a
     laugh;
Oh, winnow all my folly, and you'll find

A grain or two of truth among the chaff!
I can set a braggart quailing, with a quip,
The upstart I can wither with a whim;
He may wear a merry laugh upon his lip,
    But his laughter has an echo that is
      grim!
When they're offered to the world in merry
    guise,
    Unpleasant truths are swallowed with a
      will—
For he who'd make his fellow-creatures
    wise
    Should always gild the philosophic pill!

Lieut. And how came you to leave your
last employ?

Point. Why, sir it was in this wise. My
Lord was the Archbishop of Canterbury,
and it was considered that one of my
jokes was unsuited to His Grace's family
circle. In truth, I ventured to ask a poor
riddle, sir—Wherein lay the difference between His Grace and poor Jack Point?
His Grace was pleased to give it up, sir.
And thereupon I told him that whereas His
Grace was paid £10,000 a year for being
good, poor Jack Point was good—for nothing. 'Twas but a harmless jest, but it offended His Grace, who whipped me and
set me in the stocks for a scurril rogue,
and so we parted. I had as lief not take
post again with the dignified clergy.

Lieut. But I trust you are very careful
not to give offence. I have daughters.

Point. Sir, my jests are most carefully
selected, and anything objectionable is ex-
punged. If your honour pleases, I will try
them first on your honour's chaplain.

Lieut. Can you give me an example? Say
that I had sat me down hurriedly on something sharp?

Point. Sir I should say that you had sat
down on the spur of the moment.

Lieut. Humph! I don't think much of
that. Is that the best you can do?

Point. It has always been much admired,
sir, but we will try again.

Lieut. Well, then, I am at dinner, and
the joint of meat is but half cooked.

Point. Why then, sir, I should say that
what is *underdone* cannot be helped.

Lieut. I see. I think that manner of thing
would be somewhat irritating.

Point. At first, sir, perhaps; but use is

everything, and you would come in time
to like it.

Lieut. We will suppose that I caught you
kissing the kitchen wench under my very
nose.

Point. Under *her* very nose, good sir—
not under yours! *That* is where *I* would
kiss her. Do you take me? Oh, sir, a
pretty wit—a pretty, pretty wit!

Lieut. The maiden comes. Follow me,
friend, and we will discuss this matter at
length in my library.

Point. I am your worship's servant.
That is to say, I trust I soon shall be.
But, before proceeding to a more serious
topic, can you tell me, sir, why a cook's
brain-pan is like an overwound clock?

Lieut. A truce to this fooling—follow me.

Point. Just my luck; my best conundrum wasted!

                       [*Exeunt.*

Enter ELSIE *from Tower, led by* WILFRED,
    *who removes the bandage from her
    eyes, and exit.*

    RECITATIVE AND SONG—ELSIE

'Tis done! I am a bride! Oh, little ring,
    That bearest in thy circlet all the glad-
      ness
That lovers hope for, and that poets sing,
    What bringest thou to me but gold and
      sadness?
A bridegroom all unknown, save in this
    wise,
To-day he dies! To-day, alas, he dies!
Though tear and long-drawn sigh
    Ill fit a bride,
No sadder wife than I
    The whole world wide!
      Ah me! Ah me!
      Yet maids there be
    Who would consent to lose
      The very rose of youth,
        The flower of life,
      To be, in honest truth,
        A wedded wife,
          No matter whose!
Ah me! what profit we,
    O maids that sigh,
Though gold, though gold should live
    If wedded love must die?
Ere half an hour has rung,
    A widow I!
Ah, heaven, he is too young,
    Too brave to die!

Ah me! Ah me!
Yet wives there be
So weary worn, I trow,
  That they would scarce complain,
    So that they could
  In half an hour attain
    To widowhood,
      No matter how!
O weary wives
  Who widowhood would win,
Rejoice that ye have time
    To weary in.
      [*Exit* ELSIE *as* WILFRED *re-enters.*

Wil. (*looking after* ELSIE). 'Tis an odd freak, for a dying man and his confessor to be closeted alone with a strange singing girl. I would fain have espied them, but they stopped up the keyhole. *My* keyhole!

Enter PHOEBE *with* MERYLL. MERYLL *remains in the background, unobserved by* WILFRED.

Phoe. (*aside*). Wilfred—and alone!

Wil. Now what could he have wanted with her? That's what puzzles me!

Phoe. (*aside*). Now to get the keys from him. (*Aloud.*) Wilfred—has no reprieve arrived?

Wil. None. Thine adored Fairfax is to die.

Phoe. Nay, thou knowest that I have naught but pity for the poor condemned gentleman.

Wil. I know that he who is about to die is more to thee than I, who am alive and well.

Phoe. Why, that were out of reason, dear Wilfred. Do they not say that a live ass is better than a dead lion? No, I don't mean that!

Wil. Oh, they say that, do they?

Phoe. It's unpardonably rude of them, but I believe they put it in that way. Not that it applies to thee, who art clever beyond all telling!

Wil. Oh yes, as an assistant-tormentor.

Phoe. Nay, as a wit, as a humorist, as a most philosophic commentator on the vanity of human resolution.

[PHOEBE *slyly takes bunch of keys from* WILFRED'S *waistband and hands them to* MERYLL, *who enters the Tower, unnoticed by* WILFRED.

Wil. Truly, I have seen great resolution give way under my persuasive methods (*working a small thumbscrew*). In the nice regulation of a thumbscrew—in the hundredth part of a single revolution lieth all the difference between stony reticence and a torrent of impulsive unbosoming that the pen can scarcely follow. Ha! ha! I am a mad wag.

Phoe. (*with a grimace*). Thou art a most light-hearted and delightful companion, Master Wilfred. Thine anecdotes of the torture-chamber are the prettiest hearing.

Wil. I'm a pleasant fellow as I choose. I believe I am the merriest dog that barks. Ah, we might be passing happy together——

Phoe. Perhaps. I do not know.

Wil. For thou wouldst make a most tender and loving wife.

Phoe. Aye, to one whom I really loved. For there is a wealth of love within this little heart—saving up for—I wonder whom? Now, of all the world of men, I wonder whom? To think that he whom I am to wed is now alive and somewhere! Perhaps far away, perhaps close at hand! And I know him not! It seemeth that I am wasting time in not knowing him.

Wil. Now say that it is I—nay! suppose it for the nonce. Say that we are wed —suppose it only—say that thou art my very bride, and I thy cheery, joyous, bright, frolicsome husband—and that, the day's work being done, and the prisoners stored away for the night, thou and I are alone together—with a long, long evening before us!

Phoe. (*with a grimace*). It is a pretty picture—but I scarcely know. It cometh so unexpectedly—and yet—and yet—*were* I thy bride——

Wil. Aye!—wert thou my bride——?

Phoe. Oh, how I would love thee!

SONG—PHOEBE

Were I thy bride,
Then all the world beside
Were not too wide
  To hold my wealth of love—
Were I thy bride!
Upon thy breast
My loving head would rest,
  As on her nest
    The tender turtle dove—

Were I thy bride!
This heart of mine
Would be one heart with thine,
    And in that shrine
      Our happiness would dwell—
      Were I thy bride!
And all day long
Our lives should be a song:
    No grief, no wrong
      Should make my heart rebel—
      Were I thy bride!
    The silvery flute,
The melancholy lute,
    Were night-owl's hoot
      To my low-whispered coo—
      Were I thy bride!
    The skylark's trill
Were but discordance shrill
    To the soft thrill
      Of wooing as I'd woo—
      Were I thy bride!

MERYLL *re-enters; gives keys to* PHOEBE,
who replaces them at WILFRED'S *girdle,
unnoticed by him. Exit* MERYLL.

The rose's sigh
Were as a carrion's cry
    To lullaby
      Such as I'd sing to thee,
      Were I thy bride!
    A feather's press
Were leaden heaviness
    To my caress.
      But then, of course, you see,
      I'm not thy bride!

                [*Exit* PHOEBE.

Wil. No, thou'rt not—not yet! But,
Lord, how she woo'd! I should be no mean
judge of wooing, seeing that I have been
more hotly woo'd than most men. I have
been woo'd by maid, widow, and wife. I
have been woo'd boldly, timidly, tearfully,
shyly—by direct assault, by suggestion, by
implication, by inference, and by innuendo.
But this wooing is not of the common
order: it is the wooing of one who must
needs woo me, if she die for it!

                [*Exit* WILFRED.

Enter MERYLL, *cautiously, from Tower*

Mer. (*looking after them*). The deed is,
so far, safely accomplished. The slyboots,
how she wheedled him! What a helpless
ninny is a love-sick man! He is but as
a lute in a woman's hands—she plays upon
him whatever tune she will. But the Colonel comes. I' faith, he's just in time, for
the Yeomen parade here for his execution
in two minutes!

Enter FAIRFAX, *without beard and moustache, and dressed in Yeoman's uniform.*

Fair. My good and kind friend, thou
runnest a grave risk for me!

Mer. Tut, sir, no risk. I'll warrant none
here will recognise you. You make a brave
Yeoman, sir! So—this ruff is too high; so
—and the sword should hang thus. Here
is your halbert, sir; carry it thus. The
Yeomen come. Now remember, you are my
brave son, Leonard Meryll.

Fair. If I may not bear mine own name,
there is none other I would bear so readily.

Mer. Now, sir, put a bold face on it,
for they come.

FINALE—ACT I

Enter Yeomen of the Guard

Chorus

Oh, Sergeant Meryll, is it true—
    The welcome news we read in orders?
Thy son, whose deeds of derring-do
Are echoed all the country through,
    Has come to join the Tower Warders?
If so, we come to meet him,
That we may fitly greet him,
And welcome his arrival here
With shout on shout and cheer on cheer.
    Hurrah! Hurrah! Hurrah!

RECITATIVE—SERGEANT MERYLL

Ye Tower Warders, nursed in war's alarms,
Suckled on gunpowder, and weaned on
    glory,
Behold my son, whose all-subduing arms
Have formed the theme of many a song
    and story!
    Forgive his aged father's pride; nor
      jeer
      His aged father's sympathetic tear!
          (*Pretending to weep.*)

Chorus

    Leonard Meryll!
    Leonard Meryll!
Dauntless he in time of peril!
    Man of power,
    Knighthood's flower,
Welcome to the grim old Tower,
To the Tower, welcome thou!

RECITATIVE—FAIRFAX

Forbear, my friends, and spare me this
    ovation,

I have small claim to such consideration;
The tales that of my prowess are narrated
Have been prodigiously exaggerated!

Chorus

'Tis ever thus!
Wherever valour true is found,
True modesty will there abound.

COUPLETS

1st Yeoman

Didst thou not, oh, Leonard Meryll!
  Standard lost in last campaign,
Rescue it at deadly peril—
  Bear it safely back again?

Chorus

Leonard Meryll, at his peril,
Bore it safely back again!

2nd Yeoman

Didst thou not, when prisoner taken,
  And debarred from all escape,
Face, with gallant heart unshaken,
  Death in most appalling shape?

Chorus

Leonard Meryll, faced his peril,
Death in most appalling shape!

Fairfax (aside)

Truly I was to be pitied,
  Having but an hour to live,
I reluctantly submitted,
  I had no alternative!

(Aloud)

Oh! the tales that are narrated
  Of my deeds of derring-do
Have been much exaggerated,
Very much exaggerated,
  Scarce a word of them is true!

Chorus

They are not exaggerated, etc.

Enter PHOEBE. *She rushes to* FAIRFAX.
  Enter WILFRED.

RECITATIVE

Phoebe

Leonard!

Fairfax (puzzled)

I beg your pardon?

Phoebe

Don't you know me?
I'm little Phoebe!

Fairfax (still puzzled)

Phoebe? Is this Phoebe?
What! little Phoebe? *(Aside.)* Who the
  deuce may *she* be?
It can't be Phoebe, surely?

Wilfred

Yes, 'tis Phoebe——

Your sister Phoebe! Your own little sister!

All

Aye, he speaks the truth;
'Tis Phoebe!

Fairfax (pretending to recognise her)

Sister Phoebe!

Phoebe

Oh, my brother!

Fairfax

Why, how you've grown; I did not recognise you!

Phoebe

So many years! Oh, brother!

Fairfax

Oh, my sister!

Wilfred

Aye, hug him, girl! There are three thou
  mayst hug——
Thy father and thy brother and—myself!

Fairfax

Thyself, forsooth? And who art thou thyself?

Wilfred

Good sir, we are betrothed. (FAIRFAX *turns
  inquiringly to* PHOEBE.)

Phoebe

Or more or less——
But rather less than more!

Wilfred

To thy fond care
I do commend thy sister. Be to her
An ever-watchful guardian—eagle-eyed!
And when she feels (as sometimes she does
  feel)
Disposed to indiscriminate caress,
Be thou at hand to take those favours
  from her!

All

Be thou at hand to take those favours
  from her!

Phoebe

Yes, yes.
Be thou at hand to take those favours
  from me!

TRIO—WILFRED, FAIRFAX, AND PHOEBE

Wilfred

To thy fraternal care
  Thy sister I commend;
From every lurking snare
  Thy lovely charge defend:
  And to achieve this end,
Oh! grant, I pray, this boon—
  She shall not quit thy sight:
From morn to afternoon—

From afternoon to night—
From seven o'clock to two—
From two to eventide—
From dim twilight to 'leven at night
  She shall not quit thy side!
All
From morn to afternoon, etc.
Phoebe
So amiable I've grown,
  So innocent as well,
That if I'm left alone
  The consequences fell
No mortal can foretell.
So grant, I pray, this boon—
  I shall not quit thy sight:
From morn to afternoon—
From afternoon to night—
From seven o'clock to two—
  From two to eventide—
From dim twilight to 'leven at night
  I shall not quit thy side.
All
From morn to afternoon, etc.
Fairfax
With brotherly readiness,
  For my fair sister's sake,
At once I answer "Yes"—
  That task I undertake—
My word I never break.
I freely grant that boon,
  And I'll repeat my plight.
From morn to afternoon—   (*kiss*)
  From afternoon to night—   (*kiss*)
From seven o'clock to two—   (*kiss*)
  From two to evening meal—   (*kiss*)
From dim twilight to 'leven at night
  That compact I will seal.   (*kiss*)
All
From morn to afternoon, etc.
[*The bell of St. Peter's begins to toll. The
  Crowd enters; the block is brought
  on to the stage, and the Headsman
  takes his place. The Yeomen of the
  Guard form up. The* LIEUTENANT *en-
  ters and takes his place, and tells off*
  FAIRFAX *and two others to bring the
  prisoner to execution.* WILFRED, FAIR-
  FAX, *and two Yeomen exeunt to
  Tower.*
CHORUS (*to tolling accompaniment*)
The prisoner comes to meet his doom;
The block, the headsman, and the tomb.
The funeral bell begins to toll—
May Heaven have mercy on his soul!

SOLO—ELSIE, *with* CHORUS
Oh, Mercy, thou whose smile has shone
  So many a captive heart upon;
Of all immured within these walls,
  To-day the very worthiest falls!
Enter FAIRFAX *and two other Yeomen from
  Tower in great excitement.*
Fairfax
My lord; I know not how to tell
  The news I bear!
I and my comrades sought the prisoner's
    cell—
  He is not there!
All
  He is not there!
They sought the prisoner's cell—he is not
    there!
TRIO—FAIRFAX *and two Yeomen*
As escort for the prisoner
  We sought his cell, in duty bound;
The double gratings open were,
  No prisoner at all we found!
We hunted high, we hunted low,
  We hunted here, we hunted there—
The man we sought with anxious care
  Had vanished into empty air!
                    [*Exit* LIEUTENANT.
Girls
Now, by my troth, the news is fair,
The man has vanished into air!
All
As escort for the prisoner
  They sought his cell in duty bound, etc.
Enter WILFRED, *followed by* LIEUTENANT
Lieutenant
Astounding news! The prisoner fled!
      (*To Wilfred*)
Thy life shall forfeit be instead!
    (WILFRED *is arrested*)
Wilfred
My lord, I did not set him free,
I hate the man—my rival he!
    (WILFRED *is taken away*)
Meryll
The prisoner gone—I'm all agape!
Who could have helped him to escape?
Phoebe
Indeed I can't imagine who!
I've no idea at all—have you?
Enter JACK POINT
Dame
Of his escape no traces lurk,
Enchantment must have been at work!

Elsie (*aside to* POINT)
What have I done! Oh, woe is me!
I am his wife, and he is free!
Point
Oh, woe is *you*? Your anguish sink!
Oh, woe is *me*, I rather think!
Oh, woe is *me*, I rather think!
Yes, woe is *me*, I rather think!
  Whate'er betide
  You are his bride,
  And I am left
  Alone—bereft!
Yes, woe is *me*, I rather think!
Yes, woe is *me*, I rather think!
ENSEMBLE—LIEUTENANT *and* CHORUS
All frenzied with despair I rave,
  The grave is cheated of its due.
Who is the misbegotten knave
  Who hath contrived this deed to do?
Let search be made throughout the land,
Or $\begin{cases} \text{his} \\ \text{my} \end{cases}$ vindictive anger dread—

A thousand marks to him $\begin{cases} \text{he'll} \\ \text{I'll} \end{cases}$ hand

Who brings him here, alive or dead.
[*At the end,* ELSIE *faints in* FAIRFAX'S
  *arms; all the Yeomen and populace
  rush off the stage in different directions, to hunt for the fugitive, leaving
  only the Headsman on the stage, and*
  ELSIE *insensible in* FAIRFAX'S *arms.*
                END OF ACT I

                ACT II
SCENE.—*The same.—Moonlight*
    Two days have elapsed
Women and Yeomen of the Guard discovered
            Chorus
Night has spread her pall once more,
  And the prisoner still is free:
Open is his dungeon door,
  Useless now his dungeon key!
He has shaken off his yoke—
  How, no mortal man can tell!
Shame on loutish jailer-folk—
  Shame on sleepy sentinel!
    Enter DAME CARRUTHERS *and* KATE
        SOLO—DAME CARRUTHERS
Warders are ye?
  Whom do ye ward?
Bolt, bar, and key,
  Shackle and cord,
Fetter and chain,
  Dungeon of stone,

All are in vain—
  Prisoner's flown!
Spite of ye all, he is free—he is free!
Whom do ye ward? Pretty warders are ye!
        CHORUS OF WOMEN
Pretty warders are ye, etc.

            Chorus
            YEOMEN
Up and down, and in and out,
Here and there, and round about;
Every chamber, every house,
Every chink that holds a mouse,
Every crevice in the keep,
Where a beetle black could creep,
Every outlet, every drain,
Have we searched, but all in vain.
            WOMEN
Warders are ye?
  Whom do ye ward? etc.
                    [*Exeunt all.*
Enter JACK POINT, *in low spirits, reading
    from a huge volume.*
Point (*reads*). "The Merrie Jestes of
Hugh Ambrose. No. 7863. The Poor Wit
and the Rich Councillor. A certayne poor
wit, being an-hungered, did meet a well-
fed councillor. 'Marry, fool,' quoth the
councillor, 'whither away?' 'In truth,' said
the poor wag, 'in that I have eaten naught
these two dayes, I do wither away, and
that right rapidly!' The councillor laughed
hugely, and gave him a sausage." Humph!
the councillor was easier to please than my
new master, the Lieutenant. I would like
to take post under that councillor. Ah!
'tis but melancholy mumming when poor
heart-broken, jilted Jack Point must needs
turn to Hugh Ambrose for original light
humour!
    Enter WILFRED, *also in low spirits*
Wil. (*sighing*). Ah, Master of Point!
Point (*changing his manner*). Ha! friend
jailer! Jailer that wast—jailer that never
shalt be more! Jailer that jailed not, or
that jailed, if jail he did, so unjailerly that
'twas but jerry-jailing, or jailing in joke—
though no joke to him who, by unjailer-
like jailing, did so jeopardise his jailership.
Come, take heart, smile, laugh, wink,
twinkle, thou tormentor that tormentest
none—thou racker that rackest not—thou
pincher out of place—come, take heart, and
be merry, as I am!—(*aside, dolefully*)—
as I am!

Wil. Aye, it's well for thee to laugh. Thou hast a good post, and hast cause to be merry.

Point (bitterly). Cause? Have we not all cause? Is not the world a big butt of humour, into which all who will may drive a gimlet? See, I am a salaried wit; and is there aught in nature more ridiculous? A poor, dull, heart-broken man, who must needs be merry, or he will be whipped; who must rejoice, lest he starve; who must jest you, jibe you, quip you, crank you, wrack you, riddle you, from hour to hour, from day to day, from year to year, lest he dwindle, perish, starve, pine, and die! Why, when there's naught else to laugh at, I laugh at myself till I ache for it!

Wil. Yet I have often thought that a jester's calling would suit me to a hair.

Point. Thee? Would suit *thee,* thou death's head and cross-bones?

Wil. Aye, I have a pretty wit—a light, airy, joysome wit, spiced with anecdotes of prison cells and the torture chamber. Oh, a very delicate wit! I have tried it on many a prisoner, and there have been some who smiled. Now it is not easy to make a prisoner smile. And it should not be difficult to be a good jester, seeing that thou art one.

Point. Difficult? Nothing easier. Nothing easier. Attend, and I will prove it to thee!

SONG—POINT

Oh! a private buffoon is a light-hearted loon,
    If you listen to popular rumour;
From the morn to the night he's so joyous and bright,
    And he bubbles with wit and good humour!
He's so quaint and so terse, both in prose and in verse;
    Yet though people forgive his transgression,
There are one or two rules that all family fools
    Must observe, if they love their profession.
      There are one or two rules,
      Half a dozen, may be,
      That all family fools,
      Of whatever degree,
Must observe, if they love their profession.

If you wish to succeed as a jester, you'll need
    To consider each person's auricular:
What is all right for B would quite scandalise C
    (For C is so very particular);
And D may be dull, and E's very thick skull
    Is as empty of brains as a ladle;
While F is F sharp, and will cry with a carp
    That he's known your best joke from his cradle!
      When your humour they flout,
      You can't let yourself go;
      And it *does* put you out
      When a person says, "Oh,
I have known that old joke from my cradle!"

If your master is surly, from getting up early
    (And tempers are short in the morning),
An inopportune joke is enough to provoke
    Him to give you, at once, a month's warning.
Then if you refrain, he is at you again,
    For he likes to get value for money;
He'll ask then and there, with an insolent stare,
    "If you know that you're paid to be funny?"
      It adds to the tasks
      Of a merryman's place,
      When your principal asks,
      With a scowl on his face,
If you know that you're paid to be funny?

Comes a Bishop, maybe, or a solemn D.D.—
    Oh, beware of his anger provoking!
Better not pull his hair—don't stick pins in his chair;
    He don't understand practical joking.
If the jests that you crack have an orthodox smack,
    You may get a bland smile from these sages;
But should they, by chance, be imported from France,
    Half-a-crown is stopped out of your wages!
      It's a general rule,
      Though your zeal it may quench,
      If the family fool
      Tells a joke that's too French,

Half-a-crown is stopped out of his wages!
Though your head it may rack with a
    bilious attack,
    And your senses with toothache you're
        losing,
Don't be mopy and flat—they don't fine
    you for that,
    If you're properly quaint and amusing!
Though your wife ran away with a soldier
    that day,
    And took with her your trifle of money;
Bless your heart, they don't mind—they're
    exceedingly kind—
      They don't blame you—as long as you're
        funny!
      It's a comfort to feel,
        If your partner should fit,
      Though *you* suffer a deal,
        They don't mind it a bit—
They don't blame you—so long as you're
    funny!

Point. And so thou wouldst be a jester
eh?

Wil. Aye!

Point. Now, listen! My sweetheart, Elsie
Maynard, was secretly wed to this Fairfax
half an hour ere he escaped.

Wil. She did well.

Point. She did nothing of the kind, so
hold thy peace and perpend. Now, while
he liveth she is dead to me and I to her,
and so, my jibes and jokes notwithstand-
ing, I am the saddest and the sorriest dog
in England!

Wil. Thou art a very dull dog indeed.

Point. Now, if thou wilt swear that thou
didst shoot this Fairfax while he was trying
to swim across the river—it needs but the
discharge of an arquebus on a dark night
—and that he sank and was seen no more,
I'll make thee the very Archbishop of
jesters, and that in two days' time! Now,
what sayest thou?

Wil. I am to lie?

Point. Heartily. But thy lie must be a
lie of circumstance, which I will support
with the testimony of eyes, ears, and
tongue.

Wil. And thou wilt qualify me as a
jester?

Point. As a jester among jesters. I will
teach thee all my original songs, my self-
constructed riddles, my own ingenious par-
adoxes; nay, more, I will reveal to thee the
source whence I get them. Now, what
sayest thou?

Wil. Why, if it be but a lie thou wantest
of me, I hold it cheap enough, and I say
yes, it is a bargain!

      DUET—POINT *and* WILFRED
        Both
Hereupon we're both agreed,
  All that we two
  Do agree to
We'll secure by solemn deed,
  To prevent all
  Error mental.
        Point
You on Elsie are to call
  With a story
  Grim and gory;
        Wilfred
How this Fairfax died, and all
  I declare to
  You're to swear to.
        Both
    Tell a tale of cock and bull,
    Of convincing detail full
      Tale tremendous,
      Heaven defend us!
    What a tale of cock and bull!
        Both
In return for {your / my} own part
You are ⎱
I am ⎰ making
  Undertaking
To instruct {me / you} in the art
  (Art amazing,
  Wonder raising)
        Point
Of a jester, jesting free.
  Proud position—
  High ambition!
        Wilfred
And a lively one I'll be,
  Wag-a-wagging,
  Never flagging!
        Both
    Tell a tale of cock and bull, etc.
        [*Exeunt together.*
        Enter FAIRFAX

Fair. Two days gone, and no news of
poor Fairfax. The dolts! They seek him
everywhere save within a dozen yards of
his dungeon. So I am free! Free, but for
the cursed haste with which I hurried head-

long into the bonds of matrimony with —Heaven knows whom! As far as I remember, she should have been young; but even had not her face been concealed by her kerchief, I doubt whether, in my then plight, I should have taken much note of her. Free? Bah! The Tower bonds were but a thread of silk compared with these conjugal fetters which I, fool that I was, placed upon mine own hands. From the one I broke readily enough—how to break the other!

BALLAD—FAIRFAX

Free from his fetters grim—
Free to depart;
Free both in life and limb—
In all but heart!
Bound to an unknown bride
For good and ill;
Ah, is not one so tied
A prisoner still?
Free, yet in fetters held
Till his last hour,
Gyves that no smith can weld,
No rust devour!
Although a monarch's hand
Had set him free,
Of all the captive band
The saddest he!

Enter MERYLL

Fair. Well, Sergeant Meryll, and how fares thy pretty charge, Elsie Maynard?

Mer. Well enough, sir. She is quite strong again, and leaves us to-night.

Fair. Thanks to Dame Carruthers' kind nursing, eh?

Mer. Aye, deuce take the old witch! Ah, 'twas but a sorry trick you played me, sir, to bring the fainting girl to me. It gave the old lady an excuse for taking up her quarters in my house, and for the last two years I've shunned her like the plague. Another day of it and she would have married me! (*Enter* DAME CARRUTHERS *and* KATE.) Good Lord, here she is again! I'll e'en go. (*Going.*)

Dame. Nay, Sergeant Meryll, don't go. I have something of grave import to say to thee.

Mer. (*aside*). It's coming.

Fair. (*laughing*). I' faith, I think I'm not wanted here. (*Going.*)

Dame. Nay, Master Leonard, I've naught

to say to thy father that his son may not hear.

Fair. (*aside*). True. I'm one of the family; I had forgotten!

Dame. 'Tis about this Elsie Maynard. A pretty girl, Master Leonard.

Fair. Aye, fair as a peach blossom—what then?

Dame. She hath a liking for thee, or I mistake not.

Fair. With all my heart. She's as dainty a little maid as you'll find in a midsummer day's march.

Dame. Then be warned in time, and give not thy heart to her. Oh, *I* know what it is to give my heart to one who will have none of it!

Mer. (*aside*). Aye, *she* knows all about that. (*Aloud.*) And why is my boy to take heed of her? She's a good girl, Dame Carruthers.

Dame. Good enough, for aught I know. But she's no girl. She's a married woman.

Mer. A married woman! Tush, old lady —she's promised to Jack Point, the lieutenant's new jester.

Dame. Tush in thy teeth, old man! As my niece, Kate, sat by her bedside to-day, this Elsie slept, and as she slept she moaned and groaned, and turned this way and that way—and, "How shall I marry one I have never seen?" quoth she—then, "An hundred crowns!" quoth she—then, "Is it certain he will die in an hour?" quoth she— then, "I love him not, and yet I am his wife," quoth she! Is it not so, Kate?

Kate. Aye, aunt, 'tis even so.

Fair. Art thou sure of all this?

Kate. Aye, sir, for I wrote it all down on my tablets.

Dame. Now, mark my words: it was of this Fairfax she spake, and he is her husband, or I'll swallow my kirtle!

Mer. (*aside*). Is it true, sir?

Fair. (*aside to* MERYLL). True? Why the girl was raving! (*Aloud.*) Why should she marry a man who had but an hour to live?

Dame. Marry? There be those who would marry but for a minute, rather than die old maids.

Mer. (*aside*). Aye, I know one of them!

QUARTET—FAIRFAX, SERGEANT MERYLL, DAME
CARRUTHERS, *and* KATE.

Strange adventure! Maiden wedded
  To a groom she's never seen—
    Never, never, never seen!
Groom about to be beheaded,
  In an hour on Tower Green!
    Tower, Tower, Tower Green!
Groom in dreary dungeon lying,
Groom as good as dead, or dying,
For a pretty maiden sighing—
  Pretty maid of seventeen!
    Seven—seven—seventeen!
Strange adventure that we're trolling:
  Modest maid and gallant groom—
    Gallant, gallant, gallant groom!—
While the funeral bell is tolling,
  Tolling, tolling, Bim-a-boom!
    Bim-a, Bim-a, Bim-a-boom!
Modest maiden will not tarry;
Though but sixteen years she carry,
She must marry, she must marry,
  Though the altar be a tomb—
    Tower—Tower—Tower tomb!

[*Exeunt* DAME CARRUTHERS,
MERYLL, *and* KATE.

Fair. So my mysterious bride is no other
than this winsome Elsie! By my hand, 'tis
no such ill plunge in Fortune's lucky bag!
I might have fared worse with my eyes
open! But she comes. Now to test her
principles. 'Tis not every husband who has
a chance of wooing his own wife!

Enter ELSIE

Fair. Mistress Elsie!
Elsie. Master Leonard!
Fair. So thou leavest us tonight?
Elsie. Yes, Master Leonard. I have been
kindly tended, and I almost fear I am loth
to go.
Fair. And this Fairfax. Wast thou glad
when he escaped?
Elsie. Why, truly, Master Leonard, it is
a sad thing that a young and gallant gentleman should die in the very fullness of
his life.
Fair. Then when thou didst faint in my
arms, it was for joy at his safety?
Elsie. It may be so. I was highly
wrought, Master Leonard, and I am but a
girl, and so, when I am highly wrought, I
faint.
Fair. Now, dost thou know, I am con-
sumed with a parlous jealousy?

Elsie. Thou? And of whom?
Fair. Why, of this Fairfax, surely!
Elsie. Of Colonel Fairfax?
Fair. Aye. Shall I be frank with thee?
Elsie—I love thee, ardently, passionately!
(ELSIE *alarmed and surprised.*) Elsie, I
have loved thee these two days—which is
a long time—and I would fain join my
life to thine!
Elsie. Master Leonard! Thou art jesting!
Fair. Jesting? May I shrivel into raisins
if I jest! I love thee with a love that is a
fever—with a love that is a frenzy—with a
love that eateth up my heart! What sayest
thou? Thou wilt not let my heart be eaten
up?
Elsie (aside). Oh, mercy! What am I to
say?
Fair. Dost thou love me, or hast thou
been insensible these two days?
Elsie. I love all brave men.
Fair. Nay, there is love in excess. I thank
heaven there are many brave men in England; but if thou lovest them all, I withdraw my thanks.
Elsie. I love the bravest best. But, sir,
I may not listen—I am not free—I—I am
a wife!
Fair. Thou a wife? Whose? His name?
His hours are numbered—nay, his grave is
dug and his epitaph set up! Come, his
name?
Elsie. Oh, sir! keep my secret—it is the
only barrier that Fate could set up between
us. My husband is none other than Colonel
Fairfax!
Fair. The greatest villain unhung! The
most ill-favoured, ill-mannered, ill-natured,
ill-omened, ill-tempered dog in Christendom!
Elsie. It is very like. He is naught to
me—for I never saw him. I was blindfolded, and he was to have died within
the hour; and he did not die—and I am
wedded to him, and my heart is broken!
Fair. He was to have died, and he **did**
not die? The scoundrel! The perjured,
traitorous villain! Thou shouldst have insisted on his dying first, to make sure. 'Tis
the only way with these Fairfaxes.
Elsie. I now wish I had!
Fair. (aside.) Bloodthirsty little maiden!
(Aloud.) A fig for this Fairfax! Be mine—
he will never know—he dares not show

himself; and if he dare, what art thou to him? Fly with me, Elsie—we will be married to-morrow, and thou shalt be the happiest wife in England!

Elsie. Master Leonard! I am amazed! Is it thus that brave soldiers speak to poor girls? Oh! for shame, for shame! I am wed—not the less because I love not my husband. I am a wife, sir, and I have a duty, and—oh, sir!—thy words terrify me —they are not honest—they are wicked words, and unworthy thy great and brave heart! Oh, shame upon thee! shame upon thee!

Fair. Nay, Elsie, I did but jest. I spake but to try thee—— (*Shot heard.*)

Enter MERYLL *hastily*

Mer. (*recit.*). Hark! What was that, sir?
Fair.   Why, an arquebus—
Fired from the wharf unless I much mistake.

Mer. Strange—and at such an hour! What can it mean?

Enter CHORUS

Now what can that have been—
  A shot so late at night,
  Enough to cause a fright!
What can the portent mean?

Are foemen in the land?
  Is London to be wrecked?
  What are we to expect?
What danger is at hand?
  Let us understand
  What danger is at hand!

LIEUTENANT *enters, also* POINT *and* WILFRED
RECITATIVE
Lieutenant

Who fired that shot? At once the truth declare!

Wilfred

My lord, 'twas I—to rashly judge forbear!

Point

My lord, 'twas he—to rashly judge forbear!

DUET *and* CHORUS—WILFRED *and* POINT
Wilfred

Like a ghost his vigil keeping—

Point

Or a spectre all-appalling—

Wilfred

I beheld a figure creeping—

Point

I should rather call it crawling—

Wilfred

He was creeping—

Point

He was crawling—

Wilfred

He was creeping, creeping—

Point

Crawling!

Wilfred

He was creeping—

Point

He was crawling—

Wilfred

He was creeping, creeping—

Point

Crawling!

Wilfred

Not a moment's hesitation—
  I myself upon him flung,
With a hurried exclamation
  To his draperies I hung;
Then we closed with one another
  In a rough-and-tumble smother;
Colonel Fairfax and no other
  Was the man to whom I clung!

All

Colonel Fairfax and no other
  Was the man to whom he clung!

Wilfred

After mighty tug and tussle—

Point

It resembled more a struggle—

Wilfred

He, by dint of stronger muscle—

Point

Or by some infernal juggle—

Wilfred

From my clutches quickly sliding—

Point

I should rather call it slipping—

Wilfred

With a view, no doubt, of hiding—

Point

Or escaping to the shipping—

Wilfred

With a gasp, and with a quiver—

Point

I'd describe it as a shiver—

Wilfred

Down he dived into the river,
  And, alas, I cannot swim.

All

It's enough to make one shiver—
With a gasp and with a quiver,

Down he dived into the river;
    It was very brave of him!
                Wilfred
Ingenuity is catching;
    With the view my king of pleasing,
Arquebus from sentry snatching—
                Point
    I should rather call it seizing—
                Wilfred
        With an ounce or two of lead
        I despatched him through the head!
                All
        With an ounce or two of lead
        He despatched him through the
        head!
                Wilfred
I discharged it without winking,
Little time I lost in thinking,
Like a stone I saw him sinking—
                Point
        I should say a lump of lead.
                All
He discharged it without winking,
Little time he lost in thinking.
                Wilfred
Like a stone I saw him sinking—
                Point
        I should say a lump of lead.
                Wilfred
Like a stone, my boy, I said—
                Point
Like a heavy lump of lead.
                Wilfred
Anyhow, the man is dead,
Whether stone or lump of lead!
                All
        Anyhow, the man is dead,
        Whether stone or lump of lead!
Arquebus from sentry seizing,
With the view his king of pleasing,
        Wilfred shot him through the head,
        And he's very, very dead.
And it matters very little whether stone or
        lump of lead;
It is very, very certain that he's very, very
        dead!

RECITATIVE—LIEUTENANT

The river must be dragged—no time be
        lost;
The body must be found, at any cost.
To this attend without undue delay;
So set to work with what despatch ye
        may!
                            [*Exit*

All
Yes, yes,
We'll set to work with what despatch we
        may!
            [*Four men raise* WILFRED, *and carry
                him off on their shoulders.*

CHORUS
Hail the valiant fellow who
Did this deed of derring-do!
Honours wait on such an one;
By my head, 'twas bravely done!
Now, by my head, 'twas bravely done!
            [*Exeunt all but* ELSIE, POINT,
                    FAIRFAX, *and* PHOEBE.

Point (to ELSIE, *who is weeping).* Nay,
sweetheart, be comforted. This Fairfax was
but a pestilent fellow, and, as he had to
die, he might as well die thus as any other
way. 'Twas a good death.

Elsie. Still, he was my husband, and had
he not been, he was nevertheless a living
man, and now he is dead; and so, by your
leave, my tears may flow unbidden, Master Point.

Fair. And thou didst see all this?

Point. Aye, with both eyes at once—this
and that. The testimony of one eye is
naught—he may lie. But when it is cor-
roborated by the other, it is good evidence that none may gainsay. Here are
both present in court, ready to swear to
him!

Phoe. But art thou sure it was Colonel
Fairfax? Saw you his face?

Point. Aye, and a plaguey ill-favoured
face too. A very hang-dog face—a felon
face—a face to fright the headsman himself, and make him strike awry. Oh, a
plaguey, bad face, take my word for 't.
(PHOEBE *and* FAIRFAX *laugh.*) How they
laugh! 'Tis ever thus with simple folk—an
accepted wit has but to say "Pass the
mustard," and they roar their ribs out!

Fair. (aside). If ever I come to life
again, thou shalt pay for this, Master
Point!

Point. Now, Elsie, thou art free to choose
again, so behold me: I am young, and
well favoured. I have a pretty wit. I can
jest you, jibe you, quip you, crank you,
wrack you, riddle you——

Fair. Tush, man, thou knowest not how
to woo. 'Tis not to be done with time-
worn jests and thread-bare sophistries;

with quips, conundrums, rhymes, and para-
doxes. 'Tis an art in itself, and must be
studied gravely and conscientiously.

TRIO—ELSIE, PHOEBE, *and* FAIRFAX

Fairfax

A man who would woo a fair maid
Should 'prentice himself to the trade,
    And study all day,
    In methodical way,
How to flatter, cajole, and persuade;
He should 'prentice himself at fourteen,
And practise from morning to e'en;
    And when he's of age,
    If he will, I'll engage,
He may capture the heart of a queen!

All

    It is purely a matter of skill,
    Which all may attain if they will:
      But every Jack,
      He must study the knack
    If he wants to make sure of his Jill!

Elsie

If he's made the best use of his time,
His twig he'll so carefully lime
    That every bird
    Will come down at his word,
Whatever its plumage or clime.
He must learn that the thrill of a touch
May mean little, or nothing, or much:
    It's an instrument rare,
    To be handled with care,
And ought to be treated as such.

All

    It is purely a matter of skill, etc.

Phoebe

Then a glance may be timid or free,
It will vary in mighty degree,
    From an impudent stare
    To a look of despair
That no maid without pity can see!
And a glance of despair is no guide—
It may have its ridiculous side;
    It may draw you a tear
    Or a box on the ear;
You can never be sure till you've tried!

All

    It is purely a matter of skill, etc.

Fair. (aside to POINT*).* Now, listen to
me—'tis done thus—*(aloud)*—Mistress
Elsie, there is one here who, as thou knowest, loves thee right well!

Point (aside). That he does—right well!

Fair. He is but a man of poor estate, but
he hath a loving, honest heart. He will be
a true and trusty husband to thee, and if
thou wilt be his wife, thou shalt lie curled
up in his heart, like a little squirrel in its
nest!

Point (aside). 'Tis a pretty figure. A
maggot in a nut lies closer, but a squirrel
will do.

Fair. He knoweth that thou wast a wife
—an unloved and unloving wife, and his
poor heart was near to breaking. But now
that thine unloving husband is dead, and
thou art free, he would fain pray that thou
wouldst hearken unto him, and give him
hope that thou wouldst one day be his!

Phoe. (alarmed). He presses her hands—
and he whispers in her ear! Ods bodikins,
what does it mean?

Fair. Now, sweetheart, tell me—wilt
thou be this poor, good fellow's wife?

Elsie. If the good, brave man—*is* he a
brave man?

Fair. So men say.

Point (aside). That's not true, but let it
pass.

Elsie. If the brave man will be content
with a poor, penniless, untaught maid——

Point (aside). Widow—but let *that* pass.

Elsie. I will be his true and loving wife,
and that with my heart of hearts!

Fair. My own dear love! (*Embracing
her.*)

Phoe. (in great agitation). Why, what's
all this? Brother — brother — it is not
seemly!

Point (also alarmed, aside). Oh, I can't
let that pass! (*Aloud.*) Hold, enough, Master Leonard! An advocate should have his
fee, but methinks thou art over-paying
thyself!

Fair. Nay, that is for Elsie to say. I
promised thee I would show thee how to
woo, and herein lies the proof of the virtue
of my teaching. Go thou, and apply it elsewhere! (PHOEBE *bursts into tears.*)

QUARTET—ELSIE, PHOEBE, FAIRFAX, *and* POINT

Elsie and Fairfax

    When a wooer
      Goes a-wooing,
    Naught is truer
      Than his joy.
    Maiden hushing
      All his suing—
    Boldly blushing—
      Bravely coy!

All

Oh, the happy days of doing!
Oh, the sighing and the suing!
When a wooer goes a-wooing,
    Oh, the sweets that never cloy!

Phoebe (weeping)

When a brother
    Leaves his sister
For another,
    Sister weeps.
Tears that trickle,
    Tears that blister—
'Tis but mickle
    Sister reaps!

All

Oh, the doing and undoing,
Oh, the sighing and the suing,
When a brother goes a-wooing,
    And a sobbing sister weeps!

Point

When a jester
    Is outwitted,
Feelings fester,
    Heart is lead!
Food for fishes
    Only fitted,
Jester wishes
    He was dead!

All

Oh, the doing and undoing,
Oh, the sighing and the suing,
When a jester goes a-wooing,
    And he wishes he was dead!

[*Exeunt all but* PHOEBE,
    who remains weeping.

Phoe. And I helped that man to escape, and I've kept his secret, and pretended that I was his dearly loving sister, and done everything I could think of to make folk believe I *was* his loving sister, and this is his gratitude! Before I pretend to be sister to anybody again, I'll turn nun, and be sister to everybody—one as much as another!

Enter WILFRED

Wil. In tears, eh! What a plague art thou grizzling for now?

Phoe. Why am I grizzling? Thou hast often wept for jealousy—well, 'tis for jealousy I weep now. Aye, yellow, bilious, jaundiced jealousy. So make the most of that, Master Wilfred.

Wil. But I have never given thee cause for jealousy. The Lieutenant's cook-maid and I are but the merest gossips!

Phoe. Jealous of thee! Bah! I'm jealous of no craven cock-on-a-hill, who crows about what he'd do an he dared! I am jealous of another and a better man than thou—set that down, Master Wilfred. And he is to mary Elsie Maynard, the little pale fool—set that down, Master Wilfred—and my heart is wellnigh broken! There, thou hast it all! Make the most of it!

Wil. The man thou lovest is to marry Elsie Maynard? Why, that is no other than thy brother, Leonard Meryll!

Phoe. (*aside*). Oh, mercy! what have I said?

Wil. Why, what manner of brother is this, thou lying little jade? Speak! Who is this man whom thou hast called brother, and fondled, and coddled, and kissed!— with my connivance, too! Oh Lord! with my connivance! Ha! should it be this Fairfax! (PHOEBE *starts*.) It is! It is this accursed Fairfax! It's Fairfax! Fairfax, who——

Phoe. Whom thou hast just shot through the head, and who lies at the bottom of the river!

Wil. A—I—I may have been mistaken. We are but fallible mortals, the best of us. But I'll make sure—I'll make sure. (*Going.*)

Phoe. Stay—one word. I think it cannot be Fairfax—mind, I say I *think*—because thou hast just slain Fairfax. But whether he be Fairfax or no Fairfax, he is to marry Elsie—and—and—as thou hast shot him through the head, and he is dead, be content with that, and I will be thy wife!

Wil. Is that sure?

Phoe. Aye, sure enough, for there's no help for it! Thou art a very brute—but even brutes must marry, I suppose.

Wil. My beloved! (*Embraces her.*)

Phoe. (*aside*). Ugh!

Enter LEONARD, *hastily*

Leon. Phoebe, rejoice, for I bring glad tidings. Colonel Fairfax's reprieve was signed two days since, but it was foully and maliciously kept back by Secretary Poltwhistle, who designed that it should arrive after the Colonel's death. It hath just come to hand, and it is now in the Lieutenant's possession!

Phoe. Then the Colonel is free? Oh, kiss

me, kiss me, my dear! Kiss me, again, and again!

Wil. (dancing with fury). Ods bobs, death o' my life! Art thou mad? Am *I* mad? Are we *all* mad?

Phoe. Oh, my dear—my dear, I'm well-nigh crazed with joy! *(Kissing* LEONARD.)

Wil. Come away from him, thou hussy—thou jade—thou kissing, clinging cockatrice! And as for thee, sir, devil take thee, I'll rip thee like a herring for this! I'll skin thee for it! I'll cleave thee to the chine! I'll—oh! Phoebe! Phoebe! Who is this man?

Phoe. Peace, fool. He is my brother!

Wil. Another brother! Are there any more of them? Produce them all at once, and let me know the worst!

Phoe. This is the real Leonard, dolt; the other was but his substitute. The *real* Leonard, I say—my father's own son.

Wil. How do I know this? Has he "brother" writ large on his brow? I mistrust thy brothers! Thou art but a false jade!

[*Exit* LEONARD

Phoe. Now, Wilfred, be just. Truly I did d-ceive thee before—but it was to save a precious life—and to save it, not for me, but for another. They are to be wed this very day. Is not this enough for thee? Come—I am thy Phoebe—thy very own—and we will be wed in a year—or two—or three, at the most. Is not that enough for thee?

Enter MERYLL, *excitedly, followed by* DAME CARRUTHERS *(who listens, unobserved)*

Mer. Phoebe, hast thou heard the brave news?

Phoe. (still in WILFRED'S *arms).* Aye, father.

Mer. I'm nigh mad with joy! *(Seeing* WILFRED.) Why, what's all this?

Phoe. Oh, father, he discovered our secret through my folly, and the price of his silence is——

Wil. Phoebe's heart.

Phoe. Oh dear, no—Phoebe's hand.

Wil. It's the same thing!

Phoe. Is it?

[*Exeunt* WILFRED *and* PHOEBE.

Mer. (looking after them). 'Tis pity, but the Colonel had to be saved at any cost, and as thy folly revealed our secret, thy folly must e'en suffer for it! (DAME CARRUTHERS *comes down.)* Dame Carruthers!

Dame. So this is a plot to shield this arch-fiend, and I have detected it. A word from me, and three heads besides his would roll from their shoulders!

Mer. Nay, Colonel Fairfax is reprieved. *(Aside.)* Yet, if my complicity in his escape were known! Plague on the old meddler! There's nothing for it—*(aloud)*—Hush, pretty one! Such bloodthirsty words ill become those cherry lips! *(Aside.)* Ugh!

Dame (bashfully). Sergeant Meryll.

Mer. Why, look ye, chuck—for many a month I've—I've thought to myself— "There's snug love saving up in that middle-aged bosom for some one, and why not for thee—thats' me—so take heart and tell her—that's thee—that thou—that's me—lovest her—thee—and—and—well, I'm a miserable old man, and I've done it—and that's me!" But not a word about Fairfax! The price of thy silence is——

Dame. Meryll's heart?

Mer. No, Meryll's *hand.*

Dame. It's the same thing!

Mer. Is it?

DUET—DAME CARRUTHERS *and* SERGEANT MERYLL

Dame

Rapture, rapture
  When love's votary,
Flushed with capture,
  Seeks the notary,
    Joy and jollity
    Then is polity;
    Reigns frivolity!
Rapture, rapture!

Meryll

Doleful, doleful!
  When humanity
With its soul full
  Of satanity,
    Courting privity,
    Down declivity
    Seeks captivity!
Doleful, doleful!

Dame

Joyful, joyful!
  When virginity
Seeks, all coyful,
  Man's affinity;
    Fate all flowery,
    Bright and bowery,

Is her dowery!
Joyful, joyful!

Meryll

Ghastly, ghastly!
When man, sorrowful,
Firstly, lastly,
Of to-morrow full,
After tarrying,
Yields to harrying—
Goes a-marrying.
Ghastly, ghastly!

Both

Rapture, etc.

[*Exeunt* DAME *and* MERYLL.

FINALE

Enter Yeomen and Women
CHORUS OF WOMEN
(ELEGIACS)

Comes the pretty young bride, a-blushing,
    timidly shrinking—
  Set all thy fears aside—cheerily, pretty
    young bride!
Brave is the youth to whom thy lot thou
    art willingly linking!
  Flower of valour is he—loving as loving
    can be!
    Brightly thy summer is shining,
    Fair as the dawn of the day;

Take him, be true to him—
Tender his due to him—
Honour him, love and obey!

Enter DAME, PHOEBE, *and* ELSIE *as Bride*
TRIO—PHOEBE, ELSIE, *and* DAME CARRUTHERS

'Tis said that joy in full perfection
  Comes only once to womankind—
That, other times, on close inspection,
  Some lurking bitter we shall find.
If this be so, and men say truly,
My day of joy has broken duly.

With happiness $\begin{cases} my \\ her \end{cases}$ soul is cloyed—

This is $\begin{cases} my \\ her \end{cases}$ joy-day unalloyed!

All

Yes, yes, with happiness her soul is
  cloyed!
This is her joy-day unalloyed!

Flourish. Enter LIEUTENANT

Lieutenant

Hold, pretty one! I bring to thee
  News—good or ill, it is for thee to say.
Thy husband lives—and he is free,
  And comes to claim his bride this very
    day!

Elsie

No! no! recall those words—it cannot be!

ENSEMBLE

Kate and Chorus

Oh, day of terror! Day of tears!
Who is the man who, in his pride,
Claims thee as his bride?

Lieutenant, Meryll, and Wilfred

Come, dry these unbecoming tears,
Most joyful tidings greet thine ears,
The man to whom thou art allied
Appears to claim thee as his bride.

Dame Carruthers and Phoebe

Oh, day of terror! Day of tears!
The man to whom thou art allied
Appears to claim thee as his bride.

Elsie

Oh, Leonard, come thou to my side,
And claim me as thy loving bride!
Oh, day of terror! Day of tears!

Flourish. Enter COLONEL FAIRFAX, *hand-*
somely dressed, and attended by other
Gentlemen

Fairfax (sternly)

All thought of Leonard Meryll set aside.
Thou art mine own! I claim thee as my
  bride.

All

Thou art his own! Alas! he claims thee as
  his bride.

Elsie

A suppliant at thy feet I fall;
Thine heart will yield to pity's call!

Fairfax

Mine is a heart of massive rock,
Unmoved by sentimental shock!

All

Thy husband he!

Elsie (aside)

Leonard, my loved one—come to me.
  They bear me hence away!
But though they take me far from thee,
  My heart is thine for aye!
    My bruised heart,
    My broken heart,
Is thine, my own, for aye!

(To FAIRFAX.)
Sir, I obey!
    I am thy bride;
But ere the fatal hour
    I said the say
That placed me in thy power
    Would I had died!
Sir, I obey!
    I am thy bride!
    (Looks up and recognises FAIRFAX.)
                    Leonard!
                    Fairfax
My own!
                    Elsie
Ah! *(Embrace.)*
                Elsie and Fairfax
With happiness my soul is cloyed,
This is our joy-day unaloyed!
                    All
                Yes, yes!
With happiness their souls are cloyed,
This is their joy-day unalloyed!
            Enter JACK POINT
                    Point
Oh, thoughtless crew!
    Ye know not what ye do!
Attend to me, and shed a tear or two—
    For I have a song to sing, O!
                    All
        Sing me your song, O!
                    Point
        It is sung to the moon
        By a love-lorn loon,
Who fled from the mocking throng, O!
It's the song of a merryman, moping mum,

Whose soul was sad, and whose glance was
        glum,
Who sipped no sup, and who craved no
        crumb,
    As he sighed for the love of a ladye!
                    All
        Heighdy! heighdy!
        Misery me, lackadaydee!
He sipped no sup, and he craved no crumb,
    As he sighed for the love of a ladye!
                    Elsie
    I have a song to sing, O!
                    All
        What is your song, O!
                    Elsie
        It is sung with the ring
        Of the songs maids sing
Who love with a love life-long, O!
It's the song of a merrymaid, nestling near,
Who loved her lord—but who dropped a
        tear
At the moan of the merryman, moping
        mum,
Whose soul was sad, and whose glance was
        glum,
Who sipped no sup, and who craved no
        crumb,
    As he sighed for the love of a ladye!
                    All
        Heighdy! heighdy!
        Misery me, lackadaydee!
He sipped no sup, and he craved no crumb,
    As he sighed for the love of a ladye!
    [FAIRFAX *embraces* ELSIE *as* POINT
        falls insensible at their feet.

CURTAIN

IOLANTHE

OR

THE PEER AND THE PERI

DRAMATIS PERSONÆ

THE LORD CHANCELLOR

EARL OF MOUNTARARAT

EARL TOLLOLLER

PRIVATE WILLIS (*of the Grenadier Guards*)

STREPHON (*an Arcadian Shepherd*)

QUEEN OF THE FAIRIES

IOLANTHE (*a Fairy, Strephon's Mother*)

CELIA ⎫
LEILA ⎬ *Fairies*
FLETA ⎭

PHYLLIS (*an Arcadian Shepherdess and Ward in Chancery*)

Chorus of Dukes, Marquises, Earls, Viscounts, Barons, and Fairies

ACT I

SCENE.—*An Arcadian Landscape. A river runs around the back of the stage. A rustic bridge crosses the river.*

Enter Fairies, led by LEILA, CELIA, *and* FLETA. *They trip around the stage, singing as they dance.*

CHORUS

Tripping hither, tripping thither,
Nobody knows why or whither;
We must dance and we must sing
Round about our fairy ring!

SOLO—CELIA

We are dainty little fairies,
　Ever singing, ever dancing;
We indulge in our vagaries
　In a fashion most entrancing.
If you ask the special function
　Of our never-ceasing motion,
We reply, without compunction,
　That we haven't any notion!

CHORUS

No, we haven't any notion!
Tripping hither, etc.

SOLO—LEILA

If you ask us how we live,
Lovers all essentials give—
　We can ride on lovers' sighs,
　Warm ourselves in lovers' eyes,

Bathe ourselves in lovers' tears,
Clothe ourselves with lovers' fears,
Arm ourselves with lovers' darts,
Hide ourselves in lovers' hearts,
When you know us, you'll discover
That we almost live on lover!

CHORUS

Tripping hither, etc.

(*At the end of Chorus, all sigh wearily.*)

Celia. Ah, it's all very well, but since our Queen banished Iolanthe, fairy revels have not been what they were!

Leila. Iolanthe was the life and soul of Fairyland. Why, she wrote all our songs and arranged all our dances! We sing her songs and we trip her measures, but we don't enjoy ourselves!

Fleta. To think that five-and-twenty years have elapsed since she was banished! What could she have done to have deserved so terrible a punishment?

Leila. Something awful! She married a mortal!

Fleta. Oh! Is it injudicious to marry a mortal?

Leila. Injudicious? It strikes at the root of the whole fairy system! By our laws, the fairy who marries a mortal dies!

Celia. But Iolanthe didn't die!

Enter FAIRY QUEEN

Queen. No, because your Queen, who loved her with a surpassing love, commuted her sentence to penal servitude for life, on condition that she left her husband and never communicated with him again!

Leila. That sentence of penal servitude she is now working out, on her head, at the bottom of that stream!

Queen. Yes, but when I banished her, I gave her all the pleasant places of the earth to dwell in. I'm sure I never intended that she should go and live at the bottom of a stream! It makes me perfectly wretched to think of the discomfort she must have undergone!

Leila. Think of the damp! And her chest was always delicate.

Queen. And the frogs! Ugh! I never shall enjoy any peace of mind until I know why Iolanthe went to live among the frogs!

Fleta. Then why not summon her and ask her?

Queen. Why? Because if I set eyes on her I should forgive her at once!

Celia. Then why not forgive her? Twenty-five years—it's a long time!

Leila. Think how we loved her!

Queen. Loved her? What was your love to mine? Why, she was invaluable to me! Who taught me to cure myself inside a buttercup? Iolanthe! Who taught me to swing upon a cobweb? Iolanthe! Who taught me to dive into a dewdrop—to nestle in a nutshell—to gambol upon gossamer? Iolanthe!

Fleta. She certainly did surprising things!

Fleta. Oh, give her back to us, great Queen, for your sake if not for ours! (*All kneel in supplication.*)

Queen (*irresolute*). Oh, I should be strong, but I am weak! I should be marble, but I am clay! Her punishment has been heavier than I intended. I did not mean that she should live among the frogs—and—well, well, it shall be as you wish—it shall be as you wish!

INVOCATION—QUEEN

Iolanthe!
From thy dark exile thou art summoned!
Come to our call—
Come, Iolanthe!
Celia
Iolanthe!

Leila
Iolanthe!
All
Come to our call,
Come, Iolanthe!

[IOLANTHE *rises from the water. She is clad in waterweeds. She approaches the* QUEEN *with head bent and arms crossed.*

Iolanthe
With humbled breast
    And every hope laid low,
To thy behest,
    Offended Queen, I bow!

Queen
For a dark sin against our fairy laws
We sent thee into life-long banishment;
But mercy holds her sway within our hearts—
Rise—thou art pardoned!
Iolanthe
Pardoned!
All
Pardoned!

[*Her weeds fall from her, and she appears clothed as a fairy. The* QUEEN *places a diamond coronet on her head, and embraces her. The others also embrace her.*

CHORUS
Welcome to our hearts again,
    Iolanthe! Iolanthe!
We have shared thy bitter pain,
    Iolanthe! Iolanthe!
Every heart, and every hand
In our loving little band
Welcomes thee to Fairyland,
    Iolanthe!

Queen. And now, tell me, with all the world to choose from, why on earth did you decide to live at the bottom of that stream?

Iol. To be near my son, Strephon.

Queen. Bless my heart, I didn't know you had a son.

Iol. He was born soon after I left my husband by your royal command—but he does not even know of his father's existence.

Fleta. How old is he?

Iol. Twenty-four.

Leila. Twenty-four! No one, to look at you, would think you had a son of twenty-four! But that's one of the advantages of being immortal. We never grow old! Is he pretty?

Iol. He's extremely pretty, but he's inclined to be stout.

All (disappointed). Oh!

Queen. I see no objection to stoutness, in moderation.

Celia. And what is he?

Iol. He's an Arcadian shepherd—and he loves Phyllis, a Ward in Chancery.

Celia. A mere shepherd! and he half a fairy!

Iol. He's a fairy down to the waist—but his legs are mortal.

All. Dear me!

Queen. I have no reason to suppose that I am more curious than other people, but I confess I should like to see a person who is fairy down to the waist, but whose legs are mortal.

Iol. Nothing easier, for here he comes!

Enter STREPHON, *singing and dancing and playing on a flageolet. He does not see the Fairies, who retire up stage as he enters.*

SONG—STREPHON

Good morrow, good mother!
  Good mother, good morrow!
By some means or other,
  Pray banish your sorrow!
    With joy beyond telling
    My bosom is swelling,
    So join in a measure
    Expressive of pleasure,
For I'm to be married to-day—to-day—
  Yes, I'm to be married to-day!

Chorus (aside)

Yes, he's to be married to-day—to-day—
Yes, he's to be married to-day!

Iol. Then the Lord Chancellor has at last given his consent to your marriage with his beautiful ward, Phyllis?

Streph. Not he, indeed. To all my tearful prayers he answers me, "A shepherd lad is no fit helpmate for a Ward of Chancery." I stood in court, and there I sang him songs of Arcadee, with flageolet accompaniment—in vain. At first he seemed amused, so did the Bar; but quickly wearying of my song and pipe, bade me get out. A servile usher then, in crumpled bands and rusty bombazine, led me, still singing, into Chancery Lane! I'll go no more; I'll marry her to-day, and brave the upshot,

be it what it may! (*Sees Fairies.*) But who are these?

Iol. Oh, Strephon! rejoice with me, my Queen has pardoned me!

Streph. Pardoned you, mother? This is good news indeed.

Iol. And these ladies are my beloved sisters.

Streph. Your sisters! Then they are—my aunts!

Queen. A pleasant piece of news for your bride on her wedding day!

Streph. Hush! My bride knows nothing of my fairyhood. I dare not tell her, lest it frighten her. She thinks me mortal, and prefers me so.

Leila. Your fairyhood doesn't seem to have done you much good.

Streph. Much good! My dear aunt! it's the curse of my existence! What's the use of being half a fairy? My body can creep through a keyhole, but what's the good of that when my legs are left kicking behind? I can make myself invisible down to the waist, but that's of no use when my legs remain exposed to view? My brain is a fairy brain, but from the waist downwards I'm a gibbering idiot. My upper half is immortal, but my lower half grows older every day, and some day or other must die of old age. What's to become of my upper half when I've buried my lower half I really don't know!

Fairies. Poor fellow!

Queen. I see your difficulty, but with a fairy brain you should seek an intellectual sphere of action. Let me see. I've a borough or two at my disposal. Would you like to go into Parliament?

Iol. A fairy Member! That would be delightful!

Streph. I'm afraid I should do no good there—you see, down to the waist, I'm a Tory of the most determined description, but my legs are a couple of confounded Radicals, and, on a division, they'd be sure to take me into the wrong lobby. You see, they're two to one, which is a strong working majority.

Queen. Don't let that distress you; you shall be returned as a Liberal-Unionist, and your legs shall be our peculiar care.

Streph. (*bowing*). I see your Majesty does not do things by halves.

Queen. No, we are fairies down to the feet.

ENSEMBLE
Queen
Fare thee well, attractive stranger.
Fairies
Fare thee well, attractive stranger.
Queen
Shouldst thou be in doubt or danger,
Peril or perplexitee,
Call us, and we'll come to thee!
Fairies
Call us, and we'll come to thee!
Tripping hither, tripping thither,
Nobody knows why or whither;
We must now be taking wing
To another fairy ring!

[*Fairies and* QUEEN *trip off,* IOLANTHE, *who takes an affectionate farewell of her son, going off last.*
Enter PHYLLIS, *singing and dancing, and accompanying herself on a flageolet.*

SONG—PHYLLIS
Good morrow, good lover!
Good lover, good morrow!
I prithee discover,
Steal, purchase, or borrow
Some means of concealing
The care you are feeling,
And join in a measure
Expressive of pleasure,
For we're to be married to-day—to-day!
For we're to be married to-day!
Both
Yes, we're to be married, etc.

Streph. (*embracing her*). My Phyllis! And to-day we are to be made happy for ever.

Phyl. Well, we're to be married.

Streph. It's the same thing.

Phyl. I suppose it is. But oh, Strephon, I tremble at the step I'm taking! I believe it's penal servitude for life to marry a Ward of Court without the Lord Chancellor's consent! I shall be of age in two years. Don't you think you could wait two years?

Streph. Two years. Have you ever looked in the glass?

Phyl. No, never.

Streph. Here, look at that (*showing her a pocket mirror*), and tell me if you think it rational to expect me to wait two years?

Phyl. (*looking at herself*). No. You're quite right—it's asking too much. One must be reasonable.

Streph. Besides, who knows what will happen in two years? Why, you might fall in love with the Lord Chancellor himself by that time!

Phyl. Yes. He's a clean old gentleman.

Streph. As it is, half the House of Lords are sighing at your feet.

Phyl. The House of Lords are certainly extremely attentive.

Streph. Attentive? I should think they were! Why did five-and-twenty Liberal Peers come down to shoot over your grass-plot last autumn? It couldn't have been the sparrows. Why did five-and-twenty Conservative Peers come down to fish your pond? Don't tell me it was the gold-fish! No, no—delays are dangerous, and if we are to marry, the sooner the better.

DUET—STREPHON *and* PHYLLIS
Phyllis
None shall part us from each other,
One in life and death are we:
All in all to one another—
I to thee and thou to me!
Both
Thou the tree and I the flower—
Thou the idol; I the throng—
Thou the day and I the hour—
Thou the singer; I the song!
Strephon
All in all since that fond meeting
When in joy, I woke to find
Mine the heart within thee beating,
Mine the love that heart enshrined!
Both
Thou the stream and I the willow—
Thou the sculptor; I the clay—
Thou the ocean; I the billow—
Thou the sunrise! I the day!

[*Exeunt* STREPHON *and* PHYLLIS *together. March. Enter Procession of Peers*

Chorus
Loudly let the trumpet bray!
Tantantara!
Proudly bang the sounding brasses!
Tzing! Boom!
As upon its lordly way
This unique procession passes,
Tantantara! Tzing! Boom!
Bow, bow, ye lower middle classes!
Bow, bow, ye tradesmen, bow, ye masses!

Blow the trumpets, bang the brasses!
    Tantantara! Tzing! Boom!
We are peers of highest station,
Paragons of legislation,
Pillars of the British nation!
    Tantantara! Tzing! Boom!
Enter the LORD CHANCELLOR, *followed by*
    his train-bearer.

SONG—LORD CHANCELLOR

The Law is the true embodiment
Of everything that's excellent.
It has no kind of fault or flaw,
And I, my Lords, embody the Law.
The constitutional guardian I
Of pretty young Wards in Chancery,
All very agreeable girls—and none
Are over the age of twenty-one.
    A pleasant occupation for
    A rather susceptible Chancellor!

All

    A pleasant, etc.
        Lord Chancellor
But though the compliment implied
Inflates me with legitimate pride,
It nevertheless can't be denied
That it has its inconvenient side.
For I'm not so old, and not so plain,
And I'm quite prepared to marry again,
But there'd be the deuce to pay in the
    Lords
If I fell in love with one of my Wards!
    Which rather tries my temper, for
    I'm *such* a susceptible Chancellor!

All

    Which rather, etc.
And every one who'd marry a Ward
Must come to me for my accord,
And in my court I sit all day,
Giving agreeable girls away,
With one for him—and one for he—
And one for you—and one for ye—
And one for thou—and one for thee—
But never, oh, never a one for me!
Which is exasperating for
A highly susceptible Chancellor!

All

    Which is, etc.
        Enter LORD TOLLOLLER
Lord Toll. And now, my Lords, to the
business of the day.
Lord Ch. By all means. Phyllis, who is a
Ward of Court, has so powerfully affected
your Lordships, that you have appealed to
me in a body to give her to whichever one

of you she may think proper to select, and
a noble Lord has just gone to her cottage
to request her immediate attendance. It
would be idle to deny that I, myself, have
the misfortune to be singularly attracted
by this young person. My regard for her is
rapidly undermining my constitution. Three
months ago I was a stout man. I need say
no more. If I could reconcile it with my
duty, I should unhesitatingly award her
to myself, for I can conscientiously say that
I know no man who is so well fitted to
render her exceptionally happy. (*Peers:*
Hear, hear!) But such an award would be
open to misconstruction, and therefore, at
whatever personal inconvenience, I waive
my claim.
    Lord Toll. My Lord, I desire, on the
part of this House, to express its sincere
sympathy with your Lordship's most painful position.
    Lord Ch. I thank your Lordships. The
feelings of a Lord Chancellor who is in
love with a Ward of Court are not to be
envied. What is his position? Can he give
his own consent to his own marriage with
his own Ward? Can he marry his own
Ward without his own consent? And if he
marries his own Ward without his own
consent, can he commit himself for contempt of his own Court? And if he commit himself for contempt of his own Court,
can he appear by counsel before himself,
to move for arrest of his own judgment?
Ah, my Lords, it is indeed painful to have
to sit upon a woolsack which is stuffed
with such thorns as these!
        Enter LORD MOUNTARARAT
    Lord Mount. My Lords, I have much
pleasure in announcing that I have succeeded in inducing the young person to
present herself at the Bar of this House.
            Enter PHYLLIS
            RECIT—PHYLLIS
My well-loved Lord and Guardian dear,
You summoned me, and I am here!
        Chorus of Peers
    Oh, rapture, how beautiful!
    How gentle—how dutiful!

        SOLO—LORD TOLLOLLER
Of all the young ladies I know
    This pretty young lady's the fairest;
Her lips have the rosiest show,
    Her eyes are the richest and rarest.

Her origin's lowly, it's true,
But of birth and position I've plenty;
I've grammar and spelling for two,
And blood and behaviour for twenty!
Her origin's lowly, it's true,
I've grammar and spelling for two.
Chorus
Of birth and position he's plenty,
With blood and behaviour for twenty!
SOLO—LORD MOUNTARARAT
Though the views of the House have diverged
On every conceivable motion,
All questions of Party are merged
In a frenzy of love and devotion;
If you ask us distinctly to say
What Party we claim to belong to,
We reply, without doubt or delay,
The Party I'm singing this song to!
SOLO—PHYLLIS
I'm very much pained to refuse,
But I'll stick to my pipes and my tabors;
I can spell all the words that I use,
And my grammar's as good as my neighbours'.
As for birth—I was born like the rest,
My behaviour is rustic but hearty,
And I know where to turn for her best,
When I want a particular Party!
Chorus
Though her station is none of the best,
I suppose she was born like the rest;
And she knows where to look for her hearty,
When she wants a particular Party!
RECIT—PHYLLIS
Nay, tempt me not.
To rank I'll not be bound;
In lowly cot
Alone is virtue found!
Chorus
No, no; indeed high rank will never hurt you,
The Peerage is not destitute of virtue.
BALLAD—LORD TOLLOLLER
Spurn not the nobly born
With love affected,
Nor treat with virtuous scorn
The well-connected.
High rank involves no shame—
We boast an equal claim
With him of humble name
To be respected!
Blue blood! blue blood!

When virtuous love is sought
Thy power is naught,
Though dating from the Flood,
Blue blood!
Chorus
Blue blood! blue blood! etc.
Spare us the bitter pain
Of stern denials,
Nor with low-born disdain
Augment our trials.
Hearts just as pure and fair
May beat in Belgrave Square
As in the lowly air
O Seven Dials!
Blue blood! Blue blood!
Of what avail art thou
To serve us now?
Though dating from the Flood,
Blue blood!
Chorus
Blue blood! blue blood! etc.
RECIT—PHYLLIS
My Lords, it may not be.
With grief my heart is riven!
You waste your time on me,
For ah! my heart is given!
All
Given!
Phyllis
Yes, given!
All
Oh, horror!!!
RECIT—LORD CHANCELLOR
And who has dared to brave our high displeasure,
And thus defy our definite command?
Enter STREPHON
Strephon
'Tis I—young Strephon! mine this priceless treasure!
Against the world I claim my darling's hand!
[PHYLLIS *rushes to his arms.*
A shepherd I—
All
A shepherd he!
Strephon
Of Arcady—
All
Of Arcadee—
Strephon
Betrothed are we!
All
Betrothed are they—

Strephon
And mean to be—

All
Espoused to-day!

ENSEMBLE

Strephon
A shepherd I
Of Arcady,
Betrothed are we,
And mean to be
Espoused to-day!

The Others
A shepherd he
Of Arcadee,
Betrothed is he,
And means to be
Espoused to-day!

DUET—LORD MOUNTARARAT *and* LORD TOLLOLLER (*aside to each other*)
'Neath this blow,
  Worse than stab of dagger—
Though we mo-
  Mentarily stagger,
In each heart
  Proud are we innately—
Let's depart,
  Dignified and stately!

All
Let's depart,
  Dignified and stately!

CHORUS OF PEERS
Though our hearts she's badly bruising,
In another suitor choosing,
Let's pretend it's most amusing.
Ha! ha! ha! Tan-ta-ra!

[*Exeunt all the Peers, marching round stage with much dignity.* LORD CHANCELLOR *separates* PHYLLIS *from* STREPHON *and orders her off. She follows Peers. Manent* LORD CHANCELLOR *and* STREPHON.

Lord Ch. Now, sir, what excuse have you to offer for having disobeyed an order of the Court of Chancery?

Streph. My Lord, I know no Courts of Chancery; I go by Nature's Acts of Parliament. The bees—the breeze—the seas—the rooks—the brooks—the gales—the vales——the fountains and the mountains cry, "You love this maiden—take her, we command you!" 'Tis writ in heaven by the bright barbèd dart that leaps forth into lurid light from each grim thundercloud. The very rain pours forth her sad and sodden sympathy! When chorused Nature bids me take my love, shall I reply, "Nay, but a certain Chancellor forbids it"? Sir, you are England's Lord High Chancellor, but are you, Chancellor of birds and trees, King of the winds and Prince of thunderclouds?

Lord Ch. No. It's a nice point. I don't know that I ever met it before. But my difficulty is that at present there's no evidence before the Court that chorused Nature has interested herself in the matter.

Streph. No evidence! You have my word for it. I tell you that she bade me take my love.

Lord Ch. Ah! but, my good sir, you mustn't tell us what she told you—it's not evidence. Now an affidavit from a thunderstorm, or a few words on oath from a heavy shower, would meet with all the attention they deserve.

Streph. And have you the heart to apply the prosaic rules of evidence to a case which bubbles over with poetical emotion?

Lord Ch. Distinctly. I have always kept my duty strictly before my eyes, and it is to that fact that I owe my advancement to my present distinguished position.

SONG—LORD CHANCELLOR

When I went to the Bar as a very young man,
  (Said I to myself—said I),
I'll work on a new and original plan,
  (Said I to myself—said I),
I'll never assume that a rogue or a thief
Is a gentleman worthy implicit belief,
Because his attorney has sent me a brief
  (Said I to myself—said I!).
Ere I go into court I will read my brief through
  (Said I to myself—said I).
And I'll never take work I'm unable to do
  (Said I to myself—said I).
My learned profession I'll never disgrace
By taking a fee with a grin on my face,
When I haven't been there to attend to the case
  (Said I to myself—said I!).
I'll never throw dust in a juryman's eyes
  (Said I to myself—said I).

Or hoodwink a judge who is not over-wise
  (Said I to myself—said I).
Or assume that the witnesses summoned in
  force
In Exchequer, Queen's Bench, Common
  Pleas, or Divorce,
Have perjured themselves as a matter of
  course
  (Said I to myself—said I!).
In other professions in which men engage
  (Said I to myself—said I),
The Army, the Navy, the Church, and the
  Stage
  (Said I to myself—said I),
Professional license, if carried too far,
Your chance of promotion will certainly
  mar—
And I fancy the rule might apply to the
  Bar
  (Said I to myself—said I!).

[Exit LORD CHANCELLOR.
Enter IOLANTHE

Streph. Oh, Phyllis, Phyllis! To be taken
from you just as I was on the point of
making you my own! Oh, it's too much—
it's too much!

Iol. (*to* STREPHON, *who is in tears*). My
son in tears—and on his wedding day!

Streph. My wedding day! Oh, mother,
weep with me, for the Law has interposed
between us, and the Lord Chancellor has
separated us for ever!

Iol. The Lord Chancellor! (*Aside.*) Oh,
if he did but know!

Streph. (*overhearing her*). If he did but
know what?

Iol. No matter! The Lord Chancellor has
no power over you. Remember you are
half a fairy. You can defy him—down to
the waist.

Streph. Yes, but from the waist downwards he can commit me to prison for
years! Of what avail is it that my body
is free, if my legs are working out seven
years' penal servitude?

Iol. True. But take heart—our Queen
has promised you her special protection. I'll
go to her and lay your peculiar case before her.

Streph. My beloved mother! how can I
repay the debt I owe you?

FINALE—QUARTET

*As it commences, the Peers appear at the
back, advancing unseen and on tiptoe.*

LORD MOUNTARARAT *and* LORD TOLLOL-
LER *lead* PHYLLIS *between them, who
listens in horror to what she hears.*
    Streph. (*to Iolanthe*)
When darkly looms the day,
And all is dull and grey,
To chase the gloom away,
  On thee I'll call!

Phyl. (*speaking aside to Lord Mountararat*)
What was that?
    Lord Mountararat (*aside to Phyllis*)
I think I heard him say,
That on a rainy day,
To while the time away,
  On her he'd call!

Chorus
We think we heard him say, etc.
    [PHYLLIS *much agitated at her lover's
    supposed faithlessness.*
    Iolanthe (*to Strephon*)
When tempests wreck thy bark,
And all is drear and dark,
If thou shouldst need an Ark,
  I'll give thee one!

Phyl. (*speaking aside to* LORD TOLLOL-
LER). What was that?
    Lord Tolloller (*aside to Phyllis*)
I heard the minx remark,
She'd meet him after dark,
Inside St. James's Park,
  And give him one!

    Phyllis
The prospect's not so bad,]
My heart so sore and sad
Will never more be glad
  As summer's sun.

Iol., Lord Toll., Streph., Lord Mount.
The prospect's not so bad,
My ⎱
Thy ⎰ heart so sore and sad
May very soon be glad
  As summer's sun;

Phyl., Iol., Lord Toll., Streph., Lord Mount.
For when the sky is dark
                ⎧ my ⎫
And tempests wreck ⎨ thy ⎬ bark,
                ⎩ his ⎭
    ⎧ he should ⎫
If ⎨ I should   ⎬ need an Ark,
    ⎩ thou shouldst ⎭
She'll ⎫   ⎧ him ⎫
I'll   ⎬ give ⎨ me   ⎬ one!
       ⎭   ⎩ thee ⎭

Phyllis (revealing herself)
Ah!
[IOLANTHE *and* STREPHON *much confused.*

Phyllis
Oh, shameless one, tremble!
Nay, do not endeavour
Thy fault to dissemble,
We part—and for ever!
I worshipped him blindly,
He worships another—

Strephon
Attend to me kindly,
This lady's my mother!
Tolloller
This lady's his *what?*
Strephon
This lady's my mother!

Tenors
This lady's his *what?*

Basses
He says she's his mother!
[*They point derisively to* IOLANTHE, *laughing heartily at her. She goes for protection to* STREPHON.
Enter LORD CHANCELLOR. IOLANTHE *veils herself.*

Lord Chancellor
What means this mirth unseemly,
That shakes the listening earth?

Lord Tolloller
The joke is good extremely,
And justifies our mirth.

Lord Mountararat
This gentleman is seen,
With a maid of seventeen;
A-taking of his *dolce far niente;*
And wonders he'd achieve,
For he asks us to believe
She's his mother—and he's nearly five-and-twenty!

Lord Chancellor (sternly)
Recollect yourself, I pray,
And be careful what you say—
As the ancient Romans said, *festina lente.*
For I really do not see
How so young a girl could be
The mother of a man of five-and-twenty.

All
Ha! ha! ha! ha! ha!
Strephon
My Lord, of evidence I have no dearth—

She is—has been—my mother from my birth!
Ballad
In babyhood
Upon her lap I lay,
With infant food
She moistenèd my clay;
Had she withheld
The succour she supplied,
By hunger quelled,
Your Strephon might have died!
Lord Chancellor (much moved)
Had that refreshment been denied,
Indeed our Strephon might have died!
All (much affected)
Had that refreshment been denied,
Indeed our Strephon might have died!
Lord Mountararat
But as she's not
His mother, it appears,
Why weep these hot
Unnecessary tears?
And by what laws
Should we so joyously
Rejoice, because
Our Strephon did not die?
Oh, rather let us pipe our eye
Because our Strephon did not die!
All
That's very true—let's pipe our eye
Because our Strephon did not die!
[*All weep.* IOLANTHE, *who has succeeded in hiding her face from* LORD CHANCELLOR, *escapes unnoticed.*
Phyllis
Go traitorous one—for ever we must part:
To one of you, my Lords, I give my heart!
All
Oh, rapture!

Strephon
Hear me, Phyllis, ere you leave me.
Phyllis
Not a word—you did deceive me.
All
Not a word—you did deceive her.
[*Exit* STREPHON.

BALLAD—PHYLLIS
For riches and rank I do not long—
Their pleasures are false and vain;
I gave up the love of a lordly throng
For the love of a simple swain.
But now that simple swain's untrue,
With sorrowful heart I turn to you—
A heart that's aching,

Quaking, breaking,
As sorrowful hearts are wont to do!
The riches and rank that you befall
 Are the only baits you use,
So the richest and rankiest of you all
 My sorrowful heart shall choose.
As none are so noble—none so rich
As this couple of lords, I'll find a niche
 In my heart that's aching,
 Quaking, breaking,
For one of you two—and I don't care
 which!

ENSEMBLE

Phyllis (to Lord Mountararat and Lord
 Tolloler)
To you I give my heart so rich!
 All (puzzled)
 To which?
 Phyllis
I do not care!
To you I yield—it is my doom!
 All
 To whom?
 Phyllis
I'm not aware!
I'm yours for life if you but choose.
 All
 She's whose?
 Phyllis
That's your affair!
I'll be a countess, shall I not?
 All
 Of what?
 Phyllis
I do not care!
 All
Lucky little lady!
Strephon's lot is shady;
Rank, it seems, is vital,
"Countess" is the title,
But of what I'm not aware.

Enter STREPHON
 Strephon
Can I inactive see my fortunes fade?
 No, no!
Mighty protectress, hasten to my aid!
Enter Fairies, tripping, headed by CELIA,
 LEILA, *and* FLETA, *and followed by*
 QUEEN.

Chorus of Fairies
Tripping hither, tripping thither,
Nobody knows why or whither;
Why you want us we don't know,

But you've summoned us, and so
 Enter all the little fairies
 To their usual tripping measure!
 To oblige you all our care is—
 Tell us, pray, what is your pleasure!
 Strephon
The lady of my love has caught me talk-
 ing to another—
 Peers
 Oh, fie! our Strephon is a rogue!
 Strephon
I tell her very plainly that the lady is my
 mother—
 Peers
 Taradiddle, taradiddle, tol lol lay!
 Strephon
She won't believe my statement, and de-
 clares we must be parted,
Because on a career of double-dealing I
 have started,
Then gives her hand to one of these, and
 leaves me broken-hearted—
 Peers
 Taradiddle, taradiddle, tol lol lay!
 Queen
Ah, cruel ones, to separate two lovers from
 each other!

 Fairies
 Oh, fie! our Strephon's not a rogue!
 Queen
You've done him an injustice, for the lady
 is his mother!
 Fairies
 Taradiddle, taradiddle, tol lol lay!
 Lord Chancellor
That fable perhaps may serve his turn as
 well as any other.
(Aside.) I didn't see her face, but if they
 fondled one another,
And she's but seventeen—I don't believe it
 was his mother!
 Taradiddle, taradiddle.
 All
 Tol lol lay!
 Lord Tolloller
I have often had a use
 For a thorough-bred excuse
Of a sudden (which is English for "re-
 pente"),
 But of all I ever heard
 This is much the most absurd,
For she's seventeen, and he is five-and-
 twenty!

All

Though she is seventeen, and he's four or
    five-and-twenty!
Oh, fie! our Strephon is a rogue!
            Lord Mountararat
Now, listen, pray to me,
For this paradox will be
Carried, nobody at all *contradicente*.
Her age, upon the date
Of his birth, was *minus* eight,
If she's seventeen, and he is five-and-
    twenty!

All

To say she is his mother is an utter bit of
    folly!
Oh, fie! our Strephon is a rogue!
Perhaps his brain is addled, and it's very
    melancholy!
Taradiddle, taradiddle, tol lol lay!
I wouldn't say a word that could be reck-
    oned as injurious,

But to find a mother younger than her son
    is very curious,
And that's a kind of mother that is usu-
    ally spurious.
Taradiddle, taradiddle, tol lol lay!
            Lord Chancellor
Go away, madam;
I should say, madam,
You display, madam,
    Shocking taste.
It is rude, madam,
To intrude, madam,
With your brood, madam,
    Brazen-faced!
You come here, madam,
Interfere, madam,
With a peer, madam.
    (I am one.)
You're aware, madam,
What you dare, madam,
So take care, madam,
    And begone!

ENSEMBLE

Fairies to Queen
Let us stay, madam;
I should say, madam,
They display, madam,
    Shocking taste.
It is rude, madam,
To allude, madam,
To your brood, madam,
    Brazen-faced!
We don't fear, madam,
Any peer, madam,
Though, my dear madam,
    This is one.
They will stare, madam,
When aware, madam,
What they dare, madam—
    What they've done!

Peers
Go away, madam;
I should say, madam,
You display, madam,
    Shocking taste.
It is rude, madam,
To intrude, madam,
With your brood, madam,
    Brazen-faced!
You come here, madam,
Interfere, madam,
With a peer, madam,
    (I am one.)
You're aware, madam,
What you dare, madam,
So take care, madam,
    And begone!

Queen (furious)

Bearded by these puny mortals!
I will launch from fairy portals
All the most terrific thunders
In my armory of wonders!

Phyllis (aside)

Should they launch terrific wonders,
All would then repent their blunders.
Surely these must be immortals.
            [*Exit* PHYLLIS.

Queen

Oh! Chancellor unwary
It's highly necessary
    Your tongue to teach
    Respectful speech—
Your attitude to vary!
Your badinage so airy,
Your manner arbitrary,
    Are out of place
    When face to face
With an influential Fairy.

All the Peers (aside)
We never knew
We were talking to
An influential Fairy!
　　Lord Chancellor
A plague on this vagary,
I'm in a nice quandary!
　Of hasty tone
　With dames unknown
I ought to be more chary;
It seems that she's a fairy
From Andersen's library,
　And I took her for
　The proprietor
Of a Ladies' Seminary!
　　　Peers
　We took her for
　The proprietor
Of a Ladies' Seminary!
　　　Queen
When next your Houses do assemble,
You may tremble!
　　　Celia
Our wrath, when gentlemen offend us,
Is tremendous!
　　　Leila
They meet, who underrate our calling,
Doom appalling!
　　　Queen
Take down our sentence as we speak it,
And *he* shall wreak it!
　　　　　[*Indicating* STREPHON.
　　　Peers
Oh, spare us!
　　　Queen
Henceforth, Strephon, cast away
Crooks and pipes and ribbons so gay—
Flocks and herds that bleat and low;
Into Parliament you shall go!
　　　All
Into Parliament he shall go!
　Backed by our supreme authority,

He'll command a large majority!
Into Parliament he shall go!
　　　Queen
In the Parliamentary hive,
Liberal or Conservative—
Whig or Tory—I don't know—
But into Parliament you shall go!
　　　Fairies
Into Parliament, etc.
　　Queen (speaking through music)
Every bill and every measure
That may gratify his pleasure,
Though your fury it arouses,
Shall be passed by both your Houses!
　　　Peers
　Oh!
You shall sit, if he sees reason,
Through the grouse and salmon season;
　　　Peers
　No!
He shall end the cherished rights
You enjoy on Friday nights:
　　　Peers
　No!
He shall prick that annual blister,
Marriage with deceased wife's sister:
　　　Peers
　Mercy!
Titles shall ennoble, then,
All the Common Councilmen:
　　　Peers
　Spare us!
Peers shall teem in Christendom,
　And a Duke's exalted station
Be attainable by Com-
　Petitive Examination!
　　　Peers
　Oh, horror!
　　Fairies and Phyllis
　Their horror
They can't dissemble
Nor hide the fear that makes them tremble!

ENSEMBLE

　　　Peers
Young Strephon is the kind of lout
We do not care a fig about!
　We cannot say
　What evils may
Result in consequence.
But lordly vengeance will pursue
All kinds of common people who
　Oppose our views,
　Or boldly choose

To offer us offence.
He'd better fly at humbler game,
Or our forbearance he must claim,
　If he'd escape
　In any shape
A very painful wrench!
Your powers we dauntlessly pooh-pooh:
A dire revenge will fall on you,
　If you besiege
　Our high *prestige*—

(The word "*prestige*" is French).

Fairies, Phyllis and Strephon
With Strephon for your foe, no doubt,
A fearful prospect opens out,
    And who shall say
    What evils may
Result in consequence?
A hideous vengeance will pursue
All noblemen who venture to
    Oppose his views,
    Or boldly choose

         Peers
  Our lordly style
    You shall not quench
  With base *canaille*!
       Fairies
  (That word is French.)
        Peers
  Distinction ebbs
    Before a herd
  Of vulgar *plebs*!
       Fairies
  (A Latin word.)
        Peers
  'Twould fill with joy,
    And madness stark
  The οἱ πολλοί!
       Fairies
  (A Greek remark.)
        Peers
One Latin word, one Greek remark,
And one that's French.

        Peers
    You needn't wait:
      Away you fly!
    Your threatened hate
    We won't defy!

[FAIRIES *threaten* PEERS *with their wands.*
PEERS *kneel as begging for mercy.*
PHYLLIS *implores* STREPHON *to relent.*
*He casts her from him, and she falls
fainting into the arms of* LORD MOUNT-
ARARAT *and* LORD TOLLOLLER.
      END OF ACT I

        ACT II
SCENE.—*Palace Yard, Westminster. West-
minster Hall,* L. *Clock tower up,* R.C.
PRIVATE WILLIS *discovered on sentry,*
R. *Moonlight.*

    SONG—PRIVATE WILLIS
When all night long a chap remains
  On sentry-go, to chase monotony

To offer him offence.
'Twill plunge them into grief and shame;
His kind forbearance they must claim,
    If they'd escape
    In any shape
A very painful wrench.
Although our threats you now pooh-pooh,
A dire revenge will fall on you,
    Should he besiege
    Your high *prestige*—
(The word "*prestige*" is French).

        Fairies
  Your lordly style
    We'll quickly quench
  With base *canaille*!
        Peers
  (That word is French.)
       Fairies
  Distinction ebbs
    Before a herd
  Of vulgar *plebs*!
        Peers
  (A Latin word.)
       Fairies
  'Twill fill with joy
    And madness stark
  The οἱ πολλοί!
        Peers
  (A Greek remark.)
       Fairies
One Latin word, one Greek remark,
And one that's French.

        Fairies
    We will not wait:
      We go sky-high!
    Our threatened hate
    You won't defy!

He exercises of his brains,
  That is, assuming that he's got any.
Though never nurtured in the lap
  Of luxury, yet I admonish you,
I am an intellectual chap,
  And think of things that would astonish
    you.

  I often think it's comical—Fal, lal, la!
  Now Nature always does contrive—
    Fal, lal, la!
    That every boy and every gal
      That's born into the world alive
    Is either a little Liberal
      Or else a little Conservative!
      Fal, lal, la!

When in that House M.P.'s divide,
If they've a brain and cerebellum, too,
They've got to leave that brain outside,
And vote just as their leaders tell 'em to.
But then the prospect of a lot
Of dull M.P.'s in close proximity,
All thinking for themselves, is what
No man can face with equanimity.

Then let's rejoice with loud Fal la—
Fal lal la!
That Nature always does contrive—
Fal lal la!
That every boy and every gal
That's born into the world alive
Is either a little Liberal
Or else a little Conservative!
Fal lal la!

Enter FAIRIES, *with* CELIA, LEILA, *and*
FLETA. *They trip round stage.*

Chorus of Fairies
Strephon's a Member of Parliament!
Carries every Bill he chooses.
To his measures all assent—
Showing that fairies have their uses.
Whigs and Tories
Dim their glories,
Giving an ear to all his stories—
Lords and Commons are both in the blues!
Strephon makes them shake in their shoes!
Shake in their shoes!
Shake in their shoes!
Strephon makes them shake in their shoes!

Enter PEERS *from Westminster Hall*

Chorus of Peers
Strephon's a Member of Parliament!
Running a-muck of all abuses.
His unqualified assent
Somehow nobody now refuses.
Whigs and Tories
Dim their glories,
Giving an ear to all his stories
Carrying every Bill he may wish:
Here's a pretty kettle of fish!
Kettle of fish!
Kettle of fish!
Here's a pretty kettle of fish!

Enter LORD MOUNTARARAT *and* LORD TOLLOL-
LER *from Westminster Hall.*

Celia. You seem annoyed.
Lord Mount. Annoyed! I should think
so! Why, this ridiculous *protégé* of yours
is playing the deuce with everything! To-
night is the second reading of his Bill to
throw the Peerage open to Competitive
Examination!
Lord Toll. And he'll carry it, too!
Lord Mount. Carry it? Of course he
will! He's a Parliamentary Pickford—he
carries everything!
Leila. Yes. If you please, that's our
fault!
Lord Mount. The deuce it is!
Celia. Yes; we influence the members,
and compel them to vote just as he wishes
them to.
Leila. It's our system. It shortens the
debates.
Lord Toll. Well, but think what it all
means. I don't so much mind for myself,
but with a House of Peers with no grand-
fathers worth mentioning, the country
must go to the dogs!
Leila. I suppose it must!
Lord Mount. I don't want to say a word
against brains—I've a great respect for
brains—I often wish I had some myself—
but with a House of Peers composed
exclusively of people of intellect, what's to
become of the House of Commons?
Leila. I never thought of that!
Lord Mount. This comes of women in-
terfering in politics. It so happens that if
there is an institution in Great Britain
which is not susceptible of any improvement at all, it is the House of Peers!

SONG—LORD MOUNTARARAT
When Britain really ruled the waves—
(In good Queen Bess's time)
The House of Peers made no pretence
To intellectual eminence,
Or scholarship sublime;
Yet Britain won her proudest bays
In good Queen Bess's glorious days!
Chorus
Yes, Britain won, etc.
When Wellington thrashed Bonaparate,
As every child can tell,
The House of Peers, throughout the war,
Did nothing in particular,
And did it very well:
Yet Britain set the world ablaze
In good King George's glorious days!
Chorus
Yes, Britain set, etc.
And while the House of Peers withholds
Its legislative hand,
And noble statesmen do not itch

To interfere with matters which
    They do not understand,
As bright will shine Great Britain's rays
As in King George's glorious days!
Chorus
    As bright will shine, etc.

Leila (*who has been much attracted by
the* PEERS *during this song*). Charming persons, are they not?

Celia. Distinctly. For self-contained dignity, combined with airy condescension,
give me a British Representative Peer!

Lord Toll. Then pray stop this *protégé*
of yours before it's too late. Think of the
mischief you're doing!

Leila (*crying*). But we *can't* stop him
now. (*Aside to* CELIA.) Aren't they lovely!
(*Aloud.*) Oh, why did you go and defy
us, you great geese!

DUET—LEILA *and* CELIA
Leila
In vain to us you plead—
    Don't go!

Fairies
You break our laws—
    You are our foe:
We cry because
    We hate you so!
        You know!
You very wicked peers!
    Don't go!

[*Exeunt* LORD MOUNTARARAT, LORD TOLLOLLER, *and* PEERS. FAIRIES *gaze wistfully
after them.*

Enter FAIRY QUEEN
Queen. Oh, shame—shame upon you! Is
this your fidelity to the laws you are bound
to obey? Know ye not that it is death
to marry a mortal?

Leila. Yes, but it's not death to *wish*
to marry a mortal!

Fleta. If it were, you'd have to execute
us all!

Queen. Oh, this is weakness! Subdue it!

Celia. We know it's weakness, but the
weakness is so strong!

Leila. We are not all as tough as you
are!

Queen. Tough! Do you suppose that I
am insensible to the effect of manly beauty?

Your prayers we do not heed—
    Don't go!
It's true we sigh,
    But don't suppose
A tearful eye
    Forgiveness shows.
        Oh, no!
We're very cross indeed—
    Don't go!
Fairies
It's true we sigh, etc.
Celia
Your disrespectful sneers—
    Don't go!
Call forth indignant tears—
    Don't go!
You break our laws—
    You are our foe:
We cry because
    We hate you so!
        You know!
You very wicked Peers!
    Don't go!

Lords Mountararat and T*olloller*
Our disrespectful sneers,
    Ha! ha!
Call forth indignant tears,
    Ha! ha!
If that's the case, my dears—
Fairies
    Don't go!
Peers
    We'll go!

Look at that man! (*Referring to* SENTRY.)
A perfect picture! (*To* SENTRY.) Who are
you, sir?

Willis (*coming to* "attention"). Private
Willis, B Company, 1st Grenadier Guards.

Queen. You're a very fine fellow, sir.

Willis. I am generally admired.

Queen. I can quite understand it. (*To*
FAIRIES.) Now here is a man whose physical
attributes are simply godlike. That man has
a most extraordinary effect upon me. If I
yielded to a natural impulse, I should fall
down and worship that man. But I mortify
this inclination; I wrestle with it, and it
lies beneath my feet! That is how I treat
my regard for that man!

SONG—FAIRY QUEEN
Oh, foolish fay,
    Think you, because

His brave array
  My bosom thaws,
I'd disobey
  Our fairy laws?
Because I fly
  In realms above,
In tendency
  To fall in love,
Resemble I
  The amorous dove?
    (*Aside*)
Oh, amorous dove!
  Type of Ovidius Naso!
    This heart of mine
    Is soft as thine,
  Although I dare not say so!
    Chorus
Oh, amorous dove, etc.
On fire that glows
  With heat intense
I turn the hose
  Of common sense,
And out it goes
  At small expense!
We must maintain
  Our fairy law;
That is the main
  On which to draw—
In that we gain
  A Captain Shaw!
    (*Aside*)
  Oh, Captain Shaw!
    Type of true love kept under!
    Could thy Brigade
    With cold cascade
  Quench my great love, I wonder!
    Chorus
  Oh, Captain Shaw! etc.
    [*Exeunt* FAIRIES *and* FAIRY QUEEN,
      sorrowfully.
      Enter Phyllis

Phyl. (*half crying*). I can't think why
I'm not in better spirits. I'm engaged to
two noblemen at once. That ought to be
enough to make any girl happy. But I'm
miserable! Don't suppose it's because I care
for Strephon, for I hate him! No girl *could*
care for a man who goes about with a
mother considerably younger than himself!
Enter LORD MOUNTARARAT *and* LORD TOL-
  LOLLER.
Lord Mount. Phyllis! My darling!
Lord Toll. Phyllis! My own!
Phyl. Don't! How dare you? Oh, but

perhaps you're the two noblemen I'm en-
gaged to?
Lord Mount. I am one of them.
Lord Toll. I am the other.
Phyl. Oh, then, my darling! (*to* LORD
MOUNTARARAT). My own! (*to* LORD TOLLOL-
LER). Well, have you settled which it's
to be?
Lord Toll. Not altogether. It's a diffi-
cult position. It would be hardly delicate
to toss up. On the whole we would rather
leave it to you.
Phyl. How can it possibly concern me?
You are both Earls, and you are both rich,
and you are both plain.
Lord Mount. So we are. At least I am.
Lord Toll. So am I.
Lord Mount. No, no!
Lord Toll. I am indeed. Very plain.
Lord Mount. Well, well—perhaps you
are.
Phyl. There's really nothing to choose
between you. If one of you would forgo
his title, and distribute his estates among
his Irish tenantry, why, then, I should then
see a reason for accepting the other.
Lord Mount. Tolloller, are you prepared
to make this sacrifice?
Lord Tol. No!
Lord Mount. Not even to oblige a lady?
Lord Toll. No! not even to oblige a lady.
Lord Mount. Then, the only question is,
which of us shall give way to the other?
Perhaps, on the whole, she would be happier with me. I don't know. I may be
wrong.
Lord Toll. No. I don't know that you
are. I really believe she would. But the
awkward part of the thing is that if you
rob me of the girl of my heart, we must
fight, and one of us must die. It's a family
tradition that I have sworn to respect.
It's a painful position, for I have a very
strong regard for you, George.
Lord Mount. (*much affected*). My dear
Thomas!
Lord Toll. You are very dear to me,
George. We were boys together—at least *I*
was. If I were to survive you, my existence
would be hopelessly embittered.
Lord Mount. Then, my dear Thomas,
you must not do it. I say it again and
again—if it will have this effect upon you,
you must not do it. No, no. If one of us

is to destroy the other, let it be me!

Lord Toll. No, no!

Lord Mount. Ah, yes!—by our boyish friendship I implore you!

Lord Toll. (*much moved*). Well, well, be it so. But, no—no!—I cannot consent to an act which would crush you with unavailing remorse.

Lord Mount. But it would not do so. I should be very sad at first—oh, who would not be?—but it would wear off. I like you *very much*—but not, perhaps, as much as you like me.

Lord Toll. George, you're a noble fellow, but that tell-tale tear betrays you. No, George; you are very fond of me, and I cannot consent to give you a week's uneasiness on my account.

Lord Mount. But, dear Thomas, it would not last a week! Remember, you lead the House of Lords! on your demise I shall take your place! Oh, Thomas, it would not last a day!

Phyl. (*coming down*). Now, I do hope you're not going to fight about me, because it's really not worth while.

Lord Toll. (*looking at her*). Well, I don't believe it is!

Lord Mount. Nor I. The sacred ties of Friendship are paramount.

QUARTETTE—LORD MOUNTARARAT

Lord Tolloller, Phyllis and Private Willis

Lord Tolloller

Though p'r'aps I may incur your blame,
  The things are few
  I would not do
In Friendship's name!

Lord Mountararat

And I may say I think the same;
  Not even love
  Should rank above
True Friendship's name!

Phyllis

Then free me, pray; be mine the blame;
  Forget your craze
  And go your ways
In Friendship's name!

All

Oh, many a man, in Friendship's name,
Has yielded fortune, rank, and fame!
But no one yet, in the world so wide,
Has yielded up a promised bride!

Willis

Accept, O Friendship, all the same,

All

This sacrifice to thy dear name!

[*Exeunt* LORD MOUNTARARAT *and* LORD TOLLOLLER, *lovingly, in one direction, and* PHYLLIS *in another. Exit* SENTRY.

Enter LORD CHANCELLOR, *very miserable*

RECIT—LORD CHANCELLOR

Love, unrequited, robs me of my rest:
  Love, hopeless love, my ardent soul encumbers:
Love, nightmare-like, lies heavy on my chest,
  And weaves itself into my midnight slumbers!

SONG—LORD CHANCELLOR

When you're lying awake with a dismal headache, and repose is taboo'd by anxiety,

I conceive you may use any language you choose to indulge in, without impropriety;

For your brain is on fire—the bedclothes conspire of usual slumber to plunder you:

First your counterpane goes, and uncovers your toes, and your sheet slips demurely from under you;

Then the blanketing tickles—you feel like mixed pickles—so terribly sharp is the pricking,

And you're hot, and you're cross, and you tumble and toss till there's nothing 'twixt you and the ticking.

Then the bedclothes all creep to the ground in a heap, and you pick 'em all up in a tangle;

Next your pillow resigns and politely declines to remain at its usual angle!

Well, you get some repose in the form of a doze, with hot eye-balls and head ever aching,

But your slumbering teems with such horrible dreams that you'd very much better be waking;

For you dream you are crossing the Channel, and tossing about in a steamer from Harwich—

Which is something between a large bathing machine and a very small second-class carriage—

And you're giving a treat (penny ice and cold meat) to a party of friends and relations—

They're a ravenous horde—and they all

came on board at Sloane Square and
South Kensington Stations.
And bound on that journey you find your
attorney (who started that morning from Devon);
He's a bit undersized, and you don't feel
surprised when he tells you he's only
eleven.
Well, you're driving like mad with this
singular lad (by the by, the ship's
now a four-wheeler),
And you're playing round games, and he
calls you bad names when you tell
him that "ties pay the dealer";
But this you can't stand, so you throw up
your hand, and you find you're as
cold as an icicle,
In your shirt and your socks (the black
silk with gold clocks), crossing Salis-
bury Plain on a bicycle:
And he and the crew are on bicycles too
—which they've somehow or other
invested in—
And he's telling the tars all the particulars
of a company he's interested in—
It's a scheme of devices, to get at low
prices all goods from cough mix-
tures to cables
(Which tickled the sailors), by treating
retailers as though they were all
vegetables—
You get a good spadesman to plant a
small tradesman (first take off his
boots with a boot-tree),
And his legs will take root, and his fingers
will shoot, and they'll blossom and
bud like a fruit-tree—
From the greengrocer tree you get grapes
and green pea, cauliflower, pine-
apple, and cranberries,
While the pastrycook plant cherry brandy
will grant, apple puffs, and three-
corners, and Banburys—
The shares are a penny, and ever so many
are taken by Rothschild and Baring,
And just as a few are allotted to you, you
awake with a shudder despairing—
You're a regular wreck, with a crick in
your neck, and no wonder you snore,
for your head's on the floor, and
you've needles and pins from your
soles to your shins, and your flesh
is a-creep, for your left leg's asleep,
and you've cramp in your toes, and

a fly on your nose, and some fluff
in your lung, and a feverish tongue,
and a thirst that's intense, and a
general sense that you haven't been
sleeping in clover;
But the darkness has passed, and it's daylight at last, and the night has been
long—ditto ditto my song—and
thank goodness they're both of them
over!

[LORD CHANCELLOR *falls exhausted on a seat.*
Lords Mountararat and Tolloller come
forward.

Lord Mount. I am much distressed to
see your Lordship in this condition.

Lord Ch. Ah, my Lords, it is seldom
that a Lord Chancellor has reason to envy
the position of another, but I am free to
confess that I would rather be two Earls
engaged to Phyllis than any other half-
dozen noblemen upon the face of the globe.

Lord Toll. (*without enthusiasm*). Yes.
It's an enviable position when you're the
only one.

Lord Mount. Oh yes, no doubt—most
enviable. At the same time, seeing you
thus, we naturally say to ourselves, "This
is very sad. His Lordship is constitutionally
as blithe as a bird—he trills upon the bench
like a thing of song and gladness. His series
of judgments in F sharp minor, given
andante in six-eight time, are among the
most remarkable effects ever produced in
a Court of Chancery. He is, perhaps, the
only living instance of a judge whose decrees have received the honour of a double
encore. How can we bring ourselves to do
that which will deprive the Court of
Chancery of one of its most attractive features?"

Lord Ch. I feel the force of your remarks, but I am here in two capacities, and
they clash, my Lord, they clash! I deeply
grieve to say that in declining to entertain
my last application to myself, I presumed
to address myself in terms which render it
impossible for me ever to apply to myself
again. It was a most painful scene, my
Lord—most painful!

Lord Toll. This is what it is to have two
capacities! Let us be thankful that we are
persons of no capacity whatever.

Lord Mount. Come, come. Remember
you are a very just and kindly old gentle-

man, and you need have no hesitation in approaching yourself, so that you do so respectfully and with a proper show of deference.

Lord Ch. Do you really think so?

Lord Mount. I do.

Lord Ch. Well, I will nerve myself to another effort, and, if that fails, I resign myself to my fate!

TRIO—LORD CHANCELLOR, LORDS MOUNTARARAT *and* TOLLOLLER

Lord Mountararat

If you go in
You're sure to win—
Yours will be the charming maidie:
　Be your law
　The ancient saw,
"Faint heart never won fair lady!"

All

Faint heart never won fair lady!
　Every journey has an end—
　When at the worst affairs will mend—
　Dark the dawn when day is nigh—
　Hustle your horse and don't say die!

Lord Tolloller

He who shies
At such a prize
Is not worth a maravedi,
　Be so kind
　To bear in mind—
Faint heart never won fair lady!

All

Faint heart never won fair lady!
　While the sun shines make your hay—
　Where a will is, there's a way—
　Beard the lion in his lair—
　None but the brave deserve the fair!

Lord Chancellor

I'll take heart
And make a start—
Though I fear the prospect's shady—
　Much I'd spend
　To gain my end—
Faint heart never won fair lady!

All

Faint heart never won fair lady!
　Nothing venture, nothing win—
　Blood is thick, but water's thin—
　In for a penny, in for a pound—
　It's Love that makes the world go round!

[*Dance, and exeunt arm-in-arm together. Enter* STREPHON, *in very low spirits.*

Streph. I suppose one ought to enjoy oneself in Parliament, when one leads both Parties, as I do! But I'm miserable, poor, broken-hearted fool that I am! Oh, Phyllis, Phyllis!——

Enter PHYLLIS

Phyl. Yes.

Streph. (*surprised*). Phyllis! But I suppose I should say "My Lady." I have not yet been informed which title your ladyship has pleased to select?

Phyl. I—I haven't quite decided. You see *I* have no *mother* to advise *me*!

Streph. No. I have.

Phyl. Yes; a *young* mother.

Streph. Not very—a couple of centuries or so.

Phyl. Oh! She wears well.

Streph. She does. She's a fairy.

Phyl. I beg your pardon—a what?

Streph. Oh, I've no longer any reason to conceal the fact—she's a fairy.

Phyl. A fairy! Well, but—that would account for a good many things! Then—I suppose *you're* a fairy?

Streph. I'm half a fairy.

Phyl. Which half?

Streph. The upper half—down to the waistcoat.

Phyl. Dear me! (*Prodding him with her fingers.*) There is nothing to show it!

Streph. Don't do that.

Phyl. But why didn't you tell me this before?

Streph. I thought you would take a dislike to me. But as it's all off, you may as well know the truth—I'm only half a mortal!

Phyl. (*crying*). But I'd rather have half a mortal I do love, than have a dozen I don't!

Streph. (*crying*). But I think not—go to your half-dozen.

Phyl. (*crying*). It's only two! and I hate 'em! Please forgive me!

Streph. I don't think I ought to. Besides, all sorts of difficulties will arise. You know, my grandmother looks quite as young as my mother. So do all my aunts.

Phyl. I quite understand. Whenever I see you kissing a very young lady, I shall know it's an elderly relative.

Streph. You will? Then, Phyllis, I think we shall be very happy! (*Embracing her.*)

Phyl. We won't wait long.

Streph. No. We might change our minds. We'll get married first.

Phyl. And change our minds afterwards?

Streph. That's the usual course.

DUET—STREPHON *and* PHYLLIS

Strephon

If we're weak enough to tarry
  Ere we marry,
    You and I,
Of the feeling I inspire
  You may tire
    By and by,
For peers with flowing coffers
  Press their offers—
    That is why
I am sure we should not tarry
  Ere we marry,
    You and I!

Phyllis

If we're weak enough to tarry
  Ere we marry,
    You and I,
With a more attractive maiden,
  Jewel-laden,
    You may fly.
If by chance we should be parted,
  Broken-hearted
    I should die—
So I think we will not tarry
  Ere we marry,
    You and I.

Phyl. But does your mother know you're —I mean, is she aware of our engagement?

Enter IOLANTHE

Iol. She is; and thus she welcomes her daughter-in-law! (*Kisses her.*)

Phy. She kisses just like other people! But the Lord Chancellor?

Streph. I forgot him! Mother, none can resist your fairy eloquence; you will go to him and plead for us?

Iol. (*much agitated*). No, no; impossible!

Streph. But our happiness—our very lives—depend upon our obtaining his consent!

Phyl. Oh, madam, you cannot refuse to do this!

Iol. You know not what you ask! The Lord Chancellor is—my husband!

Streph. and Phyl. Your husband!

Iol. My husband and your father! (*Addressing* STREPHON, *who is much moved.*)

Phyl. Then our course is plain; on his learning that Strephon is his son, all objection to our marriage will be at once removed!

Iol. No; he must never know! He believes me to have died childless, and, dearly as I love him, I am bound, under penalty of death, not to undeceive him. But see—he comes! Quick—my veil!

[IOLANTHE *veils herself.* STREPHON *and* PHYLLIS *go off on tiptoe.*

Enter LORD CHANCELLOR

Lord Ch. Victory! Victory! Success has crowned my efforts, and I may consider myself engaged to Phyllis! At first I wouldn't hear of it—it was out of the question. But I took heart. I pointed out to myself that I was no stranger to myself; that, in point of fact, I had been personally acquainted with myself for some years. This had its effect. I admitted that I had watched my professional advancement with considerable interest, and I handsomely added that I yielded to no one in admiration for my private and professional virtues. This was a great point gained. I then endeavoured to work upon my feelings. Conceive my joy when I distinctly perceived a tear glistening in my own eye! Eventually, after a severe struggle with myself, I reluctantly—most reluctantly—consented.

[IOLANTHE *comes down veiled.*

RECIT—IOLANTHE

My lord, a suppliant at your feet I kneel,
Oh, listen to a mother's fond appeal!
Hear me to-night! I come in urgent need—
'Tis for my son, young Strephon, that I,
    plead!

BALLAD—IOLANTHE

He loves! If in the bygone years
  Thine eyes have ever shed
Tears—bitter, unavailing tears,
  For one untimely dead—
If, in the eventide of life,
  Sad thoughts of her arise,
Then let the memory of thy wife
  Plead for my boy—he dies!
He dies! If fondly laid aside
  In some old cabinet,
Memorials of thy long-dead bride
  Lie, dearly treasured yet,
Then let her hallowed bridal dress—
  Her little dainty gloves—

Her withered flowers—her faded tress—
Plead for my boy—he loves!

[*The* LORD CHANCELLOR *is moved by this appeal. After a pause.*

Lord Chancellor

It may not be—for so the fates decide!
Learn thou that Phyllis is my promised
bride.

Iolanthe (*in horror*)

Thy bride! No! no!

LORD CHANCELLOR

It shall be so!

Those who would separate us woe betide!

Iolanthe

My doom thy lips have spoken—
I plead in vain!

Chorus of Fairies (*without*)

Forbear! forbear!

Iolanthe

A vow already broken
I break again!

Chorus of Fairies (*without*)

Forbear! forbear!

Iolanthe

For him—for her—for thee
I yield my life.
Behold—it may not be!
I am thy wife.

Chorus of Fairies (*without*)

Aiaiah! Aiaiah! Willaloo!

Lord Chancellor (*recognizing her*)

Iolanthe! thou livest?

Iolanthe

Aye!

I live! Now let me die!

Enter FAIRY QUEEN *and* FAIRIES, IOLANTHE
kneels to her

Queen

Once again thy vows are broken:
Thou thyself thy doom hast spoken!

Chorus of Fairies

Aiaiah! Aiaiah!
Yillahalah! Willaloo!
Yillahalah! Willaloo!

Queen

Bow thy head to Destiny:
Death thy doom, and thou shalt die!

Chorus of Faries

Aiaiah! Aiaiah! etc.

PEERS *and* SENTRY *enter. The* QUEEN *raises
her spear*

Leila. Hold! If Iolanthe must die, so
must we all; for, as she has sinned, so
have we!

Queen. What?

Celia. We are all fairy duchesses, mar-
chionesses, countesses, viscountesses, and
baronesses.

Lord Mount. It's our fault. They couldn't
help themselves.

Queen. It seems they *have* helped themselves, and pretty freely, too! (*After a
pause.*) You have all incurred death; but
I can't slaughter the whole company! And
yet (*unfolding a scroll*) the law is clear—
every fairy must die who marries a mortal.

Lord Ch. Allow me, as an old Equity
draftsman, to make a suggestion. The
subtl ties of the legal mind are equal to the
emergency. The thing is really quite simple—the insertion of a single word will do
it. Let it stand that every fairy shall die
who doesn't marry a mortal, and there you
are, out of your difficulty at once!

Queen. We like your humour. Very
well! (*Altering the MS. in pencil.*) Private
Willis!

Sentry (*coming forward*). Ma'am!

Queen. To save my life, it is necessary
that I marry at once. How should you
like to be a fairy guardsman?

Sentry. Well, ma'am, I don't think much
of the British soldier who wouldn't ill-
convenience himself to save a female in
distress.

Queen. You are a brave fellow You're
a fairy from this moment. (*Wings spring
from* SENTRY's *shoulders.*) And you, my
Lords, how say you, will you join our
ranks?

[*Fairies kneel to* PEERS *and implore them
to do so*

PHYLLIS *and* STREPHON *enter*

Lord Mount. (*to Lord Tolloller*). Well,
now that the Peers are to be recruited
entirely from persons of intelligence, I
really don't see what use *we* are, down
here, do you, Tolloller?

Lord Toll. None whatever.

Queen. Good (*Wings spring from shoulders of* PEERS). Then away we go to Fairyland.

FINALE

Phyllis

Soon as we may,
Off and away!

We'll commence our journey airy—
  Happy are we—
  As you can see,
Every one is now a fairy!
      All
Every one is now a fairy!
   Iolanthe, Queen, and Phyllis
Though as a general rule we know
Two strings go to every bow,
Make up your minds that grief 'twill
    bring,
If you've two beaux to every string.
      All
Though as a general rule, etc.
   Lord Chancellor
  Up in the sky,
  Ever so high,

Pleasures come in endless series;
  We will arrange
  Happy exchange—
House of Peers for House of Peris!

      All
House of Peers for House of Peris!
  *Lords Chancellors, Mountararat, and
      Tolloller*
Up in the air, sky-high, sky-high,
Free from Wards in Chancery,
I   ⎫
He ⎬ will be surely happier; for
    ⎭
I'm ⎫
He's ⎬ such a susceptible Chancellor.
    ⎭
      All
Up in the air, etc.

CURTAIN

PATIENCE

OR

BUNTHORNE'S BRIDE

DRAMATIS PERSONÆ

COLONEL CALVERLEY		
MAJOR MURGATROYD	*(Officers of Dragoon Guards)*	
LIEUT. THE DUKE OF DUNSTABLE		

REGINALD BUNTHORNE (*a Fleshly Poet*)

ARCHIBALD GROSVENOR (*an Idyllic Poet*)

MR. BUNTHORNE'S SOLICITOR

THE LADY ANGELA
THE LADY SAPHIR
THE LADY ELLA   *(Rapturous Maidens)*
THE LADY JANE

PATIENCE (*a Dairy Maid*)

Chorus of Rapturous Maidens and Officers of Dragoon Guards

ACT I

SCENE.—*Exterior of Castle Bunthorne. Entrance to Castle by drawbridge over moat. Young ladies dressed in aesthetic draperies are grouped about the stage. They play on lutes, mandolins, etc., as they sing, and all are in the last stage of despair.* ANGELA, ELLA, *and* SAPHIR *lead them.*

Chorus

Twenty love-sick maidens we,
  Love-sick all against our will.
Twenty years hence we shall be
  Twenty love-sick maidens still.
Twenty love-sick maidens we,
And we die for love of thee.

SOLO—ANGELA

Love feeds on hope, they say, or love will die—

All

Ah, miserie!
Yet my love lives, although no hope have I!

All

Ah, miserie!
Alas, poor heart, go hide thyself away—
To weeping concords tune thy roundelay!
  Ah, miserie!

Chorus

All our love is all for one,
  Yet that love he heedeth not.
He is coy and cares for none,
  Sad and sorry is our lot!
    Ah, miserie!

SOLO—ELLA

Go, breaking heart,
  Go, dream of love requited;
Go, foolish heart,
  Go, dream of lovers plighted;
Go, madcap heart,
  Go, dream of never waking;
And in thy dream
  Forget that thou art breaking!

Chorus
Ah, miserie!

Ella
Forget that thou art breaking!

Chorus
Twenty love-sick maidens, etc.

Ang. There is a strange magic in this love of ours! Rivals as we all are in the affections of our Reginald, the very hopelessness of our love is a bond that binds us to one another!

Saph. Jealousy is merged in misery. While he, the very cynosure of our eyes

110

and hearts, remains icy insensible—what have we to strive for?

Ella. The love of maidens is, to him, as interesting as the taxes!

Saph. Would that it were! He pays his taxes.

Ang. And cherishes the receipts!

Enter LADY JANE

Saph. Happy receipts!

Jane (suddenly). Fools!

Ang. I beg your pardon?

Jane. Fools and blind! The man loves—wildly loves!

Ang. But whom? None of us!

Jane. No, none of us. His weird fancy has lighted, for the nonce, on Patience, the village milkmaid!

Saph. On Patience? Oh, it cannot be!

Jane. Bah! But yesterday I caught him in her dairy, eating fresh butter with a tablespoon. To-day he is not well!

Saph. But Patience boasts that she has never loved—that love is, to her, a sealed book! Oh, he cannot be serious!

Jane. 'Tis but a fleeting fancy—'twill quickly pass away. *(Aside.)* Oh, Reginald, if you but knew what a wealth of golden love is waiting for you, stored up in this rugged old bosom of mine, the milkmaid's triumph would be short indeed!

PATIENCE *appears on an eminence. She looks down with pity on the despondent Ladies*

RECIT—PATIENCE

Still brooding on their mad infatuation!
 I thank thee, Love, thou comest not to me!
Far happier I, free from thy ministration,
 Than dukes or duchesses who love can be!

Saphir (looking up)

'Tis Patience—happy girl! Loved by a Poet!

Patience

Your pardon, ladies. I intrude upon you. *(Going.)*

Angela

Nay, pretty child, come hither. Is it true
That you have never loved?

Patience

 Most true indeed.

Sopranos

Most marvellous!

Contraltos

And most deplorable!

SONG—PATIENCE

I cannot tell what this love may be
That cometh to all, but not to me.
It cannot be kind as they'd imply,
Or why do these ladies sigh?
It cannot be joy and rapture deep,
Or why do these gentle ladies weep?
It cannot be blissful as 'tis said,
Or why are their eyes so wondrous red?
Though everywhere true love I see
A-coming to all, but not to me
 I cannot tell what this love may be!
  For I am blithe and I am gay,
  While they sit sighing night and day.
  Think of the gulf 'twixt them and me,
  "Fa la la la!"—and "Miserie!"

Chorus

Yes, she is blithe, etc.

Patience

If love is a thorn, they show no wit
Who foolishly hug and foster it.
If love is a weed, how simple they
Who gather it, day by day!
If love is a nettle that makes you smart,
Then why do you wear it next your heart?
And if it be none of these, say I,
Ah, why do you sit and sob and sigh?
 Though everywhere, etc.

Chorus

For she is blithe, etc.

Ang. Ah, Patience, if you have never loved, you have never known true happiness! *(All sigh.)*

Pa. But the truly happy always seem to have so much on their minds. The truly happy never seem quite well.

Jane. There is a transcendentality of delirium—an acute accentuation of a supremest ecstasy—which the earthy might easily mistake for indigestion. But it is *not* indigestion—it is aesthetic transfiguration! *(To the others.)* Enough of babble. Come!

Pa. But stay, I have some news for you. The 35th Dragoon Guards have halted in the village, and are even now on their way to this very spot.

Ang. The 35th Dragoon Guards!

Saph. They are fleshly men, of full habit!

Ella. We care nothing for Dragoon Guards!

Pa. But bless me, you were all engaged to them a year ago!

Saph. A year ago!

Ang. My poor child, you don't understand these things. A year ago they were very well in our eyes, but since then our tastes have been etherealized, our perceptions exalted. (*To others.*) Come, it is time to lift up our voices in morning carol to our Reginald. Let us to his door.

[*The Ladies go off, two and two, into the Castle, singing refrain of "Twenty love-sick maidens we," and accompanying themselves on harps and mandolins.* PATIENCE *watches them in surprise, as she climbs the rock by which she entered.*

March. Enter Officers of Dragoon Guards, led by MAJOR

CHORUS OF DRAGOONS

The soldiers of our Queen
    Are linked in friendly tether;
Upon the battle scene
    They fight the foe together.
There every mother's son
    Prepared to fight and fall is;
The enemy of one
    The enemy of all is!

Enter COLONEL

SONG—COLONEL

If you want a receipt for that popular mystery,
    Known to the world as a Heavy Dragoon,
Take all the remarkable people in history,
    Rattle them off to a popular tune.
The pluck of Lord Nelson on board of the *Victory*—
Genius of Bismarck devising a plan—
The humour of Fielding (which sounds contradictory)—
Coolness of Paget about to trepan—
The science of Jullien, the eminent musico—
    Wit of Macaulay, who wrote of Queen Anne—
The pathos of Paddy, as rendered by Boucicault—
    Style of the Bishop of Sodor and Man—
The dash of a D'Orsay, divested of quackery—
Narrative powers of Dickens and Thackeray—
Victor Emmanuel—peak-haunting Peveril—

Thomas Aquinas, and Doctor Sacheverell—
Tupper and Tennyson—Daniel Defoe—
Anthony Trollope and Mr. Guizot—
Take of these elements all that is fusible,
Melt them all down in a pipkin or crucible,
Set them to simmer and take off the scum,
And a Heavy Dragoon is the residuum!

Chorus

Yes! yes! yes! yes!
    A Heavy Dragoon is the residuum!

Colonel

If you want a receipt for this soldier-like paragon,
    Get at the wealth of the Czar (if you can)—
The family pride of a Spaniard from Aragon—
    Force of Mephisto pronouncing a ban—
A smack of Lord Waterford, reckless and rollicky—
    Swagger of Roderick, heading his clan—
The keen penetration of Paddington Pollaky—
    Grace of an Odalisque on a divan—
The genius strategic of Caesar or Hannibal—
Skill of Sir Garnet in thrashing a cannibal—
Flavour of Hamlet—the Stranger, a touch of him—
Little of Manfred (but not very much of him)—
    Beadle of Burlington—Richardson's show—
    Mr. Micawber and Madame Tussaud!
        Take of these elements all that is fusible,
        Melt them all down in a pipkin or crucible,
        Set them to simmer and take off the scum,
        And a Heavy Dragoon is the residuum!

All

Yes! yes! yes! yes!
    A Heavy Dragoon is the residuum!

Col. Well, here we are once more on the scene of our former triumphs. But where's the Duke?

Enter DUKE, *listlessly, and in low spirits*

Duke. Here I am! (*Sighs.*)

Col. Come, cheer up, don't give way!

Duke. Oh, for that, I'm as cheerful as a

oor devil can be expected to be who has
he misfortune to be a duke, with a thou-
and a day!

Maj. Humph! Most men would envy
ou!

Duke. Envy *me?* Tell me, Major, are
ou fond of toffee?

Maj. Very!

Col. We are all fond of toffee.

All. We are!

Duke. Yes, and toffee in moderation is
capital thing. But to *live* on toffee—tof-
ee for breakfast, toffee for dinner, toffee
or tea—to have it supposed that you care
or nothing *but* toffee, and that you would
onsider yourself insulted if anything but
offee were offered to you—how would you
ike *that?*

Col. I can quite believe that, under those
ircumstances, even toffee would become
nonotonous.

Duke. For "toffee" read flattery, adula-
ion, and abject difference, carried to such
a pitch that I began, at last, to think that
man was born bent at an angle of forty-
ive degrees! Great Heavens, what is there
to adulate in me! Am I particularly intelligent, or remarkably studious, or excruci-
atingly witty, or unusually accomplished,
or exceptionally virtuous?

Col. You're about as commonplace a
young man as ever I saw.

All. You are!

Duke. Exactly! That's it exactly! That
describes me to a T! Thank you all very
much! Well, I couldn't stand it any longer,
so I joined this second-class cavalry regiment. In the Army, thought I, I shall be
occasionally snubbed, perhaps even bullied,
who knows? The thought was rapture,
and here I am.

Col. (*looking off*). Yes, and here are the
ladies!

Duke. But who is the gentleman with
the long hair?

Col. I don't know.

Duke. He seems popular!

Col. He *does* seem popular!

BUNTHORNE *enters, followed by Ladies, two
and two, singing and playing on harps
as before. He is composing a poem,
and quite absorbed. He sees no one,
but walks across the stage, followed
by Ladies. They take no notice of Dra-*

*goons—to the surprise and indignation
of those Officers.*

CHORUS OF LADIES

In a doleful train
  Two and two we walk all day—
For we love in vain!
  None so sorrowful as they
    Who can only sigh and say,
  Woe is me, alackaday!

CHORUS OF DRAGOONS

Now is not this ridiculous—and is not this
  preposterous?
A thorough-paced absurdity—explain it if
  you can.
Instead of rushing eagerly to cherish us
  and foster us,
  They all prefer this melancholy literary
  man.
  Instead of slyly peering at us,
    Casting looks endearing at us,
Blushing at us, flushing at us—flirting with
  a fan;
They're actually sneering at us, fleering at
  us, jeering at us!
  Pretty sort of treatment for a military
  man!
  Pretty sort of treatment for a military
  man!

Angela

Mystic poet, hear our prayer,
  Twenty love-sick maidens we—
Young and wealthy, dark and fair—
  All of county family.
  And we die for love of thee—
  Twenty love-sick maidens we!

CHORUS OF LADIES

Yes, we die for love of thee—
Twenty love-sick maidens we!

Bunthorne (*aside—slyly*)

Though my book I seem to scan
  In a rapt ecstatic way,
Like a literary man
  Who despises female clay,
I hear plainly all they say,
Twenty love-sick maidens they!

(*Officers* (*to each other*))

He hears plainly, etc.

Saphir

Though so excellently wise,
  For a moment mortal be,
Deign to raise thy purple eyes
  From thy heart-drawn poesy.
Twenty love-sick maidens see—
Each is kneeling on her knee! (*All kneel.*)

CHORUS OF LADIES
Twenty love-sick, etc.

Bunthorne (aside)
Though, as I remarked before,
Any one convinced would be

That some transcendental lore
Is monopolizing me,
Round the corner I can see
Each is kneeling on her knee!
(*Officers (to each other)*)
Round the corner, etc.

ENSEMBLE

Officers
Now is not this ridiculous, etc.

Ladies
Mystic poet, hear our prayer, etc.

Col. Angela! what is the meaning of this?
Ang. Oh, sir, leave us; our minds are but ill-tuned to light love-talk.
Maj. But what in the world has come over you all?
Jane. Bunthorne! *He* has come over us. He has come among us, and he has idealized us.
Duke. Has he succeeded in idealizing *you?*
Jane. He has!
Duke. Good old Bunthorne!
Jane. My eyes are open; I droop despairingly; I am soulfully intense; I am limp and I cling!
[*During this* BUNTHORNE *is seen in all the agonies of composition. The Ladies are watching him intently as he writhes. At last he hits on the word he wants and writes it down. A general sense of relief.*]
Bun. Finished! At last! Finished!
[*He staggers, overcome with the mental strain, into arms of* COLONEL
Col. Are you better now?
Bun. Yes,—oh, it's you—I am better now. The poem is finished, and my soul had gone out into it. That was all. It was nothing worth mentioning, it occurs three times a day. (*Sees* PATIENCE, *who has entered during this scene.*) Ah, Patience! Dear Patience! (*Holds her hand; she seems frightened.*)
Ang. Will it please you to read it to us, sir?
Saph. This we supplicate. (*All kneel.*)
Bun. Shall I?
All the Dragoons. No!
Bun. (*annoyed*—to PATIENCE). I will read it if *you* bid me!
Pa. (*much frightened*). You can if you like!

Bun. It is a wild, weird, fleshly thing; yet very tender, very yearning, very precious. It is called, "Oh, Hollow! Hollow! Hollow!"
Pa. Is it a hunting song?
Bun. A hunting song? No, it is *not* a hunting song. It is the wail of the poet's heart on discovering that everything is commonplace. To understand it, cling passionately to one another and think of faint lilies. (*They do so as he recites*)—
"OH, HOLLOW! HOLLOW! HOLLOW!"
What time the poet hath hymned
The writhing maid, lithe-limbed,
Quivering on amaranthine asphodel,
How can he paint her woes,
Knowing, as well he knows,
That all can be set right with calomel?
When from the poet's plinth
The amorous colocynth
Yearns for the aloe, faint with rapturous thrills,
How can he hymn their throes
Knowing, as well he knows,
That they are only uncompounded pills?
Is it, and can it be,
Nature has this decree,
Nothing poetic in the world shall dwell?
Or that in all her works
Something poetic lurks,
Even in colycynth and calomel?
I cannot tell.
[*Exit* BUNTHORNE
Ang. How purely fragrant!
Saph. How earnestly precious!
Pa. Well, it seems to me to be nonsense.
Saph. Nonsense, yes, perhaps—but oh, what precious nonsense!
Col. This is all very well, but you seem to forget that you are engaged to us.
Saph. It can never be. You are not Empyrean. You are not Della Cruscan. You are not even Early English. Oh, be Early

English ere it is too late! (*Officers look at each other in astonishment.*)

Jane (*looking at uniform*). Red and yellow! Primary colours! Oh, South Kensington!

Duke. We didn't design our uniforms, but we don't see how they could be improved.

Jane. No, you wouldn't. Still, there *is* a cobwebby grey velvet, with a tender bloom like cold gravy, which made Florentine fourteenth-century, trimmed with Venetian leather and Spanish altar lace, and surmounted with something Japanese—it matters not what—would at least be Early English! Come, maidens.

[*Exeunt Maidens, two and two, singing refrain of "Twenty love-sick maidens we". The Officers watch them off in astonishment.*

Duke. Gentlemen, this is an insult to the British uniform——

Col. A uniform that has been as successful in the courts of Venus as on the field of Mars!

SONG—COLONEL

When I first put this uniform on,
    I said, as I looked in the glass,
        "It's one to a million
        That any civilian
My figure and form will surpass.
    Gold lace has a charm for the fair,
    And I've plenty of that, and to spare,
        While a lover's professions,
        When uttered in Hessians,
    Are eloquent everywhere!"
        A fact that I counted upon,
        When I first put this uniform on!

CHORUS OF DRAGOONS

By a simple coincidence, few
    Could ever have counted upon,
The same thing occurred to me, too,
    When I first put this uniform on!
            Colonel
I said, when I first put it on,
    "It is plain to the veriest dunce
        That every beauty
        Will feel it her duty
To yield to its glamour at once.
They will see that I'm freely gold-laced
In a uniform handsome and chaste"—
        But the peripatetics
        Of long-haired aesthetics
Are very much more to their taste—

Which I never counted upon,
    When I first put this uniform on!
            Chorus
By a simple coincidence, few
    Could ever have reckoned upon,
I didn't anticipate that,
    When I first put this uniform on!
            [*The Dragoons go off angrily.*
Enter BUNTHORNE, *who changes his manner and becomes intensely melodramatic*

RECIT AND SONG—BUNTHORNE

Am I alone,
    And unobserved? I am!
Then let me own
    I'm an aesthetic sham!
This air severe
    Is but a mere
        Veneer!
This cynic smile
    Is but a wile
        Of guile!
This costume chaste
    Is but good taste
        Misplaced!
    Let me confess!
A languid love for lilies does *not* blight me!
Lank limbs and haggard checks do *not* delight me!
    I do *not* care for dirty greens
        By any means.
        I do *not* long for all one sees
            That's Japanese.
        I am *not* fond of uttering platitudes
            In stained-glass attitudes.
        In short, my mediaevalism's affectation,
            Born of a morbid love of admiration!

SONG

If you're anxious for to shine in the high aesthetic line as a man of culture rare,
You must get up all the germs of the transcendental terms, and plant them everywhere.
You must lie upon the daisies and discourse in novel phrases of your complicated state of mind,
The meaning doesn't matter if it's only idle chatter of a transcendental kind.
        And every one will say,
        As you walk your mystic way,
"If this young man expresses himself in terms too deep for *me*,

Why, what a very singularly deep young
man this deep young man must be!"
Be eloquent in praise of the very dull old
days which have long since passed away,
And convince 'em, if you can, that the
reign of good Queen Anne was Culture's
palmiest day.
Of course you will pooh-pooh whatever's
fresh and new, and declare it's crude
and mean,
For Art stopped short in the cultivated
court of the Empress Josephine.
   And every one will say,
   As you walk your mystic way,
"If that's not good enough for him which
is good enough for *me*,
Why, what a very cultivated kind of youth
this kind of youth must be!"
Then a sentimental passion of a vegetable
fashion must excite your languid spleen,
An attachment *à la* Plato or a bashul
young potato, or a not-too-French French
bean!
Though the Philistines may jostle, you will
rank as an apostle in the high aesthetic
band,
If you walk down Piccadilly with a poppy
or a lily in your mediaeval hand.
   And every one will say,
   As you walk your flowery way,
"If he's content with a vegetable love
which would certainly not suit *me*,
Why, what a most particularly pure young
man this pure young man must be!"
At the end of his song PATIENCE *enters.*
   He sees her
Bun. Ah! Patience, come hither. I am
pleased with thee. The bitter-hearted one,
who finds all else hollow, is pleased with
thee. For you are not hollow. *Are* you?
Pa. No, thanks, I have dined; but—I beg
your pardon—I interrupt you.
Bun. Life is made up of interruptions.
The tortured soul, yearning for solitude,
writhes under them. Oh, but my heart is
a-weary! Oh, I am a cursed thing! Don't
go.
Pa. Really, I'm very sorry——
Bun. Tell me, girl, do you ever yearn?
Pa. (*misunderstanding him*). I earn my
living.
Bun. (*impatiently*). No, no! Do you
know what it is to be heart-hungry? Do
you know what it is to yearn for the In-

definable, and yet to be brought face to
face, daily, with the Multiplication Table?
Do you know what it is to seek oceans
and to find puddles?—to long for whirl-
winds and yet to have to do the best you
can with the bellows? That's my case.
Oh, I am a cursed thing! Don't go.
Pa. If you please, I don't understand
you—you frighten me!
Bun. Don't be frightened—it's only
poetry.
Pa. Well, if that's poetry, I don't like
poetry.
Bun. (*eagerly*). Don't you? (*Aside.*) Can
I trust her? (*Aloud.*) Patience, you don't
like poetry—well, between you and me, *I*
don't like poetry. It's hollow, unsubstan-
tial—unsatisfactory. What's the use of
yearning for Elysian Fields when you
know you can't get 'em, and would only
let 'em out on building leases if you had
'em?
Pa. Sir, I——
Bun. Patience, I have long loved you.
Let me tell you a secret. I am not as
bilious as I look. If you like, I will cut
my hair. There is more innocent fun within me than a casual spectator would imagine. You have never seen me frolicsome.
Be a good girl—a very good girl—and one
day you shall. If you are fond of touch-
and-go jocularity—this is the shop for it.
Pa. Sir, I will speak plainly. In the matter of love I am untaught. I have never
loved but my great-aunt. But I am quite
certain, under any circumstances, I couldn't
possibly love *you*.
Bun. Oh, you think not?
Pa. I'm quite sure of it. Quite sure.
Quite.
Bun. Very good. Life is henceforth a
blank. I don't care what becomes of me.
I have only to ask that you will not abuse
my confidence; though *you* despise me, I
am extremely popular with the other young
ladies.
Pa. I only ask that you will leave me
and never renew the subject.
Bun. Certainly. Broken-hearted and
desolate, I go. (*Recites.*)
"Oh, to be wafted away
 From this black Aceldama of sorrow,
Where the dust of an earthy to-day
 Is the earth of a dusty to-morrow!"

It is a little thing of my own. I call it 'Heart Foam". I shall not publish it. Farewell! Patience, Patience, farewell!

[*Exit* BUNTHORNE.

Pa. What on earth does it all mean? Why does he love me? Why does he expect me to love him? He's not a relation! It frightens me!

Enter ANGELA

Ang. Why, Patience, what is the matter?

Pa. Lady Angela, tell me two things. Firstly, what on earth is this love that upsets everybody; and, secondly, how is it to be distinguished from insanity?

Ang. Poor blind child! Oh, forgive her, Eros! Why, love is of all passions the most essential! It is the embodiment of purity, the abstraction of refinement! It is the one unselfish emotion in this whirlpool of grasping greed!

Pa. Oh, dear, oh! (*Beginning to cry.*)

Ang. Why are you crying?

Pa. To think that I have lived all these years without having experienced this ennobling and unselfish passion! Why, what a wicked girl I must be! For it *is* unselfish, isn't it?

Ang. Absolutely! Love that is tainted with selfishness is no love. Oh, try, try, try to love! It really isn't difficult if you give your whole mind to it.

Pa. I'll set about it at once. I won't go to bed until I'm head over ears in love with somebody.

Ang. Noble girl! But is it possible that you have never loved anybody?

Pa. Yes, one.

Ang. Ah! Whom?

Pa. My great-aunt——

Ang. Great-aunts don't count.

Pa. Then there's nobody. At least—no, nobody. Not since I was a baby. But *that* doesn't count, I suppose.

Ang. I don't know. Tell me all about it.

DUET—PATIENCE *and* ANGELA

Long years ago—fourteen, maybe—
    When but a tiny babe of four,
Another baby played with me,
    My elder by a year or more;
A little child of beauty rare,
With marvellous eyes and wondrous hair,
Who, in my child-eyes, seemed to me
All that a little child should be!
    Ah, how we loved, that child and I!

How pure our baby joy!
How true our love—and, by the by,
    He was a little boy!

Angela

Ah, old, old tale of Cupid's touch!
I thought as much—I thought as much!
    He *was* a little boy!

Patience (*shocked*)

Pray, don't misconstrue what I say—
Remember, pray—remember, pray,
    He was a *little* boy!

Angela

No doubt! Yet, spite of all your pains,
The interesting fact remains—
    He was a *little* boy!

ENSEMBLE

Ah, yes, in ⎱ spite of all ⎰my ⎱ pains, etc.
No doubt! Yet ⎰   ⎱your⎰

[*Exit* ANGELA.

Pa. It's perfectly dreadful to think of the appalling state I must be in! I had no idea that love was a duty. No wonder they all look so unhappy! Upon my word, I hardly like to associate with myself. I don't think I'm respectable. I'll go at once and fall in love with——*Enter* GROSVENOR.) A stranger!

DUET—PATIENCE *and* GROSVENOR

Grosvenor

Prithee, pretty maiden—prithee, tell me true,
    (Hey, but I'm doleful, willow willow waly)
Have you e'er a lover a-dangling after you?
        Hey willow waly O!
        I would fain discover
        If you have a lover?
        Hey willow waly O!

Patience

Gentle sir, my heart is frolicsome and free—
    (Hey, but he's doleful, willow willow waly!)
Nobody I care for comes a-courting me—
        Hey willow waly O!
        Nobody I care for
        Comes a-courting—therefore,
        Hey willow waly O!

Grosvenor

Prithee, pretty maiden, will you marry me?
    (Hey, but he's hopeful, willow willow waly!)

I may say, at once, I'm a man of proper-
tee—

    Hey willow waly O!
    Money, I despise it;
    Many people prize it,
    Hey willow waly O!
    Patience

Gentle sir, although to marry I design—
  (Hey, but I'm hopeful, willow willow
    waly!)
As yet I do not know you, and so I must
    decline.

    Hey willow waly O!
      To other maidens go you—
      As yet I do not know you,
    Hey willow waly O!

Gros. Patience! Can it be that you don't
recognise me?

Pa. Recognise you? No, indeed I don't!

Gros. Have fifteen years so greatly
changed me?

Pa. Fifteen years? What do you mean?

Gros. Have you forgotten the friend of
your youth, your Archibald?—your little
playfellow? Oh, Chronos, Chronos, this is
too bad of you!

Pa. Archibald! Is it possible? Why, let
me look! It is! It is! It must be! Oh,
how happy I am! I thought we should
never meet again! And how you've grown!

Gros. Yes, Patience, I am much taller
and much stouter than I was.

Pa. And how you've improved!

Gros. Yes, Patience, I am very beautiful! (*Sighs.*)

Pa. But surely *that* doesn't make you
unhappy.

Gros. Yes, Patience. Gifted as I am with
a beauty which probably has not its rival
on earth, I am, nevertheless, utterly and
completely miserable.

Pa. Oh—but why?

Gross. My child-love for you has never
faded. Conceive, then, the horror of my
situation when I tell you that it is my
hideous destiny to be madly loved at first
sight by every woman I come across!

Pa. But why do you make yourself so
picturesque? Why not disguise yourself,
disfigure yourself, anything to escape this
persecution?

Gros. No, Patience, that may not be.
These gifts—irksome as they are—were
given to me for the enjoyment and delecta-

tion of my fellow-creatures. I am a trustee
for Beauty, and it is my duty to see that
the conditions of my trust are faithfully
discharged.

Pa. And you, too, are a Poet?

Gros. Yes, I am the Apostle of Simplicity. I am called "Archibald the All-
Right"—for I am infallible!

Pa. And is it possible that you condescend to love such a girl as I?

Gros. Yes, Patience, is it not strange? I
have loved you with a Florentine fourteenth-century frenzy for full fifteen years!

Pa. Oh, marvellous! I have hitherto been
deaf to the voice of love. I seem now to
know what love is! It has been revealed
to me—it is Archibald Grosvenor!

Gros. Yes, Patience, it is!

Pa. (*as in a trance*). We will never, never
part!

Gros. We will live and die together!

Pa. I swear it!

Gros. We both swear it!

Pa. (*recoiling from him*). But—oh,
horror!

Gros. What's the matter?

Pa. Why, you are perfection! A source
of endless ecstasy to all who know you!

Gros. I know I am. Well?

Pa. Then, bless my heart, there can be
nothing unselfish in loving *you!*

Gros. Merciful powers! I never thought
of that!

Pa. To monopolize those features on
which all women love to linger! It would
be unpardonable!

Gros. Why, so it would! Oh, fatal perfection, again you interpose between me
and my happiness!

Pa. Oh, if you were but a thought less
beautiful than you are!

Gros. Would that I were; but candour
compels me to admit that I'm not!

Pa. Our duty is clear; we must part,
and for ever!

Gros. Oh, misery! And yet I cannot
question the propriety of your decision.
Farewell, Patience!

Pa. Farewell, Archibald! But stay!

Gros. Yes, Patience?

Pa. Although I may not love *you*—for
you are perfection—there is nothing to
prevent your loving *me*. I am plain, homely,
unattractive!

Gros. Why, that's true!

Pa. The love of such a man as you for such a girl as I must be unselfish!

Gros. Unselfish itself!

DUET—PATIENCE *and* GROSVENOR

Patience

Though to marry you would very selfish be—

Grosvenor

Hey, but I'm doleful—willow willow waly!

Patience

You may, all the same, continue loving me—

Grosvenor

Hey willow waly O!

Both

All the world ignoring,

You'll ⎫
I'll ⎬ go on adoring—

Hey willow waly O!

[*At the end, exeunt despairingly, in opposite directions.*

FINALE—ACT I

Enter BUNTHORNE, *crowned with roses and hung about with garlands, and looking very miserable. He is led by* ANGELA *and* SAPHIR (*each of whom holds an end of the rose-garland by which he is bound*), *and accompanied by procession of Maidens. They are dancing classically, and playing on cymbals, double pipes, and other archaic instruments.*

Chorus

Let the merry cymbals sound,

Gaily pipe a Pandaean pleasure,

With a Dalphnephoric bound

Tread a gay but classic measure.

Every heart with hope is beating,

For at this exciting meeting

Fickle Fortune will decide

Who shall be our Bunthorne's bride!

Enter Dragoons, led by COLONEL, MAJOR, *and* DUKE.

They are surprised at proceedings

CHORUS OF DRAGOONS

Now tell us, we pray you,

Why thus they array you—

Oh, poet, how say you—

What is it you've done?

Duke

Of rite sacrificial,

By sentence judicial,

This seems the initial,

Then why don't you run?

Colonel

They cannot have led you

To hang or behead you,

Nor may they *all* wed you,

Unfortunate one!

CHORUS OF DRAGOONS

Then tell us, we pray you,

Why thus they array you—

Oh, poet, how say you—

What is it you've done?

RECIT—BUNTHORNE

Heart-broken at my Patience's barbarity,

By the advice of my solicitor

(*introducing his* SOLICITOR),

In aid—in aid of a deserving charity,

I've put myself up to be raffled for!

Maidens

By the advice of his solicitor

He's put himself up to be raffled for!

Dragoons

Oh, horror! urged by his solicitor,

He's put himself up to be raffled for!

Maidens

Oh, heaven's blessing on his solicitor!

Dragoons

A hideous curse on his solicitor!

[*The* SOLICITOR, *horrified at the Dragoons' curse, rushes off.*

Colonel

Stay, we implore you,

Before our hopes are blighted;

You see before you

The men to whom you're plighted!

CHORUS OF DRAGOONS

Stay, we implore you,

For we adore you;

To us you're plighted

To be united—

Stay, we implore you!

SOLO—DUKE

Your maiden hearts, ah, do not steel

To pity's eloquent appeal,

Such conduct British soldiers feel.

(*Aside to Dragoons.*)

Sigh, sigh, all sigh!

(*They all sigh.*)

To foeman's steel we rarely see

A British soldier bend the knee,

Yet, one and all, they kneel to ye—

(*Aside to Dragoons.*)

Kneel, kneel, all kneel!

(*They all kneel.*)

Our soldiers very seldom cry,
And yet—I need not tell you why—
A tear-drop dews each martial eye!
    (*Aside to Dragoons.*)
    Weep, weep, all weep!
        (*They all weep.*)

ENSEMBLE

Our soldiers very seldom cry,
And yet—I need not tell you why—
A tear-drop dews each manly eye!
    Weep, weep, all weep!
BUNTHORNE (*who has been impatient during this appeal*).
Come, walk up, and purchase with avidity,
Overcome your diffidence and natural
    timidity,
Tickets for the raffle should be purchased
    with avidity,
    Put in half a guinea and a husband you
    may gain—
Such a judge of blue-and-white and other
    kinds of pottery—
From early Oriental down to modern terra-
    cotta-ry—
Put in half a guinea—you may draw him
    in a lottery—
    Such an opportunity may not occur
    again.

Chorus

Such a judge of blue-and-white, etc.
[MAIDENS *crowd up to purchase tickets; during this* DRAGOONS *dance in single file round stage, to express their indifference.*

Dragoons

We've been thrown over, we're aware,
But we don't care—but we don't care!
There's fish in the sea, no doubt of it,
As good as ever came out of it,
And some day we shall get our share,
So we don't care—so we don't care!
[*During this the* MAIDENS *have been buying tickets. At last* JANE *presents herself.* BUNTHORNE *looks at her with aversion.*

RECIT
Bunthorne

And are *you* going a ticket for to buy?
    Jane (*surprised*)
Most certainly I am; why shouldn't I?
    Bunthorne (*aside*)
Oh, Fortune, this is hard! (*Aloud.*) Blind-
    fold your eyes;
Two minutes will decide who wins the

prize! (MAIDENS *blindfold themselves.*)
    CHORUS OF MAIDENS
Oh, Fortune, to my aching heart be kind!
Like us, thou art blindfolded, but not
    blind; (*Each uncovers one eye.*)
Just raise your bandage, thus, that you
    may see,
And give the prize, and give the prize to
    me! (*They cover their eyes again.*)
    Bunthorne
Come, Lady Jane, I pray you draw the
    first!
    Jane (*joyfully*)
He loves me best!
    Bunthorne (*aside*)
I want to know the worst!
[JANE *puts hand in bag to draw ticket.* PATIENCE *enters and prevents her doing so.*
    Patience
Hold! Stay your hand!
    All (*uncovering their eyes*)
What means this interference?
Of this bold girl I pray you make a clear-
    ance!
    Jane
Away with you, and to your milk-pails go!
    Bunthorne (*suddenly*)
She wants a ticket! Take a dozen!
    Patience
    No!
SOLO—PATIENCE (*kneeling to* BUNTHORNE)
If there be pardon in your breast
    For this poor penitent,
Who, with remorseful thought opprest,
    Sincerely doth repent;
If you, with one so lowly, still
    Desire to be allied,
Then you may take me, if you will,
    For I will be your bride!
    All
    Oh, shameless one!
      Oh, bold-faced thing!
    Away you run,
    Go, take you wing,
    You shameless one!
      You bold-faced thing!
    Bunthorne
How strong is love! For many and many
    a week
She's loved me fondly and has feared to
    speak,
But Nature, for restraint too mighty far,

Has burst the bonds of Art—and here we
are!
Patience
No, Mr. Bunthorne, no—you're wrong
again;
Permit me—I'll endeavour to explain!
SONG—PATIENCE
Patience
True love must single-hearted be—
Bunthorne
          Exactly so!
Patience
From every selfish fancy free—
Bunthorne
          Exactly so!
Patience
No idle thought of gain or joy
A maiden's fancy should employ—
True love must be without alloy.
All
          Exactly so!
Patience
Imposture to contempt must lead—
Colonel
          Exactly so!
Patience
Blind vanity's dissension's seed—
Major
          Exactly so!
Patience
It follows, then, a maiden who
Devotes herself to loving you (*indicat-
ing* BUNTHORNE)
Is prompted by no selfish view—
All
          Exactly so!
Saphir
Are you resolved to wed this shameless
one?
Angela
Is there no chance for any other?
Bunthorne (*decisively*)
None! (*Embraces* PATIENCE.)
[*Exeunt* PATIENCE *and* BUNTHORNE.
[ANGELA, SAPHIR, *and* ELLA *take* COLONEL,
DUKE, *and* MAJOR *down, while* GIRLS
gaze fondly at other OFFICERS.

SEXTETTE
I hear the soft note of the echoing voice
Of an old, old love, long dead—
It whispers my sorrowing heart "rejoice"—
For the last sad tear is shed—
The pain that is all but a pleasure will
change
For the pleasure that's all but pain,
And never, oh never, this heart will range
From that old, old love again!
(GIRLS *embrace* OFFICERS.)
Chorus
Yes, the pain that is all, etc. (*Embrace.*)
Enter PATIENCE *and* BUNTHORNE
[*As the* DRAGOONS *and* GIRLS *are embracing
enter* GROSVENOR, *reading. He takes no
notice of them, but comes slowly down,
still reading. The* GIRLS *are all strangely
fascinated by him, and gradually with-
draw from* DRAGOONS.
Angela
But who is this, whose god-like grace
Proclaims he comes of noble race?
And who is this, whose manly face
Bears sorrow's interesting trace?
ENSEMBLE—TUTTI
Yes, who is this, etc.
Grosvenor
I am a broken-hearted troubadour,
Who.e mind's aesthetic and whose tastes
are pure!
Angela
Aesthetic! He is aesthetic!
Grosvenor
Yes, yes—I am aesthetic
And poetic!
ALL THE LADIES
Then, we love you!
[*The* GIRLS *leave* DRAGOONS *and group,
kneeling, around* GROSVENOR. *Fury of*
BUNTHORNE, *who recognizes a rival.*
Dragoons
They love him! Horror!
Bunthorne and Patience
They love him! Horror!
Grosvenor
They love me! Horror! Horror! Horror!

ENSEMBLE—TUTTI

Girls
Oh, list while we a love confess
That words imperfectly express.
Those shell-like ears, ah, do not close
To blighted loves' distracting woes!

Patience
List, Reginald, while I confess
A love that's all unselfishness;
That it's unselfish, goodness knows,
You won't dispute it, I suppose?

Grosvenor

Again my cursed comeliness
Spreads hopeless anguish and distress!
Thine ears, oh Fortune, do not close
To my intolerable woes.

Dragoons

Now is not this ridiculous, etc.

END OF ACT I

ACT II

SCENE.—*A glade.* JANE *is discovered leaning on a violoncello, upon which she presently accompanies herself. Chorus of* MAIDENS *are heard singing in the distance.*

Jane. The fickle crew have deserted Reginald and sworn allegiance to his rival, and all, forsooth, because he has glanced with passing favour on a puling milkmaid! Fools! of that fancy he will soon weary—and then I, who alone am faithful to him, shall reap my reward. But do not dally too long, Reginald, for my charms are ripe, Reginald, and already they are decaying. Better secure me ere I have gone too far!

RECIT—JANE

Sad is that woman's lot who, year by year,
Sees, one by one, her beauties disappear,
When Time, grown weary of her heart-drawn sighs,
Impatiently begins to "dim her eyes"!
Compelled, at last, in life's uncertain gloamings,
To wreathe her wrinkled brow with well-saved "combings",
Reduced, with rouge, lip-salve, and pearly grey,
To "make up" for lost time as best she may!

SONG—JANE

Silvered is the raven hair,
  Spreading is the parting straight,
Mottled is the complexion fair,
  Halting is the youthful gait,
Hollow is the laughter free,
  Spectacled the limpid eye—
Little will be left of me
  In the coming by and by!
Fading is the taper waist,
  Shapeless grows the shapely limb,

Bunthorne

My jealousy I can't express,
Their love they openly confess;
His shell-like ears he does not close
To their recital of their woes.

And although severely laced,
  Spreading is the figure trim!
Stouter than I used to be,
  Still more corpulent grow I—
There will be too much of me
  In the coming by and by!

[*Exit* JANE.

Enter GROSVENOR, *followed by* MAIDENS, *two and two, each playing on an archaic instrument, as in Act I. He is reading abstractedly, as* BUNTHORNE *did in Act I, and pays no attention to them.*

CHORUS OF MAIDENS

Turn, oh, turn in this direction,
  Shed, oh, shed a gentle smile,
With a glance of sad perfection
  Our poor fainting hearts beguile!
On such eyes as maidens cherish
  Let thy fond adorers gaze,
Or incontinently perish
  In their all-consuming rays!

[*He sits—they group around him.*

Gros. (*aside*). The old, old tale. How rapturously these maidens love me, and how hopelessly! Oh, Patience, Patience, with the love of thee in my heart, what have I for these poor mad maidens but an unvalued pity? Alas, they will die of hopeless love for me, as I shall die of hopeless love for thee!

Ang. Sir, will it please you read to us?

Gros. (*sighing*). Yes, child, if you will. What shall I read?

Ang. One of your own poems.

Gros. One of my own poems? Better not, my child. *They* will not cure thee of thy love.

Ella. Mr. Bunthorne used to read us a poem of his own every day.

Saph. And, to do him justice, he read them extremely well.

Gros. Oh, did he so? Well, who am I that I should take upon myself to withhold my gifts from you? What am I but a trustee? Here is a decalet—a pure and simple thing, a very daisy—a babe might understand it. To appreciate it, it is not necessary to think of anything at all.

Ang. Let us think of nothing at all!

GROSVENOR *recites*

Gentle Jane was good as gold,
She always did as she was told;
She never spoke when her mouth was full,
Or caught bluebottles their legs to pull,
Or spilt plum jam on her nice new frock,
Or put white mice in the eight-day clock,
Or vivisected her last new doll,
Or fostered a passion for alcohol.
And when she grew up she was given in marriage
To a first-class earl who keeps his carriage!

Gros. I believe I am right in saying that there is not one word in that decalet which is calculated to bring the blush of shame to the cheek of modesty.

Ang. Not one; it is purity itself.

Gros. Here's another.

Teasing Tom was a very bad boy,
A great big squirt was his favourite toy;
He put live shrimps in his father's boots,
And sewed up the sleeves of his Sunday suits;

He punched his poor little sisters' heads,
And cayenne-peppered their four-post beds,
He plastered their hair with cobbler's wax,
And dropped hot halfpennies down their backs.

The consequence was he was lost tot*a*lly,
And married a girl in the *corps de bally!*

Ang. Marked you how grandly—how relentlessly—the damning catalogue of crime strode on, till Retribution, like a poisèd hawk, came swooping down upon the Wrong-Doer? Oh, it was terrible!

Ella. Oh, sir, you are indeed a true poet, for you touch our hearts, and they go out to you!

Gros. (*aside*). This is simply cloying. (*Aloud.*) Ladies, I am sorry to appear ungallant, but th's is Saturday, and you have been following me about ever since Monday. I should like the usual half-holiday. I shall take it as a personal favour if you will kindly allow me to close early to-day.

Saph. Oh, sir, do not send us from you!

Gros. Poor, poor girls! It is best to speak plainly. I know that I am loved by you, but I never can love you in return, for my heart is fixed elsewhere! Remember the fable of the Magnet and the Churn.

Ang. (*wildly*). But we don't know the fable of the Magnet and the Churn!

Gros. Don't you? Then I will sing it to you.

SONG—GROSVENOR

A magnet hung in a hardware shop,
And all around was a loving crop
Of scissors and needles, nails and knives,
Offering love for all their lives;
But for iron the magnet felt no whim,
Though he charmed iron, it charmed not him;
From needles and nails and knives he'd turn,
For he'd set his love on a Silver Churn!

All
A Silver Churn?

Grosvenor
A Silver Churn!
His most aesthetic,
Very magnetic
Fancy took this turn—
"If I can wheedle
A knife or a needle,
Why not a Silver Churn?"

Chorus
His most aesthetic, etc.

Grosvenor
And Iron and Steel expressed surprise,
The needles opened their well-drilled eyes,
The penknives felt "shut up", no doubt,
The scissors declared themselves "cut out",
The kettles they boiled with rage, 'tis said,
While every nail went off its head,
And hither and thither began to roam,
Till a hammer came up—and drove them home.

All
It drove them home?

Grosvenor
It drove them home!
While this magnetic,
Peripatetic
Lover he lived to learn,
By no endeavour
Can magnet ever
Attract a Silver Churn!

All
While this magnetic, etc.

[*They go off in low spirits, gazing back at him from time to time.*

Gros. At last they are gone! What is this mysterious fascination that I seem to exercise over all I come across? A curse on my fatal beauty, for I am sick of conquests!

PATIENCE *appears*

Pa. Archibald!

Gros. (*turns and sees her*). Patience!

Pa. I have escaped with difficulty from my Reginald. I wanted to see you so much that I might ask you if you still love me as fondly as ever?

Gros. Love you? If the devotion of a lifetime——(*Seizes her hand.*)

Pa. (*indignantly*). Hold! Unhand me, or I scream! (*He releases her.*) If you are a gentleman, pray remember that I am another's! (*Very tenderly.*) But you *do* love me, don't you?

Gros. Madly, hopelessly, despairingly!

Pa. That's right! I never can be yours; but that's right!

Gros. And you love this Bunthorne?

Pa. With a heart-whole ecstasy that withers, and scorches, and burns, and stings! (*Sadly.*) It is my duty.

Gros. Admirable girl! But you are not happy with him?

Pa. Happy? I am miserable beyond description!

Gros. That's right! I never can be yours; but that's right!

Pa. But go now. I see dear Reginald approaching. Farewell, dear Archibald; I cannot tell you how happy it has made me to know that you still love me.

Gros. Ah, if I only dared——(*Advances towards her.*)

Pa. Sir! this language to one who is promised to another! (*Tenderly.*) Oh, Archibald, think of me sometimes, for my heart is breaking! He is so unkind to me, and you would be so loving!

Gros. Loving! (*Advances towards her.*)

Pa. Advance one step, and as I am a good and pure woman, I scream! (*Tenderly.*) Farewell, Archibald! (*Sternly.*) Stop there! (*Tenderly.*) Think of me sometimes! (*Angrily.*) Advance at your peril! Once more, adieu!

[GROSVENOR *sighs, gazes sorrowfully at her, sighs deeply, and exit. She bursts into tears*

Enter BUNTHORNE, *followed by* JANE. *He is moody and preoccupied.*

Jane sings

In a doleful train,
  One and one I walk all day;
For I love in vain—

None so sorrowful as they
  Who can only sigh and say,
    Woe is me, alackaday!

Bun. (*seeing* PATIENCE). Crying, eh? What are you crying about?

Pa. I've only been thinking how dearly I love you!

Bun. Love me! Bah!

Jane. Love him! Bah!

Bun. (*to* JANE). Don't you interfere.

Jane. He always crushes me!

Pa. (*going to him*). What is the matter, dear Reginald? If you have any sorrow, tell it to me, that I may share it with you. (*Sighing.*) It is my duty!

Bun. (*snappishly*). Whom were you talking with just now?

Pa. With dear Archibald.

Bun. (*furiously*). With dear Archibald! Upon my honour, this is too much!

Jane. A great deal too much!

Bun. (*angrily to* JANE). Do be quiet!

Jane. Crushed again.

Pa. I think he is the noblest, purest, and most perfect being I have ever met. But I don't love him. It is true that he is devotedly attached to me, but indeed I don't love *him.* Whenever he grows affectionate, I scream. It is my duty! (*Sighing.*)

Bun. I dare say!

Jane. So do I! *I* dare say!

Pa. Why, how could I love him and love you too? You can't love two people at once!

Bun. Oh, can't you, though!

Pa. No, you can't; I only wish you could.

Bun. I don't believe you know what love is!

Pa. (*sighing*). Yes, I do. There was a happy time when I didn't, but a bitter experience has taught me.

[*Exeunt* BUNTHORNE *and* JANE.

BALLAD—PATIENCE

Love is a plaintive song,
  Sung by a suffering maid,
Telling a tale of wrong,
  Telling of hope betrayed;
Tuned to each changing note,
  Sorry when *he* is sad,
Blind to his every mote,
  Merry when he is glad!
    Love that no wrong can cure,
      Love that is always new,
    Love is the love that's pure,

That is the love that's true!
Rendering good for ill,
  Smiling at every frown,
Yielding your own self-will,
  Laughing your tear-drops down;
Never a selfish whim,
  Trouble, or pain to stir;
Everything for him,
  Nothing at all for her!
    Love that will aye endure,
      Though the rewards be few,
    That is the love that's pure,
      That is the love that's true!
[*At the end of ballad exit* PATIENCE,
  weeping.

              Enter BUNTHORNE *and* JANE
Bun. Everything has gone wrong with
me since that smug-faced idiot came here.
Before that I was admired—I may say,
loved.

Jane. Too mild—adored!

Bun. Do let a poet soliloquize! The
damozels used to follow me wherever I
went; now they all follow him!

Jane. Not all! *I* am still faithful to you.

Bun. Yes, and a pretty damozel *you* are!

Jane. No, not pretty. Massive. Cheer up!
I will never leave you, I swear it!

Bun. Oh, thank you! I know what it is;
it's his confounded mildness. They find
me too highly spiced, if you please! And
no doubt I *am* highly spiced.

Jane. Not for my taste!

Bun. (*savagely*). No, but I am for theirs.
But I will show the world I can be as
mild as he. If they want insipidity, they
shall have it. I'll meet this fellow on his
own ground and beat him on it.

Jane. You shall. And I will help you.

Bun. You will? Jane, there's a good deal
of good in you, after all!

        DUET—BUNTHORNE *and* JANE
                    Jane
So go to him and say to him, with compliment ironical—

              Bunthorne
    Sing "Hey to you—
    Good day to you"—
    And that's what I shall say!

                    Jane
"Your style is much too sanctified—your
cut is too canonical"—
              Bunthorne
    Sing "Bah to you—

    Ha! ha! to you"—
    And that's what I shall say!
                    Jane
"I was the beau ideal of the morbid young
  aesthetical—
To doubt my inspiration was regarded as
  heretical—
Until you cut me out with your placidity
  emetical."—
              Bunthorne
    Sing "Booh to you—
    Pooh, pooh to you"—
    And that's what I shall say!
                    Both
Sing "Hey to you—good day to you"—
Sing "Bah to you—ha! ha! to you"—
Sing "Booh to you—pooh-pooh to you"—
And that's what $\begin{Bmatrix} you \\ I \end{Bmatrix}$ shall say!

              Bunthorne
I'll tell him that unless he will consent to
  be more jocular—
                    Jane
    Sing "Booh to you—
    Pooh, pooh to you"—
    And that's what you should say!
              Bunthorne
To cut his curly hair, and stick an eyeglass
  in his ocular—
                    Jane
    Sing "Bah to you—
    Ha! ha! to you"—
    And that's what you should say!
              Bunthorne
To stuff his conversation full of quibble
  and of quiddity—
To dine on chops and roly-poly pudding
  with avidity—
He'd better clear away with all convenient
  rapidity.
                    Jane
    Sing "Hey to you—
    Good day to you"—
    And that's what you should say!
                    Both
Sing "Booh to you—pooh, pooh to you"—
Sing "Bah to you—ha! ha! to you"—
Sing "Hey to you—good day to you"—
And that's what $\begin{Bmatrix} I \\ you \end{Bmatrix}$ shall say!

[*Exeunt* JANE *and* BUNTHORNE *together.*
Enter DUKE, COLONEL, *and* MAJOR. *They
  have abandoned their uniforms, and
  are dressed and made up in imitation*

of Aesthetics. They have long hair, and other outward signs of attachment to the brotherhood. As they sing they walk in stiff, constrained, and angular attitudes—a grotesque exaggeration of the attitudes adopted by BUNTHORNE *and the young Ladies in Act I.*

TRIO—DUKE, COLONEL, *and* MAJOR

It's clear that mediaeval art alone retains
its zest,
To charm and please its devotees we've
done our little best.
We're not quite sure if all we do has the
Early English ring;
But, as far as we can judge, it's something
like this sort of thing:
You hold yourself like this (*attitude*),
You hold yourself like that (*attitude*),
By hook and crook you try to look both
angular and flat (*attitude*).
We venture to expect
That what we recollect,
Though but a part of true High Art, will
have its due effect.
If this is not exactly right, we hope you
won't upbraid;
You can't get high Aesthetic tastes, like
trousers, ready made.
True views on Mediaevalism Time alone
will bring,
But, as far as we can judge, it's something
like this sort of thing:
You hold yourself like this (*attitude*),
You hold yourself like that (*attitude*),
By hook and crook you try to look both
angular and flat (*attitude*).
To cultivate the trim
Rigidity of limb,
You ought to get a Marionette, and form
your style on him (*attitude*).

Col. (attitude). Yes, it's quite clear that our only chance of making a lasting impression on these young ladies is to become as aesthetic as they are.

Maj. (attitude). No doubt. The only question is how far we've succeeded in doing so. I don't know why, but I've an idea that this is not quite right.

Duke (attitude). I don't like it. I never did. I don't see what it means. I do it, but I don't like it.

Col. My good friend, the question is not whether we like it, but whether they do. They understand these things—we don't.

Now I shouldn't be surprised if this is effective enough—at a distance.

Maj. I can't help thinking, we're a little stiff at it. It would be extremely awkward if we were to be "struck" so!

Col. I don't think we shall be struck so. Perhaps we're a little awkward at first—but everything must have a beginning. Oh, here they come! 'Tention!

They strike fresh attitudes, as ANGELA *and* SAPHIR *enter*

Ang. (seeing them). Oh, Saphir—see—see! The immortal fire has descended on them, and they are of the Inner Brotherhood—perceptively intense and consummately utter. (*The* OFFICERS *have some difficulty in maintaining their constrained attitudes.*)

Saph. (in admiration). How Botticellian! How Fra Angelican! Oh, Art, we thank thee for this boon!

Col. (apologetically). I'm afraid we're not quite right.

Ang. Not supremely, perhaps, but oh, so, all-but! (*To* SAPHIR.) Oh, Saphir, are they not quite too all-but?

Saphir. They are indeed jolly utter!

Maj. (in agony). I wonder what the Inner Brotherhood usually recommend for cramp?

Col. Ladies, we will not deceive you. We are doing this at some personal inconvenience with a view of expressing the extremity of our devotion to you. We trust that it is not without its effect.

Ang. We will not deny that we are much moved by this proof of your attachment.

Saph. Yes, your conversion to the principles of Aesthetic Art in its highest development has touched us deeply.

Ang. And if Mr. Grosvenor should remain obdurate—

Saph. Which we have every reason to believe he will—

Maj. (aside, in agony). I wish they'd make haste.

Ang. We are not prepared to say that our yearning hearts will not go out to you

Col. (as giving a word of command) By sections of threes—Rapture! (*All strike a fresh attitude, expressive of aesthetic rapture.*)

Saph. Oh, it's extremely good—for beginners it's admirable.

Maj. The only question is, who will take who?

Col. Oh, the Duke chooses first, as a matter of course.

Duke. Oh, I couldn't think of it—you are really too good!

Col. Nothing of the kind. You are a great matrimonial fish, and it's only fair that each of these ladies should have a chance of hooking you. It's perfectly simple. Observe, suppose you choose Angela, I take Saphir, Major takes nobody. Suppose you choose Saphir, Major takes Angela, I take nobody. Suppose you choose neither, I take Angela, Major takes Saphir. Clear as day!

QUINTET

DUKE, COLONEL, MAJOR, ANGELA *and* SAPHIR
Duke (taking Saphir)
If Saphir I choose to marry,
  I shall be fixed up for life;
Then the Colonel need not tarry,
  Angela can be his wife.
[DUKE *dances with* SAPHIR, COLONEL *with*
  ANGELA, MAJOR *dances alone.*
  Major (dancing alone)
In that case unprecedented,
  Single I shall live and die—
I shall have to be contented
  With their heartfelt sympathy!
    All (dancing as before)
He will have to be contented
  With our heartfelt sympathy!
    Duke (taking Angela)
If on Angy I determine,
  At my wedding she'll appear
Decked in diamonds and in ermine,
  Major then can take Saphir!
[DUKE *dances with* ANGELA, MAJOR *with*
  SAPHIR, COLONEL *dances alone.*
  Colonel (dancing)
In that case unprecedented,
  Single I shall live and die—
I shall have to be contented
  With their heartfelt sympathy!
    All (dancing as before)
He will have to be contented
  With our heartfelt sympathy!
Duke (taking both Angela and Saphir)
After some debate internal,
  If on neither I decide,
Saphir then can take the Colonel,
  (*Handing* SAPHIR *to* COLONEL.)

Angy be the Major's bride!
  (*Handing* ANGELA *to* MAJOR.)
(COLONEL *dances with* SAPHIR, MAJOR *with*
  ANGELA, DUKE *dances alone.*)
  Duke (dancing)
In that case unprecedented,
  Single I must live and die—
I shall have to be contented
  With their heartfelt sympathy!
    All (dancing as before)
He will have to be contented
  With our heartfelt sympathy.
[*At the end,* DUKE, COLONEL, *and* MAJOR,
  and two girls dance off arm-in-arm.
    Enter GROSVENOR

Gros. It is very pleasant to be alone. It is pleasant to be able to gaze at leisure upon those features which all others may gaze upon at their good will! (*Looking at his reflection in hand-mirror.*) Ah, I am a very Narcissus!

Enter BUNTHORNE, *moodily*

Bun. It's no use; I can't live without admiration. Since Grosvenor came here, insipidity has been at a premium. Ah, he is there!

Gros. Ah, Bunthorne! come here—look! Very graceful, isn't it!

Bun. (*taking hand-mirror*). Allow me; I haven't seen it. Yes, it is graceful.

Gros. (*re-taking hand-mirror*). Oh, good gracious! not that—this——

Bun. You don't mean that! Bah! I am in no mood for trifling.

Gros. And what is amiss?

Bun. Ever since you came here, you have entirely monopolized the attentions of the young ladies. I don't like it, sir!

Gros. My dear sir, how can I help it? They are the plague of my life. My dear Mr. Bunthorne, with your personal disadvantages, you can have no idea of the inconvenience of being madly loved, at first sight, by every woman you meet.

Bun. Sir, until you came here I was adored!

Gros. Exactly—until I came here. That's my grievance. I cut everybody out! I assure you, if you could only suggest some means whereby, consistently with my duty to society, I could escape these inconvenient attentions, you would earn my everlasting gratitude.

Bun. I will do so at once. However popular it may be with the world at large, your personal appearance is highly objectionable to *me*.

Gros. It is? (*shaking his hand*). Oh, thank you! thank you! How can I express my gratitude?

Bun. By making a complete change at once. Your conversation must henceforth be perfectly matter-of-fact. You must cut your hair, and have a back parting. In appearance and costume you must be absolutely commonplace.

Gros. (*decidedly*). No. Pardon me, that's impossible.

Bun. Take care! When I am thwarted I am very terrible.

Gros. I can't help that. I am a man with a mission. And that mission must be fulfilled.

Bun. I don't think you quite appreciate the consequences of thwarting me.

Gros. I don't care what they are.

Bun. Suppose—I won't go so far as to say that I will do it—but suppose for one moment I were to curse you? (Grosvenor *quails*.) Ah! Very well. Take care.

Gros. But surely you would never do that? (*In great alarm.*)

Bun. I don't know. It would be an extreme measure, no doubt. Still——

Gros. (*wildly*). But you would not do it—I am sure you would not. (*Throwing himself at* BUNTHORNE'S *knees, and clinging to him.*) Oh, reflect, reflect! You had a mother once.

Bun. Never!

Gros. Then you had an aunt! (BUNTHORNE *affected.*) Ah! I see you had! By the memory of that aunt, I implore you to pause ere you resort to this last fearful expedient. Oh, Mr. Bunthorne, reflect, reflect! (*Weeping.*)

Bun. (*aside, after a struggle with himself*). I must not allow myself to be unmanned! (*Aloud.*) It is useless. Consent at once, or may a nephew's curse——

Gros. Hold! Are you absolutely resolved?

Bun. Absolutely.

Gros. Will nothing shake you?

Bun. Nothing. I am adamant.

Gros. Very good. (*Rising.*) Then I yield.

Bun. Ha! You swear it?

Gros. I do, cheerfully. I have long wished for a reasonable pretext for such a change as you suggest. It has come at last. I do it on compulsion!

Bun. Victory! I triumph!

DUET—BUNTHORNE *and* GROSVENOR

Bunthorne

When I go out of door,
Of damozels a score
  (All sighing and burning,
  And clinging and yearning)
Will follow me as before.
I shall, with cultured taste,
Distinguish gems from paste,
  And "High diddle diddle"
  Will rank as an idyll,
If I pronounce it chaste!

Both

A most intense young man,
A soulful-eyed young man,
An ultra-poetical, super-aesthetical,
Out-of-the-way young man!

Grosvenor

Conceive me, if you can,
An every-day young man:
  A commonplace type,
  With a stick and a pipe,
And a half-bred black-and-tan;
  Who thinks suburban "hops"
  More fun than "Monday Pops",
Who's fond of his dinner,
And doesn't get thinner
  On bottled beer and chops.

Both

A commonplace young man,
A matter-of-fact young man,
A steady and stolid-y, jolly Bank-holiday
Every-day young man!

Bunthorne

A Japanese young man,
A blue-and-white young man,
Francesca da Rimini, miminy, piminy,
Je-ne-sais-quoi young man!

Grosvenor

A Chancery Lane young man,
A Somerset House young man,
A very delectable, highly respectable,
Threepenny-bus young man!

Bunthorne

A pallid and thin young man,
A haggard and lank young man,
A greenery-yallery, Grosvenor Gallery,
Foot-in-the-grave young man!

Grosvenor
A Sewell & Cross young man,
A Howell & James young man,

A pushing young particle—"What's the next article?"—
Waterloo-House young man!

ENSEMBLE

Bunthorne
Conceive me, if you can,
A crotchety, cracked young man,
An ultra-poetical, super-aesthetical,
Out-of-the-way young man!

Grosvenor
Conceive me, if you can,
A matter-of-fact young man,
An alphabetical, arithmetical,
Every-day young man!

[*At the end,* GROSVENOR *dances off.*
BUNTHORNE *remains.*

Bun. It is all right! I have committed my last act of ill-nature, and henceforth I'm a changed character. (*Dances about stage, humming refrain of last air.*)
Enter PATIENCE. *She gazes in astonishment at him.*
Pa. Reginald! Dancing! And—what in the world is the matter with you?
Bun. Patience, I'm a changed man. Hitherto I've been gloomy, moody, fitful—uncertain in temper and selfish in disposition—
Pa. You have, indeed! (*sighing.*)
Bun. All that is changed. I have reformed. I have modelled myself upon Mr. Grosvenor. Henceforth I am mildly cheerful. My conversation will blend amusement with instruction. I shall still be aesthetic; but my aestheticism will be of the most pastoral kind.
Pa. Oh, Reginald! Is all this true?
Bun. Quite true. Observe how amiable I am. (*Assuming a fixed smile.*)
Pa. But, Reginald, how long will this last?
Bun. With occasional intervals for rest and refreshment, as long as I do.
Pa. Oh, Reginald, I'm so happy! (*In his*

arms.) Oh, dear, dear Reginald, I cannot express the joy I feel at this change. It will no longer be a duty to love you, but a pleasure—a rapture—an ecstasy!
Bun. My darling!
Pa. But—oh horror! (*Recoiling from him.*)
Bun. What's the matter?
Pa. Is it quite certain that you have absolutely reformed—that you are henceforth a perfect being—utterly free from defect of any kind?
Bun. It is quite certain. I have sworn it.
Pa. Then I never can be yours!
Bun. Why not?
Pa. Love, to be pure, must be absolutely unselfish, and there can be nothing unselfish in loving so perfect a being as you have now become!
Bun. But, stop a bit! I don't want to change—I'll relapse—I'll be as I was—interrupted!
Enter GROSVENOR, *followed by all the young Ladies, who are followed by Chorus of Dragoons. He has had his hair cut, and is dressed in an ordinary suit of dittoes and a pot hat. They all dance cheerfully round the stage in marked contrast to their former languor.*

CHORUS—GROSVENOR *and* GIRLS
Grosvenor
I'm a Waterloo House young man,
A Sewell & Cross young man,
A steady and stolid-y, jolly Bank-holiday,
Every-day young man!

Bun. Angela—Ella—Saphir—what—what does this mean?
Ang. It means that Archibald the All-Right cannot be all-wrong; and if the All-Right chooses to discard aestheticism, it proves that aestheticism ought to be discarded.

Girls
We're Swears & Wells young girls,
We're Madame Louise young girls,
We're prettily pattering, cheerily chattering,
Every-day young girls!

Pa. Oh, Archibald! Archibald! I'm shocked—surprised—horrified!
Gros. I can't help it. I'm not a free agent. I do it on compulsion.
Pa. This is terrible. Go! I shall never set eyes on you again. But—oh, joy!
Gros. What is the matter?

Pa. Is it quite, quite certain that you will always be a commonplace young man?

Gros. Always—I've sworn it.

Pa. Why, then, there's nothing to prevent my loving you with all the fervour at my command!

Gros. Why, that's true.

Pa. My Archibald!

Gros. My Patience! (*They embrace.*)

Bun. Crushed again!

Enter JANE

Jane (*who is still aesthetic*). Cheer up! I am still here. I have never left you, and I never will!

Bun. Thank you, Jane. After all, there is no denying it, you're a fine figure of a woman!

Jane. My Reginald!

Bun. My Jane!

Flourish. Enter COLONEL, DUKE, *and* MAJOR

Col. Ladies, the Duke has at length determined to select a bride! (*General excitement.*)

Duke. I have a great gift to bestow. Approach such of you as are truly lovely. (*All come forward, bashfully, except* JANE *and* PATIENCE.) In personal appearance you have all that is necessary to make a woman happy. In common fairness, I think I ought to choose the only one among you who has the misfortune to be distinctly plain. (*Girls retire disappointed.*) Jane!

Jane (*leaving* BUNTHORNE'S *arms*). Duke! (JANE *and* DUKE *embrace.* BUNTHORNE *is utterly disgusted.*)

Bun. Crushed again!

FINALE

Duke

After much debate internal,
 I on Lady Jane decide,
Saphir now may take the Colonel,
 Angy be the Major's bride!

[SAPHIR *pairs off with* COLONEL, ANGELA *with* MAJOR, ELLA *with* SOLICITOR.

Bunthorne

In that case unprecedented,
 Single I must live and die—
I shall have to be contented
 With a tulip or lily!
(*Takes a lily from button-hole and gazes affectionately at it.*)

All

He will have to be contented
 With a tulip or lily!
Greatly pleased with one another,
 To get married we decide.
Each of us will wed the other,
 Nobody be Bunthorne's Bride!

DANCE

CURTAIN

THE SORCERER

DRAMATIS PERSONÆ

SIR MARMADUKE POINTDEXTRE, *an Elderly Baronet*

ALEXIS, *of the Grenadier Guards—his Son*

DR. DALY, *Vicar of Ploverleigh*

NOTARY

JOHN WELLINGTON WELLS, *of J. W. Wells & Co., Family Sorcerers*

LADY SANGAZURE, *a Lady of Ancient Lineage*

ALINE, *her Daughter—betrothed to Alexis*

MRS. PARTLET, *a Pew-opener*

CONSTANCE, *her Daughter*

Chorus of Villagers

(*Twelve hours are supposed to elapse between Acts I and II*)

ACT I

SCENE.—*Exterior of* SIR MARMADUKE'S *Elizabethan Mansion.*
> *Chorus of Villagers*
> Ring forth, ye bells,
>   With clarion sound—
> Forget your knells,
>   For joys abound.
> Forget your notes
>   Of mournful lay,
> And from your throats
>   Pour joy to-day.
> For to-day young Alexis—young Alexis Pointdextre
>   Is betrothed to Aline—to Aline Sangazure,
> And that pride of his sex is—of his sex is to be next her,
>   At the feast on the green—on the green, oh, be sure!
>   Ring forth, ye bells, etc.
>   [*Exeunt the men into house.*

Enter MRS. PARTLET *with* CONSTANCE, *her daughter.*

RECITATIVE
Mrs. Partlet
Constance, my daughter, why this strange depression?
The village rings with seasonable joy,
Because the young and amiable Alexis,
Heir to the great Sir Marmaduke Point-dextre,

Is plighted to Aline, the only daughter
Of Annabella, Lady Sangazure.
You, you alone are sad and out of spirits;
What is the reason? Speak, my daughter, speak!
Constance
Oh, mother, do not ask! If my complexion
From red to white should change in quick succession,
And then from white to red, oh, take no notice!
If my poor limbs should tremble with emotion,
Pay no attention, mother—it is nothing!
If long and deep-drawn sighs I chance to utter,
Oh, heed them not, their cause must ne'er be known!

[MRS. PARTLET *motions to* CHORUS *to leave her with* CONSTANCE. *Exeunt Ladies of* CHORUS.

ARIA—CONSTANCE
When he is here,
  I sigh with pleasure—
When he is gone,
  I sigh with grief.
My hopeless fear
  No soul can measure—
His love alone
  Can give my aching heart relief!
When he is cold,
  I weep for sorrow—

131

When he is kind,
I weep for joy.
My grief untold
Knows no to-morrow—
My woe can find
No hope, no solace, no alloy!

Mrs. Partlet

Come, tell me all about it! Do not fear—
I, too, have loved; but that was long ago!
Who is the object of your young affections?

Constance

Hush, mother! He is here!

Enter DR. DALY. *He is pensive and does not
see them*

Mrs. Partlet (*amazed*)

Our reverend vicar!

Constance

Oh, pity me, my heart is almost broken!

Mrs. Partlet

My child, be comforted. To such an union
I shall not offer any opposition.
Take him—he's yours! May you and he be
happy!

Constance

But, mother dear, he is not yours to give!

Mrs. Partlet

That's true, indeed!

Constance

He might object!

Mrs. Partlet

He might.
But come—take heart—I'll probe him on
the subject.
Be comforted—leave this affair to me.

RECITATIVE—DR. DALY

The air is charged with amatory numbers—
Soft madrigals, and dreamy lovers' lays.
Peace, peace, old heart! Why waken from
its slumbers
The aching memory of the old, old days?

BALLAD

Time was when Love and I were well
acquainted.
Time was when we walked ever hand in
hand.
A saintly youth, with worldly thought untainted,
None better-loved than I in all the land!
Time was, when maidens of the noblest
station,
Forsaking even military men,
Would gaze upon me, rapt in adoration—

Ah me, I was a fair young curate then!
Had I a headache? sighed the maids assembled;
Had I a cold? welled forth the silent
tear;
Did I look pale? then half a parish
trembled;
And when I coughed all thought the end
was near!
I had no care—no jealous doubts hung o'er
me—
For I was loved beyond all other men.
Fled gilded dukes and belted earls before
me—
Ah me, I was a pale young curate then!

[*At the conclusion of the ballad,* MRS.
PARTLET *comes forward with* CONSTANCE.

Mrs. P. Good day reverend sir.

Dr. D. Ah, good Mrs. Partlet, I am
glad to see you. And your little daughter,
Constance! Why, she is quite a little woman, I declare!

Con. (*aside*). Oh, mother, I cannot speak
to him!

Mrs. P. Yes, reverend sir, she is nearly
eighteen, and as good as girl as ever stepped.
(*Aside* to Dr. D.). Ah, sir, I'm afraid
I shall soon lose her!

Dr. D. (*aside to* MRS. P.) Dear me, you
pain me very much. Is she delicate?

Mrs. P. Oh no, sir—I don't mean that
—but young girls look to get married.

Dr. D. Oh, I take you. To be sure. But
there's plenty of time for that. Four or
five years hence, Mrs. Partlet, four or
five years hence. But when the time *does*
come, I shall have much pleasure in marrying her myself—

Con. (*aside*). Oh, mother!

Dr. D. To some strapping young fellow
in her own rank of life.

Con. (*in tears*). He does *not* love me!

Mrs. P. I have often wondered, reverend
sir (if you'll excuse the liberty), that *you*
have never married.

Dr. D. (*aside*). Be still, my fluttering
heart!

Mrs. P. A clergyman's wife does so much
good in a village. Besides that, you are not
as young as you were, and before very long
you will want somebody to nurse you, and
look after your little comforts.

Dr. D. Mrs. Partlet, there is much truth

in what you say. I am indeed getting on in years, and a helpmate would cheer my declining days. Time was when it might have been; but I have left it too long—I am an old fogy, now, am I not, my dear? (*to* CONSTANCE)—a very old fogy, indeed. Ha! ha! No, Mrs. Partlet, my mind is quite made up. I shall live and die a solitary old bachelor.

Con. Oh, mother, mother! (*Sobs on* MRS. PARTLET'S *bosom.*)

Mrs. P. Come, come, dear one, don't fret. At a more fitting time we will try again—we will try again.

[*Exeunt* MRS. PARTLET *and* CONSTANCE.

Dr. D. (*looking after them*). Poor little girl! I'm afraid she has something on her mind. She is rather comely. Time was when this old heart would have throbbed in double-time at the sight of such a fairy form! But tush! I am puling! Here comes the young Alexis with his proud and happy father. Let me dry this tell-tale tear!

Enter SIR MARMADUKE *and* ALEXIS

RECITATIVE

Dr. Daly

Sir Marmaduke—my dear young friend, Alexis—

On this most happy, most auspicious plighting—

Permit me, as a true old friend, to tender My best, my very best congratulations!

Sir Marmaduke

Sir, you are most obleeging!

Alexis

Dr. Daly,

My dear old tutor, and my valued pastor, I thank you from the bottom of my heart!

(*Spoken through music*)

Dr. Daly

May fortune bless you! may the middle distance

Of your young life be pleasant as the foreground—

The joyous foreground! and, when you have reached it,

May that which now is the far-off horizon (But which will then become the middle distance),

In fruitful promise be exceeded only

By that which will have opened in the meantime,

Into a new and glorious horizon!

Sir Marmaduke

Dear Sir, that is an excellent example Of an old school of stately compliment To which I have, through life, been much addicted.

Will you obleege me with a copy of it, In clerkly manuscript, that I myself May use it on appropriate occasions?

Dr. Daly

Sir, you shall have a fairly-written copy Ere Sol has sunk into his western slumbers!

[*Exeunt* DR. DALY.

Sir M. (*to* ALEXIS, *who is in a reverie*). Come, come, my son—your *fiancée* will be here in five minutes. Rouse yourself to receive her.

Alexis. Oh rapture!

Sir M. Yes, you are a fortunate young fellow, and I will not disguise from you that this union with the House of Sangazure realizes my fondest wishes. Aline is rich, and she comes of a sufficiently old family, for she is the seven thousand and thirty-seventh in direct descent from Helen of Troy. True, there was a blot on the escutcheon of that lady—that affair with Paris—but where is the family, other than my own, in which there is no flaw? You are a lucky fellow, sir—a very lucky fellow!

Alexis. Father, I am welling over with limpid joy! No sicklying taint of sorrow overlies the lucid lake of liquid love, upon which, hand in hand, Aline and I are to float into eternity!

Sir M. Alexis, I desire that of your love for this young lady you do not speak so openly. You are always singing ballads in praise of her beauty, and you expect the very menials who wait behind your chair, to chorus your ecstasies. It is not delicate.

Alexis. Father, a man who loves as I love—

Sir M. Pooh pooh, sir! Fifty years ago I madly loved your future mother-in-law, the Lady Sangazure, and I have reason to believe that she returned my love. But were we guilty of the indelicacy of publicly rushing into each other's arms, exclaiming—

"Oh, my adored one!" "Beloved boy!" "Ecstatic rapture!" "Unmingled joy!" which seems to be the modern fashion of love-making? No! it was "Madam, I trust you are in the enjoyment of good health"—

"Sir, you are vastly polite, I protest I am mighty well"—and so forth. Much more delicate—much more respectful. But see—Aline approaches—let us retire, that she may compose herself for the interesting ceremony in which she is to play so important a part.

[*Exeunt* SIR MARMADUKE *and* ALEXIS.
Enter ALINE, *on terrace, preceded by*
Chorus of Girls.

CHORUS OF GIRLS

With heart and with voice
Let us welcome this mating:
To the youth of her choice,
   With a heart palpitating,
   Comes the lovely Aline!
May their love never cloy!
   May their bliss be unbounded!
With a halo of joy
   May their lives be surrounded!
     Heaven bless our Aline!

RECITATIVE—ALINE

My kindly friends, I thank you for this greeting,
And as you wish me every earthly joy,
I trust your wishes may have quick fulfilment!

ARIA—ALINE

Oh, happy young heart!
  Comes thy young lord a-wooing
With joy in his eyes,
   And pride in his breast—
Make much of thy prize
   For he is the best
That ever came a-suing.
   Yet—yet we must part,
     Young heart!
   Yet—yet we must part!
Oh, merry young heart,
  Bright are the days of thy wooing!
But happier far
  The days untried—
No sorrow can mar,
  When Love has tied
The knot there's no undoing.
   Then, never to part,
     Young heart!
   Then, never to part!
Enter LADY SANGAZURE

RECITATIVE—LADY SANGAZURE

My child, I join in these congratulations:
Heed not the tear that dims this aged eye!
Old memories crowd upon me. Though I sorrow,

'Tis for myself, Aline, and not for thee!
Enter ALEXIS, *preceded by Chorus of Men.*

CHORUS OF MEN AND WOMEN

With heart and with voice
Let us welcome this mating;
To the maid of his choice,
   With a heart of palpitating,
   Comes Alexis the brave!

SIR MARMADUKE *enters.* LADY SANGAZURE
and he exhibit signs of strong emotion
at the sight of each other, which they
endeavour to repress. ALEXIS *and* ALINE
rush into each other's arms.

RECITATIVE
Alexis

Oh, my adored one!
Aline

Beloved boy!
Alexis

Ecstatic rapture!
Aline

Unmingled joy!
[*They retire up.*

DUET—SIR MARMADUKE *and* LADY SANGAZURE
Sir Marmaduke (*with stately courtesy*)
Welcome joy, adieu to sadness!
  As Aurora gilds the day,
So those eyes, twin orbs of gladness,
  Chase the clouds of care away.
Irresistible incentive
  Bids me humbly kiss your hand;
I'm your servant most attentive—
  Most attentive to command!
   (*Aside with frantic vehemence*)
Wild with adoration!
Mad with fascination!
To indulge my lamentation
  No occasion do I miss!
Goaded to distraction
By maddening inaction,
I find some satisfaction
  In apostrophe like this:
"Sangazure immortal,
  "Sangazure divine,
"Welcome to my portal,
  "Angel, oh be mine!"
   (*Aloud with much ceremony*)
Irresistible incentive
  Bids me humbly kiss your hand;
I'm your servant most attentive—
  Most attentive to command!
Lady Sangazure
Sir, I thank you most politely
  For your graceful courtesee;

Compliment more true and knightly
Never yet was paid to me!
Chivalry is an ingredient
Sadly lacking in our land—
Sir, I am your most obedient,
Most obedient to command!
(*Aside with great vehemence*)
Wild with adoration!
Mad with fascination!
To indulge my lamentation
No occasion do I miss!
Goaded to distraction
By maddening inaction,
I find some satisfaction
In apostrophe like this:
"Marmaduke immortal,
"Marmaduke divine,
"Take me to thy portal,
"Loved one, oh be mine!"
(*Aloud with much ceremony*)
Chivalry is an ingredient
Sadly lacking in our land;
Sir, I am your most obedient,
Most obedient to command!
[*During this the* NOTARY *has entered, with
marriage contract.*

RECIT—NOTARY

All is prepared for sealing and for signing,
The contract has been drafted as agreed;
Approach the table, oh, ye lovers pining,
With hand and seal come execute the
deed!
[ALEXIS *and* ALINE *advance and sign,*
ALEXIS *supported by* SIR MARMADUKE,
ALINE *by her Mother.*
Chorus
See they sign, without a quiver, it—
Then to seal proceed.
They deliver it—they deliver it
As their Act and Deed!
Alexis
I deliver it—I deliver it
As my Act and Deed!
Aline
I deliver it—I deliver it
As my Act and Deed!
Chorus
With heart and with voice
Let us welcome this mating;
Leave them here to rejoice,
With true love palpitating,
Alexis the brave,
And the lovely Aline!
[*Exeunt all but* ALEXIS *and* ALINE.

Alexis. At last we are alone! My darling,
you are now irrevocably betrothed to me.
Are you not very very happy?
Aline. Oh, Alexis, can you doubt it? Do
I not love you beyond all on earth, and am
I not beloved in return? Is not true love,
faithfully given and faithfully returned,
the source of every earthly joy?
Alexis. Of that there can be no doubt.
Oh, that the world could be persuaded of
the truth of that maxim! Oh, that the
world would break down the artificial bar-
riers of rank, wealth, education, age, beauty, habits, taste, and temper, and recognise
the glorious principle, that in marriage
alone is to be found the panacea for every
ill!
Aline. Continue to preach that sweet doctrine, and you will succeed, oh, evangel of
true happiness!
Alexis. I hope so, but as yet the cause
progresses but slowly. Still I have made
some converts to the principle, that men
and women should be coupled in matrimony without distinction of rank. I have
lectured on the subject at Mechanics' Institutes, and the mechanics were unanimous
in favour of my views. I have preached in
workhouses, beershops and Lunatic Asylums, and I have been received with enthusiasm. I have addressed navvies on the
advantages that would accrue to them if
they married wealthy ladies of rank, and
not a navvy dissented!
Aline. Noble fellows! And yet there are
those who hold that the uneducated classes
are not open to argument! And what do
the countesses say?
Alexis. Why, at present, it can't be denied, the aristocracy hold aloof.
Aline. Ah, the working man is the true
Intelligence after all!
Alexis. He is a noble creature when he
is quite sober. Yes Aline, true happiness
comes of true love, and true love should
be independent of external influences. It
should live upon itself and by itself—in itself love should live for love alone!

BALLAD—ALEXIS

Love feeds on many kinds of food, I know,
Some love for rank, and some for duty:
Some give their hearts away for empty
show,
And others love for youth and beauty.

To love for money all the world is prone:
  Some love themselves, and live all lonely:
Give me the love that loves for love alone—
  I love that love—I love it only!
What man for any other joy can thirst,
  Whose loving wife adores him duly?
Want, misery, and care may do their worst,
  If loving woman loves you truly.
A lover's thoughts are ever with his own—
  None truly loved is ever lonely:
Give me the love that loves for love
    alone—
  I love that love—I love it only!

Aline. Oh, Alexis, those are noble principles!

Alexis. Yes, Aline, and I am going to take a desperate step in support of them. Have you ever heard of the firm of J. W. Wells & Co., the old-established Family Sorcerers in St. Mary Axe?

Aline. I have seen their advertisement.

Alexis. They have invented a philtre, which, if report may be believed, is simply infallible. I intend to distribute it through the village, and within half an hour of my doing so there will not be an adult in the place who will not have learnt the secret of pure and lasting happiness. What do you say to that?

Aline. Well, dear, of course a filter is a very useful thing in a house; but still I don't quite see that it is the sort of thing that places its possessor on the very pinnacle of earthly joy.

Alexis. Aline, you misunderstand me. I didn't say a filter—I said a philtre.

Aline (*alarmed*). You don't mean a love-potion?

Alexis. On the contrary— I *do* mean a love-potion.

Aline. Oh, Alexis! I don't think it would be right. I don't indeed. And then—a real magician! Oh, it would be downright wicked.

Alexis. Aline, is it, or is it not, a laudable object to steep the whole village up to its lips in love, and to couple them in matrimony without distinction of age, rank, or fortune?

Aline. Unquestionably, but—

Alexis. Then unpleasant as it must be to have recourse to supernatural aid, I must nevertheless pocket my aversion, in defer-

ence to the great and good end I have in view. (*Calling*) Hercules.

Enter a PAGE *from tent*

Page. Yes, sir.

Alexis. Is Mr. Wells there?

Page. He's in the tent, sir—refreshing.

Alexis. Ask him to be so good as to step this way.

Page. Yes, sir.

[*Exit* PAGE.

Aline. Oh, but, Alexis! A real Sorcerer! Oh, I shall be frightened to death!

Alexis. I trust my Aline will not yield to fear while the strong right arm of her Alexis is here to protect her.

Aline. It's nonsense, dear, to talk of your protecting me with your strong right arm, in face of the fact that this Family Sorcerer could change me into a guinea-pig before you could turn round.

Alexis. He *could* change you into a guinea-pig, no doubt, but it is most unlikely that he would take such a liberty. It's a most respectable firm, and I am sure he would never be guilty of so untradesmanlike an act.

Enter MR. WELLS *from tent*

Mr. W. Good day, sir. (ALINE *much terrified*)

Alexis. Good day—I believe you are a Sorcerer.

Mr. W. Yes, sir, we practise Necromancy in all its branches. We've a choice assortment of wishing-caps, divining-rods, amulets, charms, and counter-charms. We can cast you a nativity at a low figure, and we have a horoscope at three-and-six that we can guarantee. Our Abudah chests, each containing a patent Hag who comes out and prophesies disasters, with spring complete, are strongly recommended. Our Aladdin lamps are very chaste, and our Prophetic Tablets, foretelling everything—from a change of Ministry down to a rise in Unified—are much enquired for. Our penny Curse—one of the cheapest things in the trade—is considered infallible. We have some very superior Blessings, too, but they're very little asked for. We've only sold one since Christmas—to a gentleman who bought it to send to his mother-in-law—but it turned out that he was afflicted in the head and it's been returned on our hands. But our sale of penny Curses, especially on Saturday nights, is tremendous. We can't turn 'em out fast enough.

SONG—MR. WELLS

Oh! my name is John Wellington Wells,
I'm a dealer in magic and spells,
  In blessings and curses
  And ever-filled purses,
In prophecies, witches, and knells.
If you want a proud foe to "make tracks"—
If you'd melt a rich uncle in wax—
  You've but to look in
  On our resident Djinn,
Number seventy, Simmery Axe!
We've a first-class assortment of magic;
  And for raising a posthumous shade
With effects that are comic or tragic,
  There's no cheaper house in the trade.
Love-philtre—we've quantities of it;
  And for knowledge if any one burns,
We keep an extremely small prophet, a
    prophet
Who brings us unabounded returns:

    For he can prophesy
    With a wink *of* his eye,
    Peep with security
    Into futurity,
    Sum up your history,
    Clear up a mystery,
    Humour proclivity
    For a nativity—for a nativity;
    With mirrors so magical,
    Tetrapods tragical,
    Bogies spectacular,
    Answers oracular,
    Facts astronomical,
    Solemn or comical,
    And, if you want it, he
    Makes a reduction on taking a
      quantity!

        Oh!

If any one anything lacks,
  He'll find it all ready in stacks,
    If he'll only look in
    On the resident Djinn,
Number seventy, Simmery Axe!
    He can raise you hosts
      Of ghosts,
  And that without reflectors;
    And creepy things
      With wings,
  And gaunt and grisly spectres.
    He can fill you crowds
      Of shrouds,

And horrify you vastly;
  He can rack your brains
    With chains,
And gibberings grim and ghastly!
  Then, if you plan it, he
  Changes organity,
  With an urbanity,
  Full of Satanity,
  Vexes humanity
  With an inanity
  Fatal to vanity—
Driving your foes to the verge of
    insanity!
  Barring tautology,
  In demonology,
  'Lectro-biology,
  Mystic nosology,
  Spirit philology,
  High-class astrology,
  Such is his knowledge, he
  Isn't the man to require an apology!

        Oh!

My name is John Wellington Wells,
I'm a dealer in magic and spells,
  In blessings and curses
  And ever-filled purses,
In prophecies, witches, and knells.
  If any one anything lacks,
  He'll find it all ready in stacks,
    If he'll only look in
    On the resident Djinn,
  Number seventy, Simmery Axe!

Alexis. I have sent for you to consult you on a very important matter. I believe you advertise a Patent Oxy-Hydrogen Love-at-first-sight Philtre?

Mr. W. Sir, it is our leading article. (*Producing a phial.*)

Alexis. Now I want to know if you can confidently guarantee it as possessing all the qualities you claim for it in your advertisement?

Mr. W. Sir, we are not in the habit of puffing our goods. Ours is an old-established house with a large family connection, and every assurance held out in the advertisement is fully realized. (*Hurt.*)

Aline (aside). Oh, Alexis, don't offend him! He'll change us into something dreadful—I know he will!

Alexis. I am anxious from purely philanthropical motives to distribute this philtre, secretly, among the inhabitants of this vil-

lage. I shall of course require a quantity.
How do you sell it?

Mr. W. In buying a quantity, sir, we
should strongly advise you taking it in the
wood, and drawing it off as you happen
to want it. We have it in four-and-a-half
and nine gallon casks—also in pipes and
hogsheads for laying down, and we deduct
10 per cent for prompt cash.

Alexis. I should mention that I am a
Member of the Army and Navy Stores.

Mr. W. In that case we deduct 25 per
cent.

Alexis. Aline, the villagers will assemble
to carouse in a few minutes. Go and fetch
the tea-pot.

Aline. But, Alexis—

Alexis. My dear, you must obey me, if
you please. Go and fetch the tea-pot.

Aline (going). I'm sure Dr. Daly would
disapprove of it.   [*Exit* ALINE.

Alexis. And how soon does it take effect?

Mr. W. In twelve hours. Whoever drinks
of it loses consciousness for that period, and
on waking falls in love, as a matter of
course, with the first lady he meets who
has also tasted it, and his affection is at
once returned. One trial will prove the fact.

Enter ALINE *with large tea-pot*

Alexis. Good: then, Mr. Wells, I shall
feel obliged if you will at once pour as
much philtre into this tea-pot as will suf-
fice to affect the whole village.

Aline. But bless me, Alexis, many of the
villagers are married people!

Mr. W. Madam, this philtre is com-
pounded on the strictest principles. On married people it has no effect whatever. But
are you quite sure that you have nerve
enough to carry you through the fearful
ordeal?

Alexis. In the good cause I fear nothing.

Mr. W. Very good, then, we will proceed at once to the Incantation.

(*The stage grows dark*)

INCANTATION

Mr. Wells

Sprites of earth and air—
 Fiends of flame and fire—
  Demon souls,
  Come here in shoals,
 This dreadful deed inspire!

Appear, appear, appear.
  Male Voices
Good master, we are here!
  Mr. Wells
Noisome hags of night—
 Imps of deadly shade—
  Pallid ghosts,
  Arise in hosts,
 And lend me all your aid.
  Appear, appear, appear!
  Female Voices
Good master, we are here!
  Alexis (aside)
Hark, they assemble,
 These fiends of the night!
  Aline (aside)
Oh, Alexis, I tremble,
 Seek safety in flight!
  ARIA—ALINE
Let us fly to a far-off land,
 Where peace and plenty dwell—
Where the sigh of the silver strand
 Is echoed in every shell
To the joy that land will give,
 On the wings of Love we'll fly;
In innocence there to live—
 In innocence there to die!
  Chorus of Spirits
  Too late—too late,
   It may not be!
  That happy fate
   Is not for thee!
  Alexis, Aline, and Mr. Wells
  Too late—too late,
   That may not be!
  That happy fate
  Is not for $\left\{\begin{array}{l}\text{me!}\\\text{thee!}\end{array}\right.$

Mr. Wells

Now shrivelled hags, with poison bags,
 Discharge your loathsome loads!
Spit flame and fire, unholy choir!
 Belch forth your venom, toads!
Ye demons fell, with yelp and yell,
 Shed curses far afield—
Ye fiends of night, your filthy blight
 In Noisome plenty yield!

Mr. Wells (pouring phial into tea-pot—
  flash)
  Number One!

  Chorus
  It is done!
  Mr. Wells (same business)

Number Two!
> *(flash)*
> *Chorus*

One too few!
> *Mr. Wells (same business)*

Number Three!
> *(flash)*
> *Chorus*

Set us free!
Set us free—our work is done.
> Ha! ha! ha!
Set us free—our course is run!
> Ha! ha! ha!
> *Aline and Alexis (aside)*
Let us fly to a far-off land,
> Where peace and plenty dwell—
Where the sigh of the silver strand
> Is echoed in every shell.
> *Chorus of Fiends*
Ha! ha! ha! ha! ha! ha! ha! ha! ha! ha!
[Stage grows light. MR. WELLS beckons villagers. Enter villagers and all the dramatis personae, dancing joyously. MRS. PARTLET and MR. WELLS then distribute tea-cups.

> *Chorus*

Now to the banquet we press;
> Now for the eggs, the ham;
Now for the mustard and cress,
> Now for the strawberry jam!
Now for the tea of our host,
> Now for the rollicking bun,
Now for the muffin and toast,
> Now for the gay Sally Lunn!
> *Women*

The eggs and the ham, and the strawberry
jam!
> *Men*

The rollicking bun and the gay Sally Lunn!
> The rollicking, rollicking bun!
> RECIT—SIR MARMADUKE

Be happy all—the feast is spread before ye;
> Fear nothing, but enjoy yourselves, I
pray!
Eat, aye, and drink—be merry, I implore
ye,
> For once let thoughtless Folly rule the
day.
> TEA-CUP BRINDISI

Eat, drink, and be gay,
> Banish all worry and sorrow,
Laugh gaily to-day,

Weep, if you're sorry, to-morrow!
Come, pass the cup round—
> I will go bail for the liquor;
It's strong, I'll be bound,
> For it was brewed by the vicar!
> *Chorus*

None so knowing as he
> At brewing a jorum of tea,
> Ha! ha!
> A pretty stiff jorum of tea.
Trio—Mr. Wells, Aline, and Alexis (aside)
See—see—they drink—
> All thought unheeding,
The tea-cups clink,
> They are exceeding!
Their hearts will melt
> In half-an-hour—
Then will be felt
> The potion's power!
[During this verse CONSTANCE has brought a small tea-pot, kettle, caddy, and cosy to DR. DALY. He makes tea scientifically.
> *Brindisi, 2nd Verse—Dr. Daly*
> *(with the tea-pot)*
Pain, trouble, and care,
> Misery, heart-ache, and worry,
Quick, out of your lair!
> Get you all gone in a hurry!
Toil, sorrow, and plot,
> Fly away quicker and quicker—
Three spoons to the pot—
> That is the brew of your vicar!
> *Chorus*

None so cunning as he
> At brewing a jorum of tea,
> Ha! ha!
> A pretty stiff jorum of tea!
Ensemble—Alexis and Aline (aside)
Oh love, true love—unworldly, abiding!
> Source of all pleasure—true fountain of
joy,—
Oh love, true love—divinely confiding,
> Exquisite treasure that knows no alloy,—
O love, true love, rich harvest of gladness,
> Peace-bearing tillage — great garner of
bliss,—
Oh love, true love, look down on our
sadness—
> Dwell in this village—oh, hear us in this!
[It becomes evident by the strange conduct of the characters that the charm is working. All rub their eyes and stagger about the stage as if under the influence of a narcotic.

Tutti (aside)
Oh, marvelolus illusion,
Oh, terrible surprise!
  What is this strange confusion
    That veils my aching eyes?
  I must regain my senses,
    Restoring Reason's law,
  Or fearful inferences
    Society will draw!

[*Those who have partaken of the philtre
struggle in vain against its effects, and,
at the end of the chorus, fall insensible
on the stage.*

END OF ACT I

ACT II

SCENE.—*Exterior of* SIR MARMADUKE'S *mansion by moonlight. All the peasantry
are discovered asleep on the ground, as
at the end of Act I.*
Enter MR. WELLS, *on tiptoe, followed by*
ALEXIS *and* ALINE. MR. WELLS *carries a
dark lantern.*
    Trio—Alexis, Aline, and Mr. Wells
'Tis twelve, I think,
  And at this mystic hour
The magic drink
  Should manifest its power.
Oh, slumbering forms,
  How little have ye guessed
The fire that warms
  Each apathetic breast!
    Alexis
But stay, my father is not here!
    Aline
And pray where is my mother dear?
    Mr. Wells
I did not think it meet to see
A dame of lengthy pedigree,
A Baronet and K.C.B.
A Doctor of Divinity,
And that respectable Q.C.,
All fast asleep, al-fresco-ly,
And so I had them taken home
And put to bed respectably!
I trust my conduct meets your appro-
    bation.

    Alexis
Sir, you have acted with discrimination,
And shown more delicate appreciation
Than we expect in persons of your station.
    Mr. Wells
But stay—they waken, one by one—

Alexis, Mr. Wells, and Aline (aside)
  A marvelous illusion!
    A terrible surprise
  Excites a strange confusion
    Within their aching eyes—
  They must regain their senses,
    Restoring Reason's law,
  Or fearful inferences
    Society will draw!

The spell has worked—the deed is done!
I would suggest that we retire
While Love, the Housemaid, lights her
    kitchen fire!
[*Exeunt* MR. WELLS, ALEXIS, *and* ALINE, *on
tiptoe, as the villagers stretch their
arms, yawn, rub their eyes, and sit up.*
    Men
Why, where be oi, and what be oi a doin',
  A sleepin' out, just when the dews du
    rise?
    Girls
Why, that's the very way your health to
    ruin,
  And don't seem quite respectable like-
    wise!
    Men (staring at girls)
Eh, that's you!
  Only think o' that now!
    Girls (coyly)
What may you be at, now?
  Tell me, du!
    Men (admiringly)
Eh, what a nose,
  And eh, what eyes, miss!
Lips like a rose,
  And cheeks likewise, miss!
    Girls (coyly)
Oi tell you true,
  Which I've never done, sir,
Oi loike you
  As I never loiked none, sir!
    All
Eh, but oi du loike you!
    Men
If you'll marry me, I'll dig for you and
    rake for you!
    Girls
If you'll marry me, I'll scrub for you and
    bake for you!
    Men
If you'll marry me, all others I'll forsake
    for you!

All

All this will I du, if you'll marry me!

Girls

If you'll marry me, I'll cook for you and
brew for you!

Men

If you'll marry me, I've guineas not a few
for you!

Girls

If you'll marry me, I'll take you in and
du for you!

All

All this will I du, if you'll marry me!
En, but oi du loike you!

Country dance

At end of dance, enter CONSTANCE *in tears,
leading* NOTARY, *who carries an ear-
trumpet*

ARIA—CONSTANCE

Dear friends, take pity on my lot,
My cup is not of nectar!
I long have loved—as who would not?—
Our kind and reverend rector.
Long years ago my love began
So sweetly—yet so sadly—
But when I saw this plain old man,
Away my old affection ran—
I found I loved him madly.
Oh!

(*To* NOTARY)

You very, very plain old man,
I love, I love you madly!

Chorus

You very, very plain old man,
She loves, she loves you madly!

Notary

I am a very deaf old man,
And hear you very badly!

Constance

I know not why I love him so;
It is enchantment, surely!
He's dry and snuffy, deaf and slow
Ill-tempered, weak, and poorly!
He's ugly, and absurdly dressed,
And sixty-seven nearly,
He's everything that I detest,
But if the truth must be confessed,
I love him very dearly!
Oh!

(*To* NOTARY)

You're everything that I detest,
But still I love you dearly!

Chorus

You're everything that girls detest,
But still she loves you dearly!

Notary

I caught that line, but for the rest,
I did not hear it clearly!

[*During this verse* ALINE *and* ALEXIS *have
entered at back unobserved.*

Aline and Alexis

Alexis

Oh joy! oh joy!
The charm works well,
And all are now united.

Aline

The blind young boy
Obeys the spell,
Their troth they all have plighted!

ENSEMBLE

Aline and Alexis	*Constance*	*Notary*
Oh joy! oh joy!	Oh, bitter joy!	Oh joy! oh joy!
The charm works well,	No words can tell	No words can tell
And all are now	How my poor heart	My state of mind
united!	is blighted!	delighted!
The blind young boy	They'll soon employ	They'll soon employ
Obeys the spell,	A marriage bell,	A marriage bell,
Their troth they all	To say that we're	To say that we're
have plighted.	united.	united.
True happiness	I do confess	True happiness
Reigns everywhere,	A sorrow rare	Reigns everywhere,
And dwells with both	My humbled spirit	And dwells with both
the sexes,	vexes,	the sexes,
And all will bless	And none will bless	And all will bless
The thoughtful care	Example rare	Example rare
Of their beloved	Of their beloved	Of their beloved
Alexis!	Alexis!	Alexis!

[*All except* ALEXIS *and* ALINE, *exeunt lovingly.*

Aline. How joyful they all seem in their new-found happiness! The whole village has paired off in the happiest manner. And yet not a match has been made that the hollow world would not consider ill-advised!

Alexis. But we are wiser—far wiser—than the world. Observe the good that will become of these ill-assorted unions. The miserly wife will check the reckless expenditure of her too frivolous consort, the wealthy husband will shower innumerable bonnets on his penniless bride, and the young and lively spouse will cheer the declining days of her aged partner with comic songs unceasing!

Aline. What a delightful prospect for him!

Alexis. But one thing remains to be done, that my happiness may be complete. We must drink the philtre ourselves, that I may be assured of your love for ever and ever.

Aline. Oh, Alexis, do you doubt me? Is it necessary that such love as ours should be secured by artificial means? Oh, no, no, no!

Alexis. My dear Aline, time works terrible changes, and I want to place our love beyond the chance of change.

Aline. Alexis, it is already far beyond that chance. Have faith in me, for my love can never, never change!

Alexis. Then you absolutely refuse?

Aline. I do. If you cannot trust me, you have no right to love me—no right to be loved *by* me.

Alexis. Enough Aline, I shall know how to interpret this refusal.

BALLAD—ALEXIS

Thou hast the power thy vaunted love
To sanctify, all doubt above,
  Despite the gathering shade:
To make that love of thine so sure
That, come what may, it must endure
  Till time itself shall fade.
    Thy love is but a flower
    That fades within the hour!
    If such thy love, oh, shame!
    Call it by other name—
      It is not love!
Thine is the power and thine alone,
To place me on so proud a throne
  That kings might envy me!
A priceless throne of love untold,

More rare than orient pearl and gold.
  But no! Thou wouldst be free!
    Such love is like the ray
    That dies within the day:
    If such thy love, oh, shame!
    Call it by other name—
      It is not love!

Enter DR. DALY

Dr. D. (*musing*). It is singular—it is very singular. It has overthrown all my calculations. It is distinctly opposed to the doctrine of averages. I cannot understand it.

Aline. Dear Dr. Daly, what has puzzled you?

Dr. D. My dear, this village has not hitherto been addicted to marrying and giving in marriage. Hitherto the youths of this village have not been enterprising, and the maidens have been distinctly coy. Judge then of my surprise when I tell you that the whole village came to me in a body just now, and implored me to join them in matrimony with as little delay as possible. Even your excellent father has hinted to me that before very long it is not unlikely that he also may change his condition.

Aline. Oh, Alexis—do you hear that? Are you not delighted?

Alexis. Yes. I confess that a union between your mother and my father would be a happy circumstance indeed. (*Crossing to* DR. DALY.) My dear sir—the news that you bring us is very gratifying.

Dr. D. Yes—still in my eyes, it has its melancholy side. This universal marrying recalls the happy days—now, alas, gone for ever—when I myself might have—but tush! I am puling. I am too old to marry—and yet, within the last half-hour, I have greatly yearned for companionship. I never remarked it before, but the young maidens of this village are very comely. So likewise are the middle-aged. Also the elderly. All are comely—and (*with a deep sigh*) all are engaged!

Aline. Here comes your father.

Enter SIR MARMADUKE *with* MRS. PARTLET, *arm-in-arm*

Aline and Alexis (*aside*). Mrs. Partlet!

Sir M. Dr. Daly, give me joy. Alexis, my dear boy, you will, I am sure, be pleased to hear that my declining days are not unlikely to be solaced by the companionship of this good, virtuous, and amiable woman.

Alexis (*rather taken aback*). My dear father, this is not altogether what I expected. I am certainly taken somewhat by surprise. Still it can hardly be necessary to assure you that any wife of yours is a mother of mine. (*Aside to* ALINE.) It is not quite what I could have wished.

Mrs. P. (*crossing to* ALEXIS). Oh, sir, I entreat your forgiveness. I am aware that socially I am not everything that could be desired, nor am I blessed with an abundance of worldly goods, but I can at least confer on your estimable father the great and priceless dowry of a true, tender, and lovin' 'art!

Alexis (*coldly*). I do not question it. After all, a faithful love is the true source of every earthly joy.

Sir M. I knew that my boy would not blame his poor father for acting on the impulse of a heart that has never yet misled him. Zorah is not perhaps what the world calls beautiful—

Dr. D. Still she is comely—distinctly comely. (*Sighs.*)

Aline. Zorah is very good, and very clean, and honest, and quite, quite sober in her habits: and that is worth far more than beauty, dear Sir Marmaduke.

Dr. D. Yes; beauty will fade and perish, but personal cleanliness is practically undying, for it can be renewed whenever it discovers symptoms of decay. My dear Sir Marmaduke, I heartily congratulate you. (*Sighs.*)

QUINTETTE
ALEXIS, ALINE, SIR MARMADUKE, ZORAH, *and*
DR. DALY

Alexis
I rejoice that it's decided,
    Happy now will be his life,
For my father is provided
    With a true and tender wife.

ENSEMBLE
She will tend him, nurse him, mend him,
    Air his linen, dry his tears;
Bless the thoughtful fates that send him
    Such a wife to soothe his years!

Aline
No young giddy thoughtless maiden,
    Full of graces, airs, and jeers—
But a sober widow, laden

With the weight of fifty years!

Sir Marmaduke
No high-born exacting beauty,
    Blazing like a jewelled sun—
But a wife who'll do her duty,
    As that duty should be done!

Mrs. Partlet
I'm no saucy minx and giddy—
    Hussies such as them abound—
But a clean and tidy widdy
    Well be-known for miles around!

Dr. Daly
All the village now have mated,
    All are happy as can be—
I to live alone am fated:
    No one's left to marry me!

ENSEMBLE
She will tend him, etc.
[*Exeunt* SIR MARMADUKE, MRS. PARTLET, *and* ALINE, *with* ALEXIS. DR. DALY *looks after them sentimentally, then exit with a sigh.*

Enter MR. WELLS
RECITATIVE—MR. WELLS
Oh, I have wrought much evil with my spells!
    And ill I can't undo!
This is too bad of you, J. W. Wells—
    What wrong have they done you?
And see—another love-lorn lady comes—
    Alas, poor stricken dame!
A gentle pensiveness her life benumbs—
    And mine, alone, the blame!

LADY SANGAZURE *enters. She is very melancholy*
Lady Sangazure
Alas, ah me! and well-a-day!
    I sigh for love, and well I may,
    For I am very old and grey.
        But stay!
(*Sees* MR. WELLS, *and becomes fascinated by him.*)

RECITATIVE
Lady Sangazure
What is this fairy form I see before me?
Mr. Wells
Oh, horrible!—she's going to adore me!
This last catastrophe is overpowering!
Lady Sangazure
Why do you glare at one with visage lowering?
For pity's sake recoil not thus from me!
Mr. Wells
My lady, leave me—this may never be!

DUET—LADY SANGAZURE *and* MR. WELLS
Mr. Wells
Hate me! I drop my H's—have through
life!
Lady Sangazure
Love me! I'll drop them too!
Mr. Wells
Hate me! I always eat peas with a knife!
Lady Sangazure
Love me! I'll eat like you!
Mr. Wells
Hate me! I spend the day at Rosherville!
Lady Sangazure
Love me! that joy I'll share!
Mr. Wells
Hate me! I often roll down One Tree Hill!
Lady Sangazure
Love me! I'll join you there!

Lady Sangazure
Love me! my prejudices I will drop!
Mr. Wells
Hate me! that's not enough!
Lady Sangazure
Love me! I'll come and help you in the
shop!
Mr. Wells
Hate me! the life is rough!
Lady Sangazure
Love me! my grammar I will all forswear!

Mr. Wells
Hate me! abjure my lot!
Lady Sangazure
Love me! I'll stick sunflowers in my hair!
Mr. Wells
Hate me! they'll suit you not!

RECITATIVE—MR. WELLS

At what I am going to say be not en-
raged—
I may not love you—for I am engaged!
Lady Sangazure (*horrified*)
Engaged!

Mr. Wells
Engaged!
To a maiden fair,
With bright brown hair,
And a sweet and simple smile,
Who waits for me
By the sounding sea,
On a South Pacific isle.
Mr. Wells (*aside*)
A lie! No maiden waits me there!
Lady Sangazure (*mournfully*)
She has bright brown hair;
Mr. Wells (*aside*)
A lie! No maiden smiles on me!
Lady Sangazure (*mournfully*)
By the sounding sea!

ENSEMBLE

Lady Sangazure
Oh, agony, rage, despair!
The maiden has bright brown hair,
And mine is as white as snow!
False man, it will be your fault,
If I go to my family vault,
And bury my life-long woe!

Both
The family vault—the family vault.
It will certainly be $\left\{ \begin{array}{l} \text{your} \\ \text{my} \end{array} \right\}$ fault.

If $\left\{ \begin{array}{l} \text{I go} \\ \text{she goes} \end{array} \right\}$ to $\left\{ \begin{array}{l} \text{my} \\ \text{her} \end{array} \right\}$ family vault,

To bury $\left\{ \begin{array}{l} \text{my} \\ \text{her} \end{array} \right\}$ life-long woe!

[*Exit* LADY SANGAZURE, *in great anguish,
accompanied by* MR. WELLS.
Enter ALINE, RECITATIVE
Alexis! Doubt me not, my loved one! See,
Thine uttered will is sovereign law to me!

Mr. Wells
Oh, agony, rage, despair!
Oh, where will this end—oh, where?
I should like very much to know!
It will certainly be my fault,
If she goes to her family vault,
To bury her life-long woe!

All fear—all thought of ill I cast away!
It is my darling's will, and I obey!
(*She drinks the philtre.*)
The fearful deed is done,
My love is near!
I go to meet my own
In trembling fear!
If o'er us aught of ill
Should cast a shade,
It was my darling's will,
And I obeyed!

[*As* ALINE *is going off, she meets* DR. DALY,
entering pensively. He is playing on

a flageolet. Under the influence of the spell she at once becomes strangely fascinated by him, and exhibits every symptom of being hopelessly in love with him.

SONG—DR. DALY

Oh, my voice is sad and low
And with timid step I go—
For with load of love o'erladen
I enquire of every maiden,
"Will you wed me, little lady?
Will you share my cottage shady?"
Little lady answers "No!
Thank you for your kindly proffer—
Good your heart, and full your coffer;
Yet I must decline your offer—
I'm engaged to So-and-so!"
So-and-so!
So-and-so! *(flageolet solo)*
She's engaged to So-and-so!
What a rogue young hearts to pillage;
What a worker on Love's tillage!
Every maiden in the village
Is engaged to So-and-so!
So-and-so!
So-and-so! *(flageolet solo)*
All engaged to So-and-so!

[*At the end of the song* DR. DALY *sees* ALINE, *and under the influence of the potion, falls in love with her.*

ENSEMBLE—ALINE *and* DR. DALY

Oh, joyous boon! oh, mad delight;
Oh, sun and moon! oh, day and night!
Rejoice, rejoice with me!
Proclaim our joy, ye birds above—
Yet brooklets, murmur forth our love,
In choral ecstasy:

Aline

Oh, joyous boon!

Dr. Daly

Oh, mad delight!

Aline

Oh, sun and moon!

Dr. Daly

Oh, day and night!

Both

Ye birds, and brooks, and fruitful trees,
With choral joy delight the breeze—
Rejoice, rejoice with me!

Enter ALEXIS
Alexis (with rapture)

Aline, my only love, my happiness!
The philtre—you have tasted it?

Aline (with confusion)

Yes! Yes!

Alexis

Oh, joy, mine, mine for ever, and for aye!
(Embraces her.)

Aline

Alexis, don't do that—you must not!
(DR. DALY *interposes between them*)

Alexis (amazed)

Why?

DUET—ALINE *and* DR. DALY

Aline

Alas! that lovers thus should meet:
Oh, pity, pity me!
Oh, charge me not with cold deceit;
Oh, pity, pity me!
You bade me drink—with trembling awe
I drank, and, by the potion's law,
I loved the very first I saw!
Oh, pity, pity me!

Dr. Daly

My dear young friend, consolèd be—
We pity, pity you.
In this I'm not an agent free—
We pity, pity you.
Some most extraordinary spell
O'er us has cast its magic fell—
The consequence I need not tell.
We pity, pity you.

ENSEMBLE

Some most extraordinary spell
O'er $\left\{\begin{array}{c}\text{us}\\\text{them}\end{array}\right\}$ has cast its magic fell—

The consequence $\left\{\begin{array}{c}\text{we}\\\text{they}\end{array}\right\}$ need not tell.

$\left.\begin{array}{c}\text{We}\\\text{They}\end{array}\right\}$ pity, pity $\left\{\begin{array}{c}\text{thee!}\\\text{me.}\end{array}\right.$

Alexis (furiously)

False one, begone—I spurn thee,
To thy new lover turn thee!
Thy perfidy all men shall know.

Aline (wildly)

I could not help it!

Alexis (calling off)

Come one, come all!

Dr. Daly

We could not help it!

Alexis (calling off)

Obey my call!

Aline (wildly)

I could not help it!

Alexis (calling off)

Come hither, run!

Dr. Daly
We could not help it!
Alexis (calling off)
Come, every one!
Enter all the characters except LADY SAN-
GAZURE *and* MR. WELLS
Chorus
Oh, what is the matter, and what is the
    clatter?
    He's glowering at her, and threatens a
    blow!
Oh, why does he batter the girl he did
    flatter?
And why does the latter recoil from him
    so?

RECITATIVE—ALEXIS
Prepare for sad surprises—
My love Aline despises!
No thought of sorrow shames her—
Another lover claims her!
Be his, false girl, for better or for worse—
But, ere you leave me, may a lover's
    curse——
Dr. D. (coming forward). Hold! Be just.
This poor child drank the philtre at your
instance. She hurried off to meet you—but,
most unhappily, she met me instead. As
you had administered the potion to both
of us, the result was inevitable. But fear
nothing from me—I will be no man's rival.
I shall quit the country at once—and bury
my sorrow in the congenial gloom of a
Colonial Bishopric.
Alexis. My excellent old friend! *(Taking
his hand—then turning to* MR. WELLS, *who
has entered with* LADY SANGAZURE.) Oh, Mr.
Wells, what, what is to be done?
Mr. W. I do not know—and yet—there
is one means by which this spell may be
removed.
Alexis. Name it—oh, name it!
Mr. W. Or you or I must yield up his
life to Ahrimanes. I would rather it were
you. I should have no hesitation in sacrific-
ing my own life to spare yours, but we take
stock next week, and it would not be fair
on the Co.
Alexis. True. Well, I am ready!
Aline. No, no—Alexis—it must not be!
Mr. Wells, if he must die that all may be
restored to their old loves, what is to
become of me? I should be left out in the
cold, with no love to be restored to!
Mr. W. True—I did not think of that.

(To the others.) My friends, I appeal to
you, and I will leave the decision in your
hands.

FINALE
Mr. Wells
Or I or he
    Must die!
Which shall it be?
    Reply!
            Sir Marmaduke
Die thou!
    Thou art the cause of all offending
                    Dr. Daly
Die thou!
    Yield thou to this decree unbending
                    All
Die thou!
                Mr. Wells
So be it! I submit! My fate is sealed.
To public execration thus I yield!
            (Falls on trap.)
Be happy all—leave me to my despair—
I go—it matters not with whom—or
    where!
                (Gong.)
[*All quit their present partners, and rejoin
    their old lovers.* SIR MARMADUKE *leaves*
    MRS. PARTLET, *and goes to* LADY SAN-
    GAZURE. ALINE *leaves* DR. DALY, *and goes
    to* ALEXIS. DR. DALY *leaves* ALINE, *and
    goes to* CONSTANCE. NOTARY *leaves* CON-
    STANCE, *and goes to* MRS. PARTLET. *All
    the* CHORUS *make a corresponding
    change.*

                All
                Gentlemen
Oh, my adored one!
                Ladies
Unmingled joy!
                Gentlemen
Ecstatic rapture!
                Ladies
Beloved boy!
            (They embrace.)
                Sir Marmaduke
Come to my mansion, all of you! At least
We'll crown our rapture with another feast!
            ENSEMBLE
SIR MARMADUKE, LADY SANGAZURE, ALEXIS
            and ALINE
Now to the banquet we press—
    Now for the eggs and the ham—
Now for the mustard and cress—
    Now for the strawberry jam!

Chorus
Now to the banquet, etc.

DR. DALY, CONSTANCE, NOTARY, *and* MRS.

PARTLET

Now for the tea of our host—
Now for the rollicking bun—

Now for the muffin and toast—
Now for the gay Sally Lunn!
Chorus
Now for the tea, etc.
(General Dance.)
[*During the symphony* MR. WELLS *sinks through trap, amid red fire.*

CURTAIN

TRIAL BY JURY

DRAMATIS PERSONÆ

THE LEARNED JUDGE

THE PLAINTIFF

THE DEFENDANT

COUNSEL FOR THE PLAINTIFF

USHER

FOREMAN OF THE JURY

ASSOCIATE

FIRST BRIDESMAID

First produced at the Royalty Theatre, March 25, 1875

SCENE.—*A Court of Justice. Barristers, Attorneys, and Jurymen discovered.*
Chorus

Hark, the hour of ten is sounding:
Hearts with anxious fears are bounding,
Hall of Justice crowds surrounding,
  Breathing hope and fear—
For to-day in this arena,
Summoned by a stern subpœna,
Edwin, sued by Angelina,
  Shortly will appear.
Enter USHER
SOLO—USHER

Now, Jurymen, hear my advice—
All kinds of vulgar prejudice
  I pray you set aside:
With stern judicial frame of mind
From bias free of every kind,
  This trial must be tried.
Chorus

From bias free of every kind,
This trial must be tried.
[*During Chorus,* USHER *sings fortissimo,*
  "Silence in Court!"
Usher

Oh, listen to the plaintiff's case:
Observe the features of her face—
  The broken-hearted bride.
Condole with her distress of mind:
From bias free of every kind,
  This trial must be tried!
Chorus
  From bias free, etc.
Usher

And when amid the plaintiff's shrieks,
The ruffianly defendant speaks—
  Upon the other side;
What *he* may say you needn't mind—

From bias free of every kind,
  This trial must be tried!
Chorus
  From bias free, etc.
Enter DEFENDANT
RECIT—DEFENDANT

Is this the Court of the Exchequer?
All

It is!

Defendant (*aside*)
Be firm, be firm, my pecker,
Your evil star's in the ascendant!
All

Who are you?
Defendant

I'm the Defendant!
CHORUS OF JURYMEN (*shaking their fists*)
  Monster, dread our damages.
    We're the jury,
    Dread our fury!
Defendant

Hear me, hear me, if you please,
  These are very strange proceedings—
For permit me to remark
  On the merits of my pleadings,
You're at present in the dark.
[DEFENDANT *beckons to* JURYMEN—*they*
  leave the box and gather round him
  as they sing the following:
That's a very true remark—
  On the merits of his pleadings
We're at the present in the dark!
Ha! ha!—ha! ha!
SONG—DEFENDANT

When first my old, old love I knew,
  My bosom welled with joy;
My riches at her feet I threw—
  I was a love-sick boy!

No terms seemed too extravagant
　　Upon her to employ—
I used to mope, and sigh, and pant,
　　Just like a love-sick boy!
　　　　　Tink-a-Tank—Tink-a-Tank.
But joy incessant palls the sense;
　　And love, unchanged, will cloy,
And she became a bore intense
　　Unto her love-sick boy!
With fitful glimmer burnt my flame,
　　And I grew cold and coy,
At last, one morning, I became
　　Another's love-sick boy.
　　　　　Tink-a-Tank—Tink-a-Tank.

CHORUS OF JURYMEN (*advancing stealthily*)
Oh, I was like that when a lad!
　　A shocking young scamp of a rover,
I behaved like a regular cad;
　　But that sort of thing is all over.
I'm now a respectable chap
　　And shine with a virtue resplendent
And, therefore, I haven't a scrap
　　Of sympathy with the defendant!
　　　　He shall treat us with awe,
　　　　If there isn't a flaw,
Singing so merrily—Trial-la-law!
Trial-la-law—Trial-la-law!
Singing so merrily—Trial-la-law!
　　　　　[They enter the Jury-box.
　　RECIT—USHER (*on Bench*)
Silence in Court, and all attention lend.
Behold your Judge! In due submission
　　bend!
　　　Enter JUDGE *on Bench*
　　　　Chorus
　　All hail great Judge!
　　　To your bright rays
　　We never grudge
　　　Ecstatic praise.
　　　　All hail!
　　May each decree
　　　As statute rank
　　And never be
　　　Reversed in banc.
　　　　All hail!

　　　RECIT—JUDGE

For these kind words accept my thanks,
　　I pray.
A Breach of Promise we've to try to-day.
But firstly, if the time you'll not begrudge,
I'll tell you how I came to be a Judge.
　　　　All
He'll tell us how he came to be a Judge!

　　　SONG—JUDGE
When I, good friends, was called to the bar,
　　I'd an appetite fresh and hearty,
But I was, as many young barristers are,
　　An impecunious party.
I'd a swallow-tail coat of a beautiful blue—
　　A brief which I bought of a booby—
A couple of shirts and a collar or two,
　　And a ring that looked like a ruby!
　　　　Chorus
　　A couple of shirts, etc.
　　　　Judge
In Westminster Hall I danced a dance,
　　Like a semi-despondent fury;
For I thought I should never hit on a
　　chance
　　Of addressing a British Jury—
But I soon got tired of third-class journeys,
　　And dinners of bread and water;
So I fell in love with a rich attorney's
　　Elderly, ugly daughter.
　　　　Chorus
　　So he fell in love, etc.
　　　　Judge
The rich attorney, he jumped with joy,
　　And replied to my fond professions:
"You shall reap the reward of your pluck,
　　my boy
At the Bailey and Middlesex Sessions.
You'll soon get used to her looks," said he,
　　"And a very nice girl you'll find her!
She may very well pass for forty-three
　　In the dusk, with a light behind her!"
　　　　Chorus
　　She may very well, etc.
　　　　Judge
The rich attorney was good as his word;
　　The briefs came trooping gaily,
And every day my voice was heard
　　At the Sessions of Ancient Bailey.
All thieves who could my fees afford
　　Relied on my orations,
And many a burglar I've restored
　　To his friends and his relations.

　　　　Chorus
　　And many a burglar, etc.
　　　　Judge
At length I became as rich as the Gurneys—
　　An incubus then I thought her,
So I threw over that rich attorney's
　　Elderly, ugly daughter.
The rich attorney my character high
　　Tried vainly to disparage—
And now, if you please, I'm ready to try

This Breach of Promise of Marriage!
Chorus
And now if you please, etc.
Judge
For now I am a Judge!
All
And a good Judge too.
Judge
Yes, now I am a Judge!
All
And a good Judge too!
Judge
Though all my law is fudge,
Yet I'll never, never budge,
But I'll live and die a Judge!
All
And a good Judge too!
Judge (pianissimo)
It was managed by a job—
All
And a good job too!
Judge
It was managed by a job!
All
And a good job too!
Judge
It is patent to the mob,
That my being made a nob
Was effected by a job.

All
And a good job too!
Enter COUNSEL *for* PLAINTIFF. *He takes his
place in front row of Counsels' seats*

RECIT—COUNSEL
Swear thou the Jury!
Usher
Kneel, Jurymen, oh, kneel!
[*All the* JURY *kneel in the Jury-box, and so
are hidden from audience.*
Usher
Oh, will you swear by yonder skies,
Whatever question may arise,
'Twixt rich and poor, 'twixt low and high,
That you will well and truly try?
JURY (*raising their hands, which alone are
visible*)
To all of this we make reply
By the dull slate of yonder sky:
That we will well and truly try.
(*All rise with the last note*)

RECIT—COUNSEL
Where is the Plaintiff?
Let her now be brought.

RECIT—USHER
Oh, Angelina! Come thou into Court!
Angelina! Angelina!!
Enter the BRIDESMAIDS
CHORUS OF BRIDESMAIDS
Comes the broken flower—
Comes the cheated maid—
Though the tempest lower,
Rain and cloud will fade.
Take, oh take these posies:
Though thy beauty rare
Shame the blushing roses,
They are passing fair!
Wear the flowers till they fade
Happy be thy life, oh maid!
[*The* JUDGE, *having taken a great fancy to*
FIRST BRIDESMAID, *sends her a note by*
USHER, *which she reads, kisses rap-
turously, and places in her bosom.*
Enter PLAINTIFF
SOLO—PLAINTIFF
O'er the season vernal,
Time may cast a shade;
Sunshine, if eternal,
Makes the roses fade!
Time may do his duty;
Let the thief alone—
Winter hath a beauty,
That is all his own.
Fairest days are sun and shade:
I am no unhappy maid!
[*The* JUDGE *having by this time transferred
his admiration to* PLAINTIFF, *directs the*
USHER *to take the note from* FIRST
BRIDESMAID *and hand it to* PLAINTIFF
*who reads it, kisses it rapturously, and
places it in her bosom.*
CHORUS OF BRIDESMAIDS
Comes the broken flower, etc.
Judge
Oh, never, never, never, since I joined the
human race,
Saw I so exquisitely fair a face.
The Jury (*shaking their forefingers at
him*). Ah, sly dog! Ah, sly dog!
Judge (to JURY). How say you? Is she
not designed for capture?
Foreman (*after consulting with the*
JURY). We've but one word, my lord, and
that is—Rapture.
Plaintiff (*curtseying*). Your kindness
gentleman, quite overpowers!
Jury. We love you fondly and would
make you ours!

THE BRIDESMAIDS (*shaking their forefingers at* JURY)
Ah, sly dogs! Ah, sly dogs!
RECIT—COUNSEL *for* PLAINTIFF
May it please you, my lud!
Gentlemen of the jury!
Aria
With a sense of deep emotion,
I approach this painful case;
For I never had a notion
That a man could be so base,
Or deceive a girl confiding,
Vows, *etcetera*, deriding.
All
He deceived a girl confiding,
Vows, *etcetera*, deriding.
PLAINTIFF *falls sobbing on* COUNSEL'S
breast and remains there.
Counsel
See my interesting client,
Victim of a heartless wile!
See the traitor all defiant
Wear a supercilious smile!
Sweetly smiled my client on him,
Coyly woo'd and gently won him.
All
Sweetly smiled, etc.
Counsel
Swiftly fled each honeyed hour
Spent with this unmanly male!
Camberwell became a bower,
Peckham an Arcadian Vale,
Breathing concentrated otto!—
An existence *à la* Watteau.
All
Bless us, concentrated otto! etc.
Counsel
Picture, then, my client naming,
And insisting on the day:
Picture him excuses framing—
Going from her far away;
Doubly criminal to do so,
For the maid had bought her *trousseau!*
All
Doubly criminal, etc.
Counsel (*to* PLAINTIFF, *who weeps*)
Cheer up, my pretty—oh, cheer up!
Jury
Cheer up, cheer up, we love you!
COUNSEL *leads* PLAINTIFF *fondly into Witness-box; he takes a tender leave of her, and resumes his place in Court.*
(PLAINTIFF *reels as if about to faint*)

Judge
That she is reeling
Is plain to see!
Foreman
If faint you're feeling
Recline on me!
[*She falls sobbing on the* FOREMAN'S *breast.*
Plaintiff (*feebly*)
I shall recover
If left alone.
All (*shaking their fists at* DEFENDANT)
Oh, perjured lover,
Atone! atone!
Foreman
Just like a father
I wish to be.
[*Kissing her.*
Judge (*approaching her*)
Or, if you'd rather,
Recline on me!
[*She jumps on to Bench, sits down by the* JUDGE, *and falls sobbing on his breast.*
Counsel
Oh! fetch some water
From far Cologne!
All
For this sad slaughter
Atone! atone!
Jury (*shaking fists at* DEFENDANT)
Monster, monster, dread our fury—
There's the Judge, and we're the Jury!
Come! Substantial damages,
Dam—
Usher
Silence in Court!
SONG—DEFENDANT
Oh, gentlemen, listen, I pray,
Though I own that my heart has been ranging,
Of nature the laws I obey,
For nature is constantly changing.
The moon in her phases is found,
The time and the wind and the weather,
The months in succession come round,
And you don't find two Mondays together.
Consider the moral, I pray,
Nor bring a young fellow to sorrow,
Who loves this young lady to-day,
And loves that young lady to-morrow.
Bridesmaids (*rushing forward, and kneeling to* JURY)
Consider the moral, etc.

Defendant

You cannot eat breakfast all day,
　Nor is it the act of a sinner,
When breakfast is taken away,
　To turn your attention to dinner;
And it's not in the range of belief,
　That you could hold him as a glutton,
Who, when he is tired of beef,
　Determines to tackle the mutton.
　　But this I am willing to say,
　　　If it will appease her sorrow,
　　I'll marry this lady to-day,
　　　And I'll marry that lady to-morrow!
Bridesmaids (*rushing forward as before*)
　　But this he is willing to say, etc.

RECIT—JUDGE

That seems a reasonable proposition,
To which, I think, your client may agree.
Counsel
But, I submit, my lord, with all submis-
　　sion,
To marry two at once is Burglaree!
　　　　[*Referring to law book.*
In the reign of James the Second,
It was generally reckoned
As a very serious crime
To marry two wives at one time.
[*Hands book up to* JUDGE, *who reads it.*
All
　　Oh, man of learning!
QUARTETTE
Judge
A nice dilemma we have here,
That calls for all our wit:
Counsel
And at this stage, it don't appear
That we can settle it.
Defendant (*in Witness-box*)
If I to wed the girl am loth
A breach 'twill surely be—
Plaintiff
And if he goes and marries both,
It counts as Burglaree!
All
　A nice dilemma, etc.
DUET—PLAINTIFF *and* DEFENDANT
Plaintiff (*embracing him rapturously*)
I love him—I love him—with fervour un-
　ceasing
　I worship and madly adore;
My blind adoration is always increasing,
　My loss I shall ever deplore.
Oh, see what a blessing, what love and
　caressing

I've lost, and remember it, pray,
When you I'm addressing, are busy assess
　　ing
　The damages Edwin must pay!
　Defendant (*repelling her furiously*)
I smoke like a furnace—I'm always i
　liquor,
　A ruffian—a bully—a sot;
I'm sure I should thrash her, perhaps
　should kick her,
　I am such a very bad lot!
I'm not prepossessing, as you may b
　guessing,
　She couldn't endure me a day;
Recall my professing, when you are assess
　　ing
　The damages Edwin must pay!
[*She clings to him passionately; after*
　struggle, he throws her off into arms o
　COUNSEL.
　　　Jury
　We would be fairly acting,
　But this is most distracting!

RECIT—JUDGE

The question, gentlemen—is one of liquor
　You ask for guidance—this is my reply
He says, when tipsy, he would thrash an
　kick her,
　Let's make him tipsy, gentlemen, and try

Counsel
With all respect
I do object!
Plaintiff
I do object!
Defendant
I don't object!

All
With all respect
We do object!
Judge (*tossing his books and papers about*)
All the legal furies seize you!
No proposal seems to please you,
I can't stop up here all day,
I must shortly go away.
Barristers, and you, attorneys,
Set out on your homeward journeys;
Gentle, simple-minded Usher,
Get you, if you like, to Rus*her;*
Put your briefs upon the shelf,
I will marry her myself!
[*He comes down from Bench to floor o*
　Court. He embraces ANGELINA.

FINALE

Plaintiff

Oh, joy unbounded,
With wealth surrounded,
The knell is sounded
    Of grief and woe.

Counsel

With love devoted
On you he's doted
To castle moated
    Away they go.

Defendant

I wonder whether
They'll live together
In marriage tether
    In manner true?

Usher

It seems to me, sir,
Of such as she, sir,
    A judge is he, sir,
        And a good judge too.

Judge

Yes, I am a Judge.

All

And a good Judge too!

Judge

Yes, I am a Judge.

All

And a good Judge too!

Judge

Though homeward as you trudge,
You declare my law is fudge.
Yet of beauty I'm a judge.

All

And a good Judge too!

CURTAIN

RUDDIGORE

OR

THE WITCH'S CURSE

DRAMATIS PERSONÆ

MORTALS	GHOSTS
SIR RUTHVEN MURGATROYD (*disguised as Robin Oakapple, a Young Farmer*)	SIR RUPERT MURGATROYD (*the First Baronet*)
RICHARD DAUNTLESS (*his Foster-Brother—a Man-o'-war's-man*)	SIR JASPER MURGATROYD (*the Third Baronet*)
SIR DESPARD MURGATROYD, OF RUDDIGORE (*a Wicked Baronet*)	SIR LIONEL MURGATROYD (*the Sixth Baronet*)
OLD ADAM GOODHEART (*Robin's Faithful Servant*)	SIR CONRAD MURGATROYD (*the Twelfth Baronet*)
ROSE MAYBUD (*a Village Maiden*)	SIR DESMOND MURGATROYD (*the Sixteenth Baronet*)
MAD MARGARET	
DAME HANNAH (*Rose's Aunt*)	SIR GILBERT MURGATROYD (*the Eighteenth Baronet*)
ZORAH } RUTH } (*Professional Bridesmaids*)	SIR MERVYN MURGATROYD (*the Twentieth Baronet*)

AND

SIR RODERIC MURGATROYD
(*the Twenty-first Baronet*)

Chorus of Officers, Ancestors, Professional Bridesmaids, and Villagers.

ACT I

SCENE.—*The fishing village of Rederring (in Cornwall).*
ROSE MAYBUD'S *cottage is seen* L.
Enter Chorus of Bridesmaids. They range themselves in front of ROSE'S *cottage*
CHORUS OF BRIDESMAIDS
Fair is Rose as the bright May-day;
  Soft is Rose as the warm west-wind;
Sweet is Rose as the new-mown hay—
  Rose is the queen of maiden-kind!
    Rose, all glowing
      With virgin blushes, say—
    Is anybody going
      To marry you to-day?

SOLO—ZORAH
Every day, as the days roll on,
Bridesmaids' garb we gaily don,
Sure that a maid so fairly famed
Can't long remain unclaimed.
Hour by hour and day by day,
Several months have passed away,
Though she's the fairest flower that blows
No one has married Rose!

Chorus
Rose, all glowing
  With virgin blushes, say—
Is anybody going
  To marry you to-day?
Enter DAME HANNAH, *from cottage*

154

Hannah. Nay, gentle maidens, you sing well but vainly, for Rose is still heart-free, and looks but coldly upon her many suitors.

Zorah. It's very disappointing. Every young man in the village is in love with her, but they are appalled by her beauty and modesty, and won't declare themselves; so, until she makes her own choice, there's no chance for anybody else.

Ruth. This is, perhaps, the only village in the world that possesses an endowed corps of professional bridesmaids who are bound to be on duty every day from ten to four—and it is at least six months since our services were required. The pious charity by which we exist is practically wasted!

Zor. We shall be disendowed—that will be the end of it! Dame Hannah—you're a nice old person—*you* could marry if you liked. There's old Adam—Robin's faithful servant—he loves you with all the frenzy of a boy of fourteen.

Han. Nay—that may never be, for I am pledged!

All. To whom?

Han. To an eternal maidenhood! Many years ago I was betrothed to a god-like youth who woo'd me under an assumed name. But on the very day upon which our wedding was to have been celebrated, I discovered that he was no other than Sir Roderic Murgatroyd, one of the bad Baronets of Ruddigore, and the uncle of the man who now bears that title. As a son of that accursed race he was no husband for an honest girl, so, madly as I loved him, I left him then and there. He died but ten years since, but I never saw him again.

Zor. But why should you not marry a bad Baronet of Ruddigore?

Ruth. All baronets are bad; but was he worse than other baronets?

Han. My child, he was accursed.

Zor. But who cursed him? Not you, I trust!

Han. The curse is on all his line and has been, ever since the time of Sir Rupert, the first Baronet. Listen, and you shall hear the legend:

LEGEND—HANNAH

Sir Rupert Murgatroyd
His leisure and his riches

He ruthlessly employed
In persecuting witches.
With fear he'd make them quake—
He'd duck them in his lake—
  He'd break their bones
  With sticks and stones,
And burn them at the stake!
  Chorus
  This sport he much enjoyed,
  Did Rupert Murgatroyd—
    No sense of shame
    Or pity came
  To Rupert Murgatroyd!
Once, on the village green,
A palsied hag he roasted,
And what took place, I ween,
  Shook his composure boasted;
For, as the torture grim
Seized on each withered limb,
    The writhing dame
    Mid fire and flame
Yelled forth this curse on him:
"Each lord of Ruddigore,
  Despite his best endeavour,
Shall do one crime, or more,
  Once, every day, for ever!
This doom he can't defy,
However he may try,
    For should he stay
    His hand, that day
In torture he shall die!"
The prophecy came true:
Each heir who held the title
Had, every day, to do
  Some crime of import vital;
Until, with guilt o'erplied,
"I'll sin no more!" he cried,
    And on the day
    He said that say,
In agony he died!

  Chorus
And thus, with sinning cloyed,
Has died each Murgatroyd,
    And so shall fall,
    Both one and all,
Each coming Murgatroyd!
  [*Exeunt Chorus of Bridesmaids.*
Enter ROSE MAYBUD *from cottage, with
    small basket on her arm*

Han. Whither away, dear Rose? On some errand of charity, as is thy wont?

Rose. A few gifts, dear aunt, for deserving villagers. Lo, here is some peppermint rock for old gaffer Gadderby, a set of false teeth for pretty little Ruth Rowbottom, and a pound of snuff for the poor orphan girl on the hill.

Han. Ah, Rose, pity that so much goodness should not help to make some gallant youth happy for life! Rose, why dost thou harden that little heart of thine? Is there none hereaway whom thou couldst love?

Rose. And if there were such an one, verily it would ill become me to tell him so.

Han. Nay, dear one, where true love is, there is little need of prim formality.

Rose. Hush, dear aunt, for thy words pain me sorely. Hung in a plated dishcover to the knocker of the workhouse door, with naught that I could call mine own, save a change of baby-linen and a book of etiquette, little wonder if I have always regarded that work as a voice from a parent's tomb. This hallowed volume (*producing a book of etiquette*), composed, if I may believe the title-page, by no less an authority than the wife of a Lord Mayor, has been, through life, my guide and monitor. By its solemn precepts I have learnt to test the moral worth of all who approach me. The man who bites his bread, or eats peas with a knife, I look upon as a lost creature, and he who has not acquired the proper way of entering and leaving a room is the object of my pitying horror. There are those in this village who bite their nails, dear aunt, and nearly all are wont to use their pocket combs in public places. In truth I could pursue this painful theme much further, but behold, I have said enough.

Han. But is there not one among them who is faultless, in thine eyes? For example—young Robin. He combines the manners of a Marquis with the morals of a Methodist. Couldst thou not love *him?*

Rose. And even if I could, how should I confess it unto him? For lo, he is shy, and sayeth naught!

BALLAD—ROSE

If somebody there chanced to be
　Who loved me in a manner true,
My heart would point him out to me,
　And I would point him out to you.
　　　　(*Referring to book*)
But here it says of those who point—
Their manners must be out of joint—

You *may* not point—
You *must* not point—
It's manners out of joint, to point!
Had I the love of such as he,
　Some quiet spot he'd take me to,
Then he could whisper it to me,
　And I could whisper it to you.
　　　　(*Referring to book*)
But whispering, I've somewhere met,
Is contrary to etiquette:
　　　Where can it be? (*Searching book.*)
　　　Now let me see—(*Finding reference.*)
　　　　Yes, yes!
It's contrary to etiquette!
　　　(*Showing it to* HANNAH)
If any well-bred youth I knew,
　Polite and gentle, neat and trim,
Then I would hint as much to you,
　And you could hint as much to him.
　　　　(*Referring to book*)
But here it says, in plainest print,
"It's most unladylike to hint"—
You *may* not hint,
You *must* not hint—
It says you mustn't hint, in print!
And if I loved him through and through—
(True love and not a passing whim),
Then I could speak of it to you,
　And you could speak of it to him.
　　　　(*Referring to book*)
But here I find it doesn't do
To speak until you're spoken to.
　　　Where can it be? (*Searching book.*)
　　　Now let me see—(*Finding reference.*)
　　　　Yes, yes!
"Don't speak until you're spoken to!"
　　　　　[*Exit* HANNAH.

Rose. Poor aunt! Little did the good soul think, when she breathed the hallowed name of Robin, that he would do even as well as another. But he resembleth all the youths in this village, in that he is unduly bashful in my presence, and lo, it is hard to bring him to the point. But soft, he is here!

[ROSE *is about to go when* ROBIN *enters and calls her.*

Robin. Mistress Rose!
Rose. (*Surprised*). Master Robin!
Rob. I wish to say that—it is fine.
Rose. It is passing fine.
Rob. But we do want rain.
Rose. Aye, sorely! Is that all?
Rob. (*Sighing.*) That is all.

Rose. Good day, Master Robin!
Rob. Good day, Mistress Rose! (*Both oing—both stop.*)
Rose. } I crave pardon, I——
Rob. } I beg pardon, I——
Rose. You were about to say?——
Rob. I would fain consult you——
Rose. Truly?
Rob. It is about a friend.
Rose. In truth I have a friend myself.
Rob. Indeed? I mean, of course——
Rose. And I would fain consult you——
Rob. (*Anxiously.*) About him?
Rose. (*Prudishly*). About her.
Rob. (*Relieved.*) Let us consult one an-ther.

DUET—ROBIN *and* ROSE

Robin

know a youth who loves a little maid—
(Hey, but his face is a sight for to see!)
ilent is he, for he's modest and afraid—
(Hey, but he's timid as a youth can be!)

Rose

know a maid who loves a gallant youth,
(Hey, but she sickens as the days go by!)
She cannot tell him all the sad, sad truth—
(Hey, but I think that little maid will
die!)

Robin
Poor little man!
Rose
Poor little maid!
Robin
Poor little man!
Rose
Poor little maid!
Both
Now tell me pray, and tell me true,
What in the world should the { young man / maiden } do?

Robin

He cannot eat and he cannot sleep—
(Hey, but his face is a sight for to see!)
Daily he goes for to wail—for to weep——
(Hey, but he's wretched as a youth can
be!)

Rose

She's very thin and she's very pale—
(Hey, but she sickens as the days go by!)
Daily she goes for to weep—for to wail—
(Hey, but I think that little maid will
die!)

Robin
Poor iittle maid!
Rose
Poor little man!
Robin
Poor little maid!
Rose
Poor little man!
Both
Now tell me pray, and tell me true,
What in the world should the { young man / maiden } do?

Rose
If I were the youth I should offer her my
name—
(Hey, but her face is a sight for to see!)
Robin
If I were the maid I should fan his honest
flame—
(Hey, but he's bashful as a youth can
be!)
Rose
If I were the youth I should speak to her
to-day—
(Hey, but she sickens as the days go by!)
Robin
If I were the maid I should meet the lad
half way—
(For I really do believe that timid youth
will die!)
Rose
Poor little man!
Robin
Poor little maid!
Rose
Poor little man!
Robin
Poor little maid!

Both
I thank you, { miss, / sir, } for your counsel true;
I'll tell that { youth / maid } what { he / she } ought to do!

[*Exit* ROSE.

Rob. Poor child! I sometimes think that
if she wasn't quite so particular I might
venture—but no, no—even then I should
be unworthy of her!
He sits desponding. Enter OLD ADAM
Adam. My kind master is sad! Dear Sir
Ruthven Murgatroyd——
Rob. Hush! As you love me, breathe
not that hated name. Twenty years ago,

in horror at the prospect of inheriting that hideous title, and with it the ban that compels all who succeed to the baronetcy to commit at least one deadly crime per day, for life, I fled my home, and concealed myself in this innocent village under the name of Robin Oakapple. My younger brother, Despard, believing me to be dead, succeeded to the title and its attendant curse. For twenty years I have been dead and buried. Don't dig me up now.

Adam. Dear master, it shall be as you wish, for have I not sworn to obey you for ever in all things? Yet, as we are here alone, and as I belong to that particular description of good old man to whom the the truth is a refreshing novelty, let me call you by your own right title once more! (ROBIN *assents.*) Sir Ruthven Murgatroyd! Baronet! Of Ruddigore! Whew! It's like eight hours at the seaside!

Rob. My poor old friend! Would there were more like you!

Adam. Would there were indeed! But I bring you good tidings. Your foster-brother, Richard, has returned from sea—his ship the *Tom-Tit* rides yonder at anchor, and he himself is even now in this very village!

Rob. My beloved foster-brother? No, no—it cannot be!

Adam. It is even so—and see, he comes this way!

[*Exeunt together.*
Enter Chorus of Bridesmaids

Chorus

From the briny sea
  Comes young Richard, all victorious!
Valorous is he—
  His achievements all are glorious!
Let the welkin ring
With the news we bring
    Sing it—shout it—
    Tell about it—
Safe and sound returneth he,
All victorious from the sea!
Enter RICHARD. *The girls welcome him as he greets old acquaintances.*
BALLAD—RICHARD

I shipped, d'ye see, in a Revenue sloop,
  And, off Cape Finistere,
    A merchantman we see,
    A Frenchman, going free,

So we made for the bold Mounseer,
      D'ye see?
  We made for the bold Mounseer.
But she proved to be a Frigate—and she
      up with her ports,
  And fires with a thirty-two!
    It come uncommon near,
    But we answered with a cheer,
  Which paralysed the Parley-voo,
      D'ye see?
  Which paralysed the Parley-voo!
Then our Captain he up and he says, says
      he,
  "That chap we need not fear,—
    We can take her, if we like,
    She is sartin for to strike,
  For she's only a darned Mounseer,
      D'ye see?
  She's only a darned Mounseer!
But to fight a French fal-lal—it's like
      hittin' of a gal—
    It's a lubberly thing for to do;
    For we, with our faults,
    Why, we're sturdy British salts,
  While she's only a Parley-voo,
      D'ye see?
  While she's only a Parley-voo!
So we up with our helm, and we scuds
      before the breeze
  As we gives a compassionating cheer;
    Froggee answers with a shout
    As he sees us go about,
  Which was grateful of the poor Mounseer,
      D'ye see?
  Which was grateful of the poor Mounseer!
And I'll wager in their joy they kissed each
      other's cheek
  (Which is what them furriners do),
    And they blessed their lucky stars
    We were hardy British tars
  Who had pity on a poor Parley-voo,
      D'ye see?
  Who had pity on a poor Parley-voo!
      (HORNPIPE)
        [*Exeunt* CHORUS.

Enter ROBIN

Rob. Richard!
Rich. Robin!
Rob. My beloved foster-brother, and very dearest friend, welcome home again after ten long years at sea! It is such deeds as yours that cause our flag to be loved

and dreaded throughout the civilized world!

Rich. Why, lord love ye, Rob, that's but a trifle to what we *have* done in the way of sparing life! I believe I may say, without exaggeration, that the marciful little *Tom-Tit* has spared more French frigates than any craft afloat! But 'taint for a British seaman to brag, so I'll just stow my jawin' tackle and belay. (ROBIN *sighs*.) But 'vast heavin', messmate, what's brought *you* all a-cockbill?

Rob. Alas, Dick, I love Rose Maybud, and love in vain!

Rich. *You* love in vain? Come, that's too good! Why, you're a fine strapping muscular young fellow—tall and strong as a to'-gall'n'-m'st—taut as a forestay—aye, and a barrowknight to boot, if all had their rights!

Rob. Hush, Richard—not a word about my true rank, which none here suspect. Yes, I know well enough that few men are better calculated to win a woman's heart than I. I'm a fine fellow, Dick, and worthy any woman's love—happy the girl who gets me, say I. But I'm timid, Dick; shy — nervous — modest — retiring — diffident — and I cannot tell her, Dick, I cannot tell her! Ah, you've no idea what a poor opinion I have of myself, and how little I deserve it.

Rich. Robin, do you call to mind how, years ago, we swore that, come what might, we would always act upon our hearts' dictates?

Rob. Aye, Dick, and I've always kept that oath. In doubt, difficulty, and danger I've always asked my heart what I should do, and it has never failed me.

Rich. Right! Let your heart be your compass, with a clear conscience for your binnacle light, and you'll sail ten knots on a bowline, clear of shoals, rocks, and quicksands! Well, now, what does my heart say in this here difficult situation? Why, it says, "Dick," it says—(it calls me Dick acos it's known me from a babby)—"Dick," it says, "*you* ain't shy—*you* ain't modest—speak you up for him as is!" Robin, my lad, just you lay me alongside, and when she's becalmed under my lee, I'll spin her a yarn that shall sarve to fish you two together for life!

Rob. Will you do this thing for me? Can you, do you think? Yes (*feeling his pulse*). There's no false modesty about *you.* Your —what I would call bumptious self-assertiveness (I mean the expression in its complimentary sense) has already made you a bos'n's mate, and it will make an admiral of you in time, if you work it properly, you dear, incompetent old impostor! My dear fellow, I'd give my right arm for one tenth of your modest assurance!

SONG—ROBIN

My boy, you may take it from me,
That of all the afflictions accurst
   With which a man's saddled
   And hampered and addled,
A diffident nature's the worst.
Though clever as clever can be—
   A Crichton of early romance—
      You must stir it and stump it,
      And blow your own trumpet,
Or, trust me, you haven't a chance!
   If you wish in the world to advance,
   Your merits you're bound to enhance,
      You must stir it and stump it,
      And blow your own trumpet,
Or, trust me, you haven't a chance!
Now take, for example, *my* case:
   I've a bright intellectual brain—
      In all London city
      There's no one so witty—
   I've thought so again and again.
I've a highly intelligent face—
   My features cannot be denied—
      But, whatever I try, sir,
      I fail in—and why, sir?
I'm modesty personified!
   If you wish in the world to advance,
   etc.
As a poet, I'm tender and quaint—
   I've passion and fervour and grace—
      From Ovid and Horace
      To Swinburne and Morris,
They all of them take a back place.
Then I sing and I play and I paint:
   Though none are accomplished as I,
      To say so were treason:
      You ask me the reason?
I'm diffident, modest, and shy!
   If you wish in the world to advance,
   etc.

                [*Exit* ROBIN.

Rich. (*looking after him*). Ah, it's a

thousand pities he's such a poor opinion of himself, for a finer fellow don't walk! Well, I'll do my best for him. "Plead for him as though it was for your own father" —that's what my heart's a-remarkin' to me just now. But here she comes! Steady! Steady it is! (*Enter* ROSE—*he is much struck by her*.) By the Port Admiral, but she's a tight little craft! Come, come, she's not for you, Dick, and yet—she's fit to marry Lord Nelson! By the Flag of Old England, I can't look at her unmoved.

Rose. Sir, you are agitated——

Rich. Aye, aye, my lass, well said! I am agitated, true enough!—took flat aback, my girl; but 'tis naught— 'twill pass. (*Aside.*) This here heart of mine's a-dictatin' to me like anything. Question is, Have I a right to disregard its promptings?

Rose. Can I do aught to relieve thine anguish, for it seemeth to me that thou art in sore trouble? This apple—(*offering a damaged apple.*)

Rich. (*looking at it and returning it*). No, my lass, 'taint that: I'm—I'm took flat aback—I never see anything like you in all my born days. Parbuckle me, if you ain't the loveliest gal I've ever set eyes on. There—I can't say fairer than that, can I?

Rose. No. (*Aside.*) The question is, Is it meet that an utter stranger should thus express himself? (*Refers to book.*) Yes— "Always speak the truth."

Rich. I'd no thoughts of sayin' this here to you on my own account, for, truth to tell, I was chartered by another; but when I see you my heart it up and it says, says it, "This is the very lass for *you*, Dick"— 'speak up to her, Dick," it says—it calls me Dick acos we was at school together)— "tell her all, Dick," it says, "never sail under false colours—it's mean!" *That's* what my heart tells me to say, and in my rough, common-sailor fashion, I've said it, and I'm a-waiting for your reply. I'm a-tremblin', miss. Lookye here—(*holding out his hand*). That's narvousness!

Rose (*aside*). Now, how should a maiden deal with such an one? (*Consults book.*) "Keep no one in unnecessary suspense." (*Aloud.*) Behold, I will not keep you in unnecessary suspense. (*Refers to book.*) "In accepting an offer of marriage, do so

with apparent hesitation." (*Aloud.*) I take you, but with a certain show of reluctance. (*Refers to book.*) "Avoid any appearance of eagerness." (*Aloud.*) Though you will bear in mind that I am far from anxious to do so. (*Refers to book.*) "A little show of emotion will not be misplaced!" (*Aloud.*) Pardon this tear! (*Wipes her eye.*)

Rich. Rose, you've made me the happiest blue-jacket in England! I wouldn't change places with the Admiral of the Fleet, no matter who he's a-huggin' of at this present moment! But, axin' your pardon, miss (*wiping his lips with his hand*), might I be permitted to salute the flag I'm goin' to sail under?

Rose (*referring to book*). "An engaged young lady should not permit too many familiarities." (*Aloud.*) Once! (RICHARD *kisses her*.)

DUET—RICHARD *and* ROSE

Richard

The battle's roar is over,
  O my love!
Embrace thy tender lover,
  O my love!
From tempests' welter,
  From war's alarms,
O give me shelter
  Within those arms!
Thy smile alluring,
All heart-ache curing,
Gives peace enduring,
  O my love!

Rose

If heart both true and tender,
  O my love!
A life-love can engender,
  O my love!
A truce to sighing
  And tears of brine,
For joy undying
  Shall aye be mine,
And thou and I, love,
Shall live and die, love,
Without a sigh, love—
  My own, my love!

Enter ROBIN, *with* CHORUS OF BRIDESMAID

Chorus

If well his suit has sped,
Oh, may they soon be wed!
Oh, tell us, tell us, pray,
What doth the maiden say?

In singing are we justified,
Hail the Bridegroom—hail the Bride!
Let the nuptial knot be tied:
  In fair phrases,
  Hymn their praises,
Hail the Bridegroom—hail the Bride!
Rob. Well—what news? Have you spoken to her?
Rich. Aye, my lad, I have—so to speak —spoke her.
Rob. And she refuses?
Rich. Why, no, I can't truly say she do.
Rob. Then she accepts! My darling! (*Embraces her.*)

Bridesmaids

Hail the Bridegroom—hail the Bride! etc.
Rose (*aside, referring to her book*). Now, what should a maiden do when she is embraced by the wrong gentleman?
Rich. Belay, my lad, belay. You don't understand.
Rose. Oh, sir, belay, I beseech you!
Rich. You see it's like this: she accepts —but it's *me!*
Rob. You! (RICHARD *embraces* ROSE.)

Bridesmaids

Hail the Bridegroom, hail the Bride!
When the nuptial knot is tied——
Rob. (*interrupting angrily*). Hold your tongues, will you! Now then, what does this mean?
Rich. My poor lad, my heart grives for thee, but it's like this: the moment I see her, and just as I was a-goin' to mention your name, my heart it up and it says, says it—"Dick, you've fell in love with her yourself," it says; "Be honest and sailor-like—don't skulk under false colours —speak up," it says, "take her, you dog, and with her my blessin'!"
Bridesmaids

Hail the Bridegroom—hail the Bride!——
Rob. Will you be quiet! Go away! (CHORUS *make faces at him and exeunt.*) Vulgar girls!
Rich. What could I do? I'm bound to obey my heart's dictates.
Rob. Of course—no doubt. It's quite right—I don't mind—that is, not particularly—only it's—it *is* disappointing, you know.
Rose (*to* ROBIN). Oh, but, sir, I knew not that thou didst seek me in wedlock, or in very truth I should not have hearkened

unto this man, for behold, he is but a lowly mariner, and very poor withal, whereas thou art a tiller of the land, and thou hast fat oxen, and many sheep and swine, a considerable dairy farm and much corn and oil!
Rich. That's true, my lass, but it's done now, ain't it, Rob?
Rose. Still it may be that I should not be happy in thy love. I am passing young and little able to judge. Moreover, as to thy character I know naught!
Rob. Nay, Rose, I'll answer for that. Dick has won thy love fairly. Brokenhearted as I am, I'll stand up for Dick through thick and thin!
Rich. (*with emotion*). Thankye messmate! that's well said. That's spoken honest. Thankye, Rob! (*Grasps his hand.*)
Rose. Yet methinks I have heard that sailors are but worldly men, and little prone to lead serious and thoughtful lives!
Rob. And what then? Admit that Dick is *not* a steady character, and that when he's excited he uses language that would make your hair curl. Grant that—he does. It's the truth, and I'm not going to deny it. But look at his *good* qualities. He's as nimble as a pony, and his hornpipe is the talk of the Fleet!
Rich. Thankye, Rob! That's well spoken. Thankye, Rob!
Rose. But it may be that he drinketh strong waters which do bemuse a man, and make him even as the wild beasts of the desert!
Rob. Well, suppose he does, and I don't say he don't, for rum's his bane, and ever has been. He *does* drink—I won't deny it. But what of that? Look at his arms— tattooed to the shoulder! (RICH. *rolls up his sleeves.*) No, no—I won't hear a word against Dick!
Rose. But they say that mariners are but rarely true to those whom they profess to love!
Rob. Granted—granted—and I don't say that Dick isn't as bad as any of 'em. (RICH. *chuckles.*) You are, you know you are, you dog! a devil of a fellow—a regular out-and-out Lothario! But what then? You can't have everything, and a better hand at turning-in a dead-eye don't walk a deck! And what an accomplishment *that*

is in a family man! No, no—not a word
against Dick. I'll stick up for him through
thick and thin!

Rich. Thankye, Rob, thankye. You're a
true friend. I've acted accordin' to my
heart's dictates, and such orders as them
no man should disobey.

ENSEMBLE—RICHARD, ROBIN, ROSE

In sailing o'er life's ocean wide
Your heart should be your only guide;
With summer sea and favouring wind,
Yourself in port you'll surely find.

SOLO—RICHARD

My heart says, "To this maiden strike—
She's captured you.
She's just the sort of girl you like—
You know you do.
If other man her heart should gain,
I shall resign."
That's what it says to me quite plain,
This heart of mine.

SOLO—ROBIN

My heart says, "You've a prosperous lot,
With acres wide;
You mean to settle all you've got
Upon your bride."
It don't pretend to shape my acts
By word or sign;
It merely states these simple facts,
This heart of mine!

SOLO—ROSE

Ten minutes since my heart said "white"—
It now says "black."
It then said "left"—it now says "right"—
Hearts often tack.
I must obey its latest strain—
You tell me so. (*To* RICHARD.)
But should it change its mind again,
I'll let you know.

(*Turning from* RICHARD *to* ROBIN, *who embraces her.*)

ENSEMBLE

In sailing o'er life's ocean wide
No doubt the heart should be your guide;
But it is awkward when you find
A heart that does not know its mind!

[*Exeunt* ROBIN *with* ROSE L., *and* RICHARD
weeping, R.

Enter MAD MARGARET. *She is wildly dressed
in picturesuqe tatters, and is an obvious caricature of theatrical madness.*

SCENA—MARGARET

Cheerily carols the lark
Over the cot.

Merrily whistles the clerk
Scratching a blot.
But the lark
And the clerk
I remark,
Comfort me not!
Over the ripening peach
Buzzes the bee.
Splash on the billowy beach
Tumbles the sea.
But the peach
And the beach
They are each
Nothing to me!
And why?
Who am I?
Daft Madge! Crazy Meg!
Mad Margaret! Poor Peg!
He! he! he! he! he! (*chuckling*).
Mad, I?
Yes, very!
But why?
Mystery!
Don't call!
Whisht! whisht!
No crime—
'Tis only
That I'm
Love—lonely!
That's all!

BALLAD

To a garden full of posies
Cometh one to gather flowers,
And he wanders through its bowers
Toying with the wanton roses,
Who, uprising from their beds,
Hold on high their shameless heads
With their pretty lips a-pouting,
Never doubting—never doubting
That for Cytherean posies
He would gather aught but roses!
In a nest of weeds and nettles
Lay a violet, half-hidden,
Hoping that his glance unbidden
Yet might fall upon her petals.
Though she lived alone, apart,
Hope lay nestling at her heart.
But, alas, the cruel awaking
Set her little heart a-breaking,
For he gathered for his posies
Only roses—only roses!

(*Bursts into tears.*)

Enter ROSE

Rose. A maiden, and in tears? Can I do

aught to soften thy sorrow? This apple—
(*offering apple*).

Mar. (*Examines it and rejects it.*) No!
(*Mysteriously.*) Tell me, are you mad?

Rose. I? No! That is, I think not.

Mar. That's well! Then you don't love
Sir Despard Murgatroyd? All mad girls
love him. *I* love him. I'm poor Mad Margaret—Crazy Meg—Poor Peg! He! he! he!
he! (*chuckling*).

Rose. Thou lovest the bad Baronet of
Ruddigore? Oh, horrible—too horrible!

Mar. You pity me? Then be my mother!
The squirrel had a mother, but she drank
and the squirrel fled! Hush! They sing a
brave song in our parts—it runs somewhat thus: (*Sings.*)

"The cat and the dog and the little
    puppee
Sat down in a—down in a—in a——"

I forget what they sat down in, but so
the song goes! Listen—I've come to pinch
her!

Rose. Mercy, whom?

Mar. You mean "who".

Rose. Nay! it is the accusative after the
verb.

Mar. True. (*Whispers melodramatically.*)
I have come to pinch Rose Maybud!

Rose. (*Aside, alarmed.*) Rose Maybud!

Mar. Aye! I love him—he loved me
once. But that's all gone, Fisht! He gave
me an Italian glance—thus (*business*)—
and made me his. He will give *her* an
Italian glance, and make *her* his. But it
shall not be, for I'll stamp on her—stamp
on her—stamp on her! Did you ever kill
anybody? No? Why not? Listen—I killed
a fly this morning! It buzzed, and I
wouldn't have it. So it died—pop! So shall
she!

Rose. But, behold, *I* am Rose Maybud,
and I would fain not die "pop".

Mar. You are Rose Maybud?

Rose. Yes, sweet Rose Maybud!

Mar. Strange! They told me she was
beautiful. And *he* loves *you!* No, no! If I
thought that, I would treat you as the auc-
tioneer and land-agent treated the lady-
bird—I would rend you asunder!

Rose. Nay, be pacified, for behold I am
pledged to another, and lo, we are to be
wedded this very day!

Mar. Swear me that! Come to a Commissioner and let me have it on affidavit! *I*
once made an affidavit—but it died—it
died—it died! But, see, they come—Sir
Despard and his evil crew! Hide, hide—
they are all mad—quite mad!

Rose. What makes you think that?

Mar. Hush! They sing choruses in public. That's mad enough, I think! Go—hide
away, or they will seize you! Hush! Quite
softly—quite, quite softly!

    [*Exeunt together, on tiptoe.*
*Enter Chorus of Bucks and Blades, heralded
    by Chorus of Bridesmaids*

CHORUS OF BRIDESMAIDS

Welcome, gentry,
For your entry
Sets our tender hearts a-beating.
    Men of station,
    Admiration
Prompts this unaffected greeting.
    Hearty greeting offer we!

CHORUS OF BUCKS AND BLADES

    When thoroughly tired
    Of being admired
By ladies of gentle degree—degree,
    With flattery sated,
    High-flown and inflated,
Away from the city we flee—we flee!
    From charms intramural
    To prettiness rural
    The sudden transition
    Is simply Elysian,
    So come, Amaryllis,
    Come, Chloe and Phyllis,
Your slaves, for the moment, are we!

All

From charms intramural, etc.

CHORUS OF BRIDESMAIDS

    The sons of the tillage
    Who dwell in this village
Are people of lowly degree—degree.
    Though honest and active,
    They're most unattractive,
And awkward as awkward can be—can be.
    They're clumsy clodhoppers
    With axes and choppers,
    And shepherds and ploughmen
    And drovers and cowmen
    And hedgers and reapers
    And carters and keepers,
And never a lover for me!

Bridesmaids

So, welcome, gentry, etc.

BUCKS AND BLADES
When thoroughly tired, etc.
Enter SIR DESPARD MURGATROYD
SONG AND CHORUS—SIR DESPARD
Sir Despard
Oh, why am I moody and sad?
Chorus
Can't guess!
Sir Despard
And why am I guiltily mad?
Chorus
Confess!
Sir Despard
Because I am thoroughly bad!
Chorus
Oh yes—
Sir Despard
You'll see it at once in my face.
Oh, why am I husky and hoarse?
Chorus
Ah, why?
Sir Despard
It's the workings of conscience, of course.
Chorus
Fie, fie!
Sir Despard
And huskiness stands for remorse,
Chorus
Oh my!
Sir Despard
At least it does so in my case!
Sir Despard
When in crime one is fully employed—
Chorus
Like you—
Sir Despard
Your expression gets warped and destroyed:
Chorus
It do.
Sir Despard
It's a penalty none can avoid;
Chorus
How true!
Sir Despard
I once was a nice-looking youth;
But like stone from a strong catapult—
Chorus (explaining to each other)
A trice—
Sir Despard
I rushed at my terrible cult—
Chorus (explaining to each other)
That's vice—

Sir Despard
Observe the unpleasant result!
Chorus
Not nice.
Sir Despard
Indeed I am telling the truth!
Sir Despard
Oh, innocent, happy though poor!
Chorus
That's we—
Sir Despard
If I had been virtuous, I'm sure—
Chorus
Like me—
Sir Despard
I should be as nice-looking as you're!
Chorus
May be.
Sir Despard
You are very nice-looking indeed!
Oh, innocents, listen in time—
Chorus
We *doe,*
Sir Despard
Avoid an existence of crime—
Chorus
Just so—
Sir Despard
Or you'll be as ugly as I'm—
Chorus (loudly)
No! No!
Sir Despard
And now, if you please, we'll proceed.
[*All the Girls express their horror of* SIR
DESPARD. *As he approaches them they
fly from him, terror-stricken, leaving
him alone on the stage.*
Sir. D. Poor children, how they loathe
me—me whose hands are certainly steeped
in infamy, but whose heart is as the heart
of a little child. But what *is* a poor baronet
to do, when a whole picture gallery of ancestors step down from their frames and
threaten him with an excruciating death
if he hesitate to commit his daily crime?
But ha! ha! I am even with them! (*Mysteriously.*) I get my crime over the first
thing in the morning, and then, ha! ha!
for the rest of the day I do good—I do
good! (*Melodramatically.*) Two
days since, I stole a child and built an
orphan asylum. Yesterday I robbed a bank
and endowed a bishopric. To-day I carry
off Rose Maybud and atone with a cathe-

dral! This is what it is to be the sport and toy of a Picture Gallery! But I will be bitterly revenged upon them! I will give them all to the Nation, and nobody shall ever look upon their faces again!

Enter RICHARD

Rich. Ax your honour's pardon, but——

Sir. D. Ha! observed! And by a mariner! What would you with me, fellow?

Rich. Your honour, I'm a poor man-o'-war's man, becalmed in the doldrums——

Sir. D. I don't know them.

Rich. And I make bold to ax your honour's advice. Does your honour know what it is to have a heart?

Sir. D. My honour knows what it is to have a complete apparatus for conducting the circulation of the blood through the veins and arteries of the human body.

Rich. Aye, but has your honour a heart that ups and looks you in the face, and gives you quarter-deck orders that it's life and death to disobey?

Sir D. I have not a heart of that description, but I have a Picture Gallery that presumes to take that liberty.

Rich. Well, your honour, it's like this— Your honour had an elder brother——

Sir D. It had.

Rich. Who should have inherited your title and, with it, its cuss.

Sir D. Aye, but he died. Oh, Ruthven!——

Rich. He didn't.

Sir D. He did *not?*

Rich. He didn't. On the contrary, he lives in this here very village, under the name of Robin Oakapple, and he's a-going to marry Rose Maybud this very day.

Sir. D. Ruthven alive, and going to marry Rose Maybud! Can this be possible?

Rich. Now the question I was going to ask your honour is—Ought I to tell your honour this?

Sir D. I don't know. It's a delicate point. I think you ought. Mind, I'm not sure, but I think so.

Rich. That's what my heart says. It says, "Dick," it says (it calls me Dick acos it's entitled to take that liberty), "that there young gal would recoil from him if she knowed what he really were. Ought you to stand off and on, and let this young gal take this false step and never fire a shot across her bows to bring her to? No," it says, "you did *not* ought." And I won't ought, accordin'.

Sir D. Then you really feel yourself at liberty to tell me that my elder brother lives—that I may charge him with his cruel deceit, and transfer to his shoulders the hideous thraldom under which I have laboured for so many years! Free—free at last! Free to live a blameless life, and to die beloved and regretted by all who knew me!

DUET—SIR DESPARD *and* RICHARD

Richard

You understand?

Sir Despard

  I think I do;
    With vigour unshaken
    This step shall be taken.
It's neatly planned.

Richard

  I think so too;
    I'll readily bet it
    You'll never regret it!

Both

For duty, duty must be done;
The rule applies to every one,
And painful though that duty be,
To shirk the task were fiddle-de-dee!

Sir Despard

The bridegroom comes—

Richard

Likewise the bride—
    The maidens are very
    Elated and merry;
They are her chums.

Sir Despard

  To lash their pride
    Were almost a pity,
    The pretty committee!

Both

But duty, duty must be done;
The rule applies to every one,
And painful though that duty be,
To shirk the task were fiddle-de-dee!

    [*Exeunt* RICHARD *and* SIR DESPARD.

Enter Chorus of Bridesmaids and Bucks

Chorus of Bridesmaids

Hail the bride of seventeen summers:
  In fair phrases
  Hymn her praises;
Lift your song on high, all comers.
  She rejoices
  In your voices.

Smiling summer beams upon her,
Shedding every blessing on her:
   Maidens greet her—
   Kindly treat her—
You may all be brides some day!

Chorus of Bucks

Hail the bridegroom who advances,
   Agitated,
   Yet elated.
He's in easy circumstances,
   Young and lusty,
   True and trusty.

Enter ROBIN, *attended by* RICHARD *and* OLD ADAM, *meeting* ROSE, *attended by* ZORAH *and* DAME HANNAH. ROSE *and* ROBIN *embrace.*

MADRIGAL

Rose

When the buds are blossoming,
Smiling welcome to the spring,
Lovers choose a wedding day—
Life is love in merry May!

Girls

Spring is green—Fal lal la!
   Summer's rose—Fal lal la!

All

It is sad when summer goes,
   Fal la!

Men

Autumn's gold—Fal lal la!
   Winter's grey—Fal lal la!

All

Winter still is far away—
   Fal la!
Leaves in autumn fade and fall,
Winter is the end of all.
Spring and summer teem with glee:
Spring and summer, then, for me!
   Fal la!

Hannah

In the spring-time seed is sown:
In the summer grass is mown:
In the autumn you may reap:
Winter is the time for sleep.

Girls

Spring is hope—Fal lal la!
   Summer's joy—Fal lal la!

All

Spring and summer never cloy.
   Fal la!

Men

Autumn, toil—Fal lal la!
   Winter, rest—Fal lal la!

All

Winter, after all, is best—
   Fal la!

All

Spring and summer pleasure you,
Autumn, aye, and winter too—
Every season has its cheer,
Life is lovely all the year!
   Fal la!

(*Gavotte*)

After Gavotte, enter SIR DESPARD

Sir Despard

Hold, bride and bridegroom, ere you wed
   each other,
I claim young Robin as my elder brother!
His rightful title I have long enjoyed:
I claim him as Sir Ruthven Murgatroyd!

All

O wonder!

Rose (*wildly*)

Deny the falsehood, Robin, as you should,
   It is a plot!

Robin

I would, if conscientiously I could,
   But I cannot!

All

Ah, base one!

SOLO—ROBIN

As pure and blameless peasant,
   I cannot, I regret,
Deny a truth unpleasant,
   I am that Baronet!

All

He is that Baronet!

Robin

But when completely rated
   Bad Baronet am I,
That I am what he's stated
   I'll recklessly deny!

All

He'll recklessly deny!

Robin

When I'm a bad Bart. I will tell taradiddles!

All

He'll tell taradiddles when he's a bad
   Bart.

Robin

I'll play a bad part on the falsest of
   fiddles.

All

On very false fiddles he'll play a bad
   part!

Robin

But until that takes place I must be conscientious—

All

He'll be conscientious until that takes place.

Robin

Then adieu with good grace to my morals sententious!

All

To morals sententious adieu with good grace!

Zorah

Who is the wretch who hath betrayed thee?
Let him stand forth!

Richard (coming forward)

'Twas I!

All

Die, traitor!

Richard

Hold! my conscience made me!
Withhold your wrath!

SOLO—RICHARD

Within this breast there beats a heart
Whose voice can't be gainsaid.
It bade me thy true rank impart,
And I at once obeyed.
I knew 'twould blight thy budding fate—
I knew 'twould cause thee anguish great—
But did I therefore hesitate?
No! I at once obeyed!

All

Acclaim him who, when his true heart
Bade him young Robin's rank impart,
Immediately obeyed!

SOLO—ROSE *(addressing* ROBIN*)*

Farewell!
Thou hadst my heart—
'Twas quickly won!
But now we part—
Thy face I shun!
Farewell!
Go bend the knee
At Vice's shrine,
Of life with me
All hope resign.
Farewell!
(To SIR DESPARD*)*

Take me—I am thy bride!

Bridesmaids

Hail the Bridegroom—hail the Bride!
When the nuptial knot is tied;
Every day will bring some joy

That can never, never cloy!

Enter MARGARET, *who listens*

Sir Despard

Excuse me, I'm a virtuous person now—

Rose

That's why I wed you!

Sir Despard

And I to Margaret must keep my vow!

Margaret

Have I misread you?
Oh, joy! with newly kindled rapture warmed,
I kneel before you! *(Kneels)*

Sir Despard

I once disliked you; now that I've reformed,
How I adore you! *(They embrace)*

Bridesmaids

Hail the Bridegroom—hail the Bride!
When the nuptial knot is tied;
Every day will bring some joy
That can never, never cloy!

Rose

Richard, of him I love bereft,
Through thy design,
Thou art the only one that's left,
So I am thine! *(They embrace)*

Bridesmaids

Hail the Bridegroom—hail the Bride!
Let the nuptial knot be tied!

DUET—ROSE *and* RICHARD

Oh, happy the lily
When kissed by the bee;
And, sipping tranquilly,
Quite happy is he;
And happy the filly
That neighs in her pride;
But happier than any,
A pound to a penny,
A lover is, when he
Embraces his bride!

DUET—SIR DESPARD *and* MARGARET

Oh, happy the flowers
That blossom in June,
And happy the bowers
That gain by the boon,
But happier by hours
The man of descent,
Who, folly regretting,
Is bent on forgetting
His bad baronetting,
And means to repent!

TRIO—HANNAH, ADAM, *and* ZORAH

Oh, happy the blossom

That blooms on the lea,
Likewise the opossum
    That sits on a tree,
But when you come across 'em,
    They cannot compare
With those who are treading
The dance at a wedding,
While people are spreading
    The best of good fare!

SOLO—ROBIN

Oh. wretched the debtor
    Who's signing a deed!
And wretched the letter
    That no one can read!
But very much better
    Their lot it must be
Than that of the person
I'm making this verse on,
Whose head there's a curse on—
    Alluding to me!

> *Repeat ensemble with Chorus*
> (*Dance*)
> [*At the end of the dance* ROBIN *falls
> senseless on the stage. Picture.*

END OF ACT I

ACT II

SCENE.—*Picture Gallery in Ruddigore
Castle. The walls are covered with
full-length portraits of the Baronets
of Ruddigore from the time of* JAMES
I.—*the first being that of* SIR RUPERT,
*alluded to in the legend; the last that
of the last deceased Baronet,* SIR
RODERIC.

Enter ROBIN *and* ADAM *melodramatically.
They are greatly altered in appearance,* ROBIN *wearing the haggard aspect of a guilty roué;* ADAM, *that of
the wicked steward to such a man.*

DUET—ROBIN *and* ADAM
Robin

I once was as meek as a new-born lamb,
I'm now Sir Murgatroyd—ha! ha!
    With greater precision
    (Without the elision),
    Sir Ruthven Murgatroyd—ha! ha!
Adam

And I, who was once his *valley-de-sham,*
    As steward I'm now employed—ha! ha!
        The dickens may take him—
        I'll never forsake him!
    As steward I'm now employed—ha! ha!

Both

How dreadful when an innocent heart
Becomes, perforce, a bad young Bart.,
And still more hard on old Adam,
His former faithful *valley-de-sham!*
Robin

This is a painful state of things, old
    Adam!

Adam. Painful, indeed! Ah, my poor
master, when I swore that, come what
would, I would serve you in all things
for ever, I little thought to what a pass
it would bring me! The confidential adviser to the greatest villain unhung! Now,
sir, to business. What crime do you propose to commit to-day?

Rob. How should I know? As my confidential adviser, it's your duty to suggest
something.

Adam. Sir, I loathe the life you are leading, but a good old man's oath is paramount, and I obey. Richard Dauntless is
here with pretty Rose Maybud, to ask
your consent to their marriage. Poison
their beer.

Rob. No—not that—I know I'm a bad
Bart., but I'm not as bad a Bart. as all
that.

Adam. Well, there you are, you see! It's
no use my making suggestions if you don't
adopt them.

Rob. (*melodramatically*). How would it
be, do you think, were I to lure him here
with cunning wile—bind him with good
stout rope to yonder post—and then, by
making hideous faces at him, curdle the
heart-blood in his arteries, and freeze the
very marrow in his bones? How say you,
Adam, is not the scheme well planned?

Adam. It would be simply rude—nothing more. But soft—they come!

ADAM *and* ROBIN *retire up as* RICHARD *and*
    ROSE *enter, preceded by Chorus of
    Bridesmaids.*

DUET—RICHARD *and* ROSE
Richard

Happily coupled are we,
    You see—
I am a jolly Jack Tar,
    My star,
    And you are the fairest,
    The richest and rarest
Of innocent lasses you are,
    By far—

Of innocent lasses you are!
Fanned by a favouring gale,
    You'll sail
Over life's treacherous sea
    With me,
    And as for bad weather,
    We'll brave it together,
And you shall creep under my lee,
    My wee!
And you shall creep under my lee!
'?or you are such a smart little craft—
Such a neat little, sweet little craft,
    Such a bright little, tight little,
    Slight little, light little,
'?rim little, prim little craft!

Chorus

For she is such, etc.

Rose

My hopes will be blighted, I fear,
    My dear;
In a month you'll be going to sea,
    Quite free,
    And all of my wishes
    You'll throw to the fishes
As though they were never to be.
    Poor me!
As though they were never to be.
And I shall be left all alone
    To moan,
And weep at your cruel deceit,
    Complete;
    While you'll be asserting
    Your freedom by flirting
With every woman you meet,
    You cheat—
With every woman you meet!
Though I am such a smart little craft—
Such a neat little, sweet little craft,
    Such a bright little, tight little,
    Slight little, light little,
Trim little, prim little craft!

Chorus

Though she is such, etc.

Enter ROBIN

Rob. Soho! pretty one—in my power at last, eh? Know ye not that I have those within my call who, at my lightest bidding, would immure ye in an uncomfortable dungeon? (*Calling*) What ho! within there!

Rich. Hold—we are prepared for this (*producing a Union Jack*). Here is a flag that none dare defy (*all kneel*), and while this glorious rag floats over Rose May-

bud's head, the man does not live who would dare to lay unlicensed hand upon her!

Rob. Foiled—and by a Union Jack! But a time will come, and then——

Rose. Nay, let me plead with him. (*To* ROBIN.) Sir Ruthven, have pity. In my book of etiquette the case of a maiden about to be wedded to one who unexpectedly turns out to be a baronet with a curse on him is not considered. Time was when you loved me madly. Prove that this was no selfish love by according your consent to my marriage with one who, if he be not you yourself, is the next best thing—your dearest friend!

BALLAD—ROSE

In bygone days I had thy love—
    Thou hadst my heart.
But Fate, all human vows above,
    Our lives did part!
By the old love thou hadst for me—
By the fond heart that beat for thee—
By joys that never now can be,
    Grant thou my prayer!

All (kneeling)

Grant thou her prayer!

Robin (recit.)

Take her—I yield!

All (recit.)

    Oh, rapture!

Chorus

Away to the parson we go—
    Say we're solicitous very
That he will turn two into one—
    Singing hey, derry down derry!

Richard

For she *is* such a smart little craft—

Rose

Such a neat little, sweet little craft—

Richard

    Such a bright little—

Rose

        Tight little—

Richard

    Slight little—

Rose

        Light little—

Both

Trim little, slim little craft!

Chorus

For she *is* such a smart little craft, etc.
                [*Exeunt all but* ROBIN.

Rob. For a week I have fulfilled my

accursed doom! I have duly committed a crime a day! Not a great crime, I trust, but still, in the eyes of one as strictly regulated as I used to be, a crime. But will my ghostly ancestors be satisfied with what I have done, or will they regard it as an unworthy subterfuge? (*Addressing Pictures.*) Oh, my forefathers, wallowers in blood, there came at last a day when, sick of crime, you, each and every, vowed to sin no more, and so, in agony, called welcome Death to free you from your cloying guiltiness. Let the sweet psalm of that repentant hour soften your long-dead hearts, and tune your souls to mercy on your poor posterity! (*kneeling*).

[*The stage darkens for a moment. It becomes light again, and the Pictures are seen to have become animated.*

Chorus of Family Portraits

Painted emblems of a race,
All accurst in days of yore,
Each from his accustomed place
  Steps into the world once more.

[*The Pictures step from their frames and march round the stage.*

Baronet of Ruddigore,
  Last of our accursèd line,
Down upon the oaken floor—
  Down upon those knees of thine.
Coward, poltroon, shaker, squeamer,
Blockhead, sluggard, dullard, dreamer,
Shirker, shuffler, crawler, creeper,
Sniffler, snuffler, wailer, weeper,
Earthworm, maggot, tadpole, weevil!
Set upon thy course of evil,
Lest the King of Spectre-Land
Set on thee his grisly hand!

[*The Spectre of* SIR RODERIC *descends from his frame.*

Sir Roderic
Beware! beware! beware!
Robin
  Gaunt vision, who art thou
That thus, with icy glare
  And stern relentless brow,
Appearest, who knows how?

Sir Roderic
I am the spectre of the late
  Sir Roderic Murgatroyd,
Who comes to warn thee that thy fate
  Thou canst not now avoid.
Robin

Alas, poor ghost!

Sir Roderic
  The pity you
Express for nothing goes:
We spectres are a jollier crew
  Than you, perhaps, suppose!
Chorus
We spectres are a jollier crew
  Than you, perhaps, suppose!

SONG—SIR RODERIC

When the night wind howls in the chimney cowls, and the bat in the moonlight flies,
And inky clouds, like funeral shrouds, sail over the midnight skies—
When the footpads quail at the night-bird's wail, and black dogs bay at the moon,
Then is the spectres' holiday—then is the ghosts' high-noon!
Chorus

  Ha! ha!
  Then is the ghosts' high-noon!
Sir Roderic
As the sob of the breeze sweeps over the trees, and the mists lie low on the fen,
From grey tomb-stones are gathered the bones that once were women and men,
And away they go, with a mop and a mow, to the revel that ends too soon,
For cockcrow limits our holiday—the dead of the night's high-noon!
Chorus

  Ha! ha!
  The dead of the night's high-noon!
Sir Roderic
And then each ghost with his ladye-toast to their churchyard beds takes flight,
With a kiss, perhaps, on her lantern chaps, and a grisly grim "good-night";
Till the welcome knell of the midnight bell rings forth its jolliest tune,
And ushers in our next high holiday—the dead of the night's high-noon!
Chorus

  Ha! ha!
  The dead of the night's high-noon!
Rob. I recognize you now—you are the picture that hangs at the end of the gallery.
Sir Rod. In a bad light. I am.
Rob. Are you considered a good likeness?
Sir Rod. Pretty well. Flattering.

Rob. Because as a work of art you are poor.

Sir Rod. I am crude in colour, but I have only been painted ten years. In a couple of centuries I shall be an Old Master, and then you will be sorry you spoke lightly of me.

Rob. And may I ask why you have left your frames?

Sir Rod. It is our duty to see that our successors commit their daily crimes in a conscientious and workmanlike fashion. It is our duty to remind you that you are evading the conditions under which you are permitted to exist.

Rob. Really, I don't know what you'd have. I've only been a bad baronet a week, and I've committed a crime punctually every day.

Sir Rod. Let us inquire into this. Monday?

Rob. Monday was a Bank Holiday.

Sir Rod. True. Tuesday?

Rob. On Tuesday I made a false income-tax return.

All. Ha! ha!

1st Ghost. That's nothing.

2nd Ghost. Nothing at all.

3rd Ghost. Everybody does that.

4th Ghost. It's expected of you.

Sir Rod. Wednesday?

Rob. (*melodramatically*). On Wednesday I forged a will.

Sir Rod. Whose will?

Rob. My own.

Sir Rod. My good sir, you can't forge your own will!

Rob. Can't I, though! I like that! I *did*! Besides, if a man can't forge his own will, whose will can he forge?

1st Ghost. There's something in that.

2nd Ghost. Yes, it seems reasonable.

3rd Ghost. At first sight it does.

4th Ghost. Fallacy somewhere, I fancy!

Rob. A man can do what he likes with his own?

Sir Rod. I suppose he can.

Rob. Well, then, he can forge his own will, stoopid! On Thursday I shot a fox.

1st Ghost. Hear, hear!

Sir Rod. That's better (*addressing Ghosts*). Pass the fox, I think? (*They assent.*) Yes, pass the fox. Friday?

Rob. On Friday I forged a cheque.

Sir Rod. Whose cheque?

Rob. Old Adam's.

Sir Rod. But Old Adam hasn't a banker.

Rob. I didn't say I forged his banker—I said I forged his cheque. On Saturday I disinherited my only son.

Sir Rod. But you haven't got a son.

Rob. No—not yet. I disinherited him in advance, to save time. You see—by this arrangement—he'll be born ready disinherited.

Sir Rod. I see. But I don't think you can do that.

Rob. My good sir, if I can't disinherit my own unborn son, whose unborn son can I disinherit?

Sir Rod. Humph! These arguments sound very well, but I can't help thinking that, if they were reduced to syllogistic form, they wouldn't hold water. Now quite understand us. We are foggy, but we don't permit our fogginess to be presumed upon. Unless you undertake to—well, suppose we say, carry off a lady? (*Addressing Ghosts.*) Those who are in favour of his carrying off a lady? (*All hold up their hands except a Bishop.*) Those of the contrary opinion? (*Bishop holds up his hands.*) Oh, you're never satisfied! Yes, unless you undertake to carry off a lady at once—I don't care what lady—any lady—choose your lady—you perish in inconceivable agonies.

Rob. Carry off a lady? Certainly not, on any account. I've the greatest respect for ladies, and I wouldn't do anything of the kind for worlds! No, no. I'm not that kind of baronet, I assure you! If that's all you've got to say, you'd better go back to your frames.

Sir Rod. Very good—then let the agonies commence.

[*Ghosts make passes.* ROBIN *begins to writhe in agony.*

Rob. Oh! Oh! Don't do that! I can't stand it!

Sir Rod. Painful, isn't it? It gets worse by degrees.

Rob. Oh—Oh! Stop a bit! Stop it, will you? I want to speak.

[SIR RODERIC *makes signs to Ghosts, who resume their attitudes.*

Sir Rod. Better?

Rob. Yes—better now! Whew!

Sir Rod. Well, do you consent?

Rob. But it's such an ungentlemanly thing to do!

Sir Rod. As you please. (*To Ghosts.*) Carry on!

Rod. Stop—I can't stand it! I agree! I promise! It shall be done!

Sir Rod. To-day?

Rob. To-day!

Sir Rod. At once?

Rob. At once! I retract! I apologize! I had no idea it was anything like that!

Chorus

He yields! He answers to our call!
   We do not ask for more.
A sturdy fellow, after all,
   This latest Ruddigore!
All perish in unheard-of woe
   Who dare our wills defy;
We want your pardon, ere we go.
For having agonized you so—
      So pardon us—
      So pardon us—
      So pardon us—
         Or die!

Robin

I pardon you!
I pardon you!

All

He pardons us—
   Hurrah!
   [*The Ghosts return to their frames.*
Chorus

Painted emblems of a race,
   All accurst in days of yore,
Each to his accustomed place
   Steps unwillingly once more!
[*By this time the Ghosts have changed to pictures again.* ROBIN *is overcome by emotion.*

Enter ADAM

Adam. My poor master, you are not well——

Rob. Gideon Crawle, it won't do—I've seen 'em—all my ancestors—they're just gone. They say that I must do something desperate at once, or perish in horrible agonies. Go—go to yonder village—carry off a maiden—bring her here at once—any one—I don't care which—

Adam. But——

Rob. Not a word, but obey! Fly!
   [*Exit* ADAM.

RECIT. *and* SONG—ROBIN

Away, Remorse!

Compunction, hence!
Go, Moral Force!
   Go, Penitence!
To Virtue's plea
   A long farewell—
Propriety,
   I ring your knell!
Come, guiltiness of deadliest hue!
Come, desperate deeds of derring-do!
Henceforth all the crimes that I find in the
      Times,
   I've promised to perpetrate daily;
To-morrow I start, with a petrified heart,
   On a regular course of Old Bailey.
There's confidence tricking, bad coin, pocket-picking,
   And several other disgraces—
There's postage-stamp prigging, and then, thimble-rigging,
   The three-card delusion at races!
Ch! a baronet's rank is exceedingly nice,
But the title's uncommonly dear at the price!
Ye well-to-do squires, who live in the shires,
   Where petty distinctions are vital,
Who found Athenaeums and local museums,
   With views to a baronet's title—
Ye butchers and bakers and candlestick makers
   Who sneer at all things that are tradey—
Whose middle-class lives are embarrassed by wives
   Who long to parade as "My Lady",
Oh! allow me to offer a word of advice,
The title's uncommonly dear at the price!
Ye supple M.P.'s, who go down on your knees,
   Your precious identity sinking,
And vote black or white as your leaders indite
   (Which saves you the trouble of thinking),
For your country's good fame, her repute, or her shame,
   You don't care the snuff of a candle—
But you're paid for your game when you're told that your name
   Will be graced by a baronet's handle—
Oh! allow me to give *you* a word of advice—
The title's uncommonly dear at the price!
   [*Exit* ROBIN.

Enter DESPARD *and* MARGARET. *They are both dressed in sober black of formal cut, and present a strong contrast to their appearance in Act I.*

DUET

Despard

I once was a very abandoned person—

Margaret

Making the most of evil chances.

Despard

Nobody could conceive a worse 'un—

Margaret

Even in all the old romances.

Despard

I blush for my wild extravagances,
  But be so kind
  To bear in mind,

Margaret

We were the victims of circumstances!

(*Dance.*)

That is one of our blameless dances.

Margaret

I was once an exceedingly odd young lady—

Despard

Suffering much from spleen and vapours.

Margaret

Clergymen thought my conduct shady—

Despard

She didn't spend much upon linen-drapers.

Margaret

It certainly entertained the gapers.
  My ways were strange
  Beyond all range—

Despard

Paragraphs got into all the papers.

(*Dance.*)

Despard

We only cut respectable capers.

Despard

I've given up all my wild proceedings.

Margaret

My taste for a wandering life is waning.

Despard

Now I'm a dab at penny readings.

Margaret

They are not remarkably entertaining.

Despard

A moderate livelihood we're gaining.

Margaret

In fact we rule
A National School.

Despard

The duties are dull, but I'm not complaining.

(*Dance.*)

This sort of thing takes a deal of training!

Des. We have been married a week.

Mar. One happy, happy week!

Des. Our new life—

Mar. Is delightful indeed!

Des. So calm!

Mar. So unimpassioned! (*wildly*). Master, all this I owe to you! See, I am no longer wild and untidy. My hair is combed. My face is washed. My boots fit!

Des. Margaret, don't. Pray restrain yourself. Remember, you are now a district visitor.

Mar. A gentle district visitor!

Des. You are orderly, methodical, neat; you have your emotions well under control.

Mar. I have! (*wildly*). Master, when I think of all you have done for me, I fall at your feet. I embrace your ankles. I hug your knees! (*Doing so.*)

Des. Hush. This is not well. This is calculated to provoke remark. Be composed, I beg!

Mar. Ah! you are angry with poor little Mad Margaret!

Des. No, not angry; but a district visitor should learn to eschew melodrama. Visit the poor, by all means, and give them tea and barley-water, but don't do it as if you were administering a bowl of deadly nightshade. It upsets them. Then when you nurse sick people, and find them not as well as could be expected, why go into hysterics?

Mar. Why not?

Des. Because it's too jumpy for a sick-room.

Mar. How strange! Oh, Master! Master! —how shall I express the all-absorbing gratitude that—(*about to throw herself at his feet*).

Des. Now! (*warningly*).

Mar. Yes, I know, dear—it shan't occur again. (*He is seated—she sits on the ground by him.*) Shall I tell you one of poor Mad Margaret's odd thoughts? Well, then, when I am lying awake at night, and the pale moonlight streams through the latticed casement, strange fancies crowd upon my poor mad brain, and I some-times think that if we could hit upon some word for you to use whenever I am about to relapse—some word that teems with hidden meaning — like "Basingstoke" — it might recall me to my saner self. For, after all, I am only Mad Margaret! Daft Meg! Poor Meg! He! he! he!

Des. Poor child, she wanders! But soft—some one comes—Margaret—pray recollect yourself—Basingstoke, I beg! Margaret, if you don't Basingstoke at once, I shall be seriously angry.

Mar. (*recovering herself*). Basingstoke it is!

Des. Then make it so.

Enter ROBIN. *He starts on seeing them*

Rob. Despard! And his young wife! This visit is unexpected.

Mar. Shall I fly at him? Shall I tear him limb from limb? Shall I rend him asunder? Say but the word and——

Des. Basingstoke!

Mar. (*suddenly demure*). Basingstoke it is!

Des. (*aside*). Then make it so. (*Aloud.*) My brother—I call you brother still, de-spite your horrible profligacy—we have come to urge you to abandon the evil courses to which you have committed your-self, and at any cost to become a pure and blameless ratepayer.

Rob. But I've done no wrong yet.

Mar. (*wildly*). No wrong! He has done no wrong! Did you hear that!

Des. Basingstoke!

Mar. (*recovering herself*). Basingstoke it is!

Des. My brother—I still call you brother, you observe—you forget that you have been, in the eye of the law, a Bad Baronet of Ruddigore for ten years—and you are therefore responsible—in the eye of the law —for all the misdeeds committed by the unhappy gentleman who occupied your place.

Rob. I see! Bless my heart, I never thought of that! Was I very bad?

Des. Awful. Wasn't he? (*to* MARGARET).

Rob. And I've been going on like this for how long?

Des. Ten years! Think of all the atroci-ties you have committed—by attorney as it were—during that period. Remember how

you trifled with this poor child's affections —how you raised her hopes on high (don't cry, my love—Basingstoke, you know) only to trample them in the dust when they were at the very zenith of their fullness. Oh fie, sir, fie—she trusted you!

Rob. Did she? What a scoundrel I must have been! There, there—don't cry, my dear (*to* MARGARET, *who is sobbing on* ROBIN'S *breast*), it's all right now. Birming-ham, you know—Birmingham——

Mar. (*sobbing*). It's Ba—Ba—Basing-stoke!

Rob. Basingstoke! of course it is—Bas-ingstoke.

Mar. Then make it so.

Rob. There, there—it's all right—he's married you now—that is, *I've* married you (*turning to* DESPARD)—I say, which of us has married her?

Des. Oh, *I've* married her.

Rob. (*aside*). Oh, I'm glad of that. (*To* MARGARET.) Yes, *he's* married you now (*passing her over to* DESPARD), and any-thing more disreputable than my conduct seems to have been I've never even heard of. But my mind is made up—I *will* defy my ancestors. I *will* refuse to obey their behests, thus, by courting death, atone in some degree for the infamy of my career!

Mar. I knew it—I knew it—God bless you—(*hysterically*).

Des. Basingstoke!

Mar. Basingstoke it is! (*Recovers her-self.*)

PATTER-TRIO

ROBIN, DESPARD *and* MARGARET

Robin

My eyes are fully open to my awful sit-uation—
I shall go at once to Roderic and make him an oration.
I shall tell him I've recovered my forgotten moral senses,
And I don't care twopence-halfpenny for any consequences.
Now I do not want to perish by the sword or by the dagger,
But a martyr may indulge a little pardon-able swagger,
And a word or two of compliment my vanity would flatter,

But I've got to die to-morrow, so it really
doesn't matter!

Despard

So it really doesn't matter—

Margaret

So it really doesn't matter—

All

So it really doesn't matter, matter, matter,
matter, matter!

Margaret

If I were not a little mad and generally
silly
I should give you my advice upon the
subject, willy-nilly;
I should show you in a moment how to
grapple with the question,
And you'd really be astonished at the force
of my suggestion.
On the subject I shall write you a most
valuable letter,
Full of excellent suggestions when I feel a
little better,
But at present I'm afraid I am as mad as
any hatter,
So I'll keep 'em to myself, for my opinion
doesn't matter!

Despard

Her opinion doesn't matter—

Robin

Her opinion doesn't matter—

All

Her opinion doesn't matter, matter, matter,
matter, matter!

Despard

If I had been so lucky as to have a steady
brother
Who could talk to me as we are talking now to one another—
Who could give me good advice when he
discovered I was erring
(Which is just the very favour which on
you I am conferring),
My story would have made a rather interesting idyll,
And I might have lived and died a very
decent indiwiddle.
This particularly rapid, unintelligible patter
Isn't generally heard, and if it is it doesn't
matter!

Robin

If it is it doesn't matter—

Margaret

If it ain't it doesn't matter—

All

If it is it doesn't matter, matter, matter,
matter, matter!

[*Exeunt* DESPARD *and* MARGARET.

Enter ADAM

Adam (*guiltily*). Master — the deed is
done!
Rob. What deed?
Adam. She is here — alone, unpro-
tected——
Rob. Who?
Adam. The maiden. I've carried her off
—I had a hard task, for she fought like a
tiger-cat!
Rob. Great heaven, I had forgotten her!
I had hoped to have died unspotted by
crime, but I am foiled again—and by a
tiger-cat! Produce her—and leave us!

[ADAM *introduces* DAME HANNAH, *very
much excited, and exit.*

Rob. Dame Hannah! This is—this is not
what I expected.
Han. Well, sir, and what would you with
me? Oh, you have begun bravely—bravely
indeed! Unappalled by the calm dignity of
blameless womanhood, your minion has
torn me from my spotless home, and
dragged me, blindfold and shrieking,
through hedges, over stiles, and across a
very difficult country, and left me, helpless and trembling, at your mercy! Yet
not helpless, coward sir, for approach one
step—nay, but the twentieth part of one
poor inch—and this poniard (*produces
a very small dagger*) shall teach ye what
it is to lay unholy hands on old Stephen
Trusty's daughter!
Rob. Madam, I am extremely sorry for
this. It is not at all what I intended—anything more correct—more deeply respectful
than my intentions towards you, it would
be impossible for any one—however particular—to desire.
Han. Bah, I am not to be tricked by
smooth words, hypocrite! But be warned
in time, for there are, without, a hundred
gallant hearts whose trusty blades would
hack him limb from limb who dared to lay
unholy hands on old Stephen Trusty's
daughter!
Rob. And this is what it is to embark
upon a career of unlicensed pleasure!

[HANNAH, *who has taken a formidable dagger from one of the armed figures, throws her small dagger to* ROBIN.

Han. Harkye, miscreant, you have secured me, and I am your poor prisoner; but if you think I cannot take care of myself you are very much mistaken. Now then, it's one to one, and let the best man win!

[*Making for him.*

Rob. (*in an agony of terror*). Don't! don't look at me like that! I can't bear it! Roderic! Uncle! Save me!

RODERIC *enters, from his picture. He comes down the stage.*

Rod. What is the matter? Have you carried her off?

Rob. I have—she is there—look at her—she terrifies me!

Rod. (*looking at* HANNAH). Little Nannikin!

Han. (*amazed*). Roddy-doddy!

Rod. My own old love! Why, how came *you* here?

Han. This brute—he carried me off! Bodily! But I'll show him! (*about to rush at* ROBIN).

Rod. Stop! (*To* ROB.) What do you mean by carrying off this lady? Are you aware that once upon a time she was engaged to be married to me? I'm very angry—very angry indeed.

Rob. Now I hope this will be a lesson to you in future not to——

Rod. Hold your tongue, sir.

Rob. Yes, uncle.

Rod. Have you given him any encouragement?

Han. (*to* ROB.) Have I given you any encouragement? Frankly now, have I?

Rob. No. Frankly, you have not. Anything more scrupulously correct than your conduct, it would be impossible to desire.

Rod. You go away.

Rob. Yes, uncle.

[*Exit* ROBIN.

Rod. This is a strange meeting after so many years!

Han. Very. I thought you were dead.

Rod. I am. I died ten years ago.

Han. And are you pretty comfortable?

Rod. Pretty well—that is—yes, pretty well.

Han. You don't deserve to be, for I loved you all the while, dear; and it made me dreadfully unhappy to hear of all your goings-on, you bad, bad, boy!

BALLAD—HANNAH

There grew a little flower
'Neath a great oak tree:
When the tempest 'gan to lower
Little heeded she:
No need had she to cower,
For she dreaded not its power—
She was happy in the bower
   Of her great oak tree!
   Sing hey,
   Lackaday!
Let the tears fall free
For the pretty little flower and the great
   oak tree!

Both

   Sing hey,
   Lackaday! etc.
When she found that he was fickle,
   Was that great oak tree,
She was in a pretty pickle,
   As she well might be—
But his gallantries were mickle,
For Death followed with his sickle,
And her tears began to trickle
   For her great oak tree!

Both

   Sing hey,
   Lackaday! etc.
Said she, "He loved me never,
   Did that great oak tree,
But I'm neither rich nor clever,
   And so why should he?
But though fate our fortunes sever,
To be constant I'll endeavour,
Aye, for ever and for ever,
   To my great oak tree!"

Both

   Sing hey,
   Lackaday! etc.

[*Falls weeping on* RODERIC'S *bosom.*
Enter ROBIN, *excitedly, followed by all the characters and Chorus of Bridesmaids.*

Rob. Stop a bit—both of you.

Rod. This intrusion is unmannerly.

Han. I'm surprised at you.

Rob. I can't stop to apologize—an idea has just occurred to me. A Baronet of Ruddigore can only die through refusing to commit his daily crime.

Rod. No doubt.

Rob. Therefore, to refuse to commit a
ily crime is tantamount to suicide!

Rod. It would seem so.

Rob. But suicide is, itself, a crime—and
, by your own showing, you ought never
have died at all!

Rod. I see—I understand! Then I'm
actically alive!

Rob. Undoubtedly! (SIR RODERIC *em-
races* HANNAH.) Rose, when you believed
at I was a simple farmer, I believe you
ved me?

Rose. Madly, passionately!

Rob. But when I became a bad baronet,
ou very properly loved Richard instead?

Rose. Passionately, madly!

Rob. But if I should turn out *not* to be
bad baronet after all, how would you
ve me then?

Rose. Madly, passionately!

Rob. As before?

Rose. Why, of course!

Rob. My darling! (*They embrace.*)

Rich. Here, I say, belay!

Rose. Oh, sir, belay, if it's absolutely
ecessary!

Rob. Belay? Certainly not!

FINALE

Robin

Having been a wicked baronet a week,
Once again a modest livelihood I seek,

Agricultural employment
Is to me a keen enjoyment,
For I'm naturally diffident and meek!

Rose

When a man has been a naughty baronet,
And expresses his repentance and regret,
    You should help him, if you're able,
    Like the mousie in the fable,
That's the teaching of my Book of Eti-
    quette.

Richard

If you ask me why I do not pipe my eye,
Like an honest British sailor, I reply,
    That with Zorah for my missis,
    There'll be bread and cheese and kisses,
Which is just the sort of ration I enjye!

Despard and Margaret

Prompted by a keen desire to evoke,
All the blessed calm of matrimony's yoke,
We shall toddle off to-morrow,
From this scene of sin and sorrow,
For to settle in the town of Basingstoke!

All

For happy the lily
    That's kissed by the bee;
And, sipping tranquilly,
    Quite happy is he;
And happy the filly
    That neighs in her pride;
But happier than any,
A pound to a penny,
A lover is, when he
    Embraces his bride!

CURTAIN

THESPIS

OR

THE GODS GROWN OLD

DRAMATIS PERSONÆ

GODS		THESPIANS	
JUPITER		THESPIS	STUPIDAS
APOLLO	⎫	SILLIMON	SPARKEION
MARS	⎬ *Aged Deities*	TIMIDON	NICEMIS
DIANA	⎭	TIPSEION	PRETTEIA
		PREPOSTEROS	DAPHNE
MERCURY		CYMON	

ACT I

SCENE.—*The ruins of The Temple of the Gods on summit of Mount Olympus. Picturesque shattered columns, overgrown with ivy, etc.,* R. *and* L., *with entrances to temple (ruined)* R. *Fallen columns on the stage. Three broken pillars 2* R. E. *At the back of stage is the approach from the summit of the mountain. This should be "practicable" to enable large numbers of people to ascend and descend. In the distance are the summits of adjacent mountains. At first all this is concealed by a thick fog, which clears presently. Enter (through fog) Chorus of Stars coming off duty, as fatigued with their night's work.*

CHORUS OF STARS

Throughout the night
  The constellations
Have given light
  From various stations.
When midnight gloom
  Falls on all nations,
We will resume
  Our occupations.

Solo

Our light, it's true,
  Is not worth mention;
What can we do
  To gain attention,
When, night and noon,
  With vulgar glaring,
A great big Moon
  Is *always* flaring?

Chorus

Throughout the night, &c.

During Chorus Enter DIANA, *an elderl Goddess. She is carefully wrapped u in Cloaks, Shawls, etc. A Hood is ove her head, a Respirator in her mouth and Goloshes on her feet. During th chorus she takes these things off, an discovers herself dressed in the usua costume of the Lunar Diana, the God dess of the Moon.*

Dia. (*shuddering*). Ugh! How cold th nights are! I don't know how it is, bu I seem to feel the night air a great dea more than I used to. But it is time for th sun to be rising. (*Calls.*) Apollo.

Ap. (*within*). Hollo!

Dia. I've come off duty—it's time fo you to be getting up.

178

Enter APOLLO. *He is an elderly "buck" with an air of assumed juvenility, and is dressed in dressing gown and smoking cap.*

Ap. (*yawning*). I shan't go out to-day. was out yesterday and the day before and want a little rest. I don't know how it s but I seem to feel my work a great deal nore than I used to.

Dia. I'm sure these short days can't hurt ou. Why, you don't rise till six and you're n bed again by five: you should have a urn at *my* work and see how you like that –out all night!

Ap. My dear sister, I don't envy you—hough I remember when I did—but that vas when I was a younger sun. I don't hink I'm quite well. Perhaps a little change f air will do me good. I've a great mind o show myself in London this winter, hey'll be very glad to see me. No! I shan't o out to-day. I shall send them this fine, hick, wholesome fog and they won't miss ne. It's the best substitute for a blazing un—and like most substitutes, nothing at ll like the real thing. (*To fog.*) Be off with vou.

Fog clears away and discovers the scene described.

Hurried Music. MERCURY *shoots up from behind precipice at back of stage. He carries several parcels afterwards described. He sits down, very much fatigued.*

Mer. Home at last. A nice time I've had of it.

Dia. You young scamp, you've been down all night again. This is the third time you've been out this week.

Mer. Well, *you're* a nice one to blow me up for that.

Dia. I can't help being out all night.

Mer. And I can't help being down all night. The nature of Mercury requires that he should go down when the sun sets, and rise again, when the sun rises.

Dia. And what have you been doing?

Mer. Stealing on commission. There's a set of false teeth and a box of Life Pills—that's for Jupiter—An invisible peruke and a bottle of hair dye—that's for Apollo—A respirator and a pair of goloshes—that's for Cupid—A full bottomed chignon, some auricomous fluid, a box of pearl-powder,

a pot of rouge, and a hare's foot—that's for Venus.

Dia. Stealing! you ought to be ashamed of yourself!

Mer. Oh, as the god of thieves I must do something to justify my position.

Dia. and Ap. (*contemptuously*). Your position!

Mer. Oh I know it's nothing to boast of, even on earth. Up here, it's simply contemptible. Now that you gods are too old for your work, you've made me the miserable drudge of Olympus—groom, valet, postman, butler, commissionaire, maid of all work, parish beadle, and original dustman.

Ap. Your Christmas boxes ought to be something considerable.

Mer. They ought to be but they're not. I'm treated abominably. I make everybody and I'm nobody—I go everywhere and I'm nowhere—I do everything and I'm nothing. I've made thunder for Jupiter, odes for Apollo, battles for Mars, and love for Venus. I've married couples for Hymen, and six weeks afterwards, I've divorced them for Cupid—and in return I get all the kicks while they pocket the halfpence. And in compensation for robbing me of the halfpence in question, what have they done for me?

Ap. Why, they've—ha! ha! they've made you the god of thieves!

Mer. Very self-denying of them—there isn't one of them who hasn't a better claim to the distinction than I have.

SONG—MERCURY

Oh, I'm the celestial drudge,
    From morning to night I must stop at it,
On errands all day I must trudge,
    And I stick to my work till I drop at it!
In summer I get up at one
    (As a good-natured donkey I'm ranked for it),
Then I go and I light up the Sun,
    And Phœbus Apollo gets thanked for it!
    Well, well, it's the way of the world,
        And will be through all its futurity;
    Though noodles are baroned and earled,
        There's nothing for clever obscurity!

I'm the slave of the Gods, neck and heels,
    And I'm bound to obey, though I rate at 'em;

And I not only order their meals,
   But I cook 'em, and serve 'em, and wait
       at 'em.
Then I make all their nectar—I do—
   (Which a terrible liquor to rack us is)
And whenever I mix them a brew,
   Why all the thanksgivings are Bacchus's!
      Well, well, it's the way of the world,
        &c.
Then reading and writing I teach,
   And spelling-books many I've edited!
And for bringing those arts within reach,
   That donkey Minerva gets credited.
Then I scrape at the stars with a knife,
   And plate-powder the moon (on the
      days for it),
And I hear all the world and his wife
   Awarding Diana the praise for it!
      Well, well, it's the way of the world,
        &c.

[*After song—very loud and majestic music
   is heard.*

Dia. and Mer. (*looking off*). Why, who's
this? Jupiter, by Jove!
Enter JUPITER, *an extremely old man, very
   decrepit, with very thin straggling
   white beard, he wears a long braided
   dressing-gown, handsomely trimmed,
   and a silk night-cap on his head.* MER-
   CURY *falls back respectfully as he enters.*

Jup. Good day, Diana—ah Apollo—
Well, well, well, what's the matter? what's
the matter?
Dia. Why, that young scamp Mercury
says that we do nothing, and leave all the
duties of Olympus to him! Will you believe
it, he actually says that our influence on
earth is dropping down to *nil.*
Jup. Well, well—don't be hard on the
lad—to tell you the truth, I'm not sure that
he's very far wrong. Don't let it go any
further, but, between ourselves, the sacri-
fices and votive offerings have fallen off
terribly of late. Why, I can remember the
time when people offered us human sacri-
fices—no mistake about it—human sacri-
fices! think of that!
Dia. Ah! those good old days!
Jup. Then it fell off to oxen, pigs, and
sheep.
Ap. Well, there are worse things than
oxen, pigs and sheep.
Jup. So I've found to my cost. My dear

sir—between ourselves, it's dropped off from
one thing to another until it has positively
dwindled down to preserved Australian
beef! What do you think of that?
Ap. I don't like it at all.
Jup. You won't mention it—it might
go further——
Dia. It couldn't fare worse.
Jup. In short, matters have come to such
a crisis that there's no mistake about it—
something must be done to restore our
influence, the only question is, *What?*

QUARTETTE

Mercury (*coming forward in great alarm*).

Enter MARS

Oh incident unprecedented!
   I hardly can believe it's true!

Mars

Why, bless the boy, he's quite demented!
   Why, what's the matter, sir, with you?

Apollo

Speak quickly, or you'll get a warming!

Mercury

Why, mortals up the mount are swarming,
Our temple on Olympus storming,
   In hundreds—aye in thousands, too!

All

   Goodness gracious,
   How audacious;
   Earth is spacious,
      Why come here?
   Our impeding
   Their proceeding
   Were good breeding,
      That is clear.

Diana

Jupiter, hear my plea;
   Upon the mount if *they* light,
There'll be an end of me,
   I won't be seen by daylight!

Apollo

Tartarus is the place
   These scoundrels you should send to—
Should they behold my face
   My influence there's an end to!
     Jupiter (*looking over precipice*).
What fools to give themselves so much
   exertion!
     Diana (*looking over precipice*).
A government survey I'll make assertion!
     Apollo (*looking over precipice*).
Perhaps the Alpine club at their diversion!

Mercury (*looking over precipice*).
They seem to be more like a "Cook's Excursion."

All

Goodness gracious, etc.

Apollo

If, mighty Jove, you value your existence,
  Send them a thunderbolt with your regards!

Jupiter

My thunderbolts, though valid at a distance,
  Are not effective at a hundred yards.

Mercury

Let the moon's rays, Diana, strike 'em flighty,
  Make 'em all lunatics in various styles!

Diana

My Lunar rays unhappily are mighty
  Only at many hundred thousand miles.

All

Goodness gracious, etc.

[*Exeunt* JUPITER, APOLLO, DIANA, *and* MERCURY *into ruined temple.*

Enter SPARKEION *and* NICEMIS *climbing mountain at back.*

Spark. Here we are at last on the very summit, and we've left the others ever so far behind! Why, what's this?

Nice. A ruined palace! A palace on the top of a mountain. I wonder who lives here? Some mighty king, I dare say, with wealth beyond all counting, who came to live up here——

Sp. To avoid his creditors! It's a lovely situation for a country house, though it's very much out of repair.

Nice. Very inconvenient situation.

Sp. Inconvenient?

Nice. Yes—how are you to get butter, milk, and eggs up here? No pigs—no poultry—no postman. Why, I should go mad.

Sp. What a dear little practical mind it is! What a wife you will make!

Nice. Don't be too sure—we are only partly married—the marriage ceremony lasts all day.

Sp. I've no doubt at all about it. We shall be as happy as a king and queen, though we are only a strolling actor and actress.

Nice. It's very kind of Thespis to celebrate our marriage day by giving the company a pic-nic on this lovely mountain.

Sp. And still more kind to allow us to get so much ahead of all the others. Discreet Thespis! [*Kissing her.*

Nice. There now, get away, do! Remember the marriage ceremony is not yet completed.

Sp. But it would be ungrateful to Thespis's discretion not to take advantage of it by improving the opportunity.

Nice. Certainly not; get away.

Sp. On second thoughts the opportunity's so good it don't admit of improvement. There! [*Kisses her.*

Nice. How dare you kiss me before we are quite married?

Sp. Attribute it to the intoxicating influence of the mountain air.

Nice. Then we had better go down again. It is not right to expose ourselves to influences over which we have no control.

DUET—SPARKEION *and* NICEMIS

Sparkeion

Here far away from all the world,
  Dissension and derision,
With Nature's wonders all unfurled
  To our delighted vision,
    With no one here
      (At least in sight)
    To interfere
      With our delight,
  And two fond lovers sever,
    Oh do not free,
      Thine hand from mine,
    I swear to thee
      My love is thine,
  For ever and for ever!

Nicemis

On mountain top the air is keen,
  And most exhilarating,
And we say things we do not mean
  In moments less elating.
    So please to wait,
      For thoughts that crop,
    En tête-à-tête,
      On mountain top,
    May not exactly tally
      With those that you
        May entertain,
      Returning to
        The sober plain
  Of yon relaxing valley.

Sp. Very well—if you won't have anything to say to me, I know who will.

Nice. Who will?

Sp. Daphne will.

Nice. Daphne would flirt with anybody.

Sp. Anybody would flirt with Daphne. She is quite as pretty as you and has twice as much back-hair.

Nice. She has twice as much money, which may account for it.

Sp. At all events, *she* has appreciation. *She* likes good looks.

Nice. We all like what we haven't got.

Sp. She keeps her eyes open.

Nice. Yes—one of them.

Sp. Which one?

Nice. The one she doesn't wink with.

Sp. Well, I was engaged to her for six months and if she still makes eyes at me, you must attribute it to force of habit. Besides—remember—we are only half-married at present.

Nice. I suppose you mean that you are going to treat me as shamefully as you treated her. Very well, break it off if you like. *I* shall not offer any objection. Thespis used to be very attentive to me, and I'd just as soon be a manager's wife as a fifth-rate actor's!

Chorus heard, at first below, then enter DAPHNE, PRETTEIA, PREPOSTEROS, STU-PIDAS, TIPSEION, CYMON, *and other members of* THESPIS' *company climbing over rocks at back. All carry small baskets.*

CHORUS—(*with dance*)*
Climbing over rocky mountain,
Skipping rivulet and fountain,
Passing where the willows quiver,
By the ever rolling river,
    Swollen with the summer rain.
Threading long and leafy mazes,
Dotted with unnumbered daisies,
Scaling rough and rugged passes,
Climb the hardy lads and lasses,
    Till the mountain-top they gain.

First Voice
Fill the cup and tread the measure,
Make the most of fleeting leisure,
Hail it as a true ally,
    Though it perish bye and bye!

Second Voice
Every moment brings a treasure
Of its own especial pleasure,
Though the moments quickly die,
Greet them gaily as they fly!

Third Voice
Far away from grief and care,
High up in the mountain air,
Let us live and reign alone,
In a world that's all our own.

Fourth Voice
Here enthroned in the sky,
Far away from mortal eye,
We'll be gods and make decrees,
Those may honour them who please

Chorus
Fill the cup and tread the measure
    etc.

After CHORUS *and* COUPLETS *enter* THESPIS *climbing over rocks*

Thes. Bless you, my people, bless you Let the revels commence. After all, fo thorough, unconstrained, unconventiona enjoyment give me a pic-nic.

Prep. (*very gloomily*). Give him a pic-ni somebody!

Thes. Be quiet Preposteros—don't inter rupt.

Prep. Ha! ha! shut up again! But n matter.

[STUPIDAS *endeavours, in pantomime, t reconcile him. Throughout the scen* PREP, *shows symptoms of breaking ou into a furious passion, and* STUPIDA *does all he can to pacify and restrai him.*

Thes. The best of a pic-nic is that every body contributes what he pleases, and no body knows what anybody else has brough till the last moment. Now, unpack every body, and let's see what there is for every body.

Nice. I have brought you—a bottle o soda water—for the claret-cup.

Daph. I have brought you—a lettuce fo the lobster salad.

Sp. A piece of ice—for the claret-cup

Prett. A bottle of vinegar—for th lobster-salad.

Cymon. A bunch of burrage for th claret-cup!

Tips. A hard-boiled egg—for the lobster salad!

Stup. One lump of sugar for the claret cup!

Prep. He has brought one lump of suga for the claret-cup? Ha! Ha! Ha!

[*Laughing melodramatically*

*Afterwards transplanted to Act I of "The Pirates of Penzance."

Stup. Well, Preposteros, and what have you brought?

Prep. I have brought *two* lumps of the very best salt for the lobster salad.

Thes. Oh—is that all?

Prep. All! Ha! Ha! He asks if it is all! [STUPIDAS *consoles him.*

Thes. But, I say—this is capital so far as it goes—nothing could be better, but it doesn't go far enough. The claret, for instance! I don't insist on claret—or a lobster—I don't insist on lobster, but a lobster salad without a lobster, why, it isn't lobster salad. Here, Tipseion!

TIPSEION (*a very drunken bloated fellow, dressed, however, with scrupulous accuracy and wearing a large medal round his neck*). My Master

Falls on his knees to THES. *and kisses his robe.*

Thes. Get up—don't be a fool. Where's the claret? We arranged last week that you were to see to that?

Tips. True, dear master. But then I was a drunkard!

Thes. You were.

Tips. You engaged me to play convivial parts on the strength of my personal appearance.

Thes. I did.

Tips. You then found that my habits interfered with my duties as low comedian.

Thes. True——

Tips. You said yesterday that unless I took the pledge you would dismiss me from your company.

Thes. Quite so.

Tips. Good. I have taken it. It is all I have taken since yesterday. My preserver! [*Embraces him.*

Thes. Yes, but where's the wine?

Tips. I left it behind, that I might not be tempted to violate my pledge.

Prep. Minion!

[*Attempts to get at him, is restrained by* STUPIDAS.

Thes. Now, Preposteros, what *is* the matter with you?

Prep. It is enough that I am down-trodden in my profession. I will not submit to imposition out of it. It is enough that as your heavy villain I get the worst of it every night in a combat of six, I will not submit to insult in the day time. I have come out, ha! ha! to enjoy myself!

Thes. But look here, you know—virtue only triumphs at night from seven to ten —vice gets the best of it during the other twenty-three hours. Won't that satisfy you?

[STUPIDAS *endeavours to pacify him.*

Prep. (*irritated to* STUP.). Ye are odious to my sight! get out of it!

Stup. (*in great terror*). What have I done?

Thes. Now *what* is it, Preposteros, *what* is it?

Prep. I a—hate him and would have his life!

Thes. (*to* STUP.). That's it—he hates you and would have your life. Now go and be merry.

Stup. Yes, but why does he hate me?

Thes. Oh—exactly. (*To* PREP.) Why do you hate him?

Prep. Because he is a minion!

Thes. He hates you because you are a minion. It explains itself. Now go and enjoy yourselves. Ha! ha! It is well for those who *can* laugh—let them do so—there is no extra charge. The light-hearted cup and the convivial jest for them—but for me —what is there for me?

Sillimon. There is some claret-cup and lobster salad. [*Handing some.*

Thes. (*taking it*). Thank you. (*Resuming.*) What is there for me but anxiety— ceaseless, gnawing anxiety that tears at my very vitals and rends my peace of mind asunder? There is nothing whatever for me but anxiety of the nature I have just described. The charge of these thoughtless revellers is my unhappy lot. It is not a small charge, and it is rightly termed a lot, because they are many. Oh why did the gods make me a manager?

Sill. (*as guessing a riddle*). *Why* did the gods make him a manager?

Sp. Why did the *gods* make him a manager?

Dap. Why did the gods make *him* a manager?

Prett. Why did the gods make him a *manager?*

Thes. No—no—what are you talking about? what do you mean?

Dap. I've got it—don't tell us——

All. No—no—because—because——

Thes. (*annoyed*). It isn't a conundrum—it's a misanthropical question. Why cannot I join you?   [*Retires up centre.*

Dap. (*who is sitting with* SPARKEION *to the annoyance of* NICEMIS *who is crying alone*). I'm sure I don't know. We do not want you. Don't distress yourself on our account—we are getting on very comfortably—aren't we, Sparkeion?

Spar. We are so happy that we don't miss the lobster or the claret. What are lobster and claret compared with the society of those we love?   [*Embracing* DAPHNE.

Dap. Why, Nicemis, love, you are eating nothing. Aren't you happy, dear?

Nice. (*spitefully*). *You* are *quite* welcome to *my* share of *everything*. *I* intend to console *myself* with the society of my manager.

[*Takes* THESPIS' *arm affectionately.*

Thes. Here I say—this won't do, you know—I can't allow it—at least before my company—besides, you are half-married to Sparkeion. Sparkeion, here's your half-wife impairing my influence before my company. Don't you know the story of the gentleman who undermined his influence by associating with his inferiors?

All. Yes, yes,—we know it.

Prep. (*furiously*). *I* do not know it! It's ever thus! Doomed to disappointment from my earliest years——

[STUPIDAS *endeavours to console him.*

Thes. There—that's enough. Preposteros —you *shall* hear it.

SONG—THESPIS

I once knew a chap who discharged a function
On the North South East West Diddlesex junction,
He was conspicu*ous* exceeding,
For his affable ways and his easy breeding.
Although a Chairman of Directors,
He was hand in glove with the ticket inspectors,
He tipped the guards with bran-new fivers,
And sang little songs to the engine drivers.
  'Twas told to me with great compunction,
    By one who had discharged with unction,
    A Chairman of Directors' function,
    On the North South East West Diddlesex junction.

Fol diddle, lol diddle, lol lol lay.
Each Christmas Day he gave each stoker
A silver shovel and a golden poker,
He'd button-hole flowers for the ticket sorters,
And rich Bath-buns for the outside porters.
He'd mount the clerks on his first-class hunters,
And he built little villas for the road-side shunters,
And if any were fond of pigeon shooting,
He'd ask them down to his place at Tooting.
  'Twas told to me, etc.

In course of time there spread a rumour
That he did all this from a sense of humour,
So instead of signalling and stoking,
They gave themselves up to a course of joking,
Whenever they knew that he was riding,
They shunted his train on lonely siding,
Or stopped all night in the middle of a tunnel,
On the plea that the boiler was a-coming through the funnel.
  'Twas told to me, etc.

If he wished to go to Perth or Stirling,
His train through several counties whirling,
Would set him down in a fit of larking,
At four a.m. in the wilds of Barking.
This pleased his whim and seemed to strike it,
But the general Public did not like it,
The receipts fell, after a few repeatings,
And he got it hot at the annual meetings.
  'Twas told to me, etc.

He followed out his whim with vigour,
The shares went down to a nominal figure,
These are the sad results proceeding
From his affable ways and his easy breeding!
The line, with its rails and guards and peelers,
Was sold for a song to marine store dealers,
The shareholders are all in the work'us,
And he sells pipe-lights in the Regent Circus.

  'Twas told to me with much compunction,
    By one who had discharged with unction
    A Chairman of Directors' function,

On the North South East West Diddlesex
    junction,
Fol diddle lol diddle lol lol lay!
                            [*After song.*
Thes. It's very hard. As a man, I am
naturally of an easy disposition. As a
manager, I am compelled to hold myself
aloof, that my influence may not be de-
teriorated. As a man, I am inclined to
fraternize with the pauper—as a manager
I am compelled to walk about like this:
Don't know yah! Don't know yah! Don't
know yah!
[Strides haughtily about the stage, JUPITER,
    MARS, *and* APOLLO, *in full Olympian
    costume appear on the three broken
    columns. Thespians scream.*
Jupiter, Mars and Apollo (in recit.).
Presumptuous mortal!
Thes. (*same business*). Don't know yah!
Don't know yah!
*Jup., Mars and Apollo (seated on three
broken pillars, still in recit.).* Presumptuous
mortal!
Thes. I do not know you, I do not know
you.
*Jup., Mars and Apollo (standing on
ground, recit.).* Presumptuous mortal!
Thes. (*recit.*) Remove this person.
STUP. *and* PREP. *seize* APOLL. *and* MARS.
Jup. (*speaking*). Stop, you evidently
don't know me. Allow me to offer you my
card.   [*Throws flash paper.*
Thes. Ah yes, it's very pretty, but we
don't want any at present. When we do
our Christmas piece I'll let you know.
(*Changing his manner.*) Look here, you
now, this is a private party and we
haven't the pleasure of your acquaintance.
There are a good many other mountains
about, if you must have a mountain all
to yourself. Don't make me let myself
down before my company. (*Resuming.*)
Don't know yah! Don't know yah!
Jup. I am Jupiter, the King of the
Gods. This is Apollo. This is Mars.
    [*All kneel to them except* THESPIS.
Thes. Oh! then as I'm a respectable man,
and rather particular about the company
keep, I think I'll go.
Jup. No—no—stop a bit. We want to
consult you on a matter of great importance. There! Now we are alone. Who are
you?

Thes. I am Thespis of the Thessalian
Theatres.
Jup. The very man we want. Now as
a judge of what the public likes, are you
impressed with my appearance as the
father of the gods?
Thes. Well to be candid with you, I am
not. In fact, I'm disappointed.
Jup. Disappointed?
Thes. Yes, you see you're so much out
of repair. No, you don't come up to my
idea of the part. Bless you, I've played
you often.
Jup. You have!
Thes. To be sure I have.
Jup. And how have you dressed the
part?
Thes. Fine, commanding party in the
prime of life. Thunderbolt—full beard—
dignified manner—A good deal of this sort
of thing "Don't know yah! Don't know
yah! Don't know yah!"
                        [*Imitating, crosses* L.
Jup. (*much affected*). I—I'm very much
obliged to you. It's very good of you. I—
I—I used to be like that. I can't tell you
how much I feel it. And do you find I'm
an impressive character to play?
Thes. Well no, I can't say you are. In
fact, we don't use you much out of burlesque.
Jup. Burlesque! [*Offended, walks up.*
Thes. Yes, it's a painful subject, drop
it, drop it. The fact is, you are not the
gods you were—you're behind your age.
Jup. Well, but what are we to do? We
feel that we ought to do something, but
we don't know what.
Thes. Why don't you all go down to
Earth, incog., mingle with the world, hear
and see what people think of you, and
judge for yourselves as to the best means
to take to restore your influence?
Jup. Ah, but what's to become of
Olympus in the meantime?
Thes. Lor bless you, don't distress yourself about that. I've a very good company,
used to take long parts on the shortest
notice. Invest us with your powers and
we'll fill your places till you return.
Jup. (*aside*). The offer is tempting. But
suppose you fail?
Thes. Fail! Oh, we never fail in our profession. We've nothing but great successes!

Jup. Then it's a bargain?

Thes. It's a bargain.

        [*They shake hands on it.*

Jup. And that you may not be entirely without assistance, we will leave you Mercury, and whenever you find yourself in a difficulty you can consult him.

      Enter MERCURY (*trap* C.)

QUARTETTE

Jupiter

So that's arranged—you take my place, my boy,
  While we make trial of a new existence.
At length I shall be able to enjoy
  The pleasures I have envied from a distance.

Mercury

Compelled upon Olympus here to stop,
  While other gods go down to play the hero,
Don't be surprised if on this mountain top
  You find your Mercury is down at zero!

Apollo

To earth away to join in mortal acts,
  And gather fresh materials to write on,
Investigate more closely several facts,
  That I for centuries have thrown some light on!

Diana

I, as the modest moon with crescent bow,
  Have always shown a light to nightly scandal,
I must say I should like to go below,
  And find out if the game is worth the candle!

Enter all the Thespians, summoned by MERCURY

Mer. Here come your people!

Thes. People better now!

AIR—THESPIS

While mighty Jove goes down below
  With all the other deities,
I fill his place and wear his "clo,"
  The very part for me it is.
To mother earth to make a track,
  They all are spurred and booted, too,
And you will fill, till they come back,
  The parts you best are suited to.

Chorus

Here's a pretty tale for future Iliads and Odysseys,
Mortals are about to personate the gods and goddesses.

Now to set the world in order, we will work in unity.
Jupiter's perplexity is Thespis's opportunity.

SOLO—SPARKEION

Phoebus am I, with golden ray,
The god of day, the god of day,
When shadowy night has held her sway
  I make the goddess fly.
'Tis mine the task to wake the world,
In slumber curled, in slumber curled,
By me her charms are all unfurled,
  The god of day am I!

Chorus

  The god of day, the god of day,
  That part shall our Sparkeion play
    Ha! ha! &c.
  The rarest fun and rarest fare,
  That ever fell to mortal share!
    Ha! ha! &c.

SOLO—NICEMIS

I am the moon, the lamp of night.
I show a light—I show a light.
With radiant sheen I put to flight
  The shadows of the sky.
By my fair rays, as you're aware,
Gay lovers swear—gay lovers swear,
While greybeards sleep away their care,
  The lamp of night am I!

Chorus

The lamp of night—the lamp of night
Nicemis plays, to her delight.
  Ha! ha! ha! ha!
The rarest fun and rarest fare,
That ever fell to mortal share.
  Ha! ha! ha! ha!

SOLO—TIMIDON

Mighty old Mars, the God of War,
I'm destined for—I'm destined for—
A terribly famous conqueror,
  With sword upon his thigh.
When armies meet with eager shout,
And warlike rout, and warlike rout,
You'll find me there without a doubt.
  The God of War am I!

Chorus

  The God of War, the God of War.
  Great Timidon is destined for!
    Ha! ha! ha! ha!
  The rarest fun and rarest fare,
  That ever fell to mortal share.
    Ha! ha! ha! ha! &c.

SOLO—DAPHNE

When, as the fruit of warlike deeds,

The soldier bleeds, the soldier bleeds,
Calliope crowns heroic deeds,
  With immortality.
From mere oblivon I reclaim
The soldier's name, the soldier's name,
And write it on the roll of fame,
  The muse of fame am I!
                Chorus
The muse of fame, the muse of fame,
Calliope is Daphne's name,
  Ha! ha! ha! ha!
The rarest fun and rarest fare,
That ever fell to mortal share.
  Ha! ha! ha! ha!
Tutti. Here's a pretty tale!
*Enter procession of old Gods, they come
  down very much astonished at all they
  see, then passing by, ascend the plat-
  form that leads to the descent at the
  back.*
Gods (JUP., DIA., *and* APOLLO) *in corner
  are together.*
              We will go,
              Down below,
              Revels rare,
              We will share.
                Ha! ha! ha!
              With a gay
              Holiday,
              All unknown,
              And alone.
                Ha! ha! ha!
                  Tutti.
            Here's a pretty tale!
[*The Gods, including those who have
  lately entered in procession, group
  themselves on rising ground at back.
  The Thespians* (kneeling) *bid them
  farewell.*

ACT II

SCENE.—*The same scene as in Act I with
  the exception that in place of the
  ruins that filled the foreground of the
  stage, the interior of a magnificent
  temple is seen, showing the background
  of the scene of Act I, through the
  columns of the portico at the back.
  High throne L.U.E. Low seats below it.
  All the substitute gods and goddesses* (that
  is to say, Thespians) *are discovered
  grouped in picturesque attitudes about
  the stage, eating, drinking, and smoking and singing the following verses:—*

                Chorus
Of all symposia,
  The best by half,
    Upon Olympus, here, await us,
We eat Ambrosia,
  And nectar quaff—
    It cheers but don't inebriate us.
We know the fallacies
  Of human food,
    So please to pass Olympian rosy,
We built up palaces,
  Where ruins stood,
    And find them much more snug and
      cosy.
              SOLO—SILLIMON
To work and think, my dear,
  Up here, would be,
    The height of conscientious folly,
So eat and drink, my dear,
  I like to see,
    Young people gay—young people jolly.
Olympian food, my love,
  I'll lay long odds,
    Will please your lips—those rosy por-
      tals,
What is the good, my love
  Of being gods,
    If we must work like common mor-
      tals?
                Chorus
    Of all symposia, &c.
[*Exeunt all but* NICEMIS, *who is dressed as*
  DIANA, *and* PRETTEIA, *who is dressed as*
  VENUS. *They take* SILLIMON'S *arm and
  bring him down.*
Sillimon. Bless their little hearts, I can
refuse them nothing. As the Olympian stage-
manager I ought to be strict with them
and make them do their duty, but I can't.
Bless their little hearts, when I see the
pretty little craft come sailing up to me
with a wheedling smile on their pretty little
figure-heads, I can't turn my back on 'em.
I'm all bow, though I'm sure I try to be
stern!
  Prett. You certainly are a dear old thing.
  Sill. She says I'm a dear old thing!
Deputy Venus says I'm a dear old thing!
  Nice. It's her affectionate habit to describe everybody in those terms. *I* am more
particular, but still even *I* am bound to
admit that you are certainly a very dear
old thing.
  Sill. Deputy Venus says I'm a dear old

thing, and deputy Diana, who is much more particular, endorses it! Who could be severe with such deputy divinities?

Prett. Do you know, I'm going to ask you a favour.

Sill. Venus is going to ask me a favour!

Prett. You see, I am Venus.

Sill. No one who saw your face would doubt it.

Nice. (*aside*). No one who knew her *character* would.

Prett. Well Venus, you know, is married to Mars.

Sill. To Vulcan, my dear, to Vulcan. The exact connubial relation of the different gods and goddesses is a point on which we must be extremely particular.

Prett. I beg your pardon—Venus is married to Mars.

Nice. If she isn't married to Mars, she ought to be.

Sill. Then that decides it—call it married to Mars.

Prett. Married to Vulcan or married to Mars, what does it signify?

Sill. My dear, it's a matter on which I have no personal feeling whatever.

Prett. So that she is married to some one.

Sill. Exactly! so that she is married to some one. Call it married to Mars.

Prett. Now here's my difficulty. Presumptios takes the place of Mars, and Presumptios is my father!

Sill. Then why object to Vulcan?

Prett. Because Vulcan is my grandfather!

Sill. But, my dear, what an objection! You are playing a part till the real gods return. That's all! Whether you are supposed to be married to your father—or your grandfather, what does it matter? This passion for realism is the curse of the stage!

Prett. That's all very well, but I can't throw myself into a part that has already lasted a twelvemonth, when I have to make love to my father. It interferes with my conception of the characters. It spoils the part.

Sill. Well, well, I'll see what can be done. (*Exit* PRETTEIA L.U.E.) That's always the way with beginners, they've no imaginative power. A true artist ought to be superior to such considerations. (NICEMIS *comes down* R.) Well, Nicemis—I should say Diana—what's wrong with you? Don't you like your part?

Nice. Oh, immensely! It's great fun.

Sill. Don't you find it lonely out by yourself all night?

Nice. Oh, but I'm *not* alone all night!

Sill. But—I don't want to ask any injudicious questions—but who accompanies you?

Nice. Who? why Sparkeion, of course.

Sill. Sparkeion? Well, but Sparkeion is Phoebus Apollo. (*Enter* SPARKEION) He's the Sun, you know.

Nice. Of course he is; I should catch my death of cold, in the night air, if he didn't accompany me.

Sp. My dear Sillimon, it would never do for a young lady to be out alone all night. It wouldn't be respectable.

Sill. There's a good deal of truth in that. But still—the Sun—at night—I don't like the idea. The original Diana always went out alone.

Nice. I hope the original Diana is no rule for *me*. After all, what *does* it matter?

Sill. To be sure—what *does* it matter?

Sp. The sun at night, or in the daytime!

Sill. So that he shines. That's all that's necessary. (*Exit* NICEMIS R.U.E.) But poor Daphne, what will she say to this?

Sp. Oh, Daphne can console herself; young ladies soon get over this sort of thing. Did you never hear of the young lady who was engaged to Cousin Robin?

Sill. Never.

Sp. Then I'll sing it to you.

SONG—SPARKEION

Little maid of Arcadee
Sat on Cousin Robin's knee,
Thought in form and face and limb
Nobody could rival him.
He was brave and she was fair.
Truth, they made a pretty pair.
Happy little maiden, she—
Happy maid of Arcadee!
Moments fled as moments will
Happily enough, until,
After, say, a month or two,
Robin did as Robins do.
Weary of his lover's play,
Jilted her and went away.
Wretched little maiden, she—

Wretched maid of Arcadee!
To her little home she crept,
There she sat her down and wept,
Maiden wept as maidens will—
Grew so thin and pale—until
Cousin Richard came to woo!
Then again the roses grew!
Happy little maiden, she—
Happy maid of Arcadee!

[*Exit* SPARKEION.

Sill. Well, Mercury, my boy, you've had
a year's experience of us here. How do we
do it? I think we're rather an improvement on the original gods—don't you?

Mer. Well, you see, there's a good deal
to be said on both sides of the question;
you are certainly younger than the original
gods, and, therefore, more active. On the
other hand, they are certainly older than
you, and have, therefore, more experience.
On the whole I prefer *you* because your
mistakes amuse me.

SONG—MERCURY

Olympus is now in a terrible muddle,
    The deputy deities all are at fault;
They splutter and splash like a pig in a
        puddle,
    And dickens a one of 'em's earning his
        salt,
For Thespis as Jove is a terrible blunder,
    Too nervous and timid—too easy and
        weak—
Whenever he's called on to lighten or
        thunder,
    The thought of it keeps him awake for
        a week!
Then mighty Mars hasn't the pluck of a
        parrot,
    When left in the dark he will quiver
        and quail;
And Vulcan has arms that would snap like
        a carrot,
    Before he could drive in a tenpenny
        nail!
Then Venus's freckles are very repelling,
    And Venus should *not* have a squint in
        her eyes;
The learned Minerva is weak in her spell-
        ing,
    And scatters her h's all over the skies.
Then Pluto, in kindhearted tenderness
        erring,
    Can't make up his mind to let anyone
        die—

The *Times* has a paragraph ever recurring,
    "Remarkable instance of longe*vity.*"
On some it has come as a serious onus,
    To others it's quite an advantage—in
        short,
While ev'ry Life Office declares a big bonus,
    The poor undertakers are all in the
        court!
Then Cupid, the rascal, forgetting his trade
        is
    To make men and women impartially
        smart,
Will only shoot at pretty young ladies,
    And never takes aim at a bachelor's
        heart.
The results of this freak—or whatever you
        term it—
    Should cover the wicked young scamp
        with disgrace,
While ev'ry young man is as shy as a
        hermit,
    Young ladies are popping all over the
        place!
This wouldn't much matter—for bashful
        shy men,
    When skilfully handled, are certain to
        fall,
But, alas! that determined young bachelor
        Hymen
    Refuses to wed anybody at all!
He swears that Love's flame is the vilest
        of arsons,
    And looks upon marriage as quite a
        mistake;
Now, what in the world's to become of
        the parsons,
    And what of the artist who sugars the
        cake?
In short, you will see from the facts that
        I'm showing,
    The state of the case is exceedingly sad;
If Thespis's people go on as they're going,
    Olympus will certainly go to the bad!
From Jupiter downwards there isn't a dab
        in it,
    All of 'em quibble and shuffle and shirk;
A premier in Downing Street, forming a
        Cabinet,
    Couldn't find people less fit for their
        work!

Enter THESPIS, L.U.E.

Thes. Sillimon, you can retire.
Sill. Sir, I—
Thes. Don't pretend you can't when I

say you can. I've seen you do it—go! (*Exit* SILLIMON *bowing extravagantly,* THESPIS *imitates him.*) Well, Mercury, I've been in power one year to-day.

Mer. One year to-day. How do you like ruling the world?

Thes. Like it! Why it's as straightforward as possible. Why there hasn't been a hitch of any kind since we came up here. Lor! The airs you gods and goddesses give yourselves are perfectly sickening. Why it's mere child's play!

Mer. Very simple, isn't it?

Thes. Simple? Why I could do it on my head?

Mer. Ah—I daresay you will do it on your head very soon.

Thes. What do you mean by *that*, Mercury?

Mer. I mean that when you've turned the world *quite* topsy-turvy you won't know whether you're standing on your head or your heels.

Thes. Well, but, Mercury, it's all right at present.

Mer. Oh yes—as far as we know.

Thes. Well, but, you know, we know as much as anybody knows; you know, I believe, that the world's still going on.

Mer. Yes—as far as we can judge— much as usual.

Thes. Well, then, give the Father of the Drama his due, Mercury. Don't be envious of the Father of the Drama.

Mer. Well, but you see you leave so much to accident.

Thes. Well, Mercury, if I do, it's my principle. I am an easy man, and I like to make things as pleasant as possible. What did I do the day we took office? Why I called the company together and I said to them: "Here we are, you know, gods and goddesses, no mistake about it, the real thing. Well, we have certain duties to discharge, let's discharge them intelligently. Don't let us be hampered by routine and red tape and precedent, let's set the original gods an example, and put a liberal interpretation on our duties. If it occurs to any one to try an experiment in his own department, let him try it, if he fails there's no harm done, if he succeeds it is a distinct gain to society. Take it easy," I said, "and at the same time,

make experiments. Don't hurry your work, do it slowly, and do it well." And here we are after a twelvemonth, and not a single complaint or a single petition has reached me.

Mer. No—not yet.

Thes. What do you mean by "no, not yet"?

Mer. Well, you see, you don't understand these things. All the petitions that are addressed by men to Jupiter pass through my hands, and it's my duty to collect them and present them once a year.

Thes. Oh, only once a year?

Mer. Only once a year.

Thes. And the year is up—?

Mer. To-day.

Thes. Oh, then I suppose there are *some* complaints?

Mer. Yes, there *are* some.

Thes. (*disturbed*). Oh. Perhaps there are a good many?

Mer. There are a good many.

Thes. Oh. Perhaps there are a thundering lot?

Mer. There are a thundering lot.

Thes. (*very much disturbed*). Oh!

Mer. You see you've been taking it so very easy—and so have most of your company.

Thes. Oh, who has been taking it easy?

Mer. Well, all except those who have been trying experiments.

Thes. Well, but I suppose the experiments are ingenious?

Mer. Yes; they are ingenious, but on the whole ill-judged. But it's time to go and summon your court.

Thes. What for?

Mer. To hear the complaints. In five minutes they will be here. [*Exit.*

Thes. (*very uneasy*). I don't know how it is, but there is something in that young man's manner that suggests that the Father of the Gods has been taking it *too* easy. Perhaps it would have been better if I hadn't given my company so much scope. I wonder what they've been doing. I think I will curtail their discretion, though none of them appear to have much of the article. It seems a pity to deprive 'em of what little they have.

Enter DAPHNE, *weeping.*

Thes. Now then, Daphne, what's the matter with you?

Daphne. Well, you know how disgracefully Sparkeion——

Thes. (*correcting her*). Apollo——

Daphne. Apollo, then—has treated me. He promised to marry me years ago, and now he's married to Nicemis.

Thes. Now look here. I can't go into that. You're in Olympus now and must behave accordingly. Drop your Daphne—assume your Calliope.

Dap. Quite so. That's it!

[*Mysteriously.*

Thes. Oh—that is it? [*Puzzled.*

Dap. That is it, Thespis. I am Calliope, the Muse of Fame. Very good. This morning I was in the Olympian library, and I took down the only book there. Here it is.

Thes. (taking it). Lemprière's Classical Dictionary. The Olympian Peerage.

Dap. Open it at Apollo.

Thes. (*opens it*). It is done.

Dap. Read.

Thes. "Apollo was several times married, among others to Issa, Bolina, Coronis, Chymene, Cyrene, Chione, Acacallis, and Calliope."

Dap. And Calliope.

Thes. (*musing*). Ha! I didn't know he was *married* to them.

Dap. (*severely*). Sir! This is the Family Edition.

Thes. Quite so.

Dap. You couldn't expect a lady to read any other?

Thes. On no consideration. But in the original version——

Dap. I go by the Family Edition.

Thes. Then by the Family Edition, Apollo is your husband.

Enter NICEMIS *and* SPARKEION

Nice. Apollo your husband? He is my husband.

Dap. I beg your pardon. He is *my* husband.

Nice. Apollo is Sparkeion, and he's married to me.

Dap. Sparkeion is Apollo, and he's married to me.

Nice. He's my husband.

Dap. He's your brother.

Thes. Look here, Apollo, whose husband are you? Don't let's have any row about it; whose husband are you?

Sp. Upon my honour I don't know. I'm in a very delicate position, but I'll fall in with any arrangement Thespis may propose.

Dap. I've just found out that he's my husband, and yet he goes out every evening with that "thing"!

Thes. Perhaps he's trying an experiment.

Dap. I don't like my husband to make such experiments. The question is, who are we all and what is our relation to each other.

QUARTETTE

Sparkeion
You're Diana, I'm Apollo—
  And Calliope is she.
Daphne
He's your brother.
Nicemis
  You're another.
He has fairly married me,
Daphne
By the rules of this fair spot
I'm his wife, and you are not—
Sparkeion and Daphne
By the rules of this fair spot,
I'm ⎱
She's ⎰ his wife, and you are not.

Nicemis
By this golden wedding ring,
I'm his wife, and you're a "thing."
Daphne, Nicemis and Sparkeion
By this golden wedding ring,
I'm ⎱
She's ⎰ his wife, and you're a "thing."

All
Please will some one kindly tell us,
Who are our respective kin?
All of ⎰us ⎱ are very jealous,
  ⎱them⎰
Neither of ⎰us ⎱ will give in.
  ⎱them⎰
Nicemis
He's my husband I declare,
  I espoused him properlee.
Sparkeion
That is true, for I was there,
  And I saw her marry me.
Daphne
He's your brother—I'm his wife,
  If we go by Lemprière,

Sparkeion
So she is, upon my life,
  Really that seems very fair.
Nicemis
You're my husband and no other,
Sparkeion
That is true enough I swear,
Daphne
I'm his wife, and you're his brother,
Sparkeion
If we go by Lemprière.
Nicemis
It will surely be unfair,
  To decide by Lemprière.

                                        (*Crying.*)

Daphne
I will surely be quite fair,
  To decide by Lemprière,
Sparkeion and Thespsis
How you settle I don't care,
  Leave it all to Lemprière.
(*Spoken.*) The Verdict.
As Sparkeion is Apollo
Up in this Olympian clime,
Why, Nicemis, it will follow,
He's *her* husband, for the time
                    —(*indicating* DAPHNE)
When Sparkeion turns to mortal,
  Join once more the sons of men,
He may take *you* to his portal
                    —(*indicating* NICEMIS)
He will be *your* husband then.
That oh that is my decision,
  'Cording to my mental vision.
Put an end to all collision,
  That oh that is my decision.
My decision—my decision,
All
That oh that is his decision,
His decision—his decision, &c.

[*Exeunt* THES., NICE., SPARK., *and* DAPHNE,
  SPARK. *with* DAPHNE, NICEMIS *weeping
  with* THESPIS.
Mysterious Music. Enter JUPITER, APOLLO,
  and MARS, *from below, at the back of
  stage. All wear cloaks as disguise and
  all are masked.*

                    RECIT
Oh rage and fury! Oh shame and sorrow!
We'll be resuming our ranks to-morrow,
Since from Olympus we have departed,
We've been distracted and broken-hearted,
Oh wicked Thespis! Oh villain scurvy;
Through him Olympus is topsy-turvy!

Compelled to silence to grin and bear it!
He's caused our sorrow, and he shall share
  it.
Where is the monster! Avenge his blunders,
He has awakened Olympian thunders.
                    Enter MERCURY
  Jup. (*recit.*) Oh Monster!
  Ap. (*recit.*). Oh Monster!
  Mars. (*recit.*). Oh Monster!
  Mer. (*in great terror*). Please sir, **what**
have I done sir?
  Jup. What did we leave you behind for?
  Mer. Please sir, that's the question I
asked for when you went away.
  Jup. Was it not that Thespis might con-
sult you whenever he was in a difficulty?
  Mer. Well, here I've been, ready to be
consulted, chockful of reliable information
—running over with celestial maxims—advice gratis ten to four—after twelve ring
the night bell in cases of emergency.
  Jup. And hasn't he consulted you?
  Mer. Not he—he disagrees with me
about everything.
  Jup. He must have misunderstood me.
I told him to consult you whenever he was
in a fix.
  Mer. He must have thought you said
*in*sult. Why whenever I opened my mouth
he jumps down my throat. It isn't pleasant
to have a fellow constantly jumping down
your throat—especially when he always dis-
agrees with you. It's just the sort of thing
I can't digest.
  Jup. (*in a rage*). Send him here, I'll
talk to him.
  Enter THESPIS. *He is much terrified.*
  Jup. (*recit.*) Oh Monster!
  Ap. (*recit.*). Oh Monster!
  Mars (*recit.*). Oh Monster!

      THESPIS *sings in great terror, which he
        endeavours to conceal.*
  Jup. Well Sir, the year is up to-day.
  Ap. And a nice mess you've made of it.
  Mars You've deranged the whole scheme
of society.
  Thes. (*aside*). There's going to be a row!
(*Aloud and very familiarly.*) My dear boy
  —I do assure you——
  Jup. (*in recit.*). Be respectful!
  Ap. (*in recit.*). Be respectful!
  Mars (*in recit.*). Be respectful!
  Thes. I don't know what you allude to
With the exception of getting our scene-

painter to "run up" this temple, because we found the ruins draughty, we haven't touched a thing.

Jup. (*in recit.*). Oh story teller!

Ap. (*in recit.*). Oh story teller!

Mars (*in recit.*). Oh story teller!

Enter THESPIANS

Thes. My dear fellows, you're distressing yourselves unnecessarily. The court of Olympus is about to assemble to listen to the complaints of the year, if any. But there are none, or next to none. Let the Olympians assemble!

Enter THESPIANS

[THESPIS *takes chair,* JUP., AP. *and* MARS *sit below him.*

Thes. Ladies and gentlemen. It seems that it is usual for the gods to assemble once a year to listen to mortal petitions. It doesn't seem to me to be a good plan, as work is liable to accumulate; but as I'm particularly anxious not to interfere with Olympian precedent, but to allow everything to go on as it has always been accustomed to go—why, we'll say no more about it. (*Aside.*) But how shall I account for your presence?

Jup. Say we are gentlemen of the press.

Thes. That all our proceedings may be perfectly open and above-board I have communicated with the most influential members of the Athenian press, and I beg to introduce to your notice three of its most distinguished members. They bear marks emblematic of the anonymous character of modern journalism. (*Business of introduction.* THESPIS *very uneasy.*) Now then, if you're all ready we will begin.

Mer. (*brings tremendous bundles of petitions*). Here is the agenda.

Thes. What's that. The petitions?

Mer. Some of them. (*Opens one and reads.*) Ah, I thought there'd be a row about it.

Thes. Why, what's wrong now?

Mer. Why, it's been a foggy Friday in November for the last six months and the Athenians are tired of it.

Thes. There's no pleasing some people. This craving for perpetual change is the curse of the country. Friday's a very nice day.

Mer. So it is, but a Friday six months long!—it gets monotonous.

Jup., Ap. and Mars (*in recit. rising*). It's perfectly ridiculous.

Thes. (*calling them*). It shall be arranged. Cymon!

Cymon (*as Time with the usual attributes*). Sir!

Thes. (*introducing him to* THREE GODS). Allow me—Father Time—rather young at present but even Time must have a beginning. In course of Time, Time will grow older. Now then, Father Time, what's this about a wet Friday in November for the last six months.

Cym. Well, the fact is, I've been trying an experiment. Seven days in the week is an awkward number. It can't be halved. Two's into seven won't go.

Thes. (*tries it on his fingers*). Quite so—quite so.

Cym. So I abolished Saturday.

Jup., Ap. and Mars. Oh but——

[*Rising.*

Thes. Do be quiet. He's a very intelligent young man and knows what he is about. So you abolished Saturday. And how did you find it answer?

Cym. Admirably.

Thes. You hear? He found it answer admirably.

Cym. Yes, only Sunday refused to take its place.

Thes. Sunday refused to take its place?

Cym. Sunday comes after Saturday—Sunday won't go on duty after Friday, Sunday's principles are very strict. That's where my experiment sticks.

Thes. Well, but why November? come, why November?

Cym. December can't begin till November has finished. November can't finish because he's abolished Saturday. There again my experiment sticks.

Thes. Well, but why wet? Come now, why wet?

Cym. Ah, that is your fault. You turned on the rain six months ago, and you forgot to turn it off again.

Jup., Mars and Ap. (*rising—recitative*). Oh this is monstrous!

All. Order, order.

Thes. Gentlemen, pray be seated. (*To the others*) The liberty of the press, one can't help it. (*To the three gods.*) It is easily settled. Athens has had a wet Fri-

day in November for the last six months.
Let them have a blazing Tuesday in July
for the next twelve.

Jup., Mars and Ap. But——

All. Order, order.

Thes. Now then, the next article.

Mer. Here's a petition from the Peace
Society. They complain that there are no
more battles.

Mars (springing up). What!

Thes. Quiet there! Good dog—soho;
Timidon!

Tim. (as Mars). Here.

Thes. What's this about there being no
battles?

Tim. I've abolished battles; it's an experiment.

Mars (springing up). Oh come, I say——

Thes. Quiet then! (*To* TIM.) Abolished
battles?

Tim. Yes, you told us on taking office
to remember two things, to try experiments
and to take it easy. I found I couldn't take
it easy while there are any battles to attend to, so I tried the experiment and
abolished battles. And then I took it easy.
The Peace Society ought to be very much
obliged to me.

Thes. Obliged to you! Why, confound
it! since battles have been abolished war is
universal.

Tim. War universal?

Thes. To be sure it is! Now that nations can't fight, no two of 'em are on
speaking terms. The dread of fighting was
the only thing that kept them civil to each
other. Let battles be restored and peace
reign supreme.

Mer. (reads). Here's a petition from the
associated wine merchants of Mytilene.

Thes. Well, what's wrong with the associated wine merchants of Mytilene? Are
there no grapes this year?

Mer. Plenty of grapes; more than usual.

Thes. (to the gods). You observe, there
is no deception; there are more than usual.

Mer. There are plenty of grapes, only
they are full of ginger beer.

Three Gods. Oh, come I say.

[*Rising, they are put down by* THESPIS.

Thes. Eh? what. (*Much alarmed.*)
Bacchus?

Tips. (as BACCHUS). Here!

Thes. There seems to be something un-

usual with the grapes of Mytilene; they
only grow ginger beer.

Tips. And a very good thing too.

Thes. It's very nice in its way, but it is
not what one looks for from grapes.

Tips. Beloved master, a week before we
came up here, you insisted on my taking
the pledge. By so doing you rescued me
from my otherwise inevitable misery. I
cannot express my thanks. Embrace me!
                    [*Attempts to embrace him.*

Thes. Get out, don't be a fool. Look
here, you know you're the god of wine.

Tips. I am.

Thes. (very angry). Well, do you consider it consistent with your duty as the
god of wine to make the grapes yield nothing but ginger beer?

Tips. Do you consider it consistent with
my duty as a total abstainer to grow anything stronger than ginger beer?

Thes. But your duty as the god of
wine——

Tips. In every respect in which my duty
as the god of wine can be discharged consistently with my duty as a total abstainer,
I will discharge it. But when the functions clash, everything must give way to
the pledge. My preserver!
                    [*Attempts to embrace him.*

Thes. Don't be a confounded fool! This
can be arranged. We can't give over the
wine this year, but at least we can improve the ginger beer. Let all the ginger
beer be extracted from it immediately.

    Jupiter, Mars, Apollo (aside)
      We can't stand this,
      We can't stand this,
      It's much too strong,
      We can't stand this.
      It would be wrong,
      Extremely wrong,
      If we stood this,
        If we stand this,
        If we stand this,
      We can't stand this.

    Daphne, Sparkeion, Nicemis
Great Jove, this interference,
  Is more than we can stand;
Of them make a clearance,
  With your majestic hand.

        Jove
This cool audacity, it beats us hollow
  (*removing mask*) I'm Jupiter!

Mars

I'm Mars!

Apollo

I'm Apollo!

Enter DIANA *and all the other gods and goddesses.*

All (kneeling with their foreheads on the ground).

Jupiter, Mars and Apollo,
  Have quitted the dwellings of men;
The other gods quickly will follow,
  And what will become of us then.
Oh, pardon us, Jove and Apollo,
  Pardon us, Jupiter, Mars;
Oh, see us in misery wallow,
  Cursing our terrible stars.

Enter other gods.

CHORUS AND BALLET

All the Thespians.

Let us remain, we beg of you pleadingly!

Three Gods

Let them remain, they beg of us pleadingly!

Thespians.

Life on Olympus suits us exceedingly.

Gods

Life on Olympus suits them exceedingly.

Thespians

Let us remain, we pray in humility!

Gods

Let 'em remain, they pray in humility.

Thespians

If we have shown some little ability.

Gods

If they have shown some little ability.

Let us remain, etc.

Jupiter

Enough, your reign is ended;
  Upon this sacred hill
Let him be apprehended,
  And learn our awful will.
Away to earth, contemptible comedians,

And hear our curse, before we set you free;
You shall all be eminent tragedians,
  Whom no one ever goes to see!

All

We go to earth, contemptible comedians,
  We hear his curse before he sets us free,
We shall all be eminent tragedians,
  Whom no one ever, ever goes to see!

Sillimon

Whom no one—

Sparkeion

Whom no one—

Thespis

Whom *no* one—

All

Ever, ever goes to see.

[*The Thespians are driven away by the gods, who group themselves in attitudes of triumph.*

Thespis

Now, here you see the arrant folly
Of doing your best to make things jolly.
I've ruled the world like a chap in his senses,
Observe the terrible consequences.
Great Jupiter, whom nothing pleases,
Splutters and swears, and kicks up breezes,
And sends us home in a mood avengin',
In double quick time, like a railroad engine.
  And this he does without compunction,
  Because I have discharged with unction
  A highly complicated function,
  Complying with his own injunction.
    Fol, lol, lay.

Chorus

All this he does, etc.

[*The gods drive the Thespians away. The Thespians prepare to descend the mountain as the curtain falls.*

THE GONDOLIERS

OR

THE KING OF BARATARIA

DRAMATIS PERSONÆ

THE DUKE OF PLAZA-TORO (*a Grandee of Spain*)

LUIZ (*his Attendant*)

DON ALHAMBRA DEL BOLERO (*the Grand Inquisitor*)

MARCO PALMIERI

GIUSEPPE PALMIERI

ANTONIO   } (*Venetian Gondoliers*)

FRANCESCO

GIORGIO

ANNIBALE

THE DUCHESS OF PLAZA-TORO

CASILDA (*her Daughter*)

GIANETTA

TESSA

FIAMETTA   } (*Contadine*)

VITTORIA

GIULIA

INEZ (*the King's Foster-mother*)

Chorus of Gondoliers and Contadine, Men-at-Arms, Heralds, and Pages

(*An interval of three months is supposed to elapse between Acts I and II*)

Date 1750

ACT I

SCENE.—*The Piazzetta, Venice. The Ducal Palace on the right.*

FIAMETTA, GIULIA, VITTORIA, *and other Contadine discovered, each tying a bouquet of roses*

CHORUS OF CONTADINE

List and learn, ye dainty roses,
Roses white and roses red,
Why we bind you into posies
  Ere your morning bloom has fled.
By a law of maiden's making,
Accents of a heart that's aching,
Even though that heart be breaking,
  Should by maiden be unsaid:
Though they love with love exceeding,
They must seem to be unheeding—
Go ye then and do their pleading,
  Roses white and roses red!

FIAMETTA

Two there are for whom in duty,
  Every maid in Venice sighs—
Two so peerless in their beauty
  That they shame the summer skies.
We have hearts for them, in plenty,
  They have hearts, but all too few,
We, alas, are four-and-twenty!
  They, alas, are only two!
We, alas!

              Chorus
Alas!

              Fiametta
Are four-and-twenty,
They, alas!

              Chorus
Alas!

              Fiametta
Are only two.

Chorus

They, alas, are only two, alas!
Now ye know, ye dainty roses,
Why we bind you into posies,
  Ere your morning bloom has fled,
Roses white and roses red!

[*During this chorus* ANTONIO, FRANCESCO,
  GIORGIO, *and other Gondoliers have entered unobserved by the Girls—at first
  two, then two more, then four, then
  half a dozen, then the remainder of the
  Chorus.*

SOLI
Francesco

Good morrow, pretty maids; for whom
  prepare ye
These floral tributes extraordinary?

Fiametta

For Marco and Giuseppe Palmieri,
The pink and flower of all the Gondolieri.

Giulia

They're coming here, as we have heard
  but lately,
To choose two brides from us who sit
  sedately.

Antonio

Do all you maidens love them?

All

  Passionately!

Antonio

These gondoliers are to be envied greatly!

Giorgio

But what of us, who one and all adore
  you?
Have pity on our passion, we implore
  you!

Fiametta

These gentlemen must make their choice
  before you;

Vittoria

In the meantime we tacitly ignore you.

Giulia

When they have chosen two that leaves
  you plenty—
Two dozen we, and ye are four-and-twenty.

Fiametta and Vittoria

Till then, enjoy your *dolce far niente.*

Antonio

With pleasure, nobody *contradicente!*

SONG—ANTONIO *and* CHORUS

For the merriest fellows are we, tra la,
That ply on the emerald sea, tra la;
  With loving and laughing,
  And quipping and quaffing,

We're happy as happy can be, tra la—
  As happy as happy can be!
With sorrow we've nothing to do, tra la,
And care is a thing to pooh-pooh, tra la;
  And Jealousy yellow,
  Unfortunate fellow,
We drown in the shimmering blue, tra la—
  We drown in the shimmering blue!

Fiametta (looking off)

See, see, at last they come to make their
  choice—
Let us acclaim them with united voice.

[MARCO *and* GIUSEPPE *appear in gondola at
  back.*

CHORUS (*Girls*)

Hail, hail! gallant gondolieri, ben venuti!
Accept our love, our homage, and our duty.

[MARCO *and* GIUSEPPE *jump ashore—the
  Girls salute them.*

DUET—MARCO *and* GIUSEPPE,
  with CHORUS OF GIRLS

Marco and Giuseppe

Buon' giorno, signorine!

Girls

  Gondoliere carissimi!
Siamo contadine!

Marco and Giuseppe (bowing)

Servitori umilissimi!
Per chi questi fiori—
  Questi fiori bellissimi?

Girls

  Per voi, bei signori
  O eccellentissimi!

[*The Girls present their bouquets to* MARCO
  and GIUSEPPE, *who are overwhelmed
  with them, and carry them with difficulty.*

MARCO *and* GIUSEPPE (*their arms full of
  flowers*).

  O ciel'!

Girls

  Buon' giorno, cavalieri!

Marco and Giuseppe (deprecatingly).

  Siamo gondolieri.
  (*To* FIAMETTA *and* VITTORIA)
  Signorina, io t' amo!

Girls (deprecatingly).

  Contadine siamo.

Marco and Giuseppe

  Signorine!

Girls (deprecatingly).

  Contadine!

  (*Curtseying to* MARCO *and* GIUSEPPE)
  Cavalieri.

Marco and Giuseppe (deprecatingly).
>Gondolieri!
>Poveri gondolieri!
>>CHORUS
>Buon' giorno, signorine, etc.
>>DUET—MARCO *and* GIUSEPPE
>We're called *gondolieri*,
>But that's a vagary,
>It's quite honorary
>>The trade that we ply.
>For gallantry noted
>Since we were short-coated,
>To beauty devoted,
>>Giuseppe } and I;
>>Are Marco
>When morning is breaking,
>Our couches forsaking,
>To greet their awaking
>>With carols we come.
>At summer day's nooning,
>When weary lagooning,
>Our mandolins tuning,
>>We lazily thrum.
>When vespers are ringing,
>To hope ever clinging,
>With songs of our singing
>>A vigil we keep.
>When daylight is fading,
>Enwrapt in night's shading,
>With soft serenading
>>We sing them to sleep.
>We're called *gondolieri, etc.*
>>RECIT.—MARCO *and* GIUSEPPE
>>*Marco*
>And now to choose our brides!
>>*Giuseppe*
>As all are young and fair,
>And amiable besides,
>>*Both*
>We really do not care
>A preference to declare.
>>*Marco*
>A bias to disclose
>Would be indelicate—
>>*Giuseppe*
>And therefore we propose
>To let impartial Fate
>Select for us a mate!
>>*All*
>>Viva!
>>*Girls*
>A bias to disclose
>Would be indelicate—

>>*Men*
>But how do they propose
>To let impartial Fate
>Select for them a mate?
>>*Giuseppe*
>These handkerchiefs upon our eyes be good
>>enough to bind,
>>*Marco*
>And take good care that both of us are
>>absolutely blind;
>>*Both*
>Then turn us round—and we, with all con-
>>venient despatch,
>Will undertake to marry any two of you
>>we catch!
>>*All*
>>Viva!
>They undertake to marry any two of
>>{ us they catch!
>>{ them they catch!
>[*The Girls prepare to bind their eyes as
>>directed.*
>>*Fiametta (to* MARCO)
>Are you peeping?
>>Can you see me?
>>*Marco*
>Dark I'm keeping,
>>Dark and dreamy!
>>>(MARCO *slyly lifts bandage.*)
>>*Vittoria (to* GIUSEPPE)
>If you're blinded
>>Truly, say so.
>>*Giuseppe*
>All right-minded
>>Players play so! (*slyly lifts bandage*)
>>*Fiametta (detecting* MARCO)
>Conduct shady!
>>They are cheating!
>Surely they de-
>>Serve a beating! (*replaces bandage*)
>>*Vittoria (detecting* GIUSEPPE)
>This too much is;
>>Maidens mocking—
>Conduct such is
>>Truly shocking! (*replaces bandage*)
>>*All*
>>You can spy, sir!
>>Shut your eye, sir!
>You may use it by and by, sir!
>>You can see, sir!
>>Don't tell me, sir!
>That will do—now let it be, sir!

CHORUS OF GIRLS

My papa he keeps three horses,
  Black, and white, and dapple grey, sir;
Turn three times, then take your courses,
  Catch whichever girl you may, sir!

CHORUS OF MEN

My papa, etc.

MARCO *and* GIUSEPPE *turn round, as directed, and try to catch the girls. Business of blind-man's buff. Eventually* MARCO *catches* GIANETTA, *and* GIUSEPPE *catches* TESSA. *The two girls try to escape, but in vain. The two men pass their hands over the girls' faces to discover their identity.*

Giuseppe

I've at length achieved a capture!
  (*Guessing.*) This is Tessa! (*removes bandage*). Rapture, rapture!
    Marco (*guessing*).
To me Gianetta fate has granted! (*removes bandage*).
Just the very girl I wanted!
    Giuseppe (*politely to Marco*).
If you'd rather change—

Tessa

        My goodness!
This indeed is simple rudeness.
    Marco (*politely to Giuseppe*).
I've no preference whatever—

Gianetta

Listen to him! Well, I never!
  (*Each man kisses each girl.*)

Gianetta

Thank you, gallant *gondolieri!*
  In a set and formal measure
It is scarcely necessary
  To express our pleasure.
  Each of us to prove a treasure,
Conjugal and monetary,
  Gladly will devote our leisure,
Gay and gallant *gondolieri,*
  Tra, la, la, la, la, la, etc.

Tessa

Gay and gallant *gondolieri,*
  Take us both and hold us tightly,
You have luck extraordinary;
  We might both have been unsightly!
  If we judge your conduct rightly,
'Twas a choice involuntary;
  Still we thank you most politely,
Gay and Gallant *gondolieri!*
  Tra, la, la, la, la, la, etc.

CHORUS OF GIRLS

Thank you, gallant *gondolieri;*
  In a set and formal measure,
It is scarcely necessary
  To express our pleasure.
  Each of us to prove a treasure
Gladly will devote our leisure,
Gay and gallant *gondolieri!*
  Tra, la, la, la, la, la, etc.

All

Fate in this has put his finger—
  Let us bow to Fate's decree,
Then no longer let us linger,
  To the altar hurry we!
    [*They all dance off two and two*—GIANETTA *with* MARCO, TESSA *with* GIUSEPPE.
Flourish. A gondola arrives at the Piazzetta steps, from which enter the DUKE OF PLAZA-TORO, *the* DUCHESS, *their daughter* CASILDA, *and their attendant* LUIZ, *who carries a drum. All are dressed in pompous but old and faded clothes.*
Entrance of DUKE, DUCHESS, CASILDA, *and* LUIZ.

Duke

From the sunny Spanish shore,
The Duke of Plaza-Tor!—
        Duchess
And His Grace's Duchess true—
        Casilda
And His Grace's daughter, too—
        Luiz
And His Grace's private drum
To Venetia's shores have come:
        All
    If ever, ever, ever
      They get back to Spain,
    They will never, never, never
      Cross the sea again—
        Duke
Neither that Grandee from the Spanish shore,
The noble Duke of Plaza Tor'—
        Duchess
Nor His Grace's Duchess, staunch and true—
        Casilda
You may add, His Grace's daughter, too—
        Luiz
Nor His Grace's own particular drum
To Venetia's shores will come:
        All
    If ever, ever, ever
      They get back to Spain,

They will never, never, never
     Cross the sea again!

Duke. At last we have arrived at our
destination. This is the Ducal Palace, and it
is here that the Grand Inquisitor resides.
As a Castilian hidalgo of ninety-five quarterings, I regret that I am unable to pay
my state visit on a horse. As a Castilian hidalgo of that description, I should have
preferred to ride through the streets of
Venice; but owing, I presume, to an unusually wet season, the streets are in such
a condition that equestrian exercise is im-
practicable. No matter. Where is our suite?

Luiz (*coming forward*). Your Grace, I
am here.

Duch. Why do you not do yourself the
honour to kneel when you address His
Grace?

Duke. My love, it is so small a matter!
(*To* LUIZ.) Still, you may as well do it.
(LUIZ *kneels.*)

Cas. The young man seems to entertain
but an imperfect appreciation of the respect
due from a menial to a Castilian hidalgo.

Duke. My child, you are hard upon our
suite.

Cas. Papa, I've no patience with the presumption of persons in his plebian position. If he does not appreciate that position, let him be whipped until he does.

Duke. Let us hope the omission was not
intended as a slight. I should be much hurt
if I thought it was. So would he. (*To* LUIZ.)
Where are the halberdiers who were to
have had the honour of meeting us here,
that our visit to the Grand Inquisitor
might be made in becoming state?

Luiz. Your Grace, the halberdiers are
mercenary people who stipulated for a trifle
on account.

Duke. How tiresome! Well, let us hope
the Grand Inquisitor is a blind gentleman.
And the band who were to have had the
honour of escorting us? I see no band!

Luiz. Your Grace, the band are sordid
persons who required to be paid in advance.

Duch. That's so like a band!

Duke (*annoyed*). Insuperable difficulties
meet me at every turn!

Duch. But surely they know His Grace?

Luiz. Exactly—they know His Grace.

Duke. Well let us hope that the Grand

Inquisitor is a deaf gentleman. A cornet-à-
piston would be something. You do not
happen to possess the accomplishment of
tootling like a cornet-à-piston?

Luiz. Alas, no, Your Grace! But I can
imitate a farmyard.

Duke (*doubtfully*). I don't see how that
would help us. I don't see how we could
bring it in.

Cas. It would not help us in the least.
We are not a parcel of graziers come to
market, dolt!

Duke. My love, our suite's feelings! (*To*
LUIZ.) Be so good as to ring the bell and
inform the Grand Inquisitor that his Grace
the Duke of Plaza-Toro, Count Matadoro,
Baron Picadoro——

Duch. And suite——

Duke. And suite—have arrived at Venice
and seek——

Cas. Desire—

Duch. Demand!

Duke. And demand an audience.

Luiz. Your Grace has but to command.
(*Rising.*)

Duke (*much moved*). I felt sure of it—
I felt sure of it! (*Exit* LUIZ *into Ducal
Palace.*) And now my love—(*aside to*
DUCHESS) Shall we tell her? I think so—
(*aloud to* CASILDA) And now, my love, prepare for a magnificent surprise. It is my
agreeable duty to reveal to you a secret
which should make you the happiest young
lady in Venice!

Cas. A secret?

Duch. A secret which, for state reasons,
it has been necessary to preserve for twenty
years.

Duke. When you were a prattling babe
of six months old you were married by
proxy to no less a personage than the infant son and heir of His Majesty the im-
measurably wealthy King of Barataria!

Cas. Married to the infant son of the
King of Barataria? Was I consulted?
(DUKE *shakes his head.*) Then it was a
most unpardonable liberty!

Duke. Consider his extreme youth and
forgive him. Shortly after the ceremony
that misguided monarch abandoned the
creed of his forefathers, and became a
Wesleyan Methodist of the most bigoted
and persecuting type. The Grand Inquisitor,
determined that the innovation should not

be perpetuated in Barataria, caused your smiling and unconscious husband to be stolen and conveyed to Venice. A fortnight since the Methodist Monarch and all his Wesleyan Court were killed in an insurrection, and we are here to ascertain the whereabouts of your husband, and to hail you, our daughter, as Her Majesty, the reigning Queen of Barataria! (*Kneels.*)

During this speech LUIZ *re-enters*

Duch. Your Majesty! (*Kneels.*)

Duke. It is at such moments as these that one feels how necessary it is to travel with a full band.

Cas. I, the Queen of Barataria! But I've nothing to wear! We are practically penniless!

Duke. That point has not escaped me. Although I am unhappily in straitened circumstances at present, my social influence is something enormous; and a Company, to be called the Duke of Plaza-Toro, Limited, is in course of formation to work with me. An influential directorate has been secured, and I shall myself join the Board after allotment.

Cas. Am I to understand that the Queen of Barataria may be called upon at any time to witness her honoured sire in process of liquidation?

Duch. The speculation is not exempt from that drawback. If your father should stop, it will, of course, be necessary to wind him up.

Cas. But it's so undignified—it's so degrading! A Grandee of Spain turned into a public company? Such a thing was never heard of!

Duke. My child, the Duke of Plaza-Toro does not follow fashions—he leads them. He always leads everybody. When he was in the army he led his regiment. He occasionally led tnem into action. He invariably led them out of it.

SONG—DUKE OF PLAZA-TORO

In enterprise of martial kind,
　　When there was any fighting,
He led his regiment from behind—
　　He found it less exciting.
But when away his regiment ran,
　　His place was at the fore, O—
　　　　That celebrated,
　　　　Cultivated,
　　　　Underrated

Nobleman,
The Duke of Plaza-Toro!
　　　　　All
In the first and foremost flight, ha, ha!
You always found that knight, ha, ha!
　　　　That celebrated
　　　　Cultivated
　　　　Underrated
　　　　　Nobleman,
The Duke of Plaza-Toro!
　　　　　Duke
When, to evade Destruction's hand,
　　To hide they all proceeded,
No soldier in that gallant band
　　Hid half as well as he did.
He lay concealed throughout the war,
　　And so preserved his gore, O!
　　　　That unaffected,
　　　　Undetected,
　　　　Well-connected
　　　　　Warrior,
The Duke of Plaza-Toro!
　　　　　All
In every doughty deed, ha, ha!
He always took the lead, ha, ha!
　　　　That unaffected,
　　　　Undetected,
　　　　Well-connected
　　　　　Warrior,
The Duke of Plaza-Toro!
　　　　　Duke
When told that they would all be shot
　　Unless they left the service,
That hero hesitated not,
　　So marvellous his nerve is.
He sent his resignation in,
　　The first of all his corps, O!
　　　　That very knowing,
　　　　Overflowing,
　　　　Easy-going
　　　　　Paladin,
The Duke of Plaza-Toro!
　　　　　All
To men of grosser clay, ha, ha!
He always showed the way, ha, ha!
　　　　That very knowing,
　　　　Overflowing,
　　　　Easy-going
　　　　　Paladin,
The Duke of Plaza-Toro!
[*Exeunt* DUKE *and* DUCHESS *into* **Grand Ducal Palace.** *As soon as they have disappeared,* LUIZ *and* CASILDA *rush to each other's arms.*

RECIT. AND DUET—CASILDA *and* LUIZ

O rapture, when alone together
Two loving hearts and those that bear
    them
May join in temporary tether,
    Though Fate apart should rudely tear
    them.

Casilda

Necessity, Invention's mother,
Compelled me to a course of feigning—
But, left alone with one another,
    I will atone for my disdaining!
            Ah, well-beloved,
            Mine angry frown
            Is but a gown
            That serves to dress
            My gentleness!
                    Luiz
            Ah, well-beloved,
            Thy cold disdain,
            It gives no pain—
            'Tis mercy, played
            In masquerade!
                    Both
            Ah, well-beloved, etc.

Cas. O Luiz, Luiz—what have you said? What have I done? What have I allowed you to do?

Luiz. Nothing, I trust, that you will ever have reason to repent. (*Offering to embrace her.*)

Cas. (*withdrawing from him*). Nay, Luiz, it may not be. I have embraced you for the last time.

Luiz (*amazed*). Casilda!

Cas. I have just learnt, to my surprise and indignation, that I was wed in babyhood to the infant son of the King of Barataria!

Luiz. The son of the King of Barataria? The child who was stolen in infancy by the Inquisition?

Cas. The same. But of course, you know his story.

Luiz. Know his story? Why, I have often told you that my mother was the nurse to whose charge he was entrusted!

Cas. True. I had forgotten. Well, he has been discovered, and my father has brought me here to claim his hand.

Luiz. But you will not recognize this marriage? It took place when you were too young to understand its import.

Cas. Nay, Luiz, respect my principles and cease to torture me with vain entreaties. Henceforth my life is another's.

Luiz. But stay—the present and the future—*they* are another's; but the past—that at least is ours, and none can take it from us. As we may revel in naught else, let us revel in that!

Cas. I don't think I grasp your meaning.

Luiz. Yet it is logical enough. You say you cease to love me?

Cas. (*demurely*). I say I *may* not love you.

Luiz. Ah, but you do not say you *did* not love me?

Cas. I loved you with a frenzy that words are powerless to express—and that but ten brief minutes since!

Luiz. Exactly. My own—that is, until ten minutes since, my own—my lately loved, my recently adored—tell me that until, say a quarter of an hour ago, I was all in all to thee! (*Embracing her.*)

Cas. I see your idea. It's ingenious, but don't do that. (*Releasing herself.*)

Luiz. There can be no harm in revelling in the past.

Cas. None whatever, but an embrace cannot be taken to act retrospectively.

Luiz. Perhaps not!

Cas. We may recollect an embrace—I recollect many—but we must not repeat them.

Luiz. Then let us recollect a few! (*A moment's pause, as they recollect, then both heave a deep sigh.*)

Luiz. Ah, Casilda, you were to me as the sun is to the earth!

Cas. A quarter of an hour ago?

Luiz. About that.

Cas. And to think that, but for this miserable discovery, you would have been my own for life!

Luiz. Through life to death—a quarter of an hour ago!

Cas. How greedily my thirsty ears would have drunk the golden melody of those sweet words a quarter—well, it's now about twenty minutes since. (*Looking at her watch.*)

Luiz. About that. In such a matter one cannot be too precise.

Cas. And now our love, so full of life, is but a silent, solemn memory!

Luiz. Must it be so, Casilda?

Cas. Luiz, it must be so!

DUET—CASILDA *and* LUIZ

Luiz

There was a time—
   A time for ever gone—ah, woe is me!
It was no crime
   To love but thee alone—ah, woe is me!
One heart, one life, one soul,
   One aim, one goal—
Each in the other's thrall,
   Each all in all, ah, woe is me!

Both

Oh, bury, bury—let the grave close o'er
The days that were—that never will be
   more!
Oh, bury, bury love that all condemn,
And let the whirlwind mourn its requiem!

Casilda

Dead as the last year's leaves—
   As gathered flowers—ah, woe is me!
Dead as the garnered sheaves,
   That love of ours—ah, woe is me!
Born but to fade and die
   When hope was high,
Dead and as far away
   As yesterday!—ah, woe is me!

Both

Oh, bury, bury—let the grave close o'er, etc.

Re-enter from the Ducal Palace the DUKE
and DUCHESS, *followed by* DON ALHAM-
BRA DEL BOLERO, *the Grand Inquisitor.*

Duke. My child, allow me to present to
you His Distinction, Don Alhambra del
Bolero, the Grand Inquisitor of Spain. It
was His Distinction who so thoughtfully
abstracted your infant husband and brought
him to Venice.

Don Al. So this is the little lady who is
so unexpectedly called upon to assume the
functions of Royalty! And a very nice little
lady, too!

Duke. Jimp, isn't she?

Don Al. Distinctly jimp. Allow me! (*Offers his hand. She turns away scornfully.*)
Naughty temper!

Duke. You must make some allowance.
Her Majesty's head is a little turned by her
access of dignity.

Don Al. I could have wished that Her
Majesty's access of dignity had turned it
in this direction.

Duch. Unfortunately, if I am not mistaken, there appears to be some little doubt
as to His Majesty's whereabouts.

Cas. (*aside*). A doubt as to his whereabouts? Then we may yet be saved!

Don Al. A doubt? Oh dear, no—no
doubt at all! He is here, in Venice, plying
the modest but picturesque calling of a
gondolier. I can give you his address—I see
him every day! In the entire annals of our
history, there is absolutely no circumstance
so entirely free from all manner of doubt
of any kind whatever! Listen, and I'll tell
you all about it.

SONG—DON ALHAMBRA

(*with* DUKE, DUCHESS, CASILDA, *and* LUIZ)

I stole the Prince, and brought him here,
   And left him gaily prattling
With a highly respectable gondolier,
Who promised the Royal babe to rear,
And teach him the trade of a timoneer
   With his own beloved bratling.
Both of the babes were strong and stout,
   And, considering all things, clever.
Of that there is no manner of doubt—
No probable, possible shadow of doubt—
   No possible doubt whatever.

But owing, I'm much disposed to fear,
   To his terrible taste for tippling,
That highly respectable gondolier
Could never declare with a mind sincere
Which of the two was his offspring dear,
   And which the Royal stripling!
Which was which he could never make out
   Despite his best endeavour.
Of *that* there is no manner of doubt—
No probable, possible shadow of doubt—
   No possible doubt whatever.

Time sped, and when at the end of a year
   I sought that infant cherished,
That highly respectable gondolier
Was lying a corpse on his humble bier—
I dropped a Grand Inquisitor's tear—
   That gondolier had perished.
A taste for drink combined with gout,
   Had doubled him up for ever.
Of *that* there is no manner of doubt—
No probable, possible shadow of doubt—
   No possible doubt whatever.

The children followed his old career—
   (This statement can't be parried)
Of a highly respectable gondolier:
Well, one of the two (who will soon be
   here)—
But *which* of the two is not quite clear—

Is the Royal Prince you married!
Search in and out and round about,
   And you'll discover never
A tale so free from every doubt—
All probable, possible shadow of doubt—
   All possible doubt whatever!

Cas. Then do you mean to say that I am married to one of two gondoliers, but it is impossible to say which?

Don Al. Without any doubt of any kind whatever. But be reassured: the nurse to whom your husband was entrusted is the mother of the musical young man who is such a past-master of that delicately modulated instrument (*indicating the drum*). She can, no doubt, establish the King's identity beyond all question.

Luiz. Heavens, how did he know that?

Don Al. My young friend, a Grand Inquisitor is always up to date. (*To* CAS.) His mother is at present the wife of a highly respectable and old-established brigand, who carries on an extensive practice in the mountains around Cordova. Accompanied by two of my emissaries, he will set off at once for his mother's address. She will return with them, and if she finds any difficulty in making up her mind, the persuasive influence of the torture chamber will jog her memory.

RECIT.—CASILDA *and* DON ALHAMBRA

Casilda

But, bless my heart, consider my position!
   I am the wife of one, that's very clear;
But who can tell, except by intuition,
   Which is the Prince and which the Gondolier?

Don Alhambra

Submit to Fate without unseemly wrangle:
   Such complications frequently occur—
Life is one closely complicated angle:
   Death is the only true unraveller!

QUINTET—DUKE, DUCHESS, CASILDA, LUIZ,
and GRAND INQUISITOR

All

Try we life-long, we can never
   Straighten out life's tangled skein,
Why should we, in vain endeavor,
   Guess and guess and guess again?

Luiz

Life's a pudding full of plums,
Duchess
Care's a canker that benumbs.

All

Life's a pudding full of plums,
Care's a canker that benumbs.
Wherefore waste our elocution
On impossible solution?
Life's a pleasant institution,
   Let us take it as it comes!
Set aside the dull enigma,
   We shall guess it all too soon;
Failure brings no kind of stigma—
   Dance we to another tune!

Luiz

String the lyre and fill the cup,
Duchess
Lest on sorrow we should sup.
All
String the lyre and fill the cup,
Lest on sorrow we should sup.
Hop and skip to Fancy's fiddle,
Hands across and down the middle—
Life's perhaps the only riddle
   That we shrink from giving up!

[*Exeunt all into Ducal Palace except*
LUIZ, *who goes off in gondola.*
*Enter Gondoliers and Contadine, followed
by* MARCO, GIANETTA, GIUSEPPE, *and* TESSA

Chorus

   Bridegroom and bride!
   Knot that's insoluble,
   Voices all voluble
   Hail it with pride.
   Bridegroom and bride!
   We in sincerity
   Wish you prosperity,
   Bridegroom and bride!

SONG—TESSA

Tessa

When a merry maiden marries,
Sorrow goes and pleasure tarries;
   Every sound becomes a song,
   All is right, and nothing's wrong!
From to-day and ever after
Let our tears be tears of laughter.
   Every sigh that finds a vent
   Be a sigh of sweet content!
When you marry, merry maiden,
Then the air with love is laden;
   Every flower is a rose,
   Every goose becomes a swan,
   Every kind of trouble goes
   Where the last year's snows have gone!

Chorus

Sunlight takes the place of shade
When you marry, merry maid!

Tessa

When a merry maiden marries,
Sorrow goes and pleasure tarries;
   Every sound becomes a song,
   All is right, and nothing's wrong.
Gnawing Care and aching Sorrow,
Get ye gone until to-morrow;
Jealousies in grim array,
Ye are things of yesterday!
When you marry, merry maiden,
Then the air with joy is laden;
   All the corners of the earth
      Ring with music sweetly played,
   Worry is melodious mirth,
      Grief is joy in masquerade;

Chorus

Sullen night is laughing day—
All the year is merry May!

At the end of the song, DON ALHAMBRA *enters at back. The Gondoliers and Contadine shrink from him, and gradually go off, much alarmed.*

Giu. And now our lives are going to begin in real earnest! What's a bachelor? A mere nothing—he's a chrysalis. He can't be said to live—he exists.

Mar. What a delightful institution marriage is! Why have we wasted all this time? Why didn't we marry ten years ago?

Tess. Because you couldn't find anybody nice enough.

Gia. Because you were waiting for *us.*

Mar. I suppose that *was* the reason. We were waiting for you without knowing it. (DON ALHAMBRA *comes forward.*) Hallo!

Don Al. Good morning.

Giu. If this gentleman is an undertaker it's a bad omen.

Don Al. Ceremony of some sort going on?

Giu. (*aside*). He *is* an undertaker! (*Aloud.*) No—a little unimportant family gathering. Nothing in *your* line.

Don Al. Somebody's birthday I suppose?

Gia. Yes, mine!

Tess. And mine!

Mar. And mine!

Giu. And mine!

Don Al. Curious coincidence! And how old may you all be?

Tess. It's a rude question—but about ten minutes.

Don Al. Remarkably fine children! But surely you are jesting?

Tess. In other words, we were married about ten minutes since.

Don Al. Married! You don't mean to say you are married?

Mar. Oh yes, we are married.

Don Al. What, both of you?

All. All four of us.

Don Al. (*aside*). Bless my heart, how extremely awkward!

Gia. You don't mind, I suppose?

Tess. You were not thinking of either of us for yourself, I presume? Oh, Giuseppe, look at him—he was. He's heart-broken!

Don Al. No, no, I wasn't! I wasn't!

Giu. Now, my man (*slapping him on the back*), we don't want anything in your line to-day, and if your curiosity's satisfied—you can go!

Don Al. You mustn't call me your man. It's a liberty. I don't think you know who I am.

Giu. Not we, indeed! We are jolly gondoliers, the sons of Baptisto Palmieri, who led the last revolution. Republicans, heart and soul, we hold all men to be equal. As we abhor oppression, we abhor kings: as we detest vain-glory, we detest rank: as we despise effeminacy, we despise wealth. We are Venetian gondoliers—your equals in everything except our calling, and in that at once your masters and your servants.

Don Al. Bless my heart, how unfortunate! One of you may be Baptisto's son, for anything I know to the contrary; but the other is no less a personage than the only son of the late King of Barataria.

All. What!

Don Al. And I trust—I *trust* it was that one who slapped me on the shoulder and called me his man!

Giu. One of us a king! }

Mar. Not brothers! }

Tess. The King of Barataria! } *Together.*

Gia. Well, who'd have thought it! }

Mar. But which is it?

Don Al. What does it matter? As you are both Republicans, and hold kings in detestation, of course you'll abdicate at once. Good morning! (*Going.*)

Gia. and Tess. Oh, don't do that! (MARCO *and* GIUSEPPE *stop him.*)

Giu. Well, as to that, of course there are kings and kings. When I say that I detest kings, I mean I detest *bad* kings.

Don Al. I see. It's a delicate distinction.

Giu. Quite so. Now I can conceive a kind of king—an ideal king—the creature of my fancy, you know—who would be absolutely unobjectionable. A king, for instance, who would abolish taxes and make everything cheap, except gondolas——

Mar. And give a great many free entertainments to the gondoliers——

Giu. And let off fireworks on the Grand Canal, and engage all the gondolas for the occasion——

Mar. And scramble money on the Rialto among the gondoliers.

Giu. Such a king would be a blessing to his people, and if I were a king, that is the sort of king I would be.

Mar. And so would I!

Don Al. Come, I'm glad to find your objections are not insuperable.

Mar. and Giu. Oh, they're not insuperable.

Gia. and Tess. No, they're not insuperable.

Giu. Besides, we are open to conviction.

Gia. Yes; they are open to conviction.

Tess. Oh! they've often been convicted.

Giu. Our views may have been hastily formed on insufficient grounds. They may be crude, ill-digested, erroneous. I've a very poor opinion of the politician who is not open to conviction.

Tess. (*to Gia.*). Oh, he's a fine fellow!

Gia. Yes, that's the sort of politician for *my* money!

Don Al. Then we'll consider it settled. Now, as the country is in a state of insurrection, it is absolutely necessary that you should assume the reins of Government at once; and, until it is ascertained which of you is to be king, I have arranged that you will reign jointly, so that no question can arise hereafter as to the validity of any of your acts.

Mar. As one individual?

Don Al. As one individual.

Giu. (*linking himself with* MARCO). Like this?

Don Al. Something like that.

Mar. And we may take our friends with us, and give them places about the Court?

Don Al. Undoubtedly. That's always done!

Mar. I'm convinced!

Giu. So am I!

Tess. Then the sooner we're off the better.

Gia. We'll just run home and pack up a few things. (*going*)——

Don Al. Stop, stop—that won't do at all—ladies are not admitted.

All. What!

Don Al. Not admitted. Not at present. Afterwards, perhaps. We'll see.

Giu. Why, you don't mean to say you are going to separate us from our wives!

Don Al. (*aside*). This is very awkward! (*Aloud.*) Only for a time—a few months. After all, what is a few months?

Tess. But we've only been married half an hour! (*Weeps.*)

FINALE—ACT I

SONG—GIANETTA

Kind sir, you cannot have the heart
   Our lives to part
  From those to whom an hour ago
    We were united!
Before our flowing hopes you stem,
   Ah, look at them,
  And pause before you deal this blow,
    All uninvited!
You men can never understand
   That heart and hand
  Cannot be separated when
    We go a-yearning;
You see, you've only women's eyes
   To idolize
  And only women's hearts, poor men,
    To set *you* burning!
Ah me, you men will never understand
That woman's heart is one with woman's
    hand!

Some kind of charm you seem to find
   In womankind—
  Some source of unexplained delight
    (Unless you're jesting),
But what attracts you, I confess,
   I cannot guess,
  To me a woman's face is quite
    Uninteresting!
If from my sister I were torn
   It could be borne—
  I should, no doubt, be horrified,
    But I could bear it;—
But Marco's quite another thing—
   He is my King,
  He has my heart and none beside
    Shall ever share it!
Ah me, you men will never understand

That woman's heart is one with woman's
    hand!
    RECIT.—DON ALHAMBRA
Do not give way to this uncalled-for grief,
Your separation will be very brief.
  To ascertain which is the King
    And which the other,
  To Barataria's Court I'll bring
    His foster-mother;
  Her former nurseling to declare
    She'll be delighted.
  That settled, let each happy pair
    Be reunited.
    Marco, Giuseppe, Gianetta, Tessa
  Viva! His argument is strong!
  Viva! We'll not be parted long!
  Viva! It will be settled soon!
  Viva! Then comes our honeymoon!
        [*Exit* DON ALHAMBRA.
QUARTET—MARCO, GIUSEPPE, GIANETTA, TESSA
      Gianetta
Then one of us will be a Queen,
  And sit on a golden throne,
    With a crown instead,
    Of a hat on her head,
  And diamonds all her own!
With a beautiful robe of gold and green,
  I've always understood;
    I wonder whether
    She'd wear a feather?
  I rather think she should!
      All
Oh, 'tis a glorious thing, I ween,
To be a regular Royal Queen!
No half-and-half affair, I mean,
But a right-down regular Royal Queen!
      Marco
She'll drive about in a carriage and pair,
  With the King on her left-hand side,
    And a milk-white horse,
    As a matter of course,
  Whenever she wants to ride!
With beautiful silver shoes to wear
  Upon her dainty feet;
    With endless stocks
    Of beautiful frocks
  And as much as she wants to eat!
      All
Oh, 'tis a glorious thing, I ween, etc.
      Tessa
Whenever she condescends to walk,
  Be sure she'll shine at that,
    With her haughty stare
    And her nose in the air,

Like a well-born aristocrat!
At elegant high society talk
  She'll bear away the bell,
    With her "How de do?"
    And her "How are you?"
  And "I trust I see you well!"
      All
Oh, 'tis a glorious thing, I ween, etc.
      Giuseppe
And noble lords will scrape and bow,
  And double themselves in two,
    And open their eyes
    In blank surprise
  At whatever she likes to do.
And everybody will roundly vow
  She's fair as flowers in May,
    And say, "How clever!"
    At whatsoever
  She condescends to say!
      All
Oh, 'tis a glorious thing, I ween,
To be a regular Royal Queen!
No half-and-half affair, I mean,
But a right-down regular Royal Queen!
Enter Chorus of Gondoliers and Contadine
      Chorus
Now, pray, what is the cause of this re-
    markable hilarity?
  This sudden ebullition of unmitigated
    jollity?
Has anybody blessed you with a sample
    of his charity?
  Or have you been adopted by a gentle-
    man of quality?
    Marco and Giuseppe
  Replying, we sing
    As one individual,
  As I find I'm a king,
    To my kingdom I bid you all.
I'm aware you object
  To pavilions and palaces,
But you'll find I respect
  Your Republican fallacies.

      CHORUS
As they know we object
  To pavilions and palaces,
How can they respect
  Our Republican fallacies?
    MARCO *and* GIUSEPPE
      Marco
For every one who feels inclined,
Some post we undertake to find
Congenial with his frame of mind —
  And all shall equal be.

Giuseppe

The Chancellor in his peruke—
The Earl, the Marquis, and the Dook,
The Groom, the Butler, and the Cook—
    They all shall equal be!

Marco

The Aristocrat who banks with Coutts—
The Aristocrat who hunts and shoots—
The Aristocrat who cleans our boots—
    They all shall equal be!

Giuseppe

The Noble Lord who rules the State—
The Noble Lord who cleans the plate—

Marco

The Noble Lord who scrubs the grate—
    They all shall equal be!

Giuseppe

The Lord High Bishop orthodox—
The Lord High Coachman on the box—

Marco

The Lord High Vagabond in the stocks—
    They all shall equal be!

Both

For every one, etc.
    Sing high, sing low,
    Wherever they go,
        They all shall equal be!

Chorus

    Sing high, sing low,
    Wherever they go,
        They all shall equal be!
The Earl, the Marquis, and the Dook,
The Groom, the Butler, and the Cook,
The Aristocrat who banks with Coutts,
The Aristocrat who cleans the boots,
The Noble Lord who rules the State,
The Noble Lord who scrubs the grate,
The Lord High Bishop orthodox,
The Lord High Vagabond in the stocks—
For every one, etc.
    Sing high, sing low,
    Wherever they go,
        They all shall equal be!
    Then hail! O King,
        Whichever you may be,
    To you we sing,
        But do not bend the knee.
    Then hail! O King.

Marco and Giuseppe (*together*)

Come, let's away—our island crown awaits
    me—
Conflicting feelings rend my soul apart!
The thought of Royal dignity elates me,

But leaving thee behind me breaks my
    heart!
        (*Addressing* GIANETTA *and* TESSA.)

Gianetta and Tessa (*together*)

Farewell, my love; on board you must be
    getting;
But while upon the sea you gaily roam,
Remember that a heart for thee is fretting—
    The tender little heart you've left at
        home!

Gianetta

    Now, Marco dear,
    My wishes hear:
        While you're away
    It's understood
    You will be good,
        And not too gay.
    To every trace
    Of maiden grace
        You will be blind,
    And will not glance
    By any chance
        On womankind!
    If you are wise,
    You'll shut your eyes
        Till we arrive,
    And not address
    A lady less
        Than forty-five.
    You'll please to frown
    On every gown
        That you may see;
    And, O my pet,
    You won't forget
        You've married me!
And O my darling, O my pet,
Whatever else you may forget
In yonder isle beyond the sea,
Do not forget you've married me!

Tessa

You'll lay your head
Upon your bed
    At set of sun.
You will not sing
Of anything
    To any one.
You'll sit and mope
All day, I hope,
    And shed a tear
Upon the life
Your little wife
    Is passing here.
And if so be
You think of me,

Please tell the moon!
I'll read it all
In rays that fall
  On the lagoon:
You'll be so kind
As tell the wind
How you may be,
And send me words
By little birds
  To comfort me!
And O my darling, O my pet,
Whatever else you may forget,
In yonder isle beyond the sea,
Do not forget you've married me!

Quartet

Oh, my darling, O my pet, etc.
  Chorus (during which a "Xebeque" is
    hauled alongside the quay)
Then away we go to an island fair
  That lies in a Southern sea:
We know not where, and we don't much
  care,
  Wherever that isle may be.
    The Men (hauling on boat)
    One, two three,
    Haul!
    One, two three,
    Haul!
    One, two three,
    Haul!
    With a will!

All

When the breezes are a-blowing
The ship will be going,
When they don't we shall all stand still!
Then away we go to an island fair,
We know not where, and we don't much
  care,
  Wherever that isle may be.

SOLO—MARCO

Away we go
  To a balmy isle,
Where the roses blow
  All the winter while.
    All (hoisting sail)
Then away we go to an island fair
  That lies in a Southern sea:
Then away we go to an island fair,
Then away, then away, then away!
[*The men embark on the "Xebeque".*
MARCO *and* GIUSEPPE *embracing* GIA-
NETTA *and* TESSA. *The girls wave a*

farewell to the men as the curtain
falls.

END OF ACT I

ACT II

SCENE.—*Pavilion in the Court of Barataria.*
  MARCO *and* GIUSEPPE, *magnificently*
  dressed, are seated on two thrones,
  occupied in cleaning the crown and the
  sceptre. The Gondoliers are discovered,
  dressed, some as courtiers, officers of
  rank, etc., and others as private soldiers
  and servants of various degrees. All are
  enjoying themselves without reference
  to social distinctions—some playing
  cards, others throwing dice, some read-
  ing, others playing cup and ball,
  "morra", etc.

CHORUS OF MEN *with* MARCO *and* GIUSEPPE

Of happiness, the very pith
  In Barataria you may see:
A monarchy that's tempered with
  Republican Equality.
This form of government we find
The beau-ideal of its kind—
A despotism strict combined
  With absolute equality!
    Marco and Giuseppe
Two kings, of undue pride bereft,
  Who act in perfect unity,
Whom you can order right and left
  With absolute impunity.
Who put their subjects at their ease
By doing all they can to please!
And thus, to earn their bread-and-cheese,
  Seize every opportunity.
    Chorus
Of happiness, the very pith, etc.

Mar. Gentlemen, we are much obliged to
you for your expressions of satisfaction and
good feeling—I say, we are much obliged
to you for your expressions of satisfaction
and good feeling.

All. We heard you.

Mar. We are delighted, at any time, to
fall in with sentiments so charmingly expressed.

All. That's all right.

Giu. At the same time there is just one
little grievance that we should like to ven-
tilate.

All (angrily). What?

Giu. Don't be alarmed—it's not serious.
It is arranged that, until it is decided which

of us two is the actual King, we are to act as one person.

Giorgio. Exactly.

Giu. Now, although we act as *one* person, we are, in point of fact, *two* persons.

Annibale. Ah, I don't think we can go into that. It is a legal fiction, and legal fictions are solemn things. Situated as we are, we can't recognize two independent responsibilities.

Giu. No; but you can recognize two independent appetites. It's all very well to say we act as one person, but when you supply us with only one ration between us, I should describe it as a legal fiction carried a little too far.

Anni. It's rather a nice point. I don't like to express an opinion off-hand. Suppose we reserve it for argument before the full Court?

Mar. Yes, but what are we to do in the meantime?

Mar. and Giu. We want our tea.

Anni. I think we may make an interim order for double rations on their Majesties entering into the usual undertaking to indemnify in the event of an adverse decision.

Gior. That, I think, will meet the case. But you must work hard—stick to it—nothing like work.

Giu. Oh, certainly. We quite understand that a man who holds the magnificent position of King should do something to justify it. We are called "Your Majesty", we are allowed to buy ourselves magnificent clothes, our subjects frequently nod to us in the streets, the sentries always return our salutes, and we enjoy the inestimable privilege of heading the subscription lists to all the principal charities. In return for these advantages, the least we can do is to make ourselves useful about the Palace.

SONG—GIUSEPPE *with* CHORUS

Rising early in the morning,
    We proceed to light the fire,
Then our Majesty adorning
    In its workaday attire,
        We embark without delay
        On the duties of the day.
First, we polish off some batches
Of political despatches,
    And foreign politicians circumvent:
Then, if business isn't heavy,
We may hold a Royal *levée*,

Or ratify some Acts of Parliament.
Then we probably review the household
        troops—
With the usual "shalloo humps!" and
        "shalloo hoops!"
Or receive with ceremonial and state
An interesting Eastern potentate.
    After that we generally
    Go and dress our private *valet*—
(It's a rather nervous duty—he's a touchy
        little man)—
    Write some letters literary
    For our private secretary—
He is shaky in his spelling, so we help him
        if we can.
    Then, in view of cravings inner,
    We go down and order dinner;
Then we polish the Regalia and the Coro-
        nation Plate—
    Spend an hour in titivating
    All our Gentlemen-in-Waiting;
Or we run on little errands for the Min-
        isters of State.

    Oh, philosophers may sing
    Of the troubles of a King;
Yet the duties are delightful, and the privi-
        leges great;
    But the privilege and pleasure
    That we treasure beyond measure
Is to run on little errands for the Ministers
        of State.

Chorus

    Oh, philosophers may sing, etc.
After luncheon (making merry
On a bun and glass of sherry),
    If we've nothing in particular to do,
We may make a Proclamation,
Or receive a deputation—
    Then we possibly create a Peer or two.
Then we help a fellow-creature on his path
With the Garter or the Thistle or the Bath
Or we dress and toddle off in semi-state
To a festival, a function, or a *fête*.
    Then we go and stand as sentry
    At the Palace (private entry),
Marching hither, marching thither, up and
        down and to and fro,
    While the warrior on duty
    Goes in search of beer and beauty
(And it generally happens that he hasn't
        far to go).
    He relieves us, if he's able,
    Just in time to lay the table,

Then we dine and serve the coffee, and at
    half-past twelve or one,
With a pleasure that's emphatic,
We retire to our attic
With the gratifying feeling that our duty
    has been done!
Oh, philosophers may sing
Of the troubles of a King,
But of pleasures there are many and of
    worries there are none;
And the culminating pleasure
That we treasure beyond measure
Is the gratifying feeling that our duty has
    been done!

Chorus

Oh, philosophers may sing, etc.

[*Exeunt all but* MARCO *and* GIUSEPPE.

Giu. Yes, it really is a very pleasant existence. They're all so singularly kind and
considerate. You don't find them wanting
to do this, or wanting to do that, or saying
"It's my turn now." No, they let us have
all the fun to ourselves, and never seem
to grudge it.

Mar. It makes one feel quite selfish. It
almost seems like taking advantage of their
good nature.

Giu. How nice they were about the
double rations.

Mar. Most considerate. Ah! there's only
one thing wanting to make us thoroughly
comfortable.

Giu. And that is?

Mar. The dear little wives we left behind
us three months ago.

Giu. Yes, it *is* dull without female society.
We can do without everything else, but we
can't do without that.

Mar. And if we have that in perfection,
we have everything. There is only one
recipe for perfect happiness.

SONG—MARCO

Take a pair of sparkling eyes,
    Hidden, ever and anon,
      In a merciful eclipse—
Do not heed their mild surprise—
    Having passed the Rubicon,
      Take a pair of rosy lips;
Take a figure trimly planned—
    Such as admiration whets
      (Be particular in this);
Take a tender little hand,
    Fringed with dainty fingerettes,
      Press it—in parenthesis;—

Ah! Take all these, you lucky man—
Take and keep them, if you can!
Take a pretty little cot—
    Quite a miniature affair—
      Hung about with trellised vine,
Furnish it upon the spot
    With the treasures rich and rare
    I've endeavoured to define.
Live to love and love to live—
    You will ripen at your ease,
      Growing on the sunny side—
Fate has nothing more to give.
    You're a dainty man to please
      If you are not satisfied.
Ah! Take my counsel, happy man;
Act upon it, if you can!

*Enter Chorus of Contadine, running in, led
by* FIAMETTA *and* VITTORIA. *They are met
by all the Ex-Gondoliers, who welcome
them heartily.*

SCENA—CHORUS OF GIRLS, QUARTET, DUET
and CHORUS

Here we are, at the risk of our lives,
From ever so far, and we've brought your
    wives—
And to that end we've crossed the main,
And don't intend to return again!

Fiametta

Though obedience is strong,
    Curiosity's stronger—
We waited for long,
    Till we couldn't wait longer.

Vittoria

It's imprudent, we know,
    But without your society
Existence was slow,
    And we wanted variety—

All

So here we are, at the risk of our lives,
From ever so far, and we've brought your
    wives—
And to that end we've crossed the main,
And don't intend to return again!

Enter GIANETTA *and* TESSA. *They rush to
the arms of* MARCO *and* GIUSEPPE *and*
Giu. Tessa!
Tess. Giuseppe!
Gia. Marco!   }*Embrace.*
Mar. Gianetta!

TESSA *and* GIANETTA

Tessa

After sailing to this island—

Gianetta
Tossing in a manner frightful,
Tessa
We are all once more on dry land—
Gianetta
And we find the change delightful,
Tessa
As at home we've been remaining—
We've not seen you both for ages,
Gianetta
Tell me, are you fond of reigning?—
How's the food, and what's the wages?
Tessa
Does your new employment please ye?—
Gianetta
How does Royalizing strike you?
Tessa
Is it difficult or easy?—
Gianetta
Do you think your subjects like you?
Tessa
I am anxious to elicit,
Is it plain and easy steering?
Gianetta
Take it altogether, is it—
Better fun than gondoliering?
Both
We shall both go on requesting
Till you tell us, never doubt it;
Everything is interesting,
Tell us, tell us all about it!
Chorus
They will both go on requesting, etc.
Tessa
Is the populace exacting?
Gianetta
Do they keep you at a distance?
Tessa
All unaided are you acting,
Gianetta
Or do they provide assistance?
Tessa
When you're busy, have you got to
Get up early in the morning?
Gianetta
If you do what you ought not to,
Do they give the usual warning?
Tessa
With a horse do they equip you?
Gianetta
Lots of trumpeting and drumming?
Tessa
Do the Royal tradesmen tip you?

Gianetta
Ain't the livery becoming!
Tessa
Does your human being inner
Feed on everything that nice is?
Gianetta
Do they give you wine for dinner;
Peaches, sugar-plums, and ices?
Both
We shall both go on requesting
Till you tell us, never doubt it;
Everything is interesting,
Tell us, tell us all about it!
Chorus
They will both go on requesting, etc.

Mar. This is indeed a most delightful surprise!

Tess. Yes, we thought you'd like it. You see, it was like this. After you left we felt very dull and mopey, and the days crawled by, and you never wrote; so at last I said to Gianetta, "I can't stand this any longer; those two poor Monarchs haven't got any one to mend their stockings or sew on their buttons or patch their clothes—at least, I hope they haven't—let us all pack up a change and go and see how they're getting on." And she said, "Done," and they all said, "Done"; and we asked old Giacopo to lend us his boat, and *he* said, "Done"; and we've crossed the sea, and, thank goodness, *that's* done; and here we are, and—and—*I've* done!

Gia. And now—which of you is King?

Tess. And which of us is Queen?

Giu. That we shan't know until Nurse turns up. But never mind that—the question is, how shall we celebrate the commencement of our honeymoon? Gentlemen, will you allow us to offer you a magnificent banquet?

All. We will!

Giu. Thanks very much; and, ladies, what do you say to a dance?

Tess. A banquet *and* a dance! O, it's too much happiness!

CHORUS *and* DANCE
Dance a cachucha, fandango, bolero,
Xeres we'll drink—Manzanilla, Montero—
Wine, when it runs in abundance, enhances
The reckless delight of that wildest of dances.
To the pretty pitter-pitter-patter,
And the clitter-clitter-clitter-clatter—

Clitter—clitter—clatter,
Pitter—pitter—patter,
Patter, patter, patter, patter, we'll dance.
Old Xeres we'll drink—Manzanilla, Montero;
For wine, when it runs in abundance, enhances
The reckless delight of that wildest of dances!

(*Cachucha*)

The dance is interrupted by the unexpected appearance of DON ALHAMBRA, *who looks on with astonishment.* MARCO *and* GIUSEPPE *appear embarrassed. The others run off, except Drummer Boy, who is driven off by* DON ALHAMBRA.

Don Al. Good evening. Fancy ball?

Giu. No, not exactly. A little friendly dance. That's all. Sorry you're late.

Don Al. But I saw a groom dancing, and a footman!

Mar. Yes. That's the Lord High Footman.

Don Al. And, dear me, a common little drummer boy!

Giu. Oh no! That's the Lord High Drummer Boy.

Don Al. But surely, surely the servants'-hall is the place for these gentry?

Giu. Oh dear no! *We* have appropriated the servants'-hall. It's the Royal Apartment, and accessible only by tickets obtainable at the Lord Chamberlain's office.

Mar. We really must have some place that we can call our own.

Don Al. (*puzzled*). I'm afraid I'm not quite equal to the intellectual pressure of the conversation.

Giu. You see, the Monarchy has been remodelled on Republican principles.

Don Al. What!

Giu. All departments rank equally, and everybody is at the head of his department.

Don Al. I see.

Mar. I'm afraid you're annoyed.

Don Al. No. I won't say that. It's not quite what I expected.

Giu. I'm awfully sorry.

Mar. So am I.

Giu. By the by, can I offer you anything after your voyage? A plate of macaroni and a rusk?

Don Al. (*preoccupied*). No, no—nothing —nothing.

Giu. Obliged to be careful?

Don Al. Yes—gout. You see, in every Court there are distinctions that must be observed.

Giu. (*puzzled*). There are, are there?

Don Al. Why, of course. For instance, you wouldn't have a Lord High Chancellor play leapfrog with his own cook.

Mar. Why not?

Don Al. Why not! Because a Lord High Chancellor is a personage of great dignity, who should never, under any circumstances, place himself in the position of being told to tuck in his tuppenny, except by noblemen of his own rank. A Lord High Archbishop, for instance, might tell a Lord High Chancellor to tuck in his tuppenny, but certainly not a cook, gentlemen, certainly not a cook.

Giu. Not even a Lord High Cook?

Don Al. My good friend, that is a rank that is not recognized at the Lord Chamberlain's office. No, no, it won't do. I'll give you an instance in which the experiment was tried.

SONG—DON ALHAMBRA, *with* MARCO *and*
GIUSEPPE

Don Alhambra

There lived a King, as I've been told,
In the wonder-working days of old,
When hearts were twice as good as gold,
  And twenty times as mellow.
Good-temper triumphed in his face,
And in his heart he found a place
For all the erring human race
  And every wretched fellow.
When he had Rhenish wine to drink
It made him very sad to think
That some, at junket or at jink,
  Must be content with toddy.

Marco and Giuseppe

With toddy, must be content with toddy.

Don Alhambra

He wished all men as rich as he
(And he was rich as rich could be),
So to the top of every tree
  Promoted everybody.

Marco and Giuseppe

Now, that's the kind of King for me—
He wished all men as rich as he,
So to the top of every tree
  Promoted everybody!

Don Alhambra

Lord Chancellors were cheap as sprats,

And Bishops in their shovel hats
Were plentiful as tabby cats—
    In point of fact, too many.
Ambassadors cropped up like hay,
Prime Ministers and such as they
Grew like asparagus in May,
    And Dukes were three a penny.
On every side Field-Marshals gleamed,
Small beer were Lords-Lieutenant deemed,
With Admirals the ocean teemed
    All round his wide dominions.
            Marco and Giuseppe
With Admirals all round his wide domin-
    ions.

            Don Alhambra
And Party Leaders you might meet
In twos and threes in every street
Maintaining, with no little heat,
    Their various opinions.
            Marco and Giuseppe
Now that's a sight you couldn't beat—
Two Party Leaders in each street
Maintaining, with no little heat,
    Their various opinions.
            Don Alhambra
That King, although no one denies
His heart was of abnormal size,
Yet he'd have acted otherwise
    If he had been acuter.
The end is easily foretold,
When every blessed thing you hold
Is made of silver, or of gold,
    You long for simple pewter.
When you have nothing else to wear
But cloth of gold and satins rare,
For cloth of gold you cease to care—
    Up goes the price of shoddy.
            Marco and Giuseppe
Of shoddy, up goes the price of shoddy.
            Don Alhambra
In short, whoever you may be,
To this conclusion you'll agree,
When every one is somebodee,
    Then no one's anybody!
            Marco and Giuseppe
Now that's as plain as plain can be,
To this conclusion we agree—
            All
When every one is somebodee,
    Then no one's anybody!
GIANETTA *and* TESSA *enter unobserved. The
two girls, impelled by curiosity, remain
listening at the back of the stage.*
Don Al. And now I have some important

news to communicate. His Grace the Duke
of Plaza-Toro, Her Grace the Duchess, and
their beautiful daughter Casilda—I say their
beautiful daughter Casilda——
    Giu. We heard you.
    Don Al. Have arrived at Barataria, and
may be here at any moment.
    Mar. The Duke and Duchess are nothing
to us.
    Don Al. But the daughter—the beautiful
daughter! Aha! Oh, you're a lucky dog,
one of you!
    Giu. I think you're a very incomprehen-
sible old gentleman.
    Don Al. Not a bit—I'll explain. Many
years ago when you (whichever you are)
were a baby, you (whichever you are)
were married to a little girl who has grown
up to be the most beautiful young lady in
Spain. That beautiful young lady will be
here to claim you (whichever you are) in
half an hour, and I congratulate that one
(whichever it is) with all my heart.
    Mar. Married when a baby!
    Giu. But we were married three months
ago!
    Don Al. One of you—only one. The other
(whichever it is) is an unintentional big-
amist.
    Gia. and Tess. (*coming forward*). Well,
upon my word!
    Don Al. Eh? Who are these young peo-
ple?
    Tess. Who are we? Why their wives, of
course. We've just arrived.
    Don Al. Their wives! Oh dear, this is
very unfortunate! Oh dear, this complicates
matters! Dear, dear, what will Her Majesty
say?
    Gia. And do you mean to say that one
of these Monarchs was already married?
    Tess. And that neither of us will be a
Queen?
    Don Al. That is the idea I intended to
convey. (TESSA *and* GIANETTA *begin to cry.*)
    Giu. (*to* TESSA). Tessa, my dear, dear
child——
    Tess. Get away! perhaps it's you!
    Mar. (*to* GIA.). My poor, poor little
woman!
    Gia. Don't! Who knows whose husband
you are?
    Tess. And pray, why didn't you tell us
all about it before they left Venice?

Don Al. Because, if I had, no earthly temptation would have induced these gentlemen to leave two such extremely fascinating and utterly irresistible little ladies!

Tess. There's something in that.

Don Al. I may mention that you will not be kept long in suspense, as the old lady who nursed the Royal child is at present in the torture chamber, waiting for me to interview her.

Giu. Poor old girl. Hadn't you better go and put her out of her suspense?

Don Al. Oh no—there's no hurry—she's all right. She has all the illustrated papers. However, I'll go and interrogate her, and, in the meantime, may I suggest the absolute propriety of your regarding yourselves as single young ladies. Good evening!

[*Exit* DON ALHAMBRA.

Gia. Well, here's a pleasant state of things!

Mar. Delightful. One of us is married to two young ladies, and nobody knows which; and the other is married to one young lady whom nobody can identify!

Gia. And one of us is married to one of you, and the other is married to nobody.

Tess. But which of you is married to which of us, and what's to become of the other? (*About to cry.*)

Giu. It's quite simple. Observe. Two husbands have managed to acquire three wives. Three wives—two husbands. (*Reckoning up.*) That's two-thirds of a husband to each wife.

Tess. O Mount Vesuvius, here we are in arithmetic! My good sir, one can't marry a vulgar fraction!

Giu. You've no right to call me a vulgar fraction.

Mar. We are getting rather mixed. The situation entangled. Let's try and comb it out.

QUARTET—MARCO, GIUSEPPE, GIANETTA, TESSA

In a contemplative fashion,
  And a tranquil frame of mind,
Free from every kind of passion,
  Some solution let us find.
Let us grasp the situation,
  Solve the complicated plot—
Quiet, calm deliberation
  Disentangles every knot.

Tessa

I, no doubt, Giuseppe wedded—
  That's, of course, a slice of luck.
He is rather dunder-headed,
  Still distinctly, he's a duck.
    The Others
In a contemplative fashion, etc.
    Gianetta
I, a victim, too, of Cupid,
  Marco married—that is clear.
He's particularly stupid,
  Still distinctly, he's a dear.
    The Others
Let us grasp the situation, etc.

Marco

Now when we were pretty babies
  Some one married us, that's clear—
    Gianetta
And if I can catch her
I'll pinch her and scratch her,
And send her away with a flea in her ear.
    Giuseppe
He whom that young lady married,
  To receive her can't refuse.
    Tessa
If I overtake her
I'll warrant I'll make her

Marco

To Gianetta I was mated;
  I can prove it in a trice:
Though her charms are overrated,
  Still I own she's rather nice.
    The Others
In a contemplative fashion, etc.
    Giuseppe
I to Tessa, willy-nilly,
  All at once a victim fell.
She is what is called a silly,
  Still she answers pretty well.
    The Others
Let us grasp the situation, etc.

To shake in her aristocratical shoes!
    Gianetta (*to* TESSA).
If she married your Giuseppe
  You and he will have to part—

    Tessa (*to* GIANETTA).
  If I have to do it
  I'll warrant she'll rue it—
I'll teach her to marry the man of my heart!

    Tessa (*to* GIANETTA).
If she married Messer Marco
  You're a spinster, that is plain—

Gianetta (*to* TESSA).

No matter—no matter
If I can get at her
I doubt if her mother will know her
again!

All

Quiet, calm deliberation
Disentangles every knot!

[*Exeunt, pondering.*

MARCH. *Enter procession of Retainers, heralding approach of* DUKE, DUCHESS, *and* CASILDA. *All three are now dressed with the utmost magnificence.*

CHORUS OF MEN, *with* DUKE *and* DUCHESS

With ducal pomp and ducal pride
(Announce these comers,
O ye kettle-drummers!)
Comes Barataria's high-born bride.
(Ye sounding cymbals clang!)
She comes to claim the Royal hand—
(Proclaim their Graces,
O ye double basses!)
Of the King who rules this goodly land.
(Ye brazen brasses bang!)

Duke and Duchess

This polite attention touches
Heart of Duke and heart of Duchess.
Who resign their pet
With profound regret.
She of beauty was a model
When a tiny tiddle-toddle,
And at twenty-one
She's excelled by none!

Chorus

With ducal pomp and ducal pride, etc.

Duke (*to his attendants*). Be good enough to inform His Majesty that His Grace, the Duke of Plaza-Toro, Limited, has arrived, and begs——

Cas. Desires——

Duch. Demands——

Duke. And demands an audience. (*Exeunt attendants.*) And now, my child, prepare to receive the husband to whom you were united under such interesting and romantic circumstances.

Cas. But which is it? There are two of them!

Duke. It is true that at present His Majesty is a double gentleman; but as soon as the circumstances of his marriage are ascertained, he will, *ipso facto*, boil down to a single gentleman—thus presenting a unique example of an individual who becomes a single man and a married man by the same operation.

Duch. (*severely*). I have known instances in which the characteristics of both conditions existed concurrently in the same individual.

Duke. Ah, he couldn't have been a Plaza-Toro.

Duch. Oh! couldn't he, though!

Cas. Well, whatever happens, I shall, of course, be a dutiful wife, but I can never love my husband.

Duke. I don't know. It's extraordinary what unprepossessing people one can love if one gives one's mind to it.

Duch. I loved your father.

Duke. My love—that remark is a little hard, I think? Rather cruel, perhaps? Somewhat uncalled-for, I venture to believe?

Duch. It was very difficult, my dear; but I said to myself, "That man is a Duke, and I *will* love him." Several of my relations bet me I couldn't, but I did—desperately!

SONG—DUCHESS

On the day when I was wedded
To your admirable sire,
I acknowledge that I dreaded
An explosion of his ire.
I was overcome with panic—
For his temper was volcanic,
And I didn't dare revolt,
For I feared a thunderbolt!
I was always very wary,
For his fury was ecstatic—
His refined vocabulary
Most unpleasantly emphatic.
To the thunder
Of this Tartar
I knocked under
Like a martyr;
When intently
He was fuming,
I was gently
Unassuming—
When reviling
Me completely,
I was smiling
Very sweetly:
Giving him the very best, and getting back
the very worst—
That is how I tried to tame your great progenitor—at first!
But I found that a reliance

On my threatening appearance,
And a resolute defiance
Of marital interference,
And a gentle intimation
Of my firm determination
To see what I could do
To be wife and husband too
Was the only thing required
For to make his temper supple,
And you couldn't have desired
A more reciprocating couple.
Ever willing
To be wooing,
We were billing—
We were cooing;
When I merely
From him parted,
We were nearly
Broken-hearted—
When in sequel
Reunited,
We were equal-
Ly delighted.
So with double-shotted guns and colors
nailed unto the mast,
I tamed your insignificant progenitor—at
last!

Cas. My only hope is that when my
husband sees what a shady family he has
married into he will repudiate the contract
altogether.

Duke. Shady? A nobleman shady, who
is blazing in the lustre of unaccustomed
pocket-money? A nobleman shady, who
can look back upon ninety-five quarterings?
It is not every nobleman who is ninety-
five quarters in arrear—I mean, who can
look back upon ninety-five of them! And
this, just as I have been floated at a premium! Oh fie!

Duch. Your Majesty is surely unaware
that directly Your Majesty's father came
before the public he was applied for over
and over again.

Duke. My dear, Her Majesty's father
was in the habit of being applied for over
and over again—and very urgently applied
for, too—long before he was registered under the Limited Liability Act.

RECIT.—DUKE

To help unhappy commoners, and add to
their enjoyment,
Affords a man of noble rank congenial employment;

Of our attempts we offer you examples
illustrative:
The work is light, and, I may add, it's most
remunerative.

DUET—DUKE *and* DUCHESS
Duke
Small titles and orders
For Mayors and Recorders
I get—and they're highly delighted—
Duchess
They're highly delighted!
Duke
M.P.'s baronetted,
Sham Colonels gazetted,
And second-rate Aldermen knighted—
Duchess
Yes, Aldermen knighted.
Duke
Foundation-stone laying
I find very paying:
It adds a large sum to my makings—
Duchess
Large sums to his makings.
Duke
At charity dinners
The best of speech-spinners,
I get ten per cent on the takings—
Duchess
One-tenth of the takings.
Duchess
I present my lady
Whose conduct is shady
Or smacking of doubtful propriety—
Duke
Doubtful propriety.
Duchess
When Virtue would quash her,
I take and whitewash her,
And launch her in first-rate society—
Duke
First-rate society!
Duchess
I recommend acres
Of clumsy dressmakers—
Their fit and their finishing touches—
Duke
Their finishing touches.
Duchess
A sum in addition
They pay for permission
To say that they make for the Duchess—
Duke
They make for the Duchess!

Duke
Those pressing prevailers,
The ready-made tailors,
     Quote me as their great double-barrel—
          Duchess
     Their great double-barrel.
               Duke
I allow them to do so,
Though Robinson Crusoe
     Would jib at their wearing apparel—
          Duchess
     Such wearing apparel!
               Duke
I sit, by selection,
Upon the direction
     Of several Companies bubble—
          Duchess
     All Companies bubble!
               Duke
As soon as they're floated,
I'm freely bank-noted—
     I'm pretty well paid for my trouble—
          Duchess
     He's paid for his trouble!
          Duchess
At middle-class party
I play at *écarté*—
     And I'm by no means a beginner—
          Duke (significantly)
     She's not a beginner.
               Duchess
To one of my station
The remuneration—
     Five guineas a night and my dinner—
          Duke
     And wine with her dinner.
               Duchess
I write letters blatant
On medicines patent—
     And use any other you mustn't—
          Duke
     Believe me, you mustn't—
               Duchess
And vow my complexion
Derives its perfection
     From somebody's soap—which it
          doesn't—
          Duke (significantly).
     It certainly doesn't!
               Duke
We're ready as witness
To any one's fitness
     To fill any place or preferment—

Duchess
A place or preferment.
     Duchess
We're often in waiting
At junket or *fêting*,
     And sometimes attend an interment—
          Duke
     We enjoy an interment.
          Both
In short, if you'd kindle
The spark of a swindle,
     Lure simpletons into your clutches—
     Yes; into your clutches.
Or hoodwink a debtor,
You cannot do better
               Duchess
     Than trot out a Duke or a Duchess—
          Duke
     A Duke or a Duchess!

          Enter MARCO *and* GIUSEPPE

Duke. Ah! Their Majesties. Your Majesty! (*Bows with great ceremony.*)
Mar. The Duke of Plaza-Toro, I believe?
Duke. The same. (MARCO *and* GIUSEPPE *offer to shake hands with him. The* DUKE *bows ceremoniously. They endeavour to imitate him.*) Allow me to present—
Giu. The young lady one of us married?
(MARCO *and* GIUSEPPE *offer to shake hands with her.* CASILDA *curtsies formally. They endeavour to imitate her.*)
Cas. Gentlemen, I am the most obedient servant of one of you. (*Aside.*) Oh, Luiz!
Duke. I am now about to address myself to the gentleman whom my daughter married; the other may allow his attention to wander if he likes, for what I am about to say does not concern him. Sir, you will find in this young lady a combination of excellences which you would search for in vain in any young lady who had not the good fortune to be my daughter. There is some little doubt as to which of you is the gentleman I am addressing, and which is the gentleman who is allowing his attention to wander; but when that doubt is solved, I shall say (still addressing the attentive gentleman), "Take her, and may she make you happier than her mother has made me."
Duch. Sir!

Duke. If possible. And now there is a little matter to which I think I am entitled to take exception. I come here in state with Her Grace the Duchess and Her Majesty my daughter, and what do I find? Do I find, for instance, a guard of honour to receive me? No!

Mar. and Giu. No.
Duke. The town illuminated? No!
Mar. and Giu. No.
Duke. Refreshment provided? No!
Mar. and Giu. No.
Duke. A Royal salute fired? No!
Mar. and Giu. No.
Duke. Triumphal arches erected? No!
Mar. and Giu. No.
Duke. The bells set ringing?
Mar. and Giu. No.
Duke. Yes—one—the Visitors', and I rang it myself. It is not enough! It is not enough!

Giu. Upon my honour, I'm very sorry; but you see, I was brought up in a gondola, and my ideas of politeness are confined to taking off my cap to my passengers when they tip me.

Duch. That's all very well in its way, but it is not enough.

Giu. I'll take off anything else in reason.

Duke. But a Royal Salute to my daughter—it costs so little.

Cas. Papa, I don't want a salute.

Giu. My dear sir, as soon as we know which of us is entitled to take that liberty she shall have as many salutes as she likes.

Mar. As for guards of honour and triumphal arches, you don't know our people —they wouldn't stand it.

Giu. They are very off-hand with us— very off-hand indeed.

Duke. Oh, but you mustn't allow that— you must keep them in proper discipline, you must impress your Court with your importance. You want deportment—carriage——

Giu. We've got a carriage.

Duke. Manner—dignity. There must be a good deal of this sort of thing—(*business*) —and a little of this sort of thing— (*business*)—and possibly just a *Soupçon* of this sort of thing!—(*business*)—and so on. Oh, it's very useful, and most effective. Just attend to me. You are a King—I am a subject. Very good——

(*Gavotte*)
DUKE, DUCHESS, CASILDA, MARCO, GIUSEPPE
Duke
I am a courtier grave and serious
 Who is about to kiss your hand:
Try to combine a pose imperious
 With a demeanor nobly bland.
 Marco and Giuseppe
Let us combine a pose imperious
 With a demeanor nobly bland.
(MARCO *and* GIUSEPPE *endeavour to carry out his instructions.*)
 Duke
That's, if anything, *too* unbending—
 Too aggressively stiff and grand;
(*They suddenly modify their attitudes.*)
Now to the other extreme you're tending—
 Don't be so deucedly condescending!
 Duchess and Casilda
Now to the other extreme you're tending—
 Don't be so dreadfully condescending!
 Marco and Giuseppe
Oh, hard to please some noblemen seem!
 At first, if anything, *too* unbending;
Off we go to the other extreme—
 Too confoundedly condescending!
 Duke
Now a gavotte perform sedately—
 Offer your hand with conscious pride;
Take an attitude not too stately,
 Still sufficiently dignified.
 Marco and Giuseppe
Now for an attitude not too stately,
 Still sufficiently dignified.
 (*They endeavour to carry out his instructions.*)
 Duke (*beating time*).
Oncely, twicely—oncely, twicely—
 Bow impressively ere you glide.
 (*They do so.*)
Capital both—you've caught it nicely!
 That is the style of thing precisely!
 Duchess and Casilda
Capital both—they caught it nicely!
 That is the style of thing precisely!
 Marco and Giuseppe
Oh, sweet to earn a nobleman's praise!
 Capital both—we've caught it nicely!
Supposing he's right in what he says,
 This is the style of thing precisely!
[GAVOTTE. *At the end exeunt* DUKE *and* DUCHESS, *leaving* CASILDA *with* MARCO *and* GIUSEPPE.

Giu. (*to* MARCO). The old birds have

gone away and left the young chickens together. That's called tact.

Mar. It's very awkward. We really ought to tell her how we are situated. It's not fair to the girl.

Giu. Then why don't you do it?

Mar. I'd rather not—you.

Giu. I don't know how to begin. (*To* CASILDA.) A—Madam—I—we, that is, several of us——

Cas. Gentlemen, I am bound to listen to you; but it is right to tell you that, not knowing I was married in infancy, I am over head and ears in love with somebody else.

Giu. Our case exactly! *We* are over head and ears in love with somebody else! (*Enter* GIANETTA *and* TESSA.) In point of fact, with our wives!

Cas. Your wives! Then you are married?

Tess. It's not our fault.

Gia. We knew nothing about it.

Both. We are sisters in misfortune.

Cas. My good girls, I don't blame you. Only before we go any further we must really arrive at some satisfactory arrangement, or we shall get hopelessly complicated.

QUINTET AND FINALE

MARCO, GIUSEPPE, CASILDA, GIANETTA, TESSA

All

Here is a case unprecedented!
Here are a King and Queen ill-starred!
Ever since marriage was first invented
Never was known a case so hard!

Marco and Giuseppe

I may be said to have been bisected,
By a profound catastrophe!

Casilda, Gianetta, Tessa

Through a calamity unexpected
I am divisible into three!

All

O moralists all,
How can you call
Marriage a state of unitee,
When excellent husbands are bisected,
And wives divisible into three?
O moralists all,
How can you call
Marriage a state of union true?

Casilda, Gianetta, Tessa

One-third of myself is married to half of
ye or you,

Marco and Giuseppe

When half of myself has married one-third
of ye or you?

Enter DON ALHAMBRA, *followed by* DUKE,
DUCHESS, *and all the* CHORUS.

FINALE

RECIT.—DON ALHAMBRA

Now let the loyal lieges gather round—
The Prince's foster-mother has been found!
She will declare, to silver clarion's sound
The rightful King—let him forthwith be
crowned!

Chorus

She will declare, etc.

[DON ALHAMBRA *brings forward* INEZ, *the*
Prince's foster-mother.

Tessa

Speak, woman, speak—

Duke

We're all attention!

Gianetta

The news we seek—

Duchess

This moment mention.

Casilda

To us they bring—

Don Alhambra

His foster-mother.

Marco

Is he the King?

Giuseppe

Or this my brother?

All

Speak, woman, speak, etc.

RECIT.—INEZ

The Royal Prince was by the King entrusted
To my fond care, ere I grew old and
crusted;
When traitors came to steal his son reputed
My own small boy I deftly substituted!
The villains fell into the trap completely—
I hid the Prince away—still sleeping
sweetly:
I called him "son" with pardonable slyness—
His name, Luiz! Behold his Royal Highness!

[*Sensation.* LUIZ *ascends the throne*
crowned and robed as King

Cas. (*rushing to his arms*). Luiz!

Luiz. Casilda! (*Embrace.*)

All

Is this indeed the King?

Oh, wondrous revelation!
Oh, unexpected thing!
Unlooked-for situation!
Marco, Gianetta
This statement we receive
Giuseppe, Tessa
With sentiments conflicting;
Our hearts rejoice and grieve,
Each other contradicting;
To those whom we adore
We can be reunited—
In one point rather sore,
But, on the whole, delighted!

Luiz
When others claimed thy dainty hand,
I waited—waited—waited,
Duke
As prudence (so I understand)
Dictated—'tated—'tated.

Casilda
By virtue of our early vow
Recorded—'corded—'corded.

Duchess
Your pure and patient love is now
Rewarded—'warded—'warded.
All
Then hail, O King of a Golden Land,
And the high-born bride who claims his
   hand!
The past is dead, and you gain your own,
A royal crown and a golden throne!
   [*All kneel:* LUIZ *crowns* CASILDA.
All
   Once more *gondolieri*,
   Both skilful and wary,
   Free from this quandary
      Contented are we.
   From Royalty flying,
   Our gondolas plying,
   And merrily crying
      Our *"premé," "stalì!"*
So good-bye, cachucha, fandango, bolero—
   We'll dance a farewell to that measure—
Old Xeres, adieu—Manzanilla—Montero—
   We leave you with feelings of pleasure!

CURTAIN

PRINCESS IDA

OR

CASTLE ADAMANT

DRAMATIS PERSONÆ

KING HILDEBRAND

HILARION (*his Son*)

CYRIL
⎱ (*Hilarion's Friends*)
FLORIAN

KING GAMA

ARAC
GURON ⎱ (*his Sons*)
SCYNTHIUS

PRINCESS IDA (*Gama's Daughter*)

LADY BLANCHE
  (*Professor of Abstract Science*)

LADY PSYCHE (*Professor of Humanities*)

MELISSA (*Lady Blanche's Daughter*)

SACHARISSA
CHLOE ⎱ (*Girl Graduates*)
ADA

Soldiers, Courtiers, "Girl Graduates", "Daughters of the Plough", etc.

ACT I

SCENE.—*Pavilion attached to* KING HILDE-
BRAND'S PALACE. *Soldiers and Courtiers
discovered looking out through opera-
glasses, telescopes, etc.,* FLORIAN *leading.*

Chorus

Search throughout the panorama
For a sign of royal Gama,
  Who to-day should cross the water
  With his fascinating daughter—
    Ida is her name.
Some misfortune evidently
Has detained them—consequently
Search throughout the panorama
For the daughter of King Gama,
    Prince Hilarion's flame!

SOLO
Florian

Will Prince Hilarion's hopes be sadly
  blighted?
All
Who can tell?
Florian
Will Ida break the vows that she has
  plighted?

All
Who can tell?
Florian
Will she back out, and say she did no[t]
  mean them?
All
Who can tell?
Florian
If so, there'll be the deuce to pay betwee[n]
  them!
All
  No, no—we'll not despair,
  For Gama would not dare
  To make a deadly foe
  Of Hildebrand, and so,
    Search throughout, etc.
Enter KING HILDEBRAND, *with* CYRIL
Hildebrand
See you no sign of Gama?
Florian
  None, my liege!
Hildebrand
It's very odd indeed. If Gama fail
To put in an appearance at our Court
Before the sun has set in yonder west,
And fail to bring the Princess Ida here

222

To whom our son Hilarion was betrothed
At the extremely early age of one,
There's war between King Gama and our-
 selves!
(*Aside to* CYRIL) Oh, Cyril, how I dread
 this interview.
It's twenty years since he and I have met.
He was a twisted monster—all awry—
As though Dame Nature, angry with her
 work,
Had crumpled it in fitful petulance!

   Cyril
But, sir, a twisted and ungainly trunk
Often bears goodly fruit. Perhaps he was
A kind, well-spoken gentleman?

   Hildebrand
 Oh, no!
For, adder-like, his sting lay in his tongue.
His "sting" is present, though his "stung"
 is past.)

   Florian (*looking through glass*)
But stay, my liege; o'er yonder mountain's
 brow
Comes a small body, bearing Gama's arms;
And now I look more closely at it, sir,
 see attached to it King Gama's legs;
From which I gather this corollary
That that small body must be Gama's
 own!

   Hildebrand
Ha! Is the Princess with him?

   Florian
 Well, my liege,
Unless her highness is full six feet high,
And wears mustachios too—and smokes
 cigars—
And rides *en cavalier* in coat of steel—
 do not think she is.

   Hildebrand
 One never knows.
She's a strange girl, I've heard, and does
 odd things!
Come, bustle there!
For Gama place the richest robes we own—
For Gama place the coarsest prison dress—
For Gama let our best spare bed be aired—
For Gama let our deepest dungeon yawn—
For Gama lay the costliest banquet out—
For Gama place cold water and dry bread!
For as King Gama brings the Princess here,
Or brings her not, so shall King Gama
 have
Much more than everything—much less
 than nothing!

   SONG AND CHORUS
   Hildebrand
Now hearken to my strict **command**
On every hand, on every hand—
   Chorus
  To your command,
  On every hand,
 We dutifully bow!
   Hildebrand
If Gama bring the Princess here,
Give him good cheer, give him good cheer.

   Chorus
  If she come here
  We'll give him a cheer,
 And we will show you how.
Hip, hip, hurrah! hip, hip, hurrah!
Hip, hip, hurrah! hurrah! hurrah!
  We'll shout and sing
  Long live the King,
 And his daughter, too, I trow!
Then shout ha! ha! hip, hip, hurrah!
Hip, hip, hip, hip, hurrah!
For the fair Princess and her good papa,
  Hurrah! hurrah!

   Hildebrand
But if he fail to keep his troth,
Upon our oath, we'll trounce them both!
   Chorus
  He'll trounce them both,
  Upon his oath,
 As sure as quarter-day!
   Hildebrand
We'll shut him up in a dungeon cell,
And toll his knell on a funeral bell.
   Chorus
  From his dungeon cell,
  His funeral knell
 Shall strike him with dismay!
Hip, hip, hurrah! hip, hip, hurrah!
Hip, hip, hurrah! hurrah! hurrah!
  As up we string
  The faithless King,
 In the old familiar way!
We'll shout ha! ha! hip, hip, hurrah!
Hip, hip, hip, hip, hurrah!
As we make an end of her false papa,
  Hurrah! hurrah!
     [*Exeunt all.*

   Enter HILARION
   RECIT—HILARION
To-day we meet, my baby bride and I—
 But ah, my hopes are balanced by my
  fears!

What transmutations have been conjured
    by
The silent alchemy of twenty years!
BALLAD—HILARION

Ida was a twelvemonth old,
    Twenty years ago!
I was twice her age, I'm told,
    Twenty years ago!
Husband twice as old as wife
Argues ill for married life,
Baleful prophecies were rife,
    Twenty years ago!
Still, I was a tiny prince
    Twenty years ago!
She has gained upon me, since
    Twenty years ago!
Though she's twenty-one, it's true,
I am barely twenty-two—
False and foolish prophets you,
    Twenty years ago!
Enter HILDEBRAND

Hilarion

Well, father, is there news for me at last?
Hildebrand

King Gama is in sight, but much I fear
With no Princess!
Hilarion

    Alas, my liege, I've heard
That Princess Ida has forsworn the world,
And, with a band of women, shut herself
Within a lonely country house, and there
Devotes herself to stern philosophies!
Hildebrand

Then I should say the loss of such a wife
Is one to which a reasonable man
Would easily be reconciled.
Hilarion

    Oh, no!
Or I am not a reasonable man.
She is my wife—has been for twenty years!
(Holding glass.) I think I see her now.
Hildebrand

    Ha! let me look!
Hilarion

In my mind's eye, I mean—a blushing
    bride,
All bib and tucker, frill and furbelow!
How exquisite she looked as she was borne,
Recumbent, in her foster-mother's arms!
How the bride wept—nor would be com-
    forted
Until the hireling mother-for-the-nonce
Administered refreshment in the vestry.
And I remember feeling much annoyed

That she should weep at marrying with me.
But then I thought, "These brides are all
    alike.
You cry at marrying me? How much more
    cause
You'd have to cry if it were broken off!"
These were my thoughts; I kept them to
    myself,
For at that age I had not learned to speak
[Exeunt

Enter COURTIERS

Chorus

From the distant panorama
Come the sons of royal Gama.
    They are heralds evidently,
    And are sacred consequently,
      Sons of Gama, hail! oh, hail!
Enter ARAC, GURON, and SCYNTHIUS
SONG—ARAC

We are warriors three,
    Sons of Gama, Rex.
Like most sons are we,
    Masculine in sex.
All Three

    Yes, yes, yes,
Masculine in sex.
Arac

Politics we bar,
    They are not our bent;
On the whole we are
    Not intelligent.
All Three

    No, no, no,
Not intelligent.
Arac

But with doughty heart,
    And with trusty blade
We can play our part—
    Fighting is our trade.
All Three

    Yes, yes, yes,
Fighting is our trade.
All Three

Bold, and fierce, and strong, ha! ha!
    For a war we burn,
With its right or wrong, ha! ha!
    We have no concern.
Order comes to fight, ha! ha!
    Order is obeyed,
We are men of might, ha! ha!
    Fighting is our trade.
    Yes, yes, yes,
Fighting is our trade, ha! ha!

Chorus

They are men of might, ha! ha!
Fighting is their trade.
Order comes to fight, ha! ha!
Order is obeyed, ha! ha!
 Fighting is their trade!

Enter KING GAMA

SONG—GAMA

If you give me your attention, I will tell
 you what I am:
I'm a genuine philanthropist—all other
 kinds are sham.
Each little fault of temper and each social
 defect
In my erring fellow-creatures I endeavour
 to correct.
To all their little weaknesses I open people's
 eyes;
And little plans to snub the self-sufficient
 I devise;
I love my fellow-creatures—I do all the
 good I can—
Yet everybody says I'm such a disagreeable
 man!
 And I can't think why!
To compliments inflated I've a withering
 reply;
And vanity I always do my best to mor-
 tify;
A charitable action I can skilfully dissect;
And interested motives I'm delighted to
 detect;
I know everybody's income and what
 everybody earns;
And I carefully compare it with the in-
 come tax returns;
But to benefit humanity however much I
 plan,
Yet everybody says I'm such a disagreeable
 man!
 And I can't think why!
I'm sure I'm no ascetic; I'm as pleasant as
 can be;
You'll always find me ready with a crush-
 ing repartee.
I've an irritating chuckle, I've a celebrated
 sneer,
I've an entertaining snigger, I've a fascinat-
 ing leer.
To everybody's prejudice I know a thing
 or two;
I can tell a woman's age in half a minute—
 and I do.

But although I try to make myself as
 pleasant as I can,
Yet everybody says I am a disagreeable
 man!
 And I can't think why!

Enter HILDEBRAND, HILARION, CYRIL, *and*
FLORIAN

Gama

So this is Castle Hildebrand? Well, well!
Dame Rumour whispered that the place
 was grand;
She told me that your taste was exquisite,
Superb, unparalleled!
 Hildebrand (gratified).
 Oh, really, King!

Gama

But she's a liar! Why, how old you've
 grown!
Is this Hilarion? Why, you've changed
 too—
You were a singularly handsome child!
 (*To* FLORIAN)
Are you a courtier? Come, then, ply your
 trade,
Tell me some lies. How do you like your
 King?
Vile rumour says he's all but imbecile.
Now, that's not true?

Florian
 My lord, we love our King.
His wise remarks are valued by his court
As precious stones.

Gama
 And for the self-same cause.
Like precious stones, his sensible remarks
Derive their value from their scarcity!
Come now, be honest, tell the truth for
 once!
Tell it of me. Come, come, I'll harm you
 not.
This leg is crooked—this foot is ill-de-
 signed—
This shoulder wears a hump! Come, out
 with it!
Look, here's my face! Now, am I not the
 worst
Of Nature's blunders?

Cyril
 Nature never errs.
To those who know the workings of your
 mind,
Your face and figure, sir, suggest a book
Appropriately bound.

Gama (enraged).

Why, harkye, sir,
How dare you bandy words with me?

Cyril

No need
To bandy aught that appertains to you.

Gama (furiously).

Do you permit this, King?

Hildebrand

We are in doubt
Whether to treat you as an honoured
guest
Oh as a traitor knave who plights his
word
And breaks it.

Gama (quickly).

If the casting vote's with me,
I give it for the former!

Hildebrand

We shall see.
By the terms of our contract, signed and
sealed,
You're bound to bring the Princess here
to-day:
Why is she not with you?

Gama

Answer me this:
What think you of a wealthy purse-proud
man,
Who, when he calls upon a starving friend,
Pulls out his gold and flourishes his notes,
And flashes diamonds in the pauper's eyes?
What name have you for such an one?

Hildebrand

A snob.

Gama

Just so. The girl has beauty, virtue, wit,
Grace, humour, wisdom, charity and pluck.
Would it be kindly think you, to parade
These brilliant qualities before *your* eyes?
Oh no, King Hildebrand, I am no snob!

Hildebrand (furiously).

Stop that tongue,
Or you shall lose the monkey head that
holds it!

Gama

Bravo! your King deprives me of my head,
That he and I may meet on equal terms!

Hildebrand

Where is she now?

Gama

In Castle Adamant,
One of my many country houses. There
She rules a woman's University,

With full a hundred girls, who learn of her

Cyril

A hundred girls! A hundred ecstasies!

Gama

But no mere girls, my good young gentleman;
With all the college learning that you
boast,
The youngest there will prove a match for
you.

Cyril

With all my heart, if she's the prettiest

(To FLORIAN)

Fancy, a hundred matches—all alight!—
That's if I strike them as I hope to do

Gama

Despair your hope; their hearts are dead
to men.
He who desires to gain their favour must
Be qualified to strike their teeming brains
And not their hearts. They're safety
matches, sir,
And they light only on the knowledge
box—
So *you've* no chance!

Florian

And there are no males whatever in those
walls?

Gama

None, gentlemen, excepting letter mails—
And they are driven (as males often are
In other large communities) by women
Why, bless my heart, she's so particular
She'll scarcely suffer Dr. Watts's hymns—
And all the animals she owns are "hers"
The ladies rise at cockrow every morn—

Cyril

Ah, then they have male poultry?

Gama

Not at all,

(Confidentially)

The crowing's done by an accomplished
hen!

DUET—GAMA *and* HILDEBRAND

Gama

Perhaps if you address the lady
   Most politely, most politely—
Flatter and impress the lady,
   Most politely, most politely—
Humbly beg and humbly sue—
She may deign to look on you,
But your doing you must do
   Most politely, most politely!

All

Humbly beg and humbly sue, etc.
Hildebrand
Go you, and inform the lady,
  Most politely, most politely,
Is she don't, we'll storm the lady
  Most politely, most politely!
      (*To* GAMA)
You'll remain as hostage here;
Should Hilarion disappear,
We will hang you, never fear,
  Most politely, most politely!
All

He'll ⎫
I'll ⎬ remain as hostage here, etc.
You'll ⎭

GAMA, ARAC, GURON, *and* SCYNTHIUS *are marched off in custody,* HILDEBRAND *following.*

RECIT—HILARION

ome, Cyril, Florian, our course is plain,
To-morrow morn fair Ida we'll engage;
ut we will use no force her love to gain,
Nature has armed us for the war we
    wage!

TRIO—HILARION, CYRIL, *and* FLORIAN

Hilarion

Expressive glances
Shall be our lances,
  And pops of Sillery
  Our light artillery.
We'll storm their bowers
With scented showers
Of fairest flowers
  That we can buy!
    Chorus
  Oh, dainty triolet!
  Oh, fragrant violet!
  Oh, gentle heigho-let
    (Or little sigh).
On sweet urbanity,
Though mere inanity,
To touch their vanity
  We will rely!
    Cyril
When day is fading,
With serenading
  And such frivolity
  We'll prove our quality.
A sweet profusion
Of soft allusion
This bold intrusion
  Shall justify.

Chorus
Oh, dainty triolet, etc.
Florian
We'll charm their senses
With verbal fences,
  With ballads amatory
  And declamatory.
Little heeding
Their pretty pleading,
Our love exceeding
  We'll justify!
    Chorus
  Oh, dainty triolet, etc.
Re-enter GAMA, ARAC, GURON, *and* SCYN-
    THIUS *heavily ironed*
    RECIT
Gama
Must we, till then, in prison cell be thrust?
    Hildebrand
    You must!
    Gama
This seems unnecessarily severe!
    Arac, Guron, and Scynthius
      Hear, hear!
  TRIO—ARAC, GURON, *and* SCYNTHIUS
For a month to dwell
In a dungeon cell;
  Growing thin and wizen
  In a solitary prison,
Is a poor look-out
For a soldier stout,
  Who is longing for the rattle
  Of a complicated battle—
For the rum-tum-tum
Of the military drum
  And the guns that go boom! boom!
    All
The rum-tum-tum
Of the military drum, etc.
    Hildebrand
When Hilarion's bride
Has at length complied
  With the just conditions
  Of our requisitions,
You may go in haste
And indulge your taste
  For the fascinating rattle
  Of a complicated battle—
For the rum-tum-tum,
Of the military drum,
  And the guns that go boom! boom!
    All
For the rum-tum-tum-
Of the military drum, etc.

All

But till that time $\left\{\begin{array}{l}\text{we'll}\\\text{you'll}\end{array}\right\}$ here remain,

And bail $\left\{\begin{array}{l}\text{they}\\\text{we}\end{array}\right\}$ will not entertain,

Should she $\left\{\begin{array}{l}\text{his}\\\text{our}\end{array}\right\}$ mandate disobey,

$\left.\begin{array}{l}\text{Our}\\\text{Your}\end{array}\right\}$ lives the penalty will pay!

[GAMA, ARAC, GURON, *and* SCYNTHIUS *are marched off.*

END OF ACT I

ACT II

Gardens in Castle Adamant. A river runs across the back of the stage, crossed by a rustic bridge. Castle Adamant in the distance.

Girl graduates discovered seated at the feet of LADY PSYCHE

Chorus

Towards the empyrean heights
    Of every kind of lore,
We've taken several easy flights,
    And mean to take some more.
In trying to achieve success
    No envy racks our heart,
And all the knowledge we possess,
    We mutually impart.

SONG—MELISSA

Pray, what authors should she read
Who in Classics would succeed?

Psyche

If you'd climb the Helicon,
You should read Anacreon,
Ovid's *Metamorphoses*,
Likewise Aristophanes,
And the works of Juvenal:
These are worth attention, all;
But, if you will be advised,
You will get them Bowdlerized!

Chorus

Ah, we will get them Bowdlerized!

SOLO—SACHARISSA

Pray you, tell us, if you can,
What's the thing that's known as Man?

Psyche

Man will swear and Man will storm—
Man is not at all good form—
Man is of no kind of use—
Man's a donkey—Man's a goose—
Man is coarse and Man is plain—
Man is more or less insane—
Man's a ribald—Man's a rake,

Man is Nature's sole mistake!

Chorus

We'll a memorandum make—
Man is Nature's sole mistake!
And thus to empyrean height
    Of every kind of lore,
In search of wisdom's pure delight,
    Ambitiously we soar.
In trying to achieve success
    No envy racks our heart,
For all we know and all we guess,
    We mutually impart!

Enter LADY BLANCHE. *All stand up demurel[y]*

Blanche

Attention, ladies, while I read to you
The Princess Ida's list of punishments.
The first is Sacharissa. She's expelled!

All

Expelled!

Blanche

Expelled, because although she knew
No man of any kind may pass our wall[s]
She dared to bring a set of chessmen here[!]

Sacharissa (crying).

I meant no harm; they're only men o[f]
    wood!

Blanche

They're men with whom you give eac[h]
    other mate,
And that's enough! The next is Chloe.

Chloe

Ah!

Blanche

Chloe will lose three terms, for yesterda[y]
When looking through her drawing-boo[k]
    I found
A sketch of a perambulator!

All (horrified).

Oh!

Blanche

Double perambulator, shameless girl!
That's all at present. Now, attention, pray[,]
Your Principal the Princess comes to giv[e]
Her usual inaugural address
To those young ladies who joined yesterda[y]

Chorus

Mighty maiden with a mission,
    Paragon of common sense,
Running fount of erudition,
    Miracle of eloquence,
We are blind, and we would see;
We are bound, and would be free;
We are dumb, and we would talk;
We are lame, and we would walk.

Enter the PRINCESS

Mighty maiden with a mission—
Paragon of common sense;
Running fount of erudition—
Miracle of eloquence!

Princess (*Recit.*)

Minerva, oh, hear me!

ARIA

Oh, goddess wise
    That lovest light
    Endow with sight
Their unillumined eyes.
    At this my call,
    A fervent few
    Have come to woo
The rays that from thee fall.

Let fervent words and fervent thoughts be
    mine,
That I may lead them to thy sacred shrine!
Women of Adamant, fair Neophytes—
Who thirst for such instruction as we give,
Attend, while I unfold a parable.
The elephant is mightier than Man,
Yet Man subdues him. Why? The elephant
Is elephantine everywhere but here (*tap-
    ping her forehead*),
And Man, whose brain is to the elephant's
As Woman's brain to Man's—(that's rule
    of three),—
Conquers the foolish giant of the woods,
As Woman, in her turn, shall conquer Man.
In Mathematics, Woman leads the way:
The narrow-minded pedant still believes
That two and two make four! Why, we
    can prove,
We women—household drudges as we are—
That two and two make five—or three—
    or seven;
Or five-and-twenty, if the case demands!
Diplomacy? The wiliest diplomat
Is absolutely helpless in our hands,
He wheedles monarchs—Woman wheedles
    him!
Logic? Why, tyrant Man himself admits
It's waste of time to argue with a woman!
Then we excel in social qualities:
Though Man professes that he holds our
    sex
In utter scorn, I venture to believe
He'd rather pass the day with one of you,
Than with five hundred of his fellow-men!
In all things we excel. Believing this,
A hundred maidens here have sworn to
    place

Their feet upon his neck. If we succeed,
We'll treat him better than he treated us:
But if we fail, why, then let hope fail too!
Let no one care a penny how she looks—
Let red be worn with yellow—blue with
    green—
Crimson with scarlet—violet with blue!
Let all your things misfit, and you your-
    selves
At inconvenient moments come undone!
Let hair-pins lose their virtue: let the hook
Disdain the fascination of the eye—
The bashful button modestly evade
The soft embraces of the button-hole!
Let old associations all dissolve,
Let Swan secede from Edgar—Gask from
    Gask,
Sewell from Cross—Lewis from Allenby!
In other words—let Chaos come again!

(*Coming down*)

Who lectures in the Hall of Arts to-day?

Blanche

I, madam, on Abstract Philosophy.
There I propose considering, at length,
Three points—The Is, the Might Be, and
    the Must.
Whether the Is from being actual fact,
Is more important than the vague Might
    Be,
Or the Might Be, from taking wider scope,
Is for that reason greater than the Is:
And lastly, how the Is and Might Be
    stand
Compared with the inevitable Must!

Princess

The subject's deep—how do you treat it,
    pray?

Blanche

Madam, I take three possibilities,
And strike a balance, then, between the
    three:
As thus: The Princess Ida Is our head,
The Lady Psyche Might Be,—Lady
    Blanche,
Neglected Blanche, inevitably Must.
Given these three hypotheses—to find
The actual betting against each of them!

Princess

Your theme's ambitious: pray you, bear
    in mind
Who highest soar fall farthest. Fare you
    well,
You and your pupils! Maidens, follow me.
[*Exeunt* PRINCESS *and Maidens singing re-*

*frain of chorus, "And thus to em-
pyrean heights", etc. Manet* LADY
BLANCHE.

Blanche

I should command here—I was born to
    rule,
But do I rule? I don't. Why? I don't
    know.
I shall some day. Not yet. I bide my time.
I once was Some One—and the Was Will
    Be.
The Present as we speak becomes the Past,
The Past repeats itself, and so is Future!
This sounds involved. It's not. It's right
    enough.

SONG—LADY BLANCHE

Come, mighty Must!
    Inevitable Shall!
In thee I trust.
    Time weaves my coronal!
Go, mocking Is!
    Go, disappointing Was!
That I am this
    Ye are the cursed cause!
Yet humble second shall be first,
    I ween;
And dead and buried be the curst
    Has Been!
Oh, weak Might Be!
    Oh May, Might, Could, Would, Should!
How powerless ye
    For evil or for good!
In every sense
    Your moods I cheerless call
Whate'er your tense
    Ye are Imperfect, all!
Ye have deceived the trust I've shown
    In ye!
Away! The Mighty Must alone
    Shall be!

[*Exit* LADY BLANCHE.

Enter HILARION, CYRIL, *and* FLORIAN, *climbing over wall, and creeping cautiously
among the trees and rocks at the back
of the stage.*

TRIO—HILARION, CYRIL, FLORIAN

Gently, gently,
Evidently
    We are safe so far,
After scaling
Fence and paling,
    Here, at last, we are!
In this college
Useful knowledge

Everywhere one finds,
And already,
Growing steady,
    We've enlarged our minds.

Cyril

We've learnt that prickly cactus
Has the power to attract us
        When we fall.

All

        When we fall!

Hilarion

That nothing man unsettles
Like a bed of stinging nettles,
        Short or tall.

All

        Short or tall!

Florian

That bull-dogs feed on throttles—
That we don't like broken bottles
        On a wall.

All

        On a wall!

Hilarion

That spring-guns breathe defiance!
And that burglary's a science
        After all!

All

        After all!

RECIT—FLORIAN

A Woman's college! maddest folly going!
What can girls learn within its walls
    worth knowing?
I'll lay a crown (the Princess shall decide
    it)
I'll teach them twice as much in half-an-
    hour outside it.

Hilarion

Hush, scoffer; ere you sound your puny
    thunder,
List to their aims, and bow your head in
    wonder!
    They intend to send a wire
        To the moon—to the moon;
    And they'll set the Thames on fire
        Very soon—very soon;
    Then they learn to make silk purses
        With their rigs—with their rigs,
    From the ears of Lady Circe's
        Piggy-wigs—piggy-wigs.
    And weasels at their slumbers
        They trepan—they trepan;
    To get sunbeams from cu*cum*bers,
        They've a plan—they've a plan.
    They've a firmly rooted notion

They can cross the Polar Ocean,
And they'll find Perpetual Motion,
  If they can—if they can.
                All
These are the phenomena
That every pretty domina
Is hoping we shall see
At her Universitee!
                Cyril
As for fashion, they forswear it,
  So they say—so they say;
And the circle—they will square it
  Some fine day—some fine day;
Then the little pigs they're teaching
  For to fly—for to fly;
And the niggers they'll be bleaching,
  By and by—by and by!
Each newly-joined aspirant
  To the clan—to the clan—
Must repudiate the tyrant
  Known as Man—known as Man.
They mock at him and flout him,
For they do not care about him,
And they're "going to do without him"
  If they can—if they can!
                All
These are the phenomena, etc.
    In this college
    Useful knowledge
    Ev'rywhere one finds,
    And already growing steady
    We've enlarg'd our minds.
                Hilarion
So that's the Princess Ida's castle! Well,
They must be lovely girls, indeed, if it
    requires
Such walls as those to keep intruders off!
                Cyril
To keep men off is only half their charge,
And that the easier half. I much suspect
The object of these walls is not so much
To keep men off as keep the maidens in!
                Florian
But what are these? (*Examining some Col-
    legiate robes.*)
    Hilarion (looking at them).
Why, Academic robes,
Worn by the lady undergraduates
When they matriculate. Let's try them on.
    (*They do so.*)
Why, see—we're covered to the very toes.
Three lovely lady undergraduates
Who, weary of the world and all its
    wooing—

                Florian
And penitent for deeds there's no un-
    doing—
                Cyril
Looked at askance by well-conducted
    maids—
                All
Seek sanctuary in these classic shades!
    TRIO—HILARION, CYRIL, FLORIAN
                Hilarion
I am a maiden, cold and stately,
  Heartless I, with a face divine.
What do I want with a heart, innately?
  Every heart I meet is mine!
                All
  Haughty, humble, coy, or free,
    Little care I what maid may be.
  So that a maid is fair to see,
    Every maid is the maid for me!
                        (*Dance.*)
                Cyril
I am a maiden, frank and simple,
  Brimming with joyous roguery;
Merriment lurks in every dimple,
  Nobody breaks more hearts than I!
                All
  Haughty, humble, coy, or free,
    Little care I what maid may be.
  So that a maid is fair to see,
    Every maid is the maid for me!
                        (*Dance.*)
                Florian
I am a maiden, coyly blushing,
  Timid am I as a startled hind;
Every suitor sets me flushing:
  I am the maid that wins mankind!
                All
  Haughty, humble, coy, or free,
    Little care I what maid may be.
  So that a maid is fair to see,
    Every maid is the maid for me!
Enter the PRINCESS *reading. She does not
    see them*
  Flor. But who comes here? The Princess,
as I live! What shall we do?
  Hil. (*aside*). Why, we must brave it out!
(*Aloud.*) Madam, accept our humblest
reverence.
[*They bow, then, suddenly recollecting
    themselves, curtsey.*
  Prin. (*suprised*). We greet you, ladies.
What would you with us?
  Hil. (*aside*). What shall I say? (*Aloud.*)
We are three students, ma'am,

Three well-born maids of liberal estate,
Who wish to join this University.

[HILARION *and* FLORIAN *curtsey again.*
CYRIL *bows extravagantly, then, being
recalled to himself by* FLORIAN, *curt-
seys.*

Princess
If, as you say, you wish to join our ranks,
And will subscribe to all our rules, 'tis well.

Florian
To all your rules we cheerfully subscribe.

Princess
You say you're noblewomen. Well, you'll
    find
No sham degrees for noblewomen here.
You'll find no sizars here, or servitors,
Or other cruel distinctions, meant to draw
A line 'twixt rich and poor: you'll find no
    tufts
To mark nobility, except such tufts
As indicate nobility of brain.
As for your fellow-students, mark me well:
There are a hundred maids within these
    walls,
All good, all learned, and all beautiful:
They are prepared to love you: will you
    swear
To give the fullness of your love to them?

Hilarion
Upon our words and honours, ma'am, we
    will!

Princess
But we go further: will you undertake
That you will never marry any man?

Florian
Indeed we never will!

Princess
Consider well,
You must prefer our maids to all man-
    kind!

Hilarion
To all mankind we much prefer your
    maids!

Cyril
We should be dolts indeed, if we did not,
Seeing how fair——

Princess
The world is but a broken toy,
Its pleasure hollow—false its joy,
    Unreal its loveliest hue,
        Alas!
    Its pains alone are true,
        Alas!
    Its pains alone are true!

Hilarion (aside to CYRIL*).*
Take care—that's rather strong!

Princess
But have you left no lovers at your home
Who may pursue you here?

Hilarion
No, madam, none.
We're homely ladies, as no doubt you see,
And we have never fished for lover's love.
We smile at girls who deck themselves
    with gems,
False hair, and meretricious ornament,
To chain the fleeting fancy of a man,
But do not imitate them. What we have
Of hair, is all our own. Our colour, too,
Unladylike, but not unwomanly,
Is Nature's handiwork, and man has learnt
To reckon Nature an impertinence.

Princess
Well, beauty counts for naught within these
    walls;
If all you say is true, you'll pass with us
A happy, happy time!

Cyril
If, as you say,
A hundred lovely maidens wait within,
To welcome us with smiles and open arms,
I think there's very little doubt we shall!

QUARTETTE—PRINCESS, HILARION, CYRIL,
FLORIAN

Princess
The world is but a broken toy,
Its pleasure hollow—false its joy,
    Unreal its loveliest hue,
        Alas!
    Its pains alone are true,
        Alas!
    Its pains alone are true.

Hilarion
The world is everything you say,
The world we think has had its day.
    Its merriment is slow,
        Alas!
    We've tried it, and we know.
        Alas!
    We've tried it and we know.

TUTTI

Hilarion, Cyril, Florian
The world is but a broken toy,
We freely give it up with joy,
    Unreal its loveliest hue,
        Alas!
    Its pains alone are true,
        Alas!
    Its pains alone are true!

[*Exit* PRINCESS. *The three gentlemen watch
her off.* LADY PSYCHE *enters, and regards them with amazement.*

Hilarion

I'faith, the plunge is taken, gentlemen!
For, willy-nilly, we are maidens now,
And maids against our will we must re-
main!   (*All laugh heartily.*)

Psyche (*aside*).

These ladies are unseemly in their mirth.
[*The gentlemen see her and, in confusion,
resume their modest demeanour.*

Florian (*aside*).

Here's a catastrophe, Hilarion!
This is my sister! She'll remember me,
Though years have passed since she and I
have met!

Hilarion (*aside to* FLORIAN).

Then make a virtue of necessity,
And trust our secret to her gentle care.

Florian (*to* PSYCHE, *who has watched* CYRIL
in amazement).

Psyche!
Why, don't you know me? Florian!

Psyche (*amazed*).

Why, Florian!

Florian

My sister (*embraces her*).

Psyche

Oh, my dear!
What are you doing here—and who are
these?

Hilarion

I am that Prince Hilarion to whom
Your Princess is betrothed. I come to claim
Her plighted love. Your brother Florian
And Cyril came to see me safely through.

Psyche

The Prince Hilarion? Cyril too? How
strange!
My earliest playfellows!

Hilarion

Why, let me look!
Are you that learned little Psyche who
At school alarmed her mates because she
called
A buttercup "ranunculus bulbosus"?

Cyril

Are you indeed that Lady Psyche, who
At children's parties drove the conjuror
wild,
Explaining all his tricks before he did
them?

Hilarion

Are you that learned little Psyche, who
At dinner parties, brought in to dessert,
Would tackle visitors with "You don't
know
Who first determined longitude—I do—
Hipparchus 'twas—B.C. one sixty-three!"
Are you indeed that small phenomenon?

Psyche

That small phenomenon indeed am I!
But, gentlemen, 'tis death to enter here:
We have all promised to renounce man-
kind!

Florian

Renounce mankind? On what ground do
you base
This senseless resolution?

Psyche

Senseless? No.
We are all taught, and, being taught, believe
That Man, sprung from an Ape, is Ape at
heart.

Cyril

That's rather strong.

Psyche

The truth is always strong!

SONG—LADY PSYCHE

A Lady fair, of lineage high,
Was loved by an Ape, in the days gone by.
The Maid was radiant as the sun,
The Ape was a most unsightly one—
So it would not do—
His scheme fell through,
For the Maid, when his love took formal
shape,
Expressed such terror
At his monstrous error,
That he stammered an apology and made
his 'scape,
The picture of a disconcerted Ape.
With a view to rise in the social scale,
He shaved his bristles, and he docked his
tail,
He grew mustachios, and he took his tub,
And he paid a guinea to a toilet club—
But it would not do,
The scheme fell through—
For the Maid was Beauty's fairest Queen,
With golden tresses,
Like a real princess's,
While the Ape, despite his razor keen,
Was the apiest Ape that ever was seen!

He bought white ties, and he bought dress
   suits,
He crammed his feet into bright tight
   boots—
And to start in life on a brand-new plan,
He christened himself Darwinian Man!
   But it would not do,
   The scheme fell through—
For the Maiden fair, whom the monkey
      craved,
   Was a radiant Being,
   With a brain far-seeing—
While a Darwinian Man, though well-
   behaved,
At best is only a monkey shaved!

         All
While Darwinian Man, etc.
During this MELISSA *has entered unob-
      served; she looks on in amazement*
      Melissa (coming down).
      Oh, Lady Psyche!
         Psyche (terrified).
      What! you heard us then?
Oh, all is lost!

         Melissa
   Not so! I'll breathe no word!
(Advancing in astonishment to FLORIAN.)
How marvellously strange! and are you
      then
Indeed young men?

         Florian
         Well, yes, just now we are—
But hope by dint of study to become,
In course of time, young women.
      Melissa (eagerly).
                  No, no, no—
Oh, don't do that! Is this indeed a man?
I've often heard of them, but, till to-day,
Never set eyes on one. They told me men
Were hideous, idiotic, and deformed!
They're quite as beautiful as women are!
As beautiful, they're infinitely more so!
Their cheeks have not that pulpy softness
      which
One gets so weary of in womankind:
Their features are more marked—and—
      oh, their chins!
How curious! *(Feeling his chin.)*

         Florian
   I fear it's rather rough.
      Melissa (eagerly).
   Oh, don't apologize—I like it so!
QUINTETTE—PSYCHE, MELISSA, HILARION,

         CYRIL, FLORIAN
            Psyche
The woman of the wisest wit
   May sometimes be mistaken, O!
In Ida's views, I must admit,
   My faith is somewhat shaken, O!
            Cyril
On every other point than this
   Her learning is untainted, O!
But Man's a theme with which she is
   Entirely unacquainted, O!
            —acquainted, O!
            —acquainted, O!
   Entirely unacquainted, O!
            All
Then jump for joy and gaily bound,
The truth is found—the truth is found!
Set bells a-ringing through the air—
Ring here and there and everywhere—
And echo forth the joyous sound,
The truth is found—the truth is found!
            (Dance.)

            Melissa
My natural instinct teaches me
   (And instinct is important, O!)
You're everything you ought to be,
   And nothing that you oughtn't, O!
            Hilarion
That fact was seen at once by you
   In casual conversation, O!
Which is most creditable to
   Your powers of observation, O!
            —servation, O!
            —servation, O!
   Your powers of observation, O!
            All
Then jump for joy, etc.
[*Exeunt* PSYCHE, HILARION, CYRIL, *and*
   FLORIAN, MELISSA *going.*
      Enter LADY BLANCHE

            Blanche
      Melissa!
         Melissa (returning).
      Mother!

         Blanche
      Here—a word with you.
Those are the three new students?
         Melissa (confused)
                  Yes, they are.
They're charming girls.
         Blanche
               Particularly so.
So graceful, and so very womanly!

So skilled in all a girl's accomplishments!
   Melissa (confused).
  Yes—very skilled.
    Blanche
   They sing so nicely too!
    Melissa
They *do* sing nicely!
    Blanche
   Humph! It's very odd.
Two are tenors, one is a baritone!
   Melissa (much agitated).
   They've all got colds!

    Blanche
  Colds! Bah! D'ye think I'm blind?
These "girls" are men disguised!
    Melissa
      Oh no—indeed!
You wrong these gentlemen—I mean—why,
  see,
Here is an *étui* dropped by one of them
  (*picking up an étui*).
Containing scissors, needles, and——
   Blanche (opening it).
       Cigars!
Why, these *are* men! And you knew this,
  you minx!

    Melissa
Oh, spare them—they are gentlemen in-
  deed.
The Prince Hilarion (married years ago
To Princess Ida) with two trusted friends!
Consider, mother, he's her husband now,
And has been, twenty years! Consider, too,
You're only second here—you should be
  first.
Assist the Prince's plan, and when he gains
The Princess Ida, why, you *will* be first.
You will design the fashions—think of
  that—
And always serve out all the punishments!
The scheme is harmless, mother—wink at
  it!
    Blanche (aside).
The prospect's tempting! Well, well, well,
  I'll try—
Though I've not winked at anything for
  years!
'Tis but one step towards my destiny—
The mighty Must! the inevitable Shall!
  DUET—MELISSA *and* LADY BLANCHE
    Melissa
Now wouldn't you like to rule the roast,
  And guide this University?

    Blanche
  I must agree
  'Twould pleasant be.
  (Sing hey, a Proper Pride!)
    Melissa
And wouldn't you like to clear the coast
  Of malice and perversity?
    Blanche
  Without a doubt
  I'll bundle 'em out,
  Sing hey, when I preside!
    Both
Sing, hoity, toity! Sorry for some!
Sing, marry come up and $\begin{Bmatrix} my \\ her \end{Bmatrix}$ day will come!
  Sing, Proper Pride
  Is the horse to ride,
  And Happy-go-lucky, my Lady, O!
    Blanche
For years I've writhed beneath her sneers,
  Although a born Plantagenet!
    Melissa
  You're much too meek,
  Or you would speak.
  (Sing hey, I'll say no more!)
    Blanche
Her elder I, by several years,
  Although you'd ne'er imagine it.

    Melissa
  Sing, so I've heard
  But never a word
  Have I e'er believed before!

    Both
Sing, hoity, toity! Sorry for some!
Sing, marry come up and $\begin{Bmatrix} my \\ her \end{Bmatrix}$ day will come!
  Sing, she shall learn
  That a worm will turn.
  Sing Happy-go-lucky, my Lady, O!
     [*Exit* LADY BLANCHE.

    Melissa
Saved for a time, at least!
   Enter FLORIAN, *on tiptoe*
   Florian (whispering).
      Melissa—come!

    Melissa
Oh, sir! you must away from this at
  once—
My mother guessed your sex! It was my
  fault—

I blushed and stammered so that she ex-
claimed,
"Can these be men?" Then, seeing this,
"Why these——"
"Are men", she would have added, but *"are
men"*
Stuck in her throat! She keeps your secret,
sir,
For reasons of her own—but fly from this
And take me with you—that is—no—not
that!

> *Florian*

I'll go, but not without you! (*Bell.*) Why,
what's that?

> *Melissa*

The luncheon bell.

> *Florian*

> I'll wait for luncheon then!
Enter HILARION *with* PRINCESS, CYRIL *with*
PSYCHE, LADY BLANCHE *and* LADIES.
*Also "Daughters of the Plough" bear-
ing luncheon.*

> *Chorus*

Merrily ring the luncheon bell!
Here in meadow of asphodel,
Feast we body and mind as well,
So merrily ring the luncheon bell!

> SOLO—BLANCHE

Hunger, I beg to state,
Is highly indelicate,
This is a fact profoundly true,
So learn your appetites to subdue.

> *All*

> Yes, yes,
We'll learn our appetites to subdue!
> SOLO—CYRIL (*eating*)
Madame, your words so wise,
Nobody should despise,
Cursed with appetite keen I am
And I'll subdue it—
And I'll subdue it—
And I'll subdue it with cold roast
lamb!

> *All*

> Yes—yes—
We'll subdue it with cold roast lamb!
> *Chorus*
Merrily ring, etc.
> *Princess*
You say you know the court of Hilde-
brand?
There is a Prince there—I forget his
name—

> *Hilarion*

Hilarion?

> *Princess*
> Exactly—is he well?
> *Hilarion*
If it be well to droop and pine and mope,
To sigh "Oh, Ida! Ida!" all day long,
"Ida! my love! my life! Oh, come to me!"
If it be well, I say, to do all this,
Then Prince Hilarion is very well.

> *Princess*
He breathes *our* name? Well, it's a com-
mon one!
And is the booby comely?

> *Hilarion*
> Pretty well.
I've heard it said that if I dressed myself
In Prince Hilarion's clothes (supposing
this
Consisted with my maiden modesty),
I might be taken for Hilarion's self.
But what is this to you or me, who think
Of all mankind with undisguised contempt?

> *Princess*
Contempt? Why, damsel, when I think of
man,
Contempt is not the word.
> *Cyril (getting tipsy).*
> I'm sure of that,
Or if it is, it surely should not be!
> *Hilarion (aside to CYRIL).*
Be quiet, idiot, or they'll find us out.

> *Cyril*
The Prince Hilarion's a goodly lad!

> *Princess*
You know him then?
> *Cyril (tipsily).*
> I rather think I do!
We are inseparables!

> *Princess*
> Why, what's this?
You love him then?

> *Cyril*
> We do indeed—all three!

> *Hilarion*
Madam, she jests! (*Aside to* CYRIL.) Remember where you are!

> *Cyril*
Jests? Not at all! Why, bless my heart
alive,
You and Hilarion, when at the Court,
Rode the same horse!

> *Princess (horrified).*
> Astride?

Cyril
Of course! Why not?
Wore the same clothes—and once or twice,
   I think,
Got tipsy in the same good company!
Princess
Well, these are nice young ladies, on my
   word!
Cyril (tipsy).
Don't you remember that old kissing-song
He'd sing to blushing Mistress Lalage,
The hostess of the Pigeons? Thus it ran:

SONG—CYRIL

[*During symphony* HILARION *and* FLORIAN
try to stop CYRIL. *He shakes them off
angrily*

Would you know the kind of maid
  Sets my heart aflame-a?
Eyes must be downcast and staid,
  Cheeks must flush for shame-a!
    She may neither dance nor sing,
    But, demure in everything,
    Hang her head in modest way,
    With pouting lips that seem to say,
  "Oh, kiss me, kiss me, kiss me, kiss me,
    Though I die of shame-a!"
Please you that's the kind of maid
  Sets my heart aflame-a!
When a maid is bold and gay
  With a tongue goes clang-a,
Flaunting it in brave array,
  Maiden may go hang-a!
    Sunflower gay and hollyhock
    Never shall my garden stock;
    Mine the blushing rose of May,
    With pouting lips that seem to say,
  "Oh, kiss me, kiss me, kiss me, kiss me,
    Though I die for shame-a!"
Please you, that's the kind of maid
  Sets my heart aflame-a!

Princess
Infamous creature, get you hence away!
[HILARION, *who has been with difficulty restrained by* FLORIAN *during this song,
breaks from him and strikes* CYRIL
furiously on the breast.

Hilarion
Dog! there is something more to sing
  about!
Cyril (sobered).
Hilarion, are you mad?
Princess (horrified).
      Hilarion? Help!

Why, these are men! Lost! lost! **betrayed,**
  undone! (*Running on to bridge.*)
Girls, get you hence! Man-monsters, **if you
  dare**
Approach one step, I—— Ah!
(*Loses her balance, and falls into the
stream.*)

Psyche
      Oh! save her, sir!
Blanche
It's useless, sir,—you'll only catch your
  death! (HILARION *springs in.*)
Sacharissa
He catches her!

Melissa
And now he lets her go!
Again she's in his grasp—
Psyche
      And now she's not.
He seizes her back hair!
Blanche (not looking)
      And it comes off!
Psyche
No, no! She's saved!—she's saved!—she's
  saved!—she's saved!

FINALE

CHORUS OF LADIES

Oh! joy, our chief is saved,
  And by Hilarion's hand;
The torrent fierce he braved,
  And brought her safe to land!
    For his intrusion we must own
    This doughty deed may well atone!
Princess
Stand forth ye three,
  Whoe'er ye be,
And hearken to our stern decree!
Hilarion, Cyril and Florian
Have mercy, lady,—disregard your oaths!
Princess
I know not mercy, men in women's
  clothes!
  The man whose sacrilegious eyes
  Invade our strict seclusion, dies.
  Arrest these coarse intruding spies!
[*They are arrested by the "Daughters of
the Plough".*
Florian, Cyril and Ladies
Have mercy, lady—disregard your oaths!
Princess
I know not mercy, men in women's clothes!
[CYRIL *and* FLORIAN *are bound.*

SONG—HILARION

Whom thou hast chained must wear his
    chain,
  Thou canst not set him free,
He wrestles with his bonds in vain
  Who lives by loving thee!
If heart of stone for heart of fire,
  Be all thou hast to give,
If dead to me my heart's desire,
  Why should I wish to live?
      Florian, Cyril and Ladies
    Have mercy, O lady!
No word of thine—no stern command
  Can teach my heart to rove,
Then rather perish by thy hand,
  Than live without thy love!
A loveless life apart from thee
  Were hopeless slavery,
If kindly death will set me free,
  Why should I fear to die?

*[He is bound by two of the attendants, and
    the three gentlemen are marched off.*
      Enter MELISSA
        Melissa
  Madam, without the castle walls
    An armed band
  Demand admittance to our halls
    For Hildebrand!
        All
      Oh, horror!
        Princess
    Deny them!
    We will defy them!
        All
    Too late—too late!
    The castle gate
  Is battered by them!
[The gate yields. SOLDIERS *rush in.* ARAC,
    GURON, *and* SCYNTHIUS *are with them,
    but with their hands handcuffed.*

ENSEMBLE

Girls

  Rend the aid with wailing,
    Shed the shameful tear!
  Walls are unavailing,
    Man has entered here!
  Shame and desecration
    Are his staunch allies,
  Let your lamentation
    Echo to the skies!

Men

  Walls and fences scaling,
    Promptly we appear;
  Walls are unavailing,
    We have entered here.
  Female execration
    Stifle if you're wise,
  Stop your lamentation,
  Dry your pretty eyes!

  Enter HILDEBRAND
      RECIT.
      Princess
Audacious tyrant, do you dare
To beard a maiden in her lair?
      Hildebrand
    Since you inquire,
    We've no desire
To beard a maiden here, or anywhere!
      Soldiers
    No, no—we've no desire
To beard a maiden here, or anywhere!
      SOLO—HILDEBRAND
    Some years ago
    No doubt you know
(And if you don't I'll tell you so)
    You gave your troth
    Upon your oath
To Hilarion my son.
    A vow you make
    You must not break,
(If you think you may, it's a great mis-
    take),

For a bride's a bride
Though the knot were tied
    At the early age of one!
      And I'm a peppery kind of King,
      Who's indisposed for parleying
      To fit the wit of a bit of a chit,
      And that's the long and the short
        of it!
        Soldiers
For he's a peppery kind of King, etc.
    If you decide
    To pocket your pride
And let Hilarion claim his bride,
    Why, well and good,
    It's understood
We'll let bygones go by—
    But if you choose
    To sulk in the blues
I'll make the whole of you shake in your
    shoes.
    I'll storm your walls,
    And level your halls,
      In the twinkling of an eye!

For I'm a peppery Potentate,
Who's little inclined his claim to
bate,
To fit the wit of a bit of a chit,
And that's the long and the short
of it!

Soldiers

For he's a peppery kind of King, etc.

TRIO—ARAC, GURON, *and* SCYNTHIUS

We may remark, though nothing can
Dismay us,
That if you thwart this gentleman,
He'll slay us.
We don't fear death, of course—we're
taught
To shame it;
But still upon the whole we thought
We'd name it.
(*To each other.*)
Yes, yes, yes, better perhaps to name it.
Our interests we would not press
With chatter,

Three hulking brothers more or less
Don't matter;
If you'd pooh-pooh this monarch's plan,
Pooh-pooh it,
But when he says he'll hang a man,
He'll do it.
(*To each other.*)
Yes, yes, yes, devil doubt he'll do it.

Princess (*Recit.*)

Be reassured, nor fear his anger blind,
His menaces are idle as the wind.
He dares not kill you—vengeance lurks
behind!

Arac, Guron and Scynthius

We rather think he dares, but never mind!
No, no,—never, never mind!

Hildebrand

I rather think I dare, but never, never
mind!
Enough of parley—as a special boon,
We give you till to-morrow afternoon;
Release Hilarion, then, and be his bride,
Or you'll incur the guilt of fratricide!

ENSEMBLE

Princess

To yield at once to such a foe
With shame were rife;
So quick! away with him, although
He saved my life!
That he is fair, and strong, and tall,
Is very evident to all,
Yet I will die before I call
Myself his wife!

SOLO—PRINCESS
Though I am but a girl,
Defiance thus I hurl,
Our banners all

Princess

That he is fair, etc.

[*The* PRINCESS *stands, surrounded by girls
kneeling.* HILDEBRAND *and soldiers stand
on built rocks at back and sides of
stage. Picture.*

CURTAIN
END OF ACT II

ACT III

SCENE.—*Outer Walls and Courtyard of
Castle Adamant.* MELISSA, SACHARISSA,
*and ladies discovered, armed with
battleaxes.*

The Others

Oh! yield at once, 'twere better so
Than risk a strife!
And let the Prince Hilarion go—
He saved thy life!
Hilarion's fair, and strong, and tall—
A worse misfortune might befall—
It's not so dreadful, after all,
To be his wife!

On outer wall
We fearlessly unfurl.
All
Though she is but a girl, etc.

The Others

Hilarion's fair, etc.

Chorus

Death to the invader!
Strike a deadly blow,
As an old Crusader
Struck his Paynim foe!
Let our martial thunder
Fill his soul with wonder,
Tear his ranks asunder,
Lay the tyrant low!

SOLO—MELISSA
Thus our courage, all untarnished,
We're instructed to display;

But to tell the truth unvarnished,
  We are more inclined to say,
"Please you, do not hurt us."
             All
"Do not hurt us, if it please you!"
          Melissa
"Please you let us be."
             All
"Let us be—let us be!"
          Melissa
"Soldiers disconcert us."
             All
"Disconcert us, if it please you!"
          Melissa
"Frightened maids are we!"
             All
"Maids are we—maids are we!"
          Melissa
    But 'twould be an error
    To confess our terror,
    So, in Ida's name,
    Boldly we exclaim:
        Chorus
    Death to the invader!
    Strike a deadly blow,
    As as old Crusader
    Struck his Paynim foe!
Flourish. Enter PRINCESS, *armed, attended
    by* BLANCHE *and* PSYCHE
        Princess
I like your spirit, girls! We have to meet
Stern bearded warriors in fight to-day:
Wear naught but what is necessary to
Preserve your dignity before their eyes,
And give your limbs full play.
        Blanche
          One moment, ma'am,
Here is a paradox we should not pass
Without inquiry. We are prone to say,
"This thing is Needful—that, Super-
    fluous"—
Yet they invariably co-exist!
We find the Needful comprehended in
The circle of the grand Superfluous,
Yet the Superfluous cannot be bought
Unless you're amply furnished with the
    Needful.
These singular considerations are—
        Princess
Superfluous, yet not Needful—so you see
The terms may independently exist.
      (*To Ladies*)
Women of Adamant, we have to show
That women, educated to the task,

Can meet Man, face to face, on his own
    ground,
And beat him there. Now let us set to
    work:
Where is our lady surgeon?
        Sacharissa
             Madam, here!
        Princess
We shall require your skill to heal the
    wounds
Of those that fall.
      Sacharissa (*alarmed*).
        What, heal the wounded?
        Princess
                  Yes!
        Sacharissa
And cut off real live legs and arms?
        Princess
               Of course!
        Sacharissa
I wouldn't do it for a thousand pounds!
        Princess
Why, how it this? Are you faint-hearted,
    girl?
You've often cut them off in theory!
        Sacharissa
In theory I'll cut them off again
With pleasure, and as often as you like,
But not in practice.
        Princess
          Coward! get you hence,
I've craft enough for that, and courage too,
I'll do your work! My fusiliers, advance!
Why, you are armed with axes! Gilded
    toys!
Where are your rifles, pray?
        Chloe
        Why, please you, ma'am,
We left them in the armoury, for fear
That in the heat and turmoil of the fight,
They might go off!
        Princess
      "They might!" Oh, craven souls!
Go off yourselves! Thank heaven, I have a
    heart
That quails not at the thought of meeting
    men;
I will discharge your rifles! Off with you!
Where's my bandmistress?
        Ada
        Please you, ma'am, the band
Do not feel well, and can't come out to-
    day!

Princess

Why, this is flat rebellion! I've no time
To talk to them just now. But, happily,
I can play several instruments at once,
And I will drown the shrieks of those that
      fall
With trumpet music such as soldiers love!
Now stand we with respect to gunpowder?
My Lady Psyche—you who superintend
Our lab'ratory—are you well prepared
To blow these bearded rascals into shreds?

Psyche

Why, madam—

Princess

Well?

Psyche

Let us try gentler means.
We can dispense with fulminating grains
While we have eyes with which to flash our
      rage!
We can dispense with villainous saltpetre
While we have tongues with which to blow
      them up!
We can dispense, in short, with all the
      arts
That brutalize the practical polemist!

Princess (contemptuously).

I never knew a more dispensing chemist!
Away, away—I'll meet these men alone
Since all my women have deserted me!
Exeunt all but PRINCESS, *singing refrain of*
"Please you, do not hurt us", pianissimo.

Princess

So fail my cherished plans—so fails my
      faith—
And with it hope, and all that comes of
      hope!

SONG—PRINCESS

I built upon a rock,
   But ere Destruction's hand
      Dealt equal lot
      To Court and cot,
   My rock had turned to sand!
I leant upon an oak,
   But in the hour of need,
      Alack-a-day,
      My trusted stay
   Was but a bruisèd reed!
   Ah, faithless rock,
   My simple faith to mock!
   Ah, trait'rous oak,
   Thy worthlessness to cloak.
I drew a sword of steel,
   But when to home and hearth

The battle's breath
Bore fire and death,
My sword was but a lath!
I lit a beacon fire,
   But on a stormy day
      Of frost and rime,
      In wintertime,
   My fire had died away!
   Ah, coward steel,
   That fear can unanneal!
   False fire indeed,
   To fail me in my need!

She sinks on a seat. Enter CHLOE *and all*
the ladies.

Chloe

Madam, your father and your brothers
      claim
An audience!

Princess

What do they do here?

Chloe

They come
To fight for you!

Princess

Admit them!

Blanche

Infamous!
One's brothers, ma'am, are men!

Princess

So I've heard.
But all my women seem to fail me when
I need them most. In this emergency,
Even one's brothers may be turned to use.
Enter GAMA, *quite pale and unnerved.*

Gama

My daughter!

Princess

Father! thou art free!

Gama

Aye, free!
Free as a tethered ass! I come to thee
With words from Hildebrand. Those duly
      given
I must return to blank captivity.
I'm free so far.

Princess

Your message.

Gama

Hildebrand
Is loth to war with women. Pit my sons,
My three brave sons, against these popin-
      jays,
These tufted jack-a-dandy featherheads,
And on the issue let thy hand depend!

Princess

Insult on insult's head! Are we a stake
For fighting men? What fiend possesses
    thee,
That thou hast come with offers such as
    these
From such as he to such an one as I?

Gama

I am possessed
By the pale devil of a shaking heart!
My stubborn will is bent. I dare not face
That devilish monarch's black malignity!
He tortures me with torments worse than
    death,
I haven't anything to grumble at!
He finds out what particular meats I love,
And gives me them. The very choicest
    wines,
The costliest robes—the richest rooms are
    mine:
He suffers none to thwart my simplest plan,
And gives strict orders none should con-
    tradict me!
He's made my life a curse! (*weeps*)

Princess

My tortured father!

SONG—GAMA

Whene'er I poke
Sarcastic joke
  Replete with malice spiteful,
This people mild
Politely smiled,
  And voted me delightful!
Now when a wight
Sits up all night
  Ill-natured jokes devising,
And all his wiles
Are met with smiles
  It's hard, there's no disguising!
O, don't the days seem lank and long
When all goes right and nothing goes wrong,
And isn't your life extremely flat
With nothing whatever to grumble at!
  When German bands
  From music stands
Played Wagner imper*fect*ly—
  I bade them go—
  They didn't say no,
But off they went directly!
  The organ boys
  They stopped their noise
With readiness surprising,
  And grinning herds
  Of hurdy-gurds

Retired apologising!
Oh, don't the days seem lank and long, etc

  I offered gold
  In sums untold
To all who'd contradict me—
  I said I'd pay
  A pound a day
To any one who kicked me—
  I bribed with toys
  Great vulgar boys
To utter something spiteful,
  But, bless you, no!
  They *would* be so
Confoundedly politeful!
In short, these aggravating lads,
They tickle my tastes, they feed my fads
They give me this and they give me that
And I've nothing whatever to grumble at
[*He bursts into tears, and falls sobbing or
    a seat.*

Princess

My poor old father! How he must have
    suffered!
Well, well, I yield!

Gama (*hysterically*).

She yields! I'm saved, I'm saved!
                                    [*Exit*

Princess

Open the gates—admit these warriors,
Then get you all within the castle walls.
                                    [*Exit*
[*The gates are opened, and the girls moun*
    the battlements as soldiers enter. Also
    ARAC, GURON, *and* SCYNTHIUS.

Chorus of Soldiers

When anger spreads his wing,
  And all seems dark as night for it,
  There's nothing but to fight for it,
But ere you pitch your ring,
  Select a pretty site for it,
  (This spot is suited quite for it),
And then you gaily sing,
  "Oh, I love the jolly rattle
Of an ordeal by battle,
There's an end of tittle-tattle
  When your enemy is dead.
It's an arrant molly-coddle
Fears a crack upon his noddle
And he's only fit to swaddle
  In a downy feather-bed!"—

All

For a fight's a kind of thing
That I love to look upon,
  So let us sing,

Long live the King,
And his son Hilarion!
[*During this,* HILARION, FLORIAN, *and* CYRIL
*are brought out by the "Daughters of
the Plough". They are still bound and
wear the robes. Enter* GAMA.

Gama

Hilarion! Cyril! Florian! dressed as
women!
Is this indeed Hilarion?

Hilarion

Yes, it is!

Gama

Why, you look handsome in your women's
clothes!
Stick to 'em! men's attire becomes you not!
(*To* CYRIL *and* FLORIAN)
And you, young ladies, will you please to
pray
King Hildebrand to set me free again?
Hang on his neck and gaze into his eyes,
He never could resist a pretty face!

Hilarion

You dog, you'll find, though I wear
woman's garb,
My sword is long and sharp!

Gama

Hush, pretty one!
Here's a virago! Here's a termagant!
If length and sharpness go for anything,
You'll want no sword while you can wag
your tongue!

Cyril

What need to waste your words on such as
he?
He's old and crippled.

Gama

Aye, but I've three sons,
Fine fellows, young, and muscular, and
brave,
They're well worth talking to! Come, what
d'ye say?

Arac

Aye, pretty ones, engage yourselves with
us,
If three rude warriors affright you not!

Hilarion

Old as you are, I'd wring your shrivelled
neck
If you were not the Princess Ida's father.

Gama

If I were not the Princess Ida's father,
And so had not her brothers for my sons,
No doubt you'd wring my neck—in safety
too!
Come, come, Hilarion, begin, begin!
Give them no quarter—they will give you
none.
You've this advantage over warriors
Who kill their country's enemies for pay,—
You know what you are fighting for—
look there!
(*Pointing to Ladies on the battlements.*)
[*Exit* GAMA. HILARION, FLORIAN, *and* CYRIL
are led off.

SONG—ARAC

This helmet, I suppose,
Was meant to ward off blows,
    It's very hot,
    And weighs a lot,
As many a guardsman knows,
So off that helmet goes.

All

Yes, yes, yes,
So off that helmet goes!
(*Giving their helmets to attendants.*)

Arac

This tight-fitting cuirass
Is but a useless mass,
    It's made of steel,
    And weighs a deal,
A man is but an ass
Who fights in a cuirass,
So off goes that cuirass.

All

Yes, yes, yes,
So off goes that cuirass!
(*Removing cuirasses.*)

Arac

These brassets, truth to tell,
May look uncommon well,
    But in a fight
They're much too tight,
They're like a lobster shell!

All

Yes, yes, yes,
They're like a lobster shell.
(*Removing their brassets.*)

Arac

These things I treat the same (*indicating
leg pieces*).
(I quite forget their name)
    They turn one's legs
    To cribbage pegs—
Their aid I thus disclaim,
Though I forget their name!

All

Yes, yes, yes,

Their aid $\left\{ \begin{matrix} we \\ they \end{matrix} \right\}$ thus disclaim!

[*They remove their leg pieces and wear
close-fitting shape suits.
Enter* HILARION, FLORIAN, *and* CYRIL

[*Desperate fight between the three Princes
and the three Knights, during which
the Ladies on the battlements and the
Soldiers on the stage sing the following chorus.*

This is our duty plain towards
  Our Princess all immaculate,
We ought to bless her brothers' swords
  And piously ejaculate:
    Oh, Hungary!
    Oh, Hungary!
  Oh, doughty sons of Hungary!
    May all success
    Attend and bless
  Your warlike ironmongery!
Hilarion! Hilarion! Hilarion!

[*By this time,* ARAC, GURON, *and* SCYNTHIUS
  are on the ground, wounded—HILA-
  RION, CYRIL, *and* FLORIAN *stand over
  them.*

Princess (*entering through gate and followed by Ladies,* HILDEBRAND, *and*
  GAMA). Hold! stay your hands—we
  yield ourselves to you!

Ladies, my brothers all lie bleeding there!
Bind up their wounds—but look the other
  way.
      (*Coming down*).
Is this the end? (*bitterly to* LADY BLANCHE).
How say you, Lady Blanche—
Can I with dignity my post resign?
And if I do, will you then take my place?

Blanche

To answer this, it's meet that we consult
The great Potential Mysteries; I mean
The five Subjunctive Possibilities—
The May, the Might, the Would, the Could,
  the Should.
Can you resign? The prince May claim
  you; if
He Might, you Could—and if you Should,
  I Would!

Princess

I thought as much! Then, to my fate I
  yield—

So ends my cherished scheme! Oh, I had
  hoped
To band all women with my maiden
  throng,
And make them all abjure tyrannic Man!
      Hildebrand
A noble aim!

      Princess
    You ridicule it now!
But if I carried out this glorious scheme,
At my exalted name Posterity
Would bow in gratitude!
      Hildebrand
    But pray reflect—
If you enlist all women in your cause,
And make them all abjure tyrannic Man,
The obvious question then arises, "How
Is this Posterity to be provided?"
      Princess
I never thought of that! My Lady
  Blanche,
How do you solve the riddle?
      Blanche
    Don't ask me—
Abstract Philosophy won't answer it.
Take him—he is your Shall. Give in to
  Fate!
      Princess
And you desert me. I alone am staunch!
      Hilarion
Madam, you placed your trust in Woman
  —well,
Woman has failed you utterly—try Man,
Give him one chance, it's only fair—besides,
Women are far too precious, too divine,
To try unproven theories upon.
Experiments, the proverb says, are made
On humble subjects—try our grosser clay,
And mould it as you will!
      Cyril
    Remember, too,
Dear Madam, if at any time you feel
A-weary of the Prince, you can return
To Castle Adamant, and rule your girls
As heretofore, you know.
      Princess
    And shall I find
The Lady Psyche here?
      Psyche
    If Cyril, ma'am,
Does not behave himself, I think you will!
      Princess
And you, Melissa, shall I find *you* here?

Melissa

Madam, however Florian turns out,
Unhesitatingly I answer, No!

Gama

Consider this, my love, if your mamma
Had looked on matters from your point of
   view
(I wish she had), why where would you
   have been?

Blanche

There's an unbounded field of speculation,
On which I could discourse for hours!

Princess

   No doubt!
We will not trouble you. Hilarion,
I have been wrong—I see my error now.
Take me, Hilarion—"We will walk the
   world
Yoked in all exercise of noble end!
And so through those dark gates across the
   wild
That no man knows! Indeed, I love thee—
   Come!"

FINALE
Princess

With joy abiding,
Together gliding

Through life's variety,
   In sweet society,
And thus enthroning
The love I'm owning,
On this atoning
   I will rely!

Chorus

It were profanity
For poor humanity
To treat as vanity
   The sway of Love.
In no locality
Or principality
Is our mortality
   Its sway above!

Hilarion

When day is fading,
With serenading
   And such frivolity
   Of tender quality—
With scented showers
Of fairest flowers,
The happy hours
   Will gaily fly!

Chorus

It were profanity, etc.

CURTAIN

UTOPIA, LIMITED

OR

THE FLOWERS OF PROGRESS

DRAMATIS PERSONÆ

KING PARAMOUNT THE FIRST
  (*King of Utopia*)

SCAPHIO }
PHANTIS } (*Judges of the Utopian Supreme Court*)

TARARA (*the Public Exploder*)

CALYNX (*the Utopian Vice-Chamberlain*)

IMPORTED FLOWERS OF PROGRESS

LORD DRAMALEIGH
  (*a British Lord Chamberlain*)

CAPTAIN FITZBATTLEAXE (*First Life Guards*)

CAPTAIN SIR EDWARD CORCORAN, K.C.B.
  (*of the Royal Navy*)

MR. GOLDBURY
  (*a Company Promoter; afterwards Comptroller of the Utopian Household*)

SIR BAILLEY BARRE, Q.C., M.P.

MR. BLUSHINGTON (*of the County Council*)

THE PRINCESS ZARA
  (*Eldest Daughter of King Paramount*)

THE PRINCESS NEKAYA }
THE PRINCESS KALYBA } (*her Younger Sisters*)

THE LADY SOPHY
  (*their English Gouvernante*)

SALATA }
MELENE } (*Utopian Maidens*)
PHYLLA }

ACT I

SCENE.—*A Utopian Palm Grove in the gardens of* KING PARAMOUNT'S *Palace, showing a picturesque and luxuriant tropical landscape, with the sea in the distance.* SALATA, MELENE, PHYLLA, *and other Maidens discovered, lying lazily about the stage and thoroughly enjoying themselves in lotus-eating fashion.*

Opening Chorus
In lazy languor—motionless,
We lie and dream of nothingness;
  For visions come
  From Poppydom
    Direct at our command:
Or, delicate alternative,
In open idleness we live,
  With lyre and lute
  And silver flute,
    The life of Lazyland!

SOLO—PHYLLA
The song of birds
  In ivied towers;
    The rippling play
    Of waterway;
The lowing herds;
  The breath of flowers;
    The languid loves
    Of turtle doves—
These simple joys are all at hand
Upon thy shores, O Lazyland!
Chorus
  In lazy languor, etc.
  Enter CALYNX

Cal. Good news! Great news! His Majesty's eldest daughter, Princess Zara, who left our shores five years since to go to England—the greatest, the most powerful, the wisest country in the world—has taken a high degree at Girton, and is on her way home again, having achieved a complete mastery over all the elements that have tended to raise that glorious country to her present pre-eminent position among civilized nations!

Salata. Then in a few months Utopia may hope to be completely Anglicized?

Cal. Absolutely and without a doubt.

Melene (lazily). We are very well as we are. Life without a care—every want supplied by a kind and fatherly monarch, who, despot though he be, has no other thought than to make his people happy—what have we to gain by the great change that is in store for us?

Sal. What have we to gain? English institutions, English tastes, and oh, English fashions!

Cal. England has made herself what she is because, in that favoured land, every one has to think for himself. Here we have no need to think, because our monarch anticipates all our wants, and our political opinions are formed for us by the journals to which we subscribe. Oh, think how much more brilliant this dialogue would have been, if we had been accustomed to exercise our reflective powers! They say that in England the conversation of the very meanest is a coruscation of impromptu epigram!

Enter TARARA *in a great rage*

Tar. Lalabalele talala! Cyllabale lalabalica falahle!

Cal. (horrified). Stop—stop, I beg! (*All the ladies close their ears.*)

Tar. Callamalala galalate! Caritalla lalabalee kallalale poo!

Ladies. Oh, stop him! stop him!

Cal. My lord, I'm surprised at you. Are you not aware that His Majesty, in his despotic acquiescence with the emphatic wish of his people, has ordered that the Utopian language shall be banished from his court, and that all communications shall henceforth be made in the English tongue?

Tar. Yes, I'm perfectly aware of it, although—(*suddenly presenting an explosive "cracker"*). Stop—allow me.

Cal. (pulls it). Now, what's that for?

Tar. Why, I've recently been appointed Public Exploder to His Majesty, and as I'm constitutionally nervous, I must accustom myself by degrees to the startling nature of my duties. Thank you. I was about to say that although, as Public Exploder, I am next in succession to the throne, I nevertheless do my best to fall in with the royal decree. But when I am overmastered by an indignant sense of overwhelming wrong, as I am now, I slip into my native tongue without knowing it. I am told that in the language of that great and pure nation, strong expressions do not exist, consequently when I want to let off steam I have no alternative but to say, "Lalabalele molola lililah kallalale poo!"

Cal. But what is your grievance?

Tar. This—by our Constitution we are governed by a Despot who, although in theory absolute—is, in practice, nothing of the kind—being watched day and night by two Wise Men whose duty it is, on his very first lapse from political or social propriety, to denounce him to me, the Public Exploder, and it then becomes my duty to blow up His Majesty with dynamite—allow me. (*Presenting a cracker which* CALYNX *pulls.*) Thank you—and, as some compensation to my wounded feelings, I reign in his stead.

Cal. Yes. After many unhappy experiments in the direction of an ideal Republic, it was found that what may be described as a Despotism tempered by Dynamite provides, on the whole, the most satisfactory description of ruler—an autocrat who dares not abuse his autocratic power.

Tar. That's the theory—but in practice, how does it act? Now, do you ever happen to see the *Palace Peeper?* (*producing a "Society" paper*).

Cal. Never even heard of the journal.

Tar. I'm not surprised, because His Majesty's agents always buy up the whole edition; but I have an aunt in the publishing department, and she has supplied me with a copy. Well, it actually teems with circumstantially convincing details of the King's abominable immoralities! If this high-class journal may be believed, His Majesty is one of the most Heliogabalian profligates that ever disgraced an autocratic throne! And *do* these Wise Men denounce him to me? Not a bit of it! They wink at his immoralities! Under the circumstances I really think I am justified in exclaiming "Lalabalele molola lililah kalabalele poo!"

(*All horrified.*) I don't care—the occasion demands it.

[*Exit* TARARA.

March. Enter Guard, escorting SCAPHIO *and* PHANTIS

Chorus

O make way for the Wise Men!
　　They are prizemen—
Double-first in the world's university!
For though lovely this island
　　(Which is *my* land),
She has no one to match them in *her* city.
They're the pride of Utopia—
　　Cornucopia
Is each in his mental fertility.
O they never make blunder,
　　And no wonder,
For they're triumphs of infallibility.

DUET—SCAPHIO *and* PHANTIS

In every mental lore
　　(The statement smacks of vanity)
We claim to rank before
　　The wisest of humanity.
As gifts of head and heart
　　We wasted on "utility,"
We're "cast" to play a part
　　Of great responsibility.
Our duty is to spy
　　Upon our King's illicities,
And keep a watchful eye
　　On all his eccentricities.
If ever a trick he tries
　　That savours of rascality,
At our decree he dies
　　Without the least formality.
We fear no rude rebuff,
　　Or newspaper publicity;
Our word is quite enough,
　　The rest is electricity.
A pound of dynamite
　　Explodes in his auriculars;
It's not a pleasant sight—
　　We'll spare you the particulars.
Its force all men confess,
　　The King needs no admonishing—
We may say its success
　　Is something quite astonishing.
Our despot it imbues
　　With virtues quite delectable,
He minds his P's and Q's,—
　　And keeps himself respectable.
Of a tyrant polite
　　He's a paragon quite.

He's as modest and mild
　　In his ways as a child;
And no one ever met
　　With an autocrat, yet
So delightfully bland
To the least in the land!
　　So make way for the wise men, etc.

[*Exeunt all but* SCAPHIO *and* PHANTIS.
PHANTIS *is pensive.*

Sca. Phantis, you are not in your customary exuberant spirits. What is wrong?

Phan. Scaphio, I think you once told me that you have never loved?

Sca. Never! I have often marvelled at the fairy influence which weaves its rosy web about the faculties of the greatest and wisest of our race; but I thank Heaven I have never been subjected to its singular fascination. For, oh, Phantis! there is that within me that tells me that when my time *does* come, the convulsion will be tremendous! When *I* love, it will be with the accumulated fervor of sixty-six years! But I have an ideal—a semi-transparent Being, filled with an inorganic pink jelly—and I have never yet seen the woman who approaches within measurable distance of it. All are opaque—opaque—opaque!

Phan. Keep that ideal firmly before you, and love not until you find her. Though but fifty-five, I am an old campaigner in the battle-fields of Love; and, believe me, it is better to be as you are, heart-free and happy, than as I am—eternally racked with doubting agonies! Scaphio, the Princess Zara returns from England to-day!

Sca. My poor boy, I see it all.

Phan. Oh! Scaphio, she is so beautiful. Ah! you smile, for you have never seen her. She sailed for England three months before you took office.

Sca. Now tell me, is your affection requited?

Phan. I do not know—I am not sure. Sometimes I think it is, and then come these torturing doubts! I feel sure that she does not regard me with absolute indifference, for she could never look at me without having to go to bed with a sick headache.

Sca. That is surely something. Come, take heart, boy! you are young and beautiful. What more could maiden want?

Phan. Ah! Scaphio, remember she re-

turns from a land where every youth is as
a young Greek god, and where such beauty
as I can boast is seen at every turn.

Sca. Be of good cheer! Marry her, boy,
if so your fancy wills, and be sure that love
will come.

Phan. (*overjoyed*). Then you will assist
me in this?

Sca. Why, surely! Silly one, what have
you to fear? We have but to say the word,
and her father must consent. Is he not our
very slave? Come, take heart. I cannot
bear to see you sad.

Phan. Now I may hope, indeed! Scaphio,
you have placed me on the very pinnacle
of human joy!

DUET—SCAPHIO *and* PHANTIS

Scaphio

Let all your doubts take wing—
　　Our influence is great.
　If Paramount our King
　Presume to hesitate,
　　Put on the screw,
　　And caution him
　　That he will rue
　　Disaster grim
　　That must ensue
　　To life and limb,
　　Should he pooh-pooh
　This harmless whim.

Both

This harmless whim—this harmless whim,

It is, as $\begin{Bmatrix} I \\ you \end{Bmatrix}$ say, a harmless whim.

Phantis (*dancing*)

　Observe this dance
　　Which I employ
　When I, by chance,
　　Go mad with joy.
　What sentiment
　　Does this express?

[PHANTIS *continues his dance while* SCAPHIO
*vainly endeavours to discover its mean-
ing.*

　Supreme content
　　And happiness!

Both

Of course it does! Of course it does!
Supreme content and happiness!

Phantis

Your friendly aid conferred,
　I need no longer pine.
I've but to speak the word,
　And lo! the maid is mine!

I do not choose
　To be denied.
Or wish to lose
　A lovely bride—
If to refuse
　The King decide,
The Royal shoes
　Then woe betide!

Both

Then woe betide—then woe betide!
The Royal shoes then woe betide!

Scaphio (*dancing*)

　This step to use
　　I condescend
　Whene'er I choose
　　To serve a friend.
　What it implies
　Now try to guess;

[SCAPHIO *continues his dance while* PHANTIS
*is vainly endeavouring to discover its
meaning.*

　It typifies
　　Unselfishness!

Both (*dancing*)

Of course it does! Of course it does!
It typifies unselfishness!

[*Exeunt* SCAPHIO *and* PHANTIS.

March. Enter KING PARAMOUNT, *attended
by guards and nobles, and preceded by
girls dancing before him.*

Chorus

Quaff the nectar—cull the roses—
　Gather fruit and flowers in plenty!
For our King no longer poses—
　Sing the songs of *far niente!*
Wake the lute that sets us lilting,
　Dance a welcome to each comer;
Day by day our year is wilting—
　Sing the sunny songs of summer!
　　　　　La, la, la, la!

SONG—KING

A King of autocratic power we—
　A despot whose tyrannic will is law—
Whose rule is paramount o'er land and sea,
　A presence of unutterable awe!
But though the awe that I inspire
Must shrivel with imperial fire
　All foes whom it may chance to touch,
To judge by what I see and hear,
It does not seem to interfere
　With popular enjoyment, much.

Chorus

　No, no—it does not interfere
　　With our enjoyment much.

Stupendous when we rouse ourselves to strike,
Resistless when our tyrant thunder peals,
We often wonder what obstruction's like,
And how a contradicted monarch feels.
But as it is our Royal whim
Our Royal sails to set and trim
To suit whatever wind may blow—
What buffets contradiction deals
And how a thwarted monarch feels
We probably shall never know.

Chorus

No, no—what thwarted monarch feels
You'll never, never know.

RECIT.—KING

My subjects all, it is your wish emphatic
That all Utopia shall henceforth be modelled
Upon that glorious country called Great Britain—
To which some add—but others do not—Ireland.

All

It is!

King

That being so, as you insist upon it,
We have arranged that our two younger daughters
Who have been "finished" by an English Lady— *(tenderly)*
A grave and good and gracious English Lady—
Shall daily be exhibited in public,
That all may learn what, from the English standpoint,
Is looked upon as maidenly perfection!
Come hither, daughters!

Enter NEKAYA *and* KALYBA. *They are twins, about fifteen years old; they are very modest and demure in their appearance, dress, and manner. They stand with their hands folded and their eyes cast down.*

Chorus

How fair! how modest! how discreet!
How bashfully demure!
    See how they blush, as they've been taught,
    At this publicity unsought!
How English and how pure!

DUET—NEKAYA *and* KALYBA

Both

Although of native maids the cream,
We're brought up on the English scheme—
    The best of all
    For great and small
Who modesty adore.

Nekaya

For English girls are good as gold,
Extremely modest (so we're told),
Demurely coy—divinely cold—

Kalyba

    And we are that—and more.
To please papa, who argues thus—
All girls should mould themselves on us
    Because we are
    By furlongs far
    The best of all the bunch,
We show ourselves to loud applause
From ten to four without a pause—

Nekaya

Which is an awkward time because
    It cuts into our lunch.

Both

Oh, maids of high and low degree,
Whose social code is rather free,
Please look at us and you will see
What good young ladies ought to be!

Nekaya

And as we stand, like clockwork toys,
A lecturer whom papa employs
    Proceeds to praise
    Our modest ways
    And guileless character—

Kalyba

Our well-known blush—our downcast eyes—
Our famous look of mild surprise

Nekaya

(Which competition still defies)—

Kalyba

    Our celebrated "Sir!!!"
Then all the crowd take down our looks
In pocket memorandum books.
    To diagnose
    Our modest pose
    The Kodaks do their best:

Nekaya

If evidence you would possess
Of what is maiden bashfulness,
You only need a button press—

Kalyba

    And *we* do all the rest.

Enter LADY SOPHY—*an English lady of mature years and extreme gravity of demeanour and dress. She carries a lecturer's wand in her hand. She is led on by the* KING, *who expresses great regard and admiration for her.*

RECIT.—LADY SOPHY

This morning we propose to illustrate
A course of maiden courtship, from the
    start
To the triumphant matrimonial finish.
[*Through the following song the two Prin-*
cesses illustrate in gesture the descrip-
tion given by LADY SOPHY.

SONG—LADY SOPHY

Bold-faced ranger
  (Perfect stranger)
Meets two well-behaved young ladies.
  He's attractive,
  Young and active—
Each a little bit afraid is.
  Youth advances,
  At his glances
To their danger they awaken;
  They repel him
  As they tell him
He is very much mistaken.
Though they speak to him politely,
Please observe they're sneering slightly,
Just to show he's acting vainly.
This is Virtue saying plainly,
  "Go away, young bachelor,
  We are not what you take us for!"
When addressed impertinently,
English ladies answer gently,
  "Go away, young bachelor,
  We are not what you take us for!"
  As he gazes,
  Hat he raises,
Enters into conversation.
  Makes excuses—
  This produces
Interesting agitation.
  He, with daring,
  Undespairing,
Gives his card—his rank discloses.
  Little heeding
  This proceeding,
They turn up their little noses.
Pray observe this lesson vital—
When a man of rank and title
His position first discloses,
Always cock your little noses.
  When at home, let all the class
  Try this in the looking-glass.
English girls of well-bred notions
Shun all unrehearsed emotions.
  English girls of highest class
  Practise them before the glass.
  His intentions

Then he mentions.
Something definite to go on—
  Makes recitals
  Of his titles,
Hints at settlements, and so on.
  Smiling sweetly,
  They, discreetly,
Ask for further evidences:
  Thus invited,
  He, delighted,
Gives the usual references:
This is business. Each is fluttered
When the offer's fairly uttered.
"Which of them has his affection?"
He declines to make selection.
  Do they quarrel for his dross?
  Not a bit of it—they toss!
Please observe this cogent moral—
English ladies never quarrel.
  When a doubt they come across,
  English ladies always toss.

RECIT.—LADY SOPHY

The lecture's ended. In ten minutes' space
'Twill be repeated in the market-place!
[*Exit* LADY SOPHY, *followed by* NEKAYA *and*
KALYBA.

Chorus
  Quaff the nectar—cull the roses—
    Bashful girls will soon be plenty!
  Maid who thus at fifteen poses
    Ought to be divine at twenty!
      [*Exit* CHORUS. *Manent* KING.

King. I requested Scaphio and Phantis to
be so good as to favour me with an audience this morning. (*Enter* SCAPHIO *and*
PHANTIS.) Oh, here they are!

Sca. Your Majesty wished to speak with
us, I believe. You—you needn't keep your
crown on, on our account, you know.

King. I beg your pardon (*removes it*).
I always forget that! Odd, the notion of a
King not being allowed to wear one of his
own crowns in the presence of two of his
own subjects.

Phan. Yes—bizarre, is it not?

King. Most quaint. But then it's a quaint
world.

Phan. Teems with quiet fun. I often
think what a lucky thing it is that you are
blessed with such a keen sense of humour!

King. Do you know, I find it invaluable.
Do what I will, I *cannot* help looking at
the humorous side of things—for, properly
considered, everything has its humorous

side—even the *Palace Peeper* (*producing it*). See here—"Another Royal Scandal," by Junius Junior. "How long is this to last?" by Senex Senior. "Ribald Royalty," by Mercury Major. "Where is the Public Exploder?" by Mephistopheles Minor. When I reflect that all these outrageous attacks on my morality are written by me, at your command—well, it's one of the funniest things that have come within the scope of my experience.

Sca. Besides, apart from that, they have a quiet humour of their own which is simply irresistible.

King (*gratified*). Not bad, I think. Biting, trenchant sarcasm—the rapier, not the bludgeon—that's my line. But then it's so easy—I'm such a good subject—a bad King but a good Subject—ha! ha!—a capital heading for next week's leading article! (*makes a note*). And then the stinging little paragraphs about our Royal goings-on with our Royal Second Housemaid—delicately sub-acid, are they not?

Sca. My dear King, in that kind of thing no one can hold a candle to you.

Phan. But the crowning joke is the Comic Opera you've written for us—"King Tuppence, or A Good Deal Less than Half a Sovereign"—in which the celebrated English tenor, Mr. Wilkinson, burlesques your personal appearance and gives grotesque imitations of your Royal peculiarities. It's immense.

King. Ye—es—That's what I wanted to speak to you about. Now I've not the least doubt but that even *that* has its humorous side, too—if one could only see it. As a rule I'm pretty quick at detecting latent humour—but I confess I do *not* quite see where it comes in, in this particular instance. It's so horribly personal!

Sca. Personal? Yes, of course it's personal—but consider the antithetical humour of the situation.

King. Yes. I—I don't think I've quite grasped that.

Sca. No? You surprise me. Why, consider. During the day thousands tremble at your frown, during the night (from 8 to 11) thousands roar at it. During the day your most arbitrary pronouncements are received by your subjects with abject submission—during the night, they shout with joy at your most terrible decrees. It's not every monarch who enjoys the privilege of undoing by night all the despotic absurdities he's committed during the day.

King. Of course! Now I see it! Thank you very much. I was sure it had its humorous side, and it was very dull of me not to have seen it before. But, as I said just now, it's a quaint world.

Phan. Teems with quiet fun.

King. Yes. Properly considered, what a farce life is, to be sure!

SONG—KING

First you're born—and I'll be bound you
Find a dozen strangers round you.
"Hallo," cries the new-born baby,
"Where's my parents? which may they
    be?"
    Awkward silence—no reply—
    Puzzled baby wonders why!
Father rises, bows politely—
Mother smiles (but not too brightly)—
Doctor mumbles like a dumb thing—
Nurse is busy mixing something.
    Every symptom tends to show
    You're decidedly *de trop*—

All
    Ho! ho! ho! ho! ho! ho! ho! ho!
        Time's teetotum
            If you spin it,
        Gives its quotum
            Once a minute.
        I'll go bail
        You hit the nail,
        And if you fail
        The deuce is in it!
You grow up and you discover
What it is to be a lover.
Some young lady is selected—
Poor, perhaps, but well-connected,
    Whom you hail (for Love is blind)
    As the Queen of fairy kind.
Though she's plain—perhaps unsightly,
Makes her face up—laces tightly,
In her form your fancy traces
All the gifts of all the graces.
    Rivals none the maiden woo,
    So you take her and she takes you!

All
    Ho! ho! ho! ho! ho! ho! ho! ho!
        Joke beginning,
            Never ceases,
        Till your inning
            Time releases,

On your way
You blindly stray,
And day by day
    The joke increases!
Ten years later—Time progresses—
Sours your temper—thins your tresses;
Fancy, then, her chain relaxes;
Rates are facts and so are taxes.
    Fairy Queen's no longer young—
    Fairy Queen has got a tongue.
Twins have probably intruded—
Quite unbidden—just as you did—
They're a source of care and trouble—
Just as you were—only double.
    Comes at last the final stroke—
    Time has had his little joke!

All

Ho! ho! ho! ho! ho! ho! ho! ho!
Daily driven
    (Wife as drover)
Ill you've thriven—
    Ne'er in clover;
Lastly, when
Three-score and ten
    (And not till then),
        The joke is over!
Ho! ho! ho! ho! ho! ho! ho! ho!
    Then—and then
        The joke is over!
    [*Exeunt* SCAPHIO *and* PHANTIS.
        Manent KING.

King (*putting on his crown again*). It's
all very well. I always like to look on the
humorous side of things; but I do *not*
think I ought to be required to write libels
on my own moral character. Naturally, I
see the joke of it—anybody would—but
Zara's coming home to-day; she's no longer
a child, and I confess I should *not* like her
to see my Opera—though it's uncommonly
well written; and I should be sorry if the
Palace Peeper got into her hands—though
it's certainly smart—very smart indeed. It
is almost a pity that I have to buy up the
whole edition, because it's really too good
to be lost. And Lady Sophy—that blameless type of perfect womanhood! Great
Heavens, what would *she* say if the Second
Housemaid business happened to meet *her*
pure blue eye!

Enter LADY SOPHY

Lady S. My monarch is soliloquizing. I
will withdraw (*going*).

King. No—pray don't go. Now I'll give

you fifty chances, and you won't guess
whom I was thinking of.

Lady S. Alas, sir, I know too well. Ah!
King, it's an old, old story, and I'm well-
nigh weary of it! Be warned in time—
from my heart I pity you, but I am not
for you! (*going*).

King. But hear what I have to say.

Lady S. It is useless. Listen. In the course
of a long and adventurous career in the
principal European Courts, it has been revealed to me that I unconsciously exercise
a weird and supernatural fascination over
all Crowned Heads. So irresistible is this
singular property, that there is not a European Monarch who has not implored me,
with tears in his eyes, to quit his kingdom,
and take my fatal charms elsewhere. As
time was getting on it occurred to me that
by descending several pegs in the scale of
Respectability I might qualify your Majesty for my hand. Actuated by this humane motive and happening to possess Respectability enough for Six, I consented to
confer Respectability enough for Four upon
your two younger daughters—but although
I have, alas, only Respectability enough for
Two left, there is still, as I gather from the
public press of this country (*producing the
"Palace Peeper"*), a considerable balance in
my favour.

King (*aside*). Da—! (*Aloud.*) May I ask
how you came by this?

Lady S. It was handed to me by the
officer who holds the position of Public
Exploder to your Imperial Majesty.

King. And surely, Lady Sophy, surely
you are not so unjust as to place any faith
in the irresponsible gabble of the Society
press!

Lady S. (*referring to paper*). I read on
the authority of Senex Senior that your
Majesty was seen dancing with your Second Housemaid on the Oriental Platform
of the Tivoli Gardens. That is untrue?

King. Absolutely. Our Second Housemaid
has only one leg.

Lady S. (*suspiciously*). How do you
know that?

King. Common report, I give you my
honour.

Lady S. It may be so. I further read—
and the statement is vouched for by no
less an authority than Mephistopheles

Minor—that your Majesty indulges in a bath of hot rum-punch every morning. I trust I do not lay myself open to the charge of displaying an indelicate curiosity as to the mysteries of the royal dressing-room when I ask if there is any foundation for this statement?

King. None whatever. When our medical adviser exhibits rum-punch it is as a draught, not as a fomentation. As to our bath, our valet plays the garden hose upon us every morning.

Lady S. (*shocked*). Oh, pray—pray spare me these unseemly details. Well, you are a Despot—have you taken steps to slay this scribbler?

King. Well, no—I have *not* gone so far as that. After all, it's the poor devil's living, you know.

Lady S. It is the poor devil's living that surprises me. If this man lies, there is no recognized punishment that is sufficiently terrible for him.

King. That's precisely it. I—I am waiting until a punishment is discovered that will exactly meet the enormity of the case. I am in constant communication with the Mikado of Japan, who is a leading authority on such points; and, moreover, I have the ground plans and sectional elevations of several capital punishments in my desk at this moment. Oh, Lady Sophy, as you are powerful, be merciful!

DUET—KING *and* LADY SOPHY

King

Subjected to your heavenly gaze
　(Poetical phrase),
My brain is turned completely.
　　Observe me now,
　　No Monarch, I vow,
　　　Was ever so far afflicted!

Lady Sophy

I'm pleased with that poetical phrase,
　"A heavenly gaze,"
But though you put it neatly,
　　Say what you will,
　　These paragraphs still
　　　Remain uncontradicted.

Come, crush me this contemptible worm
　(A forcible term),
If he's assailed you wrongly.
　　The rage display,
　　Which, as you say,
　　　Has moved your Majesty lately.

King

Though I admit that forcible term,
　"Contemptible worm,"
Appeals to me most strongly,
　　To treat this pest
　　As you suggest
　　　Would pain my Majesty greatly.

Lady Sophy

This writer lies!

King

Yes, bother his eyes!

Lady Sophy

He lives, you say?

King

In a sort of a way.

Lady Sophy

Then have him shot.

King

Decidedly not.

Lady Sophy

Or crush him flat.

King

I cannot do that.

Both

O royal Rex,
My ⎰
Her ⎱ blameless sex
　Abhors such conduct shady.
You ⎰
I ⎱ plead in vain,
You ⎰
I ⎱ never will gain
　Respectable English lady!

[*Dance of repudiation by* LADY SOPHY.
　　Exit, followed by KING.

March. Enter all the Court, heralding the arrival of the PRINCESS ZARA, *who enters, escorted by* CAPTAIN FITZBATTLEAXE *and four Troopers, all in the full uniform of the First Life Guards.*

Chorus

Oh, maiden, rich
　In Girton lore,
That wisdom which
　We prized before,
We do confess
Is nothingness,
　Perhaps, than more.
On each of us
　Thy learning shed.
On calculus
　May we be fed
And teach us, please,

To speak with ease
All languages,
Alive and dead!
SOLO—PRINCESS *and* CHORUS
Zara

ive years have flown since I took wing—
Time flies, and his footstep ne'er re-
    tards—
m the eldest daughter of your king.
Troopers

And we are her escort—First Life
    Guards!
On the royal yacht,
    When the waves were white,
In a helmet hot
    And a tunic tight,
And our great big boots,
    We defied the storm:
For we're not recruits,
    And his uniform
well-drilled trooper ne'er discards—
nd we are her escort—First Life Guards!
Zara

hese gentlemen I present to you,
    The pride and boast of their barrack-
        yards;
hey've taken, O! such care of me!

Troopers
For we are her escort—First Life Guards!
When the tempest rose,
    And the ship went *so*—
Do you suppose
    We were ill? No, no!
Though a qualmish lot
    In a tunic tight,
And a helmet hot,
    And a breastplate bright
(Which a well-drilled trooper ne'er dis-
    cards),
We stood as her escort—First Life Guards!
Full Chorus
Knightsbridge nursemaids—serving fairies—
Stars of proud Belgravian airies;
At stern duty's call you leave them,
Though you know how that must grieve
    them!
Zara
Tantantarara-rara-rara!
Captain Fitzbattleaxe
Trumpet-call of Princess Zara!
Chorus
That's trump-call, and they're all trump
    cards—
They are her escort—First Life Guards!

ENSEMBLE

Chorus
Ladies
nightsbridge nursemaids, etc.

Men
hen the tempest rose, etc.

Full Chorus
nightsbridge nursemaids, serving fairies,
    etc.
nter KING, PRINCESSES NEKAYA *and*
KALYBA, *and* LADY SOPHY. *As the* KING
enters the escort present arms.
King. Zara! my beloved daughter! Why,
ɔw well you look and how lovely you
ιve grown! (*embraces her*).
Zara. My dear father! (*embracing him*).
nd my two beautiful little sisters! (*em-
racing them*).
Nek. Not beautiful.
Kal. Nice-looking.
Zara. But first let me present to you the
nglish warrior who commands my escort,

Princess Zara and Fitzbattleaxe (*aside*)
Oh! the hours are gold,
And the joys untold,
When my eyes behold
    My beloved Princess;
And the years will seem
But a brief day-dream,
In the joy extreme
    Of our happiness!

and who has taken, O! such care of me
during the voyage—Captain Fitzbattleaxe!
Troopers
The First Life Guards.
When the tempest rose,
    And the ship went *so*—
[CAPT. FITZBATTLEAXE *motions them to be
    silent. The Troopers place themselves
    in the four corners of the stage, stand-
    ing at ease, immovably, as if on sentry.
    Each is surrounded by an admiring
    group of young ladies, of whom they
    take no notice.*
King (*to* CAPT. FITZ.). Sir, you come
from a country where every virtue flour-
ishes. We trust that you will not criticize

too severely such shortcomings as you may detect in our semi-barbarous society.

Fitz. (*looking at* ZARA). Sir, I have eyes for nothing but the blameless and the beautiful.

King. We thank you—he is really very polite! (LADY SOPHY, *who has been greatly scandalized by the attentions paid to the Lifeguardsmen by the young ladies, marches the* PRINCESSES NEKAYA *and* KALYBA *towards an exit.*) Lady Sophy, do not leave us.

Lady S. Sir, your children are young, and, so far, innocent. If they are to remain so, it is necessary that they be at once removed from the contamination of their present disgraceful surroundings. (*She marches them off.*)

King (*whose attention has thus been called to the proceedings of the young ladies—aside*). Dear, dear! They really shouldn't. (*Aloud.*) Captain Fitzbattleaxe—

Fitz. Sir.

King. Your Troopers appear to be receiving a troublesome amount of attention from those young ladies. I know how strict you English soldiers are, and I should be extremely distressed if anything occurred to shock their puritanical British sensitiveness.

Fitz. Oh, I don't think there's any chance of that.

King. You think not? They won't be offended?

Fitz. Oh no! They are quite hardened to it. They get a good deal of that sort of thing, standing sentry at the Horse Guards.

King. It's English, is it?

Fitz. It's particularly English.

King. Then, of course, it's all right. Pray proceed, ladies, it's particularly English. Come, my daughter, for we have much to say to each other.

Zara. Farewell, Captain Fitzbattleaxe! I cannot thank you too emphatically for the devoted care with which you have watched over me during our long and eventful voyage.

DUET—ZARA *and* CAPTAIN FITZBATTLEAXE

Zara

Ah! gallant soldier, brave and true
  In tented field and tourney,
I grieve to have occasioned you
  So very long a journey.
A British warrior gives up all—
  His home and island beauty—
When summoned by the trumpet-call
  Of Regimental Duty!

All

Tantantarara-rara-rara!
Trumpet-call of Princess Zara!

ENSEMBLE

Men

A British warrior gives up all, etc.

Ladies

Knightsbridge nursemaids, etc.

Fitzbattleaxe and Zara (*aside*)

Oh, my joy, my pride,
My delight to hide,
Let us sing, aside,
  What in truth we feel.
Let us whisper low
Of our love's glad glow,
Lest the truth we show
  We would fain conceal.

Fitzbattleaxe

Such escort duty, as his due,
  To young Lifeguardsman falling
Completely reconciles him to
  His uneventful calling.
When soldier seeks Utopian glades

In charge of Youth and Beauty,
Then pleasure merely masquerades
  As Regimental Duty!

All

Tantantarara-rara-rara!
Trumpet-call of Princess Zara!

ENSEMBLE

Chorus
Men

A British warrior, etc.

Women

Knightsbridge nursemaids, etc.

Fitzbattleaxe and Zara (aside)
Oh! the hours are gold,
And the joys untold,
When my eyes behold
      My beloved Princess;
And the years will seem
But a brief day-dream,
In the joy extreme
      Of our happiness!

[*Exeunt* KING *and* PRINCESS *in one direction, Lifeguardsmen and crowd in opposite direction. Enter, at back,* SCAPHIO *and* PHANTIS, *who watch the* PRINCESS *as she goes off.* SCAPHIO *is seated, shaking violently, and obviously under the influence of some strong emotion.*

Phan. There—tell me, Scaphio, is she not beautiful? Can you wonder that I love her so passionately?

Sca. No. She is extraordinarily—miraculously lovely! Good heavens, what a singularly beautiful girl!

Phan. I knew you would say so!

Sca. What exquisite charm of manner! What surprising delicacy of gesture! Why, she's a goddess! a very goddess!

Phan. (*rather taken aback*). Yes—she's —she's an attractive girl.

Sca. Attractive? Why, you must be blind! — She's entrancing — enthralling! — intoxicating! (*Aside*) God bless my heart what's the matter with me?

Phan. (*alarmed*). Yes. You—you promised to help me to get her father's consent, you know.

Sca. Promised! Yes, but the convulsion has come, my good boy! It is she—my ideal! Why, what's this? (*staggering*). Phantis! Stop me—I'm going mad—mad with the love of her!

Phan. Scaphio, compose yourself, I beg. The girl is perfectly opaque! Besides, remember—each of us is helpless without the other. You can't succeed without my consent, you know.

Sca. And you dare to threaten? Oh, ungrateful! When you came to me, palsied with love for this girl, and implored my assistance, did I not unhesitatingly promise it? And this is the return you make? Out of my sight, ingrate! (*Aside.*) Dear! dear! what is the matter with me?

Enter CAPT. FITZBATTLEAXE *and* ZARA

Zara. Dear me. I'm afraid we are interrupting a *tête-à-tête.*

Sca. (*breathlessly*). No, no. You come very appropriately. To be brief, we—we love you—this man and I—madly—passionately!

Zara. Sir!

Sca. And we don't know how we are to settle which of us is to marry you.

Fitz. Zara, this is very awkward.

Sca. (*very much overcome*). I—I am paralysed by the singular radiance of your extraordinary loveliness. I know I am incoherent. I never was like this before—it shall not occur again. I—shall be fluent, presently.

Zara (*aside*). Oh, dear, Captain Fitzbattleaxe, what *is* to be done?

Fitz. (*aside*). Leave it to me—I'll manage it. (*Aloud.*) It's a common situation. Why not settle it in the English fashion?

Both. The English fashion? What is that?

Fitz. It's very simple. In England, when two gentlemen are in love with the same lady, and until it is settled which gentleman is to blow out the brains of the other, it is provided, by the Rival Admirers' Clauses Consolidation Act, that the lady shall be entrusted to an officer of Household Cavalry as stakeholder, who is bound to hand her over to the survivor (on the Tontine principle) in a good condition of substantial and decorative repair.

Sca. Reasonable wear and tear and damages by fire excepted?

Fitz. Exactly.

Phan. Well, that seems very reasonable. (*To* SCAPHIO.) What do you say—Shall we entrust her to this officer of House-hold Cavalry? It will give us time.

Sca. (*trembling violently*). I—I am not at present in a condition to think it out coolly—but if he *is* an officer of Household Cavalry, and if the Princess consents——

Zara. Alas, dear sirs, I have no alter-native—under the Rival Admirers' Clauses Consolidation Act!

Fitz. Good—then that's settled.

QUARTET

FITZBATTLEAXE, ZARA, SCAPHIO, *and* PHANTIS

Fitzbattleaxe

It's understood, I think, all round
That, by the English custom bound
I hold the lady safe and sound
    In trust for either rival,
Until you clearly testify
By sword or pistol, by and by,
Which gentleman prefers to die,
    And which prefers survival.

ENSEMBLE

Scaphio and Phantis

It's clearly understood, all round,
That, by your English custom bound,
He holds the lady safe and sound
    In trust for either rival,
Until we clearly testify
By sword or pistol, by and by,
Which gentleman prefers to die,
    And which prefers survival.

Zara and Fitzbattleaxe (*aside*)

We stand, I think, on safish ground,
Our senses weak it will astound
If either gentleman is found
    Prepared to meet his rival.
Their machinations we defy;
We won't be parted, you and I—
Of bloodshed each is rather shy—
    They both prefer survival.

Phantis

If I should die and he should live,
        (*Aside to* FRITZ.)
To you, without reserve, I give
Her heart so young and sensitive,
And all her predilections.

Scaphio

If he should live and I should die,
        (*Aside to* FRITZ.)
I see no kind of reason why
You should not, if you wish it, try
    To gain her young affections.

ENSEMBLE

Scaphio and Phantis (*angrily to each other*)

If I should die and you should live,
To this young officer I give
Her heart so soft and sensitive,
    And all her predilections.
If you should live and I should die,
I see no kind of reason why
He should not, if he chooses, try
    To win her young affections.

Fitzbattleaxe and Zara (*aside*)

As both of us are positive
That both of them intend to live,
There's nothing in the case to give
    Us cause for grave reflections.
As both will live and neither die
I see no kind of reason why
I should not, if I wish it, try
    To gain your young affections!

[*Exeunt* SCAPHIO *and* PHANTIS *together*

DUET—ZARA *and* FITZBATTLEAXE
Ensemble

Oh, admirable art!
    Oh, neatly-planned intention!
Oh, happy intervention—
    Oh, well-constructed plot!
When sages try to part
    Two loving hearts in fusion,
    Their wisdom's a delusion,
        And learning serves them not!

Fitzbattleaxe

Until quite plain
    Is their intent,
These sages twain
    I represent.
Now please infer
    That, nothing loth,
You're henceforth, as it were,
    Engaged to marry both—
Then take it that I represent the two—
On that hypothesis, what would you do?

Zara (aside)
What would I do? what would I do?
(*To* FITZ.)
In such a case,
Upon your breast,
My blushing face
I think I'd rest—(*doing so*).
Then perhaps I might
Demurely say—
"I find this breastplate bright
Is sorely in the way!"
Fitzbattleaxe
Our mortal race
Is never blest—
There's no such case
As perfect rest;
Some petty blight
Asserts its sway—
Some crumpled roseleaf light
Is always in the way!

[*Exit* FITZBATTLEAXE. *Manent* ZARA

Enter KING

King. My daughter! At last we are alone together.

Zara. Yes, and I'm glad we are, for I want to speak to you very seriously. Do you know this paper?

King (aside). Da—! (*Aloud.*) Oh yes—I've—I've seen it. Where in the world did you get this from?

Zara. It was given to me by Lady Sophy —my sisters' governess.

King (aside). Lady Sophy's an angel, but I do sometimes wish she'd mind her own business! (*Aloud.*) It's—ha! ha!—it's rather humorous.

Zara. I see nothing humorous in it. I only see that you, the despotic King of this country, are made the subject of the most scandalous insinuations. Why do you permit these things?

King. Well, they appeal to my sense of humour. It's the only really comic paper in Utopia, and I wouldn't be without it for the world.

Zara. If it had any literary merit I could understand it.

King. Oh, it *has* literary merit. Oh, distinctly, it has literary merit.

Zara. My dear father, it's mere ungrammatical twaddle.

King. Oh, it's not ungrammatical. I can't allow that. Unpleasantly personal, perhaps, but written with an epigrammatical point that is very rare nowadays—very rare indeed.

Zara (looking at cartoon). Why do they represent you with such a big nose?

King (looking at cartoon). Eh? Yes, it *is* a big one! Why, the fact is that, in the cartoons of a comic paper, the size of your nose always varies inversely as the square of your popularity. It's the rule.

Zara. Then you must be at a tremendous discount just now! I see a notice of a new piece called "King Tuppence," in which an English tenor has the audacity to personate you on a public stage. I can only say that I am surprised that any English tenor should lend himself to such degrading personalities.

King. Oh, he's not really English. As it happens, he's a Utopian, but he calls himself English.

Zara. Calls himself English?

King. Yes. Bless you, they wouldn't listen to any tenor who didn't call himself English.

Zara. And you permit this insolent buffoon to caricature you in a pointless burlesque! My dear father—if you were a free agent, you would never permit these outrages.

King (almost in tears). Zara—I—I admit I am not altogether a free agent. I—I am controlled. I try to make the best of it, but sometimes I find it very difficult—very difficult indeed. Nominally a Despot, I am, between ourselves, the helpless tool of two unscrupulous Wise Men, who insist on my falling in with all their wishes and threaten to denounce me for immediate explosion if I remonstrate! (*Breaks down completely.*)

Zara. My poor father! Now listen to me. With a view to remodelling the political and social institutions of Utopia, I have brought with me six Representatives of the principal causes that have tended to make England the powerful, happy, and blameless country which the consensus of European civilization has declared it to be. Place yourself unreservedly in the hands of these gentlemen, and they will reorganize your country on a footing that will enable you to defy your persecutors. They are all now washing their hands after their journey. Shall I introduce them?

King. My dear Zara, how can I thank you? I will consent to anything that will release me from the abominable tyranny of these two men. (*Calling.*) What ho! Without there! (*Enter* CALYNX.) Summon my Court without an instant's delay!

[*Exit* CALYNX.

FINALE

Enter every one, except the Flowers of Progress

Chorus

Although your Royal summons to appear
From courtesy was singularly free,
Obedient to that summons we are here—
What would your Majesty?

RECIT.—KING

My worthy people, my beloved daughter
Most thoughtfully has brought with her from England
The types of all the causes that have made
That great and glorious country what it is.

Chorus

Oh, joy unbounded!
Scaphio, Tarara, and Phantis (*aside*)
Why, what *does* this mean?

RECIT.—ZARA

Attend to me, Utopian populace,
Ye South Pacific Island viviparians;
All, in the abstract, types of courtly grace,
Yet, when compared with Britain's glorious race,
But little better than half-clothed barbarians!

Chorus

Yes! Contrasted when
With Englishmen,
Are little better than half-clothed barbarians!

Enter all the Flowers of Progress, led by FITZBATTLEAXE

SOLO—ZARA

(*Presenting* CAPT. FITZBATTLEAXE.)

When Britain sounds the trump of war
(And Europe trembles),
The army of that conqueror
In serried ranks assembles;
'Tis then this warrior's eyes and sabre gleam
For our protection—
He represents a military scheme
In all its proud perfection!

Chorus

Yes—yes—
He represents a military scheme
In all its proud perfection!
Ulahlica! Ulahlica! Ulahlica!

SOLO—ZARA

(*Presenting* SIR BAILEY BARRE, Q.C., M.P.)

A complicated gentleman allow me to present,
Of all the arts and faculties the terse embodiment,
He's a great Arithmetician who can demonstrate with ease
That two and two are three, or five, or anything you please;
An eminent Logician who can make it clear to you
That black is white—when looked at from the proper point of view;
A marvellous Philologist who'll undertake to show
That "yes" is but another and a neater form of "no."

Sir Bailey

Yes—yes—yes—
"Yes" is but another and a neater form of "no."
All preconceived ideas on any subject I can scout,
And demonstrate beyond all possibility of doubt,
That whether you're an honest man or whether you're a thief
Depends on whose solicitor has given me my brief.

Chorus

Yes—yes—yes—
That whether you're an honest man, etc.
Ulahlica! Ulahlica! Ulahlica!

SOLO—ZARA

(*Presenting* LORD DRAMALEIGH *and County Councillor.*)

What these may be, Utopians all,
Perhaps you'll hardly guess—
They're types of England's physical
And moral cleanliness.
This is a Lord High Chamberlain,
Of purity the gauge—
He'll cleanse our Court from moral stain
And purify our Stage.

Lord Dramaleigh

Yes—yes—yes—
Court reputations I revise,
And presentations scrutinize,
New plays I read with jealous eyes,
And purify the Stage.

Chorus

Court reputations, etc.

Zara

This County Councillor acclaim,
  Great Britain's latest toy—
On anything you like to name
  His talents he'll employ—
All streets and squares he'll purify
  Within your city walls,
And keep meanwhile a modest eye
  On wicked music halls.

County Councillor

Yes—yes—yes—
In towns I make improvements great,
Which go to swell the County Rate—
I dwelling-houses sanitate,
  And purify the Halls!

Chorus

In towns he makes improvements great, etc.
Ulahlica! Ulahlica! Ulahlica!

SOLO—ZARA

(*Presenting* MR. GOLDBURY.)

A Company Promoter this, with special
  education,
Which teaches what Contango means and
  also Backwardation—
To speculators he supplies a grand financial
  leaven,
Time was when *two* were company—but
  now it must be seven.

Mr. Goldbury

Yes—yes—yes—
Stupendous loans to foreign thrones
  I've largely advocated;
In ginger-pops and peppermint-drops
  I've freely speculated;
Then mines of gold, of wealth untold,
  Successfully I've floated,
And sudden falls in apple-stalls
  Occasionally quoted:
And soon or late I always call
  For Stock Exchange quotation—
No schemes too great and none too small
  For Companification!

Chorus

Yes! Yes! Yes! No schemes too great, etc.
Ulahlica! Ulahlica! Ulahlica!

Zara (*Presenting* CAPT. SIR EDWARD COR-
CORAN, R.N.)

And lastly I present
  Great Britain's proudest boast,
Who from the blows
Of foreign foes
  Protects her sea-girt coast—

And if you ask him in respectful tone,
He'll show you how you may protect your
  own!

SOLO—CAPTAIN CORCORAN

I'm Captain Corcoran, K.C.B.,
I'll teach you how we rule the sea,
  And terrify the simple Gauls;
And how the Saxon and the Celt
Their Europe-shaking blows have dealt
With Maxim gun and Nordenfelt
  (Or will, when the occasion calls).
If sailor-like you'd play your cards,
Unbend your sails and lower your yards,
  Unstep your masts—you'll never want
    'em more.
Though we're no longer hearts of oak,
Yet we can steer and we can stoke,
And, thanks to coal, and thanks to coke,
  We never run a ship ashore!

All

What never?

Captain

No, never!

All

What *never?*

Captain

Hardly ever!

All

Hardly ever run a ship ashore!
Then give three cheers, and three cheers
  more,
For the tar who never runs his ship ashore;
Then give three cheers, and three cheers
  more,
  For he never runs his ship ashore!

Chorus

All hail, ye types of England's power—
  Ye heaven-enlightened band!
We bless the day, and bless the hour
  That brought you to our land.

QUARTET

Ye wanderers from a mighty State,
Oh, teach us how to legislate—
Your lightest word will carry weight
  In our attentive ears.
Oh, teach the natives of this land
(Who are not quick to understand)
How to work off their social and
  Political arrears!

Captain Fitzbattleaxe

Increase your army!

Lord Dramaleigh

Purify your Court!

Captain Corcoran

Get up your steam and cut your canvas
short!

Sir Bailey Barre

To speak on both sides teach your slug-
gish brains!

Mr. Blushington, County Councillor

Widen your thoroughfares, and flush your
drains!

Mr. Goldbury

Utopia's much too big for one small head—
I'll float it as a Company Limited!

King

A Company Limited? What may that be?
The term, I rather think, is new to me.

Chorus

A Company Limited? etc.

Scaphio, Phantis and Tarara (aside)

What does he mean? What does he mean?
Give us a kind of clue!
What does he mean? What does he mean?
What is he going to do?

SONG—MR. GOLDBURY

Some seven men form an Association
  (If possible, all Peers and Baronets),
They start off with a public declaration
  To what extent they mean to pay their
debts.
That's called their Capital: if they are wary
  They will not quote it at a sum im-
mense.
The figure's immaterial—it may vary
  From eighteen million down to eighteen-
pence.
  I should put it rather low;
  The good sense of doing so
Will be evident at once to any debtor.
  When it's left to you to say
  What amount you mean to pay,
  Why, the lower you can put it at, the
better.

Chorus

When it's left to you to say, etc.

They then proceed to trade with all who'll
trust 'em,
  Quite irrespective of their capital
(It's shady, but it's sanctified by custom);
  Bank, Railway, Loan, or Panama Canal.
You can't embark on trading too tremen-
dous—
  It's strictly fair, and based on common
sense—
If you succeed, your profits are stupen-
dous—

And if you fail, pop goes your eighteen
pence.
  Make the money-spinner spin!
  For you only stand to win,
And you'll never with dishonesty be
twitted,
  For nobody can know,
  To a million or so,
To what extent your capital's committed

Chorus

No, nobody can know, etc.

If you come to grief, and creditors are
craving
  (For nothing that is planned by mortal
head
Is certain in this Vale of Sorrow—saving
  That one's Liability is Limited),—
Do you suppose that signifies perdition?
  If so you're but a monetary dunce—
You merely file a Winding-Up Petition,
  And start another Company at once!
  Though a Rothschild you may be
  In your own capacity,
As a Company you've come to utter sor-
row—
  But the Liquidators say,
  "Never mind—you needn't pay,"
So you start another Company to-morrow

Chorus

But the Liquidators say, etc.

RECIT.

King

Well, at first sight it strikes us as dis-
honest,
But if it's good enough for virtuous Eng-
land—
The first commercial country in the world—
It's good enough for us.

*Scaphio, Phantis and Tarara (aside to
KING)*

You'd best take care—
Please recollect *we* have not been consulted.

King (not heeding them).

And do I understand you that Great
Britain
Upon this Joint Stock principle is gov-
erned?

Mr. Goldbury

We haven't come to that, exactly—but
We're tending rapidly in that direction.
The date's not distant.

King (enthusiastically).

We will be before you!

We'll go down to Posterity renowned
As the First Sovereign in Christendom
Who registered his Crown and Country
    under
The Joint Stock Company's Act of Sixty-
    Two.

All

Ulahlica!

SOLO—KING
Henceforward, of a verity,
  With Fame ourselves we link—
We'll go down to Posterity
  Of sovereigns all the pink!

Scaphio, Phantis and Tarara (aside to
    KING)
If you've the mad temerity

Our wishes thus to blink,
You'll go down to Posterity
Much earlier than you think!
Tarara (correcting them).
He'll go *up* to Posterity,
If *I* inflict the blow!
Scaphio and Phantis (angrily).
He'll go *down* to Posterity—
  We think we ought to know!
Tarara (explaining).
He'll go *up* to Posterity,
Blown up with dynamite!
Scaphio and Phantis (apologetically).
He'll go *up* to Posterity,
Of course he will, you're right!

ENSEMBLE

King, Lady Sophy, Nekaya, Kalyba, Calynx, and Chorus	Scaphio, Phantis and Tarara *(aside)*	Fitzbattleaxe and Zara *(aside)*
Henceforward, of a verity, With fame ourselves we link— And go down to Posterity, Of sovereigns all the pink!	If he has the temerity Our wishes thus to blink, He'll go up to Posterity Much earlier than they think!	Who love with all sincerity, Their lives may safely link; And as for our Posterity— We don't care what they think!

Chorus
Let's seal this mercantile pact—
  The step we ne'er shall rue—
It gives whatever we lacked—
  The statement's strictly true.
All hail, astonishing Fact!
  All hail, Invention new—
The Joint Stock Company's Act—
  The Act of Sixty-Two!

END OF ACT I

ACT II

SCENE.—*Throne Room in the Palace. Night.*
FITZBATTLEAXE *discovered, singing to*
ZARA.

RECIT.—FITZ
Oh, Zara, my beloved one, bear with me!
Oh, do not laugh at my attempted C!
Repent not, mocking maid, thy girlhood's
    choice—
The fervour of my love affects my voice!

SONG—FITZ.
A tenor, all singers above
  (This doesn't admit of a question),
    Should keep himself quiet,
    Attend to his diet
And carefully nurse his digestion;
But when he is madly in love

It's certain to tell on his singing—
  You can't do chromatics
  With proper emphatics
When anguish your bosom is wringing!
When distracted with worries in plenty,
And his pulse is a hundred and twenty,
And his fluttering bosom the slave of mis-
    trust is,
A tenor can't do himself justice.
Now observe—(*sings a high note*),
You see, I can't do myself justice!
I could sing if my fevour were mock,
  It's easy enough if you're acting—
    But when one's emotion
    Is born of devotion
You mustn't be over-exacting.
One ought to be firm as a rock
  To venture a shake in *vibrato*,
    When fevour's expected
    Keep cool and collected
Or never attempt *agitato*.
But, of course, when his tongue is of
    leather,
And his lips appear pasted together,
And his sensitive palate as dry as a crust
    is,
A tenor can't do himself justice.
Now observe—(*sings a cadence*),

It's no use—I can't do myself justice!

Zara. Why, Arthur, what *does* it matter? When the higher qualities of the heart are all that can be desired, the higher notes of the voice are matters of comparative insignificance. Who thinks slightingly of the cocoanut because it is husky? Besides (*demurely*), you are not singing for an engagement (*putting her hand in his*), you have that already!

Fitz. How good and wise you are! How unerringly your practised brain winnows the wheat from the chaff—the material from the merely incidental!

Zara. My Girton training, Arthur. At Girton all is wheat, and idle chaff is never heard within its walls! But tell me, is not all working marvellously well? Have not our Flowers of Progress more than justified their name?

Fitz. We have indeed done our best. Captain Corcoran and I have, in concert, thoroughly remodelled the sister-services—and upon so sound a basis that the South Pacific trembles at the name of Utopia!

Zara. How clever of you!

Fitz. Clever? Not a bit. It's as easy as possible when the Admiralty and Horse Guards are not there to interfere. And so with the others. Freed from the trammels imposed upon them by idle Acts of Parliament, all have given their natural talents full play and introduced reforms which, even in England, were never dreamt of!

Zara. But perhaps the most beneficent change of all has been effected by Mr. Goldbury, who, discarding the exploded theory that some strange magic lies hidden in the number Seven, has applied the Limited Liability principle to individuals, and every man, woman, and child is now a Company Limited with liability restricted to the amount of his declared Capital! There is not a christened baby in Utopia who has not already issued his little Prospectus!

Fitz. Marvellous is the power of a Civilization which can transmute, by word, a Limited Income into an Income Limited.

Zara. Reform has not stopped here—it has been applied even to the costume of our people. Discarding their own barbaric dress, the natives of our land have unanimously adopted the tasteful fashions of England in all their rich entirety. Scaphio and Phantis have undertaken a contract to supply the whole of Utopia with clothing designed upon the most approved English models—and the first Drawing-Room under the new state of things is to be held here this evening.

Fitz. But Drawing-Rooms are always held in the afternoon.

Zara. Ah, we've improved upon that. We all look so much better by candle light! And when I tell you, dearest, that my Court train has just arrived, you will understand that I am longing to go and try it on.

Fitz. Then we must part?

Zara. Necessarily, for a time.

Fitz. Just as I wanted to tell you, with all the passionate enthusiasm of my nature, how deeply, how devotedly I love you!

Zara. Hush! Are these the accents of a heart that really feels? True love does not indulge in declamation—its voice is sweet and soft, and low. The west wind whispers when he woos the poplars!

DUET—ZARA *and* FITZBATTLEAXE

Zara

Words of love too loudly spoken
 Ring their own untimely knell;
Noisy vows are rudely broken,
 Soft the song of Philomel.
Whisper sweetly, whisper slowly,
 Hour by hour and day by day;
Sweet and low as accents holy
 Are the notes of lover's lay!

Both

Sweet and low, etc.

Fitz.

Let the conqueror, flushed with glory,
 Bid his noisy clarions bray;
Lovers tell their artless story
 In a whispered virelay.
False is he whose vows alluring
 Make the listening echoes ring;
Sweet and low when all-enduring
 Are the songs that lovers sing!

Both

Sweet and low, etc.

[*Exit* ZARA.
Enter KING, *dressed as Field-Marshal*

King. To a Monarch who has been accustomed to the uncontrolled use of his limbs, the costume of a British Field Marshal is, perhaps, at first, a little cramp ing. Are you sure that this is all right? It's not a practical joke, is it? No one has a keener sense of humour than I have, but the First Statutory Cabinet Council of Utopia Limited must be conducted with dignity and impressiveness. Now, where are the other five who signed the Articles of Association?

Fitz. Sir, they are here.

Enter LORD DRAMALEIGH, CAPTAIN CORCORAN, SIR BAILEY BARRE, MR. BLUSHINGTON, *and* MR. GOLDBURY *from different entrances.*

King. Oh! (*Addressing them.*) Gentlemen, our daughter holds her first Drawing-Room in half an hour, and we shall have time to make our half-yearly report in the interval. I am necessarily unfamiliar with the forms of an English Cabinet Council—perhaps the Lord Chamberlain will kindly put us in the way of doing the thing properly, and with due regard to the solemnity of the occasion.

Lord D. Certainly—nothing simpler. Kindly bring your chairs forward—His Majesty will, of course, preside.

[*They range their chairs across stage like Christy Minstrels.* KING *sits* C., LORD DRAMALEIGH *on his* L., MR. GOLDBURY *on his* R., CAPT. CORCORAN L. *of* LORD DRAMALEIGH, CAPT. FITZBATTLEAXE R. *of* MR. GOLDBURY, MR. BLUSHINGTON *extreme* R., SIR BAILEY BARRE *extreme* L.

King. Like this?

Lord D. Like this.

King. We take your word for it that this is all right. You are not making fun of us? This is in accordance with the practice at the Court of St. James's?

Lord D. Well, it is in accordance with the practice at the Court of St. James's Hall.

King. Oh! it seems odd, but never mind.

SONG—KING

Society has quite forsaken all her wicked courses,
Which empties our police courts, and abolishes divorces.

Chorus

Divorce is nearly obsolete in England.

King

No tolerance we show to undeserving rank and splendour;
For the higher his position is, the greater the offender.

Chorus

That's a maxim that is prevalent in England.

King

No peeress at our Drawing-Room before the Presence passes
Who wouldn't be accepted by the lower-middle classes.
Each shady dame, whatever be her rank, is bowed out neatly.

Chorus

In short, this happy country has been Anglicized completely!
It really is surprising
What a through Anglicizing
We have brought about—Utopia's quite another land;
In her enterprising movements,
She is England—with improvements,
Which we dutifully offer to our motherland!

King

Our city we have beautified—we've done it willy-nilly—
And all that isn't Belgrave Square is Strand and Piccadilly.

Chorus

We haven't any slummeries in England!

King

We have solved the labour question with discrimination polished,
So poverty is obsolete and hunger is abolished—

Chorus

We are going to abolish it in England.

King

The Chamberlain our native stage has purged, beyond a question,
Of "risky" situation and indelicate suggestion;
No piece is tolerated if it's costumed indiscreetly—

Chorus

In short, this happy country has been Anglicized completely!
It really is surprising, etc.

King

Our Peerage we've remodelled on an intellectual basis,
Which certainly is rough on our hereditary races—

Chorus

We are going to remodel it in England.

King
The Brewers and the Cotton Lords no
longer seek admission,
And Literary Merit meets with proper
recognition—
Chorus
As Literary Merit does in England!

King
Who knows but we may count among our
intellectual chickens,
Like you, an Earl of Thackeray and p'r'aps
a Duke of Dickens—
Lord Fildes and Viscount Millais (when
they come) we'll welcome sweetly—
Chorus
In short, this happy country has been
Anglicized completely!
It really is surprising, etc.
[*At the end all rise and replace their chairs.*
King. Now, then, for our first Drawing-
Room. Where are the Princesses? What an
extraordinary thing it is that since Eu-
ropean looking-glasses have been supplied
to the Royal bedrooms my daughters are
invariably late!
Lord D. Sir, their Royal Highnesses await
your pleasure in the Ante-room.
King. Oh. Then request them to do us
the favour to enter at once.
MARCH. *Enter all the Royal Household, in-
cluding (besides the Lord Chamberlain) the Vice-Chamberlain, the Master
of the Horse, the Master of the Buckhounds, the Lord High Treasurer, the
Lord Steward, the Comptroller of the
Household, the Lord-in-Waiting, the
Groom-in-Waiting, the Field Officer in
Brigade Waiting, the Gold and Silver
Stick, and the Gentlemen Ushers. Then
enter the three Princesses (their trains
carried by Pages of Honour),* LADY
SOPHY, *and the Ladies-in-Waiting.*
King. My daughters, we are about to
attempt a very solemn ceremonial, so no
giggling, if you please. Now, my Lord
Chamberlain, we are ready.
Lord D. Then, ladies and gentlemen,
places, if you please. His Majesty will take
his place in front of the throne, and will
be so obliging as to embrace all the *débu-
tantes.* (LADY SOPHY *much shocked.*)
King. What—must I really?
Lord D. Absolutely indispensable.
King. More jam for the *Palace Peeper!*

[*The* KING *takes his place in front of the
throne, the* PRINCESS ZARA *on his left,
the two younger Princesses on the left
of* ZARA.
King. Now, is every one in his place?
Lord D. Every one is in his place.
King. Then let the revels commence.
*Enter the ladies attending the Drawing-
Room. They give their cards to the
Groom-in-Waiting, who passes them
to the Lord-in-Waiting, who passes
them to the Vice-Chamberlain, who
passes them to the Lord Chamberlain,
who reads the names to the* KING *as
each lady approaches. The ladies curtsey in succession to the* KING *and the
three Princesses, and pass out. When
all the presentations have been accomplished, the* KING, *Princesses, and* LADY
SOPHY *come forward, and all the ladies
re-enter.*

RECIT.—KING
This ceremonial our wish displays
To copy all Great Britain's courtly ways.
Though lofty aims catastrophe entail,
We'll gloriously succeed or nobly fail!
Unaccompanied Chorus
Eagle high in cloudland soaring—
Sparrow twittering on a reed—
Tiger in the jungle roaring—
Frightened fawn in grassy mead—
Let the eagle, not the sparrow,
Be the object of your arrow—
Fix the tiger with your eye—
Pass the fawn in pity by.
Glory then will crown the day—
Glory, glory, anyway!
[*Then exeunt all.*
Enter SCAPHIO *and* PHANTIS, *now dressed as
judges in red and ermine robes and
undress wigs. They come down stage
melodramatically—working together.*
DUET—SCAPHIO *and* PHANTIS
Scaphio
With fury deep we burn—
Phantis
We do—
Scaphio
We fume with smothered rage—
Phantis
We do—
Scaphio
These Englishmen who rule supreme,
Their undertaking they redeem

By stifling every harmless scheme
In which we both engage—
> *Phantis*

> > They do—

> *Scaphio*
In which we both engage.
> *Phantis*
We think it is our turn—
> > *Scaphio*

> > We do—

> *Phantis*
We think our turn has come—
> > *Scaphio*

> > We do.

> *Phantis*
These Englishmen, they must prepare
To seek at once their native air.
The King as heretofore, we swear,
Shall be beneath our thumb—
> > *Scaphio*

> > He shall—

> *Phantis*
Shall be beneath our thumb—
> > *Scaphio*

> > He shall.

> *Both (with great energy).*
For this mustn't be, and this won't do,
If you'll back me, then I'll back you,
> No, this won't do,
> No, this mustn't be.

> *Enter the* KING

King. Gentlemen, gentlemen—really! This unseemly display of energy within the Royal Precincts is altogether unpardonable. Pray, what do you complain of?

Sca. (*furiously*). What do we complain of? Why, through the innovations introduced by the Flowers of Progress all our harmless schemes for making a provision for our old age are ruined. Our Matrimonial Agency is at a standstill, our Cheap Sherry business is in bankruptcy, our Army Clothing contracts are paralysed, and even our Society paper, the *Palace Peeper,* is practically defunct!

King. Defunct? Is that so? Dear, dear, I am truly sorry.

Sca. Are you aware that Sir Bailey Barre has introduced a law of libel by which all editors of scurrilous newspapers are publicly flogged—as in England? And six of our editors have resigned in succession! Now, the editor of a scurrilous paper can stand a good deal—he takes a private thrashing as a matter of course—it's considered in his salary—but no gentleman likes to be publicly flogged.

King. Naturally. I shouldn't like it myself.

Phan. Then our Burlesque Theatre is absolutely ruined!

King. Dear me. Well, theatrical property is not what it was.

Phan. Are you aware that the Lord Chamberlain, who has his own views as to the best means of elevating the national drama, has declined to license any play that is not in blank verse and three hundred years old—as in England?

Sca. And as if that wasn't enough, the County Councillor has ordered a four-foot wall to be built up right across the proscenium, in case of fire—as in England.

Phan. It's so hard on the company—who are liable to be roasted alive—and this has to be met by enormously increased salaries—as in England.

Sca. You probably know that we've contracted to supply the entire nation with a complete English outfit. But perhaps you do *not* know that, when we send in our bills, our customers plead liability limited to a declared capital of eighteenpence, and apply to be dealt with under the Winding-up Act—as in England?

King. Really, gentlemen, this is very irregular. If you will be so good as to formulate a detailed list of your grievances in writing, addressed to the Secretary of Utopia Limited, they will be laid before the Board, in due course, at their next monthly meeting.

Sca. Are we to understand that we are defied?

King. That is the idea I intended to convey.

Phan. Defied! We are defied!

Sca. (*furiously*). Take care—you know our powers. Trifle with us, and you die!

> TRIO—SCAPHIO, PHANTIS, *and* KING
> *Scaphio*
If you think that, when banded in unity,
We may both be defied with impunity,
> You are sadly misled of a verity!

> *Phantis*
If you value repose and tranquillity,
You'll revert to a state of docility,
> Or prepare to regret your temerity!

King

If my speech is unduly refractory
You will find it a course satisfactory
    At an early Board meeting to show it up.
Though if proper excuse you can trump
                any,
You may *wind* up a Limited Company,
    You cannot conveniently *blow* it up!
(SCAPHIO *and* PHANTIS *thoroughly baffled.*)
              King (dancing quietly).
Whene'er I chance to baffle you
    I, also, dance a step or two—
Of this now guess the hidden sense:
(SCAPHIO *and* PHANTIS *consider the question
as* KING *continues dancing quietly—then
                give it up.*)
    It means—complete indifference.
          Scaphio and Phantis
Of course it does—indifference!
It means complete indifference!
(KING *dancing quietly.* SCA. *and* PHAN.
            dancing furiously.)
          Scaphio and Phantis
As we've a dance for every mood
With *pas de trois* we will conclude.
What this may mean you all may guess—
It typifies remorselessness!

              King
It means unruffled cheerfulness!
[KING *dances off placidly as* SCAPHIO *and*
    PHANTIS *dance furiously.*

Phan. (*breathless*). He's right—we are
helpless! He's no longer a human being—
he's a Corporation, and so long as he con-
fines himself to his Articles of Association
we can't touch him! What are we to do?
Sca. Do? Raise a Revolution, repeal the
Act of Sixty-Two, reconvert him into an
individual, and insist on his immediate explosion! (TARARA *enters.*) Tarara, come
here; you're the very man we want.
Tar. Certainly, allow me. (*Offers a
cracker to each; they snatch them away
impatiently.*) That's rude.
Sca. We have no time for idle forms.
You wish to succeed to the throne?
Tar. Naturally.
Sca. Then you won't unless you join us.
The King has defied us, and, as matters
stand, we are helpless. So are you. We
must devise some plot at once to bring the
people about his ears.
Tar. A plot?
Phan. Yes, a plot of superhuman sub-

tlety. Have you such a thing about you?
Tar. (*feeling*). No, I think not. No.
There's one on my dressing-table.
Sca. We can't wait—we must concoct one
at once, and put it into execution without
delay. There is not a moment to spare!
    TRIO—SCAPHIO, PHANTIS, *and* TARARA
                ENSEMBLE
With wily brain upon the spot
    A private plot we'll plan,
The most ingenious private plot
    Since private plots began.
That's understood. So far we've got
And, striking while the iron's hot,
We'll now determine like a shot
The details of this private plot.
              Scaphio
I think we ought—(*whispers*).
          Phantis and Tarara
Such bosh I never heard!
              Phantis
Ah! happy thought—(*whispers*).
          Scaphio and Tarara
How utterly dashed absurd!
              Tarara
I'll tell you how—(*whispers*).
          Scaphio and Phantis
Why, what put that in your head?
              Scaphio
I've got it now(*whispers*).
          Phantis and Tarara
Oh, take him away to bed!
              Phantis
    Oh, put him to bed!
              Tarara
    Oh, put him to bed!
              Scaphio
    What! put *me* to bed?
          Phantis and Tarara
    Yes, certainly put him to bed!
              Scaphio
But, bless me, don't you see—
              Phantis
    Do listen to me, I pray—
              Tarara
It certainly seems to me—
              Scaphio
    Bah—this is the only way!
              Phantis
It's rubbish absurb you growl!
              Tarara
    You talk ridiculous stuff!
              Scaphio
You're a drivelling barndoor owl!

Phantis
You're a vapid and vain old muff!

(*All, coming down to audience.*)
So far we haven't quite solved the plot—
They're not a very ingenious lot—
 But don't be unhappy,
 It's still on the *tapis*.
We'll presently hit on a capital plot!

Scaphio
Suppose we all—(*whispers*).

Phantis
Now *there* I think you're right.
Then we might all—(*whispers*).

Tarara
That's true—we certainly might.
I'll tell you what—(*whispers*).

Scaphio
We will if we possibly can.
Then on the spot—(*whispers*).

Phantis and Tarara
Bravo! a capital plan!

Scaphio
That's exceedingly neat and new!

Phantis
Exceedingly new and neat.

Tarara
I fancy that that will do.

Scaphio
It's certainly very complete.

Phantis
Well done, you sly old sap!

Tarara
Bravo, you cunning old mole!

Scaphio
You very ingenious chap!

Phantis
You intellectual soul!

(*All, coming down and addressing audience.*)
At last a capital plan we've got.
We won't say how and we won't say what:
 It's safe in my noddle—
 Now off we will toddle,
And slyly develop this capital plot!

[*Business. Exeunt* SCAPHIO *and* PHANTIS *in one direction, and* TARARA *in the other.*

Enter LORD DRAMALEIGH *and* MR. GOLDBURY

Lord D. Well, what do you think of our first South Pacific Drawing-Room? Allowing for a slight difficulty with the trains, and a little want of familiarity with the use of the rouge-pot, it was, on the whole, a meritorious affair?

Gold. My dear Dramaleigh, it redounds infinitely to your credit.

Lord D. One or two judicious innovations, I think?

Gold. Admirable. The cup of tea and the plate of mixed biscuits were a cheap and effective inspiration.

Lord D. Yes—my idea entirely. Never been done before.

Gold. Pretty little maids, the King's youngest daughters, but timid.

Lord D. That'll wear off. Young.

Gold. That'll wear off. Ha! here they come, by George! And without the Dragon! What can they have done with her?

Enter NEKAYA *and* KALYBA, *timidly*

Nek. Oh, if you please, Lady Sophy has sent us in here, because Zara and Captain Fitzbattleaxe are going on, in the garden, in a manner which no well-conducted young ladies ought to witness.

Lord D. Indeed, we are very much obliged to her Ladyship.

Kal. Are you? I wonder why.

Nek. Don't tell us if it's rude.

Lord D. Rude? Not at all. We are obliged to Lady Sophy because she has afforded us the pleasure of seeing you.

Nek. I don't think you ought to talk to us like that.

Kal. It's calculated to turn our heads.

Nek. Attractive girls cannot be too particular.

Kal. Oh pray, pray do not take advantage of our unprotected innocence.

Gold. Pray be reassured—you are in no danger whatever.

Lord D. But may I ask—is this extreme delicacy—this shrinking sensitiveness—a general characteristic of Utopian young ladies?

Nek. Oh no; we are crack specimens.

Kal. We are the pick of the basket. *Would* you mind not coming quite so near? Thank you.

Nek. And please don't look at us like that; it unsettles us.

Kal. And we don't like it. At least, we *do* like it; but it's wrong.

Nek. We have enjoyed the inestimable privilege of being educated by a most refined and easily shocked English lady, on the very strictest English principles.

Gold. But, my dear young ladies——

Kal. Oh, don't! You mustn't. It's too affectionate.

Nek. It really does unsettle us.

Gold. Are you really under the impression that English girls are so ridiculously demure? Why, an English girl of the highest type is the best, the most beautiful, the bravest, and the brightest creature that Heaven has conferred upon this world of ours. She is frank, open-hearted, and fearless, and never shows in so favourable a light as when she gives her own blameless impulses full play!

Nek. and Kal. Oh, you shocking story!

Gold. Not at all. I'm speaking the strict truth. I'll tell you all about her.

SONG—MR. GOLDBURY

A wonderful joy our eyes to bless,
In her magnificent comeliness,
Is an English girl of eleven stone two,
And five foot ten in her dancing shoe!
　　She follows the hounds, and on she pounds—
　　　　The "field" tails off and the muffs diminish—
Over the hedges and brooks she bounds
　　Straight as a crow, from find to finish.
At cricket, her kin will lose or win—
　　She and her maids, on grass and clover,
Eleven maids out—eleven maids in—
　　And perhaps an occasional "maiden over!"

Go search the world and search the sea,
Then come you home and sing with me
There's no such gold and no such pearl
As a bright and beautiful English girl!
With a ten-mile spin she stretches her limbs,
She golfs, she punts, she rows, she swims—
She plays, she sings, she dances, too,
From ten or eleven till all is blue!
At ball or drum, till small hours come
　　(Chaperon's fan conceals her yawning)
She'll waltz away like a teetotum,
　　And never go home till daylight's dawning.
Lawn-tennis may share her favours fair—
　　Her eyes a-dance and her cheeks a-glowing—
Down comes her hair, but what does she care?
　　It's all her own and it's worth the showing!

Go search the world, etc.
Her soul is sweet as the ocean air,
For prudery knows no haven there;
To find mock-modesty, please apply
To the conscious blush and the downcast eye.
Rich in the things contentment brings,
　　In every pure enjoyment wealthy,
Blithe as a beautiful bird she sings,
　　For body and mind are hale and healthy.
Her eyes they thrill with right goodwill—
　　Her heart is light as a floating feather—
As pure and bright as the mountain rill
　　That leaps and laughs in the Highland heather!

Go search the world, etc.

QUARTET

Nekaya

Then I may sing and play?

Lord Dramaleigh

You may!

Kalyba

And I may laugh and shout?

Goldbury

No doubt!

Nekaya

These maxims you endorse?

Lord Dramaleigh

Of course!

Kalyba

You won't exclaim "Oh fie!"

Goldbury

Not I!

Goldbury

Whatever you are—be that:
　Whatever you say—be true:
　　Straightforwardly act—
　　Be honest—in fact,
　　Be nobody else but *you.*

Lord Dramaleigh

Give every answer pat—
　Your character true unfurl;
　　And when it is ripe,
　　You'll then be a type
Of a capital English girl.

All

Oh, sweet surprise—oh, dear delight,
To find it undisputed quite,
All musty, fusty rules despite,
That Art is wrong and Nature right!

Nekaya

When happy I,
　With laughter glad

I'll wake the echoes fairly,
And only sigh
  When I am sad—
    And that will be but rarely!
        Kalyba

I'll row and fish,
  And gallop, soon—
    No longer be a prim one—
And when I wish
  To hum a tune,
    It needn't be a hymn one?
     Goldbury and Lord Dramaleigh
      No, no!
It needn't be a hymn one!
        All
      (*dancing*).

Oh, sweet surprise and dear delight
To find it undisputed quite—
All musty, fusty rules despite—
That Art is wrong and Nature right!
        [*Dance, and off.*

    Enter LADY SOPHY
    RECIT.—LADY SOPHY

Oh, would some demon power the gift
  impart
To quell my over-conscientious heart—
Unspeak the oaths that never had been
  spoken,
And break the vows that never should be
  broken!

    SONG—LADY SOPHY

When but a maid of fifteen year,
  Unsought—unplighted—
Short-petticoated—and, I fear,
  Still shorter-sighted—
I made a vow, one early spring,
That only to some spotless King
Who proof of blameless life could bring
  I'd be united.
For I had read, not long before,
Of blameless kings in fairy lore,
And thought the race still flourished here—
  Well, well—
  I was a maid of fifteen year!
The KING *enters and overhears this verse*
Each morning I pursued my game
  (An early riser);
For spotless monarchs I became
  An advertiser:
But all in vain I searched each land,
So, kingless, to my native strand
Returned, a little older, and
  A good deal wiser!
I learnt that spotless King and Prince

Have disappeared some ages since—
Even Paramount's angelic grace—
  Ah, me!—
Is but a mask on Nature's face!
      [KING *comes forward.*
    RECIT.
    King
Ah, Lady Sophy—then you love me!
  For so you sing—
Lady Sophy (*indignant and surprised. Pro-
  ducing* "*Palace Peeper*").
No, by the stars that shine above me,
  Degraded King!
For while these rumours, through the city
  bruited,
Remain uncontradicted, unrefuted,
The object thou of my aversion rooted,
  Repulsive thing!
    King
  Be just—the time is now at hand
    When truth may published be.
  These paragraphs were written and
    Contributed by me!
    Lady Sophy
By you? No, no!
    King
     Yes, yes, I swear, by me!
I, caught in Scaphio's ruthless toil,
  Contributed the lot!
    Lady Sophy
And *that* is why you did not boil
  The author on the spot!
    King
And *that* is why I did not boil
  The author on the spot!
    Lady Sophy
I *couldn't* think why you did not boil!
    King
But *I* know why I did not boil
  The author on the spot!
    DUET—LADY SOPHY *and* KING
    Lady Sophy
Oh, the rapture unrestrained
  Of a candid retractation!
For my sovereign has deigned
  A convincing explanation—
And the clouds that gathered o'er
  All have vanished in the distance,
And of Kings of fairy lore
  One, at least, is in existence!
    King
Oh, the skies are blue above,
  And the earth is red and rosal,
Now the lady of my love

Has accepted my proposal!
For that *asinorum pons*
    I have crossed without assistance,
And of prudish paragons
    One, at least, is in existence!

[KING *and* LADY SOPHY *dance gracefully.
While this is going on* LORD DRAMA-
LEIGH *enters unobserved with* NEKAYA
and MR. GOLDBURY *with* KALYBA. *Then
enter* ZARA *and* CAPT. FITZBATTLEAXE.
The two girls direct ZARA'S *attention to
the* KING *and* LADY SOPHY, *who are
still dancing affectionately together. At
this point the* KING *kisses* LADY SOPHY,
*which causes the Princesses to make
an exclamation. The* KING *and* LADY
SOPHY *are at first much confused at
being detected, but eventually throw
off all reserve, and the four couples
break into a wild Tarantella, and at
the end exeunt severally.*
*Enter all the male Chorus, in great excite-
ment, from various entrances, led by*
SCAPHIO, PHANTIS, *and* TARARA, *and followed by the female Chorus.*

Chorus

Upon our sea-girt land
At our enforced command
Reform has laid her hand
    Like some remorseless ogress—
And made us darkly rue
The deeds she dared to do—
And all is owing to
    Those hated Flowers of Progress!
        So down with them!
        So down with them!
Reform's a hated ogress.
        So down with them!
        So down with them!
Down with the Flowers of Progress!

Flourish. Enter KING, *his three daughters,*
LADY SOPHY, *and the Flowers of Progress.*

King

What means this most unmannerly irrup-
    tion?
Is this your gratitude for boons conferred?

Scaphio

Boons? Bah! A fico for such boons, say
    we!
These boons have brought Utopia to a
    standstill!
Our pride and boast—the Army and the
    Navy—

Have both been reconstructed and re-
    modelled
Upon so irresistible a basis
That all the neighbouring nations have dis-
    armed—
And War's impossible! Your County Coun-
    cillor
Has passed such drastic Sanitary laws
That all the doctors dwindle, starve, and
    die!
The laws, remodelled by Sir Bailey Barre,
Have quite extinguished crime and litiga-
    tion:
The lawyers starve, and all the jails are let
As model lodgings for the working-classes!
In short—
Utopia, swamped by dull Prosperity,
Demands that these detested Flowers of
    Progress
Be sent about their business, and affairs
Restored to their original complexion!

King (*to* ZARA). My daughter, this is a
very unpleasant state of things. What is
to be done?

Zara. I don't know—I don't understand
it. We must have omitted something.

King. Omitted something? Yes, that's all
very well, but——

[SIR BAILEY BARRE *whispers to* ZARA

Zara (*suddenly*). Of course! Now I remember! Why, I had forgotten the most
essential element of all!

King. And that is?——

Zara. Government by Party! Introduce
that great and glorious element—at once
the bulwark and foundation of England's
greatness—and all will be well! No political measures will endure, because one
Party will assuredly undo all that the other
Party has done; and while grouse is to be
shot, and foxes worried to death, the legislative action of the country will be at a
standstill. Then there will be sickness in
plenty, endless lawsuits, crowded jails, in-
terminable confusion in the Army and
Navy, and in short, general and unexampled prosperity!

All. Ulahlica! Ulahlica!

Phan. (*aside*). Baffled!

Sca. But an hour *will* come!

King. Your hour has come already—
away with them, and let them wait my
will! (SCAPHIO *and* PHANTIS *are led off in*
custody.) From this moment Government

by Party is adopted, with all its attendant blessings; and henceforward Utopia will no longer be a Monarchy Limited, but, what is a great deal better, a Limited Monarchy!

Zara

There's a little group of isles beyond the wave—
  So tiny, you might almost wonder where it is—
That nation is the bravest of the brave,
  And cowards are the rarest of all rarities.
The proudest nations kneel at her command;
  She terrifies all foreign-born rapscallions;
And holds the peace of Europe in her hand
  With half a score invincible battalions!
Such, at least, is the tale
Which is borne on the gale,
  From the island which dwells in the sea.
Let up hope, for her sake,
That she makes no mistake—
  That she's all she professes to be!

King

Oh, may we copy all her maxims wise,
  And imitate her virtues and her charities;
And may we, by degrees, acclimatize
  Her Parliamentary peculiarities!
By doing so, we shall, in course of time,
  Regenerate completely our entire land—
Great Britain is that monarchy sublime,
  To which some add (but others do not) Ireland.
    Such, at least, is the tale, etc.

CURTAIN

THE GRAND DUKE

OR

THE STATUTORY DUEL

DRAMATIS PERSONÆ

RUDOLPH (*Grand Duke of Pfennig Halb-pfennig*)

ERNEST DUMMKOPF (*a Theatrical Manager*)

LUDWIG (*his Leading Comedian*)

DR. TANNHÄUSER (*a Notary*)

THE PRINCE OF MONTE CARLO

VISCOUNT MENTONE

BEN HASHBAZ (*a Costumier*)

HERALD

THE PRINCESS OF MONTE CARLO (*betrothed to* RUDOLPH)

THE BARONESS VON KRAKENFELDT (*betrothed to* RUDOLPH)

JULIA JELLICOE (*an English Comédienne*)

LISA (*a Soubrette*)

OLGA
GRETCHEN
BERTHA } (*Members of Ernest Dummkopf's Company*)
ELSA
MARTHA

Chamberlains, Nobles, Actors, Actresses, etc.

Date 1750

ACT I

SCENE.—*Market-place of Speisesaal, in the Grand Duchy of Pfennig Halbpfennig. A well, with decorated ironwork, up* L.C. GRETCHEN, BERTHA, OLGA, MARTHA, *and other members of* ERNEST DUMMKOPF'S *theatrical company are discovered, seated at several small tables, enjoying a repast in honour of the nuptials of* LUDWIG, *his leading comedian, and* LISA, *his soubrette.*

Chorus

Won't it be a pretty wedding?
  Will not Lisa look delightful?
Smiles and tears in plenty shedding—
  Which in brides of course is rightful.
  One could say, if one were spiteful,

Contradiction little dreading,
  Her bouquet is simply frightful—
Still, 'twill be a pretty wedding!
Oh, it is a pretty wedding!
  Such a pretty, pretty wedding!
        Elsa
If her dress *is* badly fitting,
  Theirs the fault who made her *trousseau.*

        Bertha
If her gloves *are* always splitting,
  Cheap kid gloves, we know, will do so.
        Olga
If upon her train she stumbled,
  On one's train one's always treading.
        Gretchen
If her hair *is* rather tumbled,
  Still, 'twill be a pretty wedding!
        Chorus
Such a pretty, pretty wedding!

Chorus

Here they come, the couple plighted—
  On life's journey gaily start them.
Soon to be for aye united,
  Till divorce or death shall part them.

[LUDWIG *and* LISA *come forward*
DUET—LUDWIG *and* LISA

Ludwig

Pretty Lisa, fair and tasty,
  Tell me now, and tell me truly,
Haven't you been rather hasty?
  Haven't you been rash unduly?
Am I quite the dashing *sposo*
  That your fancy could depict you?
Perhaps you think I'm only so-so?
        (*She expresses admiration.*)
Well, I will not contradict you!

Chorus

No, he will not contradict you!

Lisa

Who am I to raise objection?
  I'm a child, untaught and homely—
When you tell me you're perfection,
  Tender, truthful, true, and comely—
That in quarrel no one's bolder,
  Though dissensions always grieve
    you—
Why, my love, you're so much older
  That, of course, I must believe you!

Chorus

Yes, of course, she must believe you!

Chorus

If he ever acts unkindly,
Shut your eyes and love him blindly—
Should he call you names uncomely,
Shut your mouth and love him dumbly—
Should he rate you, rightly—leftly—
Shut your ears and love him deafly.
Ha! ha! ha! ha! ha! ha! ha!
  Thus and thus and thus alone
  Ludwig's wife may hold her own!

[LUDWIG *and* LISA *sit at table*
Enter NOTARY TANNHÄUSER

Not. Hallo! Surely I'm not late? (*All chatter unintelligibly in reply.*)

Not. But, dear me, you're all at breakfast! Has the wedding taken place? (*All chatter unintelligibly in reply.*)

Not. My good girls, one at a time, I beg. Let me understand the situation. As solicitor to the conspiracy to dethrone the Grand Duke—a conspiracy in which the members of this company are deeply involved—I am invited to the marriage of two of its members. I present myself in due course, and I find, not only that the ceremony has taken place—which is not of the least consequence—but the wedding breakfast is half eaten—which is a consideration of the most serious importance.

[LUDWIG *and* LISA *come down*

Lud. But the ceremony has *not* taken place. We can't get a parson!

Not. Can't get a parson! Why, how's that? They're three a penny!

Lud. Oh, it's the old story—the Grand Duke!

All. Ugh!

Lud. It seems that the little imp has selected this, our wedding day, for a convocation of all the clergy in the town to settle the details of his approaching marriage with the enormously wealthy Baroness von Krakenfeldt, and there won't be a parson to be had for love or money until six o'clock this evening!

Lisa. And as we produce our magnificent classical revival of *Troilus and Cressida* to-night at seven, we have no alternative but to eat our wedding breakfast before we've earned it. So sit down, and make the best of it.

Gret. Oh, I should like to pull his Grand Ducal ears for him, that I should! He's the meanest, the cruellest, the most spiteful little ape in Christendom!

Olga. Well, we shall soon be freed from his tyranny. To-morrow the Despot is to be dethroned.

Lud. Hush, rash girl! You know not what you say.

Olga. Don't be absurd! We're all in it—we're all tiled, here.

Lud. That has nothing to do with it. Know ye not that in alluding to our conspiracy without having first given and received the secret sign, you are violating a fundamental principle of our Association?

SONG—LUDWIG

By the mystic regulation
Of our dark Association,
Ere you open conversation
  With another kindred soul,
  You must eat a sausage-roll!
      (*Producing one.*)

All

You must eat a sausage-roll!

Ludwig

If, in turn, he eats another,
That's a sign that he's a brother—
Each may fully trust the other.
    It is quaint and it is droll,
    But it's bilious on the whole.

All

Very bilious on the whole.

Ludwig

It's a greasy kind of pasty,
Which, perhaps, a judgment hasty
Might consider rather tasty:
    Once (to speak without disguise)
    It found favour in our eyes.

All

It found favour in our eyes.

Ludwig

But when you've been six months feeding
(As we have) on this exceeding
Bilious food, it's no ill-breeding
    If at these repulsive pies
    Our offended gorges rise!

All

Our offended gorges rise!

Martha. Oh, bother the secret sign. I've eaten it until I'm quite uncomfortable! I've given it six times already to-day—and (*whimpering*) I can't eat any breakfast!

Bertha. And it's so unwholesome. Why, we should be as yellow as frogs if it wasn't for the make-up!

Lud. All this is rank treason to the cause. I suffer as much as any of you. I loathe the repulsive thing—I can't contemplate it without a shudder—but I'm a conscientious conspirator, and if you won't give the sign I will. (*Eats sausage-roll with an effort.*)

Lisa. Poor martyr! He's always at it, and it's a wonder where he puts it!

Not. Well now, about *Troilus and Cressida.* What do *you* play?

Lud. (*struggling with his feelings*). If you'll be so obliging as to wait until I've got rid of this feeling of warm oil at the bottom of my throat, I'll tell you all about it. (*LISA gives him some brandy.*) Thank you, my love; it's gone. Well, the piece will be produced upon a scale of unexampled magnificence. It is confidently predicted that my appearance as King Agamemnon, in a Louis Quatorze wig, will mark an epoch in the theatrical annals of Pfennig Halbpfennig. I endeavoured to persuade Ernest Dummkopf, our manager, to lend us the classical dresses for our marriage. Think of the effect of a real Athenian wedding procession cavorting through the streets of Speisesaal; Torches burning—cymbals banging—flutes tootling—citharæ twanging—and a throng of fifty lovely Spartan virgins capering before us, all down the High Street, singing "Eloia! Eloia! Opoponax, Eloia!" It would have been tremendous!

Not. And he declined?

Lud. He did, on the prosaic ground that it might rain, and the ancient Greeks didn't carry umbrellas! If, as is confidently expected, Ernest Dummkopf is elected to succeed the dethroned one, mark my words, he will make a mess of it.

    [*Exit* LUDWIG *with* LISA.

Olga. He's sure to be elected. His entire company has promised to plump for him on the understanding that all the places about the Court are filled by members of his troupe, according to professional precedence.

ERNEST *enters in great excitement*

Bertha (*looking off*). Here comes Ernest Dummkopf. Now we shall know all about it!

All. Well—what's the news? How is the election going?

Ern. Oh, it's a certainty—a practical certainty! Two of the candidates have been arrested for debt, and the third is a baby in arms—so, if you keep your promises, and vote solid, I'm cocksure of election!

Olga. Trust to us. But you remember the conditions?

Ern. Yes—all of you shall be provided for, for life. Every man shall be ennobled—every lady shall have unlimited credit at the Court Milliner's, and all salaries shall be paid weekly in advance!

Gret. Oh, it's quite clear he knows how to rule a Grand Duchy!

Ern. Rule a Grand Duchy? Why, my good girl, for ten years past I've ruled a theatrical company! A man who can do that can rule anything!

SONG—ERNEST

Were I a king in very truth,
And had a son—a guileless youth—
    In probable succession;
To teach him patience, teach him tact,

How promptly in a fix to act,
He should adopt, in point of fact,
    A manager's profession.
To that condition he should stoop
    (Despite a too fond mother),
With eight or ten "stars" in his troupe,
    All jealous of each other!
Oh, the man who can rule a theatrical
        crew,
Each member a genius (and some of them
        two),
And manage to humour them, little and
        great,
    Can govern this tuppenny State!
                        All
Oh, the man, etc.

Both A and B rehearsal slight
They say they'll be "all right at night"
    (They've both to go to school yet);
C in each act *must* change her dress,
D *will* attempt to "square the press";
E won't play Romeo unless
    His grandmother plays Juliet;
F claims all hoydens as her rights
    (She's played them thirty seasons);
And G must show herself in tights
    For two convincing reasons—
    Two very well-shaped reasons!
Oh, the man who can drive a theatrical
        team,
With wheelers and leaders in order supreme,
Can govern and rule, with a wave of his
        fin,
    All Europe—with Ireland thrown in!
                        All
Oh, the man, etc.

                [*Exeunt all but* ERNEST.

Ern. Elected by my fellow-conspirators
to be Grand Duke of Pfennig Halbfennig
as soon as the contemptible little occupant
of the historical throne is deposed—here is
promotion indeed! Why, instead of playing
Troilus of Troy for a month, I shall play
Grand Duke of Pfennig Halbpfennig for a
lifetime! Yet, am I happy? No—far from
happy! The lovely English *comédienne*—
the beautiful Julia, whose dramatic ability
is so overwhelming that our audiences forgive even her strong English accent—that
rare and radiant being treats my respectful
advances with disdain unutterable! And
yet, who knows? She is haughty and ambitious, and it may be that the splendid
change in my fortunes may work a cor-
responding change in her feelings towards
me!

        Enter JULIA JELLICOE
Julia. Herr Dummkopf, a word with you,
if you please.
Ern. Beautiful English maiden——
Julia. No compliments, I beg. I desire to
speak with you on a purely professional
matter, so we will, if you please, dispense
with allusions to my personal appearance,
which can only tend to widen the breach
which already exists between us.
Ern. (aside). My only hope shattered!
The haughty Londoner still despises me!
(*Aloud.*) It shall be as you will.
Julia. I understand that the conspiracy
in which we are all concerned is to develop
to-morrow, and that the company is likely
to elect you to the throne on the understanding that the posts about the Court are
to be filled by members of your theatrical
troupe, according to their professional importance.
Ern. That is so.
Julia. Then all I can say is that it places
me in an extremely awkward position.
Ern. (very depressed). I don't see how it
concerns you.
Julia. Why, bless my heart, don't you
see that, as your leading lady, I am bound
under a serious penalty to play the leading
part in all your productions?
Ern. Well?
Julia. Why, of course, the leading part in
this production will be the Grand Duchess!
Ern. My wife?
Julia. That is another way of expressing
the same idea.
Ern. (aside—delighted). I scarcely dared
even to hope for this!
Julia. Of course, as your leading lady,
you'll be mean enough to hold me to the
terms of my agreement. Oh, that's so like
a man! Well, I suppose there's no help for
it—I shall have to do it!
Ern. (aside). She's mine! (*Aloud.*) But
—do you really think you would care to
play that part? (*Taking her hand.*)
Julia (withdrawing it). Care to play it?
Certainly not—but what am I to do?
Business is business, and I am bound by
the terms of my agreement.
Ern. It's for a long run, mind—a run

that may last many, many years—no un-
derstudy—and once embarked upon there's
no throwing it up.

Julia. Oh, we're used to these long runs
in England: they are the curse of the stage
—but, you see, I've no option.

Ern. You think the part of Grand Duchess will be good enough for you?

Julia. Oh, I think so. It's a very good part
in Gerolstein, and oughtn't to be a bad one
in Pfennig Halbpfennig. Why, what did
you suppose I was going to play?

Ern. (*keeping up a show of reluctance*).
But, considering your strong personal dislike to me and your persistent rejection of
my repeated offers, won't you find it difficult to throw yourself into the part with
all the impassioned enthusiasm that the
character seems to demand? Remember,
it's a strongly emotional part, involving
long and repeated scenes of rapture, tenderness, adoration, devotion—all in luxuriant excess, and all of the most demonstra-
tive description.

Julia. My good sir, throughout my career
I have made it a rule never to allow private
feelings to interfere with my professional
duties. You may be quite sure that (however distasteful the part may be) if I undertake it, I shall consider myself professionally bound to throw myself into it with
all the ardour at my command.

Ern. (*aside—with effusion*). I'm the happiest fellow alive! (*Aloud.*) Now—would
you have any objection—to—to give me
some idea—if it's only a mere sketch—as
to how you would play it? It would be
really interesting—to me—to know your
conception of—of—the part of my wife.

Julia. How would I play it? Now, let
me see—let me see. (*Considering.*) Ah, I
have it!

BALLAD—JULIA

How would I play this part—
    The Grand Duke's Bride?
All rancour in my heart
    I'd duly hide—
    I'd drive it from my recollection
And 'whelm you with a mock affection,
    Well calculated to defy detection—
That's how I'd play this part—
    The Grand Duke's Bride.
With many a winsome smile
    I'd witch and woo;
With gay and girlish guile
    I'd frenzy you—
    I'd madden you with my caressing,
    Like turtle, her first love confessing—
    That it was "mock", no mortal would be
        guessing,
With so much winsome wile
    I'd witch and woo!
Did any other maid
    With you succeed,
I'd pinch the forward jade—
    I would indeed!
    With jealous frenzy agitated
    (Which would, of course, be simulated),
        I'd make her wish she'd never been
        created—
Did any other maid
    With you succeed!
And should there come to me,
    Some summers hence,
In all the childish glee
    Of innocence,
    Fair babes, aglow with beauty vernal,
    My heart would bound with joy diurnal!
    This sweet display of sympathy maternal,
Well, that would also be
    A mere pretence!
My histrionic art
    Though you deride,
That's how I'd play that part—
    The Grand Duke's Bride!

ENSEMBLE

Ernest

Oh joy! when two glowing young hearts,
    From the rise of the curtain,
Thus throw themselves into their parts,
    Success is most certain!
If the *rôle* you're prepared to endow
    With such delicate touches,
By the heaven above us, I vow
    You shall be my Grand Duchess!

Julia

My boy, when two glowing young hearts,
    From the rise of the curtain,
Thus throw themselves into their parts,
    Success is most certain!
The *rôle* I'm prepared to endow
    With most delicate touches,
By the heaven above us, I vow
    I will be your Grand Duchess!

[*Dance.*

Enter all the Chorus with LUDWIG, NOTARY,
and LISA—*all greatly agitated*

EXCITED CHORUS

My goodness me! what shall we do? Why,
    what
    A dreadful situation!
        (*To* LUD.)
It's all your fault, you booby you—you
    lump of indiscrimination!
I'm sure I don't know where to go—it's put
    me into such a tetter—
But this at all events I know—the sooner
    we are off, the better!

Ernest

What means this *agitato?* What d'ye seek?
As your Grand Duke elect I bid you speak!

SONG—LUDWIG

Ten minutes since I met a chap
    Who bowed an easy salutation—
Thinks I, "This gentleman, mayhap,
    Belongs to our Association."
        But, on the whole,
        Uncertain yet,
        A sausage-roll
        I took and eat—
That chap replied (I don't embellish)
By eating *three* with obvious relish.
        CHORUS (*angrily*)
        Why, gracious powers,
        No chum of ours
Could eat three sausage-rolls with relish!
        Ludwig
Quite reassured, I let him know
    Our plot—each incident explaining;
That stranger chuckled much, as though
    He thought me highly entertaining.
        I told him all,
        Both bad and good;
        I bade him call—
        He said he would:
I added much—the more I muckled,
The more that chuckling chummy
        chuckled!
        All (*angrily*).
        A bat could see
        He couldn't be
    A chum of ours if he chuckled!
        Ludwig
Well, as I bowed to his applause,
    Down dropped he with hysteric bellow—
And *that* seemed right enough, because
    I *am* a devilish funny fellow.
        Then suddenly,
        As still he squealed,

        It flashed on me
        That I'd revealed
Our plot, with all details effective,
To Grand Duke Rudolph's own detective!
        All
        What folly fell,
        To go and tell
Our plot to any one's detective!

        CHORUS
        (*Attacking* LUDWIG).
        You booby dense—
        You oaf immense,
        With no pretence
        To common sense!
        A stupid muff
        Who's made of stuff
        Not worth a puff
        Of candle-snuff!

Pack up at once and off we go, unless we're
    anxious to exhibit
Our fairy forms all in a row, strung up
    upon the Castle gibbet!
[*Exeunt Chorus. Manent* LUDWIG, LISA,
    ERNEST, JULIA, *and* NOTARY.

Julia. Well, a nice mess you've got us
into! There's an end of our precious plot!
All up—pop—fizzle—bang—done for!
    Lud. Yes, but — ha! ha! — fancy my
choosing the Grand Duke's private detective, of all men, to make a confidant of!
When you come to think of it, it's really
devilish funny!
    Ern. (*angrily*). When you come to think
of it, it's extremely injudicious to admit
into a conspiracy every pudding-headed
baboon who presents himself!
    Lud. Yes—I should never do that. If I
were chairman of this gang, I should hesitate to enrol *any* baboon who couldn't produce satisfactory credentials from his last
Zoological Gardens.
    Lisa. Ludwig is far from being a baboon.
Poor boy, he could not help giving us
away—it's his trusting nature—he was deceived.
    Julia (*furiously*). His trusting nature!
(*To* LUDWIG.) Oh, I should like to talk to
you in my own language for five minutes
—only five minutes! I know some good,
strong, energetic English remarks that
would shrivel your trusting nature into
raisins—only you wouldn't understand
them!

Lud. Here we perceive one of the disadvantages of a neglected education!

Ern. (*to* JULIA). And I suppose you'll never be my Grand Duchess now!

Julia. Grand Duchess? My good friend, if you don't produce the piece how can I play the part?

Ern. True. (*To* LUDWIG). You see what you've done.

Lud. But, my dear sir, you don't seem to understand that the man ate three sausage-rolls. Keep that fact steadily before you. Three large sausage-rolls.

Julia. Bah!—Lots of people eat sausage-rolls who are not conspirators.

Lud. Then they shouldn't. It's bad form. It's not the game. When one of the Human Family proposes to eat a sausage-roll, it is his duty to ask himself, "Am I a conspirator?" And if, on examination, he finds that he is *not* a conspirator, he is bound in honour to select some other form of refreshment.

Lisa. Of course he is. One should always play the game. (*To* NOTARY, *who has been smiling placidly through this*.) What are you grinning at, you greedy old man?

Not. Nothing—don't mind me. It is always amusing to the legal mind to see a parcel of laymen bothering themselves about a matter which to a trained lawyer presents no difficulty whatever.

All. No difficulty!

Not. None whatever! The way out of it is quite simple.

All. Simple?

Not. Certainly! Now attend. In the first place, you two men fight a Statutory Duel.

Ern. A Statutory Duel?

Julia. A Stat-tat-tatutory Duel! Ach! what a crack-jaw language this German is!

Lud. Never heard of such a thing.

Not. It is true that the practice has fallen into abeyance through disuse. But all the laws of Pfennig Halbpfennig run for a hundred years, when they die a natural death, unless, in the meantime, they have been revived for another century. The Act that institutes the Statutory Duel was passed a hundred years ago, and as it has never been revived, it expires to-morrow. So you're just in time.

Julia. But what is the use of talking to us about Statutory Duels when we none of us know what a Statutory Duel is?

Not. Don't you? Then I'll explain.

SONG—NOTARY

About a century since,
　The code of the duello
　　To sudden death
　　For want of breath
Sent many a strapping fellow.
The then presiding Prince
　(Who useless bloodshed hated),
　　He passed an Act,
　　Short and compact,
Which may be briefly stated.
Unlike the complicated laws
A Parliamentary draftsman draws,
　It may be briefly stated.

All

We know that complicated laws,
Such as a legal draftsman draws,
　Cannot be briefly stated.

Notary

By this ingenious law,
　If any two shall quarrel,
　　They may not fight
　　With falchions bright
(Which seemed to him immoral);
But each a card shall draw,
　And he who draws the lowest
　　Shall (so 'twas said)
　　Be thenceforth dead—
In fact, a legal "ghoest"
(When exigence of rhyme compels,
Orthography forgoes her spells,
　And "ghost" is written "ghoest").

All (*aside*).

With what an emphasis he dwells
Upon "orthography" and "spells"!
　That kind of fun's the lowest.

Notary

When off the loser's popped
　(By pleasing legal fiction),
　　And friend and foe
　　Have wept their woe
In counterfeit affliction,
The winner must adopt
　The loser's poor relations—
　　Discharge his debts,
　　Pay all his bets,
And take his obligations.
In short, to briefly sum the case,
The winner takes the loser's place,
　With all its obligations.

All

How neatly lawyers state a case!
The winner takes the loser's place,
   With all its obligations!
  Lud. I see. The man who draws the lowest card——
  Not. Dies, *ipso facto,* a social death. He loses all his civil rights—his identity disappears—the Revising Barrister expunges his name from the list of voters, and the winner takes his place, whatever it may be, discharges all his functions, and adopts all his responsibilities.
  Ern. This is all very well, as far as it goes, but it only protects one of us. What's to become of the survivor?
  Lud. Yes, that's an interesting point, because *I* might be the survivor.
  Not. The survivor goes at once to the Grand Duke, and, in a burst of remorse, denounces the dead man as the moving spirit of the plot. He is accepted as King's evidence, and, as a matter of course, receives a free pardon. To-morrow, when the law expires, the dead man will, *ipso facto,* come to life again—the Revising Barrister will restore his name to the list of voters, and he will resume all his obligations as though nothing unusual had happened.
  Julia. When he will be at once arrested, tried, and executed on the evidence of the informer! Candidly, my friend, I don't think much of your plot!
  Not. Dear, dear, dear, the ignorance of the laity! My good young lady, it is a beautiful maxim of our glorious Constitution that a man can only die once. Death expunges crime, and when he comes to life again, it will be with a clean slate.
  Ern. It's really very ingenious.
  Lud. (*to* NOTARY). My dear sir, we owe you our lives!
  Lisa (*aside to* LUDWIG). May I kiss him?
  Lud. Certainly not: you're a big girl now. (*To* ERNEST). Well, miscreant, are you prepared to meet me on the field of honour?
  Ern. At once. By jove, what a couple of fire-eaters we are!
  Lisa. Ludwig doesn't know what fear is.
  Lud. Oh, I don't mind this sort of duel!
  Ern. It's not like a duel with swords. I hate a duel with swords. It's not the blade I mind—it's the blood.

  Lud. And I hate a duel with pistols. It's not the ball I mind—it's the bang.
  Not. Altogether it's a great improvement on the old method of giving satisfaction.

QUINTET
LUDWIG, LISA, NOTARY, ERNEST, JULIA

Strange the views some people hold!
  Two young fellows quarrel—
Then they fight, for both are bold—
  Rage of both is uncontrolled—
Both are stretched out, stark and cold!
  Prithee, where's the moral?
    Ding dong! Ding dong!
There's an end to further action,
And this barbarous transaction
Is described as "satisfaction"!
  Ha! ha! ha! ha! satisfaction!
    Ding dong! Ding dong!
Each is laid in churchyard mould—
Strange the views some people hold!
Better than the method old,
  Which was coarse and cruel,
Is the plan that we've extolled.
Sing thy virtues manifold
(Better than refinèd gold),
  Statutory Duel!
    Sing song! Sing song!
Sword or pistol neither uses—
Playing card he lightly chooses,
And the loser simply loses!
  Ha! ha! ha! ha! simply loses.
    Sing song! Sing song!
Some prefer the churchyard mould!
Strange the views some people hold!
  Notary (*offering a card to* ERNEST).
Now take a card and gaily sing
How little you care for Fortune's rubs—
    Ernest (*drawing a card*).
  Hurrah, hurrah!—I've drawn a King!
      All
    He's drawn a King!
    He's drawn a King!
Sing Hearts and Diamonds, Spades and Clubs!
    All (*dancing*).
    He's drawn a King!
    How strange a thing!
An excellent card—his chance it aids—
Sing Hearts and Diamonds, Spades and Clubs—
Sing Diamonds, Hearts and Clubs and Spades!

    Notary (*to* LUDWIG).
Now take a card with heart of grace—

(Whatever our fate, let's play our parts).
    Ludwig (drawing a card).
Hurrah, hurrah!—I've drawn an Ace!
          All
    He's drawn an Ace!
    He's drawn an Ace!
Sing Clubs and Diamonds, Spades and
    Hearts!
        All (dancing).
    He's drawn an Ace!
    Observe his face—
Such very good fortune falls to few—
Sing Clubs and Diamonds, Spades and
    Hearts—
Sing Clubs, Spades, Hearts and Diamonds,
    too!
        Notary
That both these maids may keep their
    troth,
    And never misfortune them befall,
I'll hold 'em as trustee for both—
          All
    He'll hold 'em both!
    He'll hold 'em both!
Sing Hearts, Clubs, Diamonds, Spades and
    all!
        All (dancing).
    By joint decree
As $\left\{\begin{array}{l}\text{our}\\\text{your}\end{array}\right\}$ trustee
This Notary $\left\{\begin{array}{l}\text{we}\\\text{you}\end{array}\right\}$ will now instal—
In custody let him keep $\left\{\begin{array}{l}\text{their}\\\text{our}\end{array}\right\}$ hearts,
Sing Hearts, Clubs, Diamonds, Spades and
    all!
[Dance and exeunt LUDWIG, ERNEST, *and*
    NOTARY *with the two Girls*
March. Enter the seven Chamberlains of the
    GRAND DUKE RUDOLPH
    CHORUS OF CHAMBERLAINS
The good Grand Duke of Pfennig Halb-
    pfennig,
Though, in his own opinion, very, very big,
In point of fact he's nothing but a miser-
    able prig
Is the good Grand Duke of Pfennig Halb-
    pfennig!
Though quite contemptible, as every one
    agrees,
We must dissemble if we want our bread
    and cheese,
So hail him in a chorus, with enthusiasm
    big,

The good Grand Duke of Pfennig Halb-
    pfennig!
Enter the GRAND DUKE RUDOLPH. *He is
    meanly and miserably dressed in old
    and patched clothes, but blazes with
    a profusion of orders and decorations.
    He is very weak and ill, from low liv-
    ing.*
        SONG—RUDOLPH
A pattern to professors of monarchial
    autonomy,
I don't indulge in levity or compromising
    bonhomie,
But dignified formality, consistent with
    economy,
    Above all other virtues I particularly
        prize.
I never join in merriment—I don't see joke
    or jape any—
I never tolerate familiarity in shape any—
This, joined with an extravagant respect
    for tuppence-ha'penny,
    A keynote to my character sufficiently
        supplies.
(Speaking.) Observe. *(To Chamberlains.)*
My snuff-box!
*[The snuff-box is passed with much cere-
    mony from the Junior Chamberlain,
    through all the others, until it is pre-
    sented by the Senior Chamberlain to
    RUDOLPH, who uses it.*
    That incident a keynote to my character
        supplies.
        Rudolph
I weigh out tea and sugar with precision
    mathematical—
Instead of beer, a penny each—my orders
    are emphatical—
(Extravagance unpardonable, any more
    than that I call),
    But, on the other hand, my Ducal dig-
    nity to keep—
All Courtly ceremonial—to put it compre-
    hensively—
I rigidly insist upon (but not, I hope, of-
    fensively)
Whenever ceremonial can be practised in-
    expensively—
    And, when you come to think of it, it's
    really very cheap!
(Speaking.) Observe. *(To Chamberlains.)*
My handkerchief!
*[Handkerchief is handed by Junior Cham-
    berlain to the next in order, and so on*

until it reaches RUDOLPH, *who is much inconvenienced by the delay.*

It's sometimes inconvenient, but it's always very cheap!

Rud. My Lord Chamberlain, as you are aware, my marriage with the wealthy Baroness von Krakenfeldt will take place to-morrow, and you will be good enough to see that the rejoicings are on a scale of unusual liberality. Pass that on. (*Chamberlain whispers to Vice-Chamberlain, who whispers to the next, and so on.*) The sports will begin with a Wedding Breakfast Bee. The leading pastry-cooks of the town will be invited to compete, and the winner will not only enjoy the satisfaction of seeing his breakfast devoured by the Grand Ducal pair, but he will also be entitled to have the Arms of Pfennig Halbpfennig tattoo'd between his shoulderblades. The Vice-Chamberlain will see to this. All the public fountains of Speisesaal will run with Gingerbierheim and Currantweinmilch at the public expense. The Assistant Vice-Chamberlain will see to this. At night, everybody will illuminate; and as I have no desire to tax the public funds unduly, this will be done at the inhabitants' private expense. The Deputy Assistant Vice-Chamberlain will see to this. All my Grand Ducal subjects will wear new clothes, and the Sub-Deputy Assistant Vice-Chamberlain will collect the usual commission on all sales. Wedding presents (which, on this occasion, should be on a scale of extraordinary magnificence) will be received at the Palace at any hour of the twenty-four, and the Temporary Sub-Deputy Assistant Vice-Chamberlain will sit up all night for this purpose. The entire population will be commanded to enjoy themselves, and with this view the Acting Temporary Sub-Deputy Assistant Vice-Chamberlain will sing comic songs in the Market-place from noon to nightfall. Finally, we have composed a Wedding Anthem, with which the entire population are required to provide themselves. It can be obtained from our Grand Ducal publishers at the usual discount price, and all the Chamberlains will be expected to push the sale. (*Chamberlains bow and exeunt.*) I don't feel at all comfortable. I hope I'm not doing a foolish thing in getting married. After all, it's

a poor heart that never rejoices, and this wedding of mine is the first little treat I've allowed myself since my christening. Besides, Caroline's income is very considerable, and as her ideas of economy are quite on a par with mine, it ought to turn out well. Bless her tough old heart, she's a mean little darling! Oh, here she is, punctual to her appointment!

Enter BARONESS VON KRAKENFELDT

Bar. Rudolph! Why, what's the matter?

Rud. Why, I'm not quite myself, my pet. I'm a little worried and upset. I want a tonic. It's the low diet, I think. I am afraid, after all, I shall have to take the bull by the horns and have an egg with my breakfast.

Bar. I shouldn't do anything rash, dear. Begin with a jujube. (*Gives him one.*)

Rud. (*about to eat it, but changes his mind*). I'll keep it for supper. (*He sits by her and tries to put his arm round her waist.*)

Bar. Rudolph, don't! What in the world are you thinking of?

Rud. I was thinking of embracing you, my sugar-plum. Just as a little cheap treat.

Bar. What, here? In public? Really, you appear to have no sense of delicacy.

Rud. No sense of delicacy, Bon-bon!

Bar. No. I can't make you out. When you courted me, all your courting was done publicly in the Market-place. When you proposed to me, you proposed in the Market-place. And now that we're engaged you seem to desire that our first *tête-à-tête* shall occur in the Market-place! Surely you've a room in your Palace—with blinds—that would do?

Rud. But, my own, I can't help myself. I'm bound by my own decree.

Bar. Your own decree?

Rud. Yes. You see, all the houses that give on the Market-place belong to me, but the drains (which date back to the reign of Charlemagne) want attending to, and the houses wouldn't let—so, with a view to increasing the value of the property, I decreed that all love-episodes between affectionate couples should take place, in public, on this spot, every Monday, Wednesday, and Friday, when the band doesn't play.

Bar. Bless me, what a happy idea! So moral too! And have you found it answer?

Rud. Answer? The rents have gone up fifty per cent, and the sale of opera-glasses (which is a Grand Ducal monopoly) has received an extraordinary stimulus! So, under the circumstances, *would* you allow me to put my arm round your waist? As a source of income! Just once!

Bar. But it's so very embarrassing. Think of the opera-glasses!

Rud. My good girl, that's just what I *am* thinking of. Hang it all, we must give them *something* for their money! What's that?

Bar. (unfolding paper, which contains a large letter, which she hands to him). It's a letter which your detective asked me to hand to you. I wrapped it up in yesterday's paper to keep it clean.

Rud. Oh, it's only his report! That'll keep. But, I say, you've never been and bought a newspaper?

Bar. My dear Rudolph, do you think I'm mad? It came wrapped round my breakfast.

Rud. (relieved). I thought you were not the sort of girl to go and buy a newspaper! Well, as we've got it, we may as well read it. What does it say?

Bar. Why—dear me—here's your biography! "Our Detested Despot!"

Rud. Yes—I fancy that refers to me.

Bar. And it says—Oh, it can't be!

Rud. What can't be?

Bar. Why, it says that although you're going to marry me to-morrow, you were betrothed in infancy to the Princess of Monte Carlo!

Rud. Oh yes—that's quite right. Didn't I mention it?

Bar. Mention it! You never said a word about it!

Rud. Well, it doesn't matter, because, you see, it's practically off.

Bar. Practically off?

Rud. Yes. By the terms of the contract the betrothal is void unless the Princess marries before she is of age. Now, her father, the Prince, is stony-broke, and hasn't left his house for years for fear of arrest. Over and over again he has implored me to come to him to be married—but in vain. Over and over again he has implored me to advance him the money to enable the Princess to come to me—but in vain. I am very young, but not as young as

that; and as the Princess comes of age at two to-morrow, why at two to-morrow I'm a free man, so I appointed that hour for our wedding, as I shall like to have as much marriage as I can get for my money.

Bar. I see. Of course, if the married state is a happy state, it's a pity to waste any of it.

Rud. Why, every hour we delayed I should lose a lot of you and you'd lose a lot of me!

Bar. My thoughtful darling! Oh, Rudolph, we ought to be very happy!

Rud. If I'm not, it will be my first bad investment. Still, there *is* such a thing as a slump even in Matrimonials.

Bar. I often picture us in the long, cold, dark December evenings, sitting close to each other and singing impassioned duets to keep us warm, and thinking of all the lovely things we could afford to buy if we chose, and, at the same time, planning out our lives in a spirit of the most rigid and exacting economy!

Rud. It's a most beautiful and touching picture of connubial bliss in its highest and most rarefied development!

DUET—BARONESS *and* RUDOLPH

Baroness

As o'er our penny roll we sing,
   It is not reprehensive,
To think what joys our wealth would bring
Were we disposed to do the thing
   Upon a scale extensive.
There's rich mock-turtle—thick and clear—
   Rudolph (confidentially).
Perhaps we'll have it once a year!
   Baroness (delighted).
You *are* an open-handed dear!
   Rudolph
Though, mind you, it's expensive.
   Baroness
No doubt it *is* expensive.

   Both
How fleeting are the glutton's joys!
With fish and fowl he lightly toys,
   Rudolph
And pays for such expensive tricks
Sometimes as much as two-and-six!
   Baroness
As two-and-six?
   Rudolph
As two-and-six.

Both
Sometimes as much as two-and-six!
Baroness
It gives him no advantage, mind—
For you and he have only dined,
And you remain when once it's down
A better man by half-a-crown.
Rudolph
By half-a-crown?
Baroness
By half-a-crown.
Both
Yes, two-and-six is half-a-crown.
   Then let us be modestly merry,
   And rejoice with a derry down derry.
      For to laugh and to sing
      No extravagance bring—
   It's a joy economical, very!
Baroness
Although as you're of course aware
(I never tried to hide it)
I moisten my insipid fare
With water—which I can't abear—
Rudolph
Nor I—I can't abide it.
Baroness
This pleasing fact our souls will cheer,
With fifty thousand pounds a year
We *could* indulge in table beer!
Rudolph
Get out!
Baroness
We could—I've tried it!
Rudolph
Yes, yes, of course you've tried it!
Both
Oh, he who has an income clear
Of fifty thousand pounds a year—
Baroness
Can purchase all his fancy loves
Conspicuous hats—
Rudolph
Two-shilling gloves—
Baroness (doubtfully).
Two-shelling gloves?
Rudolph (positively).
Two-shilling gloves—
Both
Yes, think of that, two-shilling gloves!
Baroness
Cheap shoes and ties of gaudy hue,
And Waterbury watches, too—
And think that he could buy the lot
Were he a donkey—

Rudolph
Which he's *not!*
Baroness
Oh, no, he's *not!*
Rudolph
Oh, no, he's *not!*
Both (dancing).
That kind of donkey he is *not!*
   Then let us be modestly merry,
   And rejoice with a derry down derry.
      For to laugh and to sing
      Is a rational thing—
   It's a joy economical, very!
                    [*Exit* BARONESS
Rud. Oh, now for my detective's report.
(*Opens letter.*) What's this! Another con-
spiracy! A conspiracy to depose *me!* And
my private detective was so convulsed with
laughter at the notion of a conspirator
selecting him for a confidant that he was
physically unable to arrest the malefactor!
Why, it'll come off! This comes of engag-
ing a detective with a keen sense of the
ridiculous! For the future I'll employ none
but Scotchmen. And the plot is to explode to-morrow! My wedding day! Oh,
Caroline, Caroline! (*Weeps.*) This is perfectly frightful! What's to be done? I don't
know! I ought to keep cool and think, but
you *can't* think when your veins are full
of hot soda-water, and your brain's fizzing
like a firework, and all your faculties are
jumbled in a perfect whirlpool of tumbli-
cation! And I'm going to be ill! I know I
am! I've been living too low, and I'm going to be very ill indeed!

SONG—RUDOLPH

When you find you're a broken-down crit-
      ter,
Who is all of a trimmle and twitter,
With your palate unpleasantly bitter,
   As if you'd just eaten a pill—
When your legs are as thin as dividers,
And you're plagued with unruly insiders,
And your spine is all creepy with spiders,
   And you're highly gamboge in the gill—
When you've got a beehive in your head,
   And a sewing machine in each ear,
And you feel that you've eaten your bed,
   And you've got a bad headache *down
      here*—
      When such facts are about,
      And these symptoms you find
      In your body or crown—

Well, you'd better look out,
    You may make up your mind
    You had better lie down!
When your lips are all smeary—like tallow,
And your tongue is decidedly yallow,
With a pint of warm oil in your swallow,
    And a pound of tin-tacks in your chest—
When you're down in the mouth with the
        vapours,
And all over your Morris wall-papers,
    Black-beetles are cutting their capers,
    And crawly things never at rest—
When you doubt if your head is your own,
    And you jump when an open door
        slams—
Then you've got to a state which is known
    To the medical world as "jim-jams".
    If such symptoms you find
      In your body or head,
        They're not easy to quell—
    You may make up your mind
    You are better in bed,
      For you're not at all well!
[*Sinks exhausted and weeping at foot of
well.*

Enter LUDWIG

Lud. Now for my confession and full
pardon. They told me the Grand Duke was
dancing duets in the Market-place, but I
don't see him. (*Sees* RUDOLPH.) Hallo!
Who's this? (*Aside.*) Why, it *is* the Grand
Duke!

Rud. (*sobbing*). Who are you, sir, who
presume to address me in person? If you've
anything to communicate, you must fling
yourself at the feet of my Acting Temporary Sub-Deputy Assistant Vice-Chamberlain, who will fling himself at the feet of
his immediate superior, and so on, with suc-
cessive foot-flingings through the various
grades—your communication will, in course
of time, come to my august knowledge.

Lud. But when I inform your Highness
that in me you see the most unhappy, the
most unfortunate, the most completely miserable man in your whole dominion——

Rud. (*still sobbing*). *You* the most miserable man in my whole dominion? How
can you have the face to stand there and
say such a thing? Why, look at me! Look
at me! (*Bursts into tears.*)

Lud. Well, I wouldn't be a cry-baby.

Rud. A cry-baby? If you had just been
told that you were going to be deposed to-

morrow, and perhaps blown up with dynamite for all I know, wouldn't *you* be a
cry-baby? I do declare if I could only hit
upon some cheap and painless method of
putting an end to an existence which has
become insupportable, I would unhesitatingly adopt it!

Lud. You would? (*Aside.*) I see a magnificent way out of this! By Jupiter, I'll
try it! (*Aloud.*) Are you, by any chance, in
earnest?

Rud. In earnest? Why, look at me!

Lud. If you are really in earnest—if you
really desire to escape scot-free from this
impending—this unspeakably horrible catastrophe—without trouble, danger, pain, or
expense—why not resort to a Statutory
Duel?

Rud. A Statutory Duel?

Lud. Yes. The Act is still in force, but it
will expire to-morrow afternoon. You fight
—you lose—you are dead for a day. To-
morrow, when the Act expires, you will
come to life again and resume your Grand
Duchy as though nothing had happened. In
the meantime, the explosion will have taken
place and the survivor will have had to
bear the brunt of it.

Rud. Yes, that's all very well, but who'll
be fool enough to *be* the survivor?

Lud. (*kneeling*). Actuated by an overwhelming sense of attachment to your
Grand Ducal person, I unhesitatingly offer
myself as the victim of your subjects' fury.

Rud. You do? Well, really that's very
handsome. I daresay being blown up is not
nearly as unpleasant as one would think.

Lud. Oh, yes it is. It mixes one up,
awfully!

Rud. But suppose I were to lose?

Lud. Oh, that's easily arranged. (*Producing cards.*) I'll put an Ace up my sleeve—
you'll put a King up yours. When the drawing takes place, I shall seem to draw the
higher card and you the lower. And there
you are!

Rud. Oh, but that's cheating.

Lud. So it is. I never thought of that.
(*Going.*)

Rud. (*hastily*). Not that I mind. But I
say—you won't take an unfair advantage
of your day of office? You won't go tipping
people, or squandering my little savings in
fireworks, or any nonsense of that sort?

_ud._ I am hurt—really hurt—by the
estion.

_ud._ You—you wouldn't like to put
n a deposit, perhaps?

_ud._ No. I don't think I should like to
down a deposit.

_ud._ Or give a guarantee?

_ud._ A guarantee would be equally open
bjection.

_ud._ It would be more regular. Very
, I suppose you must have your own

_ud._ Good. I say—we must have a devil
quarrel!

_ud._ Oh, a devil of a quarrel!

_ud._ Just to give colour to the thing.
I give you a sound thrashing before
he people? Say the word—it's no trou-

_ud._ No, I think not, though it would
ery convincing, and it's extremely good
thoughtful of you to suggest it. Still,
vil of a quarrel!

_ud._ Oh, a devil of a quarrel!

_ud._ No half measures. Big words—
g language—rude remarks. Oh, a devil
quarrel!

_ud._ Now the question is, how shall we
mon the people?

_ud._ Oh, there's no difficulty about that.
s your heart, they've been staring at us
ugh those windows for the last half-
!

FINALE

Rudolph

e hither, all you people—
hen you hear the fearful news,
the pretty women weep'll,
en will shiver in their shoes.

Ludwig

they'll all cry "Lord, defend us!"
en they learn the fact tremendous
hat to give this man his gruel
a Statutory Duel—

Both

nis plebeian man of shoddy—
his contemptible nobody—
Your Grand Duke does not refuse!

*ring this, Chorus of men and women
have entered, all trembling with ap-
prehension under the impression that
they are to be arrested for their complicity in the conspiracy.*

Chorus

With faltering feet,
    And our muscles in a quiver,
Our fate we meet
    With our feelings all unstrung!
If our plot complete
    He has managed to diskiver,
There is no retreat—
    We shall certainly be hung!

Rudolph (*aside to* LUDWIG).

Now *you* begin and pitch it strong—walk
    into me abusively—

Ludwig (*aside to* RUDOLPH).

I've several epithets that I've reserved for
    you exclusively.
A choice selection I have here when you are
    ready *to* begin.

Rudolph

Now *you* begin——

Ludwig

No, *you* begin——

Rudolph

No, *you* begin——

Ludwig

No, *you* begin!

Chorus (*trembling*).

Has it happed as we expected?
Is our little plot detected?

DUET—RUDOLPH *and* LUDWIG

Rudolph (*furiously*).

Big bombs, small bombs, great guns and
    little ones!
Put him in a pillory!
Rack him with artillery!

Ludwig (*furiously*).

Long swords, short swords, tough swords
    and brittle ones!
Fright him into fits!
Blow him into bits!

Rudolph

You muff, sir!

Ludwig

You lout, sir!

Rudolph

Enough, sir!

Ludwig

Get out, sir! (*Pushes him.*)

Rudolph

A hit, sir?

Ludwig

Take that, sir! (*Slaps him.*)

Rudolph

It's tit, sir,

Ludwig

For tat, sir!

Chorus (appalled).

When two doughty heroes thunder,
All the world is lost in wonder;
  When such men their temper lose,
  Awful are the words they use!

Ludwig

Tall snobs, small snobs, rich snobs and
  needy ones!

Rudolph (jostling him).

Whom are you alluding to?

Ludwig (jostling him).

Where are you intruding to?

Rudolph

Fat snobs, thin snobs, swell snobs and
  seedy ones!

Ludwig

I rather think you err.
To whom do you refer?

Rudolph

To you, sir!

Ludwig

To me, sir?

Rudolph

I do, sir!

Ludwig

We'll see, sir!

Rudolph

I jeer, sir!
    (*Makes a face at* LUDWIG)
Grimace, sir!

Ludwig

Look here, sir——
    (*Makes a face at* RUDOLPH).
A face, sir!

Chorus (appalled).

When two heroes, once pacific,
Quarrel, the effect's terrific!
  What a horrible grimace!
  What a paralysing face!

All

Big bombs, small bombs, etc.

Ludwig and Rudolph (recit.).

He has insulted me, and, in a breath,
This day we fight a duel to the death!

Notary (checking them)

You mean, of course, by duel (*verbum
  sat.*),
A Statutory Duel.

All

Why, what's that?

Notary

According to established legal uses,

A card apiece each bold disput
  chooses—
Dead as a doornail is the dog who los
The winner steps into the dead m
  shoeses!

All

The winner steps into the dead m
  shoeses!

Rudolph and Ludwig

Agreed! Agreed!

Rudolph

Come, come—the pack!

Ludwig (producing one).

Behold it here!

Rudolph

I'm on the rack!

Ludwig

I quake with fear!
    (NOTARY *offers card to* LUDWIG.)

Ludwig

First draw to you!

Rudolph

If that's the case,
Behold the King! (*Drawing card from
  sleeve.*)

Ludwig (same business).

Behold the Ace!

Chorus

Hurrah, hurrah! Our Ludwig's won.
And wicked Rudolph's course is run—
So Ludwig will as Grand Duke reign
Till Rudolph comes to life again—

Rudolph

Which will occur to-morrow!
I come to life to-morrow!

Gretchen (with mocking curtsey).

My Lord Grand Duke, farewell!
  A pleasant journey, very,
To your convenient cell
  In yonder cemetery!

Lisa (curtseying).

Though malcontents abuse you,
We're much distressed to lose you!
You were, when you were living,
So liberal, so forgiving!

Bertha

So merciful, so gentle!
So highly ornamental!

Olga

And now that you've departed,
You leave us broken-hearted!

All (pretending to weep).

Yes, truly, truly, truly, truly—
  Truly broken-hearted!

ha! ha! ha! ha! ha! ha! (*Mocking him.*)
Rudolph (*furious*).
Rapscallions, in penitential fires,
  You'll rue the ribaldry that from you
    falls
To-morrow afternoon the law expires.
And then—look out for squalls!
  [*Exit* RUDOLPH, *amid general ridicule.*

Chorus
Give thanks, give thanks to wayward fate—
  By mystic fortune's sway,
Our Ludwig guides the helm of State
  For one delightful day!

  (*To* LUDWIG.)
We hail you, sir!
  We greet you, sir!
Regale you, sir!
  We treat you, sir!
    Our ruler be
    By fate's decree
  For one delightful day!

Notary
You've done it neatly! Pity that your
    powers
Are limited to four-and-twenty hours!

Ludwig
No matter, though the time will quickly
    run,
In hours twenty-four much may be done!

SONG—LUDWIG
Oh, a Monarch who boasts intellectual
    graces
  Can do, if he likes, a good deal in a
    day—
He can put all his friends in conspicuous
    places,
  With plenty to eat and with nothing to
    pay!
You'll tell me, no doubt, with unpleasant
    grimaces,
  To-morrow, deprived of your ribbons and
    laces,
You'll get your dismissal—with very long
    faces—
  But wait! on that topic I've something
    to say!
(*Dancing*). I've something to say—I've
    something to say—I've something to
    say!
Oh, our rule shall be merry—I'm not an
    ascetic—
  And while the sun shines we will get up
    our hay—

By a pushing young Monarch, of turn
    energetic,
  A very great deal may be done in a day!

Chorus
Oh, his rule will be merry, etc.
(*During this,* LUDWIG *whispers to* NOTARY,
    who writes.)
For instance, this measure (his ancestor
    drew it),
        (*alluding to* NOTARY)
  This law against duels—to-morrow will
    die—
The Duke will revive, and you'll certainly
    rue it—
  He'll give you "what for" and he'll let
    you know why!
But in twenty-four hours there's time to
    renew it—
With a century's life I've the right to imbue
    it—
It's easy to do—and, by Jingo, I'll do it!
(*Signing paper, which* NOTARY *presents.*)
  It's done! Till I perish your Monarch
    am I!
Your Monarch am I—your Monarch am I
    —your Monarch am I!
    Though I do not pretend to be very
      prophetic,
      I fancy I know what you're going to
        say—
    By a pushing young Monarch, of turn
      energetic,
      A very great deal may be done in a
        day!
    All (*astonished*).
    Oh, it's simply uncanny, his power
      prophetic—
      It's perfectly right—we *were* going
        to say,
      By a pushing, etc.
    Enter JULIA, *at back*
    Ludwig (*recit.*)
This very afternoon—at two (about)—
The Court appointments will be given out.
To each and all (for that was the condi-
    tion)
According to professional position!

All
Hurrah!
  Julia (*coming forward*).
According to professional position?

Ludwig
According to professional position!

Julia

Then, horror!

All

Why, what's the matter? What's the
  matter? What's the matter?

SONG—JULIA. (LISA *clinging to her*)

Ah, pity me, my comrades true,
Who love, as well I know you do,
  This gentle child,
    To me so fondly dear!

All

  Why, what's the matter?

Julia

Our sister love so true and deep
From many an eye unused to weep
  Hath oft beguiled
    The coy reluctant tear!

All

  Why, what's the matter?

Julia

Each sympathetic heart 'twill bruise
When you have heard the frightful news
  (O will it not?)
    That I must now impart!

All

Why, what's the matter?

Julia

Her love for him is all in all!
Ah, cursed fate! that it should fall
  Unto *my* lot
    To break my darling's heart!

All

  Why, what's the matter?

Ludwig

What means our Julia by those fateful
  looks?
Please do not keep us all on tenter-hooks—
  Now, what's the matter?

Julia

  Our duty, if we're wise,
  We never shun.
This Spartan rule applies
  To every one.
In theatres, as in life,
  Each has her line—
This part—the Grand Duke's wife
  (Oh agony!) is mine!
A maxim new I do not start—
The canons of dramatic art
Decree that this repulsive part
  (The Grand Duke's wife)
    Is mine!

All

Oh, *that's* the matter!

Lisa (*appalled, to* LUDWIG).
  Can that be so?

Ludwig

I do not know—
But time will show
If that be so.

Chorus

Can that be so? etc.

Lisa (*recit.*).
Be merciful!

DUET—LISA *and* JULIA

Lisa

Oh, listen to me, dear—
  I love him only, darling!
    Remember, oh, my pet,
    On him my heart is set!
This kindness do me, dear—
  Nor leave me lonely, darling!
    Be merciful, my pet,
    Our love do not forget!

Julia

Now don't be foolish, dear—
  You couldn't play it, darling!
    It's "leading business," pet.
    And you're but a soubrette.
So don't be mulish, dear—
  Although I say it, darling,
    It's not your line, my pet—
    I play that part, you bet!
      I play that part—
      I play that part, you bet!
  [LISA *overwhelmed with grief.*

Notary

The lady's right. Though Julia's engage-
  ment
  Was for the stage meant—
It certainly frees Ludwig from his
  Connubial promise.
Though marriage contracts—or whate'er
  you call 'em—
  Are very solemn,
Dramatic contracts (which you all adore
  so)
  Are even more so!

All

  That's very true!
Though marriage contracts, etc.

SONG—LISA

  The die is cast,
    My hope has perished!
      Farewell, O Past,
      Too bright to last,
    Yet fondly cherished!
  My light has fled,

My hope is dead,
Its doom is spoken—
My day is night,
My wrong is right
In all men's sight—
My heart is broken!

[*Exit weeping.*
Ludwig (recit.).
Poor child, where will she go? What will
she do?

Julia
That isn't in your part, you know.
Ludwig (sighing).
Quite true!
(*With an effort.*)
Depressing topics we'll not touch upon—
Let us begin as we are going on!
For this will be a jolly Court, for little
and for big!

All
Sing hey, the jolly jinks of Pfennig
Halbpfennig!
Ludwig
From morn to night our lives shall be as
merry as a grig!

All
Sing hey, the jolly jinks of Pfennig
Halbpfennig!
Ludwig
All state and ceremony we'll eternally
abolish—
We don't mean to insist upon unnecessary
polish—
And, on the whole, I rather think you'll
find our rule tollolish!

All
Sing hey, the jolly jinks of Pfennig
Halbpfennig!

Julia
But stay—your new-made Court
Without a courtly coat is—
We shall require
Some Court attire,
And at a moment's notice.
In clothes of common sort
Your courtiers must not grovel—
Your new *noblesse*
Must have a dress
Original and novel!

Ludwig
Old Athens we'll exhume!
The necessary dresses,
Correct and true
And all brand-new,

The company possesses:
Henceforth our Court costume
Shall live in song and story,
For we'll upraise
The dead old days
Of Athens in her glory!

All
Yes, let's upraise
The dead old days
Of Athens in her glory!

All
Agreed! Agreed!
For this will be a jolly Court for little and
for big! etc.

[*They carry* LUDWIG *round stage and deposit him on the ironwork of well.*
JULIA *stands by him, and the rest
group round them.*

END OF ACT I

ACT II
(THE NEXT MORNING)

SCENE.—*Entrance Hall of the Grand Ducal
Palace.*

*Enter a procession of the members of the
theatrical company (now dressed in
the costumes of* Troilus and Cressida).
*carrying garlands, playing on pipes,
citharae, and cymbals, and heralding
the return of* LUDWIG *and* JULIA *from
the marriage ceremony, which has just
taken place.*

Chorus
As before you we defile,
Eloia! Eloia!
Pray you, gentles, do not smile
If we shout, in classic style,
Eloia!
Ludwig and his Julia true
Wedded are each other to—
So we sing, till all is blue,
Eloia! Eloia!
Opoponax Eloia!
Wreaths of bay and ivy twine,
Eloia! Eloia!
Fill the bowl with Lesbian wine,
And to revelry incline—
Eloia!
For as gaily we pass on
Probably we shall, anon,
Sing a Diergeticon—
Eloia! Eloia!
Opoponax! Eloia!

RECIT—LUDWIG

Your loyalty our Ducal heartstrings
   touches:
Allow me to present your new Grand
   Duchess.
Should she offend, you'll graciously ex-
   cuse her—
And kindly recollect *I* didn't choose her!

SONG—LUDWIG

At the outset I may mention it's my
   sovereign intention
To revive the classic memories of Athens
   at its best,
For the company possesses all the necessary
   dresses
And a course of quiet cramming will
   supply us with the rest.
We've a choir hyporchematic (that is,
   ballet-operatic)
Who respond to the *choreutae* of that
   cultivated age,
And our clever chorus-master, all but cap-
   tious criticaster
Would accept as the *choregus* of the
   early Attic stage.
This return to classic ages is considered in
   their wages,
   Which are always calculated by the day
      or by the week—
And I'll pay 'em (if they'll back me) all
   in *oboloi* and *drachmae*,
   Which they'll get (if they prefer it) at
      the Kalends that are Greek!
      (*Confidentially to audience.*)
   At this juncture I may mention
   That this erudition sham
   Is but classical pretension,
      The result of steady "cram.":
   Periphrastic methods spurning,
   To this audience discerning
   I admit this show of learning
      Is the fruit of steady "cram."!

Chorus

Periphrastic methods, etc.

In the period Socratic every dining-room
   was Attic
   (Which suggests an architecture of a
      topsy-turvy kind),
There they'd satisfy their thirst on a
   recherché cold ἄριστον
   Which is what they called their lunch—
      and so may you, if you're inclined.
As they gradually got on, they'd τρέπεσθαι
   πρὸς τὸν πότον

(Which is Attic for a steady and a con-
   scientious drink).
But they mixed their wine with water—
   which I'm sure they didn't oughter—
And we modern Saxons know a trick
   worth two of that, I think!
Then came rather risky dances (under cer-
   tain circumstances)
   Which would shock that worthy gentle-
      man, the Licenser of Plays.
Corybantian mani*ac* kick—Dionysiac or
   Bacchic—
   And the Dithyrambic revels of those un-
      decorous days.
      (*Confidentially to audience.*)
   And perhaps I'd better mention,
   Lest alarming you I am,
   That it isn't our intention
      To perform a Dithyramb—
   It displays a lot of stocking,
   Which is always very shocking,
   And of course I'm only mocking
      At the prevalence of "cram."!

Chorus

It displays a lot, etc.

Ludwig

Yes, on reconsideration, there are customs
   of that nation
   Which are not in strict accordance with
      the habits of our day.
And when I come to codify, their rules I
   mean to modify,
   Or Mrs. Grundy, p'r'aps, may have a
      word or two to say.
For they hadn't mackintoshes or umbrellas
   or galoshes—
   And a shower with their dresses must
      have played the very deuce,
And it must have been unpleasing when
   they caught a fit of sneezing,
   For, it seems, of pocket-handkerchiefs
      they didn't know the use.
They wore little underclothing—scarcely
   anything—or nothing—
   And their dress of Coan silk was quite
      transparent in design—
Well, in fact, in summer weather, some-
   thing like the "altogether."
   And it's *there*, I rather fancy, I shall
      have to draw the line!
      (*Confidentially to audience.*)
   And again I wish to mention
   That this erudition sham
   Is but classical pretension,

The result of steady "cram."
Yet my classic lore agressive
(If you'll pardon the possessive)
Is exceedingly impressive
When you're passing an exam.

Chorus

Yet his classic lore, etc.

[*Exeunt Chorus. Manent* LUDWIG, JULIA, *and* LISA. LUD. (*recit.*).

Yes, Ludwig and his Julia are mated!
For when an obscure comedian, whom the law backs,
To sovereign rank is promptly elevated,
He takes it with its incidental drawbacks!
So Julia and I are duly mated!

[LISA, *through this, has expressed intense distress at having to surrender* LUDWIG.

SONG—LISA

Take care of him—he's much too good to live,
With him you must be very gentle:
Poor fellow, he's so highly sensitive,
And O, so sentimental!
Be sure you never let him sit up late
In chilly open air conversing—
Poor darling, he's extremely delicate,
And wants a deal of nursing!

Ludwig

I want a deal of nursing!

Lisa

And O, remember this—
When he is cross with pain,
A flower and a kiss—
A simple flower—a tender kiss
Will bring him round again!
His moods you must assiduously watch:
When he succumbs to sorrow tragic,
Some hardbake or a bit of butter-scotch
Will work on him like magic.
To contradict a character so rich
In trusting love were simple blindness—
He's one of those exalted natures which
Will only yield to kindness!

Ludwig

I only yield to kindness!

Lisa

And O, the bygone bliss!
And O, the present pain!
That flower and that kiss—
That simple flower—that tender kiss
I ne'er shall give again! [*Exit, weeping.*

Julia. And now that everybody has gone, and we're happily and comfortably mar-

ried, I want to have a few words with my new-born husband.

Lud. (*aside*). Yes, I expect you'll often have a few words with your new-born husband! (*Aloud.*) Well, what is it?

Julia. Why, I've been thinking that as you and I have to play our parts for life, it is most essential that we should come to a definite understanding as to how they shall be rendered. Now, I've been considering how I can make the most of the Grand Duchess.

Lud. Have you? Well, if you'll take my advice, you'll make a very fine part of it.

Julia. Why, that's quite *my* idea.

Lud. I shouldn't make it one of your hoity-toity vixenish viragoes.

Julia. You think not?

Lud. Oh, I'm quite clear about that. I should make her a tender, gentle, submissive, affectionate (but not too affectionate) child-wife—timidly anxious to coil herself into her husband's heart, but kept in check by an awe-struck reverence for his exalted intellectual qualities and his majestic personal appearance.

Julia. Oh, that is your idea of a good part?

Lud. Yes—a wife who regards her husband's slightest wish as an inflexible law, and who ventures but rarely into his august presence, unless (which would happen seldom) he should summon her to appear before him. A crushed, despairing violet, whose blighted existence would culminate (all too soon) in a lonely and pathetic death-scene! A fine part, my dear.

Julia. Yes. There's a good deal to be said for your view of it. Now there are some actresses whom it would fit like a glove.

Lud. (*aside*). I wish I'd married one of 'em!

Julia. But, you see, I *must* consider my temperament. For instance, my temperament would demand some strong scenes of justifiable jealousy.

Lud. Oh, there's no difficulty about that. You shall have *them*.

Julia. With a lovely but detested rival——

Lud. Oh, *I'll* provide the rival.

Julia. Whom I should stab—stab—stab!

Lud. Oh, I wouldn't stab her. It's been

done to death. I should treat her with a silent and contemptuous disdain, and delicately withdraw from a position which, to one of your sensitive nature, would be absolutely untenable. Dear me, I can see you delicately withdrawing, up centre and off!

Julia. Can you?

Lud. Yes. It's a fine situation—and in your hands, full of quiet pathos!

DUET—LUDWIG *and* JULIA

Ludwig

Now Julia, come,
Consider it from

This dainty point of view—
A timid tender
Feminine gender,
    Prompt to coyly coo—
Yet silence seeking,
Seldom speaking
Till she's spoken to—
A comfy, cosy,
Rosy-posy
    Innocent *ingenoo*!
        The part you're suited to—
        (To give the deuce her due)
    A sweet (O, jiminy!)
    Miminy-piminy,
    Innocent inge*noo*!

ENSEMBLE

Ludwig
The part you're suited to—
(To give the deuce her due)
A sweet (O, jiminy!)
Miminy-piminy,
Innocent inge*noo*!

Julia
You forget my special magic
(In a high dramatic sense)
Lies in situations tragic
Undeniably intense.
As I've justified promotion
In the histrionic art,
I'll submit to you my notion
Of a first-rate part.

Ludwig
Well, let us see your notion
Of a first-rate part.

Julia (*dramatically*).
I have a rival! Frenzy-thrilled,
I find you both together!
My heart stands still—with horror chilled—
Hard as the millstone nether!
Then softly, slyly, snaily, snaky—
Crawly, creepy, quaily, quaky—
I track her on her homeward way,
As panther tracks her fated prey!

(*Furiously*.)
I fly at her soft white throat—
The lily-white laughing leman!
On her agonized gaze I gloat
With the glee of a dancing demon!
My rival she—I have no doubt of her—
So I hold on—till the breath is out of her!
    —till the breath is out of her!
And then—Remorse! Remorse!

Julia
I'm much obliged to you,
I don't think that would do—
    To play (O, jiminy!)
    Miminy-piminy,
    Innocent inge*noo*!

O cold unpleasant corse,
    Avaunt! Avaunt!
That lifeless form
    I gaze upon—
That face, still warm
    But weirdly wan—
Those eyes of glass
    I contemplate—
And then, alas,
    Too late—too late!
I find she is—your Aunt!

(*Shuddering*.)
    Remorse! Remorse!
Then, mad—mad—mad!
    With fancies wild—chimerical—
Now sorrowful—silent—sad—
    Now hullaballoo hysterical!
    Ha! ha! ha! ha!
But whether I'm sad or whether I'm glad,
    Mad! mad! mad! mad!
This calls for the resources of a high-class art,
And satisfies my notion of a first-rate part!
            [*Exit* JULIA.
Enter all the Chorus, hurriedly, and in great excitement.

Chorus
Your Highness, there's a party at the door—
    Your Highness, at the door there is a party—

She says that we expect her,
But we do not recollect her,
For we never saw her countenance before!
With rage and indignation she is rife,
Because our welcome wasn't very
hearty—
She's as sulky as a super,
And she's swearing like a trooper,
O, you never heard such language in your
life!

Enter BARONESS VON KRANKENFELDT, *in a
fury.*

Baroness
With fury indescribable I burn!
With rage I'm nearly ready to explode!
There'll be grief and tribulation when I
learn
To whom this slight unbearable is owed!
For whatever may be due I'll pay it
double—
There'll be terror indescribable and
trouble!
With a hurly-burly and a hubble-
bubble
I'll pay you for this pretty episode!

All
Oh, whatever may be due she'll pay it
double!—
It's very good of her to take the
trouble—
But we don't know what she means
by "hubble-bubble"—
No doubt it's an expression *à la mode.*

Baroness (to Ludwig).
Do you know who I am?

Ludwig (examining her).
I don't;
Your countenance I can't fix, my dear.

Baroness
This proves I'm not a sham.
(*Showing pocket-handkerchief.*)

Ludwig (examining it).
It won't;
It only says "Krankenfeldt, Six," my dear.

Baroness
Express your grief profound!

Ludwig
I shan't!
This tone I never allow, my love.

Baroness
Rudolph at once produce!

Ludwig
I can't;

He isn't at home just now, my love.

Baroness (astonished).
He isn't at home just now!

All
He isn't at home just now,
(*Dancing derisively.*)
He has an appointment particular, very—
You'll find him, I think, in the town ceme-
tery;
And that's how we come to be making
so merry,
For he isn't at home just now!

Baroness
But bless my heart and soul alive, it's
impudence personified!
I've come here to be matrimonially matrimonified!

Ludwig
For any disappointment I am sorry un-
affectedly,
But yesterday that nobleman expired quite
unexpectedly—

All (sobbing).
Tol the riddle lol!
Tol the riddle lol!
Tol the riddle, lol the riddle, lol lol lay!
(*Then laughing wildly.*)
Tol the riddle, lol the riddle, lol lol lay!

Baroness
But this is most unexpected. He was well
enough at a quarter to twelve yesterday.

Ludwig
Yes. He died at half-past eleven.

Baroness
Bless me, how very sudden!

Ludwig
It *was* sudden.

Baroness
But what in the world am I to do? I was
to have been married to him to-day!

All (singing and dancing).
For any disappointment we are sorry un-
affectedly,
But yesterday that nobleman expired quite
unexpectedly—
Tol the riddle lol!

Bar. Is this Court Mourning or a Fancy
Ball?

Lud. Well, it's a delicate combination of
both effects. It is intended to express in-
consolable grief for the decease of the late
Duke and ebullient joy at the accession of
his successor. *I* am his successor. Permit me

to present you to my Grand Duchess. (*Indicating* JULIA.)

Bar. Your Grand Duchess? Oh, your Highness! (*Curtseying profoundly.*)

Julia (*sneering at her*). Old frump!

Bar. Humph! A recent creation, probably?

Lud. We were married only half an hour ago.

Bar. Exactly. I thought she seemed new to the position.

Julia. Ma'am, I don't know who you are, but I flatter myself I can do justice to *any* part on the very shortest notice.

Bar. My dear, under the circumstances you are doing admirably—and you'll improve with practice. It's so difficult to be a lady when one isn't born to it.

Julia (*in a rage, to* LUDWIG). Am I to stand this? Am I not to be allowed to pull her to pieces?

Lud. (*aside to* JULIA). No, no—it isn't Greek. Be a violet, I beg.

Bar. And now tell me all about this distressing circumstance. How did the Grand Duke die?

Lud. He perished nobly—in a Statutory Duel.

Bar. In a Statutory Duel? But that's only a civil death!—and the Act expires to-night, and then he will come to life again!

Lud. Well, no. Anxious to inaugurate my reign by conferring some inestimable boon on my people, I signalized this occasion by reviving the law for another hundred years.

Bar. For another hundred years? Then set the merry joybells ringing! Let festive epithalamia resound through these ancient halls! Cut the satisfying sandwich—broach the exhilarating Marsala—and let us rejoice to-day, if we never rejoice again!

Lud. But I don't think I quite understand. We have already rejoiced a good deal.

Bar. Happy man, you little reck of the extent of the good things you are in for. When you killed Rudolph you adopted all his overwhelming responsibilities. Know then that I, Caroline von Krakenfeldt, am the most overwhelming of them all!

Lud. But stop, stop—I've just been married to somebody else!

Julia. Yes, ma'am, to somebody else,

ma'am! Do you understand, ma'am? To somebody else!

Bar. Do keep this young woman quiet; she fidgets me!

Julia. Fidgets you!

Lud. (*aside to* JULIA). Be a violet—a crushed, despairing violet.

Julia. Do you suppose I intend to give up a magnificent part without a struggle?

Lud. My good girl, she has the law on her side. Let us both bear this calamity with resignation. If you must struggle, go away and struggle in the seclusion of your chamber.

SONG—BARONESS *and* CHORUS

Now away to the wedding we go,
    So summon the charioteers—
No kind of reluctance they show
    To embark on their married careers.
Though Julia's emotion may flow
    For the rest of her maidenly years,
        All
To the wedding we eagerly go,
    So summon the charioteers!
      Now away, etc.

[*All dance off to wedding except* JULIA.

RECIT—JULIA

So ends my dream—so fades my vision fair!
Of hope no gleam—distraction and despair!
My cherished dream, the Ducal throne to share.
That aim supreme has vanished into air!

SONG—JULIA

Broken every promise plighted—
    All is darksome—all is dreary.
Every new-born hope is blighted!
    Sad and sorry—weak and weary!
Death the Friend or Death the Foe,
Shall I call upon thee? No!
I will go on living, though
    Sad and sorry—weak and weary!
No, no! Let the bygone go by!
    No good ever came of repining:
If to-day there are clouds o'er the sky,
    To-morrow the sun may be shining!
      To-morrow, be kind,
      To-morrow, to me!
      With loyalty blind
      I curtsey to thee!
To-day is a day of illusion and sorrow,
So *viva* To-morrow, To-morrow, To-morrow!
    God save you, To-morrow!

Your servant, To-morrow!
God save you, To-morrow, To-morrow,
　　To-morrow!

[Exit JULIA.

Enter ERNEST

Ern. It's of no use—I can't wait any
longer. At any risk I must gratify my
urgent desire to know what is going on.
(*Looking off.*) Why, what's that? Surely
I see a wedding procession winding down
the hill, dressed in my *Troilus and Cressida*
costumes! That's Ludwig's doing! I see
how it is—he found the time hang heavy
on his hands, and is amusing himself by
getting married to Lisa. No—it can't be to
Lisa, for here she is!

Enter LISA

Lisa (*not seeing him*). I really cannot
stand seeing my Ludwig married twice in
one day to somebody else!

Ern. Lisa!

(LISA *sees him, and stands as if transfixed
with horror.*)

Ern. Come here—don't be a little fool—
I want you.

(LISA *suddenly turns and bolts off.*)

Ern. Why, what's the matter with the
little donkey? One would think she saw a
ghost! But if he's not marrying Lisa, whom
is he marrying? (*Suddenly.*) Julia! (*Much
overcome.*) I see it all! The scoundrel! He
had to adopt all my responsibilities, and
he's shabbily taken advantage of the situation to marry the girl I'm engaged to! But
no, it can't be Julia, for here *she* is!

Enter JULIA

Julia (*not seeing him*). I've made up my
mind. I won't stand it! I'll send in my
notice at once!

Ern. Julia! Oh, what a relief!

(JULIA *gazes at him as if transfixed.*)

Ern. Then you've not married Ludwig?
You are still true to me?

(JULIA *turns and bolts in grotesque horror.*
ERNEST *follows and stops her.*)

Ern. Don't run away! Listen to me.
Are you all crazy?

Julia (*in affected terror*). What would
you with me, spectre? Oh, ain't his eyes
sepulchral! And ain't his voice hollow!
What are you doing out of your tomb at
this time of day—apparition?

Ern. I do wish I could make you girls
understand that I'm only technically dead,
and that physically I'm as much alive as
ever I was in my life!

Julia. Oh, but it's an awful thing to be
haunted by a technical bogy!

Ern. You won't be haunted much longer.
The law must be on its last legs, and in a
few hours I shall come to life again—resume all my social and civil functions, and
claim my darling as my blushing bride!

Julia. Oh—then you haven't heard?

Ern. My love, I've heard nothing. How
could I? There are no daily papers where I
come from.

Julia. Why, Ludwig challenged Rudolph
and won, and now *he's* Grand Duke, and
he's revived the law for another century!

Ern. What! But you're not serious—
you're only joking!

Julia. My good sir, I'm a light-hearted
girl, but I don't chaff bogies.

Ern. Well, that's the meanest dodge I
ever heard of!

Julia. Shabby trick, *I* call it.

Ern. But you don't mean to say that
you're going to cry off!

Julia. I really can't afford to wait until
your time is up. You know, I've always
set my face against long engagements.

Ern. Then defy the law and marry me
now. We will fly to your native country,
and I'll play broken-English in London as
you play broken-German here!

Julia. No. These legal technicalities cannot be defied. Situated as you are, you have
no power to make me your wife. At best
you could only make me your widow.

Ern. Then be my widow—my little
dainty, winning, winsome widow!

Julia. Now what would be the good of
that? Why, you goose, I should marry
again within a month!

DUET—ERNEST *and* JULIA

Ernest

If the light of love's lingering ember
　　Has faded in gloom,
You cannot neglect, O remember,
　　A voice from the tomb!
That stern supernatural diction
Should act as a solemn restriction,
Although by a mere legal fiction
　　A voice from the tomb!

　　　　Julia (*in affected terror*).

I own that that utterance chills me—
　　It withers my bloom!

With awful emotion it thrills me—
  That voice from the tomb!
Oh, spectre, won't anything lay thee?
Though pained to deny or gainsay thee,
In this case I cannot obey thee,
  Thou voice from the tomb!

           (*Dancing.*)
So, spectre appalling,
  I bid you good-day—
Perhaps you'll be calling
  When passing this way.
Your bogydom scorning,
And all your love-lorning,
I bid you good-morning,
  I bid you good-day.
           Ernest (furious).
My offer recalling,
  Your words I obey—
Your fate is appalling
  And full of dismay.
To pay for this scorning
I give you fair warning
I'll haunt you each morning,
Each night, and each day!

[*Repeat Ensemble, and exeunt in opposite
                    directions.*
Re-enter the Wedding Procession dancing
           Chorus
Now bridegroom and bride let us toast
  In a magnum of merry champagne—
Let us make of this moment the most,
  We may not be so lucky again.
So drink to our sovereign host
  And his highly intelligent reign—
His health and his bride's let us toast
  In a magnum of merry champagne!

    SONG—BARONESS *with* CHORUS
I once gave an evening party
  (A sandwich and cut-orange ball),
But my guests had such appetites hearty
  That I couldn't enjoy it, enjoy it at all!
I made a heroic endeavour
  To look unconcerned, but in vain,
And I vow'd that I never—oh never—
  Would ask anybody again!
But there's a distinction decided—
  A difference truly immense—
When the wine that you drink is provided,
      provided,
  At somebody else's expense.
So bumpers—aye, ever so many—
  The cost we may safely ignore!
For the wine doesn't cost us a penny,
  Tho' it's Pomméry seventy-four!

           Chorus
So bumpers—aye, ever so many—etc.
Come, bumpers—aye, ever so many—
  And then, if you will, many more!
This wine doesn't cost us a penny,
  Tho' it's Pomméry, Pomméry seventy-
      four!
Old wine is a true panacea
  For ev'ry conceivable ill,
When you cherish the soothing idea
  That somebody else pays the bill!
Old wine is a pleasure that's hollow
  When at your own table you sit,
For you're thinking each mouthful you
      swallow
  Hast cost you, hast cost you a three-
      penny-bit!
So bumpers—aye, ever so many—
  And then, if you will, many more!
This wine doesn't cost us a penny,
  Tho' it's Pomméry seventy-four!
           Chorus
So, bumpers—aye, ever so many—etc.
           (*March heard*)
           Ludwig (recit.).
Why, who is this approaching,
Upon our joy encroaching?
Some rascal come a-poaching
Who's heard that wine we're broaching?
              All
  Who may this be?
  Who may this be?
Who is he? Who is he? Who is he?
           Enter HERALD
              Herald
The Prince of Monte Car*lo*,
  From Mediterranean water,
Has come here to bestow
  On you his beautiful daughter.
They've paid off all they owe,
  As every statesman oughter—
That Prince of Monte Car*lo*
  And his be-eautiful daughter!

           Chorus
    The Prince of Monte Car*lo*, etc.
              Herald
The Prince of Monte Car*lo*,
  Who is so very partickler,
Has heard that you're also
  For ceremony a stickler—
Therefore he lets you know
  by word of mouth auric'lar—
(That Prince of Monte Car*lo*
  Who is so very partick*lar*)—

Chorus
The Prince of Monte Car*lo*, etc.
Herald
That Prince of Monte Car*lo*,
From Mediterranean water,
Has come here to bestow
On you his be-eautiful daughter!
Ludwig (recit.).
His Highness we know not—nor the local-
ity
In which is situate his Principality;
But, as he guesses by some odd fatality,
This *is* the shop for cut and dried for-
mality!
Let him appear—
He'll find that we're
Remarkable for cut and dried formality.
(*Reprise of March. Exit* HERALD.
LUDWIG *beckons his Court.*)
Ludwig
I have a plan—I'll tell you all the plot of
it—
He wants formality—he shall have a lot of
it!—
(*Whispers to them, through symphony.*)
Conceal yourselves, and when I give the
cue,
Spring out on him—you all know what
to do!
(*All conceal themselves behind the draperies
that enclose the stage.*)
Pompous March. Enter the PRINCE *and*
PRINCESS OF MONTE CARLO, *attended by
six theatrical-looking nobles and the
Court Costumier.*
DUET—PRINCE *and* PRINCESS
Prince
We're rigged out in magnificent array
(Our own clothes are much gloomier)
In costumes which we've hired by the day
From a very well-known costumier.
Costumier (bowing).
I am the well-known costumier.
Princess
With a brilliant staff a Prince should make
a show
(It's a rule that never varies),
So we've engaged from the Theatre Monaco
Six supernumeraries.
Nobles
We're the supernumeraries.
All
At a salary immense,
Quite regardless of expense,

Six supernumeraries!
Prince
They do no speak, for they break our
grammar's laws,
And their language is lamentable—
And they never take off their gloves, be
cause
Their nails are not presentable.
Nobles
Our nails are not presentable!
Princess
To account for their shortcomings manifest
We explain, in a whisper bated,
They are wealthy members of the brewing
interest
To the Peerage elevated.
Nobles
To the Peerage elevated.
All
They're ⎫
We're ⎬ very, very rich,
And accordingly, as sich,
To the Peerage elevated.
Prince. Well, my dear, here we are at
last—just in time to compel Duke Rudolph
to fulfil the terms of his marriage contract.
Another hour and we should have been
too late.
Princess. Yes, papa, and if you hadn't
fortunately discovered a means of making
an income by honest industry, we should
never have got here at all.
Prince. Very true. Confined for the last
two years within the precincts of my palace
by an obdurate bootmaker who held a
warrant for my arrest, I devoted my enforced leisure to a study of the doctrine
of chances—mainly with the view of ascer-
taining whether there was the remotest
chance of my ever going out for a walk
again—and this led to the discovery of a
singularly fascinating little round game
which I have called Roulette, and by which,
in one sitting, I won no less than five thousand francs! My first act was to pay my
bootmaker—my second, to engage a good
useful working set of second-hand nobles—
and my third, to hurry you off to Pfennig
Halbpfennig as fast as a *train de luxe* could
carry us!
Princess. Yes, and a pretty job-lot of
second-hand nobles you've scraped together!
Prince (doubtfully). Pretty, you think?

Humph! I don't know. I should say tol-lol, my love—only tol-lol. They are not wholly satisfactory. There is a certain air of unreality about them—they are not convincing.

Cost. But, my goot friend, vhat can you expect for eighteenpence a day!

Prince. Now take this Peer, for instance. What the deuce do you call *him?*

Cost. Him? Oh, he's a swell—he's the Duke of Riviera.

Prince. Oh, he's a Duke, is he? Well, that's no reason why he should look so confoundedly haughty. (*To* NOBLE.) Be affable, sir! (NOBLE *takes attitude of affability.*) That's better. (*Passing to another.*) Now, who's this with his moustache coming off?

Cost. Vhy, you're Viscount Mentone, ain't you?

Noble. Blest if I know. (*Turning up sword-belt.*) It's wrote here—yes, Viscount Mentone.

Cost. Then vhy don't you say so? 'Old yerself up—you ain't carryin' sandwich boards now. (*Adjusts his moustache.*)

Prince. Now, once for all, you Peers—when His Highness arrives, don't stand like sticks, but appear to take an intelligent and sympathetic interest in what is going on. You needn't say anything, but let your gestures be in accordance with the spirit of the conversation. Now take the word from me. Affability! (*attitude*). Submission! (*attitude*). Surprise! (*attitude*). Shame! (*attitude*). Grief! (*attitude*). Joy! (*attitude*). That's better! You can do it if you like!

Princess. But, papa, where in the world is the Court? There is positively no one here to receive us! I can't help feeling that Rudolph wants to get out of it because I'm poor. He's a miserly little wretch—that's what he is.

Prince. Well, I shouldn't go so far as to say that. I should rather describe him as an enthusiastic collector of coins—of the realm—and we must not be too hard upon a numismatist if he feels a certain disinclination to part with some of his really very valuable specimens. It's a pretty hobby: I've often thought I should like to collect some coins myself.

Princess. Papa, I'm sure there's some one behind that curtain. I saw it move!

Prince. Then no doubt they are coming. Now mind, you Peers—haughty affability combined with a sense of what is due to your exalted ranks, or I'll fine you half a franc each—upon my soul I will!

[*Gong. The curtains fly back and the Court are discovered. They give a wild yell and rush on to the stage dancing wildly, with* PRINCE, PRINCESS, *and* NOBLES, *who are taken by surprise at first, but eventually join in a reckless dance. At the end all fall down exhausted.*

Lud. There, what do you think of that? That's our official ceremonial for the reception of visitors of the very highest distinction.

Prince (*puzzled*). It's very quaint—very curious indeed. Prettily footed, too. Prettily footed.

Lud. Would you like to see how we say "good-bye" to visitors of distinction? That ceremony is also performed with the foot.

Prince. Really, this tone—ah, but perhaps you have not completely grasped the situation?

Lud. Not altogether.

Prince. Ah, then I'll give you a lead over. (*Significantly.*) I am the father of the Princess of Monte Carlo. Doesn't that convey any idea to the Grand Ducal mind?

Lud. (*stolidly*). Nothing definite.

Prince (*aside*). H'm—very odd! Never mind—try again! (*Aloud.*) This is the daughter of the Prince of Monte Carlo. Do you take?

Lud. (*still puzzled*). No—not yet. Go on—don't give it up—I daresay it will come presently.

Prince. Very odd — never mind — try again. (*With sly significance.*) Twenty years ago! Little doddle doddle! *Two* little doddle doddles! Happy father—hers and yours. Proud mother—yours and hers! Hah! *Now* you take? I see you do! I see you do!

Lud. Nothing is more annoying than to feel that you're not equal to the intellectual pressure of the conversation. I wish he'd say something intelligible.

Prince. You didn't expect me?

Lud. (*jumping at it*). No, no. I grasp that—thank you very much. (*Shaking hands with him.*) No, I did *not* expect you!

Prince. I thought not. But ha! ha! at last I have escaped from my enforced restraint. (*General movement of alarm.*) (*To crowd who are stealing off.*) No, no—you misunderstand me. I mean I've paid my debts!

All. Oh! (*They return.*)

Princess (*affectionately*). But, my darling, I'm afraid that even now you don't quite realize who I am! (*Embracing him.*)

Baroness. Why, you forward little hussy, how dare you? (*Takes her away from* LUDWIG.)

Lud. You mustn't do that, my dear—never in the presence of the Grand Duchess, I beg!

Princess (*weeping*). Oh, papa, he's got a Grand Duchess!

Lud. A Grand Duchess! My good girl, I've got three Grand Duchesses!

Princess. Well, I'm sure! Papa, let's go away—this is not a respectable Court.

Prince. All these Grand Dukes have their little fancies, my love. This potentate appears to be collecting wives. It's a pretty hobby—I should like to collect a few myself. This (*admiring* BARONESS) is a charming specimen—an antique, I should say—of the early Merovingian period, if I'm not mistaken; and here's another—a Scotch lady, I think (*alluding to* JULIA), and (*alluding to* LISA) a little one thrown in. Two half-quarterns and a makeweight! (*To* LUDWIG.) Have you such a thing as a catalogue of the Museum?

Princess. But I cannot permit Rudolph to keep a museum——

Lud. Rudolph? Get along with you, I'm not Rudolph! Rudolph died yesterday!

Prince and Princess. What!

Lud. Quite suddenly—of—of—a cardiac affection.

Prince and Princess. Of a cardiac affection?

Lud. Yes, a pack-of-cardiac affection. He fought a Statutory Duel with me and lost, and I took over all his engagements—including this imperfectly preserved old lady, to whom he has been engaged for the last three weeks.

Princess. Three weeks! But I've been

engaged to him for the last twenty years!

Baroness, Lisa, and Julia. Twenty years!

Prince (*aside*). It's all right, my love—they can't get over that. (*Aloud.*) He's yours—take him, and hold him as tight as you can!

Princess. My own! (*Embracing* LUDWIG.)

Lud. Here's another!—the fourth in four-and-twenty hours! Would anybody else like to marry me? You ma'am—or you—anybody! I'm getting used to it!

Baroness. But let me tell you, ma'am——

Julia. Why, you impudent little hussy——

Lisa. Oh, here's another—here's another! (*Weeping.*)

Princess. Poor ladies, I'm very sorry for you all; but, you see, I've a prior claim. Come, away we go—there's not a moment to be lost!

CHORUS (*as they dance towards exit*)
Away to the wedding we'll go
    To summon the charioteers,
No kind of reluctance we show
    To embark on our married careers—

[*At this moment* RUDOLPH, ERNEST, *and* NOTARY *appear.*
All kneel in astonishment.

RECITATIVE

Rudolph, Ernest, and Notary
Forbear! This may not be!
    Frustrated are your plans!
With paramount decree
    The Law forbids the banns!

All. The Law forbids the banns!

Lud. Not a bit of it! I've revived the law for another century!

Rud. You didn't revive it! You couldn't revive it! You—you are an impostor, sir—a tuppenny rogue, sir! You—you never were, and in all human probability never will be—Grand Duke of Pfennig Anything!

All. What! ! !

Rud. Never—never, never! (*Aside.*) Oh, my internal economy!

Lud. That's absurd, you know. I fought the Grand Duke. He drew a King, and I drew an Ace. He perished in inconceivable agonies on the spot. Now, as that's settled, we'll go on with the wedding.

Rud. It—it isn't settled. You—you can't. I—I— (*to* NOTARY). Oh, tell him—tell him! I can't!

Not. Well, the fact is, there's been a

little mistake here. On reference to the Act that regulates Statutory Duels, I find it is expressly laid down that the Ace shall count invariably as lowest!

All. As lowest!

Rud. (*breathlessly*). As—lowest—lowest—lowest! So *you're* the ghoest—ghoest—ghoest! (*Aside.*) Oh, what *is* the matter with me inside here!

Ern. Well, Julia, as it seems that the law hasn't been revived—and as, consequently, I shall come to life in about three minutes (*consulting his watch*)——

Julia. My objection falls to the ground. (*Resignedly.*) Very well!

Princess. And am I to understand that I was on the point of marrying a dead man without knowing it? (*To* RUDOLPH, *who revives.*) Oh, my love, what a narrow escape I've had!

Rud. Oh—you are the Princess of Monte Carlo, and you've turned up just in time! Well, you're an attractive little girl, you know, but you're as poor as a rat! (*They retire up together.*)

Lisa. That's all very well, but what is to become of *me?* (*To* LUDWIG.) If you're a dead man——(*Clock strikes three.*)

Lud. But I'm not. Time's up—the Act has expired—I've come to life—the parson is still in attendance, and we'll all be married directly.

All. Hurrah!

FINALE

Happy couples, lightly treading,
    Castle chapel will be quite full!
Each shall have a pretty wedding,
    As, of course, is only rightful,
    Though the brides be fair or frightful
Contradiction little dreading,
    This will be a day delightful—
Each shall have a pretty wedding!
    Such a pretty, pretty wedding!
    Such a pretty wedding!
[*All dance off to get married as the curtain falls.*

THE END

THE BAB BALLADS

GENERAL JOHN

The bravest names for fire and flames
  And all that mortal durst,
Were General John and Private James,
  Of the Sixty-seventy-first.

General John was a soldier tried,
  A chief of warlike dons;
A haughty stride and a withering pride
  Were Major-General John's.

A sneer would play on his martial phiz,
  Superior birth to show;
"Pish!" was a favourite word of his,
  And he often said "Ho! ho!"

Full-Private James described might be,
  As a man of a mournful mind;
No characteristic trait had he
  Of any distinctive kind.

From the ranks, one day, cried Private
    James,
  "Oh! Major-General John,
I've doubts of our respective names,
  My mournful mind upon.

"A glimmering thought occurs to me
  (Its source I can't unearth),
But I've a kind of a notion we
  Were cruelly changed at birth.

"I've a strange idea that each other's names
  We've each of us here got on.
Such things have been," said Private James.
  "They have!" sneered General John.

"My General John, I swear upon
  My oath I think 'tis so——"
"Pish!" proudly sneered his General John,
  And he also said "Ho! ho!"

"My General John! my General John!
  My General John!" quoth he,
"This aristocratical sneer upon
  Your face I blush to see!

"No truly great or generous cove
  Deserving of them names,

Would sneer at a fixed idea that's drove
  In the mind of a Private James!"

Said General John, "Upon your claims
  No need your breath to waste;
If this is a joke, Full-Private James,
  It's a joke of doubtful taste.

"But, being a man of doubtless worth,
  If you feel certain quite
That we were probably changed at birth,
  I'll venture to say you're right."

So General John as Private James
  Fell in, parade upon;
And Private James, by change of names,
  Was Major-General John.

TO A LITTLE MAID

By a Policeman

Come with me, little maid!
Nay, shrink not, thus afraid—
  I'll harm thee not!
Fly not, my love, from me—
I have a home for thee—
  A fairy grot,
    Where mortal eye
    Can rarely pry,
There shall thy dwelling be!

List to me, while I tell
The pleasures of that cell,
  Oh, little maid!
What though its couch be rude—
Homely the only food
  Within its shade?
    No thought of care
    Can enter there,
No vulgar swain intrude!

Come with me, little maid,
Come to the rocky shade
  I love to sing;
Live with us, maiden rare—
Come, for we "want" thee there,
  Thou elfin thing,
    To work thy spell,
    In some cool cell
In stately Pentonville!

SIR GUY THE CRUSADER

Sir Guy was a doughty crusader,
    A muscular knight,
    Ever ready to fight,
A very determined invader,
    And Dickey de Lion's delight.

Lenore was a Saracen maiden,
    Brunette, statuesque,
    The reverse of grotesque,
Her pa was a bagman from Aden,
    Her mother she played in burlesque.

A *coryphée,* pretty and loyal,
    In amber and red,
    The ballet she led;
Her mother performed at the Royal,
    Lenore at the Saracen's Head.

Of face and of figure majestic,
    She dazzled the cits—
    Ecstaticised pits;—
Her troubles were only domestic,
    But drove her half out of her wits.

Her father incessantly lashed her,
    On water and bread
    She was grudgingly fed;
Whenever her father he thrashed her
    Her mother sat down on her head.

Guy saw her, and loved her, with reason,
    For beauty so bright
    Sent him mad with delight;
He purchased a stall for the season,
    And sat in it every night.

His views were exceedingly proper,
    He wanted to wed,
    So he called at her shed
And saw her progenitor whop her—
    Her mother sit down on her head.

"So pretty," said he, "and so trusting!
    You brute of a dad,
    You unprincipled cad,
Your conduct is really disgusting,
    Come, come, now admit it's too bad!

"You're a turbaned old Turk, and malig-
        nant—
    Your daughter Lenore
    I intensely adore,

And I cannot help feeling indignant,
    A fact that I hinted before;

"To see a fond father employing
    A deuce of a knout
    For to bang her about,
To a sensitive lover's annoying."
    Said the bagman, "Crusader, get out."

Says Guy, "Shall a warrior laden
    With a big spiky knob,
    Sit in peace on his cob
While a beautiful Saracen maiden
    Is whipped by a Saracen snob?

"To London I'll go from my charmer."
    Which he did, with his loot
    (Seven hats and a flute),
And was nabbed for his Sydenham armour
    At Mr. Ben-Samuel's suit.

Sir Guy he was lodged in the Compter,
    Her pa, in a rage,
    Died (don't know his age),
His daughter, she married the prompter,
    Grew bulky and quitted the stage.

HAUNTED

Haunted? Ay, in a social way,
By a body of ghosts in a dread array:
But no conventional spectres they—
    Appalling, grim, and tricky:
I quail at mine as I'd never quail
At a fine traditional spectre pale,
With a turnip head and a ghostly wail,
    And a splash of blood on the dicky!

Mine are horrible social ghosts,
Speeches and women and guests and hosts,
Weddings and morning calls and toasts,
    In every bad variety:
Ghosts that hover about the grave
Of all that's manly, free, and brave:
You'll find their names on the architrave
    Of that charnel-house, Society.

Black Monday—black as its school-room
        ink—
With its dismal boys that snivel and think
Of its nauseous messes to eat and drink,
    And its frozen tank to wash in.
That was the first that brought me grief,
And made me weep, till I sought relief

In an emblematical handkerchief,
　　To choke such baby bosh in.

First and worst in the grim array—
Ghosts of ghosts that have gone their way,
Which I wouldn't revive for a single day
　　For all the wealth of Plutus—
Are the horrible ghosts that school-days
　　　　scared:
If the classical ghost that Brutus dared
Was the ghost of his "Caesar" unprepared,
　　I'm sure I pity Brutus.

I pass to critical seventeen;
The ghost of that terrible wedding scene,
When an elderly Colonel stole my Queen,
　　And woke my dream of heaven.
No schoolgirl decked in her nurse-room
　　　　curls
Was my gushing innocent Queen of Pearls;
If she wasn't a girl of a thousand girls,
　　She was one of forty-seven!

I see the ghost of my first cigar,
Of the thence-arising family jar—
Of my maiden brief (I was at the Bar,
　　And I called the Judge "Your wushup!")
Of reckless days and reckless nights,
With wrenched-off knockers, extinguished
　　　　lights,
Unholy songs and tipsy fights,
　　Which I strove in vain to hush up.

Ghosts of fraudulent joint-stock banks,
Ghosts of "copy, declined with thanks,"
Of novels returned in endless ranks,
　　And thousands more, I suffer.
The only line to fitly grace
My humble tomb, when I've run my race,
Is, "Reader, this is the resting-place
　　Of an unsuccessful duffer."

I've fought them all, these ghosts of mine,
But the weapons I've used are sighs and
　　　　brine,
And now that I'm nearly forty-nine,
　　Old age is my chiefest bogy;
For my hair is thinning away at the crown,
And the silver fights with the worn-out
　　　　brown;
And a general verdict sets me down
　　As an irreclaimable fogy.

LORENZO DE LARDY

Dalilah de Dardy adored
　　The very correctest of cards,
Lorenzo de Lardy, a lord—
　　He was one of Her Majesty's Guards.

Dalilah de Dardy was fat,
　　Dalilah de Dardy was old—
(No doubt in the world about that)
　　But Dalilah de Dardy had gold.

Lorenzo de Lardy was tall,
　　The flower of maidenly pets,
Young ladies would love at his call,
　　But Lorenzo de Lardy had debts.

His money-position was queer,
　　And one of his favourite freaks
Was to hide himself, three times a year,
　　In Paris, for several weeks.

Many days didn't pass him before
　　He fanned himself into a flame,
For a beautiful "Dam du Comptwore,"
　　And this was her singular name:

Alice Eulalie Coraline
　　Euphrosine Colombina Thérèse
Juliette Stephanie Celestine
　　Charlotte Russe de la Sauce Mayonnaise.

She booked all the orders and tin,
　　Accoutred in showy fal-lal,
At a two-fifty Restaurant, in
　　The glittering Palais Royal.

He'd gaze in her orbit of blue,
　　Her hand he would tenderly squeeze,
But the words of her tongue that he knew
　　Were limited strictly to these:

"Coraline Celestine Eulalie,
　　Houp là! Je vous aime, oui, mossoo,
Combien donnez moi aujourd'hui
　　Bonjour, Mademoiselle, parlez voo."

Mademoiselle de la Sauce Mayonnaise
　　Was a witty and beautiful miss,
Extremely correct in her ways,
　　But her English consisted of this:

"Oh my! pretty man, if you please,
　　Blom boodin, biftek, currie lamb,

Bouldogue, two franc half, quite ze cheese,
  Rosbif, me spik Angleesh, godam."

A waiter, for seasons before,
  Had basked in her beautiful gaze,
And burnt to dismember Milor,
  He loved de la Sauce Mayonnaise.

He said to her, "Méchante Thérèse,
  Avec désespoir tu m'accables.
Penses-tu, de la Sauce Mayonnaise,
  Ses intentions sont honorables?

"Flirtez toujours, ma belle, si tu ôses—
  Je me vengerai ainsi, ma chère,
Je lui dirai de quoi l'on compose
  Vol au vent à la Financière!"

Lord Lardy knew nothing of this—
  The waiter's devotion ignored,
But he gazed on the beautiful miss,
  And never seemed weary or bored.

The waiter would screw up his nerve,
  His fingers he'd snap and he'd dance—
And Lord Lardy would smile and observe,
  "How strange are the customs of
      France!"

Well, after delaying a space,
  His tradesmen no longer would wait:
Returning to England apace,
  He yielded himself to his fate.

Lord Lardy espoused, with a groan,
  Miss Dardy's developing charms,
And agreed to tag on to his own,
  Her name and her newly-found arms.

The waiter he knelt at the toes
  Of an ugly and thin coryphée,
Who danced in the hindermost rows
  At the Théatre des Variétés.

Mademoiselle de la Sauce Mayonnaise
  Didn't yield to a gnawing despair
But married a soldier, and plays
  As a pretty and pert Vivandière.

BABETTE'S LOVE

Babette she was a fisher gal,
  With jupon striped and cap in crimps,
She passed her days inside the Halle,

Or catching little nimble shrimps.
Yet she was sweet as flowers in May,
With no professional bouquet.

Jacot was, of the Customs bold,
  An officer, at gay Boulogne,
He loved Babette—his love he told,
  And sighed, "Oh, soyez vous my own!"
But "Non!" said she, "Jacot, my pet,
Vous êtes trop scraggy pour Babette.

"Of one alone I nightly dream,
  An able mariner is he,
And gaily serves the Gen'ral Steam-
  Boat Navigation Companee.
I'll marry him, if he but will—
His name, I rather think, is Bill.

"I see him when he's not aware,
  Upon our hospitable coast,
Reclining with an easy air
  Upon the *Port* against a post,
A-thinking of, I'll dare to say,
His native Chelsea far away!"

"Oh, mon!" exclaimed the Customs bold,
  "Mes yeux!" he said (which means "my
      eye")
"Oh, chère!" he also cried, I'm told,
  "Par Jove," he added, with a sigh.
"Oh, mon! oh, chère! mes yeux! par Jove!
Je n'aime pas cet enticing cove!"

The *Panther's* captain stood hard by,
  He was a man of morals strict
If e'er a sailor winked his eye,
  Straightway he had that sailor licked,
Mast-headed all (such was his code)
Who dashed or jiggered, blessed or blowed.

He wept to think a tar of his
  Should lean so gracefully on posts,
He sighed and sobbed to think of this,
  On foreign, French, and friendly coasts.
"It's human natur', p'raps—if so,
Oh, isn't human natur' low!"

He called his Bill, who pulled his curl,
  He said, "My Bill, I understand
You've captivated some young gurl
  On this here French and foreign land.
Her tender heart your beauties jog—
They do, you know they do, you dog.

"You have a graceful way, I learn,
  Of leaning airily on posts,
By which you've been and caused to burn
  A tender flame on these here coasts.
A fisher gurl, I much regret—
Her age, sixteen—her name, Babette.

"You'll marry her, you gentle tar—
  Your union I myself will bless,
And when you matrimonied are,
  I will appoint her stewardess."
But William hitched himself and sighed,
And cleared his throat, and thus replied:

"Not so: unless you're fond of strife,
  You'd better mind your own affairs,
I have an able-bodied wife
  Awaiting me at Wapping Stairs;
If all this here to her I tell,
She'll larrup you and me as well.

"Skin-deep, and valued at a pin,
  Is beauty such as Venus owns—
Her beauty is beneath her skin,
  And lies in layers on her bones.
The other sailors of the crew
They always calls her 'Whopping Sue'!"

"Oho!" the Captain said, "I see!
  And is she then so very strong?"
"She'd take your honour's scruff," said he,
  "And pitch you over to Boulong!"
"I pardon you," the Captain said,
"The fair Babette you needn't wed."

Perhaps the Customs had his will,
  And coaxed the scornful girl to wed,
Perhaps the Captain and his Bill,
  And William's little wife are dead;
Or p'raps they're all alive and well:
I cannot, cannot, cannot tell.

TO MY BRIDE

(*Whoever She May Be*)

Oh! little maid!—(I do not know your
    name,
  Or who you are, so, as a safe precaution
I'll add)—Oh, buxom widow! married
    dame!
    (As one of these must be your present
      portion)
      Listen, while I unveil prophetic lore
      for you,

And sing the fate that Fortune has in
  store for you.

You'll marry soon—within a year or
    twain—
  A bachelor of *circa* two-and-thirty,
Tall, gentlemanly, but extremely plain,
  And, when you're intimate, you call him
    "Bertie."
    Neat—dresses well; his temper has been
      classified
    As hasty; but he's very quickly paci-
      fied.

You'll find him working mildly at the Bar,
  After a touch at two or three professions,
From easy affluence extremely far,
  A brief or two on Circuit—"soup" at
    Sessions;
    A pound or two from whist and back-
      ing horses,
    And, say three hundred from his own
      resources.

Quiet in harness; free from serious vice,
  His faults are not particularly shady,
You'll never find him "*shy*"—for, once or
    twice
  Already, he's been driven by a lady,
    Who parts with him—perhaps a poor
      excuse for him—
    Because she hasn't any further use for
      him.

Oh! bride of mine—tall, dumpy, dark, or
    fair!
  Oh! widow—wife, maybe, or blushing
    maiden,
I've told *your* fortune; solved the gravest
    care
  With which your mind has hitherto been
    laden.
    I've prophesied correctly, never doubt
      it;
    Now tell me mine—and please be
      quick about it!

You—only you—can tell me, an' you will,
  To whom I'm destined shortly to be
    mated,
Will she run up a heavy *modiste's* bill?
  If so, I want to hear her income stated
    (This is a point which interests me
      greatly).

To quote the bard, "Oh! have I seen
  her lately?"

Say, must I wait till husband number one
  Is comfortably stowed away at Woking?
How is her hair most usually done?
    And tell me, please, will she object to
      smoking?
      The colour of her eyes, too, you may
        mention:
        Come, Sibyl, prophesy—I'm all atten-
          tion.

SIR MACKLIN

Of all the youths I ever saw
  None were so wicked, vain, or silly,
So lost to shame and Sabbath law
  As worldly Tom, and Bob, and Billy.

For every Sabbath day they walked
  (Such was their gay and thoughtless
    natur')
In parks or gardens, where they talked
  From three to six, or even later.

Sir Macklin was a priest severe
  In conduct and in conversation,
It did a sinner good to hear
  Him deal in ratiocination.

He could in every action show
  Some sin, and nobody could doubt him.
He argued high, he argued low,
  He also argued round about him.

He wept to think each thoughtless youth
  Contained of wickedness a skinful,
And burnt to teach the awful truth,
  That walking out on Sunday's sinful.

"Oh, youths," said he, "I grieve to find
  The course of life you've been and hit
    on—
Sit down," said he, "and never mind
  The pennies for the chairs you sit on.

"My opening head is 'Kensington,'
  How walking there the sinner hardens,
Which when I have enlarged upon,
  I go to 'Secondly'—its 'Gardens.'

"My 'Thirdly' comprehendeth 'Hyde,'
  Of Secrecy the guilts and shameses;

My 'Fourthly'—'Park'—its verdure wide—
  My 'Fifthly' comprehends 'St. James's.'

"That matter settled I shall reach
  The 'Sixthly' in my solemn tether,
And show that what is true of each,
  Is also true of all, together.

"Then I shall demonstrate to you,
  According to the rules of Whately,
That what is true of all, is true
  Of each, considered separately."

In lavish stream his accents flow,
  Tom, Bob, and Billy dare not flout him;
He argued high, he argued low,
  He also argued round about him.

"Ha, ha!" he said, "you loathe your ways,
  Repentance on your souls is dawning,
In agony your hands you raise."
  (And so they did, for they were yawn-
    ing.)

To "Twenty-firstly" on they go,
  The lads do not attempt to scout him;
He argued high, he argued low,
  He also argued round about him.

"Ho, ho!" he cries, "you bow your crests—
  My eloquence has set you weeping;
In shame you bend upon your breasts!"
  (And so they did, for they were sleep-
    ing.)

He proved them this—he proved them
    that—
  This good but wearisome ascetic;
He jumped and thumped upon his hat,
  He was so very energetic.

His Bishop at this moment chanced
  To pass, and found the road encum-
    bered;
He noticed how the Churchman danced,
  And how his congregation slumbered.

The hundred and eleventh head
  The priest completed of his stricture;
"Oh, bosh!" the worthy bishop said,
  And walked him off, as in the picture.

THE YARN OF THE "NANCY BELL"

'Twas on the shores that round our coast
  From Deal to Ramsgate span,

That I found alone on a piece of stone
   An elderly naval man.

His hair was weedy, his beard was long,
   And weedy and long was he,
And I heard this wight on the shore recite,
   In a singular minor key:

"Oh, I am a cook and a captain bold,
   And the mate of the *Nancy* brig,
And a bo'sun tight, and a midshipmite,
   And the crew of the captain's gig."

And he shook his fists and he tore his hair,
   Till I really felt afraid,
For I couldn't help thinking the man had
     been drinking.
   And so I simply said:

"Oh, elderly man, it's little I know
   Of the duties of men of the sea,
And I'll eat my hand if I understand
   However you can be.

"At once a cook, and a captain bold,
   And the mate of the *Nancy* brig,
And a bo'sun tight, and a midshipmite,
   And the crew of the captain's gig."

Then he gave a hitch to his trousers, which
   Is a trick all seamen larn,
And having got rid of a thumping quid,
   He spun this painful yarn:

" 'Twas in the good ship *Nancy Bell*
   That we sailed to the Indian Sea,
And there on a reef we come to grief,
   Which has often occurred to me.

"And pretty nigh all the crew was drowned
   (There was seventy-seven o' soul),
And only ten of the *Nancy's* men
   Said 'Here!' to the muster-roll.

"There was me and the cook and the
     captain bold,
   And the mate of the *Nancy* brig,
And the bo'sun tight, and a midshipmite,
   And the crew of the captain's gig.

"For a month we'd neither wittles nor
     drink,
   Till a-hungry we did feel,
So we drawed a lot, and, accordin' shot
   The captain for our meal.

"The next lot fell to the *Nancy's* mate,
   And a delicate dish he made;
And then our appetite with the midship-
     mite
   We seven survivors stayed.

"And then we murdered the bo'sun tight,
   And he much resembled pig;
Then we wittled free, did the cook and me,
   On the crew of the captain's gig.

"Then only the cook and me was left,
   And the delicate question, 'Which
Of us two goes to the kettle?' arose
   And we argued it out as sich.

"For I loved that cook as a brother, I did,
   And the cook he worshipped me;
But we'd both be blowed if we'd either
     be stowed
   In the other chap's hold, you see.

" 'I'll be eat if you dines off me,' says Tom,
   'Yes, that,' says I, 'you'll be,'—
'I'm boiled if I die, my friend,' quoth I,
   And 'Exactly so,' quoth he.

"Says he, 'Dear James, to murder me
   Were a foolish thing to do,
For don't you see that you can't cook *me*,
   While I can—and will—cook *you!*'

"So he boils the water, and takes the salt
   And the pepper in portions true
(Which he never forgot), and some
     chopped shalot,
   And some sage and parsley too.

" 'Come here,' says he, with a proper pride,
   Which his smiling features tell,
' 'Twill soothing be if I let you see
   How extremely nice you'll smell.'

"And he stirred it round and round and
     round,
   And he sniffed at the foaming froth;
When I ups with his heels, and smothers
     his squeals
   In the scum of the boiling broth.

"And I eat that cook in a week or less,
   And—as I eating be
The last of his chops, why, I almost drops,
   For a wessel in sight I see!

"And I never larf, and I never smile,
　And I never lark nor play,
But sit and croak, and a single joke
　I have—which is to say:

" 'Oh, I am a cook and a captain bold,
　And the mate of the *Nancy* brig,
And a bo'sun tight, and a midshipmite,
　And the crew of the captain's gig!' "

THE BISHOP OF RUM-TI-FOO

From east and south the holy clan
Of Bishops gathered, to a man;
To Synod, called Pan-Anglican,
　In flocking crowds they came.
Among them was a Bishop, who
Had lately been appointed to
The balmy isle of Rum-ti-Foo,
　And Peter was his name.

His people—twenty-three in sum—
They played the eloquent tum-tum,
And lived on scalps served up in rum—
　The only sauce they knew.
When first good Bishop Peter came
(For Peter was that Bishop's name),
To humour them, he did the same
　As they of Rum-ti-Foo.

His flock, I've often heard him tell,
(His name was Peter) loved him well,
And summoned by the sound of bell,
　In crowds together came.
"Oh, massa, why you go away?
Oh, Massa Peter, please to stay."
(They called him Peter, people say,
　Because it was his name.)

He told them all good boys to be,
And sailed away across the sea,
At London Bridge that Bishop he
　Arrived one Tuesday night—
And as forthwith he homeward strode
To his Pan-Anglican abode,
He passed along the Borough Road
　And saw a gruesome sight.

He saw a crowd assembled round
A person dancing on the ground,
Who straight began to leap and bound
　With all his might and main.
To see that dancing man he stopped,
Who twirled and wriggled, skipped and
　hopped,

Then down incontinently dropped,
　And then sprang up again.

The Bishop chuckled at the sight,
"This style of dancing would delight
A simple Rum-ti-Foozleite,
　I'll learn it if I can,
To please the tribe when I get back."
He begged the man to teach his knack.
"Right Reverend Sir, in half a crack,"
　Replied that dancing man.

The dancing man he worked away,
And taught the Bishop every day—
The dancer skipped like any fay—
　Good Peter did the same.
The Bishop buckled to his task,
With *battements*, and *pas de basque*.
(I'll tell you, if you care to ask,
　That Peter was his name.)

"Come, walk like this," the dancer said,
"Stick out your toes—stick in your head,
Stalk on with quick, galvanic tread—
　Your fingers thus extend;
The attitude's considered quaint."
The weary Bishop, feeling faint,
Replied, "I do not say it ain't,
　But 'Time!' my Christian friend!"

"We now proceed to something new—
Dance as the Paynes and Lauris do,
Like this—one, two—one, two—one, two."
　The Bishop, never proud,
But in an overwhelming heat
(His name was Peter, I repeat)
Performed the Payne and Lauri feat,
　And puffed his thanks aloud.

Another game the dancer planned—
"Just take your ankle in your hand,
And try, my lord, if you can stand—
　Your body stiff and stark.
If, when revisiting your see,
You learnt to hop on shore—like me—
The novelty would striking be,
　And must attract remark."

"No," said the worthy Bishop, "No;
That is a length to which, I trow,
Colonial Bishops cannot go.
　You may express surprise
At finding Bishops deal in pride—
But, if that trick I ever tried,

I should appear undignified
In Rumti-Foozle's eyes.

"The islanders of Rum-ti-Foo
Are well-conducted persons, who
Approve a joke as much as you,
    And laugh at it as such;
But if they saw their Bishop land,
His leg supported in his hand,
The joke they wouldn't understand—
    'Twould pain them very much!"

THE PRECOCIOUS BABY

A Very True Tale.
(*To be sung to the air of the "Whistling
    Oyster."*)

An elderly person—a prophet by trade—
    With his quips and tips
    On withered old lips,
He married a young and a beautiful maid;
    The cunning old blade!
    Though rather decayed,
He married a beautiful, beautiful maid.

She was only eighteen, and as fair as could
        be,
    With her tempting smiles
    And maidenly wiles,
And he was a trifle past seventy-three:
    Now what she could see
    Is a puzzle to me,
In a prophet of seventy—seventy-three!

Of all their acquaintances bidden (or bad)
    With their loud high jinks
    And underbred winks,
None thought they'd a family have—but
        they had;
    A dear little lad
    Who drove 'em half mad,
For he turned out a horribly fast little cad.

For when he was born he astonished all by,
    With their "Law, dear me!"
    "Did ever you see."
He'd a weed in his mouth and a glass in his
        eye,
    A hat all awry—
    An octagon tie,
And a miniature—miniature glass in his eye.

He grumbled at wearing a frock and a
        cap,

With his "Oh dear, no!"
And his "Hang it! 'oo know!"
And he turned up his nose at his excellent
        pap—
    "My friends, it's a tap
    Dat is not worf a rap."
(Now this was remarkably excellent pap.)

He'd chuck his nurse under the chin, and
        he'd say,
    With his "Fal, lal, lal"—
    "'Oo doosed fine gal!"
This shocking precocity drove 'em away:
    "A month from to-day
    Is as long as I'll stay—
Then I'd wish, if you please, for to go, if
        I may."

His father, a simple old gentleman, he
    With nursery rhyme
    And "Once on a time,"
Would tell him the story of "Little Bo-P,"
    "So pretty was she,
    So pretty and wee,
As pretty, as pretty, as pretty could be."

But the babe, with a dig that would startle
        an ox,
    With his "C'ck! Oh, my!—
    Go along wiz 'oo, fie!"
Would exclaim, "I'm affaid 'oo a socking ole
        fox."
    Now a father it shocks,
    And it whitens his locks,
When his little babe calls him a shocking
        old fox.

The name of his father he'd couple and
        pair
    (With his ill-bred laugh,
    And insolent chaff)
With those of the nursery heroines rare—
    Virginia the Fair,
    Or Good Goldenhair,
Till the nuisance was more than a prophet
        could bear.

"There's Jill and White Cat" (said the bold
        little brat,
    With his loud "Ha, ha!")
    "'Oo sly ickle pa!
Wiz 'oo Beauty, Bo-Peep, and 'oo Mrs.
        Jack Sprat!
    I've noticed 'oo pat

My pretty White Cat—
I sink dear mamma ought to know about
dat!"

He early determined to marry and wive,
For better or worse
With his elderly nurse—
Which the poor little boy didn't live to
contrive:
His health didn't thrive—
No longer alive,
He died an enfeebled old dotard at five!

MORAL

Now, elderly men of the bachelor crew,
With wrinkled hose
And spectacled nose,
Don't marry at all—you may take it as
true
If ever you do
The step you will rue,
For your babes will be elderly—elderly too.

TO PHOEBE

"Gentle, modest, little flower,
Sweet epitome of May,
Love me but for half-an-hour,
Love me, love me, little fay."
Sentences so fiercely flaming
In your tiny shell-like ear,
I should always be exclaiming
If I loved you, Phoebe, dear.

"Smiles that thrill from any distance
Shed upon me while I sing!
Please ecstaticise existence,
Love me, oh thou fairy thing!"
Words like these, outpouring sadly,
You'd perpetually hear,
If I loved you, fondly, madly;—
But I do not, Phoebe, dear.

THOMAS WINTERBOTTOM HANCE

In all the towns and cities fair
On Merry England's broad expanse,
No swordsman ever could compare
With Thomas Winterbottom Hance.

The dauntless lad could fairly hew
A silken handkerchief in twain,

Divide a leg of mutton too—
And this without unwholesome strain.
On whole half-sheep, with cunning trick,
His sabre sometimes he'd employ—
No bar of lead, however thick,
Had terrors for the stalwart boy.

At Dover daily he'd prepare
To hew and slash, behind, before—
Which aggravated Monsieur Pierre,
Who watched him from the Calais shore.

It caused good Pierre to swear and dance,
The sight annoyed and vexed him so;
He was the bravest man in France—
He said so, and he ought to know.

"Regardez donc, ce cochon gros—
Ce polisson! Oh, sacré bleu!
Son sabre, son plomb, et ses gigots!
Comme cela m'ennuye, enfin, mon Dieu!

"Il sait que les foulards de soie
Give no retaliating whack—
Les gigots morts n'ont pas de quoi—
Le plomb don't ever hit you back."

But every day the zealous lad
Cut lead and mutton more and more;
And every day, poor Pierre, half mad,
Shrieked loud defiance from his shore.

Hance had a mother, poor and old,
A simple, harmless village dame,
Who crowed and clapped as people told
Of Winterbottom's rising fame.

She said, "I'll be upon the spot
To see my Tommy's sabre-play";
And so she left her leafy cot,
And walked to Dover in a day.

Pierre had a doting mother, who
Had heard of his defiant rage:
His ma was nearly eighty-two,
And rather dressy for her age.

At Hance's doings every morn,
With sheer delight *his* mother cried;
And Monsieur Pierre's contemptuous scorn
Filled *his* mamma with proper pride.

But Hance's powers began to fail—
His constitution was not strong—
And Pierre, who once was stout and hale,
Grew thin from shouting all day long.

Their mothers saw them pale and wan,
Maternal anguish tore each breast,
And so they met to find a plan
To set their offsprings' minds at rest.

Said Mrs. Hance, "Of course I shrinks
From bloodshed, ma'am, as you're aware,
But still they'd better meet, I thinks."
"Assurément!" said Madame Pierre.

A sunny spot in sunny France
Was hit upon for this affair;
The ground was picked by Mrs. Hance,
The stakes were pitched by Madame
Pierre.

Said Mrs. H., "Your work you see—
Go in, my noble boy, and win."
"En garde, mon fils!" said Madame P.
"Allons!" "Go on!" "En garde!"
"Begin!"

(The mothers were of decent size,
Though not particularly tall;
But in the sketch that meets your eyes
I've been obliged to draw them small.)

Loud sneered the doughty man of France,
"Ho! ho! Ho! ho! Ha! ha! Ha! ha!"
"The French for 'Pish!'" said Thomas
Hance.
Said Pierre, "L'Anglais, Monsieur, pour
'Bah.'"

Said Mrs. H., "Come, one! two! three!—
We're sittin' here to see all fair."
"C'est magnifique!" said Madame P.,
"Mais, parbleu! ce n'est pas la guerre!"

"Je scorn un foe si lâche que vous,"
Said Pierre, the doughty son of France.
"I fight not coward foe like you!"
Said our undaunted Tommy Hance.

"The French for 'Pooh!'" our Tommy
cried.
"L'Anglais pour 'Va!'" the Frenchman
crowed.
And so, with undiminished pride,
Each went on his respective road.

THE GHOST, THE GALLANT, THE GAEL, AND THE GOBLIN

O'er unreclaimed suburban clays
Some years ago were hobblin'
An elderly ghost of easy ways,
And an influential goblin.
The ghost was a sombre spectral shape,
A fine old five-act fogy,
The goblin imp, a lithe young ape,
A fine low-comedy bogy.

And as they exercised their joints,
Promoting quick digestion,
They talked on several curious points,
And raised this pregnant question:
"Which of us two is Number One—
The ghostie, or the goblin?"
And o'er the point they raised in fun
They fairly fell a-squabblin'.

They'd barely speak, and each, in fine,
Grew more and more reflective,
Each thought his own particular line
By far the more effective.
At length they settled some one should
By each of them be haunted,
And so arranged that either could
Exert his prowess vaunted.

"The Quaint against the Statuesque"—
By competition lawful—
The goblin backed the Quaint Grotesque,
The ghost the Grandly Awful.
"Now," said the goblin, "here's my plan—
In attitude commanding,
I see a stalwart Englishman
By yonder tailor's standing.

"The very fittest man on earth
My influence to try on—
Of gentle, p'raps of noble birth,
And dauntless as a lion!
Now wrap yourself within your shroud—
Remain in easy hearing—
Observe—you'll hear him scream aloud
When I begin appearing!"

The imp with yell unearthly—wild—
Threw off his dark enclosure:
His dauntless victim looked and smiled
With singular composure.
For hours he tried to daunt the youth,
For days, indeed, but vainly—

The stripling smiled!—to tell the truth,
  The stripling smiled inanely.

For weeks the goblin weird and wild,
  That noble stripling haunted;
For weeks the stripling stood and smiled,
  Unmoved and all undaunted.
The sombre ghost exclaimed, "Your plan
  Has failed you, goblin, plainly:
Now watch yon hardy Hieland man,
  So stalwart and ungainly.

"These are the men who chase the roe,
  Whose footsteps never falter,
Who bring with them where'er they go,
  A smack of old Sir Walter.
Of such as he, the men sublime
  Who lead their troops victorious,
Whose deeds go down to after-time,
  Enshrined in annals glorious!

"Of such as he the bard has said
  'Hech thrawfu' raltie rawkie!
Wi' thecht ta' croonie clapperhead
  And fash' wi' unco pawkie!'
He'll faint away when I appear
  Upon his native heather;
Or p'raps he'll only scream with fear,
  Or p'raps the two together."

The spectre showed himself, alone,
  To do his ghostly battling,
With curdling groan and dismal moan
  And lots of chains a-rattling!
But no—the chiel's stout Gaelic stuff
  Withstood all ghostly harrying,
His fingers closed upon the snuff
  Which upwards he was carrying.

For days that ghost declined to stir,
  A foggy shapeless giant—
For weeks that splendid officer
  Stared back again defiant.
Just as the Englishman returned
  The goblin's vulgar staring,
Just so the Scotchman boldly spurned
  The ghost's unmannered scaring.

For several years the ghostly twain
  These Britons bold have haunted,
But all their efforts are in vain—
  Their victims stand undaunted.
Unto this day the imp and ghost
  (Whose powers the imp derided)
Stand each at his allotted post—
  The bet is undecided.

KING BORRIA BUNGALEE BOO

King Borria Bungalee Boo
  Was a man-eating African swell;
His sigh was a hullabaloo,
  His whisper a horrible yell—
  A horrible, horrible yell!

Four subjects, and all of them male,
  To Borria doubled the knee,
They were once on a far larger scale,
  But he'd eaten the balance, you see
  ("Scale" and "balance" is punning, you
    see).

There was haughty Pish-Tush-Pooh-Bah,
  There was lumbering Doodle-Dum-Dey,
Despairing Alack-a-Dey-Ah,
  And good little Tootle-Tum-Teh—
  Exemplary Tootle-Tum-Teh.

One day there was grief in the crew,
  For they hadn't a morsel of meat,
And Borria Bungalee Boo
  Was dying for something to eat—
  "Come, provide me with something to
    eat!

"Alack-a-Dey, famished I feel;
  Oh, good little Tootle-Tum-Teh,
Where on earth shall I look for a meal?
  For I haven't no dinner to-day!—
  Not a morsel of dinner to-day!

"Dear Tootle-Tum, what shall we do?
  Come, get us a meal, or in truth,
If you don't we shall have to eat you,
  Oh, adorable friend of our youth!
  Thou beloved little friend of our youth!"

And he answered, "Oh, Bungalee Boo,
  For a moment I hope you will wait,—
Tippy-Wippity Tol-the-Rol-Loo
  Is the Queen of a neighbouring state—
  A remarkably neighbouring state.

"Tippy-Wippity Tol-the-Rol-Loo,
  She would pickle deliciously cold—
And her four pretty Amazons, too,
  Are enticing, and not very old—
  Twenty-seven is not very old.

"There is neat little Titty-Fol-Leh,
  There is rollicking Tral-the-Ral-Lah,

There is jocular Waggety-Weh,
　There is musical Doh-Reh-Mi-Fah—
　There's the nightingale Doh-Reh-Mi-
　　Fah!"

So the forces of Bungalee Boo
　Marched forth in a terrible row,
And the ladies who fought for Queen Loo
　Prepared to encounter the foe—
　This dreadful insatiate foe!

But they sharpened no weapons at all,
　And they poisoned no arrows—not they!
They made ready to conquer or fall
　In a totally different way—
　An entirely different way.

With a crimson and pearly-white dye
　They endeavoured to make themselves
　　fair,
With black they encircled each eye,
　And with yellow they painted their hair
　(It was wool, but they thought it was
　　hair).

And the forces they met in the field:—
　And the men of King Borria said,
"Amazonians, immediately yield!"
　And their arrows they drew to the
　　head—
　Yes, drew them right up to the head.

But jocular Waggety-Weh
　Ogled Doodle-Dum-Dey (which was
　　wrong),
And neat little Titty-Fol-Leh
　Said, "Tootle-Tum, you go along!
　You naughty old dear, go along!"

And rollicking Tral-the-Ral-Lah
　Tapped Alack-a-Dey-Ah with her fan;
And musical Doh-Reh-Mi-Fah
　Said, "Pish, go away, you bad man!
　Go away, you delightful young man!"

And the Amazons simpered and sighed,
　And they ogled, and giggled, and flushed,
And they opened their pretty eyes wide,
　And they chuckled, and flirted, and
　　blushed
　(At least, if they could, they'd have
　　blushed).

But haughty Pish-Tush-Pooh-Bah
　Said, "Alack-a-Dey, what does this
　　mean?"
And despairing Alack-a-Dey-Ah
　Said, "They think us uncommonly
　　green—
　Ha! ha! most uncommonly green!"

Even blundering Doodle-Dum-Deh
　Was insensible quite to their leers,
And said good little Tootle-Tum-Teh,
　"It's your blood that we're wanting, my
　　dears—
　We have come for our dinners, my
　　dears!"

And the Queen of the Amazons fell
　To Borria Bungalee Boo,—
In a mouthful he gulped, with a yell,
　Tippy-Wippy Tol-the-Rol-Loo—
　The pretty Queen Tol-the-Rol-Loo.

And neat little Titty-Fol-Leh
　Was eaten by Pish-Pooh-Bah,
And light-hearted Waggety-Weh
　By dismal Alack-a-Dey-Ah—
　Despairing Alack-a-Dey-Ah.

And rollicking Tral-the-Ral-Lah
　Was eaten by Doodle-Dum-Dey,
And musical Doh-Reh-Mi-Fah
　By good little Tootle-Tum-Teh—
　Exemplary Tootle-Tum-Teh!

TO THE TERRESTRIAL GLOBE

By a Miserable Wretch

Roll on, thou ball, roll on!
Through pathless realms of Space
　Roll on!
What though I'm in a sorry case?
What though I cannot meet my bills?
What though I suffer toothache's ills?
What though I swallow countless pills?
　Never *you* mind!
　　Roll on!

Roll on, thou ball, roll on!
Through seas of inky air
　Roll on!
It's true I have no shirts to wear;
It's true my butcher's bill is due;

It's true my prospects all look blue—
But don't let that unsettle you!
  Never *you* mind!
  Roll on!

                              [*It rolls on.*

GENTLE ALICE BROWN

It was a robber's daughter, and her name
  was Alice Brown,
Her father was the terror of a small Italian
  town;
Her mother was a foolish, weak, but amiable old thing;
But it isn't of her parents that I'm going
  for to sing.

As Alice was a-sitting at her window-sill
  one day,
A beautiful young gentleman he chanced
  to pass that way;
She cast her eyes upon him, and he looked
  so good and true,
That she thought, "I could be happy with a
  gentleman like you!"

And every morning passed her house that
  cream of gentlemen,
She knew she might expect him at a quarter unto ten,
A sorter in the Custom-house, it was his
  daily road
(The Custom-house was fifteen minutes'
  walk from her abode).

But Alice was a pious girl, who knew it
  wasn't wise
To look at strange young sorters with expressive purple eyes;
So she sought the village priest to whom
  her family confessed—
The priest by whom their little sins were
  carefully assessed.

"Oh, holy father," Alice said, " 'twould
  grieve you, would it not?
To discover that I was a most disreputable
  lot!
Of all unhappy sinners I'm the most unhappy one!"
The padre said, "Whatever have you been
  and gone and done?"

"I have helped mamma to steal a little
  kiddy from its dad
I've assisted dear papa in cutting up a
  little lad.
I've planned a little burglary and forged a
  little cheque,
And slain a little baby for the coral on its
  neck!"

The worthy pastor heaved a sigh, and
  dropped a silent tear—
And said, "You mustn't judge yourself too
  heavily, my dear—
It's wrong to murder babies, little corals
  for to fleece;
But sins like these one expiates at half-
  a-crown apiece.

"Girls will be girls—you're very young, and
  flighty in your mind;
Old heads upon young shoulders we must
  not expect to find:
We mustn't be too hard upon these little
  girlish tricks—
Let's see—five crimes at half-a-crown—
  exactly twelve-and-six."

"Oh, father," little Alice cried, "your kindness makes me weep,
You do these little things for me so singularly cheap—
Your thoughtful liberality I never can forget;
But oh, there is another crime I haven't
  mentioned yet!

"A pleasant-looking gentleman, with pretty
  purple eyes,
I've noticed at my window, as I've sat a-
  catching flies;
He passes by it every day as certain as can
  be—
I blush to say I've winked at him, and he
  has winked at me!"

"For shame!" said Father Paul, "my erring
  daughter! On my word
This is the most distressing news that I
  have ever heard.
Why, naughty girl, your excellent papa has
  pledged your hand
To a promising young robber, the lieutenant of his band!

"This dreadful piece of news will pain your
    worthy parents so!
They are the most remunerative customers
    I know;
For many many years they've kept starva-
    tion from my doors:
I never knew so criminal a family as yours!

"The common country folk in this insipid
    neighbourhood
Have nothing to confess, they're so ridicu-
    lously good;
And if you marry any one respectable at
    all,
Why, you'll reform, and what will then
    become of Father Paul?"

The worthy priest, he up and drew his
    cowl upon his crown,
And started off in haste to tell the news
    to Robber Brown;
To tell him how his daughter, who was
    now for marriage fit,
Had winked upon a sorter, who recipro-
    cated it.

Good Robber Brown he muffled up his
    anger pretty well,
He said, "I have a notion, and that notion
    I will tell;
I will nab this gay young sorter, terrify
    him into fits,
And get my gentle wife to chop him into
    little bits.

"I've studied human nature, and I know a
    thing or two;
Though a girl may fondly love a living
    gent, as many do,
A feeling of disgust upon her senses there
    will fall
When she looks upon his body chopped
    particularly small."

He traced that gallant sorter to a still
    suburban square;
He watched his opportunity and seized him
    unaware;
He took a life-preserver and he hit him on
    the head,
And Mrs. Brown dissected him before she
    went to bed.

And pretty little Alice grew more settled
    in her mind,
She never more was guilty of a weakness
    of the kind,
Until at length good Robber Brown be-
    stowed her pretty hand
On the promising young robber, the lieu-
    tenant of his band.

MY DREAM

The other night, from cares exempt,
I slept—and what d'you think I dreamt?
I dreamt that somehow I had come
To dwell in Topsy-Turveydom!—

Where vice is virtue—virtue, vice:
Where nice is nasty—nasty, nice:
Where right is wrong and wrong is right—
Where white is black and black is white.

Where babies, much to their surprise,
Are born astonishingly wise;
With every Science on their lips,
And Art at all their finger-tips.

For, as their nurses dandle them,
They crow binomial theorem,
With views (it seems absurd to us)
On differential calculus.

But though a babe, as I have said,
Is born with learning in his head,
He must forget it, if he can,
Before he calls himself a man.

For that which we call folly here,
Is wisdom in that favoured sphere;
The wisdom we so highly prize
Is blatant folly in their eyes.

A boy, if he would push his way,
Must learn some nonsense every day;
And cut, to carry out this view,
His wisdom teeth and wisdom too.

Historians burn their midnight oils,
Intent on giant-killers' toils;
And sages close their aged eyes
To other sages' lullabies.

Our magistrates, in duty bound,
Commit all robbers who are found;
But there the beaks (so people said)
Commit all robberies instead.

Our judges, pure and wise in tone,
Know crime from theory alone,
And glean the motives of a thief
From books and popular belief.

But there, a Judge who wants to prime
His mind with true ideas of crime,
Derives them from the common sense
Of practical experience.

Policemen march all folks away
Who practise virtue every day—
Of course, I mean to say, you know,
What we call virtue here below.

For only scoundrels dare to do
What we consider just and true,
And only good men do, in fact,
What we should think a dirty act.

But strangest of these social twirls,
The girls are boys—the boys are girls!
The men are women, too—but then,
Per contra, women all are men.

To one who to tradition clings
This seems an awkward state of things,
But if to think it out you try,
It doesn't really signify.

With them, as surely as can be,
A sailor should be sick at sea,
And not a passenger may sail
Who cannot smoke right through a gale.

A soldier (save by rarest luck)
Is always shot for showing pluck
(That is, if others can be found
With pluck enough to fire a round).

"How strange!" I said to one I saw;
"You quite upset our every law.
However can you get along
So systematically wrong?"

"Dear me," my mad informant said,
"Have you no eyes within your head?
You sneer when you your hat should doff:
Why, we begin where you leave off!

"Your wisest men are very far
Less learned than our babies are!"
I mused awhile—and then, oh me!
I framed this brilliant repartee:

"Although your babes are wiser far
Than our most valued sages are,
Your sages, with their toys and cots,
Are duller than our idiots!"

But this remark, I grieve to state,
Came just a little bit too late;
For as I framed it in my head,
I woke and found myself in bed.

Still I could wish that, 'stead of here,
My lot were in that favoured sphere!—
Where greatest fools bear off the bell
I ought to do extremely well.

THE FAIRY CURATE

Once a fairy
  Light and airy
Married with a mortal;
  Men, however,
  Never, never
Pass the fairy portal.
  Slyly stealing,
  She to Ealing
Made a daily journey;
  There she found him,
  Clients round him
(He was an attorney).

Long they tarried,
  Then they married.
When the ceremony
  Once was ended,
  Off they wended
On their moon of honey.
  Twelvemonth, maybe,
  Saw a baby
(Friends performed an orgie).
  Much they prized him,
  And baptized him
By the name of Georgie.

  Georgie grew up;
  Then he flew up
To his fairy mother.
  Happy meeting
  Pleasant greeting—
Kissing one another.
  "Choose a calling
  Most enthralling,
I sincerely urge ye."
  "Mother," said he

(Rev'rence made he),
"I would join the clergy.

"Give permission
In addition—
Pa will let me do it:
There's a living
In his giving,
He'll appoint me to it.
Dreams of coff'ring
Easter off'ring,
Tithe and rent and pew-rate,
So inflame me
(Do not blame me),
That I'll be a curate."

She, with pleasure,
Said, "My treasure,
'Tis my wish precisely.
Do your duty,
There's a beauty;
You have chosen wisely.
Tell your father
I would rather
As a churchman rank you.
You, in clover,
I'll watch over."
Georgie said, "Oh, thank you!"

Georgie scudded,
Went and studied,
Made all preparations,
And with credit
(Though he said it)
Passed examinations.
(Do not quarrel
With him, moral,
Scrupulous digestions—
'Twas his mother,
And no other,
Answered all the questions.)

Time proceeded;
Little needed
Georgie admonition:
He, elated,
Vindicated
Clergyman's position.
People round him
Always found him
Plain and unpretending;
Kindly teaching,

Plainly preaching—
All his money lending.

So the fairy,
Wise and wary,
Felt no sorrow rising—
No occasion
For persuasion,
Warning, or advising.
He, resuming
Fairy pluming
(That's not English, is it?)
Oft would fly up,
To the sky up,

Pay mamma a visit.
Time progressing,
Georgie's blessing
Grew more Ritualistic—
Popish scandals,
Tonsures—sandals—
Genuflections mystic;
Gushing meetings—
Bosom-beatings—
Heavenly ecstatics—
Broidered spencers—
Copes and censers—
Rochets and dalmatics.

This quandary
Vexed the fairy—
Flew she down to Ealing.
"Georgie, stop it!
Pray you, drop it;
Hark to my appealing:
To this foolish
Papal rule-ish
Twaddle put an ending;
This a swerve is
From our Service
Plain and unpretending."

He, replying,
Answered, sighing,
Hawing, hemming, humming,
"It's a pity—
They're so pritty;
Yet in mode becoming.
Mother tender,
I'll surrender—
I'll be unaffected—"
But his Bishop
Into *his* shop
Entered unexpected!

"Who is this, sir,—
  Ballet miss, sir?"
Said the Bishop coldly.
  " 'Tis my mother,
  And no other,"
Georgie answered boldly.
  "Go along, sir!
  You are wrong, sir,
You have years in plenty;
  While this hussy
  (Gracious mussy!)
Isn't two-and-twenty!"
  (Fairies clever
  Never, never

Grow in visage older;
  And the fairy,
  All unwary,
Leant upon his shoulder!)
  Bishop grieved him,
  Disbelieved him,
George the point grew warm on;
  Changed religion,
  Like a pigeon,[1]
And became a Mormon.

[1] "Like a bird."